MW00788061

AMERICA'S CAESAR

The Decline and Fall of Republican Government in the United States of America

by Greg Loren Durand

Volume Two

Institute for Southern Historical Review
Dahlonega, Georgia

America's Caesar:
The Decline and Fall of Republican Government
in the United States of America

Fifth Edition

Volume Two
ISBN 0 615825 63 X

Copyright © 2013
Greg Loren Durand
All Rights Reserved

The original contents of this book are the intellectual property of the author.
Reproduction of this book or pirating of any portion thereof without the express
and written permission of the author is hereby prohibited.

Printed in Dixie.

Deo Vindice!

For a catalogue listing of other available titles, please write
to the following address or visit our website:

Institute for Southern Historical Review
Post Office Box 386
Dahlonega, Georgia 30533

www.southernhistoricalreview.org

PART THREE
The Radical Republicans and the Second American Revolution

The Party seeks power entirely for its own sake. We are not interested in the good of others; we are interested solely in power. Not wealth or luxury or long life or happiness; only power, pure power. What pure power means you will understand presently.

— George Orwell

CHAPTER SIXTEEN
The Genesis of the Civil Rights Movement

War-Time Confiscation of Enemy Property

During Lincoln's war against the States, Executive power to confiscate the property of individuals sympathetic to the "enemy" was declared:

The first act authorizing the confiscation of property was that of August 6, 1861.[1]

---

1. The Act read in part as follows:

Section 1. That if, during the present or any future insurrection against the Government of the United States after the President of the United States shall have declared by proclamation that the laws of the United States are opposed and the execution thereof obstructed by combinations too powerful to be suppressed by the ordinary course of judicial proceedings or by the power vested in the marshals by law, any person, or persons, his, her, or their agent, attorney, or employee shall purchase or acquire, sell or give, any property, of whatsoever kind or description, with intent to use or employ the same, or suffer the same to be used or employed in aiding, abetting, or promoting such insurrection or resistance to the laws, or any person or persons engaged therein, or if any person or persons, being the owner or owners of any such property, shall knowingly use or employ or consent to the use or employment of the same as aforesaid, all such property is hereby declared to be lawful subject of prize and capture wherever found; and it shall be the duty of the President of the United States to cause the same to be seized, confiscated, and condemned....

Section 3. The proceedings in court shall be for the benefit of the United States and the informer equally.

Section 4. That whenever hereafter, during the present insurrection against the Government of the United States, any person claimed to be held to labor or service under the law of any State shall be required or permitted by the person to whom such labor or service is claimed to be due, or

It provided that if, during the then existing or any future insurrection against the government, after proclamation of the President that the laws of the United States are opposed by combinations too powerful to be suppressed by the ordinary machinery of government authorities for that purpose, then all that property of whatsoever kind or description used with the consent of the owner to further the interests of the insurrection should be lawful subject of prize of capture wherever found, and it was made the duty of the President to cause the same to be seized, confiscated, and condemned.... The act extended to all descriptions of property, real or personal, on land or on water. The Supreme Court decided that its enactment was in virtue of the war powers of the government. It defined no crime. It imposed no penalty. It declared nothing unlawful. It was not, therefore, a mere municipal regulation for the punishment of crime. It was aimed exclusively at the seizure and confiscation of property used, or intended to be used, to aid, abet, or promote the rebellion, then a war, or to maintain the war against the government. It treated the property as the guilty subject.[2]

Other seizure mechanisms were provided in the Captured and Abandoned Property Act of 12 March 1863.[3] Under the terms of these wartime statutes, agents of the Treasury Department entered the States of the Southern Confederacy and began to seize abandoned or otherwise considered captured property in places where U.S. troops had already swept through. Proceedings *in rem*[4] were then conducted in prize courts wherein the property was condemned and the proceeds thereof were deposited into the Treasury.[5] In the hands of

---

by the lawful agent of such person, to take up arms against the United States, or shall be required or permitted by the person to whom such labor or service is claimed to be due, or his lawful agent, to work or to be employed in or upon any fort, navy-yard, dock, armory, ship, intrenchment, or in any military or naval service whatsoever against the Government and lawful authority of the United States, then, and in every such case, the person to whom such labor or service is claimed to be due shall forfeit his claim to such labor, any law of the State or of the United States to the contrary notwithstanding. And, whenever thereafter the person claiming such labor or service shall seek to enforce his claim, it shall be a full and sufficient answer to such claim that the person whose service or labor is claimed had been employed in hostile service against the Government of the United States contrary to the provisions of this act (Statutes at Large, Volume XII, page 1266).

Section One of the above Act remains on the books at Title 50, United States Code, Section 212.

2. Birkhimer, *Military Government*, pages 182-183.

3. Statutes at Large, Volume XII, pages 820-821.

4. "A technical term used to designate proceedings or actions instituted *against the thing*, in contradistinction to personal actions, which are said to be *in personam*" (*Black's Law Dictionary* [Sixth Edition], page 793; emphasis in original).

5. Birkhimer, *Military Government*, page 196.

corrupt agents,[6] such work was very profitable indeed and by the time of the repeal of the Captured Property Act in May of 1868, the gross sales of such property seized had amounted to about $30 million with net proceeds totaling about $25 million. As discussed in a previous chapter, the primary form of property thus seized by the invading Northern army was that which was owned by Southern planters in the labor of their slaves. It was Lincoln's assertion that "the traitor against the General Government forfeits his slave at least as justly as he does any other property; and he forfeits both to the Government against which he offends. The Government, so far as there can be ownership, thus owns the forfeited slaves, and the question for Congress in regard to them is, 'Shall they be made free or sold to new masters?'"[7]

Most Americans today are completely ignorant of the true purpose of Lincoln's Emancipation Proclamation. As was discussed in Chapter Thirteen, the Proclamation only applied to the unconquered portions of the Confederate States, where Lincoln had no authority or power whatsoever to so declare freedom to the slaves, and left slavery in the Border States and the excepted counties and parishes of the South under Northern occupation "precisely as if this proclamation were not issued." No less an authority than Secretary of State Seward declared, "We show our sympathy with slavery by emancipating slaves where we cannot reach them, and holding them in bondage where we can set them free."[8] Not only did Lincoln assert the right under the "law of war" to confiscate property "whenever it helps us or hurts the enemy,"[9] but he also recognized that the Northern cause would benefit greatly should the slaves be enticed to rise up against the defenseless women, children, and elderly of the South, thereby forcing the men to withdraw from the field and return to their homes. Of course, his hopes in this regard were to be greatly disappointed.

It is important to note that the validity of the Emancipation Proclamation rested upon two premises: (1) that the Southern States were "in rebellion against the United States"; and (2) that the proclamation itself was "a fit and necessary war measure for suppressing said rebellion." Lincoln himself admitted that the proclamation had "no constitutional or legal justification, except as a military measure." If the first premise of the proclamation was false, then the second was equally spurious. Since the alleged "rebellion" was nothing more than a ruse concocted by the Republicans to justify their abandonment of the Constitution, their

---

6. Hugh McCulloch, who had replaced Salmon P. Chase as Secretary of the Treasury in 1865, observed, "I am sure I sent *some* honest agents South; but it sometimes seems very doubtful whether any of them remained honest very long" (quoted by Whitelaw Reid, *After the War: A Southern Tour, May 1, 1865 to May 1, 1866* [Cincinnati, Ohio: Moore, Wilstach, and Baldwin, 1866], pages 204-205; emphasis in original).

7. Lincoln, message to Congress, 17 July 1862; quoted by Davis, *Rise and Fall of the Confederate Government*, Volume II, pages 169-170.

8. Seward, quoted by Piatt, *Memoirs of Men Who Saved the Union*, page 150.

9. Lincoln, letter to James C. Conkling, 26 August 1863; in Basler, *Collected Works of Lincoln*, Volume VI, page 407.

destruction of the Union thereunder, and their war of conquest on the South, Lincoln's proclamation must be viewed as a revolutionary document designed to attack the very fabric of American civilization and lay the foundation for an entirely new social and political structure.

The Establishment of the Freedmen's Bureau

Even before the war had ended, a stream of legislation began to flow from Washington, D.C., the alleged purpose of which was to protect the Blacks in the enjoyment of their newly-granted status as freedmen. On 3 March 1865, over one month before General Lee surrendered the Army of Northern Virginia at Appomattox Courthouse, Virginia, Congress passed "an act to establish a bureau [the Freedmen's Bureau] for the relief of freedmen, refugees, and abandoned lands." The functions of this Bureau were to continue "during the present war of rebellion, and for one year thereafter."[10] On 5 January 1866, Republican Senator Lyman Trumbell from Illinois proposed a bill "to enlarge the powers of the Freedmen's Bureau" which would authorize the President to "divide the section of country containing such refugees and freedmen into districts, each containing one or more States" and "to divide each district into a number of sub-districts... and to assign to each sub-district at least one agent, either a citizen, officer of the army, or enlisted man...." Moreover, this bill extended "military jurisdiction and protection over all employees, agents, and officers of the bureau."[11]

Negro historian W.E. Burghardt DuBois rightly described the Freedmen's Bureau as "a new government" emanating from the War Department and exercising jurisdiction over "millions of men." It "made laws, executed them and interpreted them; it laid and collected taxes, defined and punished crime, maintained and used military force, and dictated such measures as it thought necessary and proper for the accomplishment of its varied ends."[12] This was a government existing wholly outside of the scope of the Constitution and established on the foundation of "military necessity" through which the Radicals in Congress proposed to extend the jurisdiction of the U.S. Government beyond the constitutional ten-mile square limits of Washington, D.C.[13] into the several States. As John W. Burgess stated, "It was a stiff measure even for the transition period from war to peace. It cannot be justified

---

10. Statutes at Large, Volume XIII, pages 507-509.

11. William H. Barnes, *History of the Thirty-Ninth Congress of the United States* (New York: Harper and Brothers, Publishers, 1868), pages 104-106.

12. W.E. Burghardt DuBois, "The Freedmen's Bureau," *Atlantic Monthly*, Volume LXXXVII (1901), pages 357, 358, 359.

13. U.S. Constitution, Article I, Section 8, Clause 17.

constitutionally as anything but a war measure."[14] These words were precisely those which had been used three years previously by Lincoln to describe his Emancipation Proclamation. However, whereas Lincoln had a so-called rebellion upon which to base his war measure, the Radical Republicans had no such excuse for theirs since hostilities had ceased many months before. This expansion of the powers of the Freedmen's Bureau was therefore a blatantly unconstitutional act of legislative aggression against the South and was inimical to any real restoration of peaceful relations between the two sections. Democrat Senator Thomas A. Hendricks of Indiana protested against this obvious intent with these words:

> Now, sir, it is important to note very carefully the enlargement of the powers of this bureau proposed by this bill; and in the first place, it proposes to make the bureau permanent. The last Congress would not agree to this. The bill that the Senate voted down did not limit the duration of the bureau, and it was voted down, and the bill that the Senate agreed to provided that the bureau should continue during the war and only for one year after its termination. That was the judgment of the Senate at the last session. What has occurred since to change the judgment of the Senate in this important matter?
>
> What change in the condition of the country induces the Senate now to say that this shall be a permanent bureau or department of the Government, when at the last session it said it should cease to exist within one year after the conclusion of the war? Why, sir, it seems to me that the country is now, and especially the Southern States are now in better condition than the Senate had reason to expect when the law was enacted. Civil government has been restored in almost all the Southern States; the courts are restored in many of them; in many localities they are exercising their jurisdiction within their particular localities without let or hindrance; and why I ask Senators, shall we make this bureau a perpetual and permanent institution of the Government when we refused to do it at the last session?...
>
> The next proposition of the bill is, that it shall not be confined any longer to the Southern States, but that it shall have a government over the States of the North as well as of the South. The old law allowed the President to appoint a commissioner for each of the States that had been declared to be in rebellion — one for each of the eleven seceding States, not to exceed ten in all. This bill provides that the jurisdiction of the bureau shall extend wherever, within the limits of the United States, refugees or freedmen have gone. Indiana has not been a State in insurrection, and yet there are thousands of refugees and freedmen who have gone into that State within the last three years. This bureau is to become a governing power over the State of Indiana according to the provisions of the bill. Indiana, that provides for her own paupers, Indiana that provides for the government of her own people, may, under the provision of this bill be placed under a government that our fathers never contemplated — a government that must be most distasteful to freemen....
>
> Then, sir, when this army of officers has been organized, the bill provides: "And the President of the United States, through the War Department and the commissioner,

---

14. John W. Burgess, *Reconstruction and the Constitution* (New York: Charles Scribner's Sons, 1902), page 65.

shall extend military jurisdiction and protection over all employees, agents, and officers of this bureau." Will some Senator be good enough to tell me what that means? If Indiana be declared a State within which are found refugees and freedmen, who have escaped from the Southern States, and if Indiana has a commissioner appointed to her, and if in each county of Indiana there be a sub-commissioner at a salary of $1,500 a year, with two clerks with a salary of $1,200 each, and then the War Department throws over this little army of officers in the State of Indiana its protection, what does that mean? The people of Indiana have been ground hard under the military authority and power within the last three or four years, but it was hoped that when the war would be closed the military power would be withdrawn from the State. Under this bill it may be established permanently upon the people by a body of men protected by the military power of the Government. An officer is appointed to the State of Indiana to regulate contracts which are made between the white people and the colored people of that State, and because he holds this office, not military in its character, involving no military act whatever, the military throws over him its iron shield of protection. What does that mean? If this officer shall do a great wrong and out-rage to one of the people, and the wronged citizen appeals to the court for his redress and brings his suit for damages, does the protecting shield of the War Department prevent the prosecution of that suit and the recovery of a judgment? What is the protection that is thrown over this army of office-holders? Let it be explained.[15]

Senator Hendricks then proceeded to discuss the bill's effect on the sovereignty of the Northern States:

The most remarkable sections of the bill, however, are the seventh and eighth, and to those sections I will ask for the careful attention of Senators; for I think if we can pass those two sections, and make them law, then indeed this Government can do any thing. It will be useless to speak any longer of limitations upon the powers of the General Govern-ment; it will be idle to speak of the reserved power of the States; State rights and State power will have passed away if we can do what is proposed in the seventh and eighth sections of this bill. We propose, first, to legislate against the effects of "local law, ordi-nance, police, or other regulation;" then against "custom," and lastly, against "prejudice," and to provide that "if any of the civil rights or immunities belonging to white persons" are denied to any person of color, then that person shall be taken under the military juris-diction of the Government.... The section limits its operation to "any State or district in which the ordinary course of judicial proceeding has been interrupted by the rebellion." It will be difficult to say whether in the State of Indiana and Ohio the ordinary course of judicial proceeding has or has not been interrupted. We had some war in Indiana; we had a very great raid through that State and some fighting; and I presume that in some cases the proceedings of the courts were interrupted and the courts were unable to go on with their business, so that it might be said that even in some of the Northern States this provi-sion of the bill would be applicable. Suppose that it were applicable to the State of Indiana,

---

15. Thomas A. Hendricks, quoted by Barnes, *History of the Thirty-Ninth Congress*, pages 108-109, 112.

then every man in that State, who attempted to execute the constitution and laws of the State, would be liable for a violation of the law. We do not allow to colored people there, many civil rights and immunities which are enjoyed by the white people. It became the policy of the State in 1852 to prohibit the immigration of colored people into that State.... Under that constitutional provision, and the laws enacted in pursuance of it, a colored man coming into the State since 1852 can not acquire title to real estate, can not make certain contracts, and no negro man is allowed to intermarry with a white woman. These are civil rights that are denied, and yet this bill proposes, if they are still denied in any State whose courts have been interrupted by the rebellion, the military protection of the Government shall be extended over the person who is thus denied such civil rights or immunities.

The next section of the bill provides punishments where any of these things are done, where any right is denied to a colored man which under State law is allowed to a white man. The language is very vague, and it is very difficult to say what this section will mean. If it has as broad a construction as is attempted to be given to the second section of the constitutional amendment, I would not undertake to guess what it means. Any man who shall deny to any colored man any civil rights secured to white persons, shall be liable to be taken before the officers of this bureau and to be punished according to the provisions of this section. In the first place, now that peace is restored, now that there is no war, now that men are no longer under military rule, but are under civil rule, I want to know how such a court can be organized; how it is that the citizen may be arrested without indictment, and may be brought before the officers of this bureau and tried without jury, tried without the forms which the Constitution requires....

I regard it as a very dangerous legislation. It proposes to establish a government within a government — not a republic within a republic, but a cruel despotism within a republic. In times of peace, in communities that are quiet and orderly, and obedient to the law, it is proposed to establish a government not responsible to the people, the officers of which are not selected by the people, the officers of which need not be of the people governed — a government more cruel, more despotic, more dangerous to the liberties of the people than against which our forefathers fought in the Revolution. There is nothing that these men may not do, under this bill, to oppress the people.

I have not heard, since Congress met, that any colored man has done a wrong in this country for many years; and I have scarcely heard that any white man coming in contact with colored people has done right for a number of years. Every body is expected to take sides for the colored against the white man. If I have to take sides, it will be with men of my own color and my own race....[16]

Senator Burwell C. Ritter of Kentucky — also a Democrat — stated his belief that the authors of the bill intended to establish "a colony in each of the five States above named... ultimately to drive out the entire white population of those States and fill their places with the negro race...." and that "they could not have devised a more effectual scheme for that purpose." He went on:

---

16. Hendricks, quoted by Barnes, *ibid.*, pages 116-119.

Sir, it is not to be expected that the two races will live contentedly where there are large numbers of the colored people living near to neighborhoods settled with white persons. Experience has proved to many of us that wherever large numbers of colored people live, that the white people living within five or ten miles of the place becomes sufferers to a very large extent. Now, sir, if this should be the case (as I have no doubt it will) in the States in which you propose to establish these people, the whites and blacks will disagree to such an extent that, when people find that the colored people are permanently established, they will be compelled, in self defense, to seek a home somewhere else. No doubt, Mr. Speaker, but that those who prepared this bill saw that the difficulties and disagreements to which I have just alluded would arise, and hence they require that military jurisdiction and protection shall be extended, so as to give safety in their movements; and if the white inhabitants become dissatisfied, the commissioner is prepared with authority by this bill to buy them out and put the negroes upon the land.[17]

When the bill was delivered to President Johnson, he promptly vetoed it:

The bill proposes to establish by authority of Congress military jurisdiction over all parts of the United States containing refugees and freedmen. It would by its very nature apply with most force to those parts of the United States in which the freedmen most abound, and it expressly extends the existing temporary jurisdiction of the Freedmen's Bureau, with greatly enlarged powers, over those States "in which the ordinary course of judicial proceedings has been interrupted by the rebellion." The source from which this military jurisdiction is to emanate is none other than the President of the United States, acting through the War Department and the Commissioner of the Freedmen's Bureau. The agents to carry out this military jurisdiction are to be selected either from the Army or from civil life; the country is to be divided into districts and sub-districts, and the number of salaried agents to be employed may be equal to the number of counties or parishes in all the United States where freedmen and refugees are to be found.

The subjects over which this military jurisdiction is to extend in every part of the United States include protection to "all employees, agents, and officers of this bureau in the exercise of the duties imposed" upon them by the bill; in eleven States it is further to extend over all cases affecting freedmen and refugees discriminated against "by local law, custom, or prejudice." In those eleven States the bill subjects any white person who may be charged with depriving a freedman of "any civil rights or immunities belonging to white persons" to imprisonment or fine, or both, without, however, defining the "civil rights and immunities" which are thus to be secured to the freedmen by military law. This military jurisdiction also extends to all questions that may arise respecting contracts. The agent who is thus to exercise the office of a military judge may be a stranger, entirely ignorant of the laws of the place, and exposed to the errors of judgment to which all men are liable. The exercise of power over which there is no legal supervision by so vast a number of agents as is contemplated by the bill must, by the very nature of man, be attended by acts of caprice, injustice, and passion.

---

17. Burwell C. Ritter, quoted by Barnes, *ibid.*, page 163.

The trials having their origin under this bill are to take place without the intervention of a jury and without any fixed rules of law or evidence. The rules on which offenses are to be "heard and determined" by the numerous agents are such rules and regulations as the President, through the War Department, shall prescribe. No previous presentment is required nor any indictment charging the commission of a crime against the laws; but the trial must proceed on charges and specifications. The punishment will be, not what the law declares, but such as a court-martial may think proper; and from these arbitrary tribunals there lies no appeal, no writ of error to any of the courts in which the Constitution of the United States vests exclusively the judicial power of the country.

While the territory and the classes of actions and offenses that are made subject to this measure are so extensive, the bill itself, should it become a law, will have no limitation in point of time, but will form a part of the permanent legislation of the country. I can not reconcile a system of military jurisdiction of this kind with the words of the Constitution which declare that "no person shall be held to answer for a capital or otherwise infamous crime unless on a presentment or indictment of a grand jury, except in cases arising in the land or naval forces, or in the militia when in actual service in time of war or public danger," and that "in all criminal prosecutions the accused shall enjoy the right to a speedy and public trial by an impartial jury of the State and district wherein the crime shall have been committed." The safeguards which the experience and wisdom of ages taught our fathers to establish as securities for the protection of the innocent, the punishment of the guilty, and the equal administration of justice are to be set aside, and for the sake of a more vigorous interposition in behalf of justice we are to take the risks of the many acts of injustice that would necessarily follow from an almost countless number of agents established in every parish or county in nearly a third of the States of the Union, over whose decisions there is to be no supervision or control by the Federal courts. The power that would be thus placed in the hands of the President is such as in time of peace certainly ought never to be intrusted to any one man.

Johnson further warned in his veto message that the bill would, "when put into complete operation, practically transfer the entire care, support, and control of 4,000,000 emancipated slaves to agents, overseers, or taskmasters, who, appointed at Washington, are to be located in every county and parish throughout the United States containing freedmen and refugees. Such a system would inevitably tend to a concentration of power in the executive which would enable him, if so disposed, to control the actions of this numerous class and use them for the attainment of his own political ends."[18] To put it bluntly, the ownership of the slaves was to be transferred from their Southern masters, from whom they had been confiscated, to the War Department of the U.S. Government where they would be held in perpetual bondage under a system of "military paternalism."[19]

---

18. Andrew Johnson, veto message to the Senate of the United States, 19 February 1866; quoted by Barnes, *ibid.*, pages 165-168.

19. Hummel, *Emancipating Slaves*, pages 318-319.

Without even pausing to discuss the compelling arguments against the bill, the Republican majority in Congress immediately passed it into law over the President's veto on 16 July 1866. As we will see in a later chapter, the military tribunals provided for in this bill, which were to operate under the President in his capacity as Commander-in-Chief, are still in place today, and, in fact, have completely supplanted constitutional courts throughout the country. Furthermore, the reader will clearly see here the origin of the modern American welfare State. In fact, the Freedmen's Bureau, thus set up under the jurisdiction of the War Department, appears to have been the precursor of today's Social Security Administration.[20]

The Civil Rights Act is Passed

The Freedmen's Bureau Act was followed by the Act of 9 April 1866, commonly called the Civil Rights Act, the purpose of which, according to the title, was "to protect all Persons in the United States in their Civil Rights, and furnish the Means of their Vindication." Section One read as follows:

> Be it enacted by the Senate and House of Representatives of the United States of America in Congress assembled,
> That all persons born in the United States and not subject to any foreign power, excluding Indians not taxed, are hereby declared to be citizens of the United States; and such citizens, of every race and color, without regard to any previous condition of slavery or involuntary servitude, except as a punishment for crime whereof the party shall have been duly convicted, shall have the same right, in every State and Territory in the United States, to make and enforce contracts, to sue, be parties, and give evidence, to inherit, purchase, lease, sell, hold, and convey real and personal property, and to full and equal benefit of all laws and proceedings for the security of person and property, as is enjoyed by white citizens, and shall be subject to like punishment, pains, and penalties, and to none other, any law, statute, ordinance, regulation, or custom, to the contrary notwithstanding.[21]

The additional Act of 16 July 1866 provided for the President, through the commissioner and officers of the Freedmen's Bureau, to exercise military jurisdiction over all cases and questions concerning the enjoyment of these "civil rights" by the former slaves.[22] This Act was based on the empowerment clause of the preceding Thirteenth Amendment, which gave to Congress the exclusive discretion to decide what was "appropriate legislation" for carrying out the provisions of the amendment, thereby rendering any subsequent congressional action regarding the Negro a "political question" upon which no court had the power to adjudicate.

---

20. See Chapter Twenty-Three.

21. Statutes at Large, Volume XIV, page 27.

22. *Ibid.*, page 173.

Again, a few voices, of which all but one were Democrats, were raised in Congress against the extension of citizenship to the Blacks. Senator Garrett Davis of Kentucky said:

> There never was a colony before the Declaration of Independence, and there never was a State after the Declaration of Independence, up to the time of the adoption of the Constitution, so far as I have been able to learn by the slight historical examination which I have given to the subject, that ever made or attempted to make any other person than a person who belonged to one of the nationalities of Europe a citizen. I invoke the chairman of the committee to give me an instance, to point to any history or any moment, where a negro, although that negro was born in America, was ever made a citizen of either of the States of the United States before the adoption of this Constitution. The whole material out of which citizens were made previous to the adoption of the present Constitution was from the European nationalities, from the Caucasian race, if I may use the term. I deny that a single citizen was ever made by one of the States out of the negro race. I deny that a single citizen was ever made by one of the States out of the Mongolian race. I controvert that a single citizen was ever made out of the Chinese race, out of the Hindoos, or out of any race of people but the Caucasian race of Europe.
>
> I come, then, to this position: that whenever the States, after the Declaration of Independence and before the present Constitution was adopted, legislated in relation to citizenship, or acted in their governments in relation to citizenship, the subject of that legislation or that action was the Caucasian race of Europe; that none of the inferior races of any kind were intended to be embraced or were embraced by this work of Government in manufacturing citizens....
>
> Government is a political partnership. No persons but the partners who formed the partnership are parties to the government. Here is a government formed by the white man alone. The negro was excluded from the formation of our political partnership; he had nothing to do with it; he had nothing to do in its formation.[23]

Senator Andrew J. Rogers of New Jersey protested against the bill as follows:

> This act of legislation would destroy the foundations of the Government as they were laid and established by our fathers, who reserved to the States certain privileges and immunities which ought sacredly to be preserved to them.
>
> If you had attempted to do it in the days of those who were living at the time the Constitution was made, after the birth of that noble instrument, the spirit of the heroes of the Revolution and the ghosts of the departed who laid down their lives in defense of the liberty of this country and of the rights of the States, would have come forth as witnesses against the deadly infliction and the destruction of the fundamental principle of the sovereignty of the States in violation of the Constitution, and the breaking down of the ties that bind the States, and the violation of the rights and liberties of the white men and women of America.

---

23. Garrett Davis, quoted by Barnes, *History of the Thirty-Ninth Congress*, pages 199, 202.

If you pass this bill, you will allow the negroes of this country to compete for the high office of President of the United States. Because if they are citizens at all, they come within the meaning and letter of the Constitution of the United States, which allows all natural-born citizens to become candidates for the Presidency, and to exercise the duties of that office if elected.

I am afraid of degrading this Government; I am afraid of the danger to constitutional liberty; I am alarmed at the stupendous strides which this Congress is trying to initiate; and I appeal in behalf of my country, in behalf of those that are to come after us, in generations yet unborn, as well as those now living, that conservative men on the other side should rally to the standard of sovereign and independent States, and blot out this idea which is inculcating itself here, that all the power of the States must be taken away, and the power of the Czar of Russia or the Emperor of France must be lodged in the Federal Government.

I ask you to stand by the law of the country, and to regulate these Federal and State systems upon the grand principles upon which they were intended to be regulated, that we may hand down to those who are to come after us this bright jewel of civil liberty unimpaired; and I say that the Congress or the men who will strip the people of these rights will be handed down to perdition for allowing this bright and beautiful heritage of civil liberty embodied in the powers and sovereign jurisdiction of the States to pass away from us.[24]

Senator Willard Saulsbury of Delaware perceived the bill as part of a political revolution which would inaugurate the bloodshed and horrors of a new civil war:

In my judgment the passage of this bill is the inauguration of revolution — bloodless, as yet, but the attempt to execute it by the machinery and in the mode provided in the bill will lead to revolution in blood. It is well that the American people should take warning in time and set their house in order, but it is utterly impossible that the people of this country will patiently entertain and submit to this great wrong. I do not say this because I want a revolution; Heaven knows we have had enough of bloodshed; we have had enough of strife; there has been enough of mourning in every household; there are too many new-made graves on which the grass has not yet grown for any one to wish to see the renewal of strife; but, sir, attempt to execute this act within the limits of the States of this Union, and, in my judgment, this country will again be plunged into all the horrors of civil war.[25]

Senator James McDougall of California, the only Republican voice raised in opposition to the bill, agreed with Senator Saulsbury regarding the revolutionary nature of the bill:

I agree with the Senator from Delaware that this measure is revolutionary in its character. The majority glory in their giant power, but they ought to understand that it is tyrannous to exercise that power like a giant. A revolution now is moving onward; it has

---

24. Andrew J. Rogers, quoted by Barnes, *ibid.*, pages 222-223.

25. Willard Saulsbury, quoted by Barnes, *ibid.*, page 287.

its center in the Northeast. A spirit has been radiating out from there for years past as revolutionary as the spirit that went out from Charleston, South Carolina, and perhaps its consequences will be equally fatal, for when that revolutionary struggle comes it will not be a war between the North and its power and the slaveholding population of the South; it will be among the North men themselves....[26]

Not surprisingly, these protestations and warnings were ignored by the Radical Republican majority, who had just fought a war against "the fundamental principle of the sovereignty of the States," and the bill passed in both houses of Congress and was delivered to the President for his signature. Johnson again promptly vetoed the bill, giving his reasons for doing so in his message of 27 March 1866:

> I regret that the bill which passed both houses of Congress, entitled "An act to protect all persons in the United States in their civil rights, and furnish the means for their vindication," contains provisions which I can not approve, consistently with my sense of duty to the whole people and my obligations to the Constitution of the United States. I am therefore constrained to return it to the Senate, the house in which it originated, with my objections to its becoming a law....
>
> In all our history, in all our experience as a people living under Federal and State law, no such system as that contemplated by the details of this bill has ever before been proposed or adopted. They establish, for the security of the colored race, safeguards which go infinitely beyond any that the General Government has ever provided for the white race. In fact, the distinction of race and color is, by the bill, made to operate in favor of the colored and against the white race. They interfere with the municipal legislation of the States, with the relations existing exclusively between a State and its citizens, or between inhabitants of the same State — an absorption and assumption of power by the General Government which, if acquiesced in, must sap and destroy our federative system of limited powers, and break down the barriers which preserve the rights of the States. It is another step, or rather stride, to centralization and the concentration of all legislative power in the National Government. The tendency of the bill must be to resuscitate the spirit of rebellion, and to arrest the progress of those influences which are more closely drawing around the States the bonds of union and peace.[27]

Drunk with power and filled with hatred for the White Southerner, the Radical majority once again passed the bill into law over Johnson's veto. The destruction of State sovereignty was nearing completion.

---

26. James McDougall, quoted by Barnes, *ibid.*, pages 287-288.

27. Johnson, veto message of 27 March 1866; in Richardson, *Messages and Papers of the Presidents*, Volume VIII, pages 3603, 3610-3611.

The Inferior Nature of Federal Civil Rights

It should be noted that the enjoyment of rights by "white citizens" was spoken of in the Civil Rights Act as a pre-existing condition. This historical fact could not be denied, even by the Radical Republicans during Reconstruction. From the moment of their independence from Great Britain, the former subjects of the English Crown became Citizens endowed with the right of self-government, and as such, they were viewed by law as "joint tenants in the sovereignty" possessed by their respective States.[28] The rights naturally possessed by the American people were described as "unalienable"[29] in the Declaration of Independence. Not only was it impossible for Congress, being a mere agent of the people of the States, to ascribe rights to the sovereign, but it was permanently prevented by the first ten Amendments to the Constitution from lawfully regulating or otherwise interfering with the enjoyment of these rights in any way. There was no need whatsoever of enacting a statute to protect Citizens in the free exercise of their rights, for such protection was already written into the body of the Constitution at Article IV, Section 2, which is known as the "Comity Clause": "The Citizens of each State shall be entitled to all Privileges and Immunities of Citizens in the several States."

Quite unlike a *natural* or *inalienable* right, a *civil* right is "a right given and protected by law, and a person's enjoyment thereof is regulated entirely by the law that creates it."[30] The source of the "civil rights" granted to the freedmen was not the Common Law which had been brought to this continent by the first European settlers, but the President's nearly unlimited, and wholly unconstitutional "war power" — martial law. The Republicans' assertion that the Civil Rights Act would elevate the "persons" mentioned therein to the same political status enjoyed by White State Citizens, or that such statutory units could ever be incorporated into the sovereign people of the States was a poorly concealed ruse, for it is impossible for a conferred and artificial status to ever be equal to a natural and original status. Justice Taney's observation in the *Scott v. Sandford* decision was therefore vindicated by the Radicals themselves — that Blacks in America were historically and legally viewed as "a subordinate and inferior class of beings, who had been subjugated by the dominant race, and, whether emancipated or not, yet remained subject to their authority, and had no rights or privileges but such as those who held the power and the Government might choose to grant them."

---

28. *Chisholm v. Georgia* (1793), 2 U.S. 419, 471-472, 1 L.Ed. 440, 463.

29. "Unalienable. Inalienable; incapable of being aliened, that is, sold and transferred.... Rights which can never be abridged because they are so fundamental" (*Black's Law Dictionary* [Sixth Edition], page 1523).

30. *Nickell v. Rosenfield* (1927), 82 Cal. App. 369, 375; 255 P. 760.

SUPPORTING DOCUMENT
Andrew Johnson's Veto of the Freedmen's Bureau Bill

Washington, D.C.
February 19, 1866

To the Senate of the United States:

I have examined with care the bill which originated in the Senate, and has been passed by the two houses of Congress, to amend an act entitled "An act to establish a Bureau for the relief of Freedmen and Refugees," and for other purposes. Having, with much regret, come to the conclusion that it would not be consistent with the public welfare to give my approval to the measure, I return the bill to the Senate with my objections to its becoming a law.

I might call to mind, in advance of these objections, that there is no immediate necessity for the proposed measure. The act to establish a Bureau for the relief of Freemen and Refugees, which was approved in the month of March last, has not yet expired. It was thought stringent and extensive enough for the purpose in view in time of war. Before it ceases to have effect, further experience may assist to guide us to a wise conclusion as to the policy to be adopted in time of peace.

I share with Congress the strongest desire to secure to the freedmen the full enjoyment of their freedom and property, and their entire independence and equality in making contracts for their labor; but the bill before me contains provisions which, in my opinion, are not warranted by the Constitution, and are not well suited to accomplish the end in view.

The bill proposes to establish by authority of Congress, military jurisdiction over all parts of the United States containing refugees and freedmen. It would, by its very nature, apply with most force to those parts of the United States in which the freedmen most abound; and it expressly extends the existing temporary jurisdiction of the Freeman's Bureau, with greatly enlarged powers, over those States "in which the ordinary course of judicial proceeding, has been interrupted by the rebellion." The source from which this military jurisdiction is to emanate is none other than the President of the United States, acting through the War Department and the commissioner of the Freedmen's Bureau. The agents to carry out this military jurisdiction are to be selected either from the army or from civil life; the country is to be divided into districts and sub-districts; and the number of salaried agents to be employed may be equal to the number of counties or parishes in all the United States where freedmen and refugees are to be found.

The subjects over which this military jurisdiction is to extend in every part of the United States include protection to "all employees, agents, and officers of this bureau in the exercise of the duties imposed" upon them by the bill. In eleven States it is further to extend over all cases affecting freedmen and refugees discriminated against "by local law, custom, or prejudice." In those eleven States the bill subjects any white person who may be charged with depriving a freedman of "any civil rights or immunities belonging to white persons" to imprisonment or fine, or both, without, however, defining the "civil rights and immunities" which are thus to be secured to the freedmen by military law. This military jurisdiction also extends to all questions that may arise respecting contracts. The agent who is thus to exercise the office of a military judge may be a stranger, entirely ignorant of the laws of the place, and exposed to the errors of judgment to which all men are liable. The exercise of power, over which there is no legal supervision, by so vast a number of agents as is contemplated by the bill, must, by the very nature of man, be attended by acts of caprice, injustice, and passion.

The trials, having their origin under this bill, are to take place without the intervention of a jury, and without any fixed rules of law or evidence. The rules on which offenses are to be "heard and determined" by the numerous agents, are such rules and regulations as the President, through the War Department, shall prescribe. No previous presentment is required, nor any indictment charging the commission of a crime against the laws; but the trial must proceed on charges and specifications. The punishment will be, not what the law declares, but such as a court-martial may think proper; and from these arbitrary tribunals there lies no appeal, no writ of error to any court in which the Constitution of the United States vests exclusively the judicial power of the country.

While the territory and the classes of actions and offenses that are made subject to this measure are so extensive, the bill itself, should it become a law, will have no limitation in point of time, but will form a part of the permanent legislation of the country. I can not reconcile a system of military jurisdiction of this kind with the words of the Constitution, which declare that "no person shall be held to answer for a capital or otherwise infamous crime unless upon a presentment or indictment of a grand jury, except in cases arising in the land and naval forces, or in the militia when in actual service in time of war or public danger," and that "in all criminal prosecutions the accused shall enjoy the right to a speedy and public trial, by an impartial jury of the State or district wherein the crime shall have been committed." The safeguards which the experience and wisdom of ages taught our fathers to establish as securities for the protection of the innocent, the punishment of the guilty, and the equal administration of justice, are to be set aside, and for the sake of a more vigorous interposition in behalf of justice, we are to take the risk of the many acts of injustice that would necessarily follow from an almost countless number of agents established in every parish and county in nearly a third of the States of the Union, over whose decisions there is to be no supervision or control by the Federal courts. The power that would be thus placed in the hands of the President is such as in time of peace certainly ought never to be intrusted to any one man.

If it be asked whether the creation of such a tribunal within a State is warranted as a measure of war, the question immediately presents itself whether we are still engaged in war. Let us not unnecessarily disturb the commerce and credit and industry of the country by declaring to the American people and to the world, that the United States are still in a condition of civil war. At present there is no part of our country in which the authority of the United States is disputed. Offenses that may be committed by individuals should not work a forfeiture of the rights of whole communities. The country has returned, or is returning, to a state of peace and industry, and the rebellion is in fact at an end. The measure, therefore, seems to be as inconsistent with the actual condition of the country as it is at variance with the Constitution of the United States.

If, passing from general considerations, we examine the bill in detail, it is open to weighty objections.

In time of war it was eminently proper that we should provide for those who are passing suddenly from a condition of bondage to a state of freedom. But this bill proposes to make the Freedmen's Bureau, established by the act of 1865 as one of the many great and extraordinary military measures to suppress a formidable rebellion, a permanent branch of the public administration, with its powers greatly enlarged. I have no reason to supposed, and I do not understand it to be alleged, that the act of March, 1865, has proved deficient for the purpose for which it was passed, although at that time, and for a considerable period thereafter, the Government of the United States remained unacknowledged in most of the States whose inhabitants had been involved in the rebellion. The institution of slavery, for the military destruction of which the Freedmen's Bureau was called into existence as an auxiliary, has been already effectually and finally abrogated throughout the whole country by an amendment of the Constitution of the United States, and practically its eradication has received the assent and concurrence of most of those States in which it at any time had an existence. I am not, therefore, able to discern, in the condition of the country, any thing to justify an apprehension that the powers and agencies of the Freedmen's Bureau, which were effective for the protection of freedmen and refugees during the actual continuance of hostilities and of African servitude, will now, in a time of peace and after the abolition of slavery, prove inadequate to the same proper ends. If I am correct in these views, there can be no necessity for the enlargement of the powers of the bureau, for which provision is made in the bill.

The third section of the bill authorizes a general and unlimited grant of support to the destitute and suffering refugees and freedmen, their wives and children. Succeeding sections make provision for the rent or purchase of landed estates for freedmen, and for the erection for their benefit of suitable buildings for asylums and schools, the expense to be defrayed from the Treasury of the whole people. The Congress of the United States has never heretofore thought itself empowered to establish asylums beyond the limits of the District of Columbia, except for the benefit of our disabled soldiers and sailors. It has never founded schools for any class of our own people, not even for the orphans of those who have fallen in the defense of the Union; but has left the care of education to the much more competent and efficient control of the States, of communities, of private associations, and of individuals. It has never deemed itself authorized to expend the public money for the rent or purchase of homes for the thousands, not to say millions, of the white race, who are honestly toiling from day to day for their subsistence. A system for the support of indigent persons in the United States was never contemplated by the authors of the Constitution, nor can any good reason be advanced why, as a permanent establishment, it should be founded for one class or color of our people more than another. Pending the war, many refugees and freedmen received support from the Government, but it was never intended that they should thenceforth be fed, clothed, educated, and sheltered by the United States. The idea on which the slaves were assisted to freedom was that, on becoming free, they would be a self-sustaining population. Any legislation that shall imply that they are not expected to attain a self-sustaining condition must have a tendency injurious alike to their character and their prospects.

The appointment of an agent for every county and parish will create an immense patronage; and the expense of the numerous officers and their clerks, to be appointed by the President, will be great in the beginning, with a tendency steadily to increase. The appropriations asked by the Freedmen's Bureau, as now established, for the year 1866, amount to $11,745,000. It may be safely estimated that the cost to be incurred under the pending bill will require double that amount — more than the entire sum expended in any one year under the administration of the second Adams. If the presence of agents in every parish and county is to be considered as a war measure, opposition, or even resistance, might be provoked, so that, to give effect to their jurisdiction, troops would have to be stationed within reach of every one of them, and thus a large standing force be rendered necessary. Large appropriations would therefore be required to sustain and enforce military jurisdiction in every county or parish from the Potomac to the Rio Grande. The condition of our fiscal affairs is encouraging, but, in order to sustain the present measure of public confidence, it is necessary that we practice not merely customary economy, but, as far as possible, severe retrenchment.

In addition to the objections already stated, the fifth section of the bill proposes to take away land from its former owners without any legal proceedings being first held, contrary to the provision of the Constitution which declares that no person shall "be deprived of life, liberty, or property, without due process of law." It does not appear that a part of the lands to which this section refers may not be owned by minors or persons of unsound mind, or by those who have been faithful to all their obligations as citizens of the United States. If any portion of the land is held by such persons, it is not competent for any authority to deprive them of it. If, on the other hand, it be found that the property is liable to confiscation, even then it can not be appropriated to public purposes until, by due process of law, it shall have been declared forfeited to the Government.

There is still further objection to the bill on grounds seriously affecting the class of persons to whom it is designed to bring relief; it will tend to keep the mind of the freedman in a state of uncertain expectation and restlessness, while to those among whom he lives will be a source of constant and vague apprehension.

Undoubtedly the freedman should be protected, but he should be protected by the civil authorities, especially by the exercise of all the constitutional powers of the courts of the United States and of the States. His condition is not so exposed as may at first be imagined. He is in a portion of the country where his labor can not well be spared. Competition for his services from planters, from those who are constructing or repairing railroads, and from capitalists in his vicinage or from other States, will enable him to command almost his own terms. He also possesses a perfect right to change his place of abode; and if, therefore, he does not find in one community or State a mode of life suited to his desires, or proper remuneration for his labor, he can move to another, where that labor is more esteemed and better rewarded. In truth, however, each State, induced by its own wants and interests, will do what is necessary and proper to retain within its borders all labor that is needed for the development of its resources. The laws that regulate supply and demand will retain their force, and the wages of the laborer will be regulated thereby. There is no danger that the exceedingly great demand for labor will not operate in favor of the laborer.

Neither is sufficient consideration given to the ability of the freedmen to protect and take care of themselves. It is no more than justice to them to believe that, as they have received their freedom with moderation and forbearance, so they will distinguish themselves by their industry and thrift, and soon show the world that, in a condition of freedom, they are self-sustaining, capable of selecting their own employment and their own places of abode, of insisting for themselves on a proper remuneration, and of establishing and maintaining their own asylums and schools. It is earnestly hoped that, instead of wasting away, they will, by their own efforts, establish for themselves a condition of respect, ability, and prosperity. It is certain that they can attain to that condition only through their own merits and exercise.

In this connection the query presents itself, whether the system proposed by the bill will not, when put into complete operation, practically transfer the entire care, support, and control of four million emancipated slaves to agents, overseers, or task-masters, who, appointed at Washington, are to be located in every county and parish throughout the United States containing freedmen and refugees? Such a system would inevitably tend to a concentration of power in the Executive which would enable him, if so disposed, to control the action of this numerous class and use them for attainment of his own political ends.

I can not but add another very grave objection to this bill: The Constitution imperatively declares, in connection with taxation, that each State shall have at least one Representative, and fixes the rule for the number to which, in future times, each State shall be entitled.

It also provides that the Senate of the United States shall be composed of two Senators from each State, and adds, with peculiar force, "that no State, without its consent, shall be deprived of its equal suffrage in the Senate." The original act was necessarily passed in the absence of the States chiefly affected, because their people were then contumaciously engaged in the rebellion. Now the case is changed, and some, at least, of those States are attending Congress by loyal Representatives, soliciting the allowance of the constitutional right of representation. At the time, however, of the consideration and the passing of this bill, there was no Senator or Representative in Congress from the eleven States which are to be mainly affected by its provisions. The very fact that reports were and are made against the good disposition of the people of that portion of the country is an additional reason why they need, and should have, Representatives of their own in Congress to explain their condition, reply to accusations, and assist, by their local knowledge, in the perfecting of measures immediately affecting themselves. While the liberty of deliberation would then be free, and Congress would have full power to decide according to its judgment, there could be no objection urged that the States most interested had not been permitted to be heard. The principle is firmly fixed in the minds of the American people that there should be no taxation without representation.

Great burdens have now to be borne by all the country, and we may best demand that they shall be borne without murmur when they are voted by a majority of the Representatives of the people. I would not interfere with the unquestionable right of Congress to judge, each house for itself, "of the elections, returns, and qualifications of its own members," but that authority can not be construed as including the right to shut out, in time of peace, any State from the representation to which it is entitled by the Constitution. At present, all the people of eleven States are excluded — those who were most faithful during the war not less than others. The State of Tennessee, for instance, whose authorities engaged in rebellion, was restored to all her constitutional relations to the Union by the patriotism and energy of her injured and betrayed people. Before the war was brought to a termination, they had placed themselves in relation with the General Government, had established a State government of their own; as they were not included in the Emancipation Proclamation, they, by their own act, had amended their constitution so as to abolish slavery within the limits of their State. I know no reason why the State of Tennessee, for example, should not fully enjoy "all her constitutional relations to the United States."

The President of the United States stands towards the country in a somewhat different attitude from that of any member of Congress. Each member of Congress is chosen from a single district or State; the President is chosen by the people of all the States. As eleven are not at this time represented in either branch of Congress, it would seem to be his duty, on all proper occasions, to present their just claims to Congress. There always will be differences of opinion in the community, and individuals may be guilty of transgressions of the law; but these do not constitute valid objections against the right of a State to representation. I would in nowise interfere with the discretion of Congress with regard to the qualifications of members; but I hold it my duty to recommend to you, in the interests of peace and in the interests of union, the admission of every State to its share in public legislation when, however insubordinate, insurgent, or rebellious its people may have been, it presents itself, not only in an attitude of loyalty and harmony, but in the persons of Representatives whose loyalty can not be questioned under any existing constitutional or legal test.

It is plain that an indefinite or permanent exclusion of any part of the country from representation must be attended by a spirit of disquiet and complaint. It is unwise and dangerous to pursue a course of measures which will unite a very large section of the country against another section of the country, however much the latter may preponderate. The course of emigration, the development of industry and business, and natural causes will raise up at the South men as devoted to the Union as those of any other part of the land. But if they are all excluded from Congress — if, in a permanent statute, they are declared not to be in full constitutional relations to the country — they may think they have cause to become a unit in feeling and sentiment against the Government. Under the political education of the American people, the idea is inherent and ineradicable that the consent of the majority of the whole people is necessary to secure a willing acquiescence in legislation.

The bill under consideration refers to certain of the States as though they had not "been fully restored in all their constitutional relations to the United States." If they have not, let us at once act together to secure that desirable end at the earliest possible moment. It is hardly necessary for me to inform Congress that, in my own judgment, most of these States, so far, at least, as depends upon their own action, have already been fully restored, and are to be deemed as entitled to enjoy their constitutional rights as members of the Union. Reasoning from the Constitution itself, and from the actual situation of the country, I feel not only entitled but bound to assume that, with the Federal courts restored, and those of the several States in the full exercise of their functions, the rights and interests of all classes of the people will, with the aid of the military in cases of resistance to the laws, be essentially protected against unconstitutional infringement or violation. Should this expectation unhappily fail — which I do not anticipate — then the Executive is already fully vested with the powers conferred by the act of March, 1865, establishing the Freedmen's Bureau, and hereafter, as heretofore, he can employ the land and naval forces of the country to suppress insurrection or to overcome obstructions to the laws.

In accordance with the Constitution, I return the bill to the Senate, in the earnest hope that a measure involving questions and interests so important to the country will not become a law unless, upon deliberate consideration by the people, it shall receive the sanction of an enlightened public judgment.

Andrew Johnson.

SUPPORTING DOCUMENT
Andrew Johnson's Veto of the Civil Rights Bill

Washington, D.C., March 27, 1866

To the Senate of the United States:

I regret that the bill which passed both houses of Congress, entitled "An act to protect all persons in the United States in their civil rights, and furnish the means for their vindication," contains provisions which I can not approve, consistently with my sense of duty to the whole people and my obligations to the Constitution of the United States. I am therefore constrained to return it to the Senate, the house in which it originated, with my objections to its becoming a law.

By the first section of the bill, all persons born in the United States, and not subject to any foreign power, excluding Indians not taxed, are declared to be citizens of the United States. This provision comprehends the Chinese of the Pacific States, Indians subject to taxation, the people called Gypsies, as well as the entire race designated as blacks, people of color, negroes, mulattoes, and persons of African blood. Every individual of those races, born in the United States, is by the bill made a citizen of the United States. It does not purport to declare or confer any other right of citizenship than Federal Citizenship. It does not purport to give these classes of person any status as citizens of States, except that which may result from their status as citizens of the United States. The power to confer the right of State citizenship is just as exclusively with the several States as the Power to confer the right of Federal Citizenship is with Congress.

The right of Federal Citizenship thus to be conferred on the several excepted races before mentioned is now, for the first time, proposed to be given by law. If, as is claimed by many, all persons who are native-born, already are, by virtue of the Constitution, citizens of the United States, the passage of this pending bill can not be necessary to make them such. If, on the other hand, such persons are not citizens, as may be assumed from the proposed legislation to make them such, the grave question presents itself, whether, when eleven of the thirty-six States are unrepresented in Congress, at this time it is sound policy to make our entire colored population and all other excepted classes citizens of the United States? Four millions of them have just emerged from slavery into freedom. Can it be reasonably supposed that they possess the requisite qualifications to entitle them to all privileges and immunities of citizens of the United States? Have the people of the several States expressed such a conviction? It may also be asked whether it is necessary that they should be declared citizens in order that they may be secured in the enjoyment of civil rights? Those rights proposed to be conferred by the bill are, by Federal as well as by State laws, secured to all domiciled aliens and foreigners even before the completion of the process of naturalization, and it may safely be assumed that the same enactments are sufficient to give like protection and benefits to those for whom this bill provides special legislation. Besides, the policy of the Government, from its origin to the present time, seems to have been that persons who are strangers to and unfamiliar with our institutions and our laws should pass through a certain probation, at the end of which, before attaining the coveted prize, they must give evidence of their fitness to receive and to exercise the rights of citizens as contemplated by the Constitution of the United States.

The bill, in effect, proposes a discrimination against large numbers of intelligent, worthy, and patriotic foreigners, and in favor of the negro, to whom after long years of bondage, the avenue of freedom and intelligence have now been suddenly opened. He must, of necessity, from his previous unfortunate condition of servitude, be less informed as to the nature and character of our institutions than he who coming from abroad, has to some extent at least, familiarized himself with the principles of a Government to which he voluntarily intrusts "life, liberty, and the pursuit of happiness." Yet it is now proposed by a single legislative enactment to confer the rights of citizens upon all persons of African descent, born within the extended limits of the United States, while persons of foreign birth, who make our land their home, must undergo a probation of five years, and can only then become citizens upon proof that they are of "good moral character, attached to the principles of the Constitution of the United States, and well disposed to the good order and happiness of the same."

The first section of the bill also contains an enumeration of the rights to be enjoyed by these classes, so made citizens, "in every State and Territory in the United States." These rights are, "To make and enforce contracts, to sue, be parties, and give evidence, to inherit, purchase, lease, sell, hold and convey real and personal property," and to have "full and equal benefit of all laws and proceedings for the security of persons and property as is enjoyed by white citizens." So, too, they are made subject to the same punishment, pains, and penalties in common with white citizens, and to none other. Thus a perfect equality of the white and black races is attempted to be fixed by Federal law, in every State of the Union, over the vast field of State jurisdiction covered by these enumerated rights. In no one of these can any

State ever exercise any power of discrimination between the different races.

In the exercise of State policy over matters exclusively affecting the people of each State, it has frequently been thought expedient to discriminate between the two races. By the statutes of some of the States, Northern as well as Southern, it is enacted, for instance, that no white person shall intermarry with a negro or mulatto. Chancellor Kent says, speaking of the blacks, that "marriages between them and whites are forbidden in some of the States where slavery does not exist, and they are prohibited in all slaveholding States, and when not absolutely contrary to law, they are revolting, and regarded as an offense against public decorum."

I do not say this bill repeals State laws on the subject of marriage between the two races, for as the whites are forbidden to intermarry with the blacks, the blacks can only make such contracts as the whites themselves are allowed to make, and therefore can not, under this bill, enter into the marriage contract with the whites. I cite this discrimination, however, as an instance of the State policy as to discrimination, and to inquire whether if Congress can abrogate all State laws of discrimination between the two races in the matter of real estate, of suits, and of contracts generally, Congress may not also repeal the State laws as to the contract of marriage between the two races? Hitherto every subject embraced in the enumeration of rights contained in this bill has been considered as exclusively belonging to the States. They all relate to the internal policy and economy of the respective States. They are matters which in each State concern the domestic condition of its people, varying in each according to its own peculiar circumstances, and the safety and well-being of its own citizens. I do not mean to say that upon all these subjects there are not Federal restraints, as, for instance, in the State power of legislation over contracts, there is a Federal limitation that no State shall pass a law impairing the obligations of contracts; and as to crimes, that no State shall pass an *ex post facto* law; and as to money, that no State shall make any thing but gold and silver a legal tender. But where can we find a Federal prohibition against the power of any State to discriminate, as do most of them, between aliens and citizens, between artificial persons called corporations and natural persons, in the right to hold real estate?

If it be granted that Congress can repeal all State laws discriminating between whites and blacks, in the subjects covered by this bill, why, it may be asked, may not Congress repeal in the same way all State laws discriminating between the two races on the subject of suffrage and office? If Congress can declare by law who shall hold lands, who shall testify, who shall have capacity to make a contract in a State, then Congress can by law also declare who, without regard to color or race, shall have the right to sit as a juror or as a judge, to hold office, and, finally, to vote, "in every State and Territory of the United States." As respects the Territories, they come within the power of Congress, for, as to them the law-making power is the Federal power; but as to the States, no similar provisions exist, vesting in Congress the power "to make rules and regulations" for them.

The object of the second section of the bill is to afford discriminating protection to colored persons in the full enjoyment of all the rights secured to them by the previous section. It declares "that any person who, under color of any law, statute, ordinance, regulation, or custom, shall subject, or cause to be subjected, any inhabitant of any State or Territory to the deprivation of any right secured or protected by this act, or to different punishment, pains, or penalties on account of such person having at one time been held in a condition of slavery or involuntary servitude, except as a punishment for crime whereof the party shall have been duly convicted, or by reason of his color or race, than is prescribed for the punishment of white persons, shall be deemed guilty of a misdemeanor, and, on conviction, shall be punished by fine not exceeding $1,000, or by imprisonment not exceeding one year, or both, in the direction of the court." This section seems to be designed to apply to some existing or future law of a State or Territory which may conflict with the provisions of the bill now under consideration. It provides for counteracting such forbidden legislation by imposing fine and imprisonment upon the legislators who may pass such conflicting laws, or upon such officers or agents who shall put, or attempt to put, them into execution. It means an official offense, not a common crime committed against law upon the persons or property of the black race. Such an act may deprive the black man of his property, but not of the right to hold property. It means a deprivation of the right itself, either by the State Judiciary or the State Legislature. It is therefore assumed that, under this section, members of State Legislatures who should vote for laws conflicting with the provisions of the bill; that judges of the State courts who should render judgments in antagonism with its terms; and that marshals and sheriffs, who should, as ministerial officers, execute process, sanctioned by State laws and issued by State judges, in execution of their judgments, could be brought before other tribunals, and there subjected to fine and imprisonment for the performance of the duties which State laws might impose.

Legislation thus proposed invades the judicial power of the State. It says to every State court or judge, If you decide that this act is unconstitutional; if you refuse, under the prohibition of a State law, to allow a negro to testify; if you hold that over such a subject-matter the State law is paramount, and "under color" of a State law refuse the exercise of the right to the negro, your error of judgment, however conscientious, shall subject you to fine and imprisonment. I do not apprehend that the conflicting legislation which the bill seems to contemplate is so likely to occur as to render it necessary at this time to adopt a measure of such doubtful constitutionality.

In the next place, this provision of the bill seems to be unnecessary, as adequate judicial remedies could be adopted to secure the desired end without invading the immunities of legislators, always important to be preserved in the interest of public liberty; without assailing the independence of the judiciary, always essential to the preservation of individual rights; and without impairing the efficiency of ministerial officers, always necessary for the maintenance of public peace and order. The remedy proposed by this section seems to be, in this respect, not only anomalous, but unconstitutional; for the Constitution guarantees nothing with certainty, if it does not insure to the several States the right of making and executing laws in regard to all matters arising within their jurisdiction, subject only to the restriction that, in cases of conflict with the Constitution and constitutional laws of the United States, the latter should be held to be the supreme law of the land.

The third section gives the district courts of the United States exclusive "cognizance of all crimes and offenses committed against the provisions of this act," and concurrent jurisdiction with the circuit courts of the United States of all civil and criminal cases "affecting persons who are denied or can not enforce in the courts or judicial tribunals of the State or locality where they may be any of the rights secured to them by the first section." The construction which I have given to the second section is strengthened by this third section, for it makes it clear what kind of denial or deprivation of the rights secured by the first was in contemplation. It is a denial or deprivation of such rights "in the courts or judicial tribunals of the State." It stands, therefore, clear of doubt, that the offense and the penalties provided in the second section are intended for the State judge, who, in the clear exercise of his function as a judge, not acting ministerially, but judicially, shall decide contrary to this Federal law. In other words, when a State judge, acting upon a question involving a conflict between a State law and a Federal law, and bound, according to his own judgment and responsibility, to give an impartial decision between the two, comes to the conclusion that the State law is valid and the Federal law is invalid, he must not follow the dictates of his own judgment, at the peril of fine and imprisonment. The legislative department of the Government of the United States thus takes from the judicial department of the States the sacred and exclusive duty of judicial decision, and converts the State judge into a mere ministerial officer, bound to decree according to the will of Congress.

It is clear that, in those States which deny to persons whose rights are secured by the first section of the bill any one of those rights, all criminal and civil cases affecting them will, by the provisions of the third section, come under the exclusive cognizance of the Federal tribunals. It follows that if, in any State which denies to a colored person any one of those rights, that person should commit a crime against the laws of the State — murder, arson, rape, or any other crime — all protection and punishment through the courts of the State are taken away, and he can only be tried and punished in the Federal courts. How is the criminal to be tried? If the offense is provided for and punished by Federal law, that law, and not the State law, is to govern.

It is only when the offense does not happen to be within the purview of the Federal law that the Federal courts are to try and punish him under any other law; then resort is to be had to "the common law, as modified and changed" by State legislation, "so far as the same is not inconsistent with the Constitution and laws of the United States." So that over this vast domain of criminal jurisprudence, provided by each State for the protection of its own citizens, and for the punishment of all persons who violate its criminal laws, Federal law, wherever it can be made to apply, displaces State law.

The question here naturally arises, from what source Congress derives the power to transfer to Federal tribunals certain classes of cases embraced in this section? The Constitution expressly declares that the judicial power of the United States "shall extend to all cases in law and equity arising under this Constitution, the laws of the United States, and treaties made, or which shall be made, under their authority; to all cases affecting ambassadors, other public ministers, and consuls; to all cases of admiralty and maritime jurisdiction; to controversies to which the United States shall be a party; to controversies between two or more States, between a State and citizens of another State, between citizens of different States, between citizens of the same State claiming land under grants of different States, and between a State, or the citizens thereof, and foreign States, citizens, or subjects."

Here the judicial power of the United States is expressly set forth and defined; and the act of September 24, 1789, establishing the judicial courts of the United States, in conferring upon the Federal courts jurisdiction over cases originating in State tribunals, is careful to confine them to the classes enumerated in the above recited clause of the Constitution. This section of the bill undoubtedly comprehends cases, and authorizes the exercise of powers that are not, by the Constitution, within the jurisdiction of the courts of the United States. To transfer them to those courts would be an exercise of authority well calculated to excite distrust and alarm on the part of all the States; for the bill applies alike to all of them — as well to those that have as to those that have not been engaged in rebellion.

It may be assumed that this authority is incident to the power granted to Congress by the Constitution, as recently amended, to enforce, by appropriate legislation, the article declaring that "neither slavery nor involuntary servitude, except as punishment for crime whereof the party shall have been duly convicted, shall exist within the United States, or any place subject to their jurisdiction." It can not, however, be justly claimed that, with a view to the enforcement of this article of the Constitution, there is, at present, any necessity for the exercise of all the powers which this bill confers.

Slavery has been abolished, and, at present, nowhere exists within the jurisdiction of the United States; nor has there been, nor is it likely there will be, any attempt to revive it by the people of the States. If, however, any such attempt shall be made, it will then become the duty of the General Government to exercise any and all incidental powers necessary and proper to maintain inviolate this great constitutional law of freedom.

The fourth section of the bill provides that officers and agents of the Freedmen's Bureau shall be empowered to make arrests, and also that other officers may be specially commissioned for that purpose by the President of the United States. It also authorizes circuit courts of the United States and the superior courts of the Territories to appoint, without limitation, commissioners, who are to be charged with the performance of *quasi* judicial duties. The fifth section empowers the commissioners so to be selected by the courts to appoint, in writing, under their hands, one or more suitable persons, from time to time, to execute warrants and other processes described by the bill. These numerous official agents are made to constitute a sort of police, in addition to the military, and are authorized to summon a *posse comitatus* and even to call to their aid such portion of the land and naval forces of the United States, or of the militia, "as may be necessary to the performance of the duty with which they are charged."

This extraordinary power is to be conferred upon agents irresponsible to the Government and to the people, to whose number the discretion of the commissioners is the only limit, and in whose hands such authority might be made a terrible engine of wrong, oppression, and fraud. The general statutes regulating the land and naval forces of the United States, the militia, and the execution of the laws, are believed to be adequate for every emergency which can occur in time of peace. If it should prove otherwise, Congress can, at any time, amend those laws in such a manner as, while subserving the public welfare, not to jeopard the rights, interest, and liberties of the people.

The seventh section provides that a fee of ten dollars shall be paid to each commissioner in every case brought before him, and a fee of five dollars to his deputy, or deputies, "for each person he or they may arrest and take before any such commissioner," "with such other fees as may be deemed reasonable by such commissioner," "in general for performing such other duties as may be required in the premises." All these fees are to be "paid out of the Treasury of the United States," whether there is a conviction or not; but, in case of conviction, they are to be recoverable from the defendant. It seems to me that, under the influence of such temptations, bad men might convert any law, however beneficent, into an instrument of persecution and fraud.

By the eighth section of the bill, the United States courts, which sit only in one place for white citizens, must migrate, with the marshal and district attorney (and necessarily with the clerk, although he is not mentioned), to any part of the district, upon the order of the President, and there hold a court "for the purpose of the more speedy arrest and trial of persons charged with a violation of this act;" and there the judge and the officers of the court must remain, upon the order of the President, "for the time therein designated."

The ninth section authorizes the President, or such person as he may empower for that purpose, to employ such part of the land and naval forces of the United States, or of the militia, "as shall be necessary to prevent the violation and enforce the due execution of this act." This language seems to imply a permanent military force, that is to be always at hand, and whose only business is to be the enforcement of this measure over the vast region where it is to operate.

I do not propose to consider the policy of this bill. To me the details of the bill seem fraught with evil. The white race and the black race of the South have hitherto lived together under the relation of master and slave — capital owning labor. Now, suddenly, that relation is changed, and, as to the ownership, capital and labor are divorced. They stand, now, each master of itself. In this new relation, one being necessary to the other, there will be a new adjustment, which both are deeply interested in making harmonious. Each has equal power in settling the terms, and, if left to the laws that regulate capital and labor, it is confidently believed that they will satisfactorily work out the problem. Capital, it is true, has more intelligence; but labor is never so ignorant as not to understand its own interests, not to know its own value, and not to see that capital must pay that value. This bill frustrates this adjustment. It intervenes between capital and labor, and attempts to settle questions of political economy through the agency of numerous officials, whose interest it will be to foment discord between the two races; for, as the breach widens, their employment will continue, and when it is closed, their occupation will terminate.

In all our history, in all our experience as a people living under Federal and State law, no such system as that contemplated by the details of this bill has ever before been proposed or adopted. They establish, for the security of the colored race, safeguards which go infinitely beyond any that the General Government has ever provided for the white race. In fact, the distinction of race and color is, by the bill, made to operate in favor of the colored and against the white race. They interfere with the municipal legislation of the States, with the relations existing exclusively between a State and its citizens, or between inhabitants of the same State — an absorption and assumption of power by the General Government which, if acquiesced in, must sap and destroy our federative system of limited powers, and break down the barriers which preserve the rights of the States. It is another step, or rather stride, to centralization and the concentration of all legislative power in the National Government. The tendency of the bill must be to resuscitate the spirit of rebellion, and to arrest the progress of those influences which are more closely drawing around the States the bonds of union and peace.

My lamented predecessor, in his proclamation of the 1st of January, 1863, ordered and declared that all persons held as slaves within certain States and parts of States therein designated, were and thenceforward should be free; and, further, that the Executive Government of the United States, including the military and naval authorities thereof, would recognize and maintain the freedom of such persons. This guarantee has been rendered especially obligatory and sacred by the amendment of the Constitution abolishing slavery throughout the United States. I, therefore, fully recognize the obligation to protect and defend that class of our people whenever and wherever it shall become necessary, and to the full extent compatible with the Constitution of the United States.

Entertaining these sentiments, it only remains for me to say that I will cheerfully cooperate with Congress in any measure that may be necessary for the protection of the civil rights of the freedmen, as well as those of all other classes of persons throughout the United States, by judicial process under equal and impartial laws, in conformity with the provisions of the Federal Constitution.

I now return the bill to the Senate, and regret that, in considering the bills and joint resolutions — forty-two in number — which have been thus far submitted for my approval, I am compelled to withhold my assent from a measure that has received the sanction of both houses of Congress.

Andrew Johnson.

CHAPTER SEVENTEEN
The Social Effects of the War in the South

The Attitude of the Former Slave Holders

In 1904, Southern historian Thomas Nelson Page wrote:

> Among the chief problems which have vexed the country for the last century and threaten to give yet more trouble in the future, is what is usually termed "The Negro Question." To the South, it has been for nearly forty years the chief public question, overshadowing all others, and withdrawing her from due participation in the direction and benefit of the National Government. It has kept alive sectional feeling; has inflamed partisanship; distorted party policies; barred complete reconciliation; cost hundreds of millions of money, and hundreds if not thousands of lives, and stands ever ready, like Banquo's ghost, to burst forth even at the feast.[1]

The "Negro question" still has not been sufficiently answered to this day, a century after the above words were written. "Sectional feeling" and "inflamed partisanship" remain the rotten root from whence modern racial tensions have sprung, and are the storehouse from which the proponents of "political correctness" draw their strength and the weapons which they intend to use to eradicate all traces of Southern history and heritage from the public arena.

Foremost on the docket of public censure are the planters of the old South, who are alleged to have so maltreated the emancipated slaves among them that Radical Reconstruc-

---

1. Thomas Nelson Page, *The Negro: The Southerner's Problem* (New York: Charles Scribner's Sons, 1904), pages 3-4.

tion was rendered a practical necessity to save the Negroes from ultimate extinction. Horrific tales of widespread lynchings and otherwise oppressive acts by the Ku Klux Klan and other covert organizations in the South are often appealed to as conclusive evidence of the imputed guilt. However, the recorded eyewitness accounts of even the South's enemies do not, to any large degree, substantiate these charges. For example, in his December 1865 report to the Thirty-Ninth Congress, Republican Carl Schurz wrote:

> Instances of the most touching attachment of freedmen to their old masters and mistresses have come to my notice. To a white man whom they believe to be sincerely their friend, they cling with greater affection even than to one of their own race. By some northern speculators their confidence has been sadly abused.... Those who enjoy their confidence enjoy also their affection. Centuries of slavery have not been sufficient to make them the enemies of the white race. If in the future a feeling of mutual hostility should develop itself between the races, it will probably not be the fault of those who have shown such an inexhaustible patience under the most adverse and trying circumstances.[2]

In her book, *Memorials of a Southern Planter*, Susan Dabney Smedes wrote that, for the most part, the former slaves were "very quiet and serious and more obedient and kind than they had ever been known to be."[3] Rather than widening the social gap between the races, the hardships which the war had brought upon them both, had served instead to increase their mutual dependence upon and friendship with one another:

> Something of the beautiful loyalty in them which guarded the women and children with such zeal while husbands and fathers were fighting far away persisted in the early days of their freedom. Old slaves, with fruit and gobblers and game, would sneak into the house with an instinctive sense of delicacy and leave them in the depleted larder surreptitiously. Occasionally some of these loyal creatures, momentarily intoxicated with the breath of liberty, would roam down the road towards the towns only to return with child-like faith to the old plantation. But for the suggestions of soldiers and agitators, the former masters and slaves might easily have effected a social readjustment to their mutual benefit....[4]

As Claude G. Bowers pointed out, the Whites and Blacks of the South, existing before the war in the relation of master and slave, would have, if left to themselves, naturally adapted to their new post-war relation of employer and employee with little to no difficulty.

---

2. Carl Schurz, "Report on the Condition of the South," in *Senate Executive Document No. 2* (Thirty-Ninth Congress, First Session).

3. Susan Dabney Smedes, *Memorials of a Southern Planter* (Baltimore, Maryland: Cushings and Bailey, 1888), page 228.

4. Claude G. Bowers, *The Tragic Era: The Revolution After Lincoln* (New York: Blue Ribbon Books, 1940), page 47.

The Southern planters knew that their plight was the result of Northern interference and aggression, and therefore they bore no resentment to their former slaves. Conversely, having known the kindness and care of their former masters which was bestowed upon their people from birth through old age to death, the Blacks generally had no reason to have anything but feelings of affection toward the planters, and "would have turned for leadership to the native whites, who understood them best."[5] This social harmony, as we will see, would soon perish forever in the consuming fire of Northern Radicalism, kindled as it was in the fires of jealousy and sectional hatred.

A great many of the officers of the occupying U.S. military corroborated the above descriptions of the social relations among the planters and the freedmen. Major General John W. Turner, for instance, reported on the treatment of the Blacks in Virginia: "I do not think there is a general feeling of aggression towards the negroes. The more intelligent people there, those who have landed estates, need their labor. Being dependent upon them for labor, they see the necessity of employing them, and are disposed to get along with them.... Among the lower classes of the whites there is a spirit of aggression against the negro; they are disposed to ban the negro, to kick him and cuff him, and threaten him with what they will do as soon as the Yankees go away."[6] Major Benjamin C. Truman gave the same report of the conditions in Texas and Florida:

> I have thought all along there was a necessity for the Freedmen's Bureau, but there is not so much necessity for it now as there was, especially in Texas. Texas is, by all odds, doing better than any of the other States. I talked with all the delegates particularly about the freedmen, and I did not meet a delegate or gentleman who made any complaints of the negroes whatever. They said they were doing first-rate. A great many who had been real malicious secessionists were not so generous in talking about other matters as they were about the negroes. I went all over the Brazos and Trinity lands, and a great many planters were giving the negroes two-thirds of the crops. I did not see a negro abused or ill-treated throughout the whole State. Those who owned negroes treat them very well. There are some who did not own them who are not inclined to treat them so well, but everybody is treating them well, because they need their labor. It is their policy to treat them well, even if they are inclined to do otherwise. Free labor is a success in Texas. Most of the former slaves are with their former masters everywhere in the interior....
>
> The only reason why they [the freedmen] have been moving around so much is to assure themselves that they really do possess their freedom. The whites felt a little bitter towards them nine or ten months ago. Some of them maltreated them, and great fault was found with them everywhere; but after Christmas all that died away; they are all at work. The agents of the Freedmen's Bureau, unlike those in most of the other States, make no contracts for them, but leave them to do the best they can. The negroes are not getting less

---

5. Bowers, *ibid.*, page 198.

6. John W. Turner, testimony given on 23 January 1866; in *Joint Committee on Reconstruction*, Part II: Virginia, North Carolina, and South Carolina, pages 4-5.

than $20 a month in specie and found, anywhere in the State of Texas, and in some portions of the State they are getting two-thirds the cotton crop and half the corn crop. If the season is good, and the negroes continue to work as well as they are working now, there will be a larger crop of cotton made in Texas than in any other State, and the negroes will make more money than the whites.[7]

Elsewhere, Truman testified, "It is the former slave owners who are the best friends the negro has in the South — those who, heretofore, have provided for his mere physical comfort, generally with sufficient means, though entirely neglecting his best nature, while it is the 'poor whites' that are his enemies. It is from these that he suffers most."[8] General Joseph B. Kiddoo, stationed in Texas, likewise reported:

> The better class of planters, who were former slaveholders, are, as a general thing, disposed to deal fairly with them [the freedmen]... but there is a class of men commonly known in the States as "adventurers," small planters, traveling speculators, country store-keepers... swarming the planting regions like so many buzzards seeking for prey.... It is the lower class of people that have the most bitter and vulgar hatred of the negro. The more intelligent and liberal people consider the negro set free by the arbitration of arms, and hence have no animosity towards him; while the other class hold him personally responsible and treat him accordingly.[9]

The reason for this hostility of the poor Southern Whites toward the Blacks, while not to be condoned, is nevertheless easy to understand. It was precisely the same attitude which the laboring class of Whites in the North had always had towards free Negroes — that "the presence of negroes in large numbers tends to degrade and cheapen labor, and the people have been unwilling that the white laborer shall be compelled to compete for employment with the Negro."[10] Oddly enough, the "bitterest opponents of the negro... [were] the intensely radical loyalists"[11] — the men who had fought in the Northern army against the Southern Confederacy or who had otherwise opposed it. For example, Major General Clinton B. Fisk,

7. Benjamin C. Truman, testimony given on 5 April 1866; in *ibid.*, Part IV: Florida, Louisiana, and Texas, pages 138-139.

8. Truman, "Relative to the Condition of the Southern People and the States in Which the Rebellion Existed," *Senate Executive Document 43* (Thirty-Ninth Congress, First Session; 9 August 1866).

9. J.B. Kiddoo, "Treatment of the Negroes in Texas," Senate Executive Document No. 6 (Thirty-Ninth Congress, Second Session), page 144; cited in Walter L. Fleming, *Documentary History of Reconstruction* (The Arthur H. Clarke Company, 1907), page 79.

10. Thomas A. Hendricks, *Congressional Globe* (Thirty-Ninth Congress, First Session), page 2939.

11. Testimony of Major General Clinton B. Fisk, 30 January 1866; in *Joint Committee on Reconstruction*, Part I: Tennessee, page 112.

an officer of the Freedmen's Bureau stationed in east Tennessee where the pro-Union sentiment was the strongest, reported that "the opposition of the people to freedmen and justice to the negro" was so intense that "they need the protection of the government very much...." In contrast, "the largest and wealthiest planters of the old slaveholding population" in middle and western Tennessee "more cordially co-operated" with the Bureau's work in relation to the former slaves.[12]

After conducting a tour of the Southern States following the war, John Townsend Trowbridge of Connecticut noted that there was "more prejudice against color among the middle and poorer classes — the 'Union' men of the South, who owned few or no slaves — than among the planters who owned them by scores and hundreds."[13] It should be remembered that it was predominantly these loyalists who made up the reconstructed States under Lincoln's ten percent plan[14]; the former Confederates had been disfranchised by their inability to take the "Ironclad Oath" of loyalty to the U.S. Government prescribed in the Act of 2 July 1862. This oath required candidates for public office to swear that they had "never voluntarily borne arms against the United States, voluntarily given no aid, countenance, counsel, or encouragement to persons engaged in armed hostility to the National Government, neither sought nor accepted nor attempted to exercise the functions of any office whatever under authority or pretended authority in hostility to the United States, and never yielded a voluntary support to any pretended Government within the United States, hostile or inimical thereto." As stated by James G. Blaine, "[T]he men who had been waging war against the Government could not take this oath except by committing perjury and risking its pains and penalties."[15] There were indeed some, such as Alexander Stephens, who nevertheless took this oath with the expectation that it would later be challenged as unconstitutional,[16] but, for the most part, those who fought for four years for Southern independence, or had served in some official capacity in the government of one of the Confederate States or in that of the Confederacy itself, felt themselves unable to sacrifice their personal honor by participating in the new State governments. There were some, however, who had favored secession, but had never actively participated in the conflict, and many of these men took office following the war. According to Major Truman, "The secessionists all voted to abolish

12. Fisk, in *ibid*.

13. John Townsend Trowbridge, *The South: A Tour of its Battlefields and Ruined Cities* (Hartford, Connecticut: L. Stebbins, 1866), page 239.

14. On 8 December 1863, Lincoln issued a proclamation announcing that he would recognize as the true government of any of the Southern States, with the exception of Virginia, if ten percent of the 1860 voting population would take an oath of allegiance to the U.S. Government (Richardson, *Messages and Papers of the President*, Volume VI, page 213).

15. Blaine, *Twenty Years of Congress*, Volume II, page 88.

16. Blaine, *ibid*.

slavery. I was present at four conventions, and I found that to be the fact. The loyal men were very reluctant to vote to abolish slavery, and some who finally did vote for it told me that they had made a full estimate of their losses with a view of claiming compensation."[17]

The Passage of the "Black Codes" in the South

Contrary to James G. Blaine's charge that the official acts of the reconstituted Southern States relating to the freedmen were "inspired by a spirit of apparently irreconcilable hatred of the Union,"[18] these laws, which came to be known as the "Black Codes," were enacted by the same loyalists who only reluctantly voted to abolish slavery. Blaine continued:

> As soon as the Southern Legislatures assembled, it was made evident that their members disregarded, and even derided, the opinion of those who had conquered the Rebellion and held control of the Congress of the United States. If the Southern men had intended, as their one special and desirable aim, to inflame the public opinion of the North against them, they would have proceeded precisely as they did. They treated the negro, according to a vicious phrase which had at one time wide currency, "as possessing no rights which a white man was bound to respect." Assent to the Thirteenth Amendment to the Constitution of the United States was but a gross deception so long as they accompanied it with legislation which practically deprived the negro of every trace of liberty. That which was an offense in a white man was made a misdemeanor, a heinous crime, if committed by a negro. Both in the civil and criminal code his treatment was different from that to which the white man was subjected. He was compelled to work under a series of labor laws applicable only to his own race. The laws of vagrancy were so changed as, in many of their provisions, to apply only to him, and under their operation all freedom of movement and transit was denied. The liberty to sell his time at a fair market rate was destroyed by the interposition of apprentice laws. Avenues of usefulness and skill in which he might specially excel were closed against him lest he should compete with white men. In short his liberty in all directions was so curtailed that it was a bitter mockery to refer to him in the statutes as a "freedman." The truth was, that his liberty was merely of form and not of fact, and the slavery which was abolished by the organic law of a Nation was now to be revived by the enactments of a State.[19]

Blaine was either completely blinded by his own radical prejudice or he was willing to trifle with the facts. Either way, his statements are easily rebutted. In most cases, the codes in question were merely re-enactments of the vagrancy laws which were formerly in place in the South; in others they were nearly identical to the vagrancy laws even then enforced in

---

17. Truman, in *Report on Reconstruction*, Part IV, page 140.

18. Blaine, *Twenty Years of Congress*, Volume II, page 89.

19. Blaine, *ibid.*, pages 93-94.

the New England States, and, while applicable to both Whites and Blacks, they bore far more severe penalties for the former than the latter. For example, the following law was passed in Florida on 4 November 1865:

> That upon complaint made on oath before a justice of the peace, mayor, alderman, or intendant of police, or a judge of the circuit court, that any person able to work, or otherwise to support himself in a reputable way, is wandering or strolling about, or leading an idle, or profligate, or immoral course of life, to issue his warrant to the sheriff or any constable, commanding him to arrest the party accused and bring him before such justice of the peace or other officer, and if the said officer should be satisfied by the testimony of the guilt of the accused, the said officer shall require him to enter into bond, payable to the governor of Florida and his successors in office, in such sum as the said officer may prescribe, not to exceed five hundred dollars, with sufficient security, to be approved by said officer, for his good behavior and future industry for one year; and upon his failing or refusing to give such security, he shall be committed and indicted as a vagrant, and on conviction shall be punished by a fine not exceeding five hundred dollars, and imprisoned for time not exceeding twelve months, or by being sold for a term not exceeding twelve months, at the discretion of the court....[20]

There was nothing in this law which singled out Blacks or imposed upon them a heavier penalty than it did upon Whites found in violation of its provisions, nor was there anything unreasonable about its prohibitions against vagrancy and immoral conduct. Likewise, in Mississippi, a law was passed which prohibited those persons with no lawful employment or business from "unlawfully assembling themselves together, either in the day time or night time, and all white persons so assembling themselves with freedmen, free negroes or mulattoes, on terms of equality, or living in adultery or fornication with a freed woman."[21] Blaine's claim that "that which was an offense in a white man was made a misdemeanor, a heinous crime, if committed by a negro," is contradicted by the plain language of this law, which imposed much stricter penalties and higher fines upon Whites than it did upon Blacks. White offenders were to be punished with a $200 fine and six months imprisonment; for Black offenders, however, the penalty was only a $50 fine and ten days imprisonment with the added stipulation that should the fine not be paid within five days, the sheriff was authorized to "hire out said freedman, free Negro, or mulatto, to any person who will, for the shortest period of service, pay said fine." Even with this added provision, this law was not as severe as a similar one relating to vagrant Negroes which had been passed before the war in Illinois and had only recently been repealed. Other similar laws which were then in effect throughout the North prescribed prison sentences of ninety days to three years

20. An Ordinance on Vagrancy, adopted 4 November 1865; cited in *Joint Committee on Reconstruction*, Part IV: Florida, Louisiana, Texas, pages 32-33.

21. Henry, *Story of Reconstruction*, page 102.

for Negro vagrancy, and some went even further to add public flogging of vagrant Blacks and Mulattoes. The apprenticeship laws mentioned above by Blaine were also no different in substance from what had been enforced in such Northern States as New Jersey. The reader is encouraged to refer back to the section in Chapter Six which outlined, in greater detail, these Negro laws of the North.

Another law passed by the reconstituted Mississippi legislature prohibited Negroes from possessing firearms, engaging in riots, trespassing, malicious mischief, cruel treatment of animals, making seditious public speeches, engaging in insulting gestures or in lewd language or acts, preaching the Gospel without a license, selling liquor, or "committing any other misdemeanor."[22] Denying any feelings of bitterness toward the freedmen, the committee which drafted this law stated in its report, "While some of the proposed legislation may seem rigid and stringent to the sickly modern humanitarians, they can never disturb, retard, or embarrass the good and true, useful and faithful of either race."[23] Furthermore, Governor Benjamin G. Humphreys honestly believed that with the adoption of these laws, "we may secure the withdrawal of the Federal troops."[24] As the reader can see from the above examples, and many others too numerous to enumerate here, the intent of the so-called "Black Codes" was merely the preservation of social order in the Southern States, which is the most basic duty of any government. There was no malicious singling out of freedmen for maltreatment, and no general feeling of animosity evident on the face of these laws. If anything, these legislatures were guilty of completely misjudging the attitude of the Northern people and giving an erroneous prognostication of their reaction, which was instantaneous and furious. In the words of the Chicago *Tribune*, "We tell the white men in Mississippi that the men of the North will convert the State of Mississippi into a frog pond before they will allow such laws to disgrace one foot of soil in which the bones of our soldiers sleep and over which the flag of freedom waves."[25] The sleeping Republican beast was beginning to stir.

The Blacks Are Turned Against the Whites

The amicable relations between the planters and the former slaves began to rapidly deteriorate with the arrival of more and more emissaries from the North, particularly agents

22. Henry, *ibid.*, page 103.

23. Mississippi legislative committee report of 1865; quoted by William Archibald Dunning, *Studies in Southern History and Politics* (New York: Columbia University Press, 1914), page 144.

24. Benjamin G. Humphreys, message to the State Senate and House of Representatives, 20 November 1865; in *Report on Reconstruction*, Part III, page 183.

25. Chicago *Tribune*, 1 December 1865; quoted by James Wilford Garner, *Reconstruction in Mississippi* (New York: Macmillan Company, 1901), page 104.

of the Union League. This society had been organized in Philadelphia in November of 1862 to bolster the faltering war sentiment among the Northerners following the preliminary issuance of Lincoln's Emancipation Proclamation, and it had rapidly spread across the Northern States. During the war, the Union League "sent their agents to the South and distributed leaflets to the negroes, instructing them to outrage the women and children, to force the Confederate soldiers to come home for their protection."[26] After the war had ended, the League's unethical tactics had not substantially changed. Representative Fernando Wood of New York pointed out in an official Government report that "hatred of the white race was instilled into the minds of these ignorant people by every art and vile that bad men could devise...."[27] Harriet Beecher Stowe, authoress of *Uncle Tom's Cabin*, likewise noted with much chagrin, "Corrupt politicians are already beginning to speculate on them [the freedmen] as possible capital for their schemes, and to fill their poor heads with all sorts of vagaries."[28] These people, commonly referred to as "Carpetbaggers," immediately took up the task of turning the Negroes against the Whites and instilling in their minds utopian notions of political equality and future prosperity at the expense of their former masters. Through the literature of the Union League and by word of mouth, the freedmen were generally convinced that they would be re-enslaved if the Democratic party ever came back into power. They were also promised the elective franchise with "forty acres and a mule" as the reward for voting the Republican ticket,[29] and some enterprising Northern swindlers did a thriving business selling them colored pegs with which to stake off their chosen lots.[30] Claude Bowers explained:

> The first evidence that outside influences had been at work upon the freedmen was furnished in their bizarre notions of labor, that under freedom all system ceased. At all hours of the day they could be seen laying down their implements and sauntering singing from the fields. If freedom did not mean surcease from labor, where was the boon?...
> Very soon they were eschewing labor and flocking to army camps to be fed, and here they were told, with cruel malice, that the land they had formerly cultivated as slaves

26. Susan Lawrence Davis, *Authentic History of the Ku Klux Klan, 1865-1877* (New York: American Library Service, 1924), page 172.

27. Fernando Wood, *Alleged Ku Klux Outrages* (Washington, D.C.: U.S. Government Printing Office, 1971), page 5.

28. Harriet Beecher Stowe, in Charles Edward Stowe (editor), *The Life of Harriet Beecher Stowe Compiled from Her Letters and Journals* (Boston: Houghton, Mifflin and Company, 1889), page 395.

29. Henry T. Thompson, *Ousting the Carpetbagger From South Carolina* (Columbia, South Carolina: R.L. Bryan Company, 1927), page 17.

30. Walter L. Fleming, *Documents Relating to Reconstruction* (Morgantown, West Virginia: self-published, 1904), pages 44-45.

was to be given them. Accepting it seriously, some had actually taken possession and planted corn and cotton. The assurance was given them solemnly that when Congress met, the division would be made. Quite soon they would have it on the authority of Thaddeus Stevens. Convinced of the ultimate division, they could see no sense in settling down to toil for the meager wages the impoverished planters could afford to pay....

When military orders drove them from the camps, they flocked to villages, towns, and cities, where, in the summer of 1865, they lived in idleness and squalor, huddled together in shacks, and collecting in gangs at street corners and crossroads.... Freedom — it meant idleness, and gathering in noisy groups in the streets. Soon they were living like rats in ruined houses, in miserable shacks under bridges built with refuse lumber, in the shelter of ravines and in caves in the banks of rivers. Freedom meant throwing aside all marital obligations, deserting wives and taking new ones, and in an indulgence in sexual promiscuity that soon took its toll in the victims of consumption and venereal disease. Jubilant, and happy, the negro who had his dog and a gun for hunting, a few rags to cover his nakedness, and a dilapidated hovel in which to sleep, was in no mood to discuss work.[31]

The misguided freedmen were not the only ones who used the prostrate South as a stage upon which to practice open licentiousness. A correspondent from a Northern periodical called *The Nation* traced the origin of the growing labor and racial problems to the bad influence of the occupying Northern soldiers.[32] The young Negresses who gathered at the army camps were frequently raped by the soldiers. One citizen in Georgia wrote a scathing letter to General Sherman saying, "The negro girls for miles around are gathering to the camps and debauched. It surely is not the aim of those persons who aim at the equality of colors to begin the experiment with a whole race of whores."[33] On more than a few occasions, their former masters would intervene at the peril of their own lives to protect the Blacks from their Yankee assailants.[34]

As Claude Bowers noted, "It only remained for the Federal Government to drive the disarmed people to the verge of a new rebellion by stationing negro troops in the midst of their homes. Nothing short of stupendous ignorance, or brutal malignity, can explain the arming and uniforming of former slaves and setting them as guardians over the white men and their families."[35] In South Carolina, the atrocities committed by Negro soldiers were the

31. Bowers, *Tragic Era*, pages 48-49.

32. Bowers, *ibid.*, page 51.

33. C. Mildred Thompson, *Reconstruction in Georgia* (New York: Columbia University Press, 1915), page 138.

34. John Wallace, *Carpetbag Rule in Florida* (Jacksonville, Florida: Da Costa Printing and Publishing House, 1888), page 37.

35. Bowers, *Tragic Era*, page 52.

most numerous. At Chester, for instance, a gang of these uniformed Blacks clubbed and bayoneted an elderly man. At Charleston, another gang forced their way into a house, demanding to be fed, and then, after the meal was eaten, they murdered their hostess. A male citizen of Charleston was dragged from his home to the army camp, and after he had been killed by his Negro captors, they danced on his grave.[36] In her book, *Dixie After the War*, Myrta Lockett Avary related the following horrific details of Negro atrocities against White South Carolinians:

> A white congregation was at worship in a little South Carolina church when negro soldiers filed in and began to take seats beside the ladies. The pastor had just given out his text; he stretched forth his hands and said simply, "Receive the benediction," and dismissed his people. A congregation in another country church was thrown into panic by balls crashing through boards and windows; a girl of fourteen was killed instantly. Black troops swung by, singing. Into a dwelling a squad of blacks marched, bound the owner, a prominent aged citizen, pillaged his house, and then before his eyes, bound his maiden daughter and proceeded to fight among themselves for her possession. "Though," related my informant with sharp realism, "her neck and face had been slobbered over, she stood quietly watching the conflict. At last, the victor came to her, caught her in his arms and started into an adjoining room, when he wavered and fell, she with him; she had driven a knife, of which she had in some way possessed herself, into his heart. The others rushed in and beat her until she, too, was lifeless. There was no redress."[37]

The situation in the other Southern States was no different. The following is an account of events in Tennessee:

> Friction between the native white people and the freed negroes had been growing steadily in all sections of Tennessee ever since the war. Even in the eastern part of the state, the pro-Union and Abolition stronghold, Brownlow's own newspaper, the Knoxville *Whig*, reported rapidly increasing bitterness between the races. White people, the paper said, were being wantonly insulted by negroes who "frequently elbow unprotected white women off our narrow pavements, and curse white men passing them, just to show their authority." The Republican *Banner* in Nashville reported many murders by negroes throughout the state; and in Memphis acts of violence by the negro troops garrisoned there became so frequent that the presiding judge of the county, Judge Thomas Leonard, asked that two regiments of white Federal troops be stationed in Memphis to protect the white citizens against the negro soldiers' robberies, assaults, and murders. The negro soldiers not only committed these offenses themselves, but they crowded the saloons of the city and

---

36. John S. Reynolds, *Reconstruction in South Carolina, 1865-1877* (Columbia, South Carolina: The State Company, 1905), pages 5-6.

37. Myrta Lockett Avary, *Dixie After the War* (New York: Doubleday, Page, and Company, 1906), page 267.

constituted a serious disturbing influence on the civilian negroes. This bad feeling grew so intense that in May, 1866, there was precipitated a sanguinary race riot which lasted for three days and resulted in the killing of forty-six negroes and two white men, the wounding of seventy-five others and the destruction of property to the value of $130,000, including the burning of ninety-one negro dwellings, four negro churches and twelve negro schools.[38]

So menacing had these soldiers become to the White population that, in many communities throughout the South, the women no longer dared to venture from their houses.[39] Even General Grant was appalled at the behavior of the Black soldiers and wrote in his report to President Johnson that "the presence of black troops, lately slaves, demoralizes labor.... The late slave seems to be imbued with the idea that the property of his late master should belong to him, or at least should have no protection from the colored soldier.... There is danger of collision being brought on by such cases."[40]

The Rise of the Union League

One major element of the corruption of this period, was the formation of chapters in the South of the aforementioned Union League, the purpose of which was to create a solid Republican voting bloc from the Southern Blacks:

> Meanwhile, day and night, Union League organizers were rumbling over the country roads drawing the negroes into secret clubs. There was personal persuasion in cotton fields, bar-rooms, and negro cabins, and such perfect fraternization that the two races drank whiskey from the same bottle, and the wives of some of the whites played the piano for the amusement of their black sisters. At every negro picnic, carpetbaggers mingled with the men and danced with the negro women. The time was short. An election was approaching. One July night in 1867, the fashionable Union League Club of New York, with the aristocratic John Jay in the chair, listened approvingly to a report from an organizer sent to Louisiana; and Mr. Jay announced that this was "part of the Republican programme for the next presidential campaign." The organizer in ninety days had established one hundred and twenty clubs, embracing "whites and blacks who mingled harmoniously together." It was an inspiration. Why, asked one member of the Union League Club,

---

38. Stanley F. Horn, *The Invisible Empire: The Story of the Ku Klux Klan, 1866-1871* (Boston: Houghton Mifflin Company, 1939), pages 76-77.

39. Reid, *After the War*, Volume I, page 48.

40. Grant, letter to Johnson, 18 December 1865; in *Senate Executive Document No. 2* (Thirty-Ninth Congress, First Session), pages 106, 107.

should not a club be established in every township in the South?[41]

By October of 1867, a total of eighty-eight Union League chapters had been established in South Carolina alone.[42] In North Carolina, the Union League had 80,000 members and in Louisiana, 57,300 members.[43] As pointed out by Henry T. Thompson, "Practically all the negroes in the South were members of the League,"[44] and those conservative Blacks who refused to join were in constant danger of having their property confiscated and being whipped or even lynched as traitors.[45] According to one member's testimony, the League existed "for no other purpose than to carry the elections...."[46] Thousands of ignorant freedmen, who could not even read the names on the ballots, were herded to the polls like "senseless cattle" and instructed for whom they must vote.[47] To vote the Democratic ticket was frequently a capital offense.[48] At one Republican campaign meeting held in Macon, Georgia, a notice was posted which read, "Every man that don't vote the Radical ticket this is the way we want to serve him — hang him by the neck."[49] Whites who crossed the League were also the frequent target of abuse, having their houses and barns burned in the middle of the night.

League meetings were usually conducted at night, consisting of secret initiation rites and military drills,[50] and it was not uncommon for members to disguise themselves in the regalia of the Ku Klux Klan and then "kill, whip and otherwise punish negroes who refused to do their vile bidding, and report them as outrages done by the real Ku Klux Klan."[51] According to Susan Lawrence Davis, "A spurious Ku Klux Klan was organized in the District of Columbia in 1866 and its operations and purposes were to discredit the Ku Klux

41. Bowers, *Tragic Era*, page 202.

42. Francis B. Simkins and Robert H. Woody, *South Carolina During Reconstruction* (Chapel Hill, North Carolina: University of North Carolina, 1932), page 75 (footnote).

43. Adams, *In the Course of Human Events*, page 153.

44. Thompson, *Ousting the Carpetbagger*, page 17.

45. Bowers, *Tragic Era*, page 205.

46. Simkins and Woody, *South Carolina During Reconstruction*, page 79.

47. Simkins and Woody, *ibid.*, page 80.

48. H.J. Eckenrode, *A Political History of Virginia During Reconstruction* (Baltimore, Maryland: Johns Hopkins Press, 1904), page 79; Bowers, *Tragic Era*, page 202.

49. Henry, *Story of Reconstruction*, page 322.

50. Fleming, *Documentary History of Reconstruction*, Volume II, Chapter Seven.

51. Davis, *Authentic History of the Ku Klux Klan*, page 173.

Klan of the South.... [A]ll the so-called Ku Klux outrages did not originate among the white people of the South, but with the blacks who are not Ku Klux."[52] This assertion was corroborated by Daniel Goodloe, U.S. Marshall for North Carolina for three years during Reconstruction, who said, "I have also heard of combinations of negroes calling themselves Ku Klux and committing outrages.... It has been charged that they have mobbed negroes for [voting] the [Democratic] ticket."[53] The Radical press, of course, had a field day reporting these so-called "Ku Klux outrages" in its tireless efforts to denigrate the Southern people, and a flurry of anti-Klan laws began to be passed by the Carpetbagger governments of the South. Ironically, the first indictment under the 1870 anti-Klan law of Mississippi was of Daniel Price, a Carpetbagger who had led a mob of Negroes in Klan disguise in the lynching of a Black Democrat named Adam Kennard.[54]

Not long afterward, Congress passed and President Grant approved legislation to counter the alleged Klan violence in the South. The first of these Acts provided, "If two or more persons shall band or conspire together, or go in disguise upon the public highway, or upon the premises of another, with intent to... injure, oppress, threaten or intimidate any citizen with the intention to prevent or hinder his free exercise or enjoyment of any right or privilege, granted or secured to him by the Constitution of the United States, or because of his having exercised the same; such persons shall be guilty of a felony." The second Act further provided that all persons who were connected with the conspirators would also be held responsible for any act committed, "although he was completely ignorant of the intention to commit it, and of the fact of its commission."[55] This legislation was obviously aimed at members of the various Klan chapters, threatening them with arrest merely for their being members. Although Congress conducted an extensive investigation of the alleged activities of the Klan at a cost of several million dollars, and many arrests were made, it is noteworthy that not a single conviction of any genuine Ku Klux member was obtained and no written order to commit any crime was ever found. Instead, the legislation backfired on the South's enemies, causing an outcry against the anti-Klan laws from the very people who had agitated for their enactment:

Among the men who were arrested and tried were members of the spurious Ku

---

52. Davis, *ibid.*, pages 195, 219.

53. Daniel Goodloe, quoted by Thomas Boyard, *Ku Klux Klan Organization* (Washington, D.C.: U.S. Government Printing Office, 1871), page 5.

54. Horn, *Invisible Empire*, page 154.

55. These laws are still on the books at Title 18, United States Code, Sections 241 and 242 (the same wording is at Title 42, Sections 1982 and 1983), and are frequently appealed to by "patriot" groups as safeguards of the rights of State Citizens against conspiring agents of the Government. Their real purpose was, and has always been, to protect Negroes from deprivation of their civil rights to the detriment of the rights of the States.

Klux Klan which had been formed by the "Loyal League" at Washington to foment trouble in the South. When these counterfeit Ku Klux were tried, as in the case of those prosecuted by Captain William Richardson at Huntsville, Ala., when he was employed by the real Ku Klux Klan, and obtained convictions of these men, the Federal authorities immediately freed them.

Many other citizens who were not members of the Ku Klux Klan were arrested, convicted and sent to the Federal prison.

Thirteen individuals of these spurious Ku Klux Klans were convicted in Alabama, and one pleaded guilty.

The trials and the carpet-baggers in charge of them were bitterly assailed in the Northern papers at that time, for the Northern public began to realize the injustice of the Ku Klux Laws and of the government at Washington, and to see the failure of the Law in reaching the real Ku Klux Klan, and that it was reacting against their own agents and causing them to be convicted and sent to the Federal prisons.[56]

The Purpose of the Genuine Klan

The genuine Ku Klux Klan, which acted merely as a countermeasure to the political corruption and Northern-generated racial animosity and violence that was spreading unchecked throughout the South, has borne the onus ever since of Radical propaganda from the Reconstruction era. In the minds of most Americans today, the Klan is still associated with atrocities which were actually committed in many instances by Negroes and their Radical leaders and the more popular histories continue to fan the flames with one-sided accounts of "the Klan's sadistic campaign of terror."[57] However, as is so often the case, the truth is quite different from the prevailing myth. In the words of former Confederate General John Brown Gordon of Georgia, the Klan was "an organization, a brotherhood of the property-holders, the peaceable, law-abiding citizens of the State, for self-protection."[58] Gordon further testified before the Joint Congressional Committee on Affairs in the Insurrectionary States in 1871:

The instinct of self-protection prompted that organization, the sense of insecurity and danger, particularly in those neighborhoods where the negro population largely pre-

---

56. Davis, *Authentic History of the Ku Klux Klan*, pages 145-146.

57. Eric Foner, *Reconstruction: America's Unfinished Revolution 1863-1877* (New York: Harper and Row, 1988), page 431. Foner devoted twenty pages to an enumeration of alleged Klan atrocities, some of which were quite gruesome, but never once did he mention the documented existence of the spurious Klans nor did he allow his readers to consider the possibility that the men behind the masks in the horrific incidents he cited could have been other than genuine Ku Klux.

58. John Brown Gordon, quoted by Henry, *Story of Reconstruction*, page 322.

dominated. The reasons which led up to this organization were three or four. The first and main reason was the organization of the Union League, as they called it, about which we knew nothing more than this: that the negroes would desert the plantations and go off at night in large numbers; on being asked where they had been would reply, sometimes, "We have been to the muster"; sometimes, "We have been to the lodge"; sometimes, "We have been to the meeting." We knew that the "carpetbaggers," as the people called those who came from a distance and had no interest at all with us, who were unknown to us entirely; who from all we could learn about them did not have any very exalted position at their homes — these men were organizing the colored people....

Apprehension took possession of the entire mind of the State. Men were in many instances afraid to go away from their homes and leave their wives and children, for fear of outrage. Rapes were already being committed in the country. There was this general organization of the black race on the one hand, and an entire disorganization of the white race on the other hand.

We were afraid to have a public organization; because we supposed it would be construed at once, by the authorities at Washington, as an organization antagonistic to the government of the United States. It was therefore necessary, in order to protect our families from outrage and to preserve our own lives, to have something that we could regard as a brotherhood — a combination of the best men in the country, to act purely in self-defense, to repel the attack in case we should be attacked by these people. That was the whole object of this organization.[59]

General Nathan Bedford Forrest likewise testified before the Joint Committee that "the organization was intended entirely as a protection to the people, to enforce the laws, and protect the people against outrages."[60] The veracity of these testimonies is seen in the Klan's own statement of purpose:

This is an institution of Chivalry, Humanity, Mercy, and Patriotism; embodying in its genius and its principles all that is chivalric in conduct, noble in sentiment, generous in manhood, and patriotic in purpose; its peculiar objects being:

First: To protect the weak, the innocent, and the defenseless, from the indignities, wrongs, and outrages of the lawless, the violent, and the brutal; to relieve the injured and oppressed; to succor the suffering and unfortunate, and especially the widows and orphans of Confederate soldiers.

Second: To protect and defend the Constitution of the United States, and all laws passed in conformity thereto, and to protect the States and the people thereof from all invasions from any source whatever.

Third: To aid and assist in the execution of all constitutional laws, and to protect the people from unlawful seizure, and from trial except by their peers in conformity to the

---

59. Gordon, testimony in *Report of the Joint Congressional Committee on Affairs in the Insurrectionary States* (Washington, D.C.: Government Printing Office, 1872), Volume VI, page 854.

60. Nathan Bedford Forrest, testimony in *ibid.*, Volume XIII, page 3.

laws of the land.[61]

The spread of the Klan throughout the Southern States was concurrent with the increase of aggression against their people by members of the Union League and in response to the corruption of the Carpetbaggers. On several occasions, the Klan even came to the rescue of Democratic or even conservative Republican Negroes who were targets of violence in consequence of their refusal to join with the Radicals. One such Black family who were thus saved by the interposition of the Klan were the Pooles of Florence, Alabama.[62] The Klan also assisted Government authorities in apprehending associates of Tom Clark, a deserter from both the Confederate and Northern armies who, with his band of marauders, terrorized several counties of Alabama in the early 1870s in Klan disguise.[63] The gruesome murders, rapes, and robberies committed against both Whites and Blacks by Clark and his men were all attributed to the Klan in the Northern papers.

Evidence is utterly lacking that the purpose of the Ku Klux Klan was anything but defensive in nature. Nevertheless, with the growing number of atrocities being wrongly attributed to the Klan by the Northern press, a negative and vengeful reaction from Washington was to be expected. By the time the Thirty-Ninth Congress took their seats in December of 1865, the Radical element had taken what they perceived to be the unrepentance of the Southern people as ample justification to wage a legislative war against the new outbreak of "rebellion." Flying in the face of the collected testimonies of their own military commanders throughout the South, the Joint Committee on Reconstruction, chaired by Senator William P. Fessenden of Maine, reported in early 1866:

> It appears quite clear that the anti-slavery amendments, both to the State and federal constitutions, were adopted with reluctance by the bodies which did adopt them, while in some States they have been either passed by in silence or rejected. The language of all the provisions and ordinances of these States on the subject amounts to nothing more than an unwilling admission of an unwelcome truth. As to the ordinance of secession, it is, in some cases, declared "null and void," and in others simply "repealed;" and in no instance is a refutation of this deadly heresy considered worthy of a place in the new constitution....
>
> Hardly is the war closed before the people of these insurrectionary States come forward and haughtily claim, as a right, the privilege of participating at once in that government which they had for four years been fighting to overthrow. Allowed and encouraged by the Executive to organize State governments, they at once place in power rebels, unrepentant and unpardoned, excluding with contempt those who had manifested an attachment to the Union, and preferring, in many instances, those who had rendered

---

61. Prescript of the Ku Klux Klan, quoted by Horn, *Invisible Empire*, page 38.

62. Davis, *Authentic History of the Ku Klux Klan*, page 152.

63. Davis, *ibid.*, pages 151-152.

themselves the most obnoxious.... Professing no repentance, glorying apparently in the crime they have committed, avowing still... an adherence to the pernicious doctrine of secession, and declaring that they yielded only to necessity, they insist, with unanimous voice, upon their rights as States, and proclaim that they will submit to no conditions whatever as preliminary to their resumption of power under that Constitution which they still claim the right to repudiate....

> ...[I]t is found to be clearly shown by witnesses of the highest character and having the best means of observation, that the Freedmen's Bureau, instituted for the relief and protection of freedmen and refugees, is almost universally opposed by the mass of the population, and exists in an efficient condition only under military protection.... [W]ithout its protection the colored people would not be permitted to labor at fair prices, and could hardly live in safety. They also testify that without the protection of United States troops, Union men, whether of northern or southern origin, would be obliged to abandon their homes. The feeling in many portions of the country towards emancipated slaves, especially among the uneducated and ignorant, is one of vindictive and malicious hatred. This deep-seated prejudice against color is assiduously cultivated by the public journals, and leads to acts of cruelty, oppression, and murder, which the local authorities are at no pains to prevent or punish. There is no general disposition to place the colored race, constituting at least two-fifths of the population, upon terms even of civil equality.

The report charged that because "the great mass of the people became and were insurgents, rebels, traitors, and that all of them assumed and occupied the political, legal, and practical relation of enemies of the United States," the "so-called Confederate States are not... entitled to representation in the Congress of the United States...." The committee concluded with a recommendation that changes to the "organic law" of the nation be made and bills enacted by Congress which would "determine the civil rights and privileges of all citizens in all parts of the republic" and "fix a stigma upon treason."[64] Roused by the unlawful and unconscionable acts of its own agents and lackeys, the Republican beast was now awakened and the Southern people were soon to experience its vicious bite.

---

64. *Joint Committee on Reconstruction*, pages xv, xvi, xvii, xxi.

SUPPORTING DOCUMENT

Robert Lewis Dabney's Letter to Major-General Oliver O. Howard of the Freedmen's Bureau

Prince Edward County, Virginia
12 September 1865.

Sir: Your high official trust makes you, in a certain sense, the representative man of the North, as concerns their dealing with the African race in these United States. It is as such that I venture to address you, and through you all your fellow-citizens on behalf of this recently liberated people. My purpose is humbly to remind you of your weighty charge, and to encourage you to go forward with an enlarged philanthropy and zeal in that career of beneficence toward the African which Providence has opened before you. Rarely has it fallen to the lot of one of the sons of men to receive a larger trust, or to enjoy a wider opportunity for doing good. At the beginning of the late war there were in the South nearly four millions of Africans. All these, a nation in numbers, now taken from their former guardians, are laid upon the hands of that government of which you are the special agent for their protection and guidance. To this nation of black people you are virtually father and king; your powers for their management are unlimited, and for assisting their needs you have the resources of the "greatest people on earth." Your action for the freedmen's good is restrained by no constitution or precedents, but the powers you exercise for them are as full as your office is novel. We see evidence of this in the fact that your agents, acting for the good of your charge, can seize by military arrest any one of their fellow-citizens of African descent, for no other offense than being unemployed, convey him without his consent, and without the company of his wife and family, to a distant field of industry, where he is compelled to wholesome labor for such remuneration as you may be pleased to assign. Another evidence is seen in your late order, transferring all causes and indictments in which a freedman is a party, from the courts of law of the Southern States to the bar of your own commissioners and sub-commissioners for adjudication. I beg you to believe that these instances are not cited by me for the purpose of repeating the cavils against the justice and consistency of the powers exercised in them, in which some have been heard to indulge. My purpose is not to urge with them that there is no law by which a free citizen can be rightfully abridged of his liberty of enjoying the *otium cum dignitate* so long as he abstains from crime or misdemeanor therein, merely because he wears a black skin, while the same government does not presume to interfere with the exercise of this privilege by his white fellow-citizens, even though they be those lately in rebellion against it; that this military arrest and transference to the useful though distant scene of compulsory labor, is precisely that penalty of "transportation" which Southern laws never inflicted, even on the slave, except for crime and after judicial investigation; that these commissioners for adjudicating cases to which freedmen are parties, are in reality judges at law, appointed by you, for every city and county in eleven States, and empowered to sit without jury, and to decide without regard to the precedents or statutes of the States; which would exhibit your bureau as not only an executive, but a judicial branch of the government, established without constitutional authority, and that a hundred fold more pervasive in its jurisdiction than the Supreme Court itself; and that this "order" has, by one stroke of your potent pen, deprived eight millions of white people of the right of a trial by jury, guaranteed to them by the sixth and seventh additional articles of the United States Constitution, in every case where a freedman happens to be a party against them. I repeat, that I have not adduced these instances for the purpose of urging these or such like objections (it does not become the subject to cavil against the powers exercised by his conquerors), but only to impress you with the obligation, which the fullness of your powers brings upon you, to do good to your charge upon a great scale.

I cannot believe that means will be lacking to you any more than powers. At your back stands the great, the powerful, the rich, the prosperous, the philanthropic, the Christian North, friend and liberator of the black man. It must be assumed that the zeal which waged a gigantic war for four years, which expended three thousand million of dollars, and one million of lives, in large part to free the African, will be willing to lavish anything else which may be needed for his welfare. And if the will be present, the ability is no less abundant among a people so wealthy and powerful, who exhibit the unprecedented spectacle of an emersion from a war which would have been exhausting to any other people with resources larger than when they began it, and who have found out (what all previous statesmen deemed an impossibility), that the public wealth may be actually increased by unproductive consumption. With full powers and means to do everything for the African, what may he not expect from your guardianship?

The answer which a generous and humane heart would make to this question, must of course be this: that it would seek to do for the good of its charge *everything which is possible*. But more definitely I wish to remind you that there is a *minimum* limit, which the circumstances of the case forbid you to touch. Common sense, common justice says: that *the very least you can do for them must be more than the South has accomplished*, from whose tutelage they have been taken. To this measure, at least, if not to some higher, your country, posterity, fame, and the righteous heavens, will rigidly hold you. The reason is almost too plain to be explained. If a change procured for the Africans at such a cost brings them no actual benefit, then that cost is uncompensated, and the expenditure of human weal which has been made was a blunder and a crime. Thus it becomes manifest that the measure for the task which you have before you, is the work which the South accomplished for the negro while he was a slave. The question, how much was this? is a vital one for you; it gives you your starting point from which you must advance in your career of progressive philanthropy. Listen then.

First, for the physical welfare of the negro the South has done something. A rapid increase of population and longevity are a safe index of the prosperous and sane condition of the bodies of a people. The South has so provided for the wants of the negro that his numbers have doubled themselves as rapidly as those of the whites, with no accessions by immigration. The census returns show that the South so cared for him that the percentage of congenital defects and diseases, these unfailing revealers of a depressed physical condition, idiocy, blindness, deafness, dumbness, hereditary scrofula, and such like ills, was as small as among the most prosperous Northern States. The South gave to her negro men, on an average, a half pound of bacon and three pounds of breadstuffs per day, besides his share in the products of his master's kitchen-garden, dairy and orchard; and to the women and children at a rate equally liberal. If, in some neighborhoods, the supply was less bountiful than the above, there were a hundred fold more in which it was even more abundant. The South gave to every negro, great and small, a pair of shoes every winter, and to the laboring men an additional pair at harvest. She clothed them all with a substantial suit of woolens every winter, an additional suit of cotton or flax each summer, and two shirts and two pair of socks per year, while the adults drew their hat and blanket each. She furnished each negro family with a separate cottage or cabin, and, during the severe weather, with about one-third of a cord of wood per day, to keep up those liberal fires on which his health and life so much depend. She provided, universally, such relief for his sickness that every case of serious disease was attended by a physician with nearly the same promptitude and frequency as the cases of the planters' own wives and daughters; and in all the land never was a negro fastened to his bed by illness but he received the personal, sympathizing visits fo some intelligent white person besides; master, mistress or their agent, who never went to his couch empty-handed. His dead universally received decent and Christian burial, where the bereaved survivors were soothed by the offices of Christianity. The South so shielded the negro against destitution, that from the Potomac to the Gulf, not one negro pauper was ever seen, unless he were free, and not one African poorhouse existed or was needed. Her system secured for every slave, male or female, a legal claim upon the whole property, income, and personal labor of his master, for a comfortable maintenance during any season of infirmity brought upon him by old age, the visitation of God, or his own imprudence, however protracted that season might be: a claim so sure and definite that it could be pursued by an action at law upon the slave's behalf; a claim so universally enforced and acquiesced in, that its neglect, or the death of a helpless slave through destitution, was as completely unknown among us as cannibalism. The South met that claim, which the free laboring men of other lands have so often had sorrowful occasion to argue, amid pallid famine, and with the fearful logic of insurrections and bloodshed, the claim of "the right to labor," and has met it so successfully that she has secured to every African slave capable of labor, without even one exception among all her millions, remunerative occupation, at all times, and amid all financial convulsions and depressions of business. That is, she has found at all times such occupation for all of them as has procured for them, without excessive toil, a decent maintenance during their active years, an adequate and unfailing provision for old age, a portion for their widows, and a rearing of their children. The South has so far performed these duties to the bodies of the Africans that no community of them have ever, in a single instance, amid any war, or blight, or drouth, or dearth, felt the tooth of famine on its vitals, or so much as seen the wolf, destitutions, at its door.

For the culture of the negro's mind and character, the South has also done something. She has not, indeed, fallen into the hallucination that the only processes of education are those summed up in the arts of reading and writing — facts which were not prevalent among those literacy dictators of the ancient world, the compatriots of Pericles and Plato — nor has she deemed it a likely mode to communicate these useful acts to the ebony youth, to gather three hundred of them into one pandemonium, under a single overtasked "school-marm" or bald-pated negro, and dub the seething cauldron of noise, confusion and "negro-gen gas," a "primary school." But thousands and tens of thousands has she taught to read (and offered the art to ten-fold more, who declined it from their own indolence), through the gentle and faithful agency of cultivated young masters and mistresses, a process prohibited, I boldly assert, *quicunque vult*, by no law upon the statute-book of my State, at least. But this tuition, extensive as it has been, is the merest atom and mite, in the extensive culture which she has given to the African race. She received them at the hands of British and Yankee slave traders, besotted in their primeval jungles, for the spontaneous fruits of which they lived in common. She taught the whole of them some rudiments of civilization. She taught them all the English language, a gift which, had they been introduced into the Northern States as free men, in numbers so large, they would not have received in three centuries. She taught all of them some arts of useful labor, and as large a portion of them as any other peasantry learned the mechanical arts. With the comparatively small exception of the negroes upon large estates, belonging to non-resident owners, the South has placed every negro boy and girl, during his or her growth, under the forming influence of white men and ladies, by whom they have been taught some little tinctures of the cleanliness, the decencies, the chastity, the truthfulness, the self-respect, so utterly alien to their former savage condition, and a share of courtesy and good breeding which would not disgrace any civilized people. Of the young negresses, who would otherwise have grown up the besotted victims of brutal passions, the great majority have been, at some stage of their training, introduced by the South to the parlors and chambers of their women, from whom they have learned to revere and imitate, to some degree, that grace and purity, that sweet humanity and delicacy of sentiment which glorify the Southern lady above all her sex; and under her watchful and kindly eye, has her dark-skinned sister been taught the agencies and domestic arts which make woman a blessing in her home. The boys and youths, by the same influences, have become the humble, yet affectionate, companions of their masters, and have imbibed some of their intelligence and principle. Herein was the great educational work of the South, potent and persuasive as it was simple. By her system, every man and woman of the superior race, yea, every child, was enlisted in the work of the culture of the inferior, and the whole business of domestic life was converted, by interest and affection alike, into a schooling of the mind and character.

This culture has been so far successful that the African race, lately rude savages, was raised to such a grade that, according to high military authority in the United States, they were fit to make armies as efficient as those recruited in the "great, free and enlightened North"; and in the judgment of a powerful party in that country (a party which embraces the major part of that particular corner which has the prescriptive right of knowing everything), they have been made, under Southern tutelage, fully equal to the rights and duties of voters and rulers, in the most complicated of governments. Now, feeling that it does not become a subject of that government, one recently conquered by the great North, to dispute its *dicta* on these points, I shall of course assume that they are correct. Here, then, is what the South has done for the development of the negro's mind.

Nor has our section neglected that noblest and highest interest of all races, the spiritual interest of the negro. She has diffused among the blacks a pure gospel. She gave him the Christian Sabbath, and fortified the gift with laws and penalties, capable of being executed in his behalf against his own master — laws so efficacious that enforced Sabbath labor was almost utterly unknown to him. She gave him a part in every house of worship built throughout her border (for never have I heard of one church in all these States where the slaves were not admitted along with their masters), besides building more temples for his exclusive use than the Christianity of the North has built for Pagans, in all Hindostan and China together. She has given him evangelical preaching, unmingled with the poison of Universalism, Millerisn, Socinianism, Mormonism, or with the foreign and disastrous element of politics. For nearly all the church-members of this people are connected with the great orthodox and evangelical denominations; and having been a preacher to Africans for twenty years, I have never yet heard a sermon address to them, or heard of the man who had heard it, in which the subject of abolition or pro-slavery was obtruded on their attention by a Southern minister. In one word, the South has so far cared for their souls as to bring five hundred thousand of them into the full communion of the church, thus making them at least outward and professed Christians — a ratio as large as that prevailing among the whites of the great, Christian North.

These fact concerning the work of the South for the slaves, I give without the fear of contradiction. The son of a slaveholder, an owner of slaves by inheritance, reared and educated among them, laboring for them and their masters all my professional life, I know whereof I affirm. Every intelligent citizen of the South will substantiate these statements, as within the limits of moderation, and as only a part of those which might be made.

When I claim that the South did thus much for the Africans, I am far from boasting. We ought to have done much more. Instead of pointing to it with self-laudation, it becomes us, with profound humility towards God, to confess our shortcomings towards our servants. He has been pleased, in His sovereign and fearful dispensation, to lay upon us a grievous affliction, and we know He is too just to do this except for our sins. While I am as certain as the sure word of Scripture can make me concerning any principle of social duty, that there was nothing sinful in the relation of master and slave itself, I can easily believe that our failure to fulfill some of the duties of that righteous relation is among the sins for which God's hand now makes us smart. And it does not become those who are under His discipline to boast of their good works. No; verily we have sinned; my arguments is that you must do more for the negro than we sinners of the South have done.

I have written wittingly the words, *you* must do it for them. The South cannot. Your people have effectually disable them therefor. They have done so by taking away our wealth. The South is almost utterly impoverished, and is able to do little more than to keep destitution from her own doors. But a more conclusive reason is the alienation which the armed and clerical missionaries of the North have inculcated in the breasts of these people, lately so affectionate and contented. The negroes have been diligently taught that their masters were their enemies and oppressors, that their bondage was wicked and destructive of their well-being, and especially that the religious teachings of all Southern ministers were "doctrines of devils," because they would not shout the shibboleth of abolition. The consequence is that the black race will no longer listen to the Southern people, or be guided by them. Take as evidence my own instance, which I cite precisely for the reason that it is not in the least peculiar, but reflects the common experience of all ministers and people here. Before the advent of your armies, plantation meetings were held weekly in the different quarters of the congregation, on Saturdays, in working time, cheerfully surrendered by the masters for that purpose, which brought religious instruction within two or three miles of every house. They are now all at an end. Six years ago my congregation pulled down the substantial house, built by their fathers only thirty years before, with walls as solid as living rocks, which was entirely adequate to hold the whites, and replaced it by a larger. One prominent reason was that it was not large enough to hold the servants also. They constructed in the new house three hundred commodious sittings exclusively for the blacks. Last Sabbath, under a bright and cheerful sun, those sittings were occupied during public worship by precisely three persons; and at the afternoon service, held in a chapel-of-ease, primarily for the blacks, there was not one present. Thus the North has prevented the South from doing its former work for the good of the African; consequently it must make its account to do it all itself.

But while I assert this, I would bear my emphatic testimony against the falsehood and injustice of the charge that the Southern people wish to cast off and ruin the negro, in a spirit of pique and revenge for his emancipation. That they regard this measure as neither just nor wise, is perfectly true. But they have promised to acquiesce in it as a condition of peace; that promise they intend faithfully to keep; and they universally regard slavery as finally at an end. There is nothing more manifest than that the North, amid the flame and heat of all its animosities, knows and feels that this people will not be the one to break its new covenant, hard as its conditions are; and that the freedom of the late slaves and the authority which has dictated it are secured from attack by us. And I boldly testify that this magnanimous people has not voluntarily withdrawn its humane interest from the blacks; that it earnestly desires their prosperity; that it wishes to give them employment and opportunity, and to co-operate in their maintenance as far as possible; that they do not cast off the negroes, but it is the negroes who cast them off. Yea, the people of the South are this day extending to tens of thousands of black families a generous sympathy in the midst of their own heavy losses and deep poverty, which we challenge the Christian world to surpass in its splendid philanthropy: in that we still refuse to cast off those families, although, by reason of the incumbrance of old persons, sick, and little children, their present labor is worse than worthless to us, and we know we shall receive no future recompense in the labor of the children we are thus rearing *gratis* for other men as independent of us in future as we are of them. And this is done (oftentimes in spite of a present requital of insolence, misconception, ingratitude and a petty warfare of thefts and injuries) by Southern gentlemen and ladies, who appropriate thereto a part of the avails of their own personal labors, undertaken to procure subsistence for their own children. And this is done, not in a few exceptional cases, but in a multitude of cases, in every neighborhood of every county, so that the numbers of destitute freedmen under which the able hands of your Bureau now faint, are not a tithe of those who are still maintained by the impoverished people of the South. And this is done simply because humanity makes us unwilling to thrust out those for whose happiness we have so long been accustomed to care into the hardships of their new and untried future. And unless you can expect this delicate sentiment to exhibit a permanence which would be almost miraculous under the "wear and tear" of our future poverty, I forewarn you that you must stand prepared for a tenfold increase of your present responsibilities, when these families are committed to you. That tenfold burden you must learn to bear successfully.

Having shown you the starting point of that career of beneficence to the African, from which you are solemnly bound to God and history to advance, I now return to strengthen the already irresistible argument of that obligation. If the South, with all its disadvantages, has done this modicum of good to this poor people, the North, their present guardian, with their vast advantages, must do far more. The South was the inferior section (so the North told us) in number, in wealth, in progress, in intelligence, in education, in religion. The South (so the North says) held the African under an antiquated, unrighteous and mischievous relation — that of domestic slavery. The North now has them on the new footing, which is, of course, precisely the right one. The South was their oppressor; the North is their generous liberator. The South has hag-ridden in all its energies for good (so we were instructed) by the "barbarism of slavery"; the North contains the most civilized, enlightened and efficient people on earth. Now, if you do not surpass our poor performance for the negro with this mighty contrast in your favor, how mightily will be the just reprobation which will be visited upon you by the common sentiment of mankind and by the Lord of Hosts? If you do not surpass our deeds as far as your power and greatness surpass ours, how can you stand at His bar, even beside us sinners? He has taught us that "a man is accepted according to that which he hath, and not according to that which he hath not." To this righteous rule we intend to hold you, as our successors in the guardianship of the negro.

If there are any who endeavor to lull your energies in this work, by saying that the negro, being now a free man, must take care of himself like other people; that he should be thrown on his own resources, and that, if he does not provide for his own well-being, he should be left to suffer, I beseech you, in the behalf of humanity, of justice and of your own good name, not to hearken to them. I ask you solemnly whether the freedmen have an "even start" in the race for subsistence with the other laboring men of the nation, marked as they are by difference of race and color, obstructed by stubborn prejudices, and disqualified (as you hold) for the responsibilities of self-support, to some extent, by the evil effects of their recent bondage upon their character? Is it fair, or right, or merciful to compel him to enter the *stadium*, and leave him to this fierce competition under these grave disadvantages? Again, no peasantry under the sun was ever required or was ever able to sustain themselves when connected with the soil by no tenure of any form. Under our system our slaves had the most permanent and beneficial form of tenancy; for their master's lands were bound to them by law for furnishing them homes, occupations and subsistence during the whole continuance of the master's tenure. But you have ended all this, and consigned four millions of people to a condition of homelessness. Will the North thus make gypsies of them, and then hold them responsible for the ruin which is inevitable from such a condition?

But there is another argument equally weighty. By adopting the unfeeling policy of throwing the negro upon his own resources, to sink or swim as he may, you run too great a risk of verifying the most biting reproaches and objections of your enemies. They, in case of his failure, will argue thus: That the great question in debate between the defenders of slavery and the advocates of emancipation was whether the negro was capable of self-control: that the former, who professed to be more intimately acquainted with his character, denied that he was capable of it, and solemnly warned you of the danger of his ruin, if he was intrusted with his own direction, in this country, and that you, in insisting on the experiment in spite of this warning, assumed the whole responsibility. Sir, if the freedmen should perchance fail to swim successfully, that argument would be too damaging to you and your people. You cannot afford to venture upon this risk. You are compelled by the interests of your own consistency and good name, to take effectual care that the negro shall swim; and that better than before. In the name of justice, I remonstrate against your throwing him off in his present state, by the inexorable fact that he was translated into it, neither by us, nor by himself, but by you alone; for out of that fact proceeds an obligation upon you, to make your experiment successful, which will cleave to you even to the judgment day. And out of that fact proceeds this farther obligation: that seeing you have persisted, of your own free will, in making this experiment of his liberation, you and your people are bound to bestow anything or every-thing, and to do everything, except sin, to insure that it shall be, as compared with his previous condition, a blessing to him. For, if you are not willing to do all this, were you not bound to let him alone? When the shipmaster urges landsmen to embark in his ship, and venture the perils of the deep, he thereby incurs an obligation, if a storm arises, to do everything and risk everything, even to his own life, for the rescue of his charge. If, then, you and your people should find that it will require the labors of another million of busy hands, and the expenditure of three thousand millions more of the national wealth, to obviate the evils and dangers arising to the freedmen from your experiment upon their previous condition: yea, if to do this, it is necessary to make the care and maintenance of the African the sole business and labor of the whole mighty North, you will be bound to do it at this cost.

And I beg you, sir, let no one vainly think to evade this duty which they owe you in your charge, by saying that perhaps even so profuse an expenditure as this, for the benefit of the Africans, would fail of its object; because they hold that making a prosperous career is one of those things like chewing their own food, or repenting of their own sins, which people must do for themselves, or else they are impossible to be done; and that so no amount of help can make the freedmen prosperous as such, without the right putting forth of their own spontaneity. For, do you not see that this plea surrenders you into the hands of those bitter adversaries, the Pro-Slavery men? Is this not the very thing they said? This was precisely their argument to show that philanthropy required the Africans in this country should be kept in a dependent condition. If your section acquiesces in the failure of your experiment of their liberation on this ground, what will this be but the admission of the damning charge that your measure is a blunder and a crime, aggravated by the warning so emphatic, which your opponents gave you, and to which you refused to listen?

But I feel bound, as your zealous and faithful supporter in your humane task, to give you one more caution. The objectors who watch you with so severe an eye have even a darker suggestion to make than the charge of headstrong rashness and criminal mistake in your experiment of emancipation. They are heard gloomily to insinuate that the ruin of the African (which they so persistently assert must result from the change) is not the blunder of the North, but the foreseen and intended result! Are you aware of the existence of this frightful innuendo? It is my duty to reveal it to you, that you may be put upon your guard. These stern critics are heard darkly hinting that they know Northern statesmen and presses who now admit, with a sardonic shrug, that the black man, deprived of the benignant shield of domestic servitude, must of course perish like the red man. These critics are heard inferring that the true meaning of Northern Republicanism and Free Soil is, that the white race must be free to shoulder the black race off this continent, and monopolize the sunny soil, which the God of nations gave the latter as their heritage. They take a sort of grim pleasure in pointing to the dead infants, which, they say, usually marked the liberating course of your armies through the South, in displaying the destitution and mortality which, they charge, are permitted in the vast settlements of freedmen under your care; in insinuating the rumors of official returns of a mortality already incurred in the Southwest, made to your government, so hideous that their suppression was a necessity; and in relating how the jungles which are encroaching upon the once smiling "coasts" of the Mississippi, in Louisiana, already envelope the graves of half the black population in that State! And the terrible inference from all this, which they intimate is, that the great and powerful North only permits these disasters because it intends them; that, not satisfied with the wide domain which Providence has assigned to them, they now pretend to liberate the salve whom they have seen too prosperous under his domestic servitude, in order to destroy him, and grasp, in addition, the soil which he has occupied.

Now, sir, it is incumbent on you, that the premises on which, with so dangerous a plausibility, they ground this tremendous charge, be effectually contradicted by happy and beneficent results. You must refute this monstrous indictment, and there is only one way to do it, by actually showing that you conserve and bless the African race, multiply their numbers, and confirm their prosperity on the soil, more than we have done. I repeat, the North must refute it thus. For, of course, every Northern man, while indignantly denying and abhorring it, admits (what is as plain as the sun at midday) that if the charge were indeed true, it would convict his people of the blackest public crime of the nineteenth century; a crime which would be found to involve every aggravation and every element of enormity which the nomenclature of ethics enables us to describe. It would be the deliberate, calculated, cold-blooded, selfish dedication of an innocent race of four millions to annihilation; the murder, with malice prepence, of a nation; not by the comparatively merciful process of the royal Hun, whose maxim was, that "thick grass is cut more easily than thin," summary massacre; but by the slowly eating cancer of destitution, degradation, immorality, protracting the long agony through two or three generations, thus multiplying the victims who would be permitted to be born only to sin, to suffer and to perish; and insuring the everlasting perdition of the soul, along with the body, by cunningly making their own vices the executioners of the doom. It would include the blackest guilt of treason being done under the deceitful mask of benefaction and by pretended liberators. The unrighteousness of its motive would concur with its treachery to enhance its guilt to the most stupendous height; for upon this interpretation of the purpose of the North, that motive would be, first to weaken and disable its late adversary, the South, by destroying that part of the people which was guilty of no sin against you, and then, by this union of fraud and force, to seize and enjoy the space which God gave them, and laws and constitution guaranteed. This, indeed, would be the picture which these accusers would then present of your splendid act, that you came as a pretended friend and deliverer to the African, and while he embraced you as his benefactor in all his simple confidence and joy, you thrust your sword through and through his heart, in order to reach, with a flesh wound, the hated white man who stood behind him, whom you could not otherwise reach.

Robert Lewis Dabney.

SUPPLEMENTARY ESSAY
Southern Race Relations Before and After the War
by Thomas Nelson Page

No race ever behaved better than the Negroes behaved during the war. Not only were there no massacres and no outbreaks, but even the amount of defection was not large. While the number who entered the Northern Army was considerable, it was not as great as might have been expected when all the facts are taken into account. A respectable number came from the North, while most of the others came from the sections of the South which had already been overrun by the armies of the Union and where mingled persuasion and compulsion were brought to bear. Certainly no one could properly blame them for yielding to the arguments used. Their homes were more or less broken up; organization and discipline were relaxed, and the very means of subsistence had become precarious; while on the other hand they were offered bounties and glittering rewards that drew into the armies hundreds of thousands of other nationalities. The number that must be credited to refugees who left home in the first instance for the purpose of volunteering to fight for freedom is believed by the writer to be not large; personally, he never knew of one. However large the number was, the number of those who might have gone, and yet threw in their lot with their masters and never dreamed of doing otherwise, was far larger. Many a master going off to the war intrusted his wife and children to the care of his servants with as much confidence as if they had been of his own blood. They acted rather like clansmen than like bondmen. Not only did they remain loyal, but they were nearly always faithful to any trust that had been confided to them. They were the faithful guardians of their masters' homes and families; the trusted agents and the shrewd counsellors of their mistresses. They raised the crops which fed the Confederate armies, and suffered without complaint that privation which came alike to white and black from the exactions of war. On the approach of the enemy, the trusted house servants hid the family silver and valuables, guarded horses and other property, and resisted all temptation to desert or betray. It must, of course, rest always on conjecture; but the writer believes that, had the Negroes been allowed to fight for the South, more of them would have volunteered to follow their masters than ever volunteered in the service of the Union. Many went into the field with their masters, where they often displayed not only courage but heroism, and, notwithstanding all temptations, stood by them loyally to the end. As Henry Grady once said, "A thousand torches would have disbanded the Southern Army, but there was not one."

The inference that has been drawn from this is usually one which is wholly in favor of the colored race. It is, however, rather a tribute to both races. Had slavery at the South been the frightful institution that it has ordinarily been pictured, with the slave-driver and the bloodhound always in the foreground, it is hardly credible that the failure of the Negroes to avail themselves of the opportunities for freedom so frequently offered them would have been so general and the loyalty to their masters have been so devoted.

One other reason is commonly overlooked. The instinct for command of the white race — at least, of that section to which the whites of this country belong — is a wonderful thing: the serene self-confidence which reckons no opposition, but drives straight for the highest place, is impressive. It made the race in the past; it has preserved it in our time. The Negroes knew the courage and constancy of their masters. They had had abundant proof of them for generations, and their masters were now in arms.

The failure of a servile population to rise against their masters in time of war is no new thing. History furnishes many illustrations. Plutarch tells how the besiegers of a certain city offered, not only freedom to the slaves, but added to it the promise of their masters' property and wives if they would desert them. Yet the offer was rejected with scorn. During the Revolution, freedom on the same terms was offered the slaves in Virginia and the Carolinas by the British, but with little effect, except to inflame the master to bitterer resistance. The result was the same during the Civil War.

The exactions of the war possibly brought the races nearer together than they had ever been before. There had been, in times past, some hostile feeling between the Negroes and the plain whites, due principally to the well-known arrogance of a slave population toward a poor, free, working population. This was largely dispelled during the war, on the one side by the heroism shown by the poor whites, and on the other by the kindness shown by the Negroes to their families while the men were in the army. When the war closed, the friendship between the races was never stronger; the relations were never more closely welded. The fidelity of the Negroes throughout the war was fully appreciated and called forth a warmer affection on the part of the masters and mistresses, and the care and self-denial of the whites were equally recognized by the Negroes. Nor did this relation cease with the emancipation of the Negro. The return of the masters was hailed with joy in the quarters as in the mansion. When the worn and disheartened veteran made his last mile on his return from Appomattox, it was often the group of Negroes watching for him at the plantation gate that first caught his dimmed eye and their shouts of welcome that first sounded in his ears.

A singular fact was presented which has not been generally understood. The joy with which the slaves hailed emancipation did not relax the bonds of affection between them and their former masters and mistresses. There was, of course, *ex necessitate rei*, much disorganization, and no little misunderstanding. The whites, defeated and broken, but unquelled and undismayed, were unspeakably sore; the Negroes, suddenly freed and facing an unknown condition, were naturally in a state of excitement. But the transition was accomplished without an outbreak or an outrage, and, so far as the writer's experience and information go, there were on either side few instances of insolence, rudeness or ill-temper, incident to the break-up of the old relation. This was reserved for a later time, when a new poison had been instilled into the Negro's mind and had begun to work. Such disorders as occurred were incident to the passing through the country of disbanded troops, making their way home without the means of subsistence, but even these were sporadic and temporary. For years after the war the older Negroes, men and women, remained the faithful guardians of the white women and children of their masters' families.

One reason which may be mentioned for the good-will that continued to exist during this crisis, and has borne its part in preserving kindly relations ever since, is that, among the slave-owning class, there was hardly a child who had not been rocked in a colored mammy's arms and whose first ride had not been taken with a Negro at his horse's head; not one whose closest playmates in youth had not been the young Negroes of the plantation. The entire generation which grew up during and just after the war grew up with the young Negroes, and preserved for them the feeling and sympathy which their fathers had had before them. This feeling may hardly be explained to those who had not known it. Those who have known it will need no explanation. It possibly partakes somewhat of a feudal instinct; possibly of a clan instinct. It is not mere affection; for it may exist where affection has perished and even where its object is personally detested. Whatever it is, it exists universally with those who came of the slave-holding class in the South, who knew in their youth the Negroes who belonged to their family, and, no matter what the provocation, they can no more divest themselves of it than they can of any other principle of their lives.

Such was the relation between the whites and the blacks of the South when emancipation came. It remains now to show what changes have taken place since that time; how these changes have come about, and what errors have been committed in dealing with the Race-question which still affect the two races.

The dissension which has come between the two races has either been sown since the Negro's emancipation or is inherent in the new conditions that have arisen.

When the war closed, and the emancipation of the Negroes became an established fact, the first pressing necessity in the South was to secure the means of living; for in sections where the armies had been the country had been swept clean, and in all sections the entire labor system was disorganized. The internal management of the whole South, from the general government of the Confederate States to the domestic arrangement of the simplest household among the slave-holding class, had fallen to pieces.

In most instances — indeed, in all of which the writer has any knowledge — the old masters informed their servants that their homes were still open to them, and that if they were willing to remain and work, they would do all in their power to help them. But to remain, in the first radiant holiday of freedom, was, perhaps, more than could be expected of human nature, and most of the blacks went off for a time, though later a large number of them returned. In a little while the country was filled with an army of occupation, and the Negroes, moved partly by curiosity, partly by the strangeness of the situation, and, perhaps mainly, by the lure of the rations which the Government immediately began to distribute, not unnaturally flocked to the posts of the local garrisons, leaving the fields unworked and the crops to go to destruction.

From this time began the change in the Negroes and in the old relation between them and the whites; a change not great at first, and which never became great until the Negroes had been worked on by the ignorant or designing class who, in one guise or another, became their teachers and leaders. In some places the action of military commanders had already laid the ground for serious misunderstanding by such orders as those which were issued in South Carolina for putting the Negroes in possession of what were, with some irony, termed "abandoned lands." The idea became widespread that the Government was going to divide the lands of the whites among the Negroes. Soon all over the South the belief became current that every Negro was to receive "forty acres and a mule"; a belief that undoubtedly was fostered by some of the U.S. officials. But, in the main, the military commanders acted with wisdom and commendable breadth of view, and the breach was made by civilians.

From the first, the conduct of the North toward the Negro was founded on the following principles: First, that all men are equal (whatever this may mean), and that the Negro is the equal of the white; secondly, that he needed to be sustained by the Government; and thirdly, that the interests of the Negro and the white were necessarily opposed, and the Negro needed protection against the white.

The South has always maintained that those were fundamental errors.

It appears to the writer that the position of the South on these points is sound; that, however individuals of one race may appear the equals of individuals of the other race, the races themselves are essentially unequal.

The chief trouble that arose between the two races in the South after the war grew out of the ignorance at the North of the actual conditions at the South, and the ignorance at the South of the temper and the power of the North. The North believed that the Negro was, or might be made, the actual equal of the white, and that the South not only rejected this dogma, but, further, did not accept emancipation with sincerity, and would do all in its power to nullify the work which had already been accomplished, and hold the Negroes in *quasi*-servitude. The South held that the Negro was not the equal of the white, and further held that, suddenly released from slavery, he must, to prevent his becoming a burden and a menace, be controlled and compelled to work.

In fact, as ignorance of each other brought about the conditions which produced the war between the sections, so it has brought about most of the trouble since the war.

The basic difficulty in the way of reaching a correct solution of the Negro problem is, as has been stated, that the two sections of the American people have hitherto looked at it from such widely different standpoints.

The North, for the present far removed and well buttressed against any serious practical consequences, and even against temporary discomfort from the policies and conditions it has advocated, acting on a theory, filled with a spirit of traditionary guardianship of the Negro, and reasoning from limited examples of progression and virtue, has ever insisted on one principle and one policy, founded on a conception of the absolute equality of the two races. The South, in direct contrast with the practical working of every phase of the question, affected in its daily life by every form and change that the question takes, resolutely asserts that the conception on which that policy is predicated is fundamentally erroneous, and that this policy would destroy not only the white race of the South, but even the civilization which the race has helped to establish, and for which it stands; and so, in time, would inevitably debase and destroy the nation itself.

Thus, the South holds that the question is vastly more far-reaching than the North deems it to be; that, indeed, it goes to the very foundation of race preservation. And this contention, so far from being merely a political tenet, is held by the entire white population of the South as the most passionate dogma of the white race.

This confusion of definitions has in the past resulted in untold evil, and it cannot be insisted on too often that it is of the utmost importance that the truth, whatever it is, should be established. When this shall be accomplished, and done so clearly that both sides shall accept it, the chief difficulty in the way of complete understanding between the sections will be removed. So long as the two sections are divided upon it, the question will never be settled. As soon as they unite in one view, it will settle itself on the only sound foundation — that of unimpeachable economic truth.

To this ignorance and opposition of views on the part of the two sections, unhappily, were added at the outset the misunderstandings and passions engendered by war, which prevented reason having any great part in a work which was to affect the whole future of the nation. With a fixed idea that there could be no justice toward the Negro in any dealings of their former masters, all matters relating to the Negroes were intrusted by the Government to the organization which had recently been started for this very purpose under the name of the Freedmen's Bureau. It was a subject which called for the widest knowledge and the broadest wisdom, and, unhappily, both knowledge and wisdom appeared to have been resolutely banished in the treatment of the subject.

The basis of the institution of the Freedmen's Bureau was the assumption stated: that the interests of the blacks and of the whites were necessarily opposed to each other, and that the blacks needed protection against the whites in all cases. The densest ignorance of the material on which the organization was to work prevailed, and the personnel of the organization was as unsuited to the work as could well be. With a small infusion of sensible men were mingled a considerable element of enthusiasts who felt themselves called to be the regenerators of the slaves and the scourge of their former masters, and with these, a large element of reckless adventurers who, recognizing a field for the exercise of their peculiar talents, went into the business for what they could make out of it. Measures were adopted which might have been sound enough in themselves if they had been administered with any practical wisdom. But there was no wisdom in the administration. Those who advised moderation and counselled with the whites were set aside. Bred on the idea of slavery presented in *Uncle Tom's Cabin* and inflamed by passions engendered by the war, the enthusiasts honestly believed that they were right in always taking the side of the down-trodden Negro; while the adventurers, gauging with an infallible appraisment the feelings of the North, went about their work with businesslike methods to stir up sectional strife and reap all they could from the abundant harvest. And of the two, the one did about as much mischief as the other.

No statement of any Southern white person, however pure in life, lofty in morals, high-minded in principle he might be, was accepted. His experience, his position, his character, counted for nothing. He was assumed to be so designing or so prejudiced that his counsel was valueless. It is a phase of the case which has not yet wholly disappeared, and even now we have presented to us in a large section of the country the singular spectacle of evidence being weighed rather by a man's geographical position than by his character and his opportunity for knowledge.

This self-complacent ignorance is one of the factors which prevent a complete understanding of the problem and tend to perpetuate the errors which have cost so much in the past and, unless corrected, may prove yet more expensive in the future.

The conduct of the Freedmen's Bureau misled the Negroes and caused the first breach between them and their former masters. Ignorance and truculence characterized almost every act of that unhappy time. Nearly every mistake that could be made was made on both sides. Measures that were designed with the best intentions were so administered as to bring these intentions to wreck.

On the emancipation of the slaves, the more enlightened whites of the South saw quite as clearly as any person at the North could have seen the necessity of some substitute for the former direction and training of the Negroes, and schools were started in many places by the old masters for the colored children. Teachers and money had come from the North for the education of the Negroes, and many schools were opened. But the teachers, at first devoted as many of them were, by their unwisdom alienated the good-will of the whites and frustrated much of the good which they might have accomplished. They might have been regarded with distrust in any case, for no people look with favor on the missionaries who come to instruct them as to matters of which they feel they know much more than the missionaries, and the South regarded jealously any teaching of the Negroes which looked toward equality. The new missionaries went counter to the deepest prejudice of the Southern people. They lived with the Negroes, consorting with them, and appearing with them on terms of apparent intimacy, and were believed to teach social equality, a doctrine which was the surest of all to arouse enmity then as now. The result was that hostility to the public-school system sprang up for a time. In some sections violence was resorted to by the rougher element, though it was of short duration, and was always confined to a small territory. Before long, however, this form of opposition disappeared and the public-school system became an established fact.

The next step in the alienation of the races was the formation of the secret order of the Union League. The meetings were held at night, with closed doors, and with pickets guarding the approaches, and were generally under the direction of the most hostile members of the Freedmen's Bureau. The whites regarded this movement with serious misgivings, as well they might, for, having as its basic principle the consolidation of the Negro race against the white race, it banded the Negroes in an organization which, with the exception of the Confederate Army, was the most complete that has ever been known in the South, and the fruits of which still survive today. Without going into the question of the charges that the League taught the most inflammatory doctrines, it may be asserted without fear of question that its teaching was to alienate the Negroes from the whites; to withdraw them wholly from reliance on their former masters, and to drill into their minds the imperative necessity of adherence to their new leaders, and those whom those leaders represented.

Then came the worst enemy that either race had ever had: the *post-bellum* politician. The problem was already sufficiently complicated when politics were injected into it. Well might General Lee say with a wise knowledge of men: "The real war has just begun."

No sooner had the Southern armies laid down their guns and the great armies of the North who had saved the Union disbanded, then the vultures, who had been waiting in the secure distance, gathered to the feast. The act of a madman had removed the wisest, most catholic, most conservative, and the ablest leader, one whose last thoughts almost had been to "restore the Union" by restoring the government of the Southern States along constitutional lines; and well the politicians used the unhappy tragedy for their purposes. Those who had been most cowardly in war were bravest in peace, now that peace had come. Even in Mr. Lincoln's time the radical leaders in Congress had made a strenuous fight to carry out their views, and their hostility to his plan of pacification and reconstruction was expressed with hardly less vindictiveness than they exhibited later toward his successor.

The Southern people, unhappily, acted precisely as this element wished them to act; for they were sore, unquelled, and angry. They met denunciation with defiance.

Knowing the imperative necessities of the time as no Northerner could know them; fearing the effects of turning loose a slave population of several millions, and ignorant of the deep feeling of the Northern people; the Southerners hastily enacted laws regulating labor which were certainly unwise in view of the consequences that followed, and possibly, if enforced, might have proved oppressive, though they never had a trial. Most of these laws were simply reenactments of old vagrant laws on the statute books and some still stand on the statute books; but they were enacted now expressly to control the Negroes; they showed the animus of the great body of the whites, and they aroused the deep feeling of distrust and much resentment among the Northerners. And, finally, they played into the hands of the politicians who were on the lookout for any pretext to fasten their grip on the South.

The struggle just then became intensified between the President and his opponents in Washington, with the Presidency and the control of the Government as the stake, and with the South holding the balance of power; and, unhappily, the Negroes appeared to the politicians an element that could be utilized to advantage by being made the "permanent allies" of what Mr. Stevens, Mr. Wade, and Mr. Sumner used to term "the party of the Union."

So, the Negro appeared to the politicians a useful instrument, and to the doctrinaires "a man and brother" who was the equal of his former master, and, if he were "armed with the weapon" of the ballot, would be able to protect himself and would inevitably rise to the full stature of the white.

A large part of the people of the North were undoubtedly inspired by a missionary spirit which had a high motive beneath it. But a missionary spirit undirected by knowledge of real conditions is a dangerous guide to follow. And the danger was never better illustrated than in this revolution. Doubtless, some of the politicians were inspired partly by the same idea; but the major portion had but one ruling passion — the securing of power and the down-treading of the Southern whites.

Then came the crowning error: the practical carrying out of the theories by infusing into the body politic a whole race just emerging from slavery. The most intelligent and conservative class of the whites were disfranchised; the entire adult Negro population were enfranchised. It is useless to discuss the motives with which this was done. No matter what the motives it was a national blunder; in its way as great a blunder as secession.

It is uncommonly supposed that Mr. Lincoln was the originator of this idea. The weight of his name is frequently given to it by the uninformed. Mr. Lincoln, however, was too level-headed and clear-sighted a statesman ever to have committed so great a folly. The furthest he ever went was in his letter to Governor Hahn, of Louisiana, in which he "suggested" the experiment of intrusting the ballot to "some of the colored people, for instance... the very intelligent," and as a reward for those who had fought for the Union.

In fact, for a year or two after the war no one in authority dreamed of investing the Negro race at once with the elective franchise. This came after the South had refused to tolerate the idea of the franchise being conferred on any of them, and after passions had become inflamed. The eight years of Reconstruction possibly cost the South more than the four years of war had cost her. To state it in mere figures, it may be said that when the eight years of Negro domination under carpet-bag leaders had passed, the public indebtedness of the Southern States had increased about fourfold, while the property values in all the States had shrunk, and in those States which were under the Negro rule had fallen to less than half what they had been when the South entered on that period. In Louisiana, for instance, the cost of Negro rule for four years and five months amounted to $106,020,337, besides the privileges and franchises given away to those having "pulls," and State franchises stolen. The wealth of New Orleans shrank during these eight years from $146,718,790 to $88,613,930, while real estate values in the country parishes shrank from $99,266,083 to $47,141,699.

In South Carolina and Mississippi, the other two States which were wholly under Negro rule, the condition was, if anything, worse than in Louisiana, while in the other Southern States it was not so bad, though bad enough. But the presentation of the statistics gives little idea of what the people of the South underwent while their State governments were controlled by Negroes. A wild Southern politician is said to have once truculently boasted that he would call the roll of his slaves at the foot of the Bunker Hill Monument. If the tradition is true, it was a piece of insolence which naturally offended deeply the sentiment of the people of the proud Commonwealth of Massachusetts. But his was mere gasconade. Had he been able to carry out his threat, and then had he installed his Negroes in the State-house of Massachusetts, and, by travesty of law, filled the legislative halls with thieves and proceeded to disfranchise the best and the proudest people of the Commonwealth; then had he, sustained by bayonets, during eight years ridden rough-shod over them; cut the value of their property in half; quadrupled their taxes; sold out over twenty per cent. of the landed property of the State for forfeiture; appointed over two hundred Negro trial justices who could neither read nor write, put a Negro on the bench of their highest court, and paraded through the State something like 80,000 Negro militia, armed with money stolen from the State, to insult and menace the people, while the whole South looked cooly on and declared that this treatment was just; then might there be a partial but not a complete parallel to what some of the States of the South endured under Negro rule.

It is little wonder that Governor Chamberlain, Republican and carpet-bagger though he was, should have declared as he did in writing to the New England Society, "The civilization of the Puritan and Cavalier, of the Roundhead and Huguenot, is in peril."

The South does not hold that the Negro race was primarily responsible for this travesty of government. Few reasonable men now charge the Negroes at large with more than ignorance and an invincible faculty for being worked on. But the consequences were none the less disastrous. The injury to the whites was not the only injury caused by the reconstruction system. To the Negroes, the objects of its bounty, it was no less a calamity. However high the motive may have been, no greater error could have been committed; nothing could have been more disastrous to the Negro's future than the teaching he thus received. He was taught that the white man was his enemy when he should have been taught to cultivate his friendship. He was told he was the equal of the white when he was not the equal; he was given to understand that he was the ward of the nation when he should have been trained in self-reliance; he was led to believe that the Government would sustain him when he could not be sustained. In legislation, he was taught thieving; in politics, he was taught not to think for himself, but to follow slavishly his leaders (and such leaders!); in private life, he was taught insolence. A laborer, dependent on his labor, no greater misfortune could have befallen him than estrangement from the Southern whites. To instil into his mind the belief that the Southern white was his enemy; that his interest was necessarily opposed to that of the white, and that he must thwart the white man to the utmost of his power, was to deprive him of his best friend and to array against him his strongest enemy.

To the teachings which led the Negro to feel that he was "the ward of the nation"; that he was a peculiar people whom the nation had taken under its wing and would support and foster; and that he could, by its fiat, be made the equal of the white, and would, by its strong arm, be sustained as such, may, perhaps, be traced most of the misfortunes of the Negro race, and, indeed, of the whole South, since the war. The Negro saw the experiment being tried; he saw his former master, who had been to him the type of all that was powerful and proud, and brave, and masterful, put down and held down by the United States Government, while he, himself, was set up and declared his full equal. He is quick to learn, and during this period, when he was sustained by the Government, he was as insolent as he dared to be. The only check on him was his lurking recognition of the Southerner's dominant force.

The one thing that saved the Southerners was that they knew it was not the Negroes but the Federal Government that held them in subjection. The day the bayonets were withdrawn from the South, the Negro power, which but the day before had been as arrogant and insolent as ever in the whole course of its brief authority, fell to pieces.

It is little less than amazing that the whites of the South should, after all that they went through during the period of reconstruction, have retained their kindly feeling for the Negroes, and not only retained but increased their loyalty to the Union. To the writer, it seems one of the highest tributes to the white people of the South that their patriotism should have remained so strong after all they had endured. The explanation is that the hostility of the Southern people was not directed so much against the United States or its Government, to form which they had contributed so much and in which they had taken so much pride, as against that element among the people of the North that had always opposed them, particularly where slavery was concerned. In seceding, the Southerners had acted on the doctrine enunciated by so distinguished a Northerner as John Quincy Adams in 1839, when he declared that it would be better for the States to "part in friendship from each other than to be held together by constraint," and look forward "to form again a more perfect friendship by dissolving that which could not bind, and to leave the separated parts to be reunited by the law of political gravitation to the centre," and now, slavery and secession having finally been disposed of, they naturally and necessarily gravitated back to the old feeling for the Union.

It is not less remarkable that, notwithstanding all the humiliation they had to endure during the period of Negro domination, they should still have retained their feeling of kindness for the race. The fact, however, was that they did not charge against the race in general the enormities which were committed by them during that period. However they might be outraged by their insolence and their acts, they charged it rather against the leaders than against the followers. The Southerners knew the Negroes; knew their weaknesses and their merits, and knew how easily they were misled. And it was always significant that though the Negroes universally followed their leaders and, when they felt themselves in power, conducted themselves with intolerable insolence, at other times they exhibited their old kindliness, and no sooner was the instigation removed than they were ready to resume their old relation of dependence and affection. Indeed, those who had been the worst and most revolutionary had no sooner sunk back into their former position of civility than they were forgiven and treated with good-natured tolerance.

With the overthrow of the carpet-bag governments, and the destruction of Negro domination at the South, the South began to shoot up into the light of a new prosperity. Burdened as she was by debt; staggering under disasters that had well-nigh destroyed her; scarred by the struggle through which she had gone, and scorched by the passions of that fearful time, she set herself with all her energies to recovering through the arts of peace her old place in the path of progress. The burden she has borne has been heavy, but she has carried it bravely and triumphantly.

Her property values have steadily increased. Mills have been started and manufactories established, and this not only by Southern investors, but, to a considerable extent, by Northern capital, until the South has become one of the recognized fields for investment. This, among other causes, has made the South restive under an electorate which has confined her to one political party, shut her off from ability to divide on economic questions, and which, to a certain extent, withdrew her from her due participation in the National Government. With this, another cause is the charge of the relation between the two races. It is useless to blink the question. The old relation of intimacy and affection that survived to a considerable extent even the strain and stress of the reconstruction period, and the repressive measures that followed it, has passed away, and in its place has come a feeling of indifference or contempt on the one side, and indifference or envy on the other. In some places, under some conditions, the old attitude of reliance and the old feeling of affection still remain. For example, in many families, the old relation of master and servant, of superior and retainer, may still exist. In some neighborhoods or towns, individuals of the colored race, by their ability and character, have achieved a position which has brought to them the respect and sincere good-will of the whites. A visit to the South will show anyone that, in the main, the feeling of kindness and good-will has survived all the haranguing of the politician and all the teaching of the doctrinaire. Ordinarily, the children still play together, the men work together, the elders still preserve their old good-will. The whites visit the sick and afflicted, help the unfortunate, relieve the distressed, console the bereaved, and perform the old offices of kindness. But this is, to some extent, exceptional. It is mainly confined to the very young, the old, or the unfortunate and dependent. The rule is a changed relation and a widening breach. The teaching of the younger generation of Negroes is to be rude and insolent. In the main, it is only where the whites have an undisputed authority that the old relation survives. Where the whites are so superior in numbers that no question can be raised; or again, where, notwithstanding the reversed conditions, the whites are in a position so dominant as not to admit of question, harmony prevails. When the relations are reversed there is danger of an outbreak. The Negro, misled by the teaching of his doctrinaire friends into thinking himself the equal of the white, asserts himself, and the white resents it. The consequence is a clash, and the Negro becomes the chief sufferer so invariably that it ought to throw some light on the doctrine of equality.

The preceding essay was extracted from Thomas Nelson Page, The Negro: The Southerners' Problem *(New York: Charles Scribner's Sons, 1904).*

CHAPTER EIGHTEEN
The Military Occupation of the Southern States

A State of Non-Flagrant War Continues

In 1868, Henry Clay Dean, a Democrat lawyer from Iowa, demonstrated that not all men North of the Mason-Dixon line had been fooled by Republican rhetoric or that of their late puppet, Abraham Lincoln:

> The war between the States of the Union was not a riot. It was deliberate, systematic and orderly upon the part of the Southern States. *It was not an insurrection* or rebellion, everything was done in subordination to the law and sovereign power of the States, in which it transpired with no more of violence than is common to warfare. *It was not a revolution.* It changed none of the organic laws of the States; the people armed themselves according to law to repel a threatened invasion of their country, overthrow of their government and violations of their political, legal and social rights in which they failed, and are now realizing their worst anticipated fears.
>
> It was a war between independent States, in violation of the Constitution of the United States, as interpreted by its framers; by the Supreme Court, its legal exponent and the statesmen and publicists, contemporary with its existence.
>
> The pretext for the war was the preservation of the Union — an organized Union fighting against organized States, the whole destroying its parts was the monstrous absurdity (emphasis in original).[1]

Of course, by 1865, none of these things mattered. The Northern Radicals had

---

1. Dean, *Crimes of the Civil War*, page 41.

achieved the revolution they had hoped for and had overthrown the Constitution they hated with such ferocity, leaving the Southern States and all hope of restoring "the Union as it was" to lie prostrate at their feet.

Because there had never been a congressional declaration of war, Andrew Johnson, on 2 April 1866, simply issued a Presidential Proclamation declaring the "insurrection" in all the Southern States except Texas to be "at an end, and henceforth to be so regarded."[2] On the twentieth of August of that same year, Johnson proclaimed that the "insurrection" was "at an end" in Texas as well, and that "peace, order, tranquility, and civil authority now exist, in and throughout the whole of the United States of America." The reader should recall Joint Resolution of 25 July 1861, in which Congress declared, "This war is not prosecuted upon our part in any spirit of oppression, nor for any purpose of conquest or subjugation, nor for the purpose of overthrowing or interfering with the rights or established institutions of those States, but to defend and maintain the supremacy of the Constitution and all laws made in pursuance thereof and to preserve the Union, with all the dignity, equality, and rights of the several States unimpaired; and that as soon as these objects are accomplished the war ought to cease." Based on these assurances, Johnson's proclamations should have ended all hostilities against the Southern States and restored them to their former place in the Union with their "dignity, equality, and rights... unimpaired." However, as stated by the Forty-Third Congress in 1874, the "state of war" continued:

> War was continued in those States until the President's proclamation of August 20, 1866 proclaimed "the insurrection at an end." A "state of war" continued beyond this time, more or less extensive in its theater — *"non flagrante bello sed nondum cessante bello"* (*Mrs. Alexander's Cotton*, 2 Wall. 419).
>
> A state of war does not cease with actual hostilities. "Military government may legally be continued *bello nondum cessante*, as well as *flagrante bello*".... It is easier to provoke a civil war than to restore the confidence without which peace returns but by name. Under these circumstances the reasons which justify martial law subsist.
>
> The existence of what is called "a state of war" after flagrant war has ceased is recognized on the same principle as the personal right of self-defense. This is not limited to the right to repel an attack; but so long as the purpose of renewing it remains — the *animus revertendi* — so long as the danger is imminent or probable, the party assailed may employ reasonable force against his adversary to disarm and disable him until the danger is past, and in doing this and judging of its necessity, precise accuracy as to the means is not required, but only the exercise of reasonable judgment in view of the circumstances.
>
> If after the forces under the command of Lee surrendered in April, 1865, the United States forces had been immediately withdrawn, the rebellion would possibly have resumed its hostile purposes. It was upon this theory, coupled with the constitutional duty of Congress to "guarantee to each State a republican form of government," that the recon-

---

2. Andrew Johnson, Presidential Proclamation, 2 April 1866; in Richardson, *Messages and Papers of the Presidents*, Volume VIII, page 3630.

struction acts were passed, and military as well as civil measures adopted in pursuance of them.[3]

The people of the South, economically devastated and physically and emotionally exhausted by four tragic years of war, resigned themselves to their defeat and attempted to function as States within the *de facto* military nation which had been forced upon them. In his report to President Johnson of 18 December 1865, General Grant testified to this fact: "I am satisfied the mass of thinking men in the South accept the present situation of affairs in good faith. The questions which have hitherto divided the sentiment of the people of the two sections — slavery and State-rights, or the right of the State to secede from the Union — they regard as having been settled forever by the highest tribunal, that of arms, that man can resort to."[4]

It is beyond all argument that, despite the above assertion of the Forty-Third Congress, what the President accepted as "a republican form of government" was indeed in place in each of the former "rebel" States during this period. Even the Supreme Court declared in reference to each of the Southern States, "The obligation of the state, as a member of the Union, remained perfect and unimpaired. It certainly follows that the state did not cease to be a state, nor her citizens to be citizens of the Union."[5] It was upon this basis that the Thirteenth Amendment was ratified, abolishing slavery throughout the several States.[6] However, when the Thirty-Ninth Congress proposed the Fourteenth Amendment, with its attempted elevation of the freed slaves to a political superiority over their former masters, many of whom had been disfranchised by their conquerors, Southerners once again thought it their duty to protect their posterity from the encroachments of a political party bent only on the satiation of its own lust for power. We will take a closer look at the revolutionary nature of the Fourteenth Amendment in the next chapter, but suffice it to say for now, the amendment failed to receive the approval of the required three-fourths of the States.[7] The following words of Republican Speaker of the House, Schuyler Colfax, aptly demonstrated the attitude of the Radicals toward the former "rebel States":

---

3. U.S. House of Representatives, *Report No. 262* (Forty-Third Congress, First Session, 26 March 1874).

4. Grant, report to Johnson, 18 December 1865; in *Senate Executive Document No. 2*, page 106.

5. *Texas v. White* (1867), 74 U.S. 726.

6. *Dyett v. Turner* (1968) 439 P2d 266, 269, 20 U2d 403.

7. Leander H. Perez, "The Unconstitutionality of the Fourteenth Amendment," *Congressional Record* — House, 13 June 1967, pages 15641ff; Forrest McDonald, "Was the Fourteenth Amendment Constitutionally Adopted?" *Georgia Journal of Southern Legal History*, Volume One, Number One (Spring/Summer 1991), pages 1-18.

The first session of the Thirty-ninth Congress proposed, as their plan of Reconstruction, a Constitutional Amendment. It was a bond of public justice and public safety
combined, to be embodied in our national Constitution, to show to our posterity that
patriotism is a virtue and rebellion is a crime. These terms were more magnanimous than
were ever offered in any country under like circumstances. They were kind, they were
forbearing, they were less than we had a right to demand; but in our anxiety, in our desire
to close up this question, we made the proposition. How was it received? They trampled
upon it, they spat upon it, they repudiated it, and said they would have nothing to do with
it. They were determined to have more power after the rebellion than they had before....

Though we demand no indemnity for the past, no banishment, no confiscations,
no penalties for the offended law, there is one thing we do demand, there is one thing we
have the power to demand, and that is security for the future, and that we intend to have,
not only in legislation, but imbedded in the imperishable bulwarks of our national Constitution, against which the waves of secession may dash in future but in vain. We intend to
have those States reconstructed on such enduring corner-stones that posterity shall realize
that our fallen heroes have not died in vain.[8]

In his book *Twenty Years of Congress*, James G. Blaine chose not to hide behind such
self-righteous platitudes and instead got right to the point:

In the original Constitution only three-fifths of the slaves were permitted to be
enumerated in the basis of apportionment. Two-fifths were now added and an increase of
political power to the South appeared probable as the somewhat startling result of the civil
struggle. There was an obvious injustice in giving to the white men of the South the right
to elect representatives in Congress apportioned to their section by reason of the four and
a half millions of negroes, who were enumerated in the census but not allowed to exercise
any political power. By permitting this, the Confederate soldier who fought to destroy the
Union would be endowed with a larger power of control in the National Government than
the loyal soldier who fought to maintain the Union. To allow this to be accomplished and
permanently incorporated in the working of the Government would be a mere mockery of
justice, the utter subversion of fair play between man and man.[9]

It could not have been made more evident that Reconstruction was merely the product
of "a fear that... the Confederates of the South should unite with the Democratic opponents
of the war in the North and thus obtain control of the Government...."[10] In other words, the
Republicans saw their precarious edifice, erected as it was on the graves of 600,000 Americans, about to come crashing down around them, bringing to naught over thirty years of
carefully planned agitation and intrigue. This was the real reason why, upon rejecting the

---

8. Schuyler Colfax, quoted in Barnes, *History of the Thirty-Ninth Congress*, pages 11-12.

9. Blaine, *Twenty Years of Congress*, Volume II, page 189.

10. Blaine, *ibid.*, page 190.

"magnanimous" terms set before them — the enfranchisement of the former slaves who, under the influence of agents of the Freedmen's Bureau and the Union League, were already being enticed into the Radical camp — the Whites of the South had to be disfranchised and their States destroyed. Thaddeus Stevens boldly asserted that the Southern States "ought never to be recognized as valid States, until the Constitution shall be amended... as to secure perpetual ascendancy" to the Republican party.[11] Such a goal was realized in the so-called Fourteenth Amendment.

In this battle for "perpetual ascendancy," the Negroes themselves were not the primary concern of the Republicans beyond their capacity to be used as pawns on a colossal political chessboard. This much was unabashedly admitted even by Lyman Trumbull, Senator from Illinois and author of the Civil Rights Act, when he declared, "There is a great aversion in the West — I know it is so in my State — against having free Negroes come among us. Our people want nothing to do with the Negro. We the Republican Party are the White man's party."[12] Some of the Abolitionists, however, who had a sincere, albeit fanatical, interest in the Black man's welfare, were less than enthusiastic with the path down which the dominant party had begun to travel. For example, a thoroughly disillusioned Wendell Phillips complained, "The Republican party is not inspired with any humane desire to protect the negro. It uses the bloody shirt for office, and once there, only laughs at it. Today our greatest danger is the Republican party. Wolves in sheep's clothing! Hypocrites! I hail their coming defeat, looking forward to it as the dawning of a glorious day."[13]

The Republicans' Theory of "State Suicide"

When all the presidentially-reconstructed Southern States except Tennessee rejected the Fourteenth Amendment, the doctrine of "State suicide" was resurrected in retaliation. This position, sometimes also referred to as the "forfeited rights" theory, had been propagated throughout the war by Charles Sumner and some of the other Radicals in Congress to justify their demands for a complete subjugation of the South. Founded squarely upon the historical fallacies of Story and Webster, this theory insisted that the several States were "so

---

11. Stevens, speech delivered on 18 December 1865; in *Congressional Globe* (Thirty-Ninth Congress, First Session), page 74.

12. Lyman Trumbull, quoted by Leonard P. Curry, *Blueprint for Modern America: Nonmilitary Legislation of the First Civil War Congress* (Nashville, Tennessee: Vanderbilt University Press, 1968), page 79.

13. Wendell Phillips, quoted by Edmonds, *Facts and Falsehoods*, pages 220-221. An interesting study of how the Republican party abandoned any interest in the Southern Negro is found in Stanley P. Hirshson, *Farewell to the Bloody Shirt: Northern Republicans and the Southern Negro, 1877-1893* (Chicago, Illinois: Quadrangle Press, 1968).

completely interlinked with the Union" that they were "forever dependent thereupon," and that the Constitution "must forever continue the supreme law thereof, notwithstanding the doings of any pretended governments acting singly or in confederation, in order to put an end to its supremacy."[14] According to Sumner:

> It is sometimes said that the [Southern] States themselves committed suicide, so that as States they ceased to exist, leaving their whole jurisdiction open to the occupation of the United States under [Article IV, Section 2, Clause 2 of] the Constitution. This assumption is founded on the fact that, whatever may be the existing governments in these States, they are in no respect constitutional, and since the State itself is known by the government, with which its life is intertwined, it must cease to exist constitutionally when its government no longer exists constitutionally....
>
> From approved authorities it appears that a "State"... may lose its life. Mr. Phillimore, in his recent work on International Law, says: "A State, like an individual, may die," and among the various ways, he says, "by its submission and donation of itself to another country." But in the case of our Rebel States there has been a plain submission and donation of themselves — *effective, at least, to break the continuity of government*, if not to destroy that immortality which has been claimed. Nor can it make any difference, in breaking this continuity, that the submission and donation, constituting a species of adornment, were to enemies at home rather than to enemies abroad — to Jefferson Davis rather than to Louis Napoleon. The thread is snapped in one case as much as in the other....
>
> But again it is sometimes said, that the States, by their flagrant treason, have *forfeited* their rights as States, so as to be civilly dead. It is a patent and indisputable fact, that this gigantic treason was inaugurated with all the forms of law known to the States, that it was carried forth not only by individuals, but also by States, so far as States can perpetuate treason; that the States pretended to withdraw bodily in their corporate capacities — that the Rebellion, as it showed itself, was *by* States as well as *in* States; that it was by the governments of States as well as by the people of States; and that, to the common observer, the crime was consummated by the several corporations as well as by the individuals of whom they were composed....
>
> It is enough that, for the time being, and *in the absence of a loyal government*, they can have no part and perform no function in the Union, *so that they cannot be recognized by the National Government*. The reason is plain. There are in these States no local functionaries bound by constitutional oaths, so that, in fact, there are no constitutional functionaries; and, since the State government is necessarily composed of such functionaries there can be no State government (emphasis in original).[15]

---

14. Charles Sumner, Senate resolutions dated 11 February 1862; in *Congressional Globe* (Thirty-Seventh Congress, Second Session), page 737. The reader should keep in mind that this was the very same faction that had been agitating for New England's separation from the slave States prior to the actual outbreak of the war.

15. Sumner, "Our Domestic Relations: How to Treat the Rebel States," *Atlantic Monthly* (September, 1863), Volume XII, Number 71, pages 520-521.

During a speech in the House of Representatives on 8 January 1863, Thaddeus Stevens expressed much the same opinion, "The South must be punished under the rules of war, its land confiscated.... These offending States were out of the Union and in the role of a belligerent nation to be dealt with by the laws of war and conquest.... And I hold and maintain that with regard to all the Southern states in rebellion... the Constitution has no binding influence, and no application."[16] Following the downfall of the Confederacy, his views were the same:

> Four years of bloody and expensive war, waged against the United States by eleven States, under a government called the "Confederate States of America," to which they acknowledged allegiance, have overthrown all governments within those States which could be acknowledged as legitimate by the Union. The armies of the Confederate States having been conquered and subdued, and their territory possessed by the United States, it becomes necessary to establish governments therein which shall be republican in form and principles and form a more "perfect Union" with the parent government....
>
> The slave power made war upon the nation. They declared the "more perfect Union" dissolved — solemnly declared themselves a foreign nation, alien to this republic; for four years were in fact what they claimed to be. We accepted the war which they tendered and treated them as a government capable of making war. We have conquered them, and as a conquered enemy we can give them laws; can abolish all their municipal institutions and form new ones.... If the rebel States have never been out of the Union, any attempt to reform their State institutions, either by Congress or the President, is rank usurpation.[17]

On 18 December 1865, two weeks into the first session of the Thirty-Ninth Congress, Stevens went on to say:

> Unless the law of nations is a dead letter, the late war between two acknowledged belligerents severed their original compacts, and broke all the ties that bound them together. The future condition of the conquered power depends on the will of the conqueror. They must come in as new States or remain as conquered provinces. Congress — the Senate and House of Representatives, with the concurrence of the President — is the only power that can act in the matter....
>
> If the so-called "confederate States of America" were an independent belligerent, and were so acknowledged by the United States and by Europe, or had assumed and maintained an attitude which entitled them to be considered and treated as a belligerent, then, during such time, they were precisely in the condition of a foreign nation with whom we were at war; nor need their independence as a nation be acknowledged by us to pro-

---

16. Thaddeus Stevens, *Congressional Globe* (Thirty-Seventh Congress, Third Session), page 239.

17. Stevens, speech delivered in Lancaster, Pennsylvania on 6 September 1865; quoted by New York *World*, 11 September 1865.

duce that effect....

...[I]t is something worse than ridiculous to hear men of respectable standing attempting to nullify the law of nations, and declare the Supreme Court of the United States in error, because, as the Constitution forbids it, the States could not go out of the Union in fact....

The theory that the rebel States, for four years a separate power and without representation in Congress, were all the time here in the Union, is a good deal less ingenuous and respectable than the metaphysics of Berkeley, which proved that neither the world nor any human being was in existence. If this theory were simply ridiculous it could be forgiven; but its effect is deeply injurious to the stability of the nation. I can not doubt that the late confederate States are out of the Union to all intents and purposes for which the conqueror may choose so to consider them.

But on the ground of estoppel, the United States have the clear right to elect to adjudge them out of the Union. They are estopped both by matter of record and matter *in pais*. One of the first resolutions passed by seceded South Carolina in January, 1861, is as follows: "Resolved, unanimously, That the separation of South Carolina from the Federal Union is final, and she has no further interest in the Constitution of the United States; and that the only appropriate negotiations between her and the Federal Government are as to their mutual relations as foreign States." Similar resolutions appear upon all their State and confederate government records. The speeches of their members of Congress, their generals and executive officers, and the answers of their government to our shameful suings for peace, went upon the defiant ground that no terms would be offered or received except upon the prior acknowledgment of the entire and permanent independence of the confederate States. After this, to deny that we have a right to treat them as a conquered belligerent, severed from the Union in fact, is not argument but mockery.[18]

Stevens further described the Southern States as "dead carcasses," and declared that just as "dead men cannot raise themselves," so "dead states cannot restore their own existence 'as it was.'"[19] It should be remembered that the North's premise for fighting the war was that the Southern States could never leave the Union and that they were therefore merely "in rebellion against the United States." Now it appeared that the capricious demands of lawless fanaticism could accomplish what lawful State conventions could not. The secession ordinances voted on and passed by the Southern people six years previously had been declared "legally void" by Lincoln, but a simple wave of the Republican hand was sufficient to expel those States from the "indivisible" Union. However, if Stevens was indeed correct in asserting that the State legislatures established under Presidential Reconstruction were "without any legal authority," "simulated legislative bodies," and "incapable of political action," then what business did Congress have in forwarding the Fourteenth Amendment to

18. Stevens, *Congressional Globe* (Thirty-Ninth Congress, First Session), page 73.

19. Stevens, *ibid.*, pages 72, 73.

these "extinct States"[20] for their approval? Furthermore, how could the Thirteenth Amendment, the ratification of which depended upon these same States, be viewed as anything but an utter nullity? In other words, the Southern States were considered by Congress as being in the Union when they accepted the abolition of slavery, but their status was thereafter denied when they rejected the granting of citizenship to the former slaves. If ever evidence was needed of the arbitrary and fanatical nature of a faction in possession of military power, the post-bellum antics of the Republican party are an inexhaustible source.

A Declaration of War Against State Sovereignty

On 21 December 1865, Henry J. Raymond, one of the conservative Republican Representatives from New York, declared:

> I think we have a full and perfect right to require certain conditions, in the nature of guarantees for the future, and that right rests, primarily and technically, on the surrender we may and must require at their hands. The rebellion has been defeated. A defeat always implies a surrender, and, in a political sense, a surrender implies more than the transfer of the arms used on the field of battle. It implies, in the case of civil war, a surrender of the principles and doctrines, of all the weapons and agencies, by which the war has been carried on. The military surrender was made on the field of battle, to our generals, as the agents and representatives of the Commander-in-Chief of the armies of the United States.
>
> Now, there must be at the end of the war, a similar surrender on the political field of controversy. That surrender is due as an act of justice from the defeated party to the victorious party. It is due, also, and we have a right to exact it, as a guarantee for the future. Why do we demand the surrender of their arms by the vanquished in every battle? We do it that they may not renew the contest. Why do we seek, in this and all similar cases, a surrender of the principles for which they fought? It is that they may never again be made the basis of controversy and rebellion against the Government of the United States.
>
> Now, what are those principles which should be thus surrendered? The principle of State sovereignty is one of them. It was the corner-stone of the rebellion — at once its animating spirit and its fundamental basis. Deeply ingrained as it was in the Southern heart, it must be surrendered. The ordinances in which it was embodied must not only be repealed, the principle itself must be abandoned, and the ordinances, so far as this war is concerned, be declared null and void, and that declaration must be embodied in their fundamental constitutions.[21]

Here was an open admission that the South had not been fighting for slavery at all, as has been asserted *ad nauseam* by revisionist historians for well over a century, but for the

---

20. Stevens, *ibid.*, page 74.

21. Henry J. Raymond, *ibid.*, pages 122-123.

preservation of the sovereignty of the several States. The principles which were thus demanded that the "Southern heart" surrender were simply those which the American founding fathers embodied in the constitutional compact of the Union and bequeathed to their posterity. The Republicans would not be satisfied until this repudiation was written into the State constitutions themselves and they made it clear that the Southern people would not be allowed to participate in the political affairs of the "new nation" until they had done so.

On such a convoluted political stage were played out the horrors of what came to be known as the Reconstruction period, which has rightly been referred to as "the darkest page in the saga of American history,"[22] and "a time of party abuse, of corruption, [and] of vindictive bigotry."[23] As was stated in the February 1903 issue of *Scribner's Magazine*, "Lincoln has made a precedent which future rulers will imitate. What Lincoln excused and defended will be assumed as the right for rulers to follow." The "war powers" used by Lincoln to justify armed aggression against the South from 1861-1865 were the same powers invoked by the Congress to justify the political subjugation of the South from 1867-1877. Beginning with the first Reconstruction Act, passed on 2 March 1867, the Southern States were "divided into military districts and made subject to the military authority of the United States." According to Thaddeus Stevens, "It was intended simply as a police bill to protect the loyal men from anarchy and murder, until this Congress, taking a little more time, can suit gentlemen in a bill for the admission of all those rebel States upon the basis of civil government."[24] However, the insidious nature of the Act was more honestly declared by James Garfield, who declared that it "lays its hands on the rebel governments, taking the very breath of life out of them... [and] it puts the bayonet at the breast of every rebel in the South, and leaves in the hands of Congress utterly and absolutely the work of reconstruction."[25]

Andrew Johnson stated the following in his 2 March 1867 veto of the pending bill:

> The bill places all the people of the ten States therein named under the absolute domination of military rulers....
>
> The military rule which it establishes is plainly to be used, not for any purpose of order or for the prevention of crime, but solely as a means of coercing the people into the adoption of principles and measures to which it is known that they are opposed, and upon which they have an undeniable right to exercise their own judgment.
>
> I submit to Congress whether this measure is not, in its whole character, scope, and object, without precedent and without authority, in palpable conflict with the plainest provisions of the Constitution, and utterly destructive to those great principles of liberty

---

22. Foner, *Reconstruction*, page xx.

23. Randall, *Civil War and Reconstruction*, page 689.

24. Stevens, quoted by Barnes, *History of the Thirty-Ninth Congress*, page 528.

25. James Garfield, quoted by Jabez L.M. Curry, *The Southern States of the American Union* (Richmond, Virginia: B.F. Johnson Publishing Company, 1895), page 229.

and humanity for which our ancestors on both sides of the Atlantic have shed so much blood and expended so much treasure....

The power thus given to the commanding officer over all the people of each district is that of an absolute monarch. His mere will is to take the place of all law.... He alone is permitted to determine what are rights of person or property, and he may protect them in such way as in his discretion may seem proper. It places at his free disposal all the lands and goods in his district, and he may distribute them without let or hindrance to whom he pleases. Being bound by no State law, and there being no other law to regulate the subject, he may make a criminal code of his own; and he can make it as bloody as any recorded in history or he can reserve the privilege of acting upon the impulse of his private passions in each case that arises. He is bound by no rules of evidence; there is indeed no provision by which he is authorized or required to take any evidence at all. Every thing is a crime which he chooses to call so, and all persons are condemned whom he pronounces to be guilty. He is not bound to keep any record or make any report of his proceedings. He may arrest his victims wherever he finds them, without warrant, accusation, or proof of probable cause. If he gives them a trial before he inflicts the punishment, he gives it of his grace and mercy, not because he is commanded so to do.[26]

In his official opinion of 12 June 1867, Attorney General Henry Stanbery substantiated the President's arguments:

We see, first of all, that each of these States is "made subject to the military authority of the United States"....

There can be no doubt as to the rule of construction according to which we must interpret this grant of power. It is a grant of power to military authority, over civil rights and citizens, in time of peace. It is a new jurisdiction, never granted before, by which, in certain particulars and for certain purposes, the established principle that the military shall be subordinate to the civil authority is reversed....

[This act] places the military commander on the same footing as the Congress of the United States. It assumes that "the paramount authority of the United States at any time to abolish, modify, control, or supersede," is vested in him as fully as it is reserved to Congress. He deems himself a representative of that paramount authority. He puts himself upon an equality with the law-making power of the Union; the only paramount authority in our government, so far, at least, as the enactment of laws is concerned. He places himself on higher ground than the President, who is simply an executive officer. He assumes, directly or indirectly, all authority of the States, legislative, executive, and judicial, and in effect declares, "I am the State"....

A person charged with crime in any of these military districts has rights to be protected, rights the most sacred and inviolable, and among these is the right of trial by jury, according to the laws of the land. When a citizen is arraigned before a military commission on a criminal charge he is no longer under the protection of the law, nor

---

26. Johnson, veto message of 2 March 1867; in *Congressional Globe* (Thirty-Ninth Congress, Second Session), pages 1969-1972.

surrounded with those safeguards which are provided in the Constitution. This act, passed in a time of peace, when all the courts, State and Federal, are in the undisturbed exercise of their jurisdiction, authorizes, at the discretion of a military officer, the seizure, trial, and condemnation of the citizen. The accused may be sentenced to death, and the sentence may be executed without a judge.... Military and executive authority rule throughout in the trial, the sentence, and the execution. No *habeas corpus* from any State court can be invoked; for this law declares, that "all interference, under color of State authority, with the exercise of military authority under this act, shall be null and void."[27]

The Democrats in Congress also protested against the bill as an unconstitutional peace-time extension of martial law over nearly one-half of the country. Speaking in behalf of the House minority, Charles A. Eldridge of Wisconsin voiced his objections as follows: "...[W]e are conscious that no effort of ours can prevent its passage, and the consequent accomplishment of a dissolution of the Union, and the overthrow and abandonment of our constitution of government. We can only, in the name of the Constitution, in the name of the republic, in the name of all we hold dear on earth, earnestly, solemnly protest against this action of this Congress."[28] Francis C. LeBlond of Ohio said that, if passed, the bill would prove to be "the death-knell of republican liberty upon this continent" and that it would "strike a death-blow to this Government."[29] Over in the Senate, Willard Saulsbury congratulated the President for vetoing "the most iniquitous bill that ever was presented to the Federal Congress," and went on to say, "I cannot... refrain from the expression of the hope that there may be no man, and that there may be no man within the limits of these ten States, who will participate in his own disgrace, degradation, and ruin; let them maintain their honor.... [I]f there be wrath in the vials of the Almighty, if there be arrows of vengeance in His quiver, such iniquity and injustice can not finally prove successful."[30]

Conditions in the South During Reconstruction

The above warnings went unheeded by the Radicals and the Reconstruction Act was "forced through... under whip and spur"[31] over the President's veto on the very same day the

---

27. Opinion of Attorney General Henry Stanbery (12 Op. Atty. Gen.), 12 June 1867; in *Official Opinions of the Attorney General of the United States Advising the Presidents and Heads of Departments in Relation to their Official Duties* (Washington, D.C.: U.S. Government Printing Office, 1974), Volume II, pages 186, 187, 196, 199.

28. Charles A. Eldridge, quoted by Barnes, *History of the Thirty-Ninth Congress*, page 546.

29. Francis C. LeBlond, quoted by Barnes, *ibid.*, page 547.

30. Willard Saulsbury, *Congressional Globe* (Thirty-Ninth Congress, Second Session), pages 1973.

31. Blaine, *Twenty Years of Congress*, Volume II, page 292.

latter was delivered. The dire results of the Act, and the supplemental Acts which followed it, were precisely as predicted. According to the laws of war, "The commander of the invading, occupying, or conquering army rules the country with supreme power, limited only by international law and the orders of his government."[32] In the words of Ulysses S. Grant, who was one of the military commanders placed into the field by the Act, "The law makes the district commanders their own interpreters of their power and duty under it."[33] Colonel C.C. Gilbert, who was given command of Camden, Arkansas, drew from this the conclusion that "the military are not the servants of the people... but their masters."[34] Not only were the elected civil and judicial officers of the Southern States removed by order of these commanders, and new and unelected men installed in their places, but the functions of the State legislatures were also suspended and their constitutions annulled. Anyone who dared to protest against these injustices was liable to "be punished by imprisonment at hard labor for a term not exceeding ten years nor less than two years, in the discretion of the court having jurisdiction thereof."[35] Under such a despotic rule, large numbers of Southern citizens were arrested daily on the most frivolous charges, and sometimes on no charge at all, and imprisoned in such horrible sites of torture as the Dry Tortugas:

> At the Dry Tortugas the prisoners' heads are shaved. They have to labor under a torrid sun upon a sand bank in the midst of the ocean, with balls and chains about their legs. The men who command the prisoners are amenable to the laws of neither God or man. Col. Grental, a soldier, was tied up by his thumbs, and treated with every species of cruelty and barbarity. The laws are silent and newspapers dumb. The prisoner who enters the Dry Tortugas leaves liberty, justice, hope, behind him. Large numbers of young Southern men, for any or no offense, in what is called the reconstruction period, are arrested, go through the farce of a drumhead trial, presided over by men who take a fiendish delight in torturing any Southern man or woman, nearly always found guilty, and sentenced for life to the Dry Tortugas. The lips of the Alabama journals are pinned together with bayonets. Our hands are fastened in iron cuffs. We dare not speak the whole truth. If we did our paper would be suppressed, our business ruined, our wives and children brought to want.[36]

Even some Northerners were shocked at the conditions in the South during Recon-

---

32. Birkhimer, *Military Government*, page 54.

33. Grant, quoted by *Harper's New Monthly Magazine* (New York: Harper and Brothers, 1867), Volume XXXV, page 535; Carey, *Democratic Speaker's Handbook*, page 123.

34. Colonel C.C. Gilbert, dispatch dated 8 August 1867; in *The American Annual Cyclopedia and Register of Important Events for the Year 1867* (New York: D. Appleton and Company, 1868), page 51.

35. Military criminal code, quoted by Stanbery, opinion, page 195.

36. Montgomery (Alabama) *Mail*, quoted by Edmonds, *Facts and Falsehoods*, pages 224-225.

struction. For example, the New York *Herald* stated, "Every personal right of the citizen is invaded at once. Without any process of law whatever, a man is deprived of his liberty and thrust into a cell at the mere bidding of a political or military bully. The secrecy of the telegraph and post office is violated as no man would dare violate them in despotic France."[37]

It was during this period that the aforementioned Fourteenth Amendment of 1868 and the Fifteenth Amendment of 1870 were adopted with the aid of these newly "reconstructed" States, granting statutory citizenship to the emancipated slaves and giving them the right to vote. As pointed out by Blaine, "Only a minority of Republicans were ready to demand suffrage for those who had been recently emancipated, and who, from the ignorance peculiar to servitude, were presumably unfit to be intrusted with the elective franchise."[38] Nevertheless, despite the fact that Negroes could not vote in many of the Northern States, the harsh measures imposed upon the Southern people would continue until they had extended suffrage to the former slaves, disfranchised the majority of their White population, and then drafted new State constitutions and elected new officers based upon their new electorate. In addition, each of the new States was not only required to ratify the Fourteenth Amendment, but the Amendment had to actually become a part of the federal Constitution before military rule would be lifted and the State would be entitled to representation in Congress.[39] Even then, the readmission of each of the States was left to the discretion of Congress. By making these demands, "the Radicals were driven to the absurd conclusion that the states could not qualify as members of the Union until after they had performed a function which only members can perform, *i.e.* ratify a Federal constitutional amendment."[40] It will be recalled that the States which were overthrown on the excuse that they were illegal, were the same States which had been called upon to ratify, and had actually ratified, the Thirteenth Amendment just two years earlier. As Andrew Johnson pointed out in his veto of the supplementary Reconstruction Act of 19 July 1867, "It is now too late to say that these ten political communities are not States of this Union.... [I]f this assumption that these States have no legal State governments be true, then the abolition of slavery by these illegal governments binds no one...."[41] In other words, if Stevens and the other Radicals were correct in claiming that the Southern States were not members of the Union, then the Thirteenth Amendment is not now a part of the Constitution. On the other hand, if the Thirteenth Amendment is to be accepted as valid, then the Fourteenth Amendment cannot be. When the circumstances are carefully considered, it will be admitted by any rational mind that both Amendments cannot be valid simultaneously.

37. New York *Herald*, quoted by Edmonds, *ibid.*, page 227.

38. Blaine, *Twenty Years of Congress*, Volume II, page 92.

39. Statutes at Large, Volume XIV, page 428-429.

40. Randall, *Civil War and Reconstruction*, page 787.

41. Johnson, veto of 19 July 1867 supplementary *Reconstruction Act*; in Richardson, *Messages and Papers of the Presidents*, Volume VIII, page 3738.

The adoption of the Fourteenth Amendment is one of the most atrocious debacles of American constitutional history. Not only did rump military "States" approve the amendment against the express wishes of the Southern people, but both Ohio and New Jersey subsequently reversed their positions and issued statements withdrawing their former ratification. The legislature of New Jersey declared, "The said proposed amendment not having yet received the assent of three-fourths of the States, which is necessary to make it valid, the natural and constitutional right of this State to withdraw its assent is undeniable."[42]

Because of these reversals, and the questionable nature of the reconstructed Southern States, Secretary of State William Seward, in his first proclamation of 20 July 1868, expressed some doubt as to whether the Amendment had been ratified by the required number of States. The Radicals' response was that Ohio and New Jersey did not have a right to withdraw their ratification and immediately forced a resolution through both Houses of Congress listing the purported ratification date of each State and declaring that "said fourteenth article... is declared to be part of the Constitution... and it shall be duly promulgated as such by the Secretary of State."[43] Seward capitulated to the pressure thus placed upon him and issued a second proclamation dated 28 July 1868 listing the supposed ratifications — which list differed from that of the congressional resolution — and certifying that the Amendment had "become valid to all intents and purposes as a part of the Constitution of the United States."[44] The date of Seward's second proclamation is usually that which is given to the adoption of the Fourteenth Amendment.

Senator James R. Doolittle of Wisconsin noted on 23 January 1868 that the sole purpose of Reconstruction was to "put the negro in power over the white race in all the States of the South and keep him there."[45] Once again, it needs to be stressed that the welfare of the Negro, as an end in itself, was never the primary concern of the Radicals in the Thirty-Ninth and Fortieth Congresses. Just as Johnson had warned in 1866, they used the Black man "for the attainment of [their] own political ends," and when their "fool's errand"[46] failed, they turned their backs on the freedman and left him to the mercies of a ravaged and embittered South. The following words were published in the Lemars (Iowa) *Sentinel*, a staunch Republican organ just a few years after Reconstruction was abandoned in the South:

> The Southern brigadier wants office and place, but he is willing to fight for them, or vote for them; at the drop of the hat he will shoot and cut for them; he does not whine like a whipped cur, or demand like a beggar on horseback, as the nigger does. Let the

---

42. New Jersey Acts, 27 March 1868.

43. *Congressional Globe* (Fortieth Congress, Second Session), pages 4295.

44. Statutes at Large, Volume XV, pages 708-711.

45. James R. Doolittle, *Congressional Globe* (Fortieth Congress, Second Session), page 700.

46. Albion Winegar Tourgee, *A Fool's Errand* (New York: Fords, Howard and Hulbert, 1880).

nigger first learn to vote before he asks for office. The brazen-jawed nigger is but a trifle less assuming, insolent and imperious in his demands than the lantern-jawed brigadiers; the educated nigger is a more capacious liar than his barbarian masters ever were, or dared to be.

The greatest mistake the Republican party ever made was taking the nigger at a single bound and placing on his impenetrable skull the crown of suffrage. It is a wrong to him and to us to let him wield the ballot. The nigger is necessarily an ignoramus. The free nigger, we repeat, is a fraud.[47]

The Supreme Court Denies Jurisdiction

The constitutionality of the Reconstruction Acts was brought before the Supreme Court on several occasions. In the cases of *Georgia v. Stanton* and *Mississippi v. Stanton*, both States sought injunctive relief against the Secretary of War, Edwin M. Stanton, and Generals Ulysses S. Grant, John Pope, and E.C. Ord who were empowered by the Reconstruction Acts to establish military governments in place of the existing State governments. The bill for injunction which was filed in behalf of the State of Georgia stated in part:

A State is a complete body of free persons united together for their common benefit, to enjoy peaceably what is their own, and to do justice to others. It is an artificial person. It has its affairs and its interests. It has its rules. It has its rights. A republican State, in every political, legal, constitutional, and juridical sense, as well under the law of nations, as the laws and usages of the mother country, is composed of those persons who, according to its existing constitution or fundamental law, are the constituent body. All other persons within its territory, or socially belonging to its people, as a human society, are subject to its laws, and may justly claim its protection; but they are not, in contemplation of law, any portion of the body politic known and recognized as the State. On principle it must be quite clear that the body politic is composed of those who by the fundamental law are the source of all political power, or official or governmental authority.... The State has a right to maintain its constitution or political association. And it is its duty to do what may be necessary to preserve that association. And no external power has a right to interfere with or disturb it....

The change proposed by the two acts of Congress in question is fundamental and vital. The acts seize upon a large portion — whites — of the constituent body and exclude them from acting as members of the State. It violently thrusts into the constituent body, as members thereof, a multitude of individuals — negroes — not entitled by the fundamental law of Georgia to exercise political powers. The State is to be Africanized. This will work a virtual extinction of the existing body politic, and the creation of a new, distinct, and independent body politic, to take its place and enjoy its rights and property. Such new State would be formed, not by the free will or consent of Georgia or her people, nor by the assent or acquiescence of her existing government or magistracy, but by external force.

---

47. Lemars (Iowa) *Sentinel*, 1880; quoted by Edmonds, *Facts and Falsehoods*, page 220.

Instead of keeping the guaranty against a forcible overthrow of its government by foreign invaders or domestic insurgents, this is destroying that very government by force....

Independently of this principle, the forced acquiescence of the people, under the pressure of military power, would soon work a virtual extinction of the existing political society. Each aspect of the case shows that the impending evil will produce consequences fatal to the continuance of the present State, and, consequently, that the injury would be irreparable.[48]

Jeremiah Sullivan Black, who had served as Secretary of State in the Buchanan Administration,[49] further spoke in behalf of the State of Georgia:

The defendants avow their intention to take the Government of the State of Georgia into their own hands, to nullify its laws, to control the election of its officers, to deprive its people of the right to be tried by their own courts and juries, to break up its whole social organization, to destroy its existence, and reduce it and all its people to a state of complete slavery. It is not possible to conceive how a greater wrong or more grievous injury can be committed against any large body of persons. Nor is it to be pretended that these things are to be done in pursuance of any valid law. The Constitution makes Georgia a free State, and the Act of Congress, which requires it to be enslaved, is an attempt to repeal the Constitution. The counsel for the defendants will admit that the Act of Congress is unconstitutional; and if that be true, it is of no more force than if the place it occupies on the statute book were a blank. The defendants are, therefore, guilty of a great injury against Georgia, and are committing it without the show or color of legal excuse....

If these propositions be true, the State of Georgia is a proper party in this court, complaining of an attempted infraction of its rights. No defense has yet been suggested by the defendants' counsel; no denial of the facts; no assertion that they were justified by legal authority. Was an injunction ever denied in such a case?[50]

Black, of course, was in for a big surprise. Delivering the opinion of the Court, Justice Samuel Nelson wrote:

By the second section of the third article of the Constitution "the judicial power extends to all cases, in law and equity, arising under the Constitution, the laws of the United States," *etc.*, and as applicable to the case in hand, "to controversies between a State and the citizens of another State" — which controversies, under the Judiciary Act, may be brought, in the first instance, before this court in the exercise of its original juris-

---

48. *Georgia v. Stanton* (1867), 73 U.S. 50, 65-67.

49. Black had written a lengthy legal brief in 1861 denying the power of the federal Government to militarily coerce a State. He was also the one who drafted Andrew Johnson's veto of the Reconstruction bill of 2 March 1867.

50. *Georgia v. Stanton.*

diction, and we agree that the bill filed presents a case, which, if it be the subject of judicial cognizance, would, in form, come under a familiar need of equity jurisdiction; that is, jurisdiction to grant an injunction to restrain a party from a wrong or injury to the rights of another, where the danger, actual or threatened, is irreparable, or the remedy at law inadequate. But, according to the course of proceeding under this head in equity, in order to entitle the party to the remedy, a case must be presented appropriate for the exercise of judicial power: the rights in danger, as we have seen, must be rights of persons or property, not merely political rights, which do not belong to the jurisdiction of a court, either in law or equity.

The remaining question on this branch of our inquiry is, whether, in view of the principles above stated, and which we have endeavored to explain, a case is made out in the bill of which this court can take judicial cognizance. In looking into it, it will be seen that we are called upon to restrain the defendants, who represent the executive authority of the government, from carrying into execution certain Acts of Congress, inasmuch as such execution would annul and totally abolish the existing State Government of Georgia, and establish another and different one in its place: in other words, would overthrow and destroy the corporate existence of the State, by depriving it of the means and instrumentalities whereby its existence might, and otherwise would, be maintained....

That these matters, both as stated in the body of the bill, and in the prayers for relief, call for the judgment of the court upon political questions, and upon rights, not of persons or property, but of a political character, will hardly be denied. For the rights, for the protection of which our authority is invoked, are the rights of sovereignty, of political jurisdiction, of government, of corporate existence as a State, with all its constitutional powers and privileges. No case of private rights or private property infringed, or in danger of actual or threatened infringement, is presented by the bill, in a judicial form, for the judgment of the court....

Having arrived at the conclusion that this court, for the reasons above stated, possesses no jurisdiction over the subject matter presented in the bill for relief, it is unimportant to examine the question as it respects jurisdiction over the parties.
The bill must be dismissed for want of jurisdiction (emphasis in original).[51]

Chief Justice Salmon Chase added, "Without being able to yield my assent to the grounds stated in the opinion just read for the dismissal of the complainant's bill, I concur fully in the conclusion that the case made by the bill is one of which this court has no jurisdiction."[52] The petition of Mississippi was similarly dismissed.

In Article III, Section 3, Clause 1 of the Constitution — the very Article which created the Judicial Branch of the federal Government — we are told that "treason against the United States, shall consist in levying War against them...." As demonstrated in a previous chapter, and as is evident by the plural use of "United States" in this provision, treason has no constitutional meaning if not in reference to the several States. The utter destruction

---

51. *Ibid.*, 75-77.

52. *Ibid.*, 77-78.

of a State government, especially in a presidentially-announced time of peace, would certainly qualify as "levying War" against it. The Constitution also provides in Article IV, Section 2, Clause 1 that "the Citizens of each State shall be entitled to all Privileges and Immunities of Citizens in the several States." To disfranchise thousands of Citizens of a State and to subjugate them to a foreign government without their consent was a clear violation of this provision. Furthermore, in Article IV, Section 3, Clause 1, we read that "no new State shall be formed or erected within the Jurisdiction of any other State," and finally, in Article IV, Section 4 that "the United States shall guarantee to every State in this Union a Republican Form of Government, and shall protect them against Invasion." Would it not be reasonable to assume that these blatant violations of "the supreme Law of the Land" and an apparent attempt to abrogate the Constitution itself, was, in fact, a case in law to which the jurisdiction of the Supreme Court extended? No greater example of an abrogation of duty could be given than by the above inaction of the Court during Reconstruction.

The constitutionality of the Reconstruction Acts was again brought before the Supreme Court on 2 March 1868 in the case of *Ex parte William H. McCardle*.[53] This time, the Court could not evade the issue by claiming a lack of jurisdiction, since the suit involved the personal liberty of a Citizen of Mississippi who had been arrested for criticizing the Reconstruction Acts and held by military force contrary to the Sixth Amendment to the Constitution. However, before the 5-4 ruling in favor of McCardle and against the validity of the Act under which he was being held could be published, the Radicals in Congress passed an Act on 27 March 1868 over the President's veto which deprived the Court of jurisdiction and forever placed the Reconstruction Acts beyond adjudication.[54] According to Robert C. Schenck of Ohio, this action was intended to "clip the wings" of the Court.[55] Other suggested measures were to "pack" the Court, to reduce the number of justices to three,[56] and to require a two-thirds majority agreement of the justices to effect a decision.[57] John A. Bingham of Ohio even went so far as to call for the abolition of the Court altogether.[58] McCardle's petition for a writ of *habeas corpus* was thereafter denied and the case summarily dismissed. Robert C. Grier was the only member of the Court who had the courage to protest the strong-armed tactics of Congress and the subservient response of his fellow justices:

---

53. *Ex parte McCardle* (1868), 74 U.S. 506

54. Statutes at Large, Volume XV, page 44.

55. Robert C. Schenck, quoted by Charles Warren, *The Supreme Court in United States History* (Boston: Little, Brown and Company, 1926), Volume II, pages 474-475.

56. *Congressional Globe* (Fortieth Congress, Second Session), page 484.

57. *Ibid.*, page 488.

58. Ellis P. Oberholtzer, *A History of the United States Since the Civil War* (New York: Macmillan Company, 1917), Volume I, page 465.

This case was fully argued in the beginning of this month. It is a case which involves the liberty and rights, not only of the appellant, but of millions of our fellow citizens. The country and the parties had a right to expect that it would receive the immediate and solemn attention of the court. By the postponement of this case we shall subject ourselves, whether justly or unjustly, to the imputation that we have evaded the performance of a duty imposed on us by the Constitution, and waited for Legislative interposition to suppress our action, and relieve us from responsibility. I am not willing to be a partaker of the eulogy or opprobrium that may follow. I can only say... I am ashamed that such opprobrium should be cast upon the court and that it cannot be refuted.[59]

Andrew Johnson correctly assessed the problems of Reconstruction when he addressed Congress on 9 December 1868:

Upon the reassembling of Congress it again becomes my duty to call your attention to the state of the Union and to its continued disorganized condition under the various laws which have been passed upon the subject of reconstruction....

Our own history, although embracing a period less than a century, affords abundant proof that most, if not all, of our domestic troubles are directly traceable to violations of the organic law and excessive legislation. The most striking illustrations of this fact are furnished by the enactments of the past three years upon the question of reconstruction. After a fair trial they have substantially failed and proved pernicious in their results, and there seems to be no good reason why they should longer remain upon the statute book. States to which the Constitution guarantees a republican form of government have been reduced to military dependencies, in each of which the people have been made subject to the arbitrary will of the commanding general....

The Federal Constitution — the *magna charta* of American rights, under whose wise and salutary provisions we have successfully conducted all our domestic and foreign affairs, sustained ourselves in peace and in war, and become a great nation among the powers of the earth — must assuredly be now adequate to the settlement of questions growing out of the civil war, waged alone for its vindication. This great fact is made most manifest by the condition of the country when Congress assembled in the month of December, 1865. Civil strife had ceased, the spirit of rebellion had spent its entire force, in the Southern States the people had warmed into national life, and throughout the whole country a healthy reaction in public sentiment had taken place. By the application of the simple yet effective provisions of the Constitution the executive department, with the voluntary aid of the States, had brought the work of restoration as near completion as was within the scope of its authority, and the nation was encouraged by the prospect of an early and satisfactory adjustment of all its difficulties. Congress, however, intervened, and, refusing to perfect the work so nearly consummated, declined to admit members from the unrepresented States, adopted a series of measures which arrested the progress of restoration, frustrated all that had been so successfully accomplished, and, after three years of

---

59. Robert C. Grier, quoted by Leander H. Perez, *Congressional Record — House*, 13 June 1967, page 15644.

agitation and strife, has left the country further from the attainment of union and fraternal feeling than at the inception of the Congressional plan of reconstruction. It needs no argument to show that legislation which has produced such baneful consequences should be abrogated, or else made to conform to the genuine principles of republican government.[60]

It is undeniable that the preservation of the Union of States under the Constitution — the object for which, as Johnson noted, the late war had allegedly been waged by the U.S. Government — was completely nullified by the actions of the Thirty-Ninth and Fortieth Congresses. Despite Johnson's warning, the "disorganized condition" of the country was soon to be made permanent and the States, not only in the South, but in the North as well, were systematically overthrown.

---

60. Johnson, Fourth Annual Address, 9 December 1868; in Richardson, *Messages and Papers of the Presidents*, Volume VIII, pages 3870, 3871.

SUPPORTING DOCUMENT

Andrew Johnson's Veto of the First Reconstruction Bill

Washington, D.C., March 2, 1867

To the House of Representatives of the United States:

I have examined the bill to provide for the more efficient government of the Rebel States' with care and anxiety which its transcendent importance is calculated to awaken. I am unable to give it my assent for reasons so grave that I hope a statement of them may have some influence on the minds of the patriotic and enlightened men with whom the decision must ultimately rest.

The bill places all the people of the ten States therein named under the absolute domination of military rule; and the preamble undertakes to give the reason upon which the measure is based and the ground upon which it is justified. It declares that there exists in those States no legal governments and no adequate protection for life or property, and asserts the necessity of enforcing peace and good order within their limits. This is not true as a matter of fact.

It is not denied that the States in question have each of them an actual government, with all the powers — executive, judicial, and legislative — which properly belong to a free State. They are organized like the other States of the Union, and, like them, they make, administer, and execute the laws which concern their domestic affairs. An existing *de facto* government, exercising such functions as these, is itself the law of the State upon all matters within its jurisdiction. To pronounce the supreme law making power of an established State illegal is to say that law itself is unlawful.

The provisions which these governments have made for the preservation of order, the suppression of crime, and the redress of private injuries are in substance and principle the same as those which prevail in the Northern States and in other civilized countries. They certainly have not succeeded in preventing the commission of all crime, nor has this been accomplished any where in the world.... But that people are maintaining local governments for themselves which habitually defeat the object of all government and render their own lives and property insecure is in itself utterly improbable, and the averment of the bill to that effect is not supported by any evidence which has come to my knowledge.

The bill, however, would seem to show upon its face that the establishment of peace and good order is not its real object. The fifth section declares that the preceding sections shall cease to operate in any State where certain events shall have happened. These events are, first, the selection of delegates to a State convention by an election at which Negroes shall be allowed to vote; second, the formation of a State constitution by the convention so chosen; third, the insertion into the State constitution of a provision which will secure the right of voting at all elections to Negroes and to such white men as may not be disfranchised for rebellion or felony; fourth, the submission of the constitution for ratification by their vote; fifth, the submission of the State constitution to Congress for examination and approval, and the actual approval of it by that body; sixth, the adoption of a certain amendment to the Federal Constitution by a vote of Legislature elected under the new constitution; seventh, the adoption of said amendment by a sufficient number of other States to make it a part of the Constitution of the United States. All these conditions must be fulfilled before the people of any of these States can be relieved from the bondage of military domination; but when they are fulfilled, then immediately the pains and penalties of the bill are to cease, no matter whether there be peace and order or not, and without any reference to the security of life or property.

The excuse given for the bill in the preamble is one of necessity. The military rule which it establishes is plainly to be used, not for any purpose of order or for the prevention of crime, but solely as a means of coercing the people into the adoption of principles and measures to which it is known that they are opposed, and upon which they have an undeniable right to exercise their own judgment.

I submit to Congress whether this measure is not in its whole character, scope, and object without precedent and without authority, in palpable conflict with the plainest provisions of liberty and humanity for which our ancestors on both sides of the Atlantic have shed so much blood, and expended so much treasure.

The ten States named in the bill are divided into five districts. For each district an officer of the Army, not below the rank of a brigadier-general, is to be appointed to rule over the people; and he is to be supported with an efficient military force to enable him to perform his duties and enforce his authority. Those duties and that authority, as defined by the third section of the bill, are "to protect all persons in their rights of person and property, to suppress insurrection, disorder, and violence, and to punish or cause to be punished all disturbers of the public peace or criminals." The power thus given to the commanding officer over all the people of each district is that of an absolute monarch. His mere will is to take the place of all law. The law of the States is now the only rule applicable to the subjects placed under his control, and that is completely displaced by the clause which declares all interference of State authority to be null and void. He alone is permitted to determine what are rights of person or property, and he may protect them in such a way as in his discretion may seem proper. It places at his free disposal all the lands and goods in his district, and he may distribute them without let or hindrance to whom he pleases. Being bound by no State law, and there being no other law to regulate the subject, he may make a criminal code of his own; and he can make it as bloody as any recorded in history or he can reserve the privilege of acting upon the impulse of his private passions in each case that arises. He is bound by no rules of evidence; there is indeed no provision by which he is authorized or required to take any evidence at all. Every thing is a crime which he chooses to call so, and all persons are condemned whom he pronounces to be guilty. He is not bound to keep any record or make any report of his proceedings. He may arrest his victims wherever he finds them, without warrant, accusation, or proof of probable cause. If he gives them a trial before he inflicts the punishment, he gives it of his grace and mercy, not because he is commanded so to do.

Cruel or unusual punishment is not to be inflicted, but who is to decide what is cruel and what is unusual?... Each officer may define cruelty according to his own temper, and if it is not usual, he will make it usual. Corporal punishment, imprisonment, the gag, the ball and chain, and the almost insupportable forms of torture invented for military punishment lie within the range of choice. The sentence of a commission is not to be executed without being approved by the commander, if it affects life or liberty, and a sentence of death must be approved by the President. This applies to cases in which there has been a trial and sentence. I take it to be clear, under this bill, that the military commander may condemn to death without even the form of a trial by a military commission, so that the life of the condemned may depend upon the will of two men instead of one.

It is plain that the authority here given to the military officer amounts to absolute despotism. But to make it still more unendurable, the bill provides that it may be delegated to as many subordinates as he chooses to appoint, for it declares that he shall "punish or cause to be punished." Such a power has not been wielded by any Monarch in England for more than five hundred years. In all that time no people who speak the English language have borne such servitude. It reduces the whole population of the ten States — all persons, of every color, sex and condition, and every stranger within their limits — to the most abject and degrading slavery. No master ever had a control so absolute over the slaves as this bill gives to the military officers over both white and colored persons.

I come now to a question which is, if possible, still more important. Have we the power to establish and carry into execution a measure like this? I answer, "Certainly not," if we derive our authority from the Constitution and if we are bound by the limitations which it imposes. This proposition is perfectly clear, that no branch of the Federal Government — executive, legislative, or judicial — can have any just powers except those which it derives through and exercises under the organic laws of the Union. Outside of the Constitution we have no legal authority more than private citizens, and within it we have only so much as that instrument gives us. This broad principle limits all our functions and applies to all subjects. It protects not only the citizens of States which are within the Union, but it shields every human being who comes or is brought under our jurisdiction. We have no right to do in one place more than in another that which the Constitution says we shall not do at all. If, therefore, the Southern States were in truth out of the Union, we could not treat their people in a way which the fundamental law forbids. Some persons assume that the success of our arms in crushing the opposition which was made in some of the States to the execution of the Federal laws reduced those States and all their people — the innocent as well as the guilty — to the condition of vassalage and gave us a power over them which the Constitution does not bestow or define or limit. No fallacy can be more transparent than this. Our victories subjected the insurgents to legal obedience, not to the yoke of an arbitrary despotism. When an absolute sovereign reduces his rebellious subjects, he may deal with them according to his pleasure, because he had that power before. But when a limited monarch puts down an insurrection, he must still govern according to law.

If an insurrection should take place in one of our States against the authority of the State government, and end in the overthrowing of those who planned it, would they take away the rights of all the people of the counties where it was favored by a part or a majority of the population? Could they for such a reason be wholly outlawed and deprived of their representation in the Legislature? I have always contended that the Government of the United States was sovereign within its constitutional sphere; that it executed its laws like the States themselves, by applying its coercive power directly to individuals; and that it could put down insurrection with the same effect as a State and no other. The opposite doctrine is the worst heresy of those who advocated secession, and can not be agreed to without admitting that heresy to be right.

This is a bill passed by Congress in time of peace. There is not in any one of the States brought under its operation either war or insurrection. The laws of the States and of the Federal Government are all in undisturbed and harmonious operation. The courts, State and Federal, are open and in the full exercise of their proper authority. Over every State comprised in these five military districts, life, and property are secured by State laws and Federal laws, and the National Constitution is every where in force and every where obeyed. What, then is the ground on which the bill proceeds? The title of the bill announces that it is intended "for the more efficient government" of these ten States. It is recited by way of preamble that no legal State Governments "nor adequate protection for life or property" exist in those States, and that peace and good order should be thus recitals, which prepare the way for martial law, is this, that the only foundation upon which martial law can exist under our form of Government is not stated or so much as pretended. Actual war, foreign invasion, domestic insurrection — none of these appear, and none of these in fact exist. It is not even recited that any sort of war or insurrection is threatened. Let us pause to consider, upon this question of constitutional law and power of Congress, a recent decision of the Supreme Court of the United States in *ex parte Milligan*, I will first quote from the opinion of the majority of the Court: "Martial law can not arise from a threatened invasion. The necessity must be actual and present, the invasion real, such as effectually closes the courts and deposes the civil administration."

We see that martial law comes in only when actual war closes the courts and deposes the civil authority; but this bill, in time of peace, makes martial law operate as though we were in actual war, and becomes the cause instead of the consequence of the abrogation of civil authority. One more quotation:

> It follows from what has been said on this subject that there are occasions when martial law can be properly applied. If in foreign invasion or civil war the courts are actually closed, and it is impossible to administer criminal justice according to law, then, on the theater of active military operations, where war really prevails, there is a necessity to furnish a substitute for the civil authority thus overthrown, to preserve the safety of the army and society; and as no power is left but the military, it is allowed to govern by martial rule until the laws can have their free course.

I now quote from the opinion of the minority of the Court, delivered by Chief Justice Chase: "We by no means assert that Congress can establish and apply the laws of war where no war has been declared or exists. Where peace exists, the laws of peace must prevail."

This is sufficiently explicit. Peace exists in all the territory to which this bill applies. It asserts a power in Congress, in time of peace, to set aside the laws of peace and to substitute the laws of war. The minority, concurring with the majority, declares that Congress does not possess that power.... I need not say to the representatives of the American people that their Constitution forbids the exercise of judicial power in any way but one — that is, by the ordained and established courts. It is equally well known that in all criminal cases a trial by jury is made indispensable by the express words of that instrument.

I need not say to the Representatives of the American people that their Constitution forbids the exercise of judicial power in any way but one; that is, by the ordained and established courts. It is equally well known that, in all criminal cases, a trial by jury is made indispensable by the express words of that instrument. I will not enlarge on the inestimable value of the right thus secured to every freeman, or speak of the danger to public liberty, in all parts of the country, which must ensue from a denial of it anywhere, or upon any pretense.

The Constitution also forbids the arrest of the citizen without judicial warrant, founded on probable cause. This bill authorizes an arrest without warrant, at pleasure of a military commander. The Constitution declares that "no person shall be held to answer for a capital or otherwise infamous crime unless on presentment of a grand jury." This bill holds every person not a soldier answerable for all crimes and all charges without any presentment. The Constitution declares that "no person shall be deprived of life, liberty, or property without due process of law." This bill sets aside all process of law, and makes the citizen answerable in his person and property to the will of one man, and as to his life to the will of two. Finally, the Constitution declares that "the privilege of the writ of *habeas corpus* shall not be suspended unless when, in case of rebellion or invasion, the public safety may require it"; whereas this bill declares martial law (which of itself suspends this great writ) in time of peace, and authorizes the military to make the arrest, and gives to the prisoner only one privilege, and that is trial "without unnecessary delay." He has no hope of release from custody, except the hope, such as it is, of release by acquittal before a military commission.

The United States are bound to guaranty to each State a republican form of government. Can it be pretended that this obligation is not palpably broken if we carry out a measure like this, which wipes away every vestige of republican government in ten States and puts the life, property, and honor of all people in each of them under domination of a single person clothed with unlimited authority?

Here is a bill of attainder against 9,000,000 people at once. It is based upon an accusation so vague as to be scarcely intelligible and found to be true upon no credible evidence. Not one of the 9,000,000 was heard in his own defense. The representatives of the doomed parties were excluded from all participation in the trial. The conviction is to be followed by the most ignominious punishment ever inflicted on large masses of men. It disfranchises them by hundreds of thousands and degrades them all, even those who are admitted to be guiltless, from the rank of freeman to the condition of slaves.

The purpose and object of the bill — the general intent which pervades it from beginning to end — is to change the entire structure and character of the State Governments and to compel them by force to the adoption of organic laws and regulations which they are unwilling to accept if left to themselves. The Negroes have not asked for the privilege of voting; the vast majority of them have no idea what it means. This bill not only thrusts it into their hands, but compels them, as well as the whites, to use it in a particular way. If they do not form a constitution with prescribed articles in it and afterwards elect a legislature which will act upon certain measures in a prescribed way, neither blacks nor whites can be relieved from the slavery which the bill imposes upon them. Without pausing here to consider the policy or impolicy of Africanizing the southern part of our territory, I would simply ask the attention of Congress to the manifest, well-known, and universally acknowledged rule of Constitutional law which declares that the Federal Government has no jurisdiction, authority, or power to regulate such subjects for any State. To force the right of suffrage out of the hands of white people and into the hands of the Negroes is an arbitrary violation of this principle.

This bill imposes martial law at once, and its operations will begin so soon as the General and his troops can be put in place. The dread alternative between its harsh rule and compliance with the terms of this measure is not suspended, nor are the people afforded any time for free deliberation. The bill says to them, Take martial law first, then deliberate.

The bill also denies the legality of the governments of ten of the States which participated in the ratification of the amendment to the Federal Constitution abolishing slavery forever within the jurisdiction of the United States, and practically excludes them from the Union.

That the measure proposed by this bill does violate the Constitution in the particulars mentioned and in many other ways which I forbear to enumerate is too clear to admit the least doubt. It only remains to consider whether the injunctions of that instrument ought to be obeyed or not. I think they ought to be obeyed, for reasons which I will proceed to give as briefly as possible. In the first place, it is the only system of free Government which we can hope to have as a Nation. When it ceases to be the rule of our conduct, we may perhaps take our choice between complete anarchy, a consolidated despotism, and a total dissolution of the Union; but national liberty regulated by law will have passed beyond our reach.

It was to punish the gross crime of defying the Constitution and to vindicate its supreme authority that we carried on a bloody war of four years' duration. Shall we now acknowledge that we sacrificed a million of lives and expended billions of treasure to enforce a Constitution which is not worthy of respect and preservation?

It is a part of our public history which can never be forgotten that both Houses of Congress, in July 1861, declared in the form of a solemn resolution that the war was and should be carried on for no purpose of subjugation, but solely to enforce the Constitutional rights of the States and of individuals unimpaired. This resolution was adopted and sent forth to the world unanimously by the Senate and with only two dissenting voices in the House. It was accepted by the friends of the Union in the South as well as in the North as expressing honestly and truly the object of the war. On the faith of it many thousands of persons in both sections gave their lives and their fortunes to the cause. To repudiate it now by refusing to the States and to the individuals within them the "rights" which the Constitution and laws of the Union would secure to them is a breach of our plighted honor for which I can imagine no excuse and to which I cannot voluntarily become a party.

I am thoroughly convinced that any settlement or compromise or plan of actions which is inconsistent with the principles of the Constitution will not only be unavailing, but mischievous; that it will but multiply the present evils, instead of removing them. The Constitution, in its whole integrity and vigor, throughout the length and breadth of the land, is the best of all compromises. Besides, our duty does not, in my judgment, leave us a choice between that and any other. I believe that it contains the remedy that is so much needed, and that if the coordinate branches of the Government would unite upon its provisions they would be found broad enough and strong enough to sustain in time of peace the Nation which they bore safely through the ordeal of a protracted civil war. Among the most sacred guaranties of that instrument are those which declare that "each State shall have at least one Representative," and that "no State, without its consent, shall be deprived of its equal suffrage in the Senate." Each House is made the "judge of the elections, returns and qualifications of its own members," and may, "with the concurrence of two-thirds, expel a member." Thus, as heretofore urged, "in the admission of Senators and Representatives from any and all of the States there can no just ground of apprehension that persons who are disloyal will be clothed with the powers of legislation, for this could not happen when the Constitution and the laws are enforced by a vigilant and faithful Congress." When a Senator or Representative presents his certificate of election, he may at once be admitted or rejected, or, should there be any question as to his eligibility, his credentials may be referred for investigation to the appropriate committee. If admitted to a seat, it must be upon evidence satisfactory to the House of which he thus becomes a member that he possesses the requisite constitutional and legal qualifications. If refused admission as a member for want of due allegiance to the Government, and returned to his constituents, they are admonished that none but persons loyal to the United States will be allowed a voice in the legislative councils of the Nation, and the political power and moral influence of Congress are\ thus effectively exerted in the interests of loyalty to the Government and fidelity of the Union.

And is it not far better that the work of restoration should be accomplished by simple compliance with the plain requirements of the Constitution, than by a recourse to measures which, in effect, destroy the States, and threaten the subversion of the General Government? All that is necessary to settle this simple but important question, without further agitation or delay, is a willingness, on the part of all, to sustain the Constitution, and carry its provisions into practical operation. If to-morrow either branch of Congress would declare that, upon the presentation of their credentials, members constitutionally elected, and loyal to the General Government, would be admitted to seats in Congress, while all others would be excluded, and their places remain vacant until the selection by the people of loyal and qualified persons; and if, at the same time, assurance were given that this policy would be continued until all the States were represented in Congress, it would send a thrill of joy throughout the entire land, as indicating the inauguration of a system which must speedily bring tranquility to the public mind.

While we are legislating upon subjects which are of great importance to the whole people, and which must affect all parts of the country, not only hurting the life of the present generation, but for ages to come, we should remember that all men are entitled at least to a hearing in the councils which decide upon the destiny of themselves and their children. At present ten States are denied representation, and when the Fortieth Congress assembles on the 4th day of the present month sixteen States will be without a voice in the House of Representatives. This grave fact, with the important questions before us, should induce us to pause in a course of legislation which, looking solely to the attainment of political ends, fails to consider the rights it transgresses, the law which it violates, or the institutions which it imperils.

Andrew Johnson.

SUPPORTING DOCUMENT
Opinion of Attorney General Henry Stanbery
on the First Reconstruction Act

Attorney General's Office,
June 12, 1867.

Sir: On the 24th ultimo, I had the honor to transmit for your consideration my opinion upon some of the questions arising under the reconstruction acts therein referred to. I now proceed to give my opinion on the remaining questions upon which the military commanders require instructions.

1. As to the powers and duties of these commanders.

The original act recites in its preamble, that "no legal State governments or adequate protection for life or property exists" in those ten States, and that "it is necessary that peace and good order should be enforced" in those States "until loyal and republican State governments can be legally established."

The 1st and 2d sections divide these States into five military districts, subject to the military authority of the United States, as thereinafter described, and make it the duty of the President to assign from the officers of the army a general officer to the command of each district, and to furnish him with a military force to perform his duties and enforce his authority within his district.

The 3d section declares, "that it shall be the duty of each officer, assigned as aforesaid, to protect all persons in their rights of person and property, to suppress insurrection, disorder, and violence, and to punish, or cause to be punished, all disturbers of the public peace and criminals, and to this end he may allow local civil tribunals to take jurisdiction of and try offenders, or, when in his judgment it may be necessary for the trial of offenders, he shall have power to organize military commissions or tribunals for that purpose; and all interference, under color of State authority; with the exercise of military authority under this act, shall be null and void."

The 4th section provides, "That all persons put under military arrest by virtue of this act shall be tried without unnecessary delay, and no cruel or unusual punishment shall be inflicted; and no sentence of any military commission or tribunal hereby authorized, affecting the life or liberty of any person, shall be executed, until it is approved by the officer in command of the district, and the laws and regulations for the government of the army shall not be affected by this act, except in so far as they conflict with its provisions: *Provided*, That no sentence of death under the provision of this act shall be carried into effect without the approval of the President."

The 5th section declares the qualification of voters in all elections, as well to frame the new constitution for each State, as in the elections to be held under the provisional government, until the new State constitution is ratified by Congress, and also fixes the qualifications of the delegates to frame the new constitution.

The 6th section provides, "That until the people of said rebel States shall be by law admitted by representation in the Congress of the United States, any civil governments which may exist shall be deemed provisional only, and in all respects subject to the paramount authority of the United States at any time to abolish, modify, control, or supersede the same; and in all elections to any office under such provisional governments all persons shall be entitled to vote, and none others, who are entitled to vote under the provisions of the 5th section of this act; and no person shall be eligible to any office under any such provisional government who would not be disqualified from holding office under the provisions of the third article of said constitutional amendment."

The duties devolved upon the commanding general by the supplementary act relate together to the registration of voters, and the elections to be held under the provisions of that act. And as to the duties, they are plainly enough expressed in the act, and it is not understood that any question, not heretofore considered in the opinion referred to, has arisen, or is likely to arise, in respect to them.

My attention, therefore, is directed to the powers and duties of the military commanders under the original act.

We see clearly that this act contemplates two distinct governments in each of these ten States: the one military, the other civil. The civil government is recognized as existing at the date of the act. The military government is created by the act.

Both are provisional, and both are to continue until the new State constitution is framed and the State is admitted to representation in Congress. When that event takes place, both these provisional governments are to cease. In contemplation of this act, this military authority and this civil authority are to be carried on together. The people in these States are made subject to both, and must obey both, in their respective jurisdictions.

There is, then, an imperative necessity to define as clearly as possible the line which separates the two jurisdictions, and the exact scope of the authority of each.

Now, as to the civil authority recognized by the act as the provisional civil government, it covered every department of civil jurisdiction in each of these States. It had all the characteristics and powers of a State government — legislative, judicial, and executive — and was in the full and lawful exercise of all these powers, except only that it was not entitled to representation as a State of the Union. This existing government is not set aside; it is recognized more than once by the act. It is not in any one of its departments, or as to any one of its functions, repealed or modified by this act, save only in the qualifications of voters, the qualifications of persons eligible to office, and the constitution of the State. The act does not in any other respect change the provisional government, nor does the act authorize the military authority to change it. The power of further changing it is reserved, not granted, and it is reserved to Congress, not delegated to the military commander.

Congress was not satisfied with the organic law or constitution under which this civil government was established. *That* constitution was to be changed in only one particular to make it acceptable to Congress, and that was in the matter of the elective franchise. The purpose, the sole object of this act, is to effect that change, and to effect it by the agency of the people of the State, or such of them as are made voters, by means of elections provided for in the act, and in the meantime to preserve order and to punish offenders, if found necessary, by military commissions.

We are, therefore, not at a loss to know what powers were possessed by the existing civil authority. Whatever power is not given to the military remains with the civil government. We see, first of all, that each of these States is "made subject to the military authority of the United States" — not to the military authority altogether, but with this express limitation — "as hereinafter prescribed." We must, then, examine what is hereinafter provided, to find the extent and nature of the power granted.

This, then, is what is granted to the military commander: The power or duty "to protect all persons in their rights of person and property; to suppress insurrection, disorder, and violence, and punish, or cause to be punished, all disturbers of the public peace and criminals;" and he may do this by the agency of the criminal courts of the State, or, if necessary, he may resort to military tribunals. This comprises all the powers given to the military commander.

Here is a general clause, making it the duty of the military commander to give protection to all persons in their rights of person and property. Considered by itself, and without reference to the context and to other provisions of the act, it is liable, from its generality, to be misunderstood. What sort of protection is here meant? What violations of the rights of person or of property are here intended? In what manner is this protection to be given? These questions arise at once.

It appears that some of the military commanders have understood this grant of power as all comprehensive, conferring on them the power to remove the executive and judicial officers of the State, and to appoint other officers in their places; to suspend the legislative power of the State; to take under their control, by officers appointed by themselves, the collection and disbursement of the revenues of the State; to prohibit the execution of the laws of the State by the agency of its appointed officers and agents; to change the existing laws in matters affecting purely civil and private rights; to suspend or enjoin the execution of the judgments and decrees of the established State courts; to interfere in the ordinary administration of justice in the State courts, by prescribing new qualifications for jurors, and to change, upon the ground of expediency, the existing relations of the parties to contracts, giving protection to one party by violating the rights of the other party.

I feel confident that these military officers, in all they have done, have supposed that they had full warrant for their action. Their education and training have not been of the kind to fit them for the delicate and difficult task of giving construction to such a statute as that now under consideration. They require instruction, and nearly all of them have asked for instruction, to solve their own doubts, and to furnish to them a safe ground for the performance of their duties.

There can be no doubt as to the rule of construction according to which we must interpret this grant of power. It is a grant of power to military authority, over civil rights and citizens, in time of peace. It is a new jurisdiction, never granted before, by which, in certain particulars and for certain purposes, the established principle that the military shall be subordinate to the civil authority is reversed.

The rule of construction to be applied to such a grant of power is thus stated in *Dwarris on Statutes*, p. 652: "A statute creating a new jurisdiction ought to be construed strictly." Guided by this rule, and in light of other rules of construction familiar to every lawyer, especially of those which teach us that, in giving construction to single clauses, we must look to the context and to the whole law, that general clauses are to be controlled by particular clauses, and such construction is to be put on a special clause as to make it harmonize with the other parts of the statute so as to avoid repugnancy, I proceed to the construction of this part of the act.

To consider, then, in the first place, the terms of the grant. It is of a power to protect all persons in their rights of person and property. It is not a power to create new rights, but only to protect those which exist and are established by the laws under which these people live. It is a power to preserve, not to abrogate; to sustain the existing frame of social order and civil rule, and not a power to introduce military rule in its place; in effect, it is police power; and the protection here intended is protection of persons and property against violence, unlawful force, and criminal infraction. It is given to meet the contingency recited in the preamble, of a want of "adequate protection of life and property" and the necessity also recited, "that peace and good order should be enforced."

This construction is made more apparent when we look at the immediate context, and see in what mode and by what agency this protection is to be secured. This duty or power of protection is to be performed by the suppression of insurrection, disorder, and violence, and by the punishment, either by the agency of the State courts, or by military commissions, when necessary, of all disturbers of the public peace and criminals; and it is declared, that all interference, under color of State authority, with the exercise of this military authority, shall be null and void.

The next succeeding clause provides for a speedy trial of the offender, forbids the infliction of cruel and unusual punishment, and requires that sentences of these military courts, which involve the liberty of life of the accused, shall have the approval of the commanding general, and, as to the sentence of death, the approval of the President, before execution.

All these special provisions have reference to the preservation of order and protection against violence and crime. They touch no other department or function of the civil administration, save only its criminal jurisdiction, and even as to that the clear meaning of this act is, that it is not to be interfered with by the military authority, unless when a necessity for such interferences may happen to arise. I see no authority, nor any shadow of authority, for interference with any other courts, or any other jurisdiction, than criminal courts, in the exercise of criminal jurisdiction. The existing civil authority, in all its other departments — legislative, executive, and judicial — is left untouched.

There is no provision, even under the plea of necessity, to establish, by military authority, courts of tribunals for the trial of civil cases, or for the protection of such civil rights of person or property as come within the cognizance of civil courts, as contradistinguished from criminal courts. In point of fact, there was no foundation for such a grant of power; for the civil rights act, and the freedmen's bureau act, neither of which is superseded by this act, made ample provision for the protection of all merely civil rights, where the laws or courts of these States might fail to give full, impartial protection. I find no authority anywhere in this act for the removal by the military commander of the proper officers of a State, either executive or judicial, or the appointment of persons in their places. Nothing short of an express grant of power would justify the removal or the appointment of such an officer. There is no such grant expressed or even implied. On the contrary, the act clearly enough forbids it. The regular State officials, duly elected and qualified, are entitled to hold their offices. They, too, have rights which the military commander is bound to protect, not authorized to destroy.

We find the concluding clause of the 6th section of the act that these officials are recognized, and express provision is made to perpetuate them. It is enacted that, "in all elections to any office under such provisional government, all persons shall be entitled to vote, and none others, who are entitled to vote under the provisions of the 5th section of this act; and no person shall be eligible to any office under such provisional governments who would be disqualified from holding office under the provisions of this act." This provision not only recognizes all of the officers of the provisional governments, but, in case of vacancies, very clearly points out how they are to be filled; and that happens to be in the usual way, by the people, and not by any other agency or any other power, either State or federal, civil or military.

I find it impossible, under the provisions of this act to comprehend such an official as a governor of one of these States appointed to office by one of these military commanders. Certainly he is not the governor recognized by the laws of the State, elected by the people in the State, and clothed as such with the chief executive power. Nor is he appointed as a military governor for a State, which has no lawful governor, under the pressure of an existing necessity, to exercise powers at large. The intention, no doubt, was to appoint him to fill a vacancy occasioned by a military order, and to put him in the place of the removed governor, to execute the functions of the office, as provided by law.

The law takes no cognizance of such an official, and he is clothed with no authority or color of authority. What is true as to the governor is equally true as to all the other legislative, executive, and judicial officers of the State. If the military commander can oust one from his office, he can oust them all. If he can fill one vacancy, he can fill all vacancies, and thus usurp all civil jurisdiction into his own hands, or the hands of those who hold their appointments from him and subject to his power of removal, and thus frustrate the very right secured to the people by his act. Certainly this act is rigorous enough in the power which it gives. With all its severity, the right of electing their own officials is still left with the people, and it must be preserved.

I must not be misunderstood as fixing limits of the military commander in case of an actual insurrection or riot. It may happen that an insurrection in one of these States may be so general and formidable as to require the temporary suspension of all civil government, and the establishment of martial law in its place. And the same thing may be true as to local disorder or riot, in reference to the civil government of the city or place where it breaks out. Whatever power is necessary to meet such emergencies the military commander may properly exercise.

I confine myself to the proper authority of the military commander where peace and order prevail. When peace and order do prevail, it is not allowable to displace the civil officers, and appoint others in their places, under any idea that the military commander can better perform his duties, and carry out the general purposes of the act by the agency of civil officers of his own choice rather than by the lawful incumbents. The act gives him no right to resort to such agency, but does give him the right to have "a sufficient military force" to enable him "to perform his duties and enforce his authority within the district to which he is assigned."

In the suppression of insurrection and riot the military commander is wholly independent of civil authority. So, too, in the trial and punishment of criminals and offenders, he may supersede the civil jurisdiction. His power is to be exercised in the special emergencies, and the means are put into his hands by which it is to be exercised, that is to say, "a sufficient military force to enable such officer to perform his duties and enforce his authority," and military tribunals of his own appointment to try and punish offenders. These are strictly military powers, to be executed by military authority, not by the civil authority, or by civil officers appointed by him to perform ordinary civil duties. If these emergencies do not happen, if civil order is preserved, and criminals are duly prosecuted by the regular criminal courts, the military power, though present, must remain passive. Its proper function is to preserve the peace, to act promptly when the peace is broken, and restore order. When that is done, and the civil authority may again safely resume its functions, the military power again becomes passive, but on guard and watchful.

This, in my judgment, is the whole scope of the military power conferred by this act; and, in arriving at this construction of the act, I have not found it necessary to resort to the strict construction which is allowable. The military commander is made conservator of the peace, not a legislator. His duties are military duties, executive duties; not legislative duties. He has no authority to enact or declare a new code of laws for the people within his district, under any idea that he can make a better code than the people have made for themselves. The public policy is not committed to his discretion. The Congress which passed this act undertook, in certain grave particulars, to change these laws; and, these changes being made, the Congress saw no further necessity of change, but were content to leave all the other laws in full force, but subject to this emphatic declaration: that, as to these laws, and such future changes as might be expedient, the question of expediency, and the power to alter, amend, or abolish, was reserved for "the paramount authority of the United States, at any time, to abolish, modify, control, or superseded the same." Where, then does a military commander find *his* authority "to abolish, modify, control, or supersede" any one of these laws?

The enumeration of the extraordinary power exercised by the military commanders in some of the districts would extend this opinion to an unreasonable length. A few instances must suffice. In one of these districts, the governor of a State has been deposed under a threat of military force, and another person, called a governor, has been appointed by the military commander to fill his place. Thus presenting the strange spectacle of an official intrusted with the chief power to execute the laws of the State, whose authority is not recognized by the laws he is called upon to execute.

In the same district, the judge of one of the criminal courts of the State has been summarily dealt with. The act of Congress does give authority to the military commander, in cases of necessity, to transfer the jurisdiction of a criminal court to a military tribunal. That being the specific authority over the criminal courts given by the act, no other authority over them can be lawfully exercised by the military commander. But, in this instance, the judge has, by military order, been ejected from his office, and a private citizen has been appointed by the judge in his place by military authority, and is now in the exercise of criminal jurisdiction "over all crimes, misdemeanors, and offences" committed within the territorial jurisdiction of the court.

This military appointee is certainly not authorized to try any one for an offense as a member of a military tribunal, and he has just as little authority to try and punish any offender as a judge of a criminal court of the State. It happens that this private citizen, thus placed on the bench, is to sit as the sole judge in a criminal court whose jurisdiction extends to cases involving the life of the accused. If he has any judicial power in any case, he has the same power to take cognizance of capital cases, and to sentence the accused to death, and order his execution. A strange spectacle, where the judge and the criminal may very well "change places;" for if the criminal has unlawfully taken life, so too does the judge. This is the inevitable result, for the only tribunal, the only judges, if they can be called judges, which a military commander can constitute and appoint under this act, to inflict the death penalty, is a military court composed of a board, and called in the act a "military commission."

I see no relief for the condemned against the sentence of this agent of the military commander. It is not the sort of court whose sentence of death must be first approved by the commander and finally by the President, for that is allowed only where the sentence is pronounced by a "military commission." Nor is it a sentence pronounced by the rightful court of a State, but by a court and by a judge not clothed with authority under the laws of the State, but constituted by the military authority. As the representative of this military authority, this act forbids interference, "under color of State authority," with the exercise of his functions.

In another one of these districts a military order commands the governor of the State to forbid the reassembling of the legislature, and thus suspends the proper legislative power of the State. In the same district an order has been issued "to relieve the treasurer of the State from the duties, bonds, books, papers, *etc.*, appertaining to his office," and to put an "assistant quartermaster of United States volunteers" in place of the removed treasurer; the duties of which quartermaster-treasurer are thus summed up: He is to make to the headquarters of the district "the same reports and returns required from the treasurer, and a monthly statement of receipts and expenditures; he will pay all warrants for salaries which may be or become due, and legitimate expenditures for the support of the penitentiary, State asylum, and the support of the provisional State government; but no scrip or warrants for outstanding debts of other kind than those specified will be paid without special authority from these headquarters. He will deposit funds in the same manner as though they were those of the United States."

In another of these districts a body of military edicts, issued in general and special orders regularly numbered, and in occasional circulars, have been promulgated, which already begin to assume the dimensions of a code. These military orders modify the existing law in the remedies for the collection of debts, the enforcement of judgments and decrees for the payment of money, staying proceedings instituted, prohibiting in certain cases the right to bring suit, enjoining proceedings on execution for the term of twelve months, giving new liens in certain cases, establishing homestead exemptions, declaring what shall be a legal tender, abolishing in certain cases the remedy by foreign attachment, abolishing bail, "as heretofore authorized," in cases *ex contractu*, but not in "other cases, known as actions *ex delicto*," and changing in several particulars the existing laws as to the punishment of crimes, and directing that the crimes referred to "shall be punished by imprisonment at hard labor for a term not exceeding ten years nor less than two years, in the discretion of the court having jurisdiction thereof." One of these general orders, being No. 10 of the series, contains no less than seventeen sections, embodying the various changes and modifications which have been recited.

The question at once arises in the mind of every lawyer, what power or discretion belongs to the court, having jurisdiction of any of these offences, to sentence a criminal to any other or different punishment than provided by the law which vests him with jurisdiction.

The concluding paragraph of this order, No. 10, is in these words, "Any law or ordinance heretofore in force in North Carolina or South Carolina, inconsistent with the provisions of this general order, are hereby suspended and declared inoperative." Thus announcing, not only a power to suspend the laws, but to declare them generally inoperative, and assuming full powers of legislation by the military authority. The ground upon which these extraordinary powers are based is thus set forth in military order No. 1, issued in this district: "The civil government now existing in North Carolina and South Carolina is provisional only, and in all respects subject to the paramount authority of the United States, at any time to abolish, modify, control, or supersede the same." Thus far the provisions of the act of Congress are well recited. What follows is in these words: "Locals laws and municipal regulations, not inconsistent with the Constitution and laws of the United States, or the proclamations of the President, or with such regulations as are or may be prescribed in the orders of the commanding general, are hereby declared to be in force; and, in conformity therewith, civil officers are hereby authorized to continue the exercise of their proper functions, and will be respected and obeyed by the inhabitants."

This construction of his powers, under the act of Congress, places the military commander on the same footing as the Congress of the United States. It assumes that "the paramount authority of the United States at any time to abolish, modify, control, or supersede," is vested in him as fully as it is reserved to Congress. He deems himself a representative of that paramount authority. He puts himself upon an equality with the law-making power of the Union; the only paramount authority in our government, so far, at least, as the enactment of laws is concerned. He places himself on higher ground than the President, who is simply an executive officer. He assumes, directly or indirectly, all authority of the State, legislative, executive, and judicial, and in effect declares, "I am the State."

I regret that I find it necessary to speak so plainly of this assumption of authority. I repeat what I have heretofore said, that I do not doubt that all these orders have been issued under an honest belief that they were necessary or expedient, and fully warranted by the act of Congress.

There may be evils and mischiefs in the laws which these people have made for themselves, through their own legislative bodies, which require change; but none of these can be so intolerable as the evils and mischiefs which must ensure from the sort of remedy applied. One can plainly see what will be the inevitable confusion and disorder which such disturbance of the whole civil policy of the State must produce. If these military edicts are allowed to remain, even during the brief time in which this provisional government may be in power, the seeds will be sown for such a future harvest of litigation as has never been inflicted upon any other people.

There is, in my opinion, an executive duty to be performed here, which cannot safely be avoided or delayed. For, notwithstanding the paramount authority assumed by these commanders, they are not, even as to their proper executive duties, in any sense, clothed with a paramount authority. They are, at least, subordinate executive officers. They are responsible to the President for the proper execution of their duties, and upon him rests the final responsibility. They are his selected agents. His duty is not all performed by selecting such agents as he deems competent, but the duty remains with him to see to it that they execute their duties faithfully and according to law.

It is true that this act of Congress only refers to the President in the manner of selecting and appointing these commanders; and in the matter of their powers and duties under the law, the act speaks in terms directly to them; but this does not relieve them from their responsibility to the President, nor does it relieve him from the constitutional obligation imposed upon him to see that all "the laws are faithfully executed."

It can scarcely be necessary to cite authority for so plain a proposition as this. Nevertheless, as we have a recent decision completely in point, I may as well refer to it.

Upon motion made by the State of Mississippi before the Supreme Court of the United States at its late term, for leave to file a bill against the President of the United States to enjoin him against executing the very acts of Congress now under consideration; the opinion of the court upon dismissing that motion, and it seems to have been unanimous, delivered by the chief justice. I make the following quotation from the opinion:

> Very different is the duty of the President, in the exercise of the power to see that the laws are faithfully executed, and among those laws the acts named in the bill. By the first of these acts he is required to assign generals to command in the several military districts, and to detail sufficient military force to enable such officers to discharge their duties under the law. By the supplementary act, other duties are imposed on the several commanding generals, and their duties must necessarily be performed under the supervision of the President as commander-in-chief. The duty thus imposed upon the President is in no just sense ministerial. It is purely executive and political.

Certain questions have been propounded from one of these military districts touching the construction of the power of the military commander to constitute military tribunals for the trial of offenders, which I will next consider.

Whilst the act does not in terms displace the regular criminal courts of the State, it does give the power to the military commander, when in his judgment a necessity arises, to take the administration of the criminal law into his own hands, and to try and punish offenders by means of military commissions. In giving construction to this power, we must not forget the recent and authoritative exposition given by the Supreme Court of the United States as to the power of Congress to provide for military tribunals for the trial of citizens in time of peace, and to the emphatic declaration, as to which there was no dissent or differences of opinion among the judges, that such a power was not warranted by the Constitution.

A single extract from the opinion of the minority, as delivered by the chief justice, will suffice:

> We by no means assert that Congress can establish and apply the laws of war where no war has been declared or exists; where peace exists, the laws of peace must prevail. What we do mean is, that where the nation is involved in war, and some portions of the country are invaded, and all are exposed to invasion, it is within the power of Congress to determine in what States or districts such great and imminent danger exists as

justifies the authorization of military tribunals for the trial of crimes and offences against the discipline or security of the army, or against the public safety.

Limiting myself here simply to the construction of this act of Congress, and to the question in what way it should be executed, I have no hesitation in saying, that nothing short of an absolute or controlling necessity would give any color of authority for arraigning a citizen before a military commission. A person charged with crime in any of these military districts has rights to be protected, rights the most sacred and inviolable, and among these is the right of trial by jury, according to the laws of the land. When a citizen is arraigned before a military commission on a criminal charge he is no longer under the protection of the law, nor surrounded with those safeguards which are provided in the Constitution. This act, passed in a time of peace, when all the courts, State and Federal, are in the undisturbed exercise of their jurisdiction, authorizes, at the discretion of a military officer, the seizure, trial, and condemnation of the citizen. The accused may be sentenced to death, and the sentence may be executed without a judge. A sentence which forfeits all the property of the accused requires no approval. If it affects the liberty of the accused, it requires the approval of the commanding general; and if it affects his life, it requires the approval of the general and of the President. Military and executive authority rule throughout in the trial, the sentence, and the execution. No *habeas corpus* from any State court can be invoked; for this law declares, that "all interferences, under color of State authority, with the exercise of military authority under this act, shall be null and void."

I repeat it, that nothing short of an absolute necessity can give any color of authority to a military commander to call into exercise such a power. It is a power the exercise of which may involve him, and every one concerned, in the greatest responsibilities. The occasion for its exercise should be reported at once to the Executive, for such instructions as may be deemed necessary and proper.

Questions have arisen whether, under this power, these military commissions can take cognizance of offences committed before the passage of the act, and whether they can try and punish for acts not made crimes or offences by Federal or State law. I am clearly of the opinion that they have no jurisdiction as to either. They can take cognizance of no offence that has not happened after the law took effect. Inasmuch as the tribunal to punish, and the measure or degree of punishment, are established by this act, we must construe it to be prospective, and not retroactive. Otherwise, it would take the character of an *ex post facto* law. Therefore, in the absence of any language which gives the act a retrospective character, I do not hesitate to say it cannot apply to past offences.

There is no legislative power given under this military bill to establish a new criminal code. The authority given is to try and punish criminals and offenders, and this proceeds upon the idea that crimes and offences have been committed; but no person can be called a criminal or an offender for doing an act which, when done, was not prohibited by law.

But, as to the measure of punishment, I regret to be obliged to say that it is left altogether to the military authorities, with only this limitation: that the punishment to be inflicted shall not be cruel or unusual. The military commission may try the accused, fix the measure of punishment, even to the penalty of death, and direct the execution of the sentence. It is only when the sentence affects the "life or liberty" of the person that it need be approved by the commanding general, and only cases where it affects the life of the accused that it needs also the approval of the President. As to the crimes or offenses against the laws of the United States, the military authority can take no cognizance of them, nor in any way interfere with the regular administration of justice by the appropriate Federal courts....

I am sir, very respectfully,
Your obedient servant,
Henry Stanbery.

CHAPTER NINETEEN
The Purpose of the Fourteenth Amendment

"U.S. Citizens" Have No Inalienable Rights

This [Fourteenth] article of amendment to the Constitution of the United States and its companion the Fifteenth Amendment which relates to the ballot... are considered to be the Negro's charter of liberty....

The great moral values held by the words "equal protection of the laws," "due process of law," and "the right of suffrage" were given to them [the former slaves] by the white man's long travail. They were earned by the white man. They are the heritage of the civilization which he built....

The Negroes in the South in 1868 knew nothing about these things. The defeat of the South on the field of battle freed the Negro from involuntary servitude. But the Fourteenth Amendment, even if lawfully adopted, could not change his nature or make him into a white man with a black skin. The attempt to do this was revolutionary and flew into the face of history....

The real reason for these two amendments rests upon a much cruder foundation. It was twofold: To take revenge on the South through the impoverishment and disfranchisement of its leaders and to build up a permanently strong Republican Party in the South through the use of Negro votes. The Republican leaders were not primarily concerned with the welfare of the Negro, but they welcomed the opportunity to use him for their own ends.[1]

---

1. Charles Wallace Collins, *Whither Solid South? A Study in Politics and Race Relations* (New Orleans, Louisiana: Pelican Publishing Company, 1947), pages 94-96.

We have seen both the historical and legal background of the so-called Fourteenth Amendment, which was forcibly added to the Constitution by military power rather than by ratification of the States. Drafted by Lincoln-appointed Chief Justice of the Supreme Court, Salmon Portland Chase, this amendment was a masterpiece of deception. For the purposes of this chapter, we will focus our discussion mainly on the first clause which reads, "All persons born or naturalized in the United States, and subject to the jurisdiction thereof, are citizens of the United States and of the State wherein they reside. No State shall make or enforce any law which shall abridge the privileges or immunities of citizens of the United States; nor shall any State deprive any person of life, liberty, or property, without due process of law; nor deny any person within its jurisdiction the equal protection of the laws." The "United States" referred to in this amendment was not the several sovereign States "in Congress assembled" under the Constitution, but rather the centralized military despotism created by the Freedmen's Bureau Act and the Civil Rights Act — a fact which the Radicals in Congress were very vocal in declaring and to which all legislation subsequently based on the purported amendment attests. For example, according to the Gold Reserve Act of 1934, "...[T]he term 'United States' means the Government of the United States."[2] Thus, the name of the Union of States has been transferred to the *creature* of that Union and, in violation of all known rules of grammar, a clearly plural noun is now interpreted as though it were singular. This is also evident in the fact that the word "thereof" in the jurisdiction clause is singular in nature — "Every person born or naturalized in the United States subject to *its* jurisdiction is a citizen" (emphasis added)[3] — whereas the wording of the jurisdiction clause of the previous Thirteenth Amendment, ratified *before* Reconstruction, was clearly plural — "Neither slavery nor involuntary servitude... shall exist within the United States, or any place subject to *their* jurisdiction" (emphasis added). The difference in phraseology is due to the fact that the Thirteenth Amendment was ratified by the several State legislatures acting in some semblance of a republican capacity under Presidential Reconstruction, whereas the Fourteenth was "ratified" by military satellites of Washington, D.C. set up in the South after the operating State governments had been overthrown.

According to *Black's Law Dictionary*, "The Fourteenth Amendment of the Constitution of the United States, ratified [sic] in 1868, creates or at least recognizes for the first time a citizenship of the United States, as distinct from that of the states."[4] A series of judicial rulings in the 1870s substantiates this assertion. According to the ruling of the California Supreme Court in *Van Valkenburg v. Brown*:

> No white person born within the limits of the United States and subject to *their* jurisdiction, or born without those limits and subsequently naturalized under *their* laws,

---

2. Gold Reserve Act (1934), Chapter 6, Section 15.

3. Title 26, *Code of Federal Regulations*, Section 1.1-1(c), "Who is a citizen."

4. *Black's Law Dictionary* (Sixth Edition), page 657.

owes his status of citizenship to the recent amendments to the Federal Constitution [the Thirteenth, Fourteenth, and Fifteenth].

The purpose of the Fourteenth Amendment of the Constitution of the United States was to confer the status of citizenship upon a numerous class of persons domiciled within the limits of the United States who could not be brought within the operation of the naturalization laws because native born, and whose birth, though native, had at the same time left them without the status of citizenship. Such persons were not white persons, but in the main were of African blood, who had been held in slavery in this country, or having themselves never been held in slavery, were the native-born descendants of slaves (emphasis added).[5]

The following year, the U.S. Supreme Court declared in the famous *Slaughter House Cases*:

The main purpose of the thirteenth, fourteenth, and fifteenth amendments was the freedom of the African race....

The first section of the fourteenth article, to which our attention is more specifically invited, opens with a definition of citizenship — not only citizenship of the United States, but citizenship of the states.... The distinction between citizenship of the United States and citizenship of a state is clearly recognized and established....

Of the privileges and immunities of the citizens of the United States, and, of the privileges and immunities of the citizen of the state, and what they respectively are, we will presently consider; but we wish to state here that it is only the former which are placed by this clause under the protection of the fourteenth article of the federal Constitution, and that the latter, whatever they may be, are not intended to have any additional protection by this paragraph of the amendment.[6]

The ruling in *Strauder v. West Virginia* was similar: "The fourteenth amendment, although prohibitory in terms, confers a positive immunity or right to the colored race — the right to exemption from unfriendly legislation against them distinctively as colored."[7] Again, in *United States v. Susan B. Anthony*: "The Fourteenth Amendment creates and defines citizenship of the United States. It had long been contended, and had been held by many learned authorities, and had never been judicially decided to the contrary, that there was no such thing as a citizen of the United States, except by first becoming a citizen of some state.... The rights of citizens of the state, as such, are not under consideration in the Fourteenth Amendment. They stand as they did before the adoption of the Fourteenth Amendment and are fully guaranteed by other provisions."[8]

---

5. *Van Valkenburg v. Brown* (1872), 43 Cal. 43, 47.

6. *Slaughter House Cases* (1873), 83 U.S. 36, 16 Wall. 36, 21 L.Ed. 394.

7. *Strauder v. West Virginia* (1879), 100 U.S. 303, 35 L.Ed. 664.

8. *United States v. Susan B. Anthony* (1873), 24 Fed. Cas. 829.

Why were the "rights of citizens of the state... not under consideration" in the Fourteenth Amendment? Simply because the sole purpose of this alleged amendment was to create — or rather to permanently establish — an entirely new political status in order to deal with the infusion into the legal system of a class of people who were separate from, and had no means of access to, the citizenship of the Constitution. Although "the people of [a] State, as successors of its former sovereign, are entitled to all the rights which formerly belonged to the King by his prerogative,"[9] the "privileges and immunities of citizens of the United States... are only such as arise out of the nature and essential character of the national government...."[10] In the case of *Tashiro v. Jordan*, a California court stated that "citizenship of the United States does not entitle the citizen to privileges and immunities of the citizen of a state, since privileges and immunities of the one are not the same as the other."[11] In *Cleveland Raceways, Inc. v. Bowers*, the Ohio supreme court declared that "the privileges and immunities protected by the Fourteenth Amendment... are not those fundamental privileges and immunities inherent in state citizenship but only those which owe their existence to the federal government, its national character, its Constitution, or its laws."[12] Even more recently, the U.S. District Court in Colorado stated, "The privileges and immunities clause of the Fourteenth Amendment protects very few rights because it neither incorporates any of the Bill of Rights nor protects all rights of individual citizens. Instead, this provision protects only those rights peculiar to being a citizen of the federal government; it does not protect those rights which relate to state citizenship."[13]

Just what are these "rights which relate to state citizenship" — rights which, as we read above, are "fully guaranteed by other provisions" besides the Fourteenth Amendment? They can be none other than those enumerated in the first eight amendments to the Constitution:

> The individual may stand upon his constitutional rights as a citizen. He is entitled to carry on his private business in his own way. His power to contract is unlimited. He owes no duty to the State or to his neighbors to divulge his business, or to open his doors

9. *Lansing v. Smith* (1829), 21 D. 89, 4 Wend. 9. This political sovereignty was enjoyed by the people in their collective capacity, not as individuals. There is not now, nor ever has been, such a thing as "individual sovereignty," as claimed by many in the so-called Patriot movement. As a member of society, a White American male was a co-tenant in the sovereignty of his State; as an individual, however, he was a subject of that sovereignty.

10. *Twining v. New Jersey* (1908), 211 U.S. 78, 53 L.Ed. 97. It should be kept in mind that there was no "national government" prior to 1861, but a *general* (federal) Government of the several United States.

11. *K. Tashiro et. al. v. Jordan, Secretary of State, et. al.* (1927) 256 Cal. 545.

12. *Cleveland Raceways, Inc. v. Bowers* (Ohio, 1958), 163 N.E. 2d 73.

13. *Jones v. Temmer* (U.S. District Court, Colorado, 1993), 829 F.Supp. 1226.

to an investigation, so far as it may tend to incriminate him. He owes no such duty to the State, since he receives nothing therefrom, beyond the protection of his life and property. His rights are such as existed by the law of the land long antecedent to the organization of the State, and can only be taken from him by due process of law, and in accordance with the Constitution. Among his rights are a refusal to incriminate himself, and the immunity of him and his property from arrest or seizure except under a warrant of the law. He owes nothing to the public so long as he does not trespass upon their rights.[14]

It cannot be misconstrued what the courts, from the U.S. Supreme Court down to the State courts, have been openly and consistently stating for well over a century: the freed slaves were never given access to the same inalienable rights which had been enjoyed by White Citizens from the beginning of the American Republic. For example, in the *Twining v. New Jersey* case, the Supreme Court stated that "an exemption from compulsory self-incrimination is what is described as a fundamental right belonging to all who live under a free government, and incapable of impairment by legislation or judicial decision; it is, so far as the states are concerned, a fundamental right inherent in state citizenship, and is a privilege or immunity of that citizenship only," whereas "immunity from self-incrimination is not, as a fundamental right of national citizenship, included in the privileges and immunities of citizens of the United States."[15] The Court went on to declare, "The right of trial by jury in civil cases, guaranteed by the 7th Amendment, and the right to bear arms, guaranteed by the 2nd Amendment, have been distinctly held not to be privileges and immunities of citizens of the United States... and in effect the same decision was made in respect of the guaranty against prosecution, except by indictment of a grand jury, contained in the 5th Amendment, and in respect of the right to be confronted with witnesses, contained in the 6th Amendment...."[16]

The first clause of the Fourteenth Amendment does not embrace "the personal rights enumerated in the first eight Amendments, because those rights were not within the meaning of the clause 'privileges and immunities of citizens of the United States.'" In addition, citizens under this Amendment cannot even be certain that they will be guaranteed "due process of law" because "this court has always declined to give a comprehensive definition of it, and has preferred that its full meaning should be gradually ascertained by the process of inclusion and exclusion in the course of the decisions of cases as they arise."[17] In other words, whereas State Citizens, who were once protected by the Constitution and the Common Law, had sev-

---

14. *Hale v. Hankel* (1906), 201 U.S. 43, 74.

15. *Twining v. New Jersey*, 211 U.S. 78, 97.

16. *Ibid.*, 98-99; citing *Walker v. Sauvinet*, 92 U.S. 90 , 23 L. ed. 678; *Presser v. Illinois*, 116 U.S. 252 , 29 L. ed. 615, 6 Sup. Ct. Rep. 580; *Hurtado v. California*, 110 U.S. 516 , 28 L. ed. 232, 4 Sup. Ct. Rep. 111, 292; *West v. Louisiana*, 191 U.S. 258 , 48 L. ed. 965, 24 Sup. Ct. Rep. 650.

17. *Ibid.*

eral centuries of legal history from which to extract a precise definition of "due process of
law," the statutory "persons" created by the Fourteenth Amendment are left at the whim of
a "make it up as you go" legal system in which a fair trial is whatever the judge decides it
will be.

U.S. citizens, who by definition are only residents, not Citizens, of a State, also are
denied the most basic of Common Law rights which English and American freemen have
enjoyed for hundreds of years. To state that the Fourteenth Amendment created a rightless
political status (slavery) would not be an exaggeration. In fact, "The only absolute and unqualified right of a United States citizen is to residence within the territorial boundaries of
the United States."[18]

"U.S. Citizenship" is a Legal Fiction

It is beyond dispute that before the Civil Rights Act, there had been no such thing as
a citizen of the United States in the sense given in the Fourteenth Amendment. Men were
Citizens of their respective States, and then in reference to the Union of the several States,
they were Americans. Even the naturalization of aliens was accomplished by the State legislatures or by State courts. No one in the first seventy-five years of the American Republic
dreamed that such a creature as a citizen of the U.S. Government would ever come into existence:

> By metaphysical refinement, in examining our form of government, it might be
> correctly said that there is no such thing as a citizen of the United States. But constant
> usage — arising from convenience, and perhaps, necessity, and dating from the formation
> of the Confederacy — has given substantial existence to the idea which the term conveys.
> A citizen of any one of the States of the Union, is held to be, and called a citizen of the
> United States, although technically and abstractly there is no such thing.
>
> To conceive a citizen of the United States who is not a citizen of some one of the
> States, is totally foreign to the idea, and inconsistent with the proper construction and com-
> mon understanding of the expression as used in the Constitution, which must be deduced
> from its various other provisions. The object then to be obtained, by the exercise of the
> power of naturalization, was to make citizens of the respective states.[19]

> The Constitution nowhere defines the meaning of the word "citizen," either by
> way of inclusion or exclusion.... [I]t must be interpreted in the light of the common law,
> the principles and history of which were familiarly known to the framers of the Constitu-
> tion.[20]

---

18. *U.S. v. Valentine* (1968), 288 F.Supp. 957.

19. *Ex parte Knowles* (1855), 5 Cal. 300, 302.

20. *United States v. Wong Kim Ark* (1898), 169 U.S. 654.

Most people confuse the "Citizen of the United States," mentioned in the body of the Constitution with the "citizen of the United States" described in the Fourteenth Amendment, and assume that since similar language is employed, they must refer to one and the same "person." However, there is not a single law dictionary, statute or court case that would support the belief that the current "U.S. citizenship" has always been in existence and that the "person" found within this martial venue enjoys the same political status as a Citizen of one of the several States. In light of the fact that the general Government was the creation of the sovereign people of the several States, it would be impossible for a legal creation *of* the creation to ever be truly elevated to an equality with the creator.

According to the U.S. Supreme Court, "An unconstitutional act is not a law. It confers no rights. It imposes no duties. It affords no protection. It creates no office. It is in legal contemplation as inoperative as though it had never been passed. Therefore an unconstitutional act purporting to create an office gives no validity to the acts of a person acting under color of its authority."[21] It could also be asserted that neither does an unconstitutional act create a citizenship. If the Civil Rights Act of 1866, which was, without a doubt, completely unconstitutional, "confers no rights... imposes no duties... affords no protection... [and] creates no office," what exactly then *was* "created or at least recognized for the first time" by its offspring, the Fourteenth Amendment? Simply put, the purported amendment did nothing more than establish a taxable franchise of the *de facto* military corporation which is now seated in the District of Columbia — a legal fiction which possesses no real substance in law but which nevertheless becomes "paramount and dominant" over whatever other political status may be claimed by the individual under its jurisdiction.[22] The reader should note the following definitions:

> Legal fiction. Assumption of fact made by court as basis for deciding a legal question. A situation contrived by the law to permit a court to dispose of a matter....[23]

> *Fictio*.... In Roman law, a fiction; and assumption or supposition of the law. Such was properly a term of pleading, and signified a false averment on the part of the plaintiff which the defendant was not allowed to traverse; as that the plaintiff was a Roman citizen, when in truth he was a foreigner. The object of the fiction was to give the court jurisdiction.[24]

> Fictitious. Founded on a fiction; having the character of a fiction; pretended; counterfeit. Feigned, imaginary, not real, false, not genuine, nonexistent. Arbitrarily in-

21. *Norton v. Shelby County* (1886), 6 S.Ct. 1121.

22. *Colgate v. Harvey* (1935), 296 U.S. 404, 427; 80 L.Ed. 299.

23. *Black's Law Dictionary* (Sixth Edition), page 894.

24. *Ibid.*, page 623.

vented and set up, to accomplish an ulterior object.[25]

In his veto of the Civil Rights bill, Andrew Johnson perceived the "ulterior object" of the creation of a statutory "Federal citizenship" to be to "sap and destroy our federative system of limited powers and break down the barriers which preserve the rights of the States" and to take "another step, or rather stride, toward centralization and the concentration of all legislative powers in the National Government."[26] That Johnson was correct in his assessment of the situation was substantiated by James G. Blaine, who declared that the Reconstruction legislation "heartily recognized the supreme sovereignty of the National Government as having been indisputably established by the overthrow of the Rebellion which was undertaken to confirm the adverse theory of State-rights."[27] Blaine further remarked, "As the vicious theory of State-rights had been constantly at enmity with the true spirit of Nationality, the Organic Law of the Republic should be so amended that no standing-room for th[at] heresy would be left."[28] Here we have an open admission from a Republican member of Congress not only that the creation of "U.S. citizenship" by the Civil Rights Act was intended to be an assault on the "Organic Law of the Republic" — the Constitution — but that it had been the South, not the North, which had fought in the late war to confirm the principles set forth in that document, particularly in the Tenth Amendment. Clearly, Blaine and his cohorts were the true perpetrators of "rebellion," not the people of the Southern States.

The Fourteenth Amendment is Anti-Republican

Since the Fourteenth Amendment is a product of the Republican party, it may sound strange, even contradictory, to label it "anti-republican." However, the contradiction lies instead with the political faction which assumed the name "Republican" in 1854 when, in fact, its leading members both advocated and actually accomplished an overthrow of the principles of true republicanism in America. In the Declaration of Independence, we read that a free people have both the right *and* the duty to alter and even to abolish an oppressive government and to "institute new government, laying its foundation on such principles and organizing its powers in such form, as to them shall seem most likely to effect their safety and happiness." Governments thus "deriving their just powers from the consent of the governed" are said to be republican and are the only form of government allowed by the Constitution: "The Union is an association of the people of republics; its preservation is calculated to de-

---

25. *Ibid.*, page 624.

26. Johnson, in Richardson, *Messages and Papers of the Presidents*, Volume VIII, page 3611.

27. Blaine, *Twenty Years of Congress*, Volume II, page 300.

28. Blaine, *ibid.*, page 303.

pend on the preservation of those republics. The people of each pledge themselves to preserve that form of government in all. Thus each becomes responsible to the rest, that no other form of government shall prevail in it, and all are bound to preserve it in every one."[29]

In sharp contrast, as the U.S. Supreme Court declared in 1884, the "person" defined in the first clause of the Fourteenth Amendment "is not merely subject in some respect or degree to the jurisdiction of the United States, *but completely subject*" (emphasis added).[30] By definition, a subject is "one that owes allegiance to a sovereign and is governed by his laws."[31] Furthermore, subjection is the "obligation of one or more persons to act at the discretion or according to the judgment and will of others" and "the term is little used, in this sense, in countries enjoying a republican form of government."[32] Since the primary characteristic of a State, "in the ordinary sense of the Constitution," is "a political community of free citizens,"[33] there can be no doubt that a body politic formed by statutory "persons" who are in complete subjection to the U.S. Government cannot be a true State, and certainly cannot be republican in form as required by the Constitution. Though it may bear the name of "State," such an entity would be more properly designated as a territory, or an administrative subdivision, of the centralized Government in Washington, D.C. Those who vote in the elections of such a "State" are merely voicing their opinion regarding Government policy, and their will may be, and, in fact, often is, overturned by the sovereign will of their master.

According to one authoritative source, "The Federal Civil Rights Act is in derogation of the common law and must be strictly construed."[34] This, of course, would also apply to everything proceeding from the Civil Rights Act, including the Fourteenth Amendment. Clearly, to be "in derogation of the common law" is to be in derogation of the Constitution, which is firmly rooted in the Common Law. "U.S. citizenship" in this context is therefore not really citizenship at all — at least not in the constitutional sense of the term — but is instead a consensual contract[35] which originates outside of the Constitution and which estab-

---

29. Rawle, *View of the Constitution*, page 295.

30. *Elk v. Wilkins* (1884) 112 U.S. 94.

31. *Black's Law Dictionary* (Sixth Edition), page 1425.

32. *Ibid.*

33. *State of Texas v. White* (1868), 74 U.S. 700.

34. Francis Rawle (editor), *Bouvier's Law Dictionary* (Kansas City, Missouri: Vernon Law Book Company, 1914), Volume I, page 500.

35. "Consensual contracts are such as are founded upon and completed by the mere agreement of the contracting parties, without any external formality or symbolic act to fix the obligation" (*Black's Law Dictionary* [Sixth Edition], page 323). Mere acquiescence is sufficient for such a contract to impose duties, for "*longa patientia trahitur ad consensum.* Long sufferance is construed as consent" (*ibid.*, page 942).

lishes the relationship of sovereign and subject (master and slave) between the contracting parties; as such, it cannot lawfully be attached to any free people at the mere whim of either the U.S. Government or any of its countless agencies.[36] To attempt to enlarge the scope of the Civil Rights Act beyond its original intent to secure civil rights to the Negro freedmen would amount to levying a war of annihilation against the several States by politically murdering their Citizens. This, in the clear language of Article III, Section 3, Clause 1 of the Constitution, would be treason and yet thousands of Americans every year acquiesce in this colossal crime when they declare themselves to be "completely subject" to an illegitimate Government by registering to vote, or when they accept any of the other benefits which are held out as enticements for them to abandon their birthright.

The Continuing Effects of Reconstruction

Having examined the meaning behind the first section of the Fourteenth Amendment, let us now focus on the fifth and last section which reads: "The Congress shall have power to enforce, by appropriate legislation, the provisions of this article." This section, which also appears in the Thirteenth and Fifteenth Amendments, escapes the notice of most people, but it is nevertheless pregnant with meaning and is therefore of monumental importance in understanding the intent of the authors of the amendment. When one reads Article I, Section 8, Clause 18 of the Constitution, it will be seen that Congress was already given all the legislative authority needed "to make all Laws which shall be necessary and proper for carrying into Execution the foregoing Powers, and all other Powers vested in the Government of the United States, or in any Department or officer thereof." There was no need whatsoever for an additional empowerment clause to be added to the Fourteenth Amendment unless additional power was being claimed by Congress outside of the Constitution. Furthermore, since the Constitution was intended to be the "supreme Law of the Land," the powers claimed under this and other Reconstruction amendments must have arisen from a source other than the organic law. We have already seen that this source was military necessity, or martial law.

Unfortunately, the revolutionary nature of the Fourteenth Amendment goes beyond the establishment of a permanent venue of martial law. This amendment also took a giant step toward the abolition of the independent judicial system established under Article III of the Constitution. This attack on the Judicial Branch of the Government is found in the words "appropriate legislation" which precluded judicial review of any law passed by Congress in relation to the freedmen. This phrase "was added out of abundant caution. It authorizes congress to select, from time to time, the means that might be deemed appropriate to the end. It employs a phrase which had been enlightened by well-considered judicial application. Any exercise of legislative power within its limits involves a legislative [political], and not a judi-

---

36. "*Beneficium invito non datur*. A privilege or benefit is not granted against one's will" (*ibid.*, page 157).

cial question."[37] This explains why "the federal courts actually refuse to hear argument on the invalidity of the 14th Amendment."[38] Thus was set up within this country a legal situation never for a moment imagined by the founders — the Legislative Branch as its own judge and a virtually impotent Judicial Branch unable to gainsay any action of Congress claimed to be "appropriate" to force and perpetuate Radical Reconstruction on the States.

In his book *The Era of Reconstruction 1865-1877*, Kenneth M. Stampp wrote:

> Radical idealism was in part responsible for two of the most momentous enactments of the reconstruction years: the Fourteenth Amendment to the federal Constitution which gave Negroes citizenship and promised them equal protection of the laws, and the Fifteenth Amendment which gave them the right to vote. The fact that these amendments could not have been adopted under any other circumstances, or at any other time, before or since, may suggest the crucial importance of the reconstruction era in American history. Indeed, without radical reconstruction, it would be impossible to this day for the federal government to protect Negroes from legal and political discrimination.[39]

What were the circumstances under which the Fourteenth and Fifteenth Amendments were adopted? Again, it was "'a state of war' after flagrant war has ceased" when "[m]ilitary government may legally be continued." It was a time when the States were said to have "committed suicide, so that as states they cease to exist, leaving their whole jurisdiction open to the occupation of the United States under the Constitution." It was a time when the States had been reduced "to the condition of territories" and the disenfranchised Citizens thereof had been reduced "to abject subjection to the sway of the government." Finally, it was "a grant of power to military authority, over civil rights and citizens, in time of peace" and "a new jurisdiction, never granted before, by which, in certain particulars and for certain purposes, the established principle that the military shall be subordinate to the civil authority is reversed." Consequently, the continued enforcement of the provisions of the Reconstruction amendments is a clear and open declaration of war against the American people and serves to put them on notice that they remain under martial law, or at least its more mild form of martial rule, to this day. Without this state of affairs, "it would be impossible... for the federal government to protect Negroes from legal and political discrimination."

It has been admitted that "the revolutionary Fourteenth Amendment... still functions as an instrument of revolution."[40] Indeed, the "new jurisdiction" established by this bogus

---

37. *United States v. Rhodes* (1998), 27 Fed.Cas. 785, 793.

38. Perez, "The Unconstitutionality of the Fourteenth Amendment," page 15646.

39. Kenneth M. Stampp, *The Era of Reconstruction, 1865-1877* (New York: Random House, 1965), pages 12-13.

40. Henry Steele Commager and Richard B. Morris, "Editors' Introduction" in Foner, *Reconstruction*, page xvii.

amendment is antithetical to the republican form of government which the federal Government is bound to guarantee to the several States of the Union. However, if the States, as lawfully constituted bodies politic, have been destroyed by eliminating their Citizens and repopulating their respective territories with alien residents, then the Union established by our forefathers also does not exist and the Government, no longer having any duties to the States to perform, is freed from all constitutional restraints which it does not impose upon itself. The clay has not only said to the potter, "What hast thou done?" but has also risen in revolt and declared itself sovereign over its master:

> They [the Radical Republicans during Reconstruction] knew what they intended by the vague terms of section one of the Amendment. They knew that it could be interpreted so as to extend far beyond the negro race question. They desired to nationalize all civil rights, to make the Federal power supreme, and to bring the private life of every citizen directly under the eye of Congress.... This result was to be obtained by disenfranchising the whites and enfranchising the blacks.... It meant the death knell of the doctrine of State's rights — the ultimate nationalization of all civil rights and the consequent abolition of State control over the private rights and duties of the individual. It meant the passing over of the police power of the State, into the police power of the national government, thereby giving Congress undefined and unlimited powers whereby it would be enabled to enter fields of legislation from which hitherto it had been barred....
>
> [The Fourteenth Amendment] is a set-back to proper government. This operation of the Fourteenth Amendment runs counter to the ideals expressed in the Preamble to the Constitution itself. It does anything but promote domestic tranquility....
>
> The same force in the Republican Party which secured the adoption of the Amendment has also given us its ideal of the purpose and scope of that constitutional measure by the laws thereunder enacted. They meant to change the form of the American Commonwealth. The States were to exist only in name. Their legislatures and their courts were to be reduced to impotency. The citizens of the States were now to live directly under the surveillance of the Federal Government, looking to it for protection in his private affairs and fearing its avenging power should he transgress the least of its commandments....
>
> No longer was the National Government to be one of delegated powers, and no part of the sovereign power was to be held any longer by the States. Section one of the Fourteenth Amendment was intended ultimately to create out of the former Union one centralized consolidated government with the supreme power vested in the Federal authorities in Washington. Such was the ideal of the Radicals....[41]

The claim that the Fourteenth Amendment elevated the Blacks to social and political equality with the Whites is a farce. Instead, what has happened over time, is that both Whites and Blacks have been equally subjugated beneath the heel of an unlimited and unaccountable military despotism. There is an agenda behind the "politically correct" dogma propagated by

---

41. Charles Wallace Collins, *The Fourteenth Amendment and the States* (Boston: Little, Brown and Company, 1912), pages 10-11, 20, 45-46, 159, 161.

the Government-controlled media and by the NAACP and other Government-funded race-agitating groups — an agenda of deception and cover-up. The traditional heritage, culture, and symbols of the old South are being attacked with an unprecedented ferocity today because they are powerful reminders of the principles upon which true liberty in this country was founded, the most important of which is the right of a people to govern themselves. Ignorance of history has been the political undoing of the American people, who have surrendered the freedoms purchased with the blood of their forefathers in favor of a form of martial slavery more oppressive than anything that allegedly existed in the antebellum South. The second Reconstruction of the Twenty-First Century may very well accomplish what the first Reconstruction of the Nineteenth Century merely began — the permanent erasure of the memory of free republican government from the American mind.

SUPPORTING DOCUMENT

The Unconstitutionality of the Fourteenth Amendment
by Hon. Leander H. Perez
Congressional Record — 13 June 1967

The purported Fourteenth Amendment to the U.S. Constitution is and should be held to be ineffective, invalid, null, void, and unconstitutional for the following reasons:

1. The Joint Resolution proposing said Amendment was not submitted to or adopted by a Constitutional Congress as required by Article 1, Section 3, and Article V of the U.S. Constitution.

2. The Joint Resolution was not submitted to the President for his approval as required by Article 1, Section 5 of the Constitution.

3. The proposed Fourteenth Amendment was rejected by more than one fourth of all the States in the Union, and it was never ratified by three fourths of all the States in the Union as required by Article V, Section 1 of the Constitution.

The U.S. Constitution provides: "The Senate of the United States shall be composed of two Senators from each State...."[1] No State, without its consent, shall be deprived of its equal suffrage in the Senate.[2] The fact that twenty-three Senators had been unlawfully excluded from the U.S. Senate in order to secure a two thirds vote for the adoption of the Joint Resolution proposing the Fourteenth Amendment is shown by Resolutions of protest adopted by the following State Legislatures.

The New Jersey Legislature by Resolution on March 27, 1868, protested as follows:

---

1. U.S. Constitution, Article 1, Section 3.

2. *Ibid.*, Article V.

       The said proposed amendment not having yet received the assent of three fourths of the States, which is necessary to make it valid, the natural and constitutional right of this State to withdraw its assent is undeniable....

       That it being necessary by the Constitution that every amendment to the same should be proposed by two thirds of both houses of Congress, the authors of said proposition, for the purpose of securing the assent of the requisite majority, determined to, and did, exclude from the said two houses eighty representatives from eleven States of the Union, upon the pretense that there were no such States in the Union; but, finding that two thirds of the remainder of the said houses could not be brought to assent to the said proposition, they deliberately formed and carried out the design of mutilating the integrity of the United States Senate, and without any pretext or justification, other than the possession of the power, without the right, and in the palpable violation of the Constitution, ejected a member of their own body, representing this State, and thus practically denied to New Jersey its equal suffrage in the Senate, and thereby nominally secured the vote of two thirds of the said house.[3]

The Alabama Legislature protested against being deprived of representation in the Senate of the U.S. Congress.[4] The Texas Legislature, by Resolution on October 15, 1866, protested as follows:

       The Amendment to the Constitution proposed by this joint resolution as Article XIV is presented to the Legislature of Texas for its action thereon, under Article V of that Constitution. This Article V, providing the mode of making amendments to that instrument, contemplates the participation by all the States through their representatives in Congress, in proposing amendments. As representatives from nearly one third of the States were excluded from the Congress proposing the amendments, the constitutional requirement was not complied with; it was violated in letter and in spirit; and the proposing of these amendments to States which were excluded from all participation in their initiation in Congress, is a nullity.[5]

The Arkansas Legislature, by Resolution on December 17, 1866, protested as follows:

       The Constitution authorized two thirds of both houses of Congress to propose amendments; and, as eleven States were excluded from deliberation and decision upon the one now submitted, the conclusion is inevitable that it is not proposed by legal authority, but in palpable violation of the Constitution.[6]

---

3. *New Jersey Acts*, 27 March 1868.

4. *Alabama House Journal*, 1866, pages 210-213.

5. *Texas House Journal*, 1866, page 577.

6. *Arkansas House Journal*, 1866, page 287.

The Georgia Legislature, by Resolution on November 9, 1866, protested as follows:

> Since the reorganization of the State government, Georgia has elected Senators and Representatives. So has every other State. They have been arbitrarily refused admission to their seats, not on the ground that the qualifications of the members elected did not conform to the fourth paragraph, second section, first Article of the Constitution, but because their right of representation was denied by a portion of the States having equal but not greater rights than themselves. They have in fact been forcibly excluded; and, inasmuch as all legislative power granted by the States to the Congress is defined, and this power of exclusion is not among the powers expressly or by implication defined, the assemblage, at the capital, of representatives from a portion of the States, to the exclusion of the representatives of another portion, cannot be a constitutional Congress, when the representation of each State forms an integral part of the whole.
>
> This amendment is tendered to Georgia for ratification, under that power in the Constitution which authorizes two thirds of the Congress to propose amendments. We have endeavored to establish that Georgia had a right, in the first place, as a part of the Congress, to act upon the question, "Shall these amendments be proposed?" Every other excluded State had the same right. The first constitutional privilege has been arbitrarily denied. Had these amendments been submitted to a constitutional Congress, they would never have been proposed to the States. Two thirds of the whole Congress never would have proposed to eleven States voluntarily to reduce their political power in the Union, and at the same time, disfranchise the larger portion of the intellect, integrity, and patriotism of eleven co-equal States.[7]

The Florida Legislature, by Resolution on December 5, 1866, protested as follows:

> Let this alteration be made in the organic system and some new and more startling demands may or may not be required by the predominant party previous to allowing the ten States now unlawfully and unconstitutionally deprived of their right of representation as guaranteed by the Constitution of this country and there is no act, not even that of rebellion, can deprive them.[8]

The South Carolina Legislature, by Resolution on November 27, 1866, protested as follows:

> Eleven of the Southern States, including South Carolina, are deprived of their representation in Congress. Although their Senators and Representatives have been duly elected and have presented themselves for the purpose of taking their seats, their credentials have, in most instances, been laid upon the table without being read, or have been referred to a committee, who have failed to make any report on the subject. In short, Congress has refused to exercise its Constitutional functions, and decide either upon the elec-

---

7. *Georgia House Journal*, 1866, pages 66-67.

8. *Florida House Journal*, 1866, page 76.

tion, the return, or the qualification of these selected by the States and people to represent us. Some of the Senators and Representatives from the Southern States were prepared to take the test oath, but even these have been persistently ignored, and kept out of the seats to which they were entitled under the Constitution and laws.

Hence this amendment has not been proposed by "two thirds of both Houses" of a legally constituted Congress, and is not, Constitutionally or legitimately, before a single Legislature for ratification.[9]

The North Carolina Legislature, by Resolution on December 6, 1866, protested as follows:

The Federal Constitution declares in substance, that Congress shall consist of a House of Representatives, composed of members apportioned among the respective States in the ratio of their population and of a Senate, composed of two members from each State. And in the Article which concerns Amendments, it is expressly provided that "no State, without its consent, shall be deprived of its equal suffrage in the Senate." The contemplated Amendment was not proposed to the States by a Congress thus constituted. At the time of its adoption, the eleven seceding States were deprived of representation both in the Senate and House, although they all, except the State of Texas, had Senators and Representatives duly elected and claiming their privileges under the Constitution. In consequence of this, these States had no voice on the important question of proposing the Amendment. Had they been allowed to give their votes, the proposition would doubtless have failed to command the required two thirds majority....

If the votes of these States are necessary to a valid ratification of the Amendment, they were equally necessary on the question of proposing it to the States; for it would be difficult, in the opinion of the Committee, to show by what process in logic, men of intelligence, could arrive at a different conclusion.[10]

Article I, Section 7 of the United States Constitution provides that not only every bill have been passed by the House of Representatives and the Senate of the United States Congress, but that:

Every order, resolution, or vote to which the concurrence of the Senate and House of Representatives may be necessary (except on a question of adjournment) shall be presented to the President of the United States; and before the same shall take effect, shall be approved by him, or being disapproved by him shall be repassed by two thirds of the Senate and House of Representatives, according to the rules and limitations prescribed in the case of a bill.

9. *South Carolina House Journal*, 1866, pages 33-34.

10. *North Carolina Senate Journal*, 1866-67, pages 92-93.

The Joint Resolution proposing the Fourteenth Amendment[11] was never presented to the President of the United States for his approval, as President Andrew Johnson stated in his message on June 22, 1866. Therefore the Joint Resolution did not take effect.

Pretermitting the ineffectiveness of said Resolution, as demonstrated above, fifteen States out of the then thirty-seven States of the Union rejected the proposed Fourteenth Amendment between the date of its submission to the States by the Secretary of State on June 16, 1866, and March 24, 1868, thereby further nullifying said Resolution and making it impossible for its ratification by the constitutionally required three fourths of such States, as shown by the rejections thereof by the Legislatures of the following States: Texas rejected the Fourteenth Amendment on October 27, 1866.[12] Georgia rejected it on November 9, 1866.[13] Florida rejected it on December 6, 1866. [14]Alabama rejected it on December 7, 1866.[15] Arkansas rejected it on December 17, 1866.[16] North Carolina rejected it on December 17, 1866.[17] South Carolina rejected it on December 20, 1866.[18] Kentucky rejected it on January 8, 1867.[19] Virginia rejected it on January 9, 1867.[20] Louisiana rejected it on February 6, 1867.[21] Delaware rejected it on February 7, 1867.[22] Maryland rejected it on March 23, 1867.[23]

---

11. Statutes at Large, Volume XIV, pages 358ff.

12. *Senate Journal* (Thirty-Ninth Congress, First Session), page 563; *House Journal*, 1866, page 889.

13. *House Journal*, 1866, pages 578-584; *Senate Journal*, 1866, page 471.

14. *House Journal*, 1866, page 68; *Senate Journal*, 1866, page 72.

15. *House Journal*, 1866, page 76; *Senate Journal*, 1866, page 8.

16. *House Journal*, 1866, pages 210-213; *Senate Journal*, 1866, page 183.

17. *House Journal*, 1866-67, page 183; *Senate Journal*, 1866-67, page 138.

18. *House Journal*, 1866, pages 288-291; *Senate Journal*, 1866, page 262.

19. *House Journal*, 1866, page 284; *Senate Journal*, 1866, page 230.

20. *House Journal*, 1867, page 60; *Senate Journal*, 1867, page 62.

21. *House Journal*, 1866-67, page 108; *Senate Journal*, 1866-67, page 101.

22. James M. McPherson, *The Struggle For Equality: Abolitionists and the Negro in the Civil War and Reconstruction* (Princeton, New Jersey: Princeton University Press, 1964), page 194; *American Annual Cyclopedia and Register of Important Events of the Year 1867* (New York: D. Appleton and Company, 1870), page 452.

23. *House Journal*, 1867, page 223; *Senate Journal*, 1867, page 176.

Mississippi rejected it on January 31, 1868.[24] Ohio rejected it on January 15, 1868.[25] New Jersey rejected it on March 24, 1868.[26]

There is no question that all of the Southern States which rejected the Fourteenth Amendment had legally constituted governments, were fully recognized by the Federal Government, and were functioning as member States of the Union at the time of their rejection. President Andrew Johnson in his veto message of March 2, 1867, pointed out: "It is not denied that the States in question have each of them an actual government with all the powers, executive, judicial, and legislative, which properly belong to a free State. They are organized like the other States of the Union, and, like them, they make, administer, and execute the laws which concern their domestic affairs."[27]

If further proof were needed that these States were operating under legally constituted governments as member States of the Union, the ratification of the Thirteenth Amendment on December 8, 1865 undoubtedly supplies this official proof. If the Southern States were *not* member States of the Union, the Thirteenth Amendment would not have been submitted to their Legislatures for ratification.

The Thirteenth Amendment to the United States Constitution was proposed by Joint Resolution of Congress[28] and was approved February 1, 1865 by President Abraham Lincoln, as required by Article I, Section 7 of the United States Constitution. The President's signature is affixed to the Resolution. The Thirteenth Amendment was ratified by twenty-seven States of the then thirty-six States of the Union, including the Southern States of Virginia, Louisiana, Arkansas, South Carolina, North Carolina, Alabama, and Georgia. This is shown by the Proclamation of the Secretary of State on December 18, 1865.[29] Without the votes of these seven Southern State Legislatures the Thirteenth Amendment would have failed. There can be no doubt but that the ratification by these seven Southern States of the Thirteenth Amendment again established the fact that their Legislatures and State governments were duly and lawfully constituted and functioning as such under their State constitutions.

Furthermore, on April 2, 1866, President Andrew Johnson issued a proclamation that stated, "The insurrection which heretofore existed in the States of Georgia, South Carolina, Virginia, North Carolina, Tennessee, Alabama, Louisiana, Arkansas, Mississippi, and Florida is at an end, and is henceforth to be so regarded."[30] On August 20, 1866, President Johnson

---

24. *House Journal*, 1867, page 1141; *Senate Journal*, 1867, page 808.

25. James M. McPherson, *Struggle For Equality*, page 194.

26. *House Journal*, 1868, pages 44-50; *Senate Journal*, 1868, pages 22-38.

27. *Minutes of the Assembly*, 1868, page 743; *Senate Journal*, 1868, page 356.

28. *House Journal* (Thirty-Ninth Congress, Second Session), page 563.

29. Statutes at Large, Volume XIII, page 567.

30. *Ibid.*, page 774.

issued another proclamation[31] pointing out the fact that the Senate and House of Representatives had adopted identical Resolutions on July 22[32] and July 25, 1861,[33] that the Civil War forced by disunionists of the Southern States, was not waged for the purpose of conquest or to overthrow the rights and established institutions of those States, but to defend and maintain the supremacy of the Constitution and to preserve the Union with all the equality and rights of the several States unimpaired, and that as soon as these objects were accomplished, the war ought to cease. The President's proclamation on April 2, 1866[34] declared that the insurrection in the other Southern States, except Texas, no longer existed. On August 20, 1866, the President proclaimed that the insurrection in the State of Texas had been completely ended. He continued, "And I do further proclaim that the said insurrection is at an end, and that peace, order, tranquility, and civil authority now exist, in and throughout the whole of the United States of America."[35]

The State of Louisiana rejected the Fourteenth Amendment on February 6, 1867, making it the tenth State to have rejected the same, or more than one fourth of the total number of thirty-six States of the Union as of that date. Because this left less than three fourths of the States to ratify the Fourteenth Amendment, it failed of ratification in fact and in law, and it could not have been revived except by a new Joint Resolution of the Senate and House of Representatives in accordance with the constitutional requirement.

Faced with the positive failure of ratification of the Fourteenth Amendment, both Houses of Congress passed over the veto of the President three Acts, known as the Reconstruction Acts, between the dates of March 2 and July 19, 1867. The third of said Acts[36] was designed to illegally remove with "Military force" the lawfully constituted State Legislatures of the ten Southern States of Virginia, North Carolina, South Carolina, Georgia, Florida, Alabama, Mississippi, Arkansas, Louisiana, and Texas. In President Andrew Johnson's veto message on the Reconstruction Act of March 2, 1867, he pointed out these unconstitutionalities:

> If ever the American citizen should be left to the free exercise of his own judgment, it is when he is engaged in the work of forming the fundamental law under which he is to live. That work is his work, and it cannot be properly taken out of his hands. All this legislation proceeds upon the contrary assumption that the people of these States shall

---

31. Presidential Proclamation No. 153 in *General Records of the United States* (G.S.A. National Archives and Records Service).

32. Statutes at Large, Volume XIV, page 814.

33. *House Journal* (Thirty-Seventh Congress, First Session), page 123.

34. *Senate Journal* (Thirty-Seventh Congress, First Session), page 91ff.

35. Statutes at Large, Volume XIII, page 763.

36. *Ibid.*, Volume XIV, page 811.

have no constitution, except such as may be arbitrarily dictated by Congress, and formed under the restraint of military rule. A plain statement of facts makes this evident.

In all these States there are existing constitutions, framed in the accustomed way by the people. Congress, however, declares that these constitutions are not "loyal and republican" and requires the people to form them anew. What, then, in the opinion of Congress, is necessary to make the constitution of a State "loyal and republican"? The original act answers this question: "It is universal negro suffrage" — a question which the federal Constitution leaves exclusively to the States themselves. All this legislative machinery of martial law, military coercion, and political disfranchisement is avowedly for that purpose and none other. The existing constitutions of the ten States, conform to the acknowledged standards of loyalty and republicanism. Indeed, if there are degrees in republican forms of government, their constitutions are more republican now, than when these States — four of which were members of the original thirteen — first became members of the Union.[37]

In President Johnson's veto message regarding the Reconstruction Act of July 19, 1867, he pointed out various unconstitutionalities as follows:

The veto of the original bill of the 2d of March was based on two distinct grounds — the interference of Congress in matters strictly appertaining to the reserved powers of the States, and the establishment of military tribunals for the trial of citizens in time of peace....

A singular contradiction is apparent here. Congress declares these local State governments to be illegal governments, and then provides that these illegal governments shall be carried on by federal officers, who are to perform the very duties on its own officers by this illegal State authority. It certainly would be a novel spectacle if Congress should attempt to carry on a legal State government by the agency of its own officers. It is yet more strange that Congress attempts to sustain and carry on an illegal State government by the same federal agency....

It is now too late to say that these ten political communities are not States of this Union. Declarations to the contrary made in these three acts are contradicted again and again by repeated acts of legislation enacted by Congress from the year 1861 to the year 1867.

During that period, while these States were in actual rebellion, and after that rebellion was brought to a close, they have been again and again recognized as States of the Union. Representation has been apportioned to them as States. They have been divided into judicial districts for the holding of district and circuit courts of the United States, as States of the Union only can be distracted. The last act on this subject was passed July 23, 1866, by which every one of these ten States was arranged into districts and circuits.

They have been called upon by Congress to act through their legislatures upon at least two amendments to the Constitution of the United States. As States they have ratified one amendment, which required the vote of twenty-seven States of the thirty-six then composing the Union. When the requisite twenty-seven votes were given in favor of that

---

37. *Ibid.*, pages 814.

amendment, it was proclaimed to be a part of the *Constitution* of the United States, and slavery was declared no longer to exist within the United States or any place subject to their jurisdiction. If these seven States were not legal States of the Union, it follows as an inevitable consequence that in some of the States slavery yet exists. It does not exist in these seven States, for they have abolished it also in their State constitutions; but Kentucky not having done so, it would still remain in that State. But, in truth, if this assumption that these States have no legal State governments be true, then the abolition of slavery by these illegal governments binds no one, for Congress now denies to these States the power to abolish slavery by denying them the power to elect a legal State legislature, or to frame a constitution for any purpose, even for such a purpose as the abolition of slavery.

As to the other constitutional amendment having reference to suffrage, it happens that these States have not accepted it. The consequence is, that it has never been proclaimed or understood, even by Congress, to be a part of the Constitution of the United States. The Senate of the United States has repeatedly given its sanction to the appointment of judges, district attorneys, and marshals for every one of these States; yet, if they are not legal States, not one of these judges is authorized to hold a court. So, too, both houses of Congress have passed appropriation bills to pay all these judges, attorneys, and officers of the United States for exercising their functions in these States. Again, in the machinery of the internal revenue laws, all these States are distracted, not as "Territories," but as "States."

So much for continuous legislative recognition. The instances cited, however, fall far short of all that might be enumerated. Executive recognition, as is well known, has been frequent and unwavering. The same may be said as to judicial recognition through the Supreme Court of the United States.

To me these considerations are conclusive of the unconstitutionality of this part of the bill before me, and I earnestly commend their consideration to the deliberate judgment of Congress.

(And now to the Court.) Within a period of less than a year, the legislation of Congress has attempted to strip the executive department of the government of its essential powers. The Constitution, and the oath provided in it, devolve upon the President the power and duty to see that the laws are faithfully executed. The Constitution, in order to carry out this power, gives him the choice of the agents, and makes them subject to his control and supervision. But in the execution of these laws the constitutional obligation upon the President remains, but the powers to exercise that constitutional duty is effectually taken away. The military commander is, as to the power of appointment, made to take the place of the President, and the General of the Army the place of the Senate; and any attempt on the part of the President to assert his own constitutional power may, under pretense of law, be met by official insubordination. It is to be feared that these military officers, looking to the authority given by these laws rather than to the letter of the Constitution, will recognize no authority but the commander of the district and the General of the Army.

If there were no other objection than this to this proposed legislation, it would be sufficient.[38]

No one can contend that the Reconstruction Acts were ever upheld as being valid and constitutional. They were brought into question, but the courts either avoided decision or were prevented by Congress from finally adjudicating upon their constitutionality. In *Mississippi v. President Andrew Johnson*,[39] where the suit sought to enjoin the President of the United States from enforcing provisions of the Reconstruction Acts, the U.S. Supreme Court held that the President could not be adjoined because for the Judicial Department of the government to attempt to enforce the performance of the duties of the President might be justly characterized, in the language of Chief Justice Marshall, as "an absurd and excessive extravagance." The Court further said that if it granted the injunction against the enforcement of the Reconstruction Acts, and if the President refused obedience, it was needless to observe that the Court was without power to enforce its process.

In a joint action, the States of Georgia and Mississippi brought suit against the President and the Secretary of War. The Court said:

> The bill then sets forth that the intent and design of the Acts of Congress, as apparent on their face and by their terms, are to overthrow and annul this existing State government, and to erect another and different government in its place, unauthorized by the Constitution and in defiance of its guaranties; and that, in furtherance of this intent and design, the defendants, the Secretary of War, the General of the Army, and Major General Pope, acting under orders of the President, are about setting in motion a portion of the army to take military possession of the State, and threaten to subvert her government and subject her people to military rule; that the State is holding inadequate means to resist the power and force of the Executive Department of the United States; and she therefore insists that such protection can, and ought to be afforded by a decree or order of this court in the premises.[40]

The applications for injunction by these two States to prohibit the Executive Department from carrying out the provisions of the Reconstruction Acts directed to the overthrow of their government, including this dissolution of their State Legislatures, were denied on the grounds that the organization of the government into three great departments — the Executive, Legislative, and Judicial — carried limitations of the powers of each by the Constitution. This case went the same way as the previous case of Mississippi against President Johnson and was dismissed without adjudicating upon the constitutionality of the Reconstruction Acts.

---

38. *House Journal* (Fortieth Congress, First Session), page 232.

39. *Mississippi v. President Andrew Johnson* (1867), 4 Wall. 475-502.

40. 6 Wall. 50-78, 154 U.S. 554.

In another case, *ex parte William H. McCradle*,[41] a petition for the writ of *habeas corpus* for unlawful restraint by military force of a Citizen not in the military service of the United States was before the United States Supreme Court. After the case was argued and taken under advisement, and before conference in regarding the decision to be made, Congress passed an emergency act,[42] vetoed by the President and repassed over his veto, repealing the jurisdiction of the U.S. Supreme Court in such case. Accordingly, the Supreme Court dismissed the appeal without passing upon the constitutionality of the Reconstruction Acts, under which the non-military Citizen was held without benefit of writ of *habeas corpus*, in violation of Article I, Section 9 of the U.S. Constitution. That Act of Congress placed the Reconstruction Acts beyond judicial recourse and avoided tests of constitutionality.

It is recorded that one of the Supreme Court Justices, Grier, protested against the action of the Court as follows:

> This case was fully argued in the beginning of this month. It is a case which involves the liberty and rights, not only of the appellant, but of millions of our fellow citizens. The country and the parties had a right to expect that it would receive the immediate and solemn attention of the court. By the postponement of this case we shall subject ourselves, whether justly or unjustly, to the imputation that we have evaded the performance of a duty imposed on us by the Constitution, and waited for Legislative interposition to suppress our action, and relieve us from responsibility. I am not willing to be a partaker of the eulogy or opprobrium that may follow. I can only say... I am ashamed that such opprobrium should be cast upon the court and that it cannot be refuted.

The ten States were organized into Military Districts under the unconstitutional Reconstruction Acts, their lawfully constituted Legislatures were illegally removed by "military force," and were replaced by rump, so-called Legislatures, seven of which carried out military orders and pretended to ratify the Fourteenth Amendment as follows: Arkansas on April 6, 1868;[43] North Carolina on July 2, 1868;[44] Florida on June 9, 1868;[45] Louisiana on July 9, 1868;[46] South Carolina on July 9, 1868;[47] Alabama on July 13, 1868;[48] Georgia on July 21,

---

41. *Ex parte William H. McCardle*, 7 Wall. 506-515.

42. Act of Congress, March 27, 1868; Statutes at Large, Volume XV, page 44.

43. *House Journal* (Thirty-Ninth Congress, Second Session), pages 563ff.

44. *Ibid.* (Fortieth Congress, First Session), pages 232ff.

45. James M. McPherson, *Struggle For Equality*, page 53.

46. *House Journal*, 1868, page 15; *Senate Journal*, 1868, page 15.

47. *House Journal*, 1868, page 9; *Senate Journal*, 1868, page 8.

48. *Senate Journal*, 1868, page 21.

1868.[49]

Of the above seven States whose Legislatures were removed and replaced by rump, so-called Legislatures, six Legislatures of the States of Louisiana, Arkansas, South Carolina, Alabama, North Carolina, and Georgia had ratified the Thirteenth Amendment as shown by the Secretary of State's Proclamation of December 18, 1865, without which ratifications, the Thirteenth Amendment could not and would not have been ratified because said six States made a total of twenty-seven out of thirty-six States, or exactly three fourths of the number required by Article V of the Constitution for ratification.

Furthermore, governments of the States of Louisiana and Arkansas had been re-established under a Proclamation issued by President Abraham Lincoln dated December 8, 1863.[50] The government of North Carolina had been re-established under a Proclamation issued by President Andrew Johnson dated May 29, 1865.[51] The government of Georgia had been re-established under a Proclamation issued by President Johnson dated June 17, 1865.[52] The government of Alabama had been re-established under a Proclamation issued by President Johnson dated June 21, 1865.[53] The government of South Carolina had been re-established under a Proclamation issued by President Johnson dated June 30, 1865.[54]

These three Reconstruction Acts, under which the above state Legislatures were illegally removed and unlawful rump, or so-called Legislatures were substituted in a mock effort to ratify the Fourteenth Amendment, were unconstitutional, null and void, *ab initio*, and all acts done thereunder were also null and void, including the purported ratification of the Fourteenth Amendment by said six Southern puppet Legislatures of Arkansas, North Carolina, Louisiana, South Carolina, Alabama, and Georgia.

Those *Reconstruction Acts* of Congress and all acts and things unlawfully done thereunder were in violation of Article IV, Section 4 of the United States Constitution, which required the United States to guarantee a republican form of government. They violated Article 1, Section 3, and Article V of the Constitution which entitled every State in the Union to two Senators because under provisions of these unlawful Acts of Congress, ten States were deprived of having two Senators, or equal suffrage in the Senate.

The Secretary of State expressed doubt as to whether three fourths of the required States had ratified the Fourteenth Amendment, as shown by his Proclamation of July 20,

---

49. *House Journal*, 1868, page 50; *Senate Journal*, 1868, page 12.

50. Francis Newton Thorpe, *The Federal and State Constitutions* (Washington, D.C.: Government Printing Office, 1906), Volume I, pages 288-306; *ibid.*, Volume XI, pages 1429-1448.

51. Thorpe, *ibid.*, Volume V, pages 2799-2800.

52. Thorpe, *ibid.*, Volume II, pages 809-822.

53. Thorpe, *ibid.*, Volume I, pages 116-132.

54. Thorpe, *ibid.*, Volume VI, pages 3269-3281.

1868.[55] Promptly on July 21, 1868, a Joint Resolution was adopted by the Senate and House of Representatives declaring that three fourths of the several States of the Union had indeed ratified the Fourteenth Amendment.[56] That Resolution, however, included the purported ratifications by the unlawful puppet Legislatures of five States — Arkansas, North Carolina, Louisiana, South Carolina, and Alabama — which had previously rejected the Fourteenth Amendment by action of their lawfully constituted Legislatures, as shown above. This Joint Resolution assumed to perform the function of the Secretary of State in whom Congress, by Act of April 20, 1818, had vested the function of issuing such Proclamation declaring the ratification of Constitutional Amendments.

The Secretary of State bowed to the action of Congress and issued his Proclamation of July 28, 1868,[57] in which he stated that he was acting under authority of the Act of April 20, 1818, but pursuant to said Resolution of July 21, 1868. He listed three fourths or so of the then thirty-seven States as having ratified the Fourteenth Amendment, including the purported ratification by the unlawful puppet Legislatures of the states of Arkansas, North Carolina, Louisiana, South Carolina, and Alabama. Without said five purported ratifications there would have been only twenty-five States left to ratify out of thirty-seven when a minimum of twenty-eight States was required by three fourths of the States of the Union.

The Joint Resolution of Congress and the resulting Proclamation of the Secretary of State also included purported ratifications by the States of Ohio and New Jersey, although the Proclamation recognized the fact that the Legislatures of said States, several months previously, had withdrawn their ratifications and effectively rejected the Fourteenth Amendment in January, 1868 and April, 1868. Therefore, deducting these two States from the purported ratification of the Fourteenth Amendment, only twenty-three State ratifications at most could be claimed — five less than the required number required to ratify the Amendment.

From all of the above documented historic facts, it is inescapable that the Fourteenth Amendment was never validly adopted as an article of the Constitution, that it has no legal effect, and it should be declared by the Courts to be unconstitutional, and therefore, null, void, and of no effect.

The defenders of the Fourteenth Amendment contend that the U.S. Supreme Court has decided finally upon its validity. In what is considered the leading case, *Coleman v. Miller*, the U.S. Supreme Court did not uphold the validity of the Fourteenth Amendment. In that case, the Court brushed aside constitutional questions as though they did not exist. For instance, the Court made the following statement:

> The legislatures of Georgia, North Carolina, and South Carolina had rejected the

---

55. Statutes at Large, Volume XIV, pages 428ff; 15 Statutes at Large, pages 14ff.

56. *Ibid.*, Volume XV, page 706.

57. *House Journal* (Fortieth Congress, Second Session), page 1126.

amendment in November and December, 1866. New governments were erected in those
States (and in others) under the direction of Congress. The new legislatures ratified the
amendment, that of North Carolina on July 4, 1868, that of South Carolina on July 9, 1868,
and that of Georgia on July 21, 1868.[58]

The Court gave no consideration to the fact that Georgia, North Carolina, and South
Carolina were three of the original States of the Union with valid and existing constitutions
on an equal footing with the other original States and those later admitted into the Union.
Congress certainly did not have the right to remove those State governments and their Legislatures under unlawful military power set up by the unconstitutional Reconstruction Acts,
which had for their purpose the destruction and removal of legal State governments and the
nullification of the Constitution.

The fact that these three States and seven other Southern States had existing constitutions, were recognized as States of the Union, again and again, had been divided into judicial
districts for holding their district and circuit courts of the United States, had been called by
Congress to act through their Legislatures upon two Amendments — the Thirteenth and the
Fourteenth — and by their ratifications had actually made possible the adoption of the Thirteenth, as well as their State governments having been re-established under Presidential Proclamations, as shown by President Johnson's veto message and proclamations, were all
brushed aside by the Court in *Coleman v. Miller* by the statement, "New governments were
erected in those States (and in others) under the direction of Congress," and that these new
legislatures ratified the Amendment.

The U.S. Supreme Court overlooked that it previously had held that at no time were
these Southern States out of the Union.[59] In *Coleman v. Miller*, the Court did not adjudicate
upon the invalidity of the Acts of Congress which set aside those State constitutions and
abolished their state Legislatures. The Court simply referred to the fact that their legally constituted Legislatures had rejected the Fourteenth Amendment and that the "new legislatures"
had ratified it. The Court further overlooked the fact that the State of Virginia was also one
of the original States with its constitution and Legislature in full operation under its civil
government at the time.

In addition, the Court also ignored the fact that the other six Southern States, which
were given the same treatment by Congress under the unconstitutional Reconstruction Acts,
all had legal constitutions and a republican form of government in each State, as was recognized by Congress by its admission of those stated into the Union. The Court certainly must
take judicial cognizance of the fact that before a new State is admitted by Congress into the
Union, Congress enacts an Enabling Act to enable the inhabitants of the territory to adopt a
constitution to set up a republican form of government as a condition precedent to the admis-

58. *Coleman v. Miller*, 307 U.S. 448, 59 S.Ct. 972.

59. *White v. Hart* (1871), 13 Wall. 646, 654.

sion of the State into the Union, and upon approval of such constitution, Congress then passes the Act of Admission of such stated. All this was ignored and brushed aside by the Supreme Court in the *Coleman v. Miller* case. However, the Court inadvertently stated:

> Whenever official notice is received at the Department of State that any amendment to the Constitution of the United States has been adopted, according to the provisions of the Constitution, the Secretary of State shall forthwith cause the amendment to be published, with his certificate, specifying the States by which the same may have been adopted, and that the same has become valid, to all intents and purposes, as a part of the Constitution of the United States.

In *Hawke v. Smith*, the U.S. Supreme Court unmistakingly held:

> The fifth article is a grant of authority by the people to Congress. The determination of the method of ratification is the exercise of a national power specifically granted by the Constitution; that power is conferred upon Congress, and is limited to two methods, by action of the Legislatures of three fourths of the States. *Dodge v. Woolsey*, 18 How. 331, 15 L.Ed. 401. The framers of the Constitution might have adopted a different method. Ratification might have been left to a vote of the people, or to some authority of government other than that selected. The language of the article is plain, and admits of no doubt in its interpretation. It is not the function of courts or legislative bodies, National or State, to alter the method which the Constitution has fixed.[60]

We submit that in none of the cases in which the Court avoided the constitutional issues involved, did it pass upon the constitutionality of that Congress which purported to adopt the Joint Resolution for the Fourteenth Amendment, with eighty Representatives and twenty-three Senators forcibly ejected or denied their seats and their votes on said Resolution, in order to pass the same by a two thirds vote, as pointed out in the New Jersey Legislature Resolution of March 27, 1868.

Such a fragmentary Congress also violated the constitutional requirements of Article V that no State, without its consent, shall be deprived of its equal suffrage in the Senate. There is no such thing as giving life to an Amendment illegally proposed or never legally ratified by three-fourths of the States. There is no such thing as Amendment by laches, no such thing as Amendment by waiver, no such thing as Amendment by acquiescence, and no such thing as Amendment by any other means whatsoever except the means specified in Article V of the Constitution itself. It does not suffice to say that there have been hundreds of cases decided under the Fourteenth Amendment to offset the constitutional deficiencies in its proposal or ratification as required by Article V. If hundreds of litigants did not question the validity of the Fourteenth Amendment, or question the same perfunctorily without submitting documentary proof of the facts of record which made its purported adoption un-

---

60. *Hawke v. Smith* (1920), 253 U.S. 221, 40 S.Ct. 227.

constitutional, their failure cannot change the Constitution for the millions in America.

The same thing is true of laches; the same thing is true of acquiescence; the same thing is true of ill-considered court decisions. To ascribe constitutional life to an alleged Amendment which never came into being according to the specified methods laid down in Article V cannot be done without doing violence to Article V itself. This is true, because the only question open to the courts is whether the alleged Fourteenth Amendment became a part of the Constitution through a method required by Article V. Anything beyond that which a court is called upon to hold in order to validate an Amendment, would be equivalent to writing into Article V another mode of the Amendment process which has never been authorized by the people of the United States of America.

On this point, therefore, the question is: Was the Fourteenth Amendment proposed and ratified in accordance with Article V? In answering this question, it is of no real moment that decisions have been rendered in which the parties did not contest or submit proper evidence, or the Court assumed that there was a Fourteenth Amendment. If a statute never in fact passed in Congress, through some error of administration and printing got in the published reports of the statutes, and if under such supposed statute courts had levied punishment upon a number of persons charged under it, and if the error in the published volume was discovered and the fact became known that no such statute had ever passed in Congress, it is unthinkable that the courts would continue to administer punishment in similar cases, on a non-existent statute because prior decisions had done so. If that be true as to a statute we need only realize the greater truth when the principle is applied to the solemn question of the contents of the Constitution. While the defects in the method of proposing and the subsequent method of computing "ratification" has been brief above, it should be noted that the failure to comply with Article V began with the first action by Congress. The very Congress which proposed the alleged Fourteenth Amendment under the first part of Article V was itself, at that very time, violating the last part as well as the first part of Article V of the Constitution.

There is one, and only one, provision of the Constitution of the United States which is forever immutable, which can never be changed or expunged. The courts cannot alter it, the executives cannot question it, the Congress cannot change it, and the States themselves, though they act in perfect concert, cannot amend it in any manner whatsoever, whether they act through conventions called for the purpose or through their Legislatures. Not even the unanimous vote of every voter in the United States of America could amend this provision. It is a perpetual fixture in the Constitution, so perpetual and so fixed that if the people of the United States of America desired to change or exclude it, they would be compelled to abolish the Constitution and start afresh.

The unalterable provision is this: "No State, without its consent, shall be deprived of its equal suffrage in the Senate." A State, by its own consent, may waive this right of equal suffrage, but that is the only legal method by which a failure to accord this immutable right of equal suffrage in the Senate can be justified. Certainly not by forcible ejection and denial by a majority in Congress, as was done for the adoption of the Joint Resolution for the Fourteenth Amendment. Statements by the Court in the *Coleman v. Miller* case that Congress was left in complete control of the mandatory process, and therefore it was a political affair for Congress to decide if an Amendment had been ratified, does not square with Article V of the Constitution which shows no intention to leave Congress in charge of deciding such matters. Even a constitutionally recognized Congress is given but one volition in Article V, and that is to vote whether to propose an Amendment on its own initiative. The remaining steps by Congress are mandatory. Congress shall propose Amendments; if the Legislatures of two thirds of the States make application, Congress shall call a convention. For the Court to give Congress any power beyond that which is found in Article V is to write new material into Article V. It would be inconceivable that the Congress of the United States could propose, compel submission to, and then give life to an invalid Amendment by resolving that its effort had succeeded regardless of compliance with the positive provisions of Article V. It should need no further citation to sustain the proposition that neither the Joint Resolution proposing the Fourteenth Amendment nor its ratification by the required three fourths of the States in the Union were in compliance with the requirements of Article V of the Constitution.

When the mandatory provisions of the Constitution are violated, the Constitution itself strikes with nullity the Act that did violence to its provisions. Thus, the Constitution strikes with nullity the purported Fourteenth Amendment. The courts, bound by oath to support the Constitution, should review all of the evidence herein submitted and measure the facts proving violations of the mandatory provisions of Article V of the Constitution, and finally render judgment declaring said purported Amendment never to have been adopted as required by the Constitution. The Constitution makes it the sworn duty of the judges to uphold the Constitution which strikes with nullity the Fourteenth Amendment. As Chief Justice Marshall pointed out for a unanimous Supreme Court in *Marbury v. Madison*:

> The framers of the Constitution contemplated the instrument as a rule for the government of courts, as well as of the legislature....
> Why does a judge swear to discharge his duties agreeably to the constitution of the United States, if that Constitution forms no rule for his government?...
> If such be the real state of things, that is worse than solemn mockery. To prescribe, or to take this oath, becomes equally a crime....
> Thus, the particular phraseology of the Constitution of the United States confirms and strengthens the principle, supposed to be essential to all written constitutions.... that courts, as well as other departments, are bound by that instrument.[61]

The Federal courts actually refuse to hear argument on the invalidity of the Fourteenth Amendment, even when the evidence above is presented squarely by the pleadings. Only an aroused public sentiment in favor of preserving the Constitution and our institutions and freedoms under constitutional government, and the future security of our country, will

---

61. *Marbury v. Madison*, I Cranch, 136, 179.

break the political barrier which now prevents judicial consideration of the unconstitutionality of the Fourteenth Amendment.

SUPPLEMENTARY ESSAY
There is No "Fourteenth Amendment"
by David Lawrence

1. Outside the South, six States — New Jersey, Ohio, Kentucky, California, Delaware and Maryland — failed to ratify the proposed amendment.

2. In the South, ten States — Texas, Arkansas, Virginia, North Carolina, South Carolina, Georgia, Alabama, Florida, Mississippi and Louisiana — by formal action of their legislatures, rejected it under the normal processes of civil law.

3. A total of 16 legislatures out of 37 failed legally to ratify the "Fourteenth Amendment."

4. Congress — which had deprived the Southern States of their seats in the Senate — did not lawfully pass the resolution of submission in the first instance.

5. The Southern States which had rejected the amendment were coerced by a federal statute passed in 1867 that took away the right to vote or hold office from all citizens who had served in the Confederate Army. Military governors were appointed and instructed to prepare the roll of voters. All this happened in spite of the presidential proclamation of amnesty previously issued by the President. New legislatures were thereupon chosen and forced to "ratify" under penalty of continued exile from the Union. In Louisiana, a General sent down from the North presided over the State legislature.

6. Abraham Lincoln had declared many times that the Union was "inseparable" and "indivisible." After his death, and when the war was over, the ratification by the Southern States of the Thirteenth Amendment, abolishing slavery, had been accepted as legal. But Congress in the 1867 law imposed the specific conditions under which the Southern States would be "entitled to representation in Congress."

7. Congress, in passing the 1867 law that declared the Southern States could not have

their seats in either the Senate or House in the next session unless they ratified the "Four-teenth Amendment," took an unprecedented step. No such right — to compel a State by an act of Congress to ratify a constitutional amendment — is to be found anywhere in the Con-stitution. Nor has this procedure ever been sanctioned by the Supreme Court of the United States.

8. President Andrew Johnson publicly denounced this law as unconstitutional. But it was passed over his veto.

9. Secretary of State Seward was on the spot in July 1868 when the various "ratifica-tions" of a spurious nature were placed before him. The legislatures of Ohio and New Jersey had notified him that they rescinded their earlier action of ratification. He said in his official proclamation that he was not authorized as Secretary of State "to determine and decide doub-tful questions as to the authenticity of the organization of State legislatures or as to the power of any State legislature to recall a previous act or resolution of ratification." He added that the amendment was valid "if the resolutions of the legislatures of Ohio and New Jersey, ratifying the aforesaid amendment, are to be deemed as remaining of full force and effect, notwithstanding the subsequent resolutions of the legislatures of these States." This was a very big "if." It will be noted that the real issue, therefore, is not only whether the forced "ratification" by the ten Southern States was lawful, but whether the withdrawal by the legis-latures of Ohio and New Jersey — two Northern States — was legal. The right of a State, by action of its legislature, to change its mind at any time before the final proclamation of ratifi-cation is issued by the Secretary of State has been confirmed in connection with other consti-tutional amendments.

10. The Oregon Legislature in October 1868 — three months after the Secretary's proclamation was issued — passed a rescinding resolution, which argued that the "Four-teenth Amendment" had not been ratified by three fourths of the States and that the "ratifications" in the Southern States were "usurpations, unconstitutional, revolutionary and void" and that, "until such ratification is completed, any State has a right to withdraw its assent to any proposed amendment."

What do the historians say about all this? The *Encyclopedia Americana* states: "Re-construction added humiliation to suffering.... Eight years of crime, fraud, and corruption followed and it was State legislatures composed of Negroes, carpetbaggers and scalawags who obeyed the orders of the generals and ratified the amendment."

W.E. Woodward, in his famous work, *A New American History*, published in 1936, says:

> To get a clear idea of the succession of events let us review [President Andrew] Johnson's actions in respect to the ex-Confederate States.
>
> In May, 1865, he issued a Proclamation of Amnesty to former rebels. Then he established provisional governments in all the Southern States. They were instructed to call Constitutional Conventions. They did. New State governments were elected. White men only had the suffrage [the Fifteenth Amendment establishing equal voting rights had not yet been passed]. Senators and Representatives were chosen, but when they appeared

at the opening of Congress they were refused admission. The State governments, however, continued to function during 1866.

Now we are in 1867. In the early days of that year [Thaddeus] Stevens brought in, as chairman of the House Reconstruction Committee, a bill that proposed to sweep all the Southern State governments into the wastebasket. The South was to be put under military rule.

The bill passed. It was vetoed by Johnson and passed again over his veto. In the Senate it was amended in such fashion that any State could escape from military rule and be restored to its full rights by ratifying the Fourteenth Amendment and admitting black as well as white men to the polls.

In challenging its constitutionality, President Andrew Johnson said in his veto message: "I submit to Congress whether this measure is not in its whole character, scope and object without precedent and without authority, in palpable conflict with the plainest provisions of the Constitution, and utterly destructive of those great principles of liberty and humanity for which our ancestors on both sides of the Atlantic have shed so much blood and expended so much treasure."

Many historians have applauded Johnson's words. Samuel Eliot Morison and Henry Steele Commager, known today as "liberals," wrote in their book, *The Growth of the American Republic*: "Johnson returned the bill with a scorching message arguing the unconstitutionality of the whole thing, and most impartial students have agreed with his reasoning."

James Truslow Adams, another noted historian, writes in his *History of the United States*: "The Supreme Court had decided three months earlier, in the *Milligan* case, ... that military courts were unconstitutional except under such war conditions as might make the operation of civil courts impossible, but the President pointed out in vain that practically the whole of the new legislation was unconstitutional.... There was even talk in Congress of impeaching the Supreme Court for its decisions! The legislature had run amok and was threatening both the Executive and the Judiciary."

Actually, President Johnson was impeached, but the move failed by one vote in the Senate.

The Supreme Court, in case after case, refused to pass on the illegal activities involved in "ratification." It said simply that they were acts of the "political departments of the Government." This, of course, was a convenient device of avoidance. The Court has adhered to that position ever since Reconstruction Days.

Andrew C. McLaughlin, whose *Constitutional History of the United States* is a standard work, writes: "Can a State which is not a State and not recognized as such by Congress, perform the supreme duty of ratifying an amendment to the fundamental law? Or does a State — by congressional thinking — cease to be a State for some purposes but not for others?"

This is the tragic history of the so-called "Fourteenth Amendment" — a record that is a disgrace to free government and a "government of law." Isn't the use of military force to override local government what we deplored in Hungary?

It is never too late to correct injustice. The people of America should have an opportunity to pass on an amendment to the Constitution that sets forth the right of the Federal Government to control education and regulate attendance at public schools either with federal power alone or concurrently with the States. That's the honest way, the just way to deal with the problem of segregation or integration in the schools. Until such an amendment is adopted, the "Fourteenth Amendment" should be considered as null and void. There is only one supreme tribunal — it is the people themselves. Their sovereign will is expressed through the procedures set forth in the Constitution itself.

The preceding essay was extracted from U.S. News & World Report, *27 September 1957.*

PART FOUR
The Triumph of Democratic Socialism in the Twentieth Century

> When plunder becomes a way of life for a group of men living together in society, they create for themselves in the course of time a legal system that authorizes it and a moral code that glorifies it.
>
> — Frederick Bastiat

CHAPTER TWENTY
The "New Nation" Enters the First World War

There is No Longer a Federal Government

In his book entitled *Abraham Lincoln and the Second American Revolution*, modern historian James M. McPherson wrote:

> [After the war] the old decentralized federal republic became a new national polity that taxed the people directly, created an internal revenue bureau to collect these taxes, expanded the jurisdiction of federal courts, established a national currency and a national banking structure.
>
> The United States went to war in 1861 to preserve the *Union*; it emerged from war in 1865 having created a *nation*. Before 1861 the two words "United States" were generally used as a plural noun: "The United States *are* a republic." After 1865 the United States became a singular noun. The loose union of states became a nation (emphasis in original).[1]

McPherson, who does not take sides with the South, perhaps admitted more than he intended in the above statement. The vast majority of Americans today are completely blind to the fact that there was no restoration of "the Union as it was" when the Southern States were subjugated in 1865, but rather the permanent establishment of a centralized military despotism which, although styled the "United States," bears no more relation to the Govern-

---

1. James M. McPherson, *Abraham Lincoln and the Second American Revolution* (New York: Oxford University Press, 1990), page viii.

ment of the United States of America under the Constitution than did that political body to the former Government under the Articles of Confederation. Prior to the 1860s, the Union was not a self-existent entity, but merely a condition arising from the common consent of the participating States. As such, the Union could neither create States — the new States were admitted by Congress to the Union *after* being created by the inhabitants of the Territories — nor compel their submission by force once admitted — a war between the States was only made possible by States acting in combination outside of the constitutionally-created Union against their sister States. The Government created by the Constitution was established to govern this voluntary association of States, and to represent them abroad; it was therefore their common agent, never their master. As Supreme Court Justice Story pointed out in 1833, "The Federal Government... as a creature of that compact [the Constitution], must be bound by its creators, the several States in the Union and the citizens thereof, having no existence but under the Constitution, nor any rights but as that instrument confers."[2] Echoing this view, Jefferson Davis wrote:

> In the nature of things, no union can be formed except by separate, independent, and distinct parties. Any other combination is not a union; and, upon the destruction of any of these elements in the parties, the union *ipso facto* ceases. If the Government is the result of a union of States, then these States must be separate, sovereign, and distinct, to be able to form a union, which is entirely an act of their own volition. Such a government as ours had no power to maintain its existence any longer than the contracting parties pleased to cohere, because it was founded on the great principle of voluntary federation, and organized "to establish justice and insure domestic tranquility." Any departure from this principle by the General Government not only perverts and destroys its nature, but furnishes a just cause to the injured State to withdraw from the union. A new union might subsequently be formed, but the original one could never by coercion be restored. Any effort on the part of the others to force the seceding State to consent to come back is an attempt at subjugation. It is a wrong which no lapse of time or combination of circumstances can ever make right. A forced union is a political absurdity.[3]

Likewise, Alexander H. Stephens wrote:

> The very object in forming all Confederated Republics is to create a *new* and an *entirely artificial* or conventional *State* or *Nation*, which springs from their joint Sovereignties, and which has no existence apart from them, and which is but the Corporate Agent of all those Sovereignties creating it, and through which alone they are to be known to Foreign Powers, during the continuance of the Confederation. This Conventional Nation

---

2. Story, *Commentaries on the Constitution*, Volume I, page 318. This statement proves that Story was able to accurately discuss the constitutional compact of States under the Constitution when he was not under the spell of his opposing consolidationist theory.

3. Davis, *Rise and Fall of the Confederate Government*, Volume II, page 322.

is but a Political Corporation. It has no *original* or *inherent* powers whatever. All its powers are derived — all are specific — all are limited — all are delegated — all may be resumed — all may be forfeited by misuser, as well as non-user. It is created by the separate Republics forming it. They are the Creators. It is but their Creature — subject to their will and control. They barely delegate the exercise of certain Sovereign powers to their common agent, retaining to themselves, separately, all that absolute, ultimate Sovereignty, by which this common agent, with all its delegated powers, is created. The new Conventional State or Nation thus formed is brought into being by the will of the several States or Nations forming it, and by the same will it may cease to exist, as to any or all of them, while the separate Sovereignties of its Creators may survive, and live on forever....

...[T]he Government itself, with all its power as well as machinery, was founded upon Compact between separate and distinct Sovereign States. If this be so, as has been conclusively established, then the Government, so constructed, must of necessity be Federal, and purely Federal, in its character (emphases in original).[4]

In this view, Davis and Stephens were sustained by none other than Alexander Hamilton himself. According to Hamilton, the States "possess inherent advantages, which will ever give them an influence and ascendancy over the National Government, and will forever preclude the possibility of Federal encroachments." To therefore strike at the sovereignty of the States, and to destroy their governments, would deliver a fatal blow to the federal Government itself and would amount to its own "political suicide." Such an action, in Hamilton's opinion, would be the end of American liberty: "The States can never lose their powers till the whole people of America are robbed of their liberties. These must go together; they must support each other, or meet one common fate."[5] Given his oft-expressed love of consolidation, Hamilton's observations carry all the more weight because he spoke of things as they were, not as he had desired them to be.

In the words of the Supreme Court, "The people of each State compose a State, having its own government, and endowed with all the functions essential to separate and independent existence.... In many articles of the Constitution the necessary existence of the States, and, within their proper spheres, the independent authority of the States, is distinctly recognized. The States disunited might continue to exist, but without the States in Union there could be no such political body as the United States."[6] It follows then, upon a dissolution of the voluntary Union, a destruction of the Constitution, and an overthrow of the sovereign States, that the federal Government of the United States can no longer exist in organic

4. Stephens, *Constitutional View of the War Between the States*, Volume I, pages 483, 485.

5. Hamilton, in Elliott, *Debates in the Several State Conventions*, Volume II, pages 239, 355.

6. *Lane County v. Oregon* (1869), 7 Wallace 71, 76.

law[7] as a corporation *de jure*; if it continues, it must necessarily take on a "life" of its own under color of law[8] as a corporation *de facto* with its own internal codes, rules, and regulations. It has been judicially declared that "where congress creates a corporation merely by virtue of its authority to legislate for a particular territory, and not by a general act, the corporation is a foreign one in any state or territory other than that in which it was created."[9] It comes as no surprise, therefore, that Title 28, United States Code, Section 3002(15)(a) clearly defines the "United States" as "a Federal corporation" and that elsewhere we are told, "The United States government is a foreign corporation with respect to a State."[10] *Black's Law Dictionary* defines a corporation as "an artificial person or legal entity."[11] Thus, the U.S. Government, with its permanent seat in the District of Columbia,[12] is a fiction comprised of other fictions ("U.S. citizens"), not the lawful government comprised of real people (State Citizens) it was before the 1860s:

> This self-formed corporate body has not merely an *esprit de corps*, but a oneness of will and purpose characteristic alike of a corporation, an oligarchy, or an autocrat; and the federal legislature, executive and judiciary, which were established as three absolutely independent institutions, to watch, and, if necessary, check one another, are now so unified as to act with one mind and will: thus practically changing them into a vast and chronic conspiracy against the people's liberty, as any gang of men, acting with one mind in the hiding places of the constitution and government, and constantly influenced by power and money, will gradually become.
>
> Under the forms of a republican federation, then, we have a consolidated empire, and a corporate despot, just as the Romans had "an absolute monarchy disguised in the form of a commonwealth" (Gibbon). The parallelism will hereafter more fully appear.[13]

It is this corporate despot that has continued its subjugation of the people of both North and South through its municipal franchises, the fifty reconstructed "States." That these are not the organic and sovereign States which comprised the original Union but are, by their

---

7. "Organic law. The fundamental law, or constitution, of a state or nation, written or unwritten. That law or system of laws or principles which defines and establishes the organization of its government" (*Black's Law Dictionary* [Sixth Edition], page 1099).

8. "Color of law. The appearance or semblance, without the substance, of legal right" (*Ibid.*, page 265).

9. *Daly v. National Life Insurance Company* (1878), 64 Ind. 1.

10. *In re Merriam*, 36 N.E. 505, 141 N.Y. 479, affirmed 16 S.Ct. 1073, 163 U.S. 625, 41 L.Ed. 287.

11. *Black's Law Dictionary* (Sixth Edition), page 340.

12. Title 4, United States Code, Section 71.

13. Sage, *Republic of Republics*, pages 11-12.

very nature, foreign political entities which are only nominally republican, is evident from the fact that their elective franchises consist exclusively of U.S. citizens who, although they reside in one of the States, nevertheless have their legal domicile in Washington, D.C. and owe "unqualified allegiance" to the Government seated there.[14] Furthermore, the new State constitutions were all framed post-Reconstruction by these foreign residents and, at least in the South, contain provisions which openly repudiate State sovereignty and the right of the American people to self-determination:

> With the shots "heard round the world," Americans rebelled against an oppressive foreign authority. Then, after a generation as semi-independent states, they entered into a compact as "the People" in order, as the Preamble to the Constitution reads, to "secure the Blessings of Liberty to ourselves and our Posterity." The purpose of the 1789 Constitution was to charter a government of limited powers that could never become a tyrannical overlord. To guard against government's tendency toward self-aggrandizement, the framers not only expressly delimited the powers of Congress but tried in the Bill of Rights to carve out certain areas of freedom — speech, press, assembly, religion, arms — that would remain beyond the federal government's reach. They would remain vested in "the People," who preceded and superseded the Constitution they established....
>
> The recognition that the People are one group, an American nation, makes possible the sustained campaign to convert the elitist Constitution of 1789 into an egalitarian constitution of popular suffrage — that is, a constitution that bases democratic rule on the majority of *all* the people....
>
> Nationhood, equality, and democracy — these are the ideas that forge a new Constitution. But Lincoln was a good lawyer, and lawyers always seek to camouflage conceptual transformations as the continuous outgrowth of language used in the past. That's why he invoked government "by the people" to capture the new principle of democratic rule. But the significance of the People had changed. They no longer exist as the guarantors of the Constitution, the bestowers of legitimacy. States and individuals can no longer set themselves apart from the nation. The people exist exclusively as voters, as office holders and as beneficiaries of legislation.
>
> The relevant concept in the new Constitution, then, is not "We the People" but "We the citizens of the nation" — and this transformation is apparent in the post-Civil War amendments. The Fourteenth Amendment, for example, gives us our first concept of national citizenship. "All persons born or naturalized in the United States, and subject to the jurisdiction thereof" are henceforth citizens. Prior to the Civil War, we allowed each state to define for itself who could become a citizen of the state and, on that basis, a citizen of the country. The new definition of who belongs to the polity marks a new beginning (emphasis in original).[15]

Thus, according to this writer, the so-called "Civil War" somehow breathed life into

---

14. *U.S. v. Macintosh* (1931), 283 U.S. 605, at 625, 51 S.Ct. 570, at 575.

15. George P. Fletcher, "Unsound Constitution," *The New Republic*, 23 June 1997, pages 14-15.

the empty shell of the Story-Webster theory of the "people in the aggregate." It does not seem to bother such modern legal experts that the "campaign to convert the elitist Constitution of 1789 into an egalitarian constitution of popular suffrage" was, in reality, a lawless and bloody revolution which would have made Robespierre envious.

Additionally, over the last decade or so, the foreign residents of the States have begun to remove the old boundaries from their constitutions. For example, the acting Mississippi State Legislature proposed and adopted the following resolution in 1990:

> That the following amendment to the Mississippi Constitution of 1890 be submitted to the qualified electors of the state for ratification or rejection at an election to be held on the first Tuesday after the first Monday of November, 1990:
> Repeal Section 3, Mississippi Constitution of 1890, which reads as follows:
> Section 3. The limits and boundaries of the State of Mississippi are as follows, to wit: [description of boundaries omitted]....
> BE IT FURTHER RESOLVED, That the explanation of the amendment for the ballot shall read as follows: "This proposed constitutional amendment repeals the section which establishes the boundaries of the state."[16]

It should be noted that since a State is legally defined as "a people permanently occupying a fixed territory,"[17] and "a political community of free citizens, occupying a territory of defined boundaries,"[18] it follows that a "State" with no boundaries cannot really be a State at all.

The Congress established by Article I of the Constitution consisted of a House of Representatives, composed of elected representatives of "the People of the several States,"[19] and a Senate, composed of "two Senators from each State" acting as representatives of the State government which selected them.[20] Since all political power descended from the sovereignty of the people of the States, it is obvious that the members of Congress could not be other than State Citizens — a Congress composed of statutory "persons" has no lawful standing to make law under the Constitution, but may only decide matters of public policy. That Congress continues to operate in this provisional character to this day is openly declared in the list of Titles in Volume One of the United States Code. Title II — "The Congress" — is marked with an asterisk and a footnote at the bottom of the page reads, "Exists By Resolution." The difference between resolution and law is "that the former is used whenever the

---

16. Mississippi Senate Concurrent Resolution 520.

17. *Black's Law Dictionary* (Sixth Edition), page 1407.

18. *Texas v. White*, 74 U.S. 700.

19. U.S. Constitution, Article I, Section 2, Clause 2.

20. *Ibid.*, Section 3, Clause 1.

legislative body passing it wishes merely to express an opinion as to some given matter or thing and is only to have a temporary effect on such particular thing, while by a 'law' it is intended to permanently direct and control matters applying to persons or things in general."[21] Of course, Congress is not alone in facing this problem of legitimacy; today, not a single office in the land, from the President down to the lowliest notary public, is occupied by a State Citizen as required by the United States Constitution and the constitutions of the several ante-bellum States. Indeed, it would be correct to say that such Citizens have long since gone out of existence and with them went the Republic.

The President as "Supreme Dictator"

> Not only did [Lincoln] do things that were regarded by most people as within the exclusive field of Congress's power, but he went further and asserted his competence to do things in an emergency that Congress could never do at all, maintaining that his designation as Commander in Chief allowed him to adopt measures that in normal times could only be effected by an amendment to the Constitution. This was a revolutionary and unique reading of the war clauses of that document, an unparalleled precedent for some equally extraordinary crisis act by a future President of the United States.[22]

The "executive war power" that was invented and utilized by Lincoln lay somewhat dormant from the close of Reconstruction to the first World War. During this time, the reconstructed States were allowed to maintain an appearance of their former glory and the centralized Government in Washington was content to play the part of a benevolent and unobtrusive overseer. Moreover, the four-month Spanish-American conflict of 1898 healed the breach between North and South, and by the close of the Nineteenth Century many Southerners were willing to put the tragic past behind them and accept their place in the new nation without further complaint. In the words of Southern historian Jabez L.M. Curry, "The spirit of nationality and of devotion to the Union is as strong in Georgia as in Massachusetts...."[23] Even

---

21. *Black's Law Dictionary* (Sixth Edition), page 1310.

22. Clinton L. Rossiter, *Constitutional Dictatorship: Crisis Government in the Modern Democracies* (Princeton, New Jersey: Princeton University Press, 1948), page 234. Rossiter's usage of the phrase "constitutional dictatorship" is based on his assumption that the Constitution allows for the President to seize control over the Government in times of crisis. As such, his book was basically an apology for the dictatorial actions of Abraham Lincoln, and later of Woodrow Wilson, and Franklin Delano Roosevelt, but it is nevertheless a valuable resource for anyone who wishes to understand the mindset which drove these men and now drives the Government which they created. A more up-to-date treatise on the subject is Martin S. Sheffer, *The Judicial Development of Presidential War Powers* (Westport, Connecticut: Praeger Publishers, 1999).

23. Curry, *Southern States of the American Union*, page 235.

former Confederate military heroes, such as John Brown Gordon, likened the War Between the States to the Christian Church's baptism on the Day of Pentecost, stating their expectation that "the Republic, rising from its baptism of blood with a national life more robust, a national union more complete, and a national influence ever widening, shall go forever forward in its benign mission to humanity."[24]

However, with the entry of the United States into the first World War, the Government under the Administration of Woodrow Wilson cast aside all pretenses of its "benign mission to humanity," and returned with renewed vigor to its former policy of denying the American people the right to govern themselves:

> Faced with the exigencies of World War I, Wilson found it necessary to expand executive emergency powers enormously. In many respects, this expansion of powers in wartime was based on precedents set by Lincoln decades earlier. Unlike Lincoln, however, Wilson relied heavily on Congress for official delegations of authority no matter how broadly these might be.
>
> Wilson's exercise of power in the First World War provided a model for future Presidents and their advisors. During the preparedness period of 1915-1916, the submarine crisis in the opening months of 1917, and the period of direct involvement of U.S. armed forces from April 1917 to November 1918, Wilson utilized powers as sweeping as Lincoln's. Because governmental agencies were more highly organized and their jurisdictions wider, presidential powers were considerably more effective than ever before.[25]

At the height of the war, it was said of Wilson, "What the United States needs and what it must have if it is to win the war is a supreme dictator, with sole control of and sole responsibility for every phase of war activity.... The sooner it comes the better for all of us.... For supreme dictator at the present moment, there is but one possible man — the President of the United States."[26] Wilson himself, when he was still a professor of politics at Princeton University, had taught that the President could ignore the constitutional separation of the Executive and Legislative powers at his own discretion — not only in times of crisis, but in

---

24. John Brown Gordon, *Reminiscences of the Civil War* (New York: Charles Scribner's Sons, 1903), page 465.

25. United States Senate, "Introduction," *Emergency Powers Statutes: Provisions of Federal Law Now in Effect Delegating to the Executive Authority in Time of National Emergency: Report of the Special Committee on the Termination of the National Emergency* (United States Senate Report No. 93-549, Ninety-Third Congress, First Session; Washington, D.C.: U.S. Government Printing Office, November 19, 1973; #24-509), page 3.

26. Warren G. Harding, quoted by New York *Times*, 10 February 1918; cited by Rossiter, *Constitutional Dictatorship*, page 254.

peacetime as well — by becoming the "originator of policies."[27] As President, his views were not substantially different for he "always regarded the forthright suggestion of desired legislation as one of his principal functions."[28]

The two most noteworthy Acts which were passed by Congress during this period at Wilson's bidding were the Trading With the Enemy Act of 1917 and the Sedition Act of 1918. The first of these Acts designated as an enemy of the United States Government "any individual, partnership, or other body of individuals, of any nationality, resident within the territory... of any nation with which the United States is at war,"[29] and basically prohibited trade among such persons within foreign territory occupied by the U.S. military, except by special license granted by the President.[30] Resurrecting the old heavy-handed censorship that had been attempted by the Federalists in 1798, the second Act "punished expressions of opinion which, irrespective of their likely consequences, were 'disloyal, profane, scurrilous or abusive' of the American form of Government, flag or uniform; and under it Americans were persecuted for criticizing the Red Cross, the YMCA and even the budget."[31] Even the Committee on Public Information, which was the propaganda arm of the Wilson Administration, had to admit that "few more sweeping measures have ever found their way to the national statute book."[32]

Journalist Walter Lippmann denounced the Wilson Administration for having "instituted a reign of terror in which honest thought is impossible, in which moderation is discountenanced and in which panic supplants reason."[33] Henry Lewis Mencken, editor of the Baltimore *Evening Sun*, likewise described this legislation as "a system of espionage altogether without precedent in American history, and not often matched in the history of Russia, Austria and Italy. It has, as a matter of daily routine, hounded men and women in cynical violation of their constitutional rights, invaded the sanctuary of domicile, manufactured evidence

---

27. Woodrow Wilson, *Constitutional Government in the United States* (New York: Columbia University Press, 1908), page 73; see also Norman J. Small, *Some Constitutional Interpretations of the Presidency* (Baltimore, Maryland: John Hopkins Press, 1932), pages 46-54.

28. Rossiter, *Constitutional Dictatorship*, page 244.

29. *Trading With the Enemy Act*, 6 October 1917, Section 2(a); Statutes at Large, Volume XL, page 411.

30. *Ibid.*, Section 5(b).

31. Paul Johnson, *Modern Times* (New York: Harper and Row, 1983), page 204.

32. Frederic L. Paxson, Edward S. Corwin, and Samuel B. Harding (editors), *War Cyclopedia: A Handbook for Ready Reference on the Great War* (Washington, D.C.: Government Printing Office, 1918), page 88.

33. Walter Lippmann, letter to Secretary of War Newton Baker, 23 July 1920; quoted by Johnson, *Modern Times*, page 204.

against the innocent, flooded the land with agents and provocateurs, raised neighbor against neighbor, filled the public press with inflammatory lies and fostered all the worst poltrooneries of sneaking and malicious wretches."[34] Mencken was mistaken on only one count: this "system of espionage" was not, in fact, "altogether without precedent in American history." It had been practiced with reckless abandon against the Northern Democrats by the Republicans during the War of 1861, and it was now the Democrats' opportunity to return the favor.

Another notable feature of the Wilson years was the passage of the Selective Service Act of 18 May 1917. This was the first time that conscription was ever used by the U.S. Government to send soldiers overseas and was a gross violation of the Constitution, which only allowed for the calling forth of the State militia "to execute the Laws of the Union, suppress Insurrections and repel Invasions."[35] Despite this defect, nearly ten million men between the ages of twenty-one and thirty-one years had been registered for the draft by the fifth of June. That number more than doubled by the following year when the eligible age bracket was broadened to include men between the ages of eighteen and forty-eight years. Agents of the American Protection League, newly created under the auspices of the Department of Justice and boasting a membership of about 250,000 by mid-1918, descended on the major cities, eager to earn the $50 bounty which the Government had placed upon the head of any draft-dodger. An amended form of the Selective Service Act remains on the books at Title 50, United States Code, Section 460.[36]

It was Wilson's promise that the "supreme dictatorship" which he had established would be terminated at the close of the war, but when Congress passed a bill in the summer of 1920 repealing sixty wartime measures delegating emergency powers to the President, Wilson killed the bill by a pocket veto.[37] Most notably, the Trading With the Enemy Act, with its Executive war power to regulate the commercial activities of "enemies" during wartime, was left in place.[38] This fact prompted U.S. Supreme Court Justice Charles E. Hughes to issue the following warning in 1920: "We went to war for liberty and democracy, with the result that we fed the autocratic appetite. We have seen war powers, which are essential to

---

34. Henry Lewis Menchen, quoted by Johnson, *op. cit.*, page 206.

35. U.S. Constitution, Article I, Section 8, Clause 15.

36. At the time of this writing, a bill — H.R.163 and S.89 — is before Congress which will expand conscription to include females.

37. United States Senate, *A Brief History of the Emergency Powers in the United States* (Special Committee on National Emergencies and Delegated Emergency Powers, Ninety-Third Congress, Second Session, July 1974), page 4. According to *Black's Law Dictionary*, a "pocket veto" is an "act of the President in retaining a legislative bill without approving or rejecting it at the end of the legislative session and, in effect, vetoing it by such inactivity" (page 1155).

38. U.S. Senate, *Emergency Powers Statutes*, page 5.

the preservation of the nation in time of war, exercised broadly after the military emergency has passed and in conditions for which they were never intended, and we may well wonder, in view of the precedents now established, whether constitutional government as heretofore maintained in this republic could survive another great war even victoriously waged.'[39] Justice Hughes did not have to wonder for long.

39. Charles E. Hughes, quoted by the New York *Times*, June 22, 1920, page 11.

SUPPORTING DOCUMENT

George William Norris' Speech in the Senate Opposing the Entry of the United States into World War One
Congressional Record — 4 April 1917

While I am most emphatically and sincerely opposed to taking any step that will force our country into the useless and senseless war now being waged in Europe, yet, if this resolution passes, I shall not permit my feeling of opposition to its passage to interfere in any way with my duty either as a senator or as a citizen in bringing success and victory to American arms. I am bitterly opposed to my country entering the war, but if, notwithstanding my opposition, we do enter it, all of my energy and all of my power will be behind our flag in carrying it on to victory.

The resolution now before the Senate is a declaration of war. Before taking this momentous step, and while standing on the brink of this terrible vortex, we ought to pause and calmly and judiciously consider the terrible consequences of the step we are about to take. We ought to consider likewise the route we have recently traveled and ascertain whether we have reached our present position in a way that is compatible with the neutral position which we claimed to occupy at the beginning and through the various stages of this unholy and unrighteous war.

No close student of recent history will deny that both Great Britain and Germany have, on numerous occasions since the beginning of the war, flagrantly violated in the most serious manner the rights of neutral vessels and neutral nations under existing international law, as recognized up to the beginning of this war by the civilized world.

The reason given by the President in asking Congress to declare war against Germany is that the German government has declared certain war zones, within which, by the use of submarines, she sinks, without notice, American ships and destroys American lives. The first war zone was declared by Great Britain. She gave us and the world notice of it on the 4th day of November, 1914. The zone became effective November 5, 1914. This zone so declared by Great Britain covered the whole of the North Sea. The first German war zone was declared on the 4th day of February, 1915, just three months after the British war zone was declared. Germany gave fifteen days' notice of the establishment of her zone, which became effective on the 18th day of February, 1915. The German war zone covered the English Channel and the high seawaters around the British Isles.

It is unnecessary to cite authority to show that both of these orders declaring military zones were illegal and contrary to international law. It is sufficient to say that our government has officially declared both of them to be illegal and has officially protested against both of them. The only difference is that in the case of Germany we have persisted in our protest, while in the case of England we have submitted.

What was our duty as a government and what were our rights when we were confronted with these extraordinary orders declaring these military zones? First, we could have defied both of them and could have gone to war against both of these nations for this violation of international law and interference with our neutral rights. Second, we had the technical right to defy one and to acquiesce in the other. Third, we could, while denouncing them both as illegal, have acquiesced in them both and thus remained neutral with both sides, although not agreeing with either as to the righteousness of their respective orders. We could have said to American shipowners that, while these orders are both contrary to international law and are both unjust, we do not believe that the provocation is sufficient to cause us to go to war for the defense of our rights as a neutral nation, and, therefore, American ships and American citizens will go into these zones at their own peril and risk.

Fourth, we might have declared an embargo against the shipping from American ports of any merchandise to either one of these governments that persisted in maintaining its military zone. We might have refused to permit the sailing of any ship from any American port to either of these military zones. In my judgment, if we had pursued this course, the zones would have been of short duration. England would have been compelled to take her mines out of the North Sea in order to get any supplies from our country. When her mines were taken out of the North Sea then the German ports upon the North Sea would have been accessible to American shipping and Germany would have been compelled to cease her submarine warfare in order to get any supplies from our nation into German North Sea ports.

There are a great many American citizens who feel that we owe it as a duty to humanity to take part in this war. Many instances of cruelty and inhumanity can be found on both sides. Men are often biased in their judgment on account of their sympathy and their interests. To my mind, what we ought to have maintained from the beginning was the strictest neutrality. If we had done this I do not believe we would have been on the verge of war at the present time. We had a right as a nation, if we desired, to cease at any time to be neutral. We had a technical right to respect the English war zone and to disregard the German war zone, but we could not do that and be neutral. I have no quarrel to find with the man who does not desire our country to remain neutral. While many such people are moved by selfish motives and hopes of gain, I have no doubt but that in a great many instances, through what I believe to be a misunderstanding of the real condition, there are many honest, patriotic citizens who think we ought to engage in this war and who are behind the President in his demand that we should declare war against Germany. I think such people err in judgment and to a great extent have been misled as to the real history and the true facts by the almost unanimous demand of the great combination of wealth that has a direct financial interest in our participation in the war. We have loaned many hundreds of millions of dollars to the allies in this controversy. While such action was legal and countenanced by international law, there is no doubt in my mind but the enormous amount of money loaned to the allies in this country has been instrumental in bringing about a public sentiment in favor of our country taking a course that would make every bond worth a hundred cents on the dollar and making the payment of every debt certain and sure. Through this instrumentality and also through the instrumentality of others who have not only made millions out of the war in the manufacture of munitions, *etc*, and who would expect to make millions more if our country can be drawn into the catastrophe, a large number of the great newspapers and news agencies of the country have been controlled and enlisted in the greatest propaganda that the world has ever known, to manufacture sentiment in favor of war. It is now demanded that the American citizens shall be used as insurance policies to guarantee the safe delivery of munitions of war to belligerent nations. The enormous profits of munition manufacturers, stockbrokers, and bond dealers must be still further increased by our entrance into the war. This has brought us to the present moment, when Congress, urged by the President and backed by the artificial sentiment, is about to declare war and engulf our country in the greatest holocaust that the world has ever known.

In showing the position of the bondholder and the stockbroker I desire to read an extract from a letter written by a member of the New York Stock Exchange to his customers. This writer says: "Regarding the war as inevitable, Wall Street believes that it would be preferable to this uncertainty about the actual date of its commencement. Canada and Japan are at war, and are more prosperous than ever before. The popular view is that stocks would have a quick, clear, sharp reaction immediately upon outbreak of hostilities, and that then they would enjoy an old-fashioned bull market such as followed the outbreak of war with Spain in 1898. The advent of peace would force a readjustment of commodity prices and would probably mean a postponement of new enterprises. As peace negotiations would be long drawn out, the period of waiting and uncertainty for business would be long. If the United States does not go to war it is nevertheless good opinion that the preparedness program will compensate in good measure for the loss of the stimulus of actual war."

Here we have the Wall Street view. Here we have the man representing the class of people who will be made prosperous should we become entangled in the present war, who have already made millions of dollars, and who will make many hundreds of millions more if we get into the war. Here we have the cold-blooded proposition that war brings prosperity to that class of people who are within the viewpoint of this writer. He expresses the view, undoubtedly, of Wall Street, and of thousands of men elsewhere, who see only dollars coming to them through the handling of stocks and bonds that will be necessary in case of war. "Canada and Japan," he says, "are at war, and are more prosperous than ever before."

To whom does the war bring prosperity? Not to the soldier who for the munificent compensation of $16 per month shoulders his musket and goes into the trench, there to shed his blood and to die if necessary; not to the broken-hearted widow who waits for the return of the mangled body of her husband; not to the mother who weeps at the death of her brave boy; not to the little children who shiver with cold; not to the babe who suffers from hunger; nor to the millions of mothers and daughters who carry broken hearts to their graves. War brings no prosperity to the great mass of common and patriotic citizens. It increases the cost of living of those who toil and those who already must strain every effort to keep soul and body together. War brings prosperity to the stock gambler on Wall Street — to those who are already in possession of more wealth than can be realized or enjoyed. Again this writer says that if we can not get war, "it is nevertheless good opinion that the preparedness program will compensate in good measure for the loss of the stimulus of actual war." That is, if we can not get war, let us go as far in that direction as possible. If we can not get war, let us cry for additional ships, additional guns, additional munitions, and everything else that will have a tendency to bring us as near as possible to the verge of war. And if war comes, do such men as these shoulder the musket and go into the trenches?

Their object in having war and in preparing for war is to make money. Human suffering and the sacrifice of human life are necessary, but Wall Street considers only the dollars and the cents. The men who do the fighting, the people who make the sacrifices, are the ones who will not be counted in the measure of this great prosperity that he depicts. The stock brokers would not, of course, go to war, because the very object they have in bringing on the war is profit, and therefore they must remain in their Wall Street offices in order to share in that great prosperity which they say war will bring. The volunteer officer, even the drafting officer, will not find them. They will be concealed in their palatial offices on Wall Street, sitting behind mahogany desks, covered up with clipped coupons — coupons soiled with the sweat of honest toil, coupons stained with mothers' tears, coupons dyed in the lifeblood of their fellow men.

We are taking a step today that is fraught with untold danger. We are going into war upon the command of gold. We are going to run the risk of sacrificing millions of our countrymen's lives in order that other countrymen may coin their lifeblood into money. And even if we do not cross the Atlantic and go into the trenches, we are going to pile up a debt that the toiling masses that shall come many generations after us will have to pay. Unborn millions will bend their backs in toil in order to pay for the terrible step we are now about to take. We are about to do the bidding of wealth's terrible mandate. By our act we will make millions of our countrymen suffer, and the consequences of it may well be that millions of our brethren must shed their lifeblood, millions of broken-hearted women must weep, millions of children must suffer with cold, and millions of babes must die from hunger, and all because we want to preserve the commercial right of American citizens to deliver munitions of war to belligerent nations.

SUPPLEMENTARY ESSAY
Imperatorial Sovereignty
by Francis Lieber

The Caesars of the first centuries claimed their power as bestowed upon them by the people, and went so far as to assume the praetorians, with an accommodating and intimidated senate, as the representatives, for the time, of the people. The Caesars never rested their power upon divine right, nor did they boldly adopt the Asiatic principle in all its nakedness, that power — the sword, the bow-string, the mere possession of power — is the only foundation of the right to wield it. The *majestas populi* had been transferred to the emperor. Such was their theory. Julius, the first of the Caesars, made himself sole ruler by the popular element, against the institutions of the country.

If it be observed here that these institutions had become effete, that the Roman city-government was impracticable for an extensive empire, and that the civil wars had proved how incompatible the institutions of Rome had become with the actual state of the people, it will be allowed — not to consider the common fact that governments or leaders first do everything to corrupt the people or plunge them into civil wars, and then, "taking advantage of their own wrong," use the corruption and bloodshed as a proof of the necessity to upset the government — it will be allowed, I say, that at any rate Caesar did not establish liberty, or claim to be the leader of a free state, and that he made his appearance at the close of a long period of freedom, marking the beginning of the most fearful decadence which stands on record; and that, unfortunately, the rulers vested with this imperatorial sovereignty never prepare a better state of things with reference to civil dignity and healthful self-government. They may establish peace and police; they may silence civil war, but they also destroy those germs from which liberty might sprout forth at a future period. However long Napoleon I. might have reigned, his whole path must have led him farther away from that of an Alfred, who allowed self-government to take root, and respected it where he found it. We can never arrive at the top of a steeple by descending deeper into a pit.

Whatever Caesar's greatness may have been, he did not, at any rate, usher in a new and prosperous era, either of liberty or popular grandeur. What is the Roman empire after Caesar? Count the good rulers, and weigh them against the unutterable wretchedness resulting from the worst of all combinations — of lust of power, voluptuousness, avarice, and cruelty — and forming a stream of increasing demoralization, which gradually swept down in its course everything noble that had remained of better times.

The Roman empire did, undoubtedly, much good, by spreading institutions which adhered to it in spite of itself, as seeds adhere to birds, and are carried to great distances; but it did this in spite, and not in consequence of the imperatorial sovereignty.

How, in view of all these facts of Roman history and of Napoleon I., the French have been able once more boastfully to return to the forms and principles of imperatorial sovereignty, and once more to confound an apparently voluntary divestment of all freedom with liberty, is difficult to be understood by any one who is accustomed to self-government. Whatever allowance we may make on the ground of vanity, both because it may please the ignorant to be called upon to vote *yes* or *no*, regarding an imperial crown, and because it may please them more to have an imperial government than one that has no such sounding name; whatever may be ascribed to military recollections — and, unfortunately, in history people only see prominent facts, as at a distance we see only the steeples of a town, and not the dark lanes and crowding misery which may be around them; whatever allowance may be made, and however well we may know that the whole could never have been effected without a wide-spread centralized government and an enormous army — it still remains surprising to us that the French, or at least those who now govern, please themselves in the imperatorial forms of Rome, and in presenting popular absolutism as a desirable phase of democracy. As though Tacitus had written like a contented man, and not with despair in his breast, breathed into many lines of his melancholy annals!

Yet so it is. Mr. Troplong, now president of the senate, said on a solemn occasion, after the sanguinary second of December, when he was descanting on the services rendered by Louis Napoleon: "The Roman democracy conquered in Caesar and in Augustus the era of its tardy *avenement*." If imperatorial sovereignty were to be the lasting destiny of France, and not a phase, French history would consist of a long royal absolutism; a short struggle for liberty, with the long fag-end of Roman history — the *avenement* of democracy is it own destroyer, the imperatorial sovereignty, but without the long period of Roman republicanism.

So little, indeed, has imperatorial sovereignty to do with liberty, that we find even the earliest Asiatics ascribing the origin of their despotic power to unanimous election. I do not allude only to the case of Daioces, related by Herodotus, but to the mythological books of Asiatic nations. The following extract from the Mongolian cosmogony, whose mythos extends over a vast part of the East, is so curious and so striking an instance of "the *avenement* of democracy" — though not a tardy one — and so clear a conception of imperatorial sovereignty without a suspicion of liberty, as a matter of course, since the whole refers to Asia, that the reader will not be dissatisfied with the extract:

> At this time [that is, after evil had made its appearance on earth] a living being appeared of great beauty and excellent aspect, and of a candid and honest soul and clear intellect. This being confirmed the righteous possessors in their property, and obliged the unrighteous possessors to give up what they had unjustly acquired. Thereupon the fields were distributed according to equal measure, and to every one was done even justice. Then all elected him for their chief, and yielded allegiance to him with these words: We elect thee for our chief, and we will never trespass thy ordinances. On account of this unanimous election, he is called in the Indian language Ma-ha-Ssamati-Radsha; in Thibetian, Mangboi-b Kurbai-r Gjabbo; and in Mongolian, Olana-ergukdeksen Chagran [the many-elected Monarch].

"In the name of the people," are the words with which commenced the first decree of Louis Napoleon, issued after the second of December, when he had made himself master of France, and in which he called upon all the French to state whether he should have unlimited power for ten years. If it was not their will, the decree said, there was no necessity of violence, for in that case he would resign his power. This was naive. But theories or words proclaimed before the full assumption of imperatorial sovereignty are of as little importance as after it. Where liberty is not a fact and a daily recurring reality, it is not liberty. The word *Libertas* occurs frequently on the coins of Nero, and still more the sentimental words, *Fides Mutua, Liberalitas Augusta, Felicitas Publica.*

Why, it may still be asked, did the Caesars recur to the people as the source of their power, and why did the civilians say that the emperor was legislator, and power-holder, inasmuch as the *majestas* of the Roman people, who had been legislators and power-holders, had been conferred upon him? Because, partly, the first Caesars, at any rate the very first, had actually ascended the steps of power with the assistance of some popular element, cheered on somewhat like a diademed tribune; because there was and still is no other actual source of power imaginable than the people, whether they positively give it, or merely acquiesce in the imperatorial power, and because, as to the historical fact by which power in any given case is acquired, we must never forget that the ethical element and that of intellectual consistency are so inbred in man that, wherever humanity is developed, a constant desire is observable to make actions, however immoral or inconsistent, at least theoretically agree with them. No proclamation of war has ever avowed, I believe, that war was simply undertaken because he who issued the proclamation had the power and meant to use it *fas aut nefas.* Even Attila called himself the scourge of God.

No matter what the violence of facts had been, however rudely the shocks of events have succeeded one another, the first thing that men do after these events have taken place is invariably to bring them into some theoretical consistency, and to attempt to give some reasonable account of them. This is the intellectual demand ever active in man. The other, equally active, is the ethical demand. No man, though he commanded innumerable legions, could stand up before a people and say, "I owe my crown to the murder of my mother, to the

madness of the people, or to slavish place-men." To appear merely respectable in an intellectual and ethical point of view, requires some theoretical decorum. The purer the generally
acknowledged code of morality, or the prevailing religion is, or the higher the general mental
system which prevails at the time, the more assiduous are also those who lead the public
events, to establish, however hypocritically, this apparent agreement between their acts and
theory, as well as morals. It is a tribute, though impure, paid to truth and morality.

It has been said in the preceding pages that imperatorial sovereignty must be always
the most stringent absolutism, especially when it rests theoretically on election by the whole
people, and that the transition from an uninstitutional popular absolutism to the imperatorial
sovereignty is easy and natural. At the time of the so-called French republic of 1848, it was
a common way of expressing the idea then prevailing, to call the people *le peuple-roi* (the
king-people), and an advocate, defending certain persons before the high court of justiciary
sitting at Versailles in 1849, for having invaded the chamber of representatives, and consequently having violated the constitution, used this remarkable expression, "the people" (confounding of course a set of people, a gathering of a part of the inhabitants of a single city,
with *the* people) "never violate the constitution."

Where such ideas prevail, the question is not about a change of ideas, but simply
about the lodgement of power. The minds and souls are already thoroughly familiarized with
the idea of absolutism, and destitute of the idea of self-government. This is also one of the
reasons why there is so much similarity between monarchical absolutism, and such for instance as we see in Russia, and communism, as it was preached in France; and it explains
why absolutism, having made rapid strides under the Bourbons before the first revolution,
has terminated every successive revolution with a still more compressive absolutism and
centralism, except indeed the revolution of 1830. This revolution was undertaken to defend
parliamentary government, and may be justly called a counter-revolution on the part of the
people against a revolution attempted and partially carried by the government. It explains
further how Louis Napoleon after the second of December, and later when he desired to place
the crown of uncompromising absolutism on his head, could appeal to the universal suffrage
of all France — he that had previously curtailed it, with the assistance of the chamber of
representatives. This phenomenon, however, must be explained also by the system of centralism, which prevails in France. I shall offer a few remarks on this topic after having treated
of some more details appertaining to the subject immediately in hand.

The idea of the *peuple-roi* (it would perhaps have been more correct to say *peuple-
czar*) also tends to explain the otherwise inconceivable hatred against the *burgeoisie*, by
which the French understand the aggregate of those citizens who inhabit towns and live upon
a small amount of property or by traffic. The communists and the French so-called democrats
entertained a real hatred against the *burgeoisie*; the proclamation, occasionally issued by
them, openly avowed it; and the government, when it desired to establish unconditional absolutism in form as well as principle, fanned this hatred. Yet no nation can exist without this
essential element of society. In reading the details of French history of the year 1848 and the
next succeeding years, the idea is formed upon our mind that a vast multitude of the French

were bent on establishing a real and unconditional aristocracy of the *ouvrier* — the workman.

If the imperatorial sovereignty is founded upon an actual process of election, whether this consist in a mere form or not, it bears down all opposition, nay all dissent, however lawful it may be, by a reference to the source of its power. It says, "I am the people, and whoever dissents from me is an enemy to the people. *Vox Populi vox Dei*. My divine right is the voice of God, which spake in the voice of the people. The government is the true representative of the people."

The eight millions of votes, more or less, which elevated the present French emperor, first to the decennial presidency and then to the imperial throne, are a ready answer to all objections. If private property is confiscated by a decree; if persons are deported without trial; if the jury trial is shorn of its guarantees, the answer is always the same. The emperor is the unlimited central force of the French democracy; thus the theory goes. He is the incarnation of the popular power, and if any of the political bodies into which the imperatorial power may have subdivided itself, like a Hindoo god, should happen to indicate an opinion of its own, it is readily given to understand that the government is in fact the people. Such bodies cannot, of course, be called institutions; for they are devoid of independence and every element of self-government. The president of the French legislative corps in 1858, found it necessary, on the opening of the session, to assure his colleagues, in an official address, that their body was by no means without some importance in the political system, as many seem to suppose.

The source of imperatorial power, however, is hardly ever what it is pretended to be, because, if the people have any power left, it is not likely that they will absolutely denude themselves of it, surely not in any modern and advanced nation. The question in these cases is not whether they love liberty, but simply whether they love power — and every one loves power. On the one hand, we have to observe that no case exists in history in which the question, whether imperatorial power shall be conferred upon an individual, is put to the people, except after a successful conspiracy against the existing powers or institutions, or a *coup d'etat*, if the term be preferred, on the part of the imperatorial candidate; and, on the other hand, a state of things in which so great a question is actually left to the people is wholly unimaginable. There may be a so-called interregnum during the conclave, when the cardinals elect a pope, but a country cannot be imagined in a state of perfect interregnum while the question is deciding whether a hereditary empire shall be established. It is idle to feign believing that this is possible, most especially so where the question is to be decided not by representatives, but by universal suffrage, and that, too, in a country where the executive power spreads over every inch of the territory, and is characterized by the most consistent centralism. The two last elections of Louis Napoleon prove what is here stated. Ministers, prefects, bishops, were openly and officially influencing the elections; not to speak of the fact that large elections concerning persons in power, which allow to vote only yes or no, have really little meaning, as the history of France abundantly proves.

When such a vote is put to the people under circumstances which have been indicated, the first question which presents itself, is: And what if the vote turn out No? Will the

candidate, already at the head of the army, the executive, and of every other branch; whose
initials are paraded everywhere, and whose portrait is in the courts of justice, some of which
actually have styled themselves imperial; and who has been addressed Sire; who has an enormous civil list — will he make a polite bow, give the keys to some one else, and walk his
way? And to whom was he to give the government? The question was not, as Mr. de
Laroche-Jacquelin had proposed, Shall A or B rule us? Essentially this question would not
have been better; but there would have been apparently some sense in it. The question simply
was: Shall B rule us? — Yes or No. It is surprising that some persons can actually believe
reflecting people may thus be duped.

The Caesar always exists before the imperatorial government is acknowledged and
openly established. Whether the praetorians or legions actually proclaim the Caesar or not,
it is always the army that makes him. A succeeding ballot is nothing more than a trimming
belonging to more polished or more timid periods, or it may be a tribute to that civilization
which does not allow armies to occupy the place they hold in barbarous or relapsing times,
at least not openly so.

First to assume the power and then to direct the people to vote, whether they are satisfied with the act or not, leads psychologically to a process similar to that often pursued by
Henry VIII., and according to which it became a common saying: First clap a man into prison
for treason, and you will soon have abundance of testimony. It was the same in the witch-
trials.

The process of election becomes peculiarly unmeaning, because the power already
assumed allows no discussion. There is no free press.

Although no reliance can be placed on wide-spread elections, whose sole object is
to ratify the assumption of imperatorial sovereignty, and when therefore it already dictatori-
ally controls all affairs, it is not asserted that the dictator may not at times be supported by
large masses, and possibly assume the imperatorial sovereignty with the approbation of a
majority. I have repeatedly acknowledged it; but it is unquestionably true that generally in
times of commotion, and especially in uninstitutional countries, minorities rule, for it is minorities that actually contend. Yet, even where this is not the case, the popularity of the
Caesar does in no way affect the question. Large, unarticulated masses are swayed by temporary opinions or passions, as much so as individuals, and it requires but a certain skill to seize
upon the proper moment to receive their acclamation, if they are willing and consider themselves authorized to give away by one sudden vote, all power and liberty, not only for their
own lifetime, but for future generations. In the institutional government alone, substantial
public opinion can be generated and brought to light.

It sometimes happens that arbitrary power or centralism recommends itself to popular
favor by showing that it intends to substitute a democratic equality for oligarchic or oppressive, unjust institutions, and the liberal principle may seem to be on the side of the levelling
ruler. This was doubtless the case when in the sixteenth and seventeenth century the power
of the crown made itself independent on the continent of Europe. Instead of transforming the
institutions, or of substituting new ones, the governments leveled them to the ground, and

that unhappy centralization was the consequence which now draws every attempt at liberty back into its vortex. At other times, monarchs or governments disguise their plans to destroy liberty in the garb of liberty itself. Thus James II. endeavored to break through the restraints of the constitution, or perhaps ultimately to establish the catholic religion in England, by proclaiming liberty of conscience for all, against the established church. Austria at one time urged measures, apparently liberal for the peasants, against the Gallician monks. In such cases, governments are always sure to find numerous persons that do not look beyond the single measure, nor to the means by which it is carried out; yet the legality and constitutionality of these means are of great, and frequently of greater importance than the measure itself. Even historians are frequently captivated by the apparently liberal character of a single measure, forgetting that the dykes of an institutional government once being broken through, the whole country may soon be flooded by an irresistible tide of arbitrary power. We have a parallel in the criminal trial, in which the question how we arrive at the truth is of equal importance with the object of arriving at truth. *Nullum bonum nisi bene.*

On the other hand, all endeavors to throw more and more unarticulated power into the hands of the primary masses, to deprive a country more and more of a gradually evolving character; in one word, to introduce an ever-increasing direct, unmodified popular power, amount to an abandonment of self-government, and an approach to imperatorial sovereignty, whether there be actually a Caesar or not — to popular absolutism, whether the absolutism remain for any length of time in the hands of a sweeping majority, subject, of course, to a skillful leader, as in Athens after the Peloponesian war, or whether it rapidly pass over into the hands of a broadly named Caesar. Imperatorial sovereignty may be at a certain period more plausible than the sovereignty founded upon divine right, but they are both equally hostile to self-government, and the only means to resist the inroads of power is, under the guidance of providence and a liberty-wedded people, the same means which in so many cases have withstood the inroads of the barbarians, namely, the institution — the self-sustaining and organic systems of laws.

The preceding essay was extracted from Francis Lieber, Civil Liberty and Self-Government *(Philadelphia, Pennsylvania: J.B. Lippincott and Company, 1859).*

CHAPTER TWENTY-ONE
The Deception of the New Deal

"We Could Never Go Back to the Old Order"

In his 1949 essay entitled, "Emergencies and the Presidency," Albert L. Sturm made the following observation: "Emergency powers are not solely derived from legal sources. The extent of their invocation and use is also contingent upon the personal conception which the incumbent of the Presidential office has of the Presidency and the premises upon which he interprets his legal powers. In the last analysis, the authority of a President is largely determined by the President himself."[1] It was the emergency powers latent in the Trading With the Enemy Act that were assumed by Franklin Delano Roosevelt when he took office a little over a decade later during the crisis of the Great Depression. As Clinton Rossiter noted, "[T]he crisis government of 1933 was marked by an unprecedented breakdown of the constitutional barriers separating Congress and the President."[2] Indeed, Roosevelt's views, expressed in his first Inaugural Address of 4 March 1933, bore a striking similarity to that of his predecessor in the 1860s:

> It is to be hoped that the normal balance of Executive and Legislative authority may be wholly adequate to meet the unprecedented task before us. But it may be that an unprecedented demand and need for undelayed action may call for a temporary departure from that normal balance of public procedure.

---

1. Albert L. Sturm, "Emergencies and the Presidency," *Journal of Politics*, February 1949, pages 125-126.

2. Rossiter, *Constitutional Dictatorship*, page 256.

I am prepared under my constitutional duty to recommend the measures that a stricken Nation in the midst of a stricken world may require. These measures, or such other measures as the Congress may build out of its experience and wisdom, I shall seek, within my constitutional authority, to bring to a speedy adoption.

But in the event that the Congress shall fail to take one of these two courses, and in the event that the national emergency is still critical, I shall not evade the clear course of duty that will then confront me. I shall ask the Congress for the one remaining instrument to meet the crisis — broad Executive power to wage a war against the emergency, as great as the power that would be given to me if we were in fact invaded by a foreign foe. And when the war is won, the power under which I act will automatically revert to the people of the United States — to the people to whom these powers belong.[3]

The day after delivering this address, Roosevelt issued a Presidential Proclamation calling Congress into special session to discuss unspecified "public interests." However, before Congress had the chance to convene, he shut down the nation's banks on the sixth of March, and then, after deceptively altering the 1917 Trading With the Enemy Act in his proposed legislation, he duped Congress into declaring the American people to be enemies of the U.S. Government on the ninth of March, which directly resulted in the confiscation of their property in gold. How all this was accomplished was a stroke of despotic genius. In Presidential Proclamation 2039, Roosevelt stated:

Whereas there have been heavy and unwarranted withdrawals of gold and currency from our banking institutions for the purpose of hoarding; and

Whereas continuous and increasingly extensive speculative activity abroad in foreign exchange has resulted in severe drains on the Nation's stocks of gold; and

Whereas these conditions have created a national emergency; and

Whereas it is in the best interest of all bank depositors that a period of respite be provided with a view to preventing further hoarding of coin, bullion or currency or speculation in foreign exchange and permitting the application of appropriate measures to protect the interests of our people; and

Whereas it is provided in Section 5(b) of the Act of October 6, 1917, (40 Stat. L. 411) as amended, "That the President may investigate, regulate, or prohibit, under such rules and regulations as he may prescribe, by means of licenses or otherwise, any transactions in foreign exchange and the export, hoarding, melting, or earmarkings of gold or silver coin or bullion or currency ***"; and

Whereas it is provided in Section 16 of the said Act "that whoever shall willfully violate any of the provisions of this Act or of any license, rule, or regulation issued thereunder, and whoever shall willfully violate, neglect, or refuse to comply with any order of the President issued in compliance with the provisions of this Act, shall, upon conviction,

---

3. Franklin D. Roosevelt, inaugural address, 4 March 1933; in Samuel Irving Rosenman (editor), *The Public Papers and Addresses of Franklin D. Roosevelt* (New York: Random House, 1938), Volume II, page 16.

be fined not more that $10,000, or, if a natural person, imprisoned for not more than ten years or both; ***";

Now, therefore, I, Franklin D. Roosevelt, President of the United States of America, in view of such national emergency and by virtue of the authority vested in me by said Act and in order to prevent the export, hoarding, or earmarking of gold or silver coin or bullion or currency, do hereby proclaim, order, direct and declare that from Monday, the sixth day of March, to Thursday, the ninth day of March, Nineteen Hundred and Thirty Three, both dates inclusive, there shall be maintained and observed by all banking institutions and all branches thereof located in the United States of America, including the territories and insular possessions, a bank holiday, and that during said period all banking transactions shall be suspended. During such holiday, excepting as hereinafter provided, no such banking institution or branch shall pay out, export, earmark, or permit the withdrawal or transfer in any manner or by any device whatsoever, of any gold or silver coin or bullion or currency or take any other action which might facilitate the hoarding thereof; nor shall any such banking institution or branch pay out deposits, make loans or discounts, deal in foreign exchange, transfer credits from the United States to any place abroad, or transact any other banking business whatsoever.

Pertinent sections of the Bank Holiday Act, which Roosevelt and his advisors authored, are as follows:

An act to provide relief in the existing national emergency in banking and for other purposes.

Be it enacted by the Senate and House of Representatives of the United States of America in Congress assembled, That the Congress hereby declares that a serious emergency exists and that it is imperatively necessary speedily to put into effect remedies of uniform national application.

TITLE I

Section 1. The actions, regulations, rules, licenses, orders and proclamations heretofore or hereafter taken, promulgated, made, or issued by the President of the United States or the Secretary of the Treasury since March 4, 1933, pursuant to the authority conferred by subdivision (b) of section 5 of the Act of October 6, 1917, as amended, are hereby approved and confirmed.

Sec. 2. Subdivision (b) of section 5 of the Act of October 6, 1917 (40 Stat. L. 411), as amended, is hereby amended to read as follows:

"(b) During time of war or during any other period of national emergency declared by the President, the President may, through any agency that he may designate, or otherwise, investigate, regulate, or prohibit, under such rules and regulations as he may prescribe, by means of licenses or otherwise, any transactions in foreign exchange, transfers of credit between or payments by banking institutions as defined by the President, and exporting, hoarding, melting, or earmarking of gold or silver coin or bullion or currency, by any person within the United States or any place subject to the jurisdiction thereof...."

It should be noted that the original Trading With the Enemy Act defined "enemy" in Section 2(a) as "any individual, partnership, or other body of individuals, of any nationality, resident within the territory (including that occupied by the military and naval forces) of any nation with which the United States is at war, or resident *outside* the United States and doing business within such territory...." (emphasis added) "Citizens of the United States" were expressly excluded from the definition of "enemy" in Section 2(c). However, Roosevelt's proclamation and his bill for a bank holiday clearly applied the term "enemy" to any person conducting business "*within* the United States or any place subject to the jurisdiction thereof" (emphasis added).[4] Consequently, while the original Trading With the Enemy Act was intended by Congress to define, regulate, and punish war-time trading with a foreign enemy without a license, Roosevelt's rewording changed its scope to the definition, regulation, and punishment of trading *among* the enemy — the American people themselves — during a national emergency.

Furthermore, "hoarding," or merely possessing, gold was made illegal by the Emergency Banking Relief Act of 9 March 1933[5] and all gold held by private persons in the United States was required to be surrendered to the Government, even though the actual wording of the Trading With the Enemy Act, which Roosevelt pretended to quote for his authority in his initial proclamation, said nothing at all about hoarding. Such was the convenient addition which Roosevelt used to pin the blame for the economic crisis on the American people, rather than on the corrupt Federal Reserve System, where it belonged,[6] and to justify the subsequent confiscation of the "enemy's" property.[7] To add insult to injury, the Gold Reserve Act of 1934 removed the gold backing of Federal Reserve Notes, as provided for in Section 16 of the Federal Reserve Act of 1913. Section 2 of the Gold Reserve Act stated:

> Upon the approval of this Act all right, title, and interest... in and to any and all gold coin and gold bullion shall pass to and are vested in the United States....
>
> Any gold withheld, acquired, transported, melted or treated, imported, exported, or earmarked or held in custody, in violation of this Act or of any regulation issued hereunder, or licenses issued pursuant thereto, shall be forfeited to the United States, and may be seized and condemned by like proceedings as those provided by law for the forfeiture, seizure, and condemnation of property imported into the United States contrary to law; and

---

4. *Bank Holiday Act*, Section 2(b).

5. Statutes at Large, Volume XLVIII, page 2; Title 12, United States Code, Section 248.

6. See Chapter Twenty-Two.

7. Even when such Roosevelt defenders as Clinton Rossiter have admitted the "questionable authority of section 5b of the Trading With the Enemy Act" and that FDR had acted "undoubtedly beyond the [war-time] purview of the Act of 1917" (*Constitutional Dictatorship*, pages 257, 258), they invariably neglect to point out these deceptive alterations in the actual wording of the Act.

in addition any person failing to comply with the provisions of this Act or of any such regulations or licenses, shall be subject to a penalty equal to twice the value of the gold in respect of which such failure occurred.[8]

This Act left the people with mere interest-bearing debt-instruments, or "direct obligations of the United States," to use as money. Later, in 1964, silver certificates were also removed from circulation by Executive Order and the content of the coins was changed from silver to nickel-clad copper. There is currently now no constitutional money in circulation in the United States.

It was clear from his hasty actions that Roosevelt never had any intention of maintaining the "normal balance of Executive and Legislative authority," but that he desired to force Congress to comply with a predetermined agenda. In its report of 19 November 1973, the U.S. Senate stated:

> In actual fact, it could appear that the President called the Congress into special session to sanction his emergency banking action and then continued the meeting for as long as it suited the mutual purposes of the two branches. When the proclamation for the gathering was issued on March 5, no purpose for the assembly was specifically indicated or even alluded to generally. Roosevelt knew what he wanted to do but had no Legislative plans. Before arriving in Washington, he had rough drafts of two presidential proclamations: one calling a special session of Congress; the other declaring a bank holiday and controlling the export of gold by invoking forgotten provisions of the wartime Trading With the Enemy Act. The bank holiday proclamation was issued on March 6. Between the evening after the inauguration and the opening of Congress, William Woodin, Roosevelt's Treasury Secretary, Raymond Moley, a Roosevelt assistant, and a few others wrote the Emergency Banking Bill. When Congress convened, the House had no copies of the measure and had to rely upon the Speaker reading from a draft text. After thirty-eight minutes of debate, the House passed the Bill. That evening, the Senate followed suit.
>
> The emergency banking measure extended government assistance to private bankers to reopen their banks. The Bill validated actions the President had already taken, gave him complete control over gold movements, penalized hoarding, authorized the issue of new [non-redeemable] Federal Reserve Bank notes, and arranged for the reopening of banks with liquid assets and the reorganization of the rest.[9]

One important detail which is missing in the above report is that Roosevelt's banking bill had not even been completed when Congress convened at noon on the ninth of March. As John T. Flynn pointed out in his book *The Roosevelt Myth*, "A folded newspaper was tossed into the hopper to serve as a bill until the document could be completed."[10] The copy

---

8. Gold Reserve Act, Section 2(a), 4.

9. U.S. Senate, *Emergency Powers Statutes*.

10. John T. Flynn, *The Roosevelt Myth* (San Francisco, California: Fox and Wilkes, 1998), page 10.

from which the Speaker of the House of Representatives read on the floor was merely a rough draft; the Senate did not even have that much to work from, and yet, both Houses passed the unfinished bill into law. Representative Louis T. McFadden of Pennsylvania later complained of this irregularity with these words: "Mr. Speaker, I regret that the membership of the House has had no opportunity to consider or even read this bill. The first opportunity I had to know what this legislation is was when it was read from the Clerk's desk. It is an important banking bill. It is a dictatorship over finance in the United States. It is complete control over the banking system in the United States."[11] The truth of McFadden's observation would soon become very apparent to all Americans.

A year after his inauguration, Roosevelt wrote his book entitled *On Our Way*, in which he attempted to justify himself in the eyes of the American people. In his own words, the proclaimed emergency "related to far more than banks," for "it covered the whole economic and therefore the whole social structure of the country."[12] Roosevelt was correct in pointing out that his grab for power was not limited to the banking system. In fact, immediately after seizing control of the banks and money of the American people, he proceeded to seize control of agriculture and industry as well through the Agriculture Adjustment Act (AAA) of 12 May 1933 and the National Industrial Recovery Act (NIRA) of 16 June 1933. Both of these Acts, having the phrase "national emergency" in their titles, were based on the same Trading With the Enemy war powers as was the preceding Bank Holiday Act. It was Roosevelt's assertion that the crisis could only be overcome "by a complete reorganization and a measured control of the economic structure.... It called for a long series of new laws, new administrative agencies."[13] He went on to solicit the "understanding on the part of the people," and concluded, "We could never go back to the old order."[14] Combined with the amended Trading With the Enemy Act, the various Acts of Congress passed at Roosevelt's behest gave him nearly absolute control over the economic and social structure of the nation. Consequently, his "New Deal" was, in reality, a complete and deliberate destruction of the last remaining vestiges of constitutional government in America — the "old order" — and the permanent establishment of an Executive dictatorship on its ruins. Contrary to the clear wording of Article I, Section 9, Clause 3 of the U.S. Constitution, Roosevelt's usurpation of power was "remedied"[15] by Congress' *ex post facto* passage of the Emergency Banking Act,

---

11. Louis T. McFadden, *Congressional Record — House*, 9 March 1933, page 80.

12. Franklin Delano Roosevelt, *On Our Way* (New York: The John Day Company, 1934), page 35.

13. Roosevelt, *ibid.*, page 36.

14. Roosevelt, *ibid.*

15. *United States v. Briddle* (1962, D.C. Cal.) 212 F.Supp. 584. What is interesting about this particular case is the court admitted that "the President was not authorized to declare a bank holiday by the *Trading With the Enemy Act*, but the lack of authority was remedied by the passage of 12 USCS, Section 95b." It was constitutionally impossible for the Congress to so "remedy" a violation

the following clause of which remains on the books to this day at Title 12, United States Code, Section 95(b): "The actions, regulations, rules, licenses, orders and proclamations heretofore or hereafter taken, promulgated, made, or issued by the President of the United States or the Secretary of the Treasury since March 4, 1933, pursuant to the authority conferred by subsection (b) of section 5 of the [Trading With the Enemy] Act of October 6, 1917, as amended, are hereby approved and confirmed."

The Supreme Court Opposes the "New Deal"

A provision of the Constitution, it is hardly necessary to say, does not admit of two distinctly opposite interpretations. It does not mean one thing at one time and an entirely different thing at another time.... This view, at once so rational in its application to the written word, and so necessary to the stability of constitutional principles, though from time to time challenged, has never, unless recently, been put within the realm of doubt by the decisions of this court. The true rule was forcefully declared in *Ex parte Milligan*, 4 Wall. 2, 120, 121, in the face of circumstances of national peril and public unrest and disturbance far greater than any that exist to-day. In that great case this court said that the provisions of the Constitution there under consideration had been expressed by our ancestors in such plain English words that it would seem the ingenuity of man could not evade them, but that after the lapse of more than seventy years they were sought to be avoided. "Those great and good men," the Court said, "foresaw that troublous times would arise, when rules and people would become restive under restraint, and seek by sharp and decisive measures to accomplish ends deemed just and proper; and that the principles of constitutional liberty would be in peril, unless established by irrepealable law. The history of the world had taught them that what was done in the past might be attempted in the future." And then, in words the power and truth of which have become increasingly evident with the lapse of time, there was laid down the rule without which the Constitution would cease to be the "supreme law of the land," binding equally upon governments and governed at all times and under all circumstances, and become a mere collection of political maxims to be adhered to or disregarded according to the prevailing sentiment or the legislative and judicial opinion in respect of the supposed necessities of the hour: "The Constitution of the United States is a law for rulers and people, equally in war and in peace, and covers with the shield of its protection all classes of men, at all times, and under all circumstances. No doctrine, involving more pernicious consequences, was ever invented by the wit of man than that any of its provisions can be suspended during any of the great exigencies of government. Such a doctrine leads directly to anarchy or despotism...."

Chief Justice Taney, in *Dred Scott v. Sandford*, 19 How, 393, 426, said that, while the Constitution remains unaltered, it must be construed now as it was understood at the time of its adoption; that it is not only the same in words but the same in meaning, "and

---

of the Constitution and the trust of the people, and, had the Government still been bound by that document, Roosevelt would have been a prime candidate for impeachment.

as long as it continues to exist in its present form, it speaks not only in the same words, but with the same meaning and intent with which it spoke when it came from the hands of its framers, and was voted on and adopted by the people of the United States. Any other rule of construction would abrogate the judicial character of this court, and make it the mere reflex of the popular opinion or passion of the day." And in *South Carolina v. United States*, 199 U.S. 437, 448 , 449 S., 26 S.Ct. 110, 111, 4 Ann.Cas. 737, in an opinion by Mr. Justice Brewer, this court quoted these words with approval and said: "The Constitution is a written instrument. As such its meaning does not alter. That which it meant when adopted, it means now.... Those things which are within its grants of power, as those grants were understood when made, are still within them; and those things not within them remain still excluded." The words of Judge Campbell, speaking for the Supreme Court of Michigan in *People ex rel. Twitchell v. Blodgett*, 13 Mich. 127, 139, 140, are peculiarly apposite. "But it may easily happen," he said, "that specific provisions may, in unforeseen emergencies, turn out to have been inexpedient. This does not make these provisions any less binding. Constitutions can not be changed by events alone. They remain binding as the acts of the people in their sovereign capacity, as the framers of Government, until they are amended or abrogated by the action prescribed by the authority which created them. It is not competent for any department of the Government to change a constitution, or declare it changed, simply because it appears ill adapted to a new state of things."[16]

So wrote Justice George Sutherland of the U.S. Supreme Court in 1934. As was the case with Lincoln, the Court was a formidable foe with which Roosevelt had to contend, for a majority of the justices opposed his emergency legislation at nearly every opportunity. For example, in the 1934 *Home Building and Loan Association v. Blaisdell* decision, Chief Justice Hughes attacked the very foundation of the New Deal with the following observations: "Emergency does not create power. Emergency does not increase granted power or remove or diminish the restrictions imposed upon power granted or reserved. The Constitution was adopted in a period of grave emergency. Its grants of power to the federal government and its limitations of the power of the States were determined in the light of emergency, and they are not altered by emergency. What power was thus granted and what limitations were thus imposed are questions which have always been, and always will be, the subject of close examination under our constitutional system."[17]

In the 1935 *United States v. Butler* decision, the Court struck down the Agricultural Adjustment Act because it gave to the Government power to tax the people far beyond the constitutional "general welfare" limitation. In effect, the AAA was a thinly disguised socialist plan to redistribute the wealth of the country from one class of citizens to another:

A tax, in the general understanding and in the strict constitutional sense, is an exaction for the support of government; the term does not connote the expropriation of

---

16. *Home Building and Loan Association v. Blaisdell* (1934), 29 U.S. 398, at 448-451.

17. *Ibid.*, at 425.

money from one group to be expended for another, as a necessary means in a plan of regulation, such as the plan for regulating agricultural production set up in the Agricultural Adjustment Act....

The regulation of a farmer's activities under the statute, though in form subject to his own will, is in fact coercion through economic pressure; his right of choice is illusory. Even if a farmer's consent were purely voluntary, the Act would stand no better. At best it is a scheme for purchasing with federal funds submission to federal regulation of a subject reserved to the states.[18]

The Court went on to warn that the policies reflected in the AAA, as well as other New Deal legislation, "would furnish the means whereby the provisions of the Constitution, sedulously framed to define and limit the powers of the United States and preserve the powers of the States," could be "subverted, the independence of the individual states obliterated, and the United States converted into a central government exercising uncontrolled police power in every state of the Union, superseding all local control or regulation of the affairs or concerns of the states."[19]

Another example of this "uncontrolled police power" which was created by Roosevelt and his advisors was the National Industrial Recovery Act. Under this Act, each industry in the country was organized into a Government-supervised trade association called a "code authority," and then, under these code authorities — a total of 700 of them created by 13,000 pages of administrative orders[20] — all commercial production, wages, and prices were regulated by the National Recovery Administration (NRA). Prior to its passage, Representative Ernest W. Marland of Oklahoma protested these drachonian measures with this warning:

No law has been written which so much affected human rights, human happiness and human destiny since the writing of the Magna Carta on the field of Runnymeade 718 years ago as will the passage of the National Industrial Act. It may mean that by the passage of this act we shall have repealed the great charter of human rights which guaranteed government by law instead of government by discretion which had hitherto prevailed. By this National Industrial Recovery Act we will confer upon the President of the United States wider discretionary powers of government than have ever been held by any but an absolute monarch.[21]

As usual, such voices of dissent were in the minority and the bill was enacted on 16 June 1933. A tailor by the name of Jack Magid was the first victim of the new law — he was

---

18. *United States v. Butler* (1936), 297 U.S. 1, 77.

19. *Ibid.*

20. Rossiter, *Constitutional Dictatorship*, page 262.

21. Ernest W. Marland, *Congressional Record — House*, Volume LXXVI, Part Six, pages 5698.

arrested and thrown into jail for pressing a suit of clothes for thirty-five cents rather than forty cents as fixed by the Tailors' Code.[22] However, the price-fixing of the NRA soon produced a formidable black market which in turn required a large police force to combat. In the garment industry, for example, code enforcers would "enter a man's factory, send him out, line up his employees, subject them to minute interrogation, take over his books on the instant."[23] Moreover, since night work was prohibited, "squadrons of these private coat-and-suit police went through the district at night, battering down doors with axes looking for men who were committing the crime of sewing together a pair of pants at night."[24] The NRA was finally abandoned by the Roosevelt Administration because "the American people were not yet conditioned to regimentation on such a scale"[25] and "it attempted to do too much in too short a time."[26] In other words, the NRA was too strong a dose of totalitarianism and the American people choked on it. Roosevelt learned thereafter to give his "medicine" in smaller doses.

How instructive are the following words of Justice Robert H. Jackson, who wrote the concurring opinion in the *Youngstown Steel* case:

> The appeal, however, that we declare the existence of inherent power *ex necessitate* to meet an emergency asks us to do what many think would be wise, although it is something the forefathers omitted. They knew what emergencies were, knew the pressures they engender for authoritative action, knew, too, how they afford a ready pretext for usurpation. We may also suspect that they suspected that emergency powers would tend to kindle emergencies. Aside from suspension of the privilege of the writ of *habeas corpus* in time of rebellion or invasion, when the public safety may require it, they made no express provision for exercise of extraordinary authority because of a crisis. I do not think we rightfully may so amend their work, and, if we could, I am not convinced it would be wise to do so, although many modern nations have forthrightly recognized that war and economic crises may upset the normal balance between liberty and authority. Their experience with emergency powers may not be irrelevant to the argument here that we should say that the Executive, of his own volition, can invest himself with undefined emergency powers.[27]

---

22. Flynn, *Roosevelt Myth*, page 41.

23. Flynn, *ibid.*

24. Flynn, *ibid.*

25. Flynn, *ibid.*

26. Ernest K. Lindley, *Half Way With Roosevelt* (New York: Viking Press, 1946), page 151.

27. *Youngstown Sheet & Tube Co. v. Sawyer* (1952), 343 U.S. 579.

Roosevelt Attempts to "Pack" the Court

It was Roosevelt's bitter complaint that "we have been relegated by the Supreme Court to the horse-and-buggy definition of interstate commerce."[28] Faced with an impending decision by the Court on both the Social Security Act and the National Labor Relations Act, Roosevelt immediately went to work with Attorney-General Homer Cummings on a Court Reform bill under "the most absolute secrecy" to "streamline" the Supreme Court "in order that it also may function in accord with modern necessities."[29] The essence of the bill would give Roosevelt the power to appoint an additional justice to the Court for every one of the current justices who were over the age of seventy, but were refusing to retire. In his presentation message to Congress of 5 February 1937, Roosevelt wrote, "In exceptional cases, of course, judges, like other men, retain to an advanced age full mental and physical vigor. Those not so fortunate are often unable to perceive their own infirmities.... A lower mental or physical vigor leads men to avoid an examination of complicated and changed conditions. Little by little, new facts become blurred through old glasses fitted, as it were, for the needs of another generation; older men, assuming that the scene is the same as it was in the past, cease to explore or inquire into the present or the future."[30]

Roosevelt initially justified his proposal by claiming that it would assist the "aged, overworked justices" to deal with a growing backlog of cases. However, this excuse was immediately rebutted by Chief Justice Hughes, who informed Congress that the Court's docket was completely up-to-date. At this point, Roosevelt changed his tactic to an all-out attack on the integrity of the justices, blaming them for "cast[ing] doubts on the ability of the elected Congress to protect us against catastrophe by meeting squarely our modern social and economic conditions." He described the American form of government as a "three-horse team provided by the Constitution to the American people so that their field might be plowed" and said, "Two of the horses, the Congress and the executive, are pulling in unison today; the third [the Court] is not." He went on: "When the Congress has sought to stabilize national agriculture, to improve the conditions of labor, to safeguard business against unfair competition, to protect our national resources, and in many other ways, to serve our clearly national needs, the majority of the Court has been assuming the power to pass on the wisdom of these acts of the Congress — and to approve or disapprove the public policy written into these laws.... We have, therefore, reached the point as a nation where we must take action to save the Constitution from the Court and the Court from itself." His plan would "bring

---

28. Roosevelt, remarks at a press conference on 31 May 1935; in Rosenman, *Papers and Addresses of Franklin D. Roosevelt*, Volume IV, page 221.

29. Flynn, *Roosevelt Myth*, page 97.

30. Roosevelt, message to Congress of 5 February 1937; quoted by William E. Leuchtenburg, *The Supreme Court Reborn: The Constitutional Revolution in the Age of Roosevelt* (New York: Oxford University Press, 1995), pages. 133-134.

into the judicial system a steady and continuing stream of new and younger blood" and would "save our national Constitution from hardening of the judicial arteries."[31]

The primary targets of Roosevelt's criticisms were James McReynolds, Pierce Butler, Willis Van Devanter, and George Sutherland — the four conservative justices who consistently opposed him. However, there were two others — the moderate Chief Justice Hughes and the liberal Louis D. Brandeis — who were also over seventy. Thus, if the bill were passed by Congress, the number of justices on the Supreme Court would increase from nine to fifteen — the six new members, of course, being appointed by Roosevelt himself.

For Roosevelt, who had become emboldened by his recent landslide re-election, the ensuing backlash in the press against what many derided as an attempt at "court packing," was somewhat unexpected. One political cartoon showed a tiny Supreme Court justice fleeing to escape being crushed by a gigantic Executive thumb. Another depicted the President ascending steps labeled "Government Reorganization" and "Supreme Court Revision," to a throne marked "Dictator." His plan was also repeatedly likened to the dictatorships of Stalin, Hitler, and Mussolini. For example, the following editorial appeared in the Chicago *Tribune*:

> The change which Mr. Roosevelt has proposed is revolutionary. The word is used advisedly. The essential difference between free government in America and dictatorial government in Europe is the independence of our three branches of government. Mussolini dominates not only the executive branch of government but the law making and the judicial branches as well. Otherwise he would be no dictator. Precisely the same description applies to Hitler and Stalin. They are dictators because they write the laws, they put them into effect and there is no independent judiciary to which the citizens can appeal against the autocrat.
>
> Mr. Roosevelt is the chief executive by election and he holds congress in the hollow of his hand. How lightly he regards its theoretical independence in framing the nation's laws is indicated by the fact that he gave them a draft of his judiciary bill with orders to pass it. If the bill is passed by a supine congress, as he expects, he will have control over the courts, too. From that moment the will of the President will be the constitution of the United States. And his successors will take the same view of the matter. Power once seized is rarely relinquished.[32]

The Washington *Star* of the tenth of February opined:

> If the American people accept this last audacity of the President without letting out a yell to high heaven, they have ceased to be jealous of their liberties and are ripe for ruin. This is the beginning of pure personal government....
> The Executive is already powerful by reason of his overwhelming victory in

31. Roosevelt, "Fireside Chat" of 9 March 1937.

32. "The Future of the Supreme Court," Chicago *Tribune*, 7 February 1937.

November, and will be strengthened even more if the reorganization plan for the administration, presented some weeks ago, is adopted. We have, to all intents and purposes, a one party Congress, dominated by the President. Although nearly 40 percent of the voters repudiated the New Deal at the polls, they have less than 20 percent representation in both houses of Congress. And now the Supreme Court is to have a majority determined by the President and by a Senate which he dominates. When that happens we will have a one-man Government. It will all be constitutional. So, he claims, is Herr Hitler....

And let us not be confused by the words "liberal" and "conservative" or misled into thinking that the expressed will of the majority is the essence of democracy. By that definition Hitler, Stalin and Mussolini are all great democratic leaders. The essence of democracy is the protection of minorities. Nor has a majority of this generation the right to mortgage a majority of the next. In the Constitution of the United States is incorporated the rights of the people, rights enjoyed by every American citizen in perpetuity, which cannot be voted away by any majority, ever. Majorities are temporary things. The Supreme Court is there to protect the fundamental law even against the momentary "will of the people." That is its function. And it is precisely because nine men can walk out and say: "You can't do that!" that our liberties are protected against the mob urge that occasionally arises. The Court has been traditionally divorced from momentary majorities.[33]

Even the Congress, which had previously been so compliant, proved to be an obstacle which Roosevelt could not overcome and he was forced to abandon his proposed bill in July of that same year. However, due to the resignation of Willis Van Devanter later that year, and the resignations and deaths of four more justices over the next two years, Roosevelt eventually succeeded in "packing" the Court anyway. He initially appointed Felix Frankfurter, Hugo Black, Stanley Reed and William O. Douglas to fill the vacancies — men who had little or no prior judicial experience[34] but who were all liberals upon whom he could rely to push his agenda through.[35] By 1941, even the moderate Chief Justice Hughes was gone

---

33. Dorothy Thompson, editorial, Washington *Star*, 10 February 1937.

34. Black was a trial lawyer in the 1920s in Birmingham, Alabama.

35. Felix Frankfurter immigrated with his Jewish family to the United States from Vienna, Austria in 1894. Even though he initially spoke no English, he graduated from Harvard Law School in 1906 and went on to join its faculty in 1914. During his time at Harvard, he was vilified as a Communist and many alumni demanded that he be fired for his radical political views. He was a regular contributor in the 1920s to the Progressive (Socialist) periodical, *The New Republic*, and was one of the principal authors of Roosevelt's New Deal legislation.

Hugo Black, a former member of the 1920s incarnation of the Ku Klux Klan and a Southern Populist, had been a supporter of FDR's "court packing" plan and an outspoken critic of the Hughes Court. The Populists, also known as "the People's party," claimed to be the ideological descendants of Thomas Jefferson, but were, in reality, a socialist labor movement which, according to their 1892

and four more justices were appointed — Frank Murphy, James F. Byrnes, Robert H. Jackson, and Wiley B. Rutledge. With no more conservatives left to stand in Roosevelt's way, this newly "revitalized" Court immediately went to work to reverse dozens of prior decisions which stood as obstacles to New Deal socialism. Like the Congress had in 1933, the Court thereafter "rubber-stamped" everything that Roosevelt wished to do, often resorting to convoluted interpretations of the interstate commerce clause in the Constitution to justify the expansion of Executive power into the local matters of the States. For example, this Court, with Harlan F. Stone at the helm, ruled in *Kirschbaum v. Walling* that the elevator operator in a privately-owned building in New Jersey was engaged in interstate commerce and therefore subject to Government regulation because one of the businesses in the building sold its products in other States.[36] In *Wickard v. Filburn*, the Court upheld a Government-imposed

---

and 1896 platforms, opposed American industrialization, and advocated Government-ownership of public transportation and utilities, a graduated income tax in defiance of the Supreme Court's ruling in the 1895 *Pollack v. Farmers' Loan and Trust Company* decision (finally realized in the Sixteenth Amendment), popular election of the President and U.S. Senators (the latter realized by the Seventeenth Amendment), and, finally, called for a general expansion of the power of the central Government. The Populist philosophy was commonly referred to as "agrarianism" and the most famous of their number was Theodore Roosevelt. Populism is generally viewed by historians as the groundbreaker for the New Deal.

Stanley Reed was a former attorney from Kentucky and a liberal Democrat who, as U.S. Solicitor General, argued for the constitutionality of the original New Deal before the Hughes Court. Denying that the Constitution was a "gaoler to preserve the status quo," Reed supported FDR's confiscation of gold from the American people and the nation's departure from the gold standard in 1935. He is often identified by historians as a "moderate" because he moved somewhat slower than his fellow justices.

William O. Douglas was a former professor at Columbia and Yale Law schools, but left that profession to serve on FDR's Securities and Exchange Commission in 1933. He was also a staunch supporter of the New Deal, and at the age of 40, was the youngest and would become the longest-serving justice on the Court. Douglas' liberal philosophy was best described by judicial historian Henry J. Abraham as follows: "The Douglas human rights posture would not be checked by the verbiage of the Constitution: if that document and its Bill of Rights did not provide the kind of protection for the individual Douglas deemed necessary to bring about equal justice under law as he perceived it, well, he would find it" (*Justices, Presidents, and Senators: A History of the U.S. Supreme Court Appointments from Washington to Clinton* [Lanham, Maryland: Rowman and Littlefield, 1999]). Douglas himself admitted that "at the constitutional level where we work, 90 percent of any decision is emotional. The rational part of us supplies the reasons for supporting our predilections" (quoted by Robert Dowlet, "The Right to Arms: Does the Constitution or the Predilection of Judges Reign?" *Oklahoma Law Review* [1983], Vol. 36, No. 1). Not retiring until 1975, he was one of the justices responsible for the 1973 decision in *Roe v. Wade*, which struck down the anti-abortion law of Texas, and consequently similar laws in nearly all of the States, as an unconstitutional deprivation of a woman's "right of privacy."

36. *A.B. Kirschbaum v. Walling* (1942), 316 U.S. 517.

fine on a farmer who had, without a license, planted twelve acres of wheat which he fed to animals raised on his own farm to be used as food for his own family. Roscoe Filburn insisted that his actions did not involve interstate commercial activity, but the Court countered that if he had not used his own wheat for feed, he would have purchased wheat from another source, which could possibly have affected the price of wheat in other States.[37]

Another accomplishment of the Roosevelt-controlled Supreme Court was the appointment of an advisory committee to develop a unified system of procedural rules for the official establishment and operation of a uniform "summary judgment" civil court system to uphold and enforce the new administrative measures. These rules, known as the *Federal Rules of Civil Procedure* of 1938, when adopted by all the States, had the effect of abolishing courts of Common Law throughout the country and instituting in their place a court system under the authority of the President as Commander-in-Chief. Thus, it is no longer necessary for citizens to be indicted for crimes by a grand jury of their peers, as guaranteed in the Fifth Amendment of the Constitution, but they are now summarily tried before quasi-military tribunals for offenses in violation of the codes, rules, and regulations created by a myriad of unelected bureaucrats under the control of the Executive. Even in the case of a jury trial, the members of the jury are rarely the peers of the accused, and are carefully screened and instructed to find according to Government policy in all cases whatsoever. This will be discussed at greater length in a later chapter.

In a speech against the bill which would become the Agricultural Adjustment Act, delivered in the House of Representatives on 22 March 1933, James M. Beck of Pennsylvania stated:

> I think of all the damnable heresies that have ever been suggested in connection with the Constitution, the doctrine of emergency is the worst. It means that when Congress declares an emergency, there is no Constitution. This means its death. It is the very doctrine that the German chancellor [Adolf Hitler] is invoking today in the dying hours of the parliamentary body of the German republic, namely, that because of an emergency, it should grant to the German chancellor absolute power to pass any law, even though the law contradicts the constitution of the German republic. Chancellor Hitler is at least frank about it. We pay the Constitution lipservice, but the result is the same....
>
> But the Constitution of the United States, as a restraining influence in keeping the federal government within the carefully prescribed channels of power, is moribund, if not dead. We are witnessing its death-agonies, for when this bill becomes a law, if unhappily it becomes a law, there is no longer any workable Constitution to keep the Congress within the limits of its Constitutional powers.[38]

Beck was only partially correct: since April of 1861, it has not been necessary for

---

37. *Wickard v. Filburn* (1942), 317 U.S. 131.

38. James M. Beck, *Congressional Record — House*, Volume LXXVI, Part One, pages 754-755.

Congress to declare an emergency in order to "suspend" the Constitution — that is the assumed prerogative of the President of the United States in his capacity as Commander-in-Chief of the military. It is beyond dispute that the political sovereignty, which Roosevelt himself acknowledged was the rightful possession of the people of the several States, was once again usurped in the 1930s and thereafter permanently retained by the Executive branch of the U.S. Government. We shall see how the lives, property, and financial transactions of the American people are almost entirely subject to the control of the President who, as pointed out in 1862 by Benjamin Robbins Curtis, has the "power to delegate his mastership to such satraps as he may select." The foul tree of despotism which was planted in American soil over one hundred and fifty years ago by Lincoln, watered by the radical Republicans during Reconstruction, and fertilized by Roosevelt, has at last come to full fruition — America is now a socialist police State, the people have been reduced to abject slavery, and the Constitution has become little more than a curiosity in the museum of historical relics:

> Constitutional dictatorship is a dangerous thing.... The most obvious danger of constitutional dictatorship, or of any of its institutions, is the unpleasant possibility that such dictatorship will abandon its qualifying adjective and become permanent and unconstitutional. Too often in a struggling constitutional state have the institutions of emergency power served as efficient weapons for a *coup d'etat*....
>
> [Another risk] inherent in the constitutional employment of dictatorial institutions is the simple fact that changes less than revolutionary, but nonetheless changes, will be worked in the permanent structure of government and society. No constitutional government ever passed through a period in which emergency powers were used without undergoing some degree of permanent alteration, always in the direction of an aggrandizement of the power of the state.[39]

---

39. Rossiter, *Constitutional Dictatorship*, pages 294, 295.

SUPPORTING DOCUMENT
Louis T. McFadden's Speech
in the House of Representatives
Congressional Record — 9 March 1933

Mr. Chairman, the United States is bankrupt: it has been bankrupted by the corrupt and dishonest Federal Reserve. It has repudiated its debts to its own citizens. Its chief foreign creditor is Great Britain, and a British bailiff has been at the White House and British Agents are in the United States Treasury making inventories and arranging terms of liquidation!

Mr. Chairman, the Federal Reserve has offered to collect the British claims in full from the American public by trickery and corruption, if Great Britain will help to conceal its crimes. The British are shielding their agents, the Federal Reserve, because they do not wish that system of robbery to be destroyed here. They wish it to continue for their benefit! By means of it, Great Britain has become the financial mistress of the world. She has regained the position she occupied before the World War.

For several years she has been a silent partner in the business of the Federal Reserve. Under threat of blackmail, or by their bribery, or by their native treachery to the people of the United States, the officials in charge of the Federal Reserve unwisely gave Great Britain immense gold loans running into hundreds of millions of dollars. They did this against the law! Those gold loans were not single transactions. They gave Great Britain a borrowing power in the United States of billions. She squeezed billions out of this Country by means of her control of the Federal Reserve.

As soon as the Hoover Moratorium was announced, Great Britain moved to consolidate her gains. After the treacherous signing away of American rights at the seven-power conference at London in July, 1931, which put the Federal Reserve under the control of the Bank of International Settlements, Great Britain began to tighten the hangman's noose

755

around the neck of the United States.

She abandoned the gold standard and embarked upon a campaign of buying up the claims of foreigners against the Federal Reserve in all parts of the world. She has now sent her bailiff, Ramsey MacDonald, here to get her war debt to this country canceled. But she has a club in her hands! She has title to the gambling debts which the corrupt and dishonest Federal Reserve incurred abroad.

Ramsey MacDonald, the labor party deserter, has come here to compel the President to sign on the dotted line, and that is what Roosevelt is about to do! Roosevelt will endeavor to conceal the nature of his action from the American people. But he will obey the International Bankers and transfer the war debt that Great Britain should pay to the American people, to the shoulders of the American taxpayers.

Mr. Chairman, the bank holiday in the several States was brought about by the corrupt and dishonest Federal Reserve. These institutions manipulated money and credit, and caused the States to order bank holidays.

These holidays were frame-ups! They were dress rehearsals for the national bank holiday which Franklin D. Roosevelt promised Sir Ramsey MacDonald that he would declare.

There was no national emergency here when Franklin D. Roosevelt took office excepting the bankruptcy of the Federal Reserve — a bankruptcy which has been going on under cover for several years and which has been concealed from the people so that the people would continue to permit their bank deposits and their bank reserves and their gold and the funds of the United States Treasury to be impounded in these bankrupt institutions.

Under cover, the predatory International Bankers have been stealthily transferring the burden of the Federal Reserve debts to the people's Treasury and to the people themselves. They have been using the farms and the homes of the United States to pay for their thievery! That is the only national emergency that there has been here since the depression began.

The week before the bank holiday was declared in New York State, the deposits in New York savings banks were greater than the withdrawals. There were no runs on New York banks. There was no need of a bank holiday in New York, or of a national holiday.

Roosevelt did what the International Bankers ordered him to do! Do not deceive yourself, Mr. Chairman, or permit yourself to be deceived by others into the belief that Roosevelt's dictatorship is in any way intended to benefit the people of the United States: he is preparing to sign on the dotted line! He is preparing to cancel the war debts by fraud! He is preparing to internationalize this Country and to destroy our Constitution itself in order to keep the Federal Reserve intact as a money institution for foreigners!

Mr. Chairman, I see no reason why citizens of the United States should be terrorized into surrendering their property to the International Bankers who own and control the Federal Reserve. The statement that gold would be taken from its lawful owners if they did not voluntarily surrender it to private interests shows that there is an antichrist in our Government. The statement that it is necessary for the people to give their gold — the only real money — to the banks in order to protect the currency, is a statement of calculated dishonesty!

By his unlawful usurpation of power on the night of March 5, 1933, and by his proclamation, which in my opinion was in violation of the Constitution of the United States, Roosevelt divorced the currency of the United States from gold, and the United States currency is no longer protected by gold. It is therefore sheer dishonesty to say that the people's gold is needed to protect the currency.

Roosevelt ordered the people to give their gold to private interests — that is, to banks, and he took control of the banks so that all the gold and gold values in them, or given into them, might be handed over to the predatory International Bankers who own and control the Federal Reserve. Roosevelt cast in his lot with the usurers. He agreed to save the corrupt and dishonest Federal Reserve at the expense of the people of the United States. He took advantage of the people's confusion and weariness and spread the dragnet over the United States to capture everything of value that was left in it. He made a great haul for the International Bankers.

The Prime Minister of England came here for money! He came here to collect cash! He came here with Federal Reserve Currency and other claims against the Federal Reserve which England had bought up in all parts of the world. And he has presented them for redemption in gold.

Mr. Chairman, I am in favor of compelling the Federal Reserve to pay their own debts. I see no reason why the general public should be forced to pay the gambling debts of the International Bankers.

By his action in closing the banks of the United States, Roosevelt seized the gold value of forty billions or more of bank deposits in the United States banks. Those deposits were deposits of gold values. By his action he has rendered them payable to the depositors in paper only, if payable at all, and the paper money he proposes to pay out to bank depositors and to the people generally in lieu of their hard earned gold values in itself, and being based on nothing into which the people can convert it, the said paper money is of negligible value altogether.

It is the money of slaves, not of free men. If the people of the United States permit it to be imposed upon them at the will of their credit masters, the next step in their downward progress will be their acceptance of orders on company stores for what they eat and wear. Their case will be similar to that of starving coal miners. They, too, will be paid with orders on company stores for food and clothing, both of indifferent quality and be forced to live in company-owned houses from which they may be evicted at the drop of a hat. More of them will be forced into conscript labor camps under supervision.

At noon on the 4th of March, 1933, Franklin D. Roosevelt, with his hand on the Bible, took an oath to preserve, protect and defend the Constitution of the United States. At midnight on the 5th of March, 1933, he confiscated the property of American citizens. He took the currency of the United States off the gold standard of value. He repudiated the internal debt of the Government to its own citizens. He destroyed the value of the American dollar. He released, or endeavored to release, the Federal Reserve from their contractual liability to redeem Federal Reserve currency in gold or lawful money on a parity with gold. He depreciated the value of the national currency.

The people of these United States are now using unredeemable paper slips for money. The Treasury cannot redeem that paper in gold or silver. The gold and silver of the Treasury has unlawfully been given to the corrupt and dishonest Federal Reserve. And the Administration has since had the effrontery to raid the Country for more gold for the private interests by telling our patriotic citizens that their gold is need to protect the currency. It is not being used to protect the currency! It is being used to protect the corrupt and dishonest Federal Reserve!

The directors of these institutions have committed criminal offense against the United States Government, including the offense of making false entries on their books, and the still more serious offense of unlawfully abstracting funds from the United States Treasury! Roosevelt's gold raid is intended to help them out of the pit they dug for themselves when they gambled away the wealth and savings of the American people.

The International Bankers set up a dictatorship here because they wanted a dictator who would protect them. They wanted a dictator who would issue a proclamation giving the Federal Reserve an absolute and unconditional release from their special currency in gold, or lawful money of any Federal Reserve Bank.

Has Roosevelt released any other class of debtors in this Country from the necessity of paying their debts? Has he made a proclamation telling the farmers that they need not pay their mortgages? Has he made a proclamation to the effect that mothers of starving children need not pay their milk bills? Has he made a proclamation relieving householders from the necessity of paying rent? Not he! He has issued one kind of proclamation only, and that is a proclamation to relieve international bankers and the foreign debtors of the United States Government.

Mr. Chairman, the gold in the banks of this country belongs to the American people who have paper money contracts for it in the form of national currency. If the Federal Reserve cannot keep their contracts with United States citizens to redeem their paper money in gold, or lawful money, then the Federal Reserve must be taken over by the United States Government and their officers must be put on trial.

There must be a day of reckoning. If the Federal Reserve have looted the Treasury so that the Treasury cannot redeem the United States currency for which it is liable in gold, then the Federal Reserve must be driven out of the Treasury.

Mr. Chairman, a gold certificate is a warehouse receipt for gold in the Treasury, and the man who has a gold certificate is the actual owner of a corresponding amount of gold stacked in the Treasury subject to his order. Now comes Roosevelt who seeks to render the money of the United States worthless by unlawfully proclaiming that it may *not* be converted into gold at the will of the holder.

Roosevelt's next haul for the International Bankers was the reduction in the pay of all Federal employees. Next in order are the veterans of all wars, many of whom are aged and infirm, and others sick and disabled. These men had their lives adjusted for them by acts of

Congress determining the amounts of the pensions, and, while it is meant that every citizen should sacrifice himself for the good of the United States, I see no reason why those poor people, these aged Civil War veterans and war widows and half-starved veterans of the World War, should be compelled to give up their pensions for the financial benefit of the International vultures who have looted the Treasury, bankrupted the Country and traitorously delivered the United States to a foreign foe.

There are many ways of raising revenue that are better than that barbaric act of injustice. Why not collect from the Federal Reserve the amount they owe the U.S. Treasury in interest on all the Federal Reserve currency they have taken from the Government? That would put billions of dollars into the U.S. Treasury. If Franklin D. Roosevelt is as honest as he pretends to be, he will have that done immediately. And in addition, why not compel the Federal Reserve to disclose their profits and to pay the Government its share? Until this is done, it is rank dishonesty to talk of maintaining the credit of the U.S. Government.

My own salary as a member of Congress has been reduced, and while I am willing to give my part of it that has been taken away from me to the U.S. Government, I regret that the United States has suffered itself to be brought so low by the vultures and crooks who are operating the roulette wheels and faro tables in the Federal Reserve, that is now obliged to throw itself on the mercy of its legislators and charwomen, its clerks, and its poor pensioners and to take money out of our pockets to make good the defalcations of the International Bankers who were placed in control of the Treasury and given the monopoly of U.S. Currency by the misbegotten Federal Reserve.

I am well aware of the International Bankers who drive up to the door of the United States Treasury in their limousines and look down with scorn upon members of Congress because we work for so little, while they draw millions a year. The difference is that we earn, or try to earn, what we get — and they steal the greater part of their takings.

I do not like to see vivisections performed on human beings. I do not like to see the American people used for experimental purposes by the credit masters of the United States. They predicted among themselves that they would be able to produce a condition here in which American citizens would be completely humbled and left starving and penniless in the streets. The fact that they made that assertion while they were fomenting their conspiracy against the United States shows that they like to see a human being, especially an American, stumbling from hunger when he walks.

Something should be done about it, they say. Five-cent meals, or something! But Franklin D. Roosevelt will not permit the House of Representatives to investigate the condition of the Federal Reserve. Franklin D. Roosevelt will not do that. He has certain International Bankers to serve. They now look to him as the man *higher up* who will protect them from the just wrath of an outraged people.

The International Bankers have always hated our pensioners. A man with a small pension is a ward of the Government. He is not dependent upon them for a salary or wages. They cannot control him. They do not like him. It gave them great pleasure, therefore, to slash the veterans.

But Franklin D. Roosevelt will never do anything to embarrass his financial supporters. He will cover up the crimes of the Federal Reserve. Before he was elected, Mr. Roosevelt advocated a return to the earlier practices of the Federal Reserve, thus admitting its corruptness. The Democratic platform advocated a change in the personnel of the Federal Reserve. These were campaign bait. As a prominent Democrat lately remarked to me, "There is no new deal. The same old crowd is in control."

The claims of foreign creditors of the Federal Reserve have no validity in law. The foreign creditors were the receivers — and the willing receivers — of stolen goods! They have received through their banking fences immense amounts of currency, and that currency was unlawfully taken from the United States Treasury by the Federal Reserve.

England discovered the irregularities of the Federal Reserve quite early in its operations and through fear, apparently, the Federal Reserve have for years suffered themselves to be blackmailed and dragooned into permitting England to share in the business of the Federal Reserve.

The Federal Reserve have unlawfully taken many millions of dollars of the public credit of the United States and have given it to foreign sellers on the security of the debt paper of foreign buyers in purely foreign transactions, and when the foreign buyers refused to meet their obligations and the Federal Reserve saw no honest way of getting the stolen goods back into their possession, they decided by control of the executive to make the American people pay their losses!

They likewise entered into a conspiracy to deprive the people of the United States of their title to the war debts and not being able to do that in the way they intended, they are now engaged in an effort to debase the American dollar so that foreign governments will have their debts to this country cut in two, and then by means of other vicious underhanded arrangements, they propose to remit the remainder.

So far as the United States is concerned, the gambling counters have no legal standing. The U.S. Treasury cannot be compelled to make good the gambling ventures of the corrupt and dishonest Federal Reserve. Still less should the bank deposits of the United States be used for that purpose. Still less should the national currency have been made irredeemable in gold so that the gold which was massed and stored to redeem the currency for American citizens may be used to pay the gambling debts of the Federal Reserve for England's benefit.

The American people should have their gold in their own possession where it cannot be held under secret agreement for any foreign-controlled bank, or world bank, or foreign nation. Our own citizens have the prior claim to it. The paper money they have in their possession deserves redemption far more than U.S. currency and credit which was stolen from the U.S. Treasury and bootlegged abroad.

Why should the foreigners be made preferred creditors of the bankrupt United States? Why should the United States be treated as bankrupt at all? This Government has immense sums due it from the Federal Reserve. The directors of these institutions are men of great wealth. Why should the guilty escape the consequences of their misdeeds? Why should the people of the United States surrender the value of their gold bank deposits to pay off the gambling debts of these bankers? Why should Roosevelt promise foreigners that the United States will play the part of a good neighbor, "meeting its obligations"?

Let the Federal Reserve meet their own obligations. Every member of the Federal Reserve should be compelled to disgorge, and every acceptance banker and every discount corporation which has made illegal profits by means of public credit unlawfully bootlegged out of the U.S. Treasury and hired out by the crooks and vultures of the Federal Reserve should be compelled to disgorge.

Gambling debts due to foreign receivers of stolen goods should not be paid by sacrificing our title to our war debts, the assets of the U.S. Treasury which belong to all the people of the United States and which it is our duty to preserve inviolate in the people's Treasury. The U.S. Treasury cannot be made liable for them. The Federal Reserve currency must be redeemed by the Federal Reserve banks or else these Federal Reserve banks must be liquidated.

We know from assertions made here by the Hon. John N. Garner, Vice-President of the United States, that there is a condition in the U.S. Treasury which would cause American citizens, if they knew what it was, to lose all confidence in their government. That is a condition that Roosevelt will not have investigated. He has brought with him from Wall Street, James Warburg, the son of Paul M. Warburg. Mr. Warburg is the head of the Bank of Manhattan Company. Mr. Warburg, alien born, and the son of an alien who did not become naturalized here until several years after this Warburg's birth, is a son of a former partner of Kuhn, Loeb and Company, an grandson of another partner, a nephew of a former partner, and a nephew of a present partner. He holds no office in our Government, but I am told that he is in daily attendance at the Treasury, and that he has private quarters there! In other words, Mr. Chairman, Kuhn, Loeb and Company now control and occupy the U.S. Treasury.

The text of the Executive order which seems to place an embargo on shipments of gold permits the Secretary of the Treasury, a former director of the Federal Reserve of New York, the practices of which have been corrupt, to issue licenses at his discretion for the export of gold coin, or bullion, earmarked or held in trust for a recognized foreign government or foreign central bank for international settlement. Now, Mr. Chairman, if gold held in trust for those foreign institutions may be sent to them, I see no reason why gold held in trust for Americans as evidenced by their gold certificates and other currency issued by the U.S. Government should not be paid to them.

I think that American citizens should be entitled to treatment at least as good as that which the present administration is extending to foreign governments, foreign central banks, and the bank of International Settlements. I think a veteran of the World War, with a $20.00 gold certificate, is at least as much entitled to receive his own gold for it as any international banker in the city of New York of London.

By the terms of this Executive order, gold may be exported if it is actually required, for the fulfillment of any contract entered into prior to the date of this order by an applicant who, in obedience to the Executive order of April 5, 1933, has delivered gold coin, gold bullion, or gold certificates. This means that gold may be exported to pay the obligations abroad of the Federal Reserve which were incurred prior to the date of the order, namely, April 20, 1933.

If a European bank should send $100,000,000 in Federal Reserve currency to a bank in this country for redemption, that bank could easily ship gold to Europe in exchange for that currency. Such Federal Reserve currency would represent "contracts" entered into prior to the date of the order. If the Bank of International Settlements or any other foreign bank holding any of the present gambling debt paper of the Federal Reserve should draw a draft for the settlement of such obligation, gold would be shipped to them because the debt contract would have been entered into prior to the date of the order.

Mr. Speaker, I rise to a question of constitutional privilege.

Whereas, I charge Eugene Meyer, Roy A. Young, Edmund Platt, Eugene B. Black, Adolph Casper Miller, Charles S. Hamlin, George R. James, Andrew W. Mellon, Ogden L. Mills, William H. Woodin, John W. Poole, J.F.T. O'Connor, members of the Federal Reserve Board; F.H. Curtis, J.H. Chane, R.L. Austin, George De Camp, L.B. Williams, W.W. Hoxton, Oscar Newton, E.M. Stevens, J.S. Wood, J.N. Payton, M.L. McClure, C.C. Walsh, Isaac B. Newton, Federal Reserve agents, jointly and severally, with violations of the Constitution and laws of the United States, and whereas I charge them with having taken funds from the U.S. Treasury which were not appropriated by the Congress of the United States, and I charge them with having unlawfully taken over $80,000,000,000 from the U.S. Government in the year 1928, the said unlawful taking consisting of the unlawful creation of claims against the U.S. Treasury to the extent of over $80,000,000,000 in the year 1928; and I charge them with similar thefts committed in 1929, 1930, 1931, 1932, and 1933, and in years previous to 1928, amounting to billions of dollars; and

Whereas I charge them, jointly and severally, with having unlawfully created claims against the U.S. Treasury by unlawfully placing U.S. Government credit in specific amounts to the credit of foreign governments and foreign central banks of issue; private interests and commercial and private banks of the United States and foreign countries, and branches of foreign banks doing business in the United States, to the extent of billions of dollars; and with having made unlawful contracts in the name of the U.S. Government and the U.S. Treasury; and with having made false entries on books of account; and

Whereas I charge them, jointly and severally, with having taken Federal Reserve Notes from the U.S. Treasury and with having issued Federal Reserve Notes and with having put Federal Reserve Notes into circulation without obeying the mandatory provision of the Federal Reserve Act which requires the Federal Reserve Board to fix an interest rate on all issues of Federal Reserve Notes supplied to Federal Reserve Banks, the interest resulting therefrom to be paid by the Federal Reserve Banks to the Government of the United States for the use of the Federal Reserve Notes, and I charge them of having defrauded the U.S. Government and the people of the United States of billions of dollars by the commission of this crime; and

Whereas I charge them, jointly and severally, with having purchased U.S. Government securities with U.S. Government credit unlawfully taken and with having sold the said U.S. Government securities back to the people of the United States for gold or gold values and with having again purchased U.S. Government securities with U.S. Government credit unlawfully taken and with having again sold the said U.S. Government securities for gold or gold values, and I charge them with having defrauded the U.S. Government and the people of the United States by this rotary process; and

Whereas I charge them, jointly and severally, with having unlawfully negotiated U.S. Government securities, upon which the Government liability was extinguished, as collateral security for Federal Reserve Notes and with having substituted such securities for gold which was being held as collateral security for Federal Reserve Notes, and with having by the process defrauded the U.S. Government and the people of the United States, and I charge them with the theft of all the gold and currency they obtained by this process; and

Whereas I charge them, jointly and severally, with having unlawfully issued Federal Reserve currency on false, worthless and fictitious acceptances and other circulating evidence of debt, and with having made unlawful advances of Federal Reserve currency, and with having unlawfully permitted renewals of acceptances and renewals of other circulating evidences of debt, and with having permitted acceptance bankers and discount dealer corporations and other private bankers to violate the banking laws of the United States; and

Whereas I charge them, jointly and severally, with having conspired to have evidences of debt to the extent of $1,000,000,000 artificially created at the end of February, 1933 and early in March, 1933, and with having made unlawful issues and advances of Federal Reserve currency on the security of said artificially created evidences of debt for a sinister purpose, and with having assisted in the execution of said sinister purpose; and

Whereas I charge them, jointly and severally, with having brought about a repudiation of the currency obligations of the Federal Reserve Banks to the people of the United States, and with having conspired to obtain a release for the Federal Reserve Board and the Federal Reserve Banks from their contractual liability to redeem all Federal Reserve currency in gold or lawful money at the Federal Reserve Bank and with having defrauded the holders of Federal Reserve currency, and with having conspired to have the debts and losses of the Federal Reserve Board and the Federal Reserve Banks unlawfully transferred to the Government and the people of the United States; and

Whereas I charge them, jointly and severally, with having unlawfully substituted Federal Reserve currency and other irredeemable paper currency for gold in the hands of the people after the decision to repudiate the Federal Reserve currency and the national currency was made known to them, and with thus having obtained money under false pretenses; and

Whereas I charge them, jointly and severally, with having brought about a repudiation of the national currency of the United States in order that the gold value of the said currency might be given to private interests, foreign governments, foreign central banks of issues, and the Bank of International Settlements, and the people of the United States to be left without gold or lawful money and with no currency other than a paper currency irredeemable in gold, and I charge them with having done this for the benefit of private interests, foreign governments, foreign central banks of issue, and the Bank of International Settlements; and

Whereas I charge them, jointly and severally, with conniving with the Edge Law banks, and other Edge Law institutions, accepting banks, and discount corporations, foreign central banks of issue, foreign commercial banks, foreign corporations, and foreign individuals with funds unlawfully taken from the U.S. Treasury; and I charge them with having unlawfully permitted and made possible "new financing" for foreigners at the expense of the U.S. Treasury to the extent of billions of dollars and with having unlawfully permitted and made possible the bringing into the United States of immense quantities of foreign securities, created in foreign countries for export to the United States, and with having unlawfully permitted the said foreign securities to be imported into the United States instead of gold, which was lawfully due to the United States on trade balances and otherwise, and with having unlawfully permitted and facilitated the sale of the said foreign securities in the United States; and

Whereas I charge them, jointly and severally, with having unlawfully exported U.S. coins and currency for a sinister purpose, and with having deprived the people of the United States of their lawful circulating medium of exchange, and I charge them with having arbitrarily and unlawfully reduced the amount of money and currency in circulation in the United States to the lowest rate per capita in the history of the Government, so that the great mass of the people have been left without a sufficient medium of exchange, and I charge them with concealment and evasion in refusing to make known the amount of U.S. money in coins and paper currency exported and the amount remaining in the United States, as a result of which refusal the Congress of the United States is unable to ascertain where the U.S. coins and issues of currency are at the present time, and what amount of U.S. currency is now held abroad; and

Whereas I charge them, jointly and severally, with having arbitrarily and unlawfully raised and lowered the rates of money and with having arbitrarily increased and diminished the volume of currency in circulation for the benefit of private interests at the expense of the Government and the people of the United States, and with having unlawfully manipulated money rates, wages, salaries and property values both real and personal, in the United States, by unlawful operations in the open discount market and by resale and repurchase agreements unsanctioned by law; and

Whereas I charge them, jointly and severally, with having brought about the decline in prices on the New York Stock Exchange and other exchanges in October, 1929, by unlawful manipulation of money rates and the volume of U.S. money and currency in circulation; by theft of funds from the U.S. Treasury by gambling in acceptances and U.S. Government securities; by service rendered to foreign and domestic speculators and politicians, and by unlawful sale of U.S. gold reserves abroad, and whereas I charge that the unconstitutional inflation law imbedded in the so-called Farm Relief Act by which the Federal Reserve Banks are given permission to buy U.S. Government securities to the extent of $3,000,000,000 and to draw forth currency from the people's Treasury to the extent of $3,000,000,000 is likely to result in connivance on the part of said accused with others in the purchase by the Federal Reserve of the U.S. Government securities to the extent of $3,000,000,000 with the U.S. Government's own credit unlawfully taken — it being obvious that the Federal Reserve do not intend to pay anything of value to the U.S. Government for the said U.S. Government securities, no provision for payment in gold or lawful money appearing in the so-called *Farm Relief Bill* — and the U.S. Government will thus be placed in a position of conferring a gift of $3,000,000,000 in U.S. Government securities on the Federal Reserve to enable them to pay more on their bad debts to foreign governments, foreign central banks of issue, private interests, and private and commercial banks, both foreign and domestic, and the Bank of International Settlements, and whereas the U.S. Government will thus go into debt to the extent of $3,000,000,000 and will then have an additional claim for $3,000,000,000 in currency unlawfully created against it and whereas no private interest should be permitted to buy U.S. Government securities with the Government's own credit unlawfully taken and whereas currency should not be issued for the benefit of said private interests so acquired, and whereas it has been publicly stated and not denied that the inflation amendment of the Farm Relief Act is the matter of benefit which was secured by Ramsey MacDonald, the Prime Minister of Great Britain, upon the occasion of his latest visit to the White House and U.S. Treasury, and whereas there is grave danger that the accused will employ the provision creating U.S. Government securities to the extent of $3,000,000,000 and three millions in currency to be issuable thereupon for the benefit of themselves and their foreign principals, and that they will convert the currency so obtained to the uses of Great Britain by secret arrangements with the Bank of England of which they are the agents, and for which they maintain an account and perform services at the expense of the U.S. Treasury and that they will likewise confer benefits upon the Bank of International Settlements for which they maintain an account and perform services at the expense of the U.S. Treasury; and

Whereas I charge them, jointly and severally, with having concealed the insolvency of the Federal Reserve and with having failed to report the insolvency of the Federal Reserve to the Congress and with having conspired to have the said insolvent institutions continue in operation, and with having permitted the said insolvent institutions to receive U.S. Government funds and other deposits, and with having permitted them to exercise control over the gold reserves of the United States and with having permitted them to transfer upward of $100,000,000,000 of their debts and losses to the general public and the Government of the United States, and with having permitted foreign debts of the Federal Reserve to be paid with the property, the savings, the wages, and the salaries of the people of the United States, and with the farms and the homes of the American people, and whereas I charge them with forcing the bad debts of the Federal Reserve upon the general public covertly and dishonestly and with taking the general wealth and savings of the people of the United States under false pretenses, to pay the debts of the Federal Reserve to foreigners; and

Whereas I charge them, jointly and severally, with violations of the Federal Reserve Act and other laws; with maladministration of the Federal Reserve Act; and with evasions of the Federal Reserve law and other laws; and with having unlawfully failed to report violations of law on the part of the Federal Reserve Banks which, if known, would have caused the Federal Reserve Banks to lose their charters; and

Whereas I charge them, jointly and severally, with failure to protect and maintain the gold reserves and the gold stock and gold coinage of the United States and with having sold the gold reserves of the United States to foreign governments, foreign central banks of issue, foreign commercial and private banks, and other foreign institutions and individuals at a profit to themselves, and I charge them with having sold gold reserves of the United States so that between 1924 and 1928 the United States gained no gold on net account but suffered a decline in its percentage of central gold reserves from 45.9 percent in 1924 to 37.5 percent in 1928 notwithstanding the fact that the United States had a favorable balance of trade throughout that period; and

Whereas I charge them, jointly and severally, with having conspired to concentrate U.S. Government securities and thus the national debt of the United States in the hands of foreigners and international money lenders and with having conspired to transfer to foreigners and international money lenders title to and control of the financial resources of the United States; and

Whereas I charge them, jointly and severally, with having fictitiously paid installments on the national debt with Government credit unlawfully taken; and

Whereas I charge them, jointly and severally, with the loss of the U.S. Government funds intrusted to their care; and

Whereas I charge them, jointly and severally, with having destroyed independent banks in the United States and with having thereby caused losses amounting to billions of dollars to the depositors of the said banks, and to the general public of the United States; and

Whereas I charge them, jointly and severally, with the failure to furnish true reports of the business operations and the true conditions of the Federal Reserve to the Congress and the people, and having furnished false and misleading reports to the Congress of the United States; and

Whereas I charge them, jointly and severally, with having published false and misleading propaganda intended to deceive the American people and to cause the United States to lose its independence; and

Whereas I charge them, jointly and severally, with unlawfully allowing Great Britain to share in the profits of the Federal Reserve at the expense of the Government and the people of the United States; and

Whereas I charge them, jointly and severally, with having entered into secret agreements and illegal transactions with Montague Norman, Governor of the Bank of England; and

Whereas I charge them, jointly and severally, with swindling the U.S. Treasury and the people of the United States in pretending to have received payment from Great Britain of the amount due on the British war debt to the United States in December, 1932; and

Whereas I charge them, jointly and severally, with having conspired with their foreign principals and others to defraud the U.S. Government and to prevent the people of the United

States from receiving payment of the war debts due to the United States from foreign nations; and

Whereas I charge them, jointly and severally, with having robbed the U.S. Government and the people of the United States by their theft and sale of the gold reserves of the United States and other unlawful transactions, and with having created a deficit in the U.S. Treasury, which has necessitated to a large extent the destruction of our national defense and the reduction of the U.S. Army and the U.S. Navy and other branches of the national defense; and

Whereas I charge them, jointly and severally, of having reduced the United States from a first class power to one that is dependent, and with having reduced the United States from a rich and powerful nation to one that is internationally poor; and

Whereas I charge them, jointly and severally, with the crime of having treasonably conspired and acted against the peace and security of the United States and with having treasonably conspired to destroy constitutional Government in the United States.

Resolved, That the Committee on the Judiciary is authorized and directed as a whole or by subcommittee, to investigate the official conduct of the Federal Reserve agents to determine whether, in the opinion of the said committee, they have been guilty of any high crime or misdemeanor which in the contemplation of the Constitution requires the interposition of the constitutional powers of the House. Such Committee shall report its findings to the House, together with such resolution or resolutions of impeachment or other recommendations it deems proper.

For the purposes of this resolution the Committee is authorized to sit and act during the present Congress at such times and places in the District of Columbia or elsewhere, whether or not the House is sitting, has recessed or has adjourned, to hold such clerical, stenographical, and other assistants, to require the attendance of such witnesses and the production of such books, papers, and documents, to take such testimony, and to have such printing and binding done, and to make such expenditures as it deems necessary.

SUPPLEMENTARY ESSAY
Executive Control of the Social and Economic Life of the States
by Sterling E. Edmunds

The people of the United States have been too close to the political drama that has been unfolding in the affairs of their government, and too bewildered by phrases deliberately chosen to delude them, to understand the cataclysmic significance of what has happened, but to the future historian the period of 1933-1940 will clearly mark the end of a political cycle for the North Americans, in the final failure of the most successful experiment ever made by man in civil society to govern himself without a master.

The historian will trace its beginnings in the revolt of a few million colonists against the oppressions of the English Crown in the late Eighteenth Century, and their erection of a unique system of government, having for its primary object a realization of the innate worth and dignity of the individual, by emancipating him from the inveterate ambition, vanity, and folly of his rulers, through substituting freedom for force as the underlying principle of the system. The results will be recorded as having excited the hope and envy of the world as an example in which a small and sturdy group, favorably situated geographically in a new land, wrought themselves into the mightiest and most prosperous nation on earth and governed themselves as freemen for a century and a half.

Those who formed this peculiar system of government had earnestly studied the history of the rise and fall of civil societies in search of a formula for a permanent order of freedom. They saw that man invariably counted for little more than the beasts of the field under all political forms in which power was centralized in his rulers, whether they appeared as autocracies, aristocracies, oligarchies, theocracies or democracies. And they will be credited by the historian with having deducted the political maxim, that the freedom of the individual is possible only under a polity in which governmental power is limited and divided and kept so. Not centralization but decentralization was the great essential principle. As Thomas Jefferson wrote in a spirit of warning, in 1816: "What has destroyed the liberty and rights of man in every government that has ever existed under the sun? The generalizing and concentrating all cares and powers into one body, no matter whether of the autocrats of Russia and France or of the aristocrats of a Venetian Senate."

In the system constructed by the Americans were thirteen independent States, just freed by arms from alien rule as colonies, which formed a Union. Then they delegated to a common federal government certain of their powers to deal with matters concerning their interrelations and with foreign affairs. And these certain powers which the federal government might exercise were reduced to writing and enumerated in a Constitution of the United States, with provision for a solemn oath to be taken by the Chief Executive "before he enter upon the execution of his office," to "preserve, protect and defend" it.

Thus the powers of the federal government were not only limited, in the hope of escaping the common degradation of other peoples, but the powers that were delegated were divided and allocated to three co-ordinate, co-equal and independent branches. All power to enact the laws, dealing with but twenty enumerated subjects, to be found in Section 8 of Article I, was placed with the legislative branch, or Congress, exclusively; all power to enforce or execute the laws thus enacted was placed with the Executive exclusively; and all power to interpret and to decide the intent and meaning of the laws under the limited grants of power, was placed with the judiciary branch, or the federal courts. Such was the framework erected upon the principles of decentralization, limitation, and division of governmental power over the citizen. In a note written in his *Annals*, in 1792, Jefferson recorded:

"I said to President Washington that if the equilibrium of the three great bodies, the Legislative, Executive and Judiciary, could be preserved, if the Legislature could be kept independent, I should never fear the result of such a government; but that I could not but be uneasy when I saw the Executive had swallowed up the Legislative branch."

But it was not enough to erect a government of limited authority over the citizen as a mere paper instrument, as will be noted from the examples of failure of the score of American republics to the south that were formed in imitation and on the constitutional pattern of the government of the United States. From the time of their independence from European rule, in spite of their constitutional forms, they oscillated between anarchy and despotism, remaining republics in name only.

Obviously, if man is to restrain the control which government may exercise over him, and escape anarchy in liberty becoming license, he must assume the high moral duties and practice the difficult virtues of self-control and self-reliance, to make possible self-government in the mass. And the same capacity and willingness to control ambition and greed must be practiced by those who are chosen to wield governmental power over him. That is the hard price that man must pay for ordered freedom in civil society.

It will be written for the instruction of those who come after us, that in the years

1933-1940, the outstanding experiment of the North Americans in seeking to preserve a free political system by means of limitation and division, or decentralization of governmental authority, came to an end, and that a new cycle began in which they again found themselves the mere pawns and playthings of centralized power. And in the analysis of the failure, the impartial historian will not hesitate to ascribe it to the loss of those qualities of character in the mass and in government, without which the constitutional paper forms are lifeless and vain.

He will note many social and political phenomena that are familiar accompaniments in the record of like vicissitudes among other peoples whose civilizations have flourished and declined, particularly among the Romans. He will first mark what Ferrero declares to be "the disease that killed the Roman Empire," which he terms "excessive urbanization," the piling up of population in great cities, drawn from the peace and quiet industry of the country by the infinite but frivolous attractions of urban life. Then came the periodic economic crises, and the impoverishment of large numbers of the improvident classes, in the midst of continuing luxury, with widespread discontent.

Before the Roosevelt era this problem was met without danger. It was localized in the cities and, while relieved to some extent by private charity, was allowed to solve itself in the natural way, of forcing those unable to find employment of free support to return to work in the fields, whence they came. It was a hard solution for many, but it preserved the spirit of self-respect and self-reliance in all who thus surrounded their own difficulties. It was implicit in the free system that each man, through the exercise of prudence, must care for himself; that society needed the active cooperation and productive energy of each citizen, and that the provision which a man made for himself and his family was the measure of his worth and self-respect. His failure so to provide, while provoking pity, also carried the stigma of neglect of obligations to himself and to the community.

In the great economic depression in the third decade of this century, the central government, recognizing the millions of unemployed to be voting citizens, who, through public largess, might be permanently attached to the new course the Roosevelt administration had embarked upon, proclaimed it the duty of the federal government to feed, house and clothe all unable to care for themselves. "The people must not be allowed to starve" had a kind-hearted meaning, which all politicians readily approved.

This was the artificial expedient adopted by declining Rome, of treating poverty as a national, instead of as an individual concern, with vast public works for the unemployed, regardless of their utility, and the distribution of money and food for all who applied. There was no inducement to look carefully into the qualifications of recipients, since numbers were important. The evil was thus only intensified by reversing the current and stimulating a continuing exodus from country to city, until almost one-fifth of the population was exempted from the necessity of seeking self-support.

The corrupting effects were seen not only in the making of chronic paupers of millions of citizens congested in the cities, but in demoralizing the Mayors of cities and the Governors of State, in their constant journeyings to the capital, like mendicants, to solicit of the President as large portions as possible of the immense sums which he was permitted to dole out. Excessive taxation supplied barely a half of the demands of this profligacy, the remainder was supplied regularly by new borrowing and new public debt, with no concern over future repayment.

Among the people themselves there naturally resulted a spirit of carelessness and indolence, with no interest more serious than the pursuit of entertainment and amusement, in the theaters and at games, as an escape from boredom.

History discloses the apparent paradox that the periods in which man has most lavishly adorned his great cities are not periods of continued healthy growth, but are periods of decline. The magnificent temples and other buildings of the ancients are, in fact, symbols of decadence. So the years 1933-1940 will be mentioned as a time of splendid adornment of the capital of Washington, with great new public buildings displacing private structures throughout the city to house the hundreds of thousands of new federal officials appointed to enforce the new order of universal regulation and care of the affairs of the people.

The old simplicity of a federal government going about its limited duties without fuss will be seen to have given way to stir and bustle in the assumption of new powers, and repeated harangues by radio, arraigning as popular enemies every element of opposition to the full realization of presidential supremacy. This was accompanied by preferment for the sycophant and exclusion from all appointive offices of citizens of independence and worth.

And the chronicler will record, too, a remarkable coincidence in which almost simultaneously, a like experiment on the American model, made by another great and numerous people in Europe, came to a like end after a brief trial. And the immediate instruments in both transformations will be identified as two magnetic and ambitious men, who carried out *coups d'etat* against the republic of which they were the elected constitutional heads, strangely coupling the names of Franklin Roosevelt and Adolf Hitler as the two chief actors in this historical human drama.

In each of the two countries in 1933, there were present the same disintegrating forces among the peoples themselves making for success in any attempted *coup d'etat* — unsettled economic conditions and economic distress, class division and factionalism, unbalanced budgets and accumulating debt, unsound currencies, and a cleverly encouraged and accepted delusion that a strong one-man government could bestow happiness and do for the people what they felt hopeless to do for themselves. In Germany there was the added factor of a national feeling of impotence under injustice arising out of the harsh terms imposed upon her in the late treaty of peace of 1919.

Hitler, leading a people enjoying constitutional liberty, but who for centuries were accustomed to authoritarian rule, could and did destroy limited constitutional government in Germany by one open and daring stroke. His National Socialist party won almost complete control of the Reichstag in the election of March 5, 1933, with a popular vote of 17,269,629 to 13,590,258. On the same day this "rubber stamp" legislative body of his creatures, passed an enabling act clothing him with supreme power as Reich's chancellor, thus putting an end to the fourteen-year-old Weimar Constitution and the German Republic. All constitutional rights of the people were swallowed up in the new "Third Reich."

Roosevelt, head of the Democratic party, was elected to the Presidency of the United States in 1932 by a popular vote of 22,821,857 to Mr. Hoover's 15,761,841, and his party's candidates won 322 of the 435 seats in the lower House, with 68 of the 96 seats in the Senate. He appointed no man of recognized ability or attachment to our free institutions to his Cabinet posts. Among those he did appoint were four not of his party, who were associated with the elder La Follette, in his Progressive and Socialist campaign for the Presidency in 1924. He also surrounded himself with a group of young radicals as a sort of inner Cabinet, as his special personal advisers. It was they who secretly concerted and drafted the plan for the overthrow of constitutional government, which he put into execution.

Being the elected head of a people long practiced in and the hereditary possessors of personal and political freedom, he could not proceed in the forthright manner chosen by Hitler, but adopted the more adroit course of disguise and pretense.

There were three principal obstacles to any successful assault upon the existing limited constitutional system. First was the Constitution itself, which contained provisions for its own further limitation or expansion of power by amendments proposed by Congress to the legislatures or to conventions in the States, requiring the approval of three-fourths for ratification; or by the calling of a national constitutional convention on the application of the legislatures of two-thirds of the States, to propose amendments to be similarly ratified. The very purpose of the amending clause was to provide a peaceable way to make any change urgently desired by the people and to obviate revolution and violence, the only alternative left to other peoples, and customarily used to right their grievances against the oppressions of government.

Second, there was the Supreme Court of the United States constantly on guard to prevent usurpation of power by declaring null and void all acts of Congress and all executive acts outside of the written authority permitted in the Constitution.

And finally, there was the economic system of private industry and commerce, which it was intended to subject to political control, from which no complaint submission could be expected.

The first step in the plot was a "smearing" campaign by hundreds of administration press agents, to disparage and discredit the Constitution, the Supreme Court, and business generally. Hence, we heard much of the Constitution being "antiquated" and "outmoded," and "slush over the Constitution." The President himself joined in this assault at a press conference by terming the Constitution something suited to "the horse and buggy days." The Supreme Court was held up to public view as "Nine Old Men," equally out of step with the times. And the great institutions of private industry, the source of livelihood to our millions of workers at wages paid nowhere else in the world, became "economic royalists" and an "economic autocracy," actuated solely by greed in its exploitation of the workers. Those persons who came to the defense of the Constitution and the Court were called "old fogies" and "reactionaries."

And to gain the popular ear, new catch-phrases such as "emergency," "social justice," "social security," "planned economy," "collective bargaining," "ever-normal granary" filled the press and masked the course of the revolutionary change. It was with Roosevelt as Gibbons relates of Augustus, that mankind is governed by names, and he was not deceived in his expectation that the Senate and people would submit to slavery, provided they were respectfully assured that they still enjoyed their ancient freedom.

By 1933 the stage was set for the series of legislative acts, drafted behind the backs of the people by the young radical advisers, which were so to change the nature of our limited dual system as to release the federal government from the restraints of the Constitution, and to subordinate the States and the people to an all-embracing central executive authority. In rapid succession bills were sent to Congress for presidential control of banking, public utilities, the security exchanges, and in the deceptively-named National Industrial Recovery Act and the Agricultural Adjustment Act, the President was given complete power over the industrial and agricultural life of the nation, with authority to compel cooperation in industry, to fix prices and wages and hours, in place of the former free, competitive system. In the N.I.R.A. was also provision for $3,000,000,000 to be given to the President to use in his discretion in relief and public works. And, in the Emergency Agricultural Relief Act, levying taxes on processors of agricultural commodities, to be paid to farmers, was a further provision empowering the President to issue $3,000,000,000 of unsecured paper money.

Under the N.I.R.A., the Administrator, the appointee of the President, was empowered to set aside the anti-trust laws and compel industry to enter into regulated combinations in restraint of trade. When Representative Edward W. Pou of North Carolina reported the bill for passage in the House on May 25, 1933, he said, not in shame, but with a note of satisfaction:

"It is very true that under this bill — and I shall not attempt to discuss its merits — the President of the United States is made a dictator over industry for the time being, but it is a benign dictatorship; it is a dictatorship dedicated to the welfare of all the American people."

A servile Congress, like Hitler's Reichstag, permitted the immediate enactment of these measures, practically without debate. Then followed the gold control act, repudiating and annulling public and private contracts to pay debts in gold, and devaluing the dollar; the federal emergency relief act, home owners' loan corporation act, revival of the Reconstruction Finance Corporation, subsistence homestead act, the Tennessee Valley public utility government monopoly act, crop credit loans to farmers act, communications act, compulsory railroad pension act, tobacco control act, the Guffey coal act, to fix prices and wages and hours in mining; the creation of the farm mortgage corporation with authority to borrow $2,000,000,000 to relieve farm debtors; national housing act, loans to industry act, as part of 714 acts approved by Congress in that year. The authority of Congress had sunk into such contempt that these legislative acts centering despotic power in the President, were, in effect, executive decrees sent to Congress for mere registration. The Executive had swallowed up the Legislative branch.

In the Gold Control Act, the first of the series, the President was given dictatorial power over all forms of money and authority to devalue the dollar as much as fifty percent. All gold was called in from the people, with severe penalties for hoarding and exportation. The execution of contracts payable in gold was prohibited, and promises in United States bonds so to pay were repudiated. Meantime the content of the dollars we had previously known, with 25.8 grains of gold, was reduced to 15-5/21 grains, giving the government all of the gold and a paper profit of about $15 an ounce on all the gold called in, or a total of about $2,000,000,000. This $2,000,000,000 was turned over to the Treasury Department as a "Stabilization Fund" to be used to support the price of government bonds and to rig the market in maintaining prices, during a period of reckless borrowing.

All of these acts were calculated to attach and render acquiescent certain large classes of voters through subsidies in various forms, and to confuse and strangle the private activities and enterprise of citizens in various fields of industry and commerce which their intelligence and energies had built up under our traditional free system. To execute these several new powers conferred on the President, new boards or commissions were created, to be filled by his appointees. Invariably they were staffed with persons who were known to be hostile to the system of free enterprise and favorable to political control of private industry and commerce, under what was termed "a planned national economy."

The Tennessee Valley Authority was created in 1933 as a government utility monopoly, operating in Tennessee, North Carolina, Georgia, Alabama, Mississippi and Kentucky, in competition with private utility plants. Being financed out of the federal Treasury with hundreds of millions of dollars, paying no taxes and caring nothing for deficits, it has already compelled one great private utility to sell out or go broke, and is a like menace to other private utilities in those six States.

It will illuminate the utterly alien character of this government enterprise to refer to a decision of the Supreme Court of the United States, handed down in 1905. In the case of *South Carolina vs. U.S.*, South Carolina established a State liquor monopoly, and the question was on the right of the federal government to tax its operations. The court held that, when a State engaged in business ordinarily of a private character it could be taxed; that if this were not so, a State might take over all private business and defeat taxation for the support of the government in the whole field of internal revenue. Continuing, it said:

"There is a large and growing movement in the country in favor of the acquisition and management by the public of what are termed public utilities, including not merely therein, the supply of gas and water, but the entire railroad system. Would a State by taking into possession these public utilities lose its republican form of government?...

"Moreover, at the time of the adoption of the Constitution, there probably was not one person in the country who seriously contemplated the possibility of government, whether State or national, ever descending from its primitive plant of a body politic, to take up the work of the individual as a body corporate.... Certain it is that if the possibility of a government usurping the ordinary business of individuals, driving them out of the market, and maintaining place and power by means of what would have been called, in heated invective of the time — a 'legion of mercenaries,' had been in the public mind, the Constitution would not have been adopted, or an inhibition of such power would have been placed among Madison's amendments.... If we look upon the Constitution in the light of the common law we are led to the same conclusion. All avenues of trade were open to the individual. The government did not attempt to exclude him from any. Whatever restraints were put upon him were police regulations to control his conduct in business and not to exclude him therefrom. The government was no competitor, nor did it assume to carry on any business, which ordinarily is carried on by individuals. Indeed, every attempt at monopoly arose, whether from the government of the Sovereign or otherwise. The framers of the Constitution were not anticipating that a State would attempt to monopolize any business heretofore carried on by individuals."

Yet the federal government is now engaged in many businesses, ordinarily considered of a private character, in competition with the citizen. An investigation into the subject by the Shannon Committee of the lower House of Congress in 1932 revealed this competition is carried on in not less than two hundred fields of business. Two outstanding instances are in water transportation and in the manufacture and sale of electricity. The Inland Waterways Corporation is thus depriving the railroads of tonnage which it carries at lower rates on the Mississippi River and its tributaries, while the huge electrical project, the Tennessee Valley Authority, is purposely seeking to destroy private utility plants in its territory.

But when it comes to the matter of taxation by the States of these federal ventures into private business the Supreme Court forbids it. In a recent T.V.A. case it was held that the federal government was engaged in "flood control" on navigable streams, and that the incidental production and sale of electrical power from dams was the excuse of a governmental function and not subject to taxation by the States. Thus the federal government may tax any venture into Socialism by the States but may itself strip the States of taxable property in displacing private enterprise with no right in the States to tax such operations.

The ventures of the federal government into house-building, called "slum-clearance," is another field in which private industry is suffering from government competition, with the building projects now held to be proper government functions.

In the Securities and Exchange Act of 1933, under the pretext of protecting the purchaser of securities, a new commission is given power to starve industry and prevent the raising of new capital for extension of plant. All manufacturing and other concerns desiring to raise additional capital through the issuance of new securities must first obtain the approval of this commission. The stock exchange and brokerage houses likewise come in for regulation in the handling, and the buying and selling of any securities. In addition, there is particular provision for control by the commission in the matter of public utility corporations, both as to their finances and to their corporate interrelations.

In the Federal Communications Act of 1934, the President assumed control over interstate communications by wire and radio, through a commission to which all radio stations must apply regularly for rents of six-months licenses to operate. The result has been a censorship on whatever opponents of the President and his policies may wish freely to broadcast, with none upon the President, who may use the radio at his pleasure and without cost.

That the Federal Communications Commission has been guilty of a glaring act of oppression and repression of private enterprise is seen in its decision in March, 1940, forbidding the Radio Corporation of America to manufacture and sell television sets to the public, which would open up an entire new industry based upon years of costly research and provide new employment for an incalculable number of persons now wishing employment.

In 1933 came the National Labor Relations Act to enforce "collective bargaining," giving a partisan federal Labor Board arbitrary power over employers, in behalf of organized workers, with the power to summon, prosecute and decide, and impose heavy financial burdens in the form of "back pay," in cases of its own charges of vague "unfair" practices; and, further, to compel workers to join the unions of favored labor leaders.

The act, following a campaign of vituperation painting the employer as the enemy and sordid exploiter of the employees, forbids any intercourse or discussion of their relations between them, which might be initiated by the employer, as an "unfair" practice. Thus a condition of permanent hostility is legally imposed upon their relations. Meantime the law defines an "employee" as "any individual, whose work has ceased in consequence of or in connection with any current labor dispute or because of any unfair labor practice and who has not obtained any other regular and substantially equivalent employment." The employee is thus given a property right in his job, even after striking, in connection with which he is entitled to "back pay."

In 1938 a companion piece to the Labor Board Act was passed under the title, the Wages and Hours Act, fixing minimum wages and maximum hours for large classes of workers in the States, alleging in the preamble of the act that the existence of living conditions below certain standards is a burden on interstate commerce, and "interferes with the orderly marketing of goods."

For the year of October, 1938 to October, 1939, the act provided for minimum wages of 25 cents an hour and a 44-hour week; for 1940-1941, 30 cents an hour and a 42-hour week, and thereafter, 40 cents an hour and a 40-hour week, with time-and-a-half for overtime, or 60 cents an hour. The act caused an immediate loss of jobs to thousands of workers in small concerns which could not meet the new burden upon the payroll in addition to the payroll taxes imposed by the Social Security Act.

The National Labor Relations Act and the Wages and Hours Act are both given the semblance of being constitutional by limiting their application to workers engaged in "interstate commerce," as a means of removing burdens upon such commerce by preventing labor disputes, which they, in fact, have fostered. But this limitation of the acts has been rendered nugatory by the Roosevelt Supreme Court, in construing "interstate commerce" to include manufacturing as well as transportation. Thus, in the case of *Labor Board vs Fainblatt*, a women's clothing manufacturer, decided in October, 1939, the court said that an "employer is subject to the National Labor Relations Board although not himself engaged in commerce," and that the power of Congress over interstate commerce is one for "the protection of interstate commerce from interference due to activities which are wholly intrastate;" wherefore, all business activities in the States are brought under federal control.

In a vigorous dissenting opinion Mr. Justice McReynolds pointed out that the court had long held that manufacturing is not commerce but transformation; that buying and selling and transportation among the States constituted interstate commerce. By such attenuated reasoning, he said, the court "permits a disruption of the federal system." And then he added this remarkable indictment of the new court:

"The present decision and the reasoning offered to support it will inevitably intensify bewilderment. The resulting curtailment of the independence of the States and the tremendous enlargement of federal power denote the serious impairment of the very foundation of our federated system. Perhaps the change of direction, no longer capable of concealment, will give potency to the efforts of those who apparently hope to end a system of government found inhospitable to their ultimate designs."

And even where employers have signed contracts with local unions for a longer hour week at a flat rate, suits are now being instigated claiming enormous sums as "back pay" calculated on the hours worked beyond the 44 or 42 hours, as overtime with time-and-a-half-pay.

The fixing of wages and hours by government has always tended to create unemployment in enforcing new economies upon employers, thus creating an evil outweighing any benefits conferred. Its greatest evil, however, lies in denying to free men the right freely to make their own contracts of employment.

The Social Security Act comprehends ten separate programs for levying and distributing new taxes on industry and the workers, namely, old age and survivors insurance, unemployment pensions, aid to the blind, aid to mothers and children, maternal and child welfare, material and child health services, services to crippled children, child welfare services, public health services, vocational rehabilitation. These new taxes amounted to $631,223,715.09 in 1939, and to $703,400,000 in 1940.

The word "services" means the personal attention to mothers and children and others by a new army of federal agents specializing in various social, recreational and health fields, sent out into the States.

The old age and survivors insurance and the unemployment compensation plans are patterned after the social legislation devised by Bismarck between 1883 and 1889, in an attempt to allay socialist agitation in Germany, by partly meeting their demands. In the old age plan the employer and employee are taxed an equal percentage on the payroll and on the wage, respectively, starting at 1 percent and rising to 3 percent. These sums are remitted quarterly by the employer to the federal government, and, presumably, constitute a trust fund to be guarded for future application to pensions for those who reach 65 years of age or for payments at death. Actually, this trust fund of millions has been used largely to meet a part of the current deficit spending by the federal government.

The unemployment compensation plan levies a straight federal payroll tax of 3 percent on the employer, in addition to all other taxes. As a means of inducing the States to levy a like payroll tax on the employers for the same purpose, the act provides that any State setting up a Social Security Board which meets federal standards, will have its administrative expenses paid by the federal government. This means much more easy money and more patronage for the politicians of the States and has been readily adopted by all.

The act further provides that if a State has an employment tax law approved by the National Social Security Board, each employer may credit against his federal tax the taxes levied by the State for its unemployment fund up to 90 percent of the federal tax. These taxes must be paid whether the employer is making a profit or losing money. Meantime, the powers of the Federal Trade Commission to harass business with questionnaires and investigations, were expanded to include the field of advertising, and to suppress whatever it considered "unfair."

In 1938, in connection with the alleged "strike" of capital and his "spending for prosperity" campaign, President Roosevelt asked for $3,000,000,000; and, in further pursuit of his policy to discredit private enterprise, he requested an investigation of "concentrated economic power" and monopoly in the United States. Congress promptly constituted a body, known as the Temporary National Economic Committee, with twelve members: three of the Senate, three of the House, and six of the executive departments. The course of the investigation, largely guided by radical Roosevelt appointees from the departments, is showing deep interest in the billions of assets of the great insurance companies, invested as security for their millions of policy-holders. The report, which is yet to be made, can scarcely be anything but a further condemnation of the citizen in his right freely to labor and trade and pursue his own material well-being, known as the system of "free enterprise." Common prudence should prompt the citizen to manifest far greater alarm over "concentrated political power" than over concentrated economic power. The latter is plainly necessary in large assets for large undertakings: The former usually means their confiscation.

At the same time, through the taxing power and the billions of dollars borrowed and voted to the President for use in his discretion for "Relief," from which he distributed subsidies and pensions, he announced that he was seeking "the redistribution of wealth" to bring about "the more abundant life." Among these subsidies are those to farmers to effectuate crop control, amounting to about $1,000,000,000 a year.

All students know that these two aspects of Roosevelt's program — government control of industrial production and commerce and labor, and the exercise of the power to take from one and give to another — constitute the two main pillars of State Socialism. The common definition of Socialism or Social Democracy is:

"...a political and economic theory of social reorganization, the essential feature of which is governmental control of economic activities, to the end that competition shall give way to cooperation and that the opportunities of life and the rewards of labor shall be equitably apportioned."

Yet the President was probably not intentionally becoming the great American Socialist leader, however much his policies won for him the active support of Socialists and Communists. Having never been under the necessity of earning a living or paying a wage he had had no experience with the practical operation of our system of private economy and its cooperative demands. He was a theorist like all the professors and young college graduates with whom he surrounded himself.

In his attitude of hostility toward all successor business men, the psychologist would probably find it based upon the common vice of envy and a desire to exhibit what he conceived to be his own superiority, through his exercise of political power over them, however questionably obtained. That in arraying the mass of employees against their employers in the process, he was wrecking the best example of self-government ever built up by the free men, to satisfy his ambitions, was of no concern.

The Constitution provides in Article V the means of orderly change and to attempt it otherwise is a "high crime and misdemeanor" calling for impeachment. Yet Donald Richberg, a confidant of the President and later Administrator of the N.I.R.A., admitted that the Roosevelt program was of revolutionary character, when he said:

"In this favored nation of ours we are attempting possibly the greatest experiment in history. Revolution by the sword and bayonet is nothing new. Revolution by pen and voice is something different. The violent overthrow of parliaments and rulers is nothing new, but the peaceful transition of all departments of government from one fundamental concept of a politico-economic system to another is different."

But what Mr. Richberg lauded as a "peaceful transition" was, in fact, brought about by the greatest violence to the Constitution itself. In daring alone to bring about a new "politico-economic" system through legislation unauthorized by the Constitution, President Roosevelt destroyed the exclusive right of the people themselves to amend the Constitution in any manner they please, and transferred that power to himself. The amending power of the people is now useless, and in its place, new accession of power in the federal government will be made by the government itself by legislative construction, based upon precedents of usurpation which Mr. Roosevelt has established. This peaceable means for change in the fundamental law may now be said to be closed to the people, and we shall have no alternative in the future but that of other peoples for redress of grievances, namely, violence; and we, therefore, enter upon that "endless cycle of oppression, rebellion, reformation; oppression, rebellion, reformation again; and so on forever," which Thomas Jefferson affirmed was the only remaining choice if the avenue of orderly amendment were shut.

Thus step by step, Roosevelt seized power personally which, from the foundation of our government, had been judicially determined as forbidden to the federal government, and compounded the limited dual system into an unlimited unitary one. Flushed with his success he was bold enough to tell Congress, on January 3, 1934, that he had brought about "a permanent readjustment of many of our social and economic arrangements;" and, on January 4, 1935, that he had effected "a new order of things." And, in commenting on the "new order of things," he confessed his work of destroying our constitutional guarantee, with the justification pretended by every man who has overturned a free government, namely, the welfare of the people, saying:

"They (the people) realize that in 34 months we have built up new instruments of public power. In the hands of a people's government this power is wholesome and proper, but in the hands of political puppets of economic autocracy such power would provide shackles for the liberties of the people."

These "new instruments of public power" are, of course, the numerous new alphabetical boards and commissions, created under his "must" legislation and filled by his appointees as personal agents for his personal rule. Each agency is a petty tyranny in its own particular field, combining within itself the three essential powers of government: the legislative, the executive and the judicial; the power to make rules and regulations with the force of law, the power to enforce its own rules and regulations, and the power to inflict penalties for any failure of the citizen to comply with its decision, free from any right in the victim to obtain redress in the courts. This right is defeated by clauses in the acts creating the agencies, which though permitting appeal, deny to the courts the right to reverse a board decision if there is a scintilla of evidence to support its "findings of facts." As the boards dispatch their examiners charged with the duty of finding certain evidence in support of certain favored interests or policies, a wholly partial decision results which the courts may not disturb.

As the President views it, the United States is divided into two hostile camps engaged in a social and economic war. They are industry, or the employing class, and the worker, or employee class. The employing class, which provides wages for the employee and taxes to support the government, constitutes an "economic autocracy" that must be destroyed. And through the "new instruments of public power" the President has put "shackles" on its liberty, through various measures adopted by his administrative lieutenants to blacken its name, to prevent it from obtaining capital to expand and increase employment, and to prevent its normal functioning, while at the same time loading it down with new and crushing taxes.

The conviction is widely held, and with reason, that it is the deliberate purpose thus to make all private business unprofitable, as a prelude to its expropriation by government as the sole operator and employer, under the false plea that the system of free men in a free economy is no longer capable of sustaining the general welfare of the country. However fantastic this may seem, it has been publicly professed by some of the alien-minded and anti-American presidential lieutenants brought in to operate the "new instruments of public power."

The arbitrary, capricious and partial conduct of these new boards and the widespread complaints that have followed, induced the American Bar Association to propose a general statute, applicable to all administrative boards, restoring to the citizen his right of appeal to the courts with power to pass on the law and the facts, and to reverse any decision not based upon a preponderance of the evidence, and to set aside any rule or regulation found contrary to law or violating any constitutional rights of the complaining citizen.

Such a bill was sponsored by the late United States Senator Logan of Kentucky, and introduced in 1939. It was passed without a dissenting vote, but immediate pressure put upon the Senate compelled a hurried recall of the bill and its recommittal to the Judiciary Committee, where it has since remained.

However, the companion bill, exempting the interstate Commerce Commission, the Federal Trade Commission, the Federal Reserve Board and the federal lending agencies, came up for debate in the House in April, 1940, where congressional "yes-men" used every effort to cause its rejection, and predicted that the President would veto it, if it were passed. The President himself let it be known, at a press conference on April 5, that he opposed any interference with his new boards and commissions by the courts, nor did he wish the courts to pass on the legality of their decisions. It would slow up the machinery of government, he said. Yet the House was courageous enough to pass the bill on April 19, by a vote of 280 to 97, and send it on to the Senate for reconsideration.

If the independence of the courts had not been seriously compromised during the Roosevelt era through many appointments of judges who share the President's alien philosophy of government, the Logan bill would go a long way toward destroying one-man government and again making ours a government of laws. In the *Pottsville Broadcasting* case, decided by the Supreme Court in 1939, for example, we find the pedantic new Associate Justice Frankfurter saying:

"To assimilate the relations of these administrative bodies and the courts to the relationship of lower and upper courts is to disregard the origin and purposes of the movement for administrative regulation.... Unless these vital differentiations between the functions of judicial and administrative tribunals are observed, courts will stray outside their province and read the laws of Congress through the distorting lenses of inapplicable legal doctrine."

Why this was couched in such bewildering language, only Justice Frankfurter knows. He might have said in simple English for all to understand:

"It is no function of the courts to restrain administrative boards."

And that is the view of the President.

One contemporary historian, and only one, Mr. Mark Sullivan, appeared at the time to understand what was happening in Washington as the President's legislative program unfolded in the succession of bills he sent to Congress. In a dispatch to the New York *Herald Tribune*, he said:

"The country has not even a faint realization of what is taking place at Washington. By laws so numerous that even members of Congress do not follow them, so intricate that only close study can understand them, and in some cases carrying hidden meanings and unrevealed intentions on the part of the writers of the laws, there is being imposed upon our country not merely an enormous number of regulations attended by criminal penalties, but actually a new system, a whole new philosophy of society and government."

On May 27, 1935, the Supreme Court, in a unanimous decision, declared the National Industrial Recovery Act unconstitutional as an unwarranted attempt on the part of the federal government to reach into the States and control manufacturing and internal commerce, which were reserved to the States in the division of power by the Constitution. And it said particularly:

"If the commerce clause were construed to reach all enterprises and transactions which could be said to have an indirect effect upon interstate commerce, the federal authority would embrace practically all of the activities of the people and the authority of the State over its domestic concerns would exist only by inference of the federal government... It is not the province of the court to consider the economic advantages or disadvantages of such a centralized system. It is sufficient to say that the federal Constitution does not provide for it."

This decision merely confirmed a long line of decisions declaring that the constitutional power of Congress to regulate interstate commerce became operative when an object of interstate commerce began to move in interstate transportation and ceased when the object came to rest at the end of its journey. As Woodrow Wilson had affirmed in his Columbia University lectures in 1907:

"If the federal power (to regulate interstate commerce) does not end with the regulation of the actual movements of trade, it ends nowhere, and the line between State and federal jurisdiction is obliterated."

President Roosevelt was so deeply wounded in his vanity by the decision holding the act unconstitutional that he devoted more than an hour on the radio in a harangue to the people, in further disparagement of the Supreme Court.

On May 18, 1936, the Guffey Coal Act was declared unconstitutional on the same ground, that mining was also a subject that was exclusively within the reserved powers of the States to regulate, if they wished. But the second decision revealed a division of 5 to 3 in the Court, Justices Cardoza, Brandeis, and Stone, upholding the Roosevelt measure. And on June 6, 1936, the Agricultural Adjustment Act was also declared void as an attempted usurpation of the reserved powers of the States. Again Justices Cardoza, Brandeis and Stone dissented. The coup d'etat appeared to have been defeated.

On the eve of his reelection in 1936, in a campaign radio address to the nation, the President revealed a defiant impatience with those leaders of private industry who had sought a remedy in the Courts against his new and arbitrary power over them, in a multiplicity of suits, and had finally frustrated him in the Supreme Court. He wantonly stigmatized these citizens as "economic royalists." They had "met their match" in the last four years, he declared, and, in the next four years they would "meet their master."

To one of President Roosevelt's ambition and purpose, his reelection in 1936 by the great majority of 27,476,673 to 16,679,583, constituted a "popular mandate," or a ratification of his setting aside the old limited constitutional order and his inauguration of an unlimited unitary system in its place. In taking the oath of office for his second term, on the main portico of the capitol, his head bared in the rain, he "reconsecrated" his government to leadership of "the American people forward along the road over which they have chosen to advance." And history afforded him what seemed to be a supporting precedent for popular ratification of unconstitutional executive acts, which his young personal advisers had no doubt called to his attention. It was in 1848, on the formation of the Republic of France, that Louis Napoleon was elected constitutional President for a term of four years, and by the Constitution, he was ineligible to reelection. As the end of his term approached in 1851, he dismissed the National Assembly, announced the end of the Republic and inauguration of the Second Empire, with himself as Emperor, which the people of France ratified at an election on December 20 and 21, in voting away their liberties, 7,437,216 to 640,737.

But a persisting majority of "Nine Old Men" of the Supreme Court would ignore the "popular mandate" as a mere fiction and would confirm no change in the government brought about other than by the orderly process prescribed in the Constitution itself. How to overcome this obstacle was the problem of the moment. Another precedent, this time from English history, was available as the solution. It was in the reign of James II, likewise distinguished for a persistent effort to overturn the English constitution. Although James' predecessor, Charles II, had taken an oath in 1672, to abide by the laws concerning the dispensing power (laws forbidding appointment of Catholics to office), James was determined to name Catholics not only to civil and military, but even to spiritual, offices. In 1686, as a first attempt to release himself from the law, he sought an opinion from the courts of common law that he possessed the power to appoint Catholics "in particular cases," and he summoned the judges before him.

As Macaulay relates, four of the judges demurred. Jones, the Chief Justice of Common Pleas, "a man who had never before shrunk from any drudgery, however cruel and servile," now held in the royal closet language which might have become the lips of the purest magistrates in our history. He was plainly told that he must give up his opinion or his place.

"For my place," he answered, "I care little. I am old and worn out in the services of the Crown; but I am mortified to find that your Majesty thinks me capable of giving a judgment which none but an ignorant or a dishonest man can give."

"I am determined," said the King, "to have twelve judges who will be all of my mind as to this matter."

"Your Majesty," answered Jones, "may find twelve judges of your mind but hardly twelve lawyers."

Jones was dismissed from office, as were Montague, Chief Baron of the Exchequer, and Judges Neville and Charlton, and the court was packed, one of the new judges being Christopher Milton, younger brother of the great poet. The King also dismissed his Solicitor General Finch and his Attorney General Sawyer, who equally refused to endorse his course.

Thomas Powis, "an obscure barrister," was appointed Solicitor General to succeed Finch, and undertook to argue for the dispensing power before the packed court, with mock parties at interest. By a decision of eleven to one, the King's power to appoint Catholics "in particular cases," was affirmed. The one dissenting judge is stated to have acted collusively, to give some semblance of independence in the court. James lost his throne and fled to France within the same year that records this perfidy to the courts and constitution of England.

But President Roosevelt's Attorney General Cummings was more loyal than King James; Attorney General Sawyer. He not only drew the bill to pack the Supreme Court with the addition of six new partisan Justices, but appeared before the Senate Judiciary Committee on March 10, 1937, to defend it as necessary, on the ground that the Court was overburdened with work, an argument which the Chief Justice himself proved false in a letter to the Chairman of the Senate Committee a few days later.

To the President's surprise, something of a rebellion swept the country against "the forward movement" along the road he assumed "the people had chosen to advance," and Congress failed him. Almost immediately following this failure, however, fate played into the President's hands and success came to him through enough vacancies, caused by death and resignation, to give him a majority of the Court through new appointments.

Practically every one of President Roosevelt's laws that was declared unconstitutional by the Supreme Court that he found on taking office in 1932, has been resubmitted and passed by a continuing docile Congress, with a mere change of form or name. And all that have been challenged by citizens and reached the newly-reconstituted Court have been pronounced constitutional. As the result of these recent decisions, the President, through his nominees and administrators, may be said now to control local industry, manufacturing, retail distribution, mining, planting and growing crops, prices and wages, and hours of labor, throughout the country. The *coup d'etat* against the States and against the limited constitutional system is finally judicially confirmed, with a minority of two, the valiant survivors of the "Nine Old Men," still holding their ground and dissenting. It is implicit in some of the new Court's decisions, also, that the federal government may apply the public money of the taxpayer to any purpose, public or private, foreign or domestic, it sees fit. The President seems to have made certain that the Constitution may no longer be successfully invoked to limit the unrestrained exercise of national power for the full domestic development of Social Democracy, as the new philosophy of our society and government.

No lawyer can today advise his client with any assurance as to the continuing validity of any principle of constitutional law, and he is even more at sea as to that immense and vague volume enacted, not by Congress, but by administrative boards, with which his main practice is now concerned. Until Congress passed the Federal Register Act in 1938, to compile all of these rules and regulations as a code of "administrative law," much of it was unpublished and secret and withheld from both lawyer and client. In April, 1940, this code was published, embracing all rules and regulations that had legal effect on June 1, 1938. And it consisted of seventeen volumes, each containing between 1000 and 1200 pages.

This same confusion that exists in our system of internal law has been introduced by President Roosevelt into our foreign policies. Until the Roosevelt era the United States had pursued with safety and credit the foreign policies laid down by Washington, Jefferson, Monroe and all of their successors, up to Woodrow Wilson. The two principal ones were (1) "minding our own business," expressed technically as non-intervention in the affairs of other nations, and (2) forbidding European interference in American political affairs. They embraced cultivating impartially peace, commerce and honest friendship with all nations and avoiding entangling alliances. There was a third policy of constant striving for the progressive improvement and clarification of the principles of international law in the promotion of peaceable processes in the settlement of international disputes.

The new Roosevelt foreign policies appear to repudiate all of the foregoing. In the place of non-intervention in the affairs of other nations he has adopted the policy of direct interference, even to the point of lending large sums of money to particular favored nations as belligerents, as in the case of China and Finland.

There is nowhere to be found in the Constitution any authority under which the President may lend the money of American taxpayers in gambling upon favorites in foreign wars, but that is what this particular Roosevelt policy consists of. And in the close financial understanding of the Roosevelt administration with Great Britain and France, and in the cooperation that is lent to sustain their financial structures, there exists what is, in fact, a financial alliance that may logically develop into military cooperation when they again call for help, as they did with their "backs to the wall" in 1917. And let it not be forgotten that this is what Great Britain and France confidently calculated upon in their new war against the old enemy.

Instead of pursuing the policy of impartially cultivating peace, commerce and honest friendship with all nations, he and certain heads of his departments have blatantly cultivated enmity in publicly making invidious distinctions between the "totalitarian governments" and the "Democracies." In the place of seeking to promote the progress of law he has placed his reliance upon force in the ordering of international affairs. Such a policy of constant war as a means of promoting peace, was enunciated by President Roosevelt in a radio address to the nation from Chicago, on October 5, 1937, when he said:

"The peace-loving nations must make a concerted effort in opposition to those violations of treaties and those ignorings of humane instincts which are today creating a state of international anarchy and instability from which there is no escape through mere isolation and neutrality.... There must be positive endeavors to preserve peace."

Then the President proposed the "quarantine" of "international lawlessness" by concerted action, presumably through boycotts and embargoes on our commerce with "lawless" nations. The President actually lent himself to the solicitation of Great Britain to inject the United States into the Italian war in Ethiopia in 1935, by embargoing the shipment of oil to Italy. This was such unneutral conduct as to amount to an act of war, but it exemplifies one of the President's new foreign policies.

At the time of the enunciation of President Roosevelt's policy of universal interference in the broils of others, the Brussels Conference was in session to see what could be done to stop Japanese military action in China. All of the delegations of the other governments represented urged the United States "to take the lead," but the popular reaction to the President's Chicago address admonished him that the people would not support him in a war with Japan, and the United States delegation was not committed.

In his report to the House of Commons on December 20, 1937, Prime Minister Chamberlain said that the Brussels Conference proved that "There was only one way the (Sino-Japanese) conflict could be brought to an end — that is, not by peace, but by force," that is to say, by war. Mr. Chamberlain added that while the Brussels Conference was disappointing "to all friends of peace," presumably because the United States would not "take the lead" in war against Japan, there was one satisfactory feature — "throughout the Conference we found ourselves in complete and harmonious agreement with the delegation of the United States in all matters discussed." And this "complete and harmonious agreement" between the

Roosevelt and British policies appears to have continued unbroken, with no public revelation of how far we are involved. It would logically include coming to the aid of the "Democracies," if considered necessary, and thus again "making the world safe" for them.

The prudent and enlightened doctrine of Neutrality, developed largely from our own contributions toward the growth of law, is one of passing no judgment and playing no favorites in the wars of others, while insisting upon our rights. This policy has been scrapped by the President, in favor of a new one of taking sides in all wars, because, as he told Congress in his message in January, 1939:

"We have learned that when we deliberately try to legislate neutrality, our neutrality laws may operate unevenly and unfairly — may actually give aid to an aggressor and deny it to his victim. The instinct of self-preservation should warn us that we ought not to let that happen again."

This statement embodies a policy having no relation to any principle of law, but rather scuttles law for an unrestrained course of whim and caprice. The President states unequivocally that he wishes the power to pass judgment upon the justice of all future wars, and to discriminate against the belligerent he doesn't like, whom he calls the "aggressor," in favor of the one he does like, whom he calls the "victim." That is a simple policy of international meddling. Under the universally accepted principles of international law, no neutral State may adjust its attitude of conduct toward either belligerent in any war by any idea it may have of the merits of the controversy, except by frankly and honestly becoming an ally of the one it favors. To play favorites without becoming a co-belligerent is dishonest as well as unlawful, for which the law itself provides both hostile and peaceable remedies. The belligerent thus discriminated against may declare such unneutral conduct an act of war and treat the neutral State accordingly, or it may rightfully claim pecuniary damages, which only a lawless nation could refuse to entertain. We ourselves established this principle of pecuniary liability for unneutral conduct in international law, and, in 1871, in the *Alabama* claims, collected $15,500,000 in damages from Great Britain for her acts of favoritism to the Confederacy during the Civil War.

It is one of the distinctive glories of our past that, as a young and weak nation, we dated to challenge the might of England's naval power in defense of the rights of all neutral nations to pursue their peaceful commerce on the high seas, which, from the time of Grotius, were recognized by all but England as the common property of all nations and free for the common use and enjoyment of all. And out of our courageous support of this principle came the doctrine of "the freedom of the seas," finally recognized even by Great Britain, in the great law-making treaties, The Hague Conventions of 1899 and 1907. The persistent violations of the principle by Great Britain and Germany in 1914-1918 met with constant protest from our government until we became a co-belligerent and condoned them as a temporary beneficiary of the lawless blockade against the German people.

In the present war renewed violations of "the freedom of the seas" by Great Britain are not only not protested against but under the new Roosevelt policy, the principle is abandoned altogether, and our ships are forbidden to assert it in any seas which Great Britain may unlawfully close. Meantime the government has also supinely submitted to the seizure of our neutral mails, which were declared in The Hague Convention of 1907 to be "inviolable."

In the new Roosevelt policy of "concerted" action, with two or three other great powers to enforce our ideas of international justice — always colored by self-interest — the whole idea of the progressive development of a system of international law for the rule of a Society of Nations, large and small but legally equal before it, is destroyed. Yet this is the goal toward which all enlightened modern statesmen have striven, with our earnest participation, as giving the only promise of an ultimate international order of peace with justice.

As the rule of law has been displaced by the rule of force and caprice in our national system, so the new reliance in international policy is not upon law but upon superior force. It is a policy which will plant millions of new little white crosses over the graves of young Americans throughout Europe and the Orient in the days ahead.

The usurpations of power the President has practiced have become precedents, upon which new precedents will be built for new usurpations. That is the natural method of expansion of power in all governments. It is possible for some heroic figure, like Kleisthenes, to arise and create in the people and force upon leading politicians "that rare and difficult sentiment which we may term 'a constitutional morality,'" as Grote relates of a period of regeneration of the subsidized and demoralized Athenians. But the complaisance of our people toward governmental usurpations setting aside their most cherished rights and contributing to their moral degradation, leaves one wondering whether they are longer capable of that righteous wrath toward representatives who have betrayed them, out of which might come their deliverance. Then, too, there are interested classes of millions of beneficiaries of the sinister policy of attaching great masses of voters through financial dependence upon the public treasury.

The form of constitutional government remains; its substance has all but disappeared. While the violation of law does not repeal law, a series of violations of a constitution of government, premeditated and lasting over a period of seven years, and submitted to, if not acquiesced in by other departments of government and by a large part of the people, is, in fact, a form of repeal which will be more dearly seen when it becomes complete.

So, too, the States, once self-governing and autonomous in a limited federal dual system, remain in name. But they are fast being reduced to mere geographical divisions under the guidance and direction of thousands of agents sent out by the central authority.

The Republic of Germany was a short-lived experiment among a people not practiced in recent centuries in self-government. It might have changed in time by the choice of its people to an authoritarian form. But it can be said of the Republic of the United States of America, that it lasted longer than any other republic ever set up; that its basic principles of the sovereignty and indefeasible rights of the citizen against government, leaving his energies free, made possible the development of a higher degree of comfort and happiness and virtue in its people than anywhere before found on the earth, and that, like a star falling into the immensity of time, it will be recorded as the most luminous attempt ever made by man to govern himself without an overlord.

In the centralization of unrestrained power over the citizen in the President, the most cherished principle of Anglo-American liberty we once enjoyed, that man may freely labor and trade and acquire and be protected in the fruits of his labor, has, of course, vanished. This principle of limitation upon royal power, came into being for the first time in the world's history in the Charter of Liberties of Henry I in 1100, and was reaffirmed in a like charter of Henry II in 1154. In 1215 it was embodied in Chapter 39 of Magna Charta, extorted from King John at Runnymede in these words: "No freeman shall be taken or imprisoned or be disseised of his freehold or of his liberties or his free customs or be outlawed or exiled or otherwise destroyed but by lawful judgment of his peers or by the law of the land." And to maintain these rights Englishmen were compelled to force thirty-two written reconfirmations of them by six of their arbitrary Kings before they became fixed in their fundamental law. Many may think that rights protected by law are a free gift from Heaven; actually they can be won and preserved only by manly and constant resistance to the natural aggressive tendency of all government at all times to suppress them. The only means thus far known to political science for a reconciliation of liberty with government lie in the imposition of restraints upon governmental power, embodies in written constitutions, with an alert citizenry watchful to repel encroachments. Writing of the limitations imposed upon the powers of our federal government in the new Constitution, when commending it to the people of the States for ratification in 1788, James Madison said:

> It may be a reflection on human nature, that such devices should be necessary to control the abuses of government. But what is government itself, but the greatest of all reflections on human nature. If men were angels, no government would be necessary.
>
> In framing a government which is to be administered by men over men, the great difficulty lies in this: you must first enable the government to control the governed; and in the next place oblige it to control itself.

The expansive English guarantee, found in Chapter 39 of Magna Charta, was transplanted in our federal Constitution in Amendments V and XIV and in the constitution of every State in the Union. It appears in the phraseology, "no person shall be deprived of life, liberty or property without due process of law," the term "due process of law" being the equivalent of "the law of the land." Generally, due process of law is defined as a pledge of individual rights and liberties, designed to secure to every person those fundamental and inalienable rights of life, liberty and property, inherent in every man, against the invading power of government. But the guarantee is also found in our State constitutions, in some such language as is used in that of Missouri: "That all persons have a natural right to life, liberty and the enjoyment of the gains of their own industry; that to give security to these things is the principal office of government, and that when government does not confer this security it fails of its chief design."

Mr. Justice Matthews of the Supreme Court, said of the term "due process of law," that it is one of those grand monuments, showing the victorious progress of the race in securing to men the blessings of civilization under the reign of just and equal laws, so that, in the famous language of the Massachusetts Bill of Rights, the Commonwealth "may be a government of laws and not of men." The phrase embraces innumerable protective principles, not the least important of which is the citizen's right of access to his independent courts at all times to defeat any arbitrary action of government or its officials.

The apparent conflict between this vital right to life, liberty and property, and the necessary power of the government to tax, was reconciled in that other great complementary Anglo-Saxon principle, that taxes may be levied but the proceeds must be applied, not to private or class interests, but to public purposes only, which also disappeared in the Roosevelt *coup d'etat*.

The historic position of our once-free system, as to the citizen's immunity against spoliation by government, may be illustrated in a concrete and pertinent case arising in a United States District Court in 1891, in which *Richard V. Sauer of Uvalde County, Texas*, a German immigrant, sought naturalization as an American citizen. On being interrogated by Judge Paschal, he stated that he was a Socialist, and that he favored the taking of land from all who owned more than 200 acres, and its distribution among those who had none.

"Thereupon," reported Judge Paschal, "I stated that, in the judgment of the court the principles of Socialism are directly at war with and antagonistically to the principles of the Constitution of the United States of America, and absolutely inconsistent with his being 'well disposed to the good order and happiness of the people and government of the United States.'"

"I further explained to him that private property could not, under the Constitution, be taken by the government for private use, and that this was a fundamental principle of the government and one of the most sacred and guarded rights of the citizen. He repelled the suggestions with derision and scorn."

And Sauer was denied citizenship.

A full discussion of what has been legislatively superimposed upon our unique system of free government in "economic" control, by all of the new federal corporations, commissions, boards, bureaus, and other administrative agencies created or reformed, would require volumes, but an outstanding interpretative symbol, or germ plasm, in the field of "social readjustment," is to be found in a single bureau, the history of which will illuminate what has happened in the social aspect of "the new order of things." And that symbol is the innocent-sounding and appealingly-named feminist instrumentality, located in the Department of Labor, and known as the Children's Bureau. The "new order" is, in fact, the fulfillment and triumph of the socialistic aims pursued with unceasing tenacity and intelligence by this Children's Bureau since the day of its creation by Congress in 1912.

The preceding essay was extracted from Sterling E. Edmunds, The Roosevelt Coup d'Etat of 1933-40: The History of the Most Successful Experiment Ever Made by Man to Govern Himself Without a Master *(Boise, Idaho: Gospel Ministries, [1940] 1995).*

CHAPTER TWENTY-TWO
The Nature of the Federal Reserve System

The Establishment of a Central Bank in America

It has been said that, "In politics, nothing happens by accident. If it happens, you can bet it was planned that way." In the preceding chapter, we have seen *what* happened during the banking emergency of the early 1930s; we will now take a look at *how* and *why* it happened. To do this, we will need to first go back in time to the late 1700s.

As discussed in Chapter One, the Federalist faction present at the Philadelphia Convention was led by Alexander Hamilton, who advocated not only a strong, centralized government, but also a large public debt. In fact, he suggested that "a national debt, if it is not excessive, will be to us a national blessing" and that "it will be a powerful cement to our nation."[1] It was also Hamilton's opinion that "no plan could succeed which does not unite the interest and credit of rich individuals with that of the state."[2] Necessary to the contracting of this debt was a central banking system of which Hamilton was the chief proponent.

In stark contrast to the Hamiltonian economic school was the Jeffersonian, which was wholly opposed to a central bank and an extended, multi-generational debt. In the words of Thomas Jefferson, who was Secretary of State under the Washington Administration:

It is a wise ruler never to borrow a dollar without laying a tax at the same instant

---

1. Alexander Hamilton, letter to Robert Morris, 30 April 1781; in Harold C. Syrett (editor), *The Papers of Alexander Hamilton* (New York: Columbia University Press, 1961), Volume II, page 635.

2. Hamilton, quoted by Arthur M. Schlesinger, Jr., *The Age of Jackson* (New York: Mentor Books, 1945), pages 6-7; Wilfred E. Binkley, *American Political Parties* (New York: Alfred A. Knopf, 1943), page 40.

for paying the interest and the principal within a given term.... The earth belongs to the living, not the dead.... We may consider each generation as a distinct nation, with a right to... bind themselves, but not the succeeding generations....

The modern theory of the perpetuation of debt has drenched the earth with blood, and crushed its inhabitants under burdens ever accumulating....

We shall consider ourselves unauthorized to saddle posterity with our debts, and morally bound to pay them ourselves.[3]

Jefferson pointed out that Congress had not been delegated the authority by the Constitution to create a central bank, and that the ability to establish a bank was therefore reserved by the States under the Tenth Amendment. He insisted that the de-centralization of public credit was as essential to the well-being of the Union as was the de-centralization of political power. He also said, "A private central bank issuing the public currency is a greater threat to the liberties of the people than a standing army."[4] Jefferson perceived Article I, Section 8, Clause 2 of the Constitution to be pregnant with grave danger for the country and therefore advocated a constitutional amendment "taking from the federal government their power of borrowing."[5]

By 1791, the Hamiltonian school had prevailed against the Jeffersonian school and the Bank of the United States, designed by Hamilton himself, was granted a twenty-year charter by Congress. The Bank had a monopoly in the issuance of notes, which could be used to pay taxes and duties to the Government. The Bank's charter required that these notes be redeemable in gold or silver (specie), but at the same time, it was not required to back 100 percent of its notes with specie — a fractional reserve loophole which would eventually lead to an inflation of the currency. The cause and nature of inflation will be explained in greater detail later in this chapter.

The Bank charter also provided that 80 percent of its capital would be held by private investors, with the Government contributing only 20 percent. However, this investment could be immediately loaned back to the Government at six percent interest. Furthermore, as noted by John Kenneth Galbraith, "Foreigners could own shares but not vote them."[6] This seemingly innocent provision opened the door to complete foreign ownership over time of the

---

3. Thomas Jefferson, in Andrew Lipscomb and Albert Ellery Bergh (editors), *The Writings of Thomas Jefferson* (Washington, D.C.: Jefferson Memorial Association, 1903), Volume XIII, pages 269, 270, 272, 358.

4. Jefferson, in Paul Leicester Ford (editor), *The Writings of Thomas Jefferson* (New York: G.P. Putnam and Sons, 1899), Volume X, page 31.

5. Jefferson, letter to John Taylor, 26 November 1798; in Lipscomb and Bergh, *Writings of Thomas Jefferson*, Volume X, page 64.

6. John Kenneth Galbraith, *Money: Whence It Came, Where It Went* (Boston: Houghton Mifflin Company, 1975), page 72.

institution through which the Government was to receive a large portion of its revenue. According to Gustavus Myers, "Under the surface, the Rothschilds have long had a powerful influence in dictating American financial laws. The law records show that they were powers in the old Bank of the United States."[7] The Rothschild family would play a key role in a major event in American history seventy years later.

The Bank, of course, proved to be a disaster, just as Jefferson had predicted. With the creation of millions of unbacked notes, prices rose over 70 percent in just five years. Public dissatisfaction with the Bank rose steadily and when its charter was up for renewal in 1811, the measure was defeated by only one vote in each House of Congress. On 24 January 1811, the first Bank of the United States closed its doors and banking in America passed back exclusively to the several States. However, with the resulting financial chaos of the second war with Great Britain in 1812, it was not long before a second central bank was proposed. In 1816, a twenty-year charter was granted by Congress to the Second Bank of the United States, which was nearly identical to the first. As with the first, a substantial amount of the stock in this second bank was provided by foreign investors — in the beginning, a full one-third.[8] Immediately, the money supply was expanded over $27 million in unbacked paper currency and prices again began to rise to dizzying heights:

> Starting in July 1818, the government and the BUS began to see what dire straits they were in; the enormous inflation of money and credit, aggravated by the massive fraud, had put the BUS in danger of going under and illegally failing to maintain specie payments. Over the next year, the BUS began a series of enormous contractions, forced curtailment of loans, contractions of credit in the south and west.... The contraction of money and credit swiftly brought to the United States its first widespread economic and financial depression. The first nationwide "boom-bust" cycle had arrived in the United States....
>
> The result of this contraction was a rash of defaults, bankruptcies of business and manufacturers, and a liquidation of unsound investments during the boom.[9]

Andrew Jackson's Opposition to the Bank

The most formidable foe with whom the Second Bank of the United States had to contend was Andrew Jackson, who was elected President in 1828 on a strong anti-central bank Democratic platform. When Congress attempted to pass a bill granting the Bank an

---

7. Gustavus Myers, *History of the Great American Fortunes* (New York: Random House, 1936), page 556.

8. Herman E. Krooss (editor), *Documentary History of Banking and Currency in the United States* (New York: Chelsea House, 1983), Volume III, page 25.

9. Murry N. Rothbard, *The Mystery of Banking* (New York: Richardson and Snyder, 1983), pages 204-205.

early renewal of its charter on 4 July 1832, Jackson promptly vetoed the bill with these words: "It is not our own citizens only who are to receive the bounty of our Government. More than eight millions of the stock of this bank are held by foreigners. By this act the American Republic proposes virtually to make them a present of some millions of dollars.... It appears that more than a fourth part of the stock is held by foreigners and the residue is held by a few hundred of our own citizens, chiefly of the richest class."[10] Foreign ownership meant foreign intrigue and interference in American affairs, said Jackson:

> Is there no danger to our liberty and independence in a bank that in its nature has so little to bind it to our country?... [Is there no] cause to tremble for the purity of our elections in peace and for the independence of our country in war?... The course which would be pursued by a bank almost wholly owned by the subjects of a foreign power, and managed by those whose interests, if not affections, would run in the same direction there can be no doubt.... Controlling our currency, receiving our public monies, and holding thousands of our citizens in dependence, it would be more formidable and dangerous than a naval and military power of the enemy.[11]

Jackson also argued, as did Jefferson before him, that the centralization of credit led directly to the centralization of political power, which was contrary to both the spirit and letter of the Constitution.

When Jackson was re-elected in 1832, four years remained to the Bank's charter. However, Jackson declared full-scale war against it by ordering the removal of most of the Government's deposits from the Bank and their diffusion throughout various State banks. The Government's expenses were then paid from the remaining deposits until they too were depleted. "You are a den of vipers," Jackson accused the Bank's supporters. "I intend to rout you out and by the Eternal God I will rout you out."[12] It was not long before Jackson had paid off the debt incurred by the War of 1812, and for the first time in its history — unfortunately also the *last* time — the federal Government was nearly debt-free[13] with a surplus in the Treasury of over $37 million, which was to be distributed back to the States in four quarterly payments beginning on 1 January 1837.[14] Not surprisingly, Jackson was the victim of an

---

10. Andrew Jackson, veto of the Bank of the United States bill, 10 July 1832; in Richardson, *Messages and Papers of the Presidents*, Volume II, page 577.

11. Jackson, in Richardson, *ibid.*, page 581.

12. Jackson, quoted by Herman J. Viola, *Andrew Jackson* (New York: Chelsea House, 1986), page 86.

13. The total national debt in 1835 was $351,289 and $291,089 the following year (McHenry, *Cotton Trade*, page 174).

14. The fourth installment of this sum was never distributed due to the financial panic of 1837, which sent the federal Government spiraling back into debt. By the end of the year, the national debt

assassination attempt on the steps of the Capitol on 30 January 1835. Richard Lawrence, the would-be assassin whose two pistols both misfired, admitted privately to friends years later that he had been hired and promised protection by certain unnamed European persons.[15]

The Bank's charter expired in 1836 and was not renewed. Thus, the old Jeffersonian school finally defeated the Hamiltonian, and the central banking system in the United States was committed to the grave, where it remained until it was resurrected a quarter of a century later by the Lincoln Administration.

"A First Mortgage Upon the Property of the United States"

As mentioned before, the U.S. Treasury was officially bankrupt when war erupted between the North and South in 1861. In addition, the year prior to the outbreak of the war saw the expenses of the federal Government at $67 million. In only twelve months, this figure had risen to $475 million, and by the end of the war, to $1.3 billion. It was estimated that the war was costing the Government an astronomical $2 million a day and by its end, the annual deficit had risen to $2.6 billion. Having no central bank with the ability to print currency, Abraham Lincoln had nowhere to turn to finance his crusade against Southern secession. Lincoln authorized his Secretary of the Treasury to borrow money from private financiers at rates as high as 19 percent per year, but as these sources grew more and more costly, Lincoln finally turned to the printing of fiat currency himself — United States Bank Notes — to make up the shortfall. His rationale was as follows:

> Government, possessing power to create and issue currency and credit as money and enjoying the right to withdraw currency and credit from circulation by taxation and otherwise, need not and should not borrow capital at interest as a means of financing government work and public enterprise. The government should create, issue, and circulate all the currency and credit needed to satisfy the spending power of the government and the buying power of consumers. The privilege of creating and issuing money is not only the supreme prerogative of government, but it is the government's greatest creative opportunity.[16]

Lincoln's assertions were clearly contradicted by the plain wording of Article 1,

---

had risen to $1.8 million, to $4.8 million the following year, and nearly $12 million the next. With the exception of the years 1840 and 1841, the national debt would never again be less than $15 million, and by the outbreak of the war between the States in 1861, it had skyrocketed to over $334 million (McHenry, *ibid.*, pages 174, 183).

15. Robert J. Donovan, *The Assassins* (New York: Harper and Brothers, 1952), page 83.

16. Lincoln, quoted by Robert L. Owen, *National Economy and the Banking System* (Washington, D.C.: U.S. Government Printing Office, 1939), page 91.

Section 8, Clause 4 of the Constitution, but as with other constitutional prohibitions, he saw this one as optional in times of "national emergency." Initially, $150 million worth of these "greenbacks" were issued, but by the end of the war, over $430 million were in circulation. Unlike those of the First and Second Banks of the United States which had to be borrowed by the Government before they were considered to be money, Lincoln's notes were declared "legal tender for all debts, public and private" by the Act of Congress of 25 February 1862. This Act was amended on the eleventh of June of that same year, adding the phrase "except duties on imports and interest on the public debt, which from that time forward should be paid in coin." While it was a "Federal offense" punishable by imprisonment for private citizens to refuse to accept payment in greenbacks, the Government itself collected revenue from the people in gold. That same year, the Bureau of Internal Revenue was also created to collect a new income tax, which was also payable in gold. Later, the Credit Strengthening Act was passed by the Fortieth Congress and signed into law by President Ulysses S. Grant on 18 March 1869. This law required all Government obligations to banking institutions to be paid in gold, while its obligations to private individuals were to be paid in currency. Thus can be seen a subtle scheme to confiscate the gold from the Northern people which pre-dated a similar scheme instituted by Roosevelt seven decades later.

There were those individuals, however, who were not pleased with Lincoln's issuance of greenbacks. A memorandum entitled *The Hazard Circular*, which was distributed throughout the business world of New England in 1862, stated the complaint as follows:

> Slavery is likely to be abolished by the war power and chattel slavery destroyed. This I and my European friends are in favor of; for slavery is but the owning of labor and carries with it the care of the laborer, while the European plan, led on by England, is capital control of labor by controlling wages. This can be done by controlling the money. The great debt that capitalists will see to it is made out of the war must be used as a means to control the volume of money. To accomplish this the bonds must be used as a banking basis. We are now waiting for the Secretary of the Treasury to make this recommendation to Congress. It will not do to allow the greenback, as it is called, to circulate as money any length of time, as we cannot control that. But we can control the bonds and through them the bank issues.[17]

In Chapter Eleven, the plan proposed by a New England financier to replenish the depleted Treasury was briefly discussed. After some coaxing from Lincoln, Secretary of the Treasury Salmon P. Chase reworked the proposal and presented it to Congress. The National Banking Act was thereafter passed into law on 25 February 1863. Basically, the Government would issue Coupon Treasury Notes, which drew 7.5 percent semi-annual interest payments, and were convertible after three years into six percent 5-20 and 10-40 gold-bearing bonds.

---

17. *The Hazard Circular*, quoted by Charles A. Lindburgh, *Banking and Currency and the Money Trust* (Washington, D.C.: National Capital Press, 1913), page 102.

These bonds were funded by pledging the property and future labor of the American people as security, and thus were admitted to be "a first mortgage upon the property of the United States."[18] In addition, they were exempted from taxation.

In tandem with the issuance of bonds, the de-centralized banks of the several States in the North were consolidated into a national system and were given the ability to issue bank notes, backed 90 percent with these bonds with only a 10 percent specie reserve requirement. Thus, the banks were offered the opportunity to collect double interest — first, on the purchased bonds *and* second, on the issued currency. As would be expected, there was a mad scramble to purchase the Government's bonds and there was the appearance of sudden prosperity in the North. In reality, this prosperity was a thin covering of a massive public debt which could never be paid off, "because to do so meant there would be no bonds to back the national bank notes. To pay off the debt was to destroy the money supply."[19] The Hamiltonian school of economics had once again triumphed over the Jeffersonian, and being embroiled in a full-scale sectional war, the people were in no position to complain.

Just as was the case with both incarnations of the Bank of the United States, one of the principal investors in this new banking system was the Rothschild family of Europe. The following letter was sent from the Rothschild investment house located in London to a banking firm in New York City:

Rothschild Brothers, Bankers,
London, June 25th, 1863

Messrs. Ikleheimer, Morton, and Vandergould,
No. 3 Wall St.,
New York, U.S.A.

Dear Sir:

A Mr. John Sherman has written us from a town in Ohio, U.S.A., as to the profits that may be made in the National Banking business under a recent act of your Congress, a copy of which act accompanied his letter. Apparently this act has been drawn upon the plan formulated here last summer by the British Bankers Association and by the Association recommended to our American friends as one that if enacted into law, would prove highly profitable to the banking fraternity throughout the world.

Mr. Sherman declares that there has never been such an opportunity for capitalists to accumulate money, as that presented by this act, and that the old plan of State Banks is so unpopular, that the new scheme will, by contrast, be most favorably regarded, notwithstanding the fact that it gives the National Banks an almost absolute control of the National finance. "The few who can understand the system," he says, "Will either be so interested

---

18. Dean, *Crimes of the Civil War*, page 230.

19. Galbraith, *Money: Whence It Came*, page 90.

in its profits, or so dependent of its favors that there will be no opposition from that class, while on the other hand, the great body of people, mentally incapable of comprehending the tremendous advantages that capital derives from the system, will bear its burdens without complaint and perhaps without even suspecting that the system is inimical to their interest."

Please advise fully as to this matter and also state whether or not you will be of assistance to us, if we conclude to establish a National Bank in the City of New York. If you are acquainted with Mr. Sherman we will be glad to know something of him. If we avail ourselves of the information he furnished, we will, of course, make due compensation.

Awaiting your reply, we are
Your respectful servants,
Rothschild Brothers.[20]

The John Sherman mentioned in this letter was a Republican Senator from Ohio who was largely responsible for pushing the national bank scheme and the later Fourteenth Amendment through the Senate. It was Sherman's belief that America should "nationalize as much as possible" and that "all private interests, all local interests, all banking interests, the interests of individuals, everything, should be subordinate now to the interest of the Government."[21] He was also the brother of the infamous Northern General, William Tecumseh Sherman, who literally blazed a wide trail through Georgia and the two Carolinas, thus destroying their economies and forcing them into massive debt and dependence upon the new national system.

According to a statement attributed to German Chancellor Otto von Bismark, the Rothschilds were also responsible, at least to some degree, for orchestrating the events which brought about the sectional war in the first place:

The division of the United States into federations of equal force was decided long before the Civil War by the high financial powers of Europe. These bankers were afraid that the United States, if they remained in one block and as one nation, would attain economic and financial independence, which would upset their financial domination over Europe and the world. Of course, in the "inner circle" of finance, the voice of the Rothschilds prevailed. They saw an opportunity for prodigious booty if they could substitute two feeble democracies, burdened with debt to the financiers... in place of a vigorous Republic sufficient unto herself. Therefore, they sent their emissaries into the field to

20. Rothschild Brothers to Messrs. Ikleheimer, Morton, and Vandergould, 25 June 1863; quoted by Owen, *National Economy*, pages 99-100.

21. John Sherman, quoted by Heather Cox Richardson, *The Greatest Nation on the Earth: Republican Economic Policies During the Civil War* (Cambridge, Massachusetts: Harvard University Press, 1997), page 87.

exploit the question of slavery and to drive a wedge between the two parts of the Union.... The rupture between the North and the South became inevitable; the masters of European finance employed all their forces to bring it about and to turn it to their advantage.[22]

After the national banking system was installed and its perpetual, multi-generational debt was firmly grafted onto the economy, Chase resigned from his position as Secretary of the Treasury and was appointed by Lincoln to the Supreme Court, filling the position just vacated by the death of Chief Justice Roger B. Taney. This appointment was an ingenious strategic move on Lincoln's part; having been the chief architect of the national banking system, Chase was now in a position to place upon it the judicial stamp of approval. He would later draft the Fourteenth Amendment, the fifth and last section of which placed the unconstitutionally contracted war debt, and hence, the new banking system erected upon it, beyond the scope of judicial review. This latter section was no doubt added to prevent the public repudiation called for by leading Democrats, such as Henry Clay Dean:

> ...[T]here is no fact in the history of this war debt more startling than this: that the great body of these bankers and bondholders were, at the beginning of the war, but poor men; many of them helpless bankrupts, and many of the pretended loans were mere collusions between bankers and government officers, entered into for the purpose of creating money for the one and power for the other, at the expense of the people, who would be required to raise standing armies from their children to support this power and contribute taxes from their labor to maintain the funding system.
>
> This has always been the case in the history of paper money inflations; that the pretended benefactors of government have been simply swindlers, who have imposed upon the people their worthless promises to pay in lieu of specie as the pretext for their robbery.
>
> This is true, with scarcely an exception, in every country, that the government is never assisted by paper in any war. Those who issue it amass fortunes by the issue. To this one our country has not been an exception.
>
> In the history of insolvent estates, bankrupts, merchants, contested debts and repudiated obligations, which make up the assets of the last six years, it must not startle mankind that the honest people have thrown off the yoke rudely placed upon them by reckless and unscrupulous tyrants.[23]

The Federal Reserve System and How It Works

The nation operated under Chase's banking system for over fifty years, the only substantial change being the removal in June of 1874 of the 10 percent specie reserve re-

---

22. Otto von Bismark, quoted in *La Vielle France* (17-24 March 1921), Number 216, pages 13-16; cited by G. Edward Griffin, *The Creature From Jekyll Island* (Westlake Village, California: American Media, 1998), page 374.

23. Dean, *Crimes of the Civil War*, pages 267-268.

quirement. Then, with the passage of the Federal Reserve Act of 23 December 1913, the alleged power of the U.S. Government to issue paper currency was delegated to a privately owned banking cartel — the Federal Reserve. It is a common misconception, no doubt generated by its deceptive name, that the Federal Reserve is part of the U.S. Government. However, as the Ninth District Court was forced to admit as recently as 1982, "...[W]e conclude that the [Federal] Reserve Banks are not federal instrumentalities... but are independent, privately owned and locally controlled corporations."[24] According to a report prepared by the House Subcommittee on Domestic Finance, "the Federal Reserve is 'independent' in its policy-making. The Federal Reserve neither requires nor seeks the approval of any branch of Government for its policies. The System itself decides what ends its policies are aimed at and then takes whatever action it sees fit to reach those ends."[25] Furthermore, William P.G. Harding, a former Senator from Ohio and later Governor of the Federal Reserve Board, admitted in testimony during a Senate hearing in 1921, "The Federal Reserve Bank is an institution owned by the stockholding member banks. From a legal standpoint these banks are private corporations, organized under a special act of Congress, namely, the Federal Reserve Act. They are not in the strict sense of the word Government banks. The Government has not a dollar's worth of stock in it."[26] Instead, the owners of the Federal Reserve were, and are, the heirs to the bondholders and financiers of Lincoln's war against the South, whose right to collect payment from the United States Government and its citizens "shall not be questioned" under the alleged Fourteenth Amendment.

The Federal Reserve System (hereafter "the Fed") is made up of twelve regional banks, each presided over by a governor. Though it has the appearance of a diversified system, the New York Fed acts as the decision-making center and the other eleven banks are "so many expensive mausoleums erected to salve the local pride and quell the Jacksonian fears of the hinterland."[27] In other words, it is a central bank concealed by a thin disguise of de-centralization. In addition, while the Fed pays taxes on its real estate, its other financial assets are exempted from Federal and State taxes.[28]

Section 16 of the original Federal Reserve Act of 1913 provided for the issuance of Federal Reserve Notes, but it did not make them "legal tender"; they were fully redeemable

---

24. *Lewis v. U.S.* (1982), 680 F.2d 1239.

25. House Subcommittee on Domestic Finance, *Questions and Answers on Money: A Supplement to A Primer on Money* (Eighty-Eighth Congress, Second Session).

26. William P.G. Harding, quoted by Eustace Mullins, *Secrets of the Federal Reserve* (Staunton, Virginia: Bankers Research Institute, 1984), page 157. Harding's term as Governor of the Board was cut short in 1923 when he mysteriously died from what many suspected was poisoning. His wife refused to allow an autopsy.

27. Ferdinand Lundberg, *America's Sixty Families* (New York: Vanguard Press, 1937), page 122.

28. Title 12, United States Code, Section 531.

in either gold or "lawful money." That was all changed when the Gold Reserve Act of 1934 amended Section 16 to render Federal Reserve Notes (hereafter "FRNs") redeemable in "lawful money" only: "Federal Reserve notes are legal tender under 31 USC 5103, and are therefore 'lawful money'.... Federal Reserve notes have become practically the only form of paper currency in circulation. Consequently, if a holder of Federal Reserve notes presents them for redemption in lawful money at the Treasury or at a Federal Reserve Bank, he is most likely to receive in exchange lawful money in the form of other Federal Reserve notes."[29]

The atrocious scam of the Fed system is seen clearly in how the "money" supply is made to expand and contract at the will of this private corporation. This expansion and contraction is known as inflation and deflation. When the Fed decides to inject more FRNs into circulation, it contacts the U.S. Government's Bureau of Engraving and Printing and orders the bills at a cost of less than two cents each, regardless of the denomination.[30] In reality, however, there is actually no cost to the Fed at all, for the printing job is merely paid for with a check behind which there are absolutely no funds on deposit anywhere. This was openly admitted by the Fed itself in the publication *Putting It Simply*: "When you or I write a check there must be sufficient funds in our account to cover that check, but when the Federal Reserve writes a check there is no bank deposit on which that check is drawn. When the Federal Reserve writes a check, it is creating money."[31] What is a crime for the average citizen to do, the Fed does on a routine basis and even boasts about it.

The Fed then uses the newly printed FRNs — which cost it nothing — to purchase securities (bonds, or T-bills) from the U.S. Treasury Department. These securities are interest-bearing debt instruments which themselves are unbacked by anything but the Government's promise-to-pay and its ability to make good on that promise by future taxation. The FRNs which are thus put into circulation are evidences of this debt which the citizens of the United States now owe to the Fed. In other words, the U.S. Government prints paper money, but cannot use it until it borrows it, with interest, from a non-governmental, privately-owned banking cartel. However, it needs to be noted that FRNs only make up a small percentage of the circulating funds in the United States. The bulk of the money supply is created by individual bank loans and by the writing of checks. How this works is also very simple: the individual banks in the system are required by the Federal Reserve to hold as little as ten percent of their deposits in reserve. That means that if someone deposits 100.00[32] into their local bank, that deposit, though now a liability because the bank must pay out the full 100.00

---

29. Russell L. Munk, Assistant General Counsel (International Affairs), Department of the Treasury, statement issued 26 October 1989.

30. House of Representatives, *Money Facts*, Chapter Three.

31. *Putting It Simply* (Boston: Federal Reserve Bank of Boston, 1984), page 17.

32. The dollar symbol has been omitted purposefully to differentiate fiat money from actual money.

to the depositor on demand, is also simultaneously transformed into an asset of 90.00 which the bank may then loan out at interest. Every loan eventually itself becomes a bank deposit, which creates even more assets which the bank may again loan out at interest. These loans obviously cannot be made from the same funds which were deposited, because those funds are still owed to the depositors. Thus, every deposit merely serves as the basis for the creation of 90 percent more in "checkbook money." In other words, the banks not only have the ability to create money out of absolutely nothing, but they then are privileged to collect interest from those whose "credit history" qualifies them to borrow this imaginary money. Furthermore, as the process plays itself out, the money supply will be inflated many times the amount of the original loan, thereby driving the prices for goods and services up as well.

When the Fed decides to contract the money supply, as it did in the years just prior to the Great Depression, one of the ways it does this is simply by redeeming its T-bills or selling them on the open market. Another way is to curtail the availability of credit by raising interest rates for bank loans in the private sector, thereby reducing the amount of checkbook money in circulation. The people are caught in a hopeless "catch twenty-two" between a high level of debt and a "sound" economy, or a low level of debt and a crippling recession. Using either its power of inflation or deflation, the Fed, at absolutely no cost to itself, has become the financial master over approximately 300 million indentured servants.[33] It should be obvious that since neither the Government nor the vast majority of the people have any money of their own which was not directly created by the printing and borrowing of FRNs, or indirectly created through a bank loan, it is entirely impossible to pay off the national debt, much less to even pay on the principle. In fact, every cent which is collected from the people through taxation is applied to the interest alone. Not only that, but every cent which the people pay the Fed was itself borrowed from a bank within the Fed system — with additional interest.

Federal Reserve Notes Are Monetized Debt

Most people today believe that Federal Reserve Notes are money and that they may be used to purchase goods or services, and to pay debts. However, we have just seen that FRNs are evidences of a debt owed to the Fed by the U.S. Government. By definition, money "does not embrace notes... [or] evidences of debt...."[34] Moreover, although FRNs are "in the likeness of noninterest bearing promissory notes payable [in money — *i.e.* dollars of gold or silver] to the bearer on demand," they are in reality nothing more than "direct obligations of the United States."[35] It is logically impossible to pay a debt with a debt, which is what actu-

---

33. United States Population Clock Projection: www.census.gov/cgi-bin/popclock.

34. *Black's Law Dictionary* (Sixth Edition), page 1005.

35. *Ibid.*, page 613.

ally is believed to happen when a FRN is used as if it were money in the modern financial world. According to Joint Resolution 192, also known as the *Abrogation of the Gold Clause* of 5 June 1933, "any obligation which purports to give the obligee a right to require payment in gold or a particular kind of coin or currency, or in an amount in money of the United States measured thereby, is declared to be against public policy." In other words, it is "public policy" that debts not be *paid*, but only *discharged*. The distinction between a "debt discharged" and a "debt paid" was explained in *Stanek v. White*: "When discharged the debt still exists though divested of its character as a legal obligation during the operation of the discharge. Something of the original vitality of the debt continues to exist which may be transferred, even though the transferee takes it subject to its disability incident to the discharge. The fact that it carries something which may be a consideration for a new promise to pay, so as to make an otherwise worthless promise a legal obligation, makes it subject of transfer by assignment."[36] Thus, when someone "discharges" their debt today with Federal Reserve Notes — or with a check or some other instrument denominated in FRNs — the debt still exists and is merely passed down the line to the next person, and ultimately to the following generation. It is therefore no more legally or mathematically possible to actually pay one's personal debts than it is to pay the national debt. In fact, if all debts — personal, corporate, and national — were extinguished, there would no longer be any "money" in circulation. The cliche "passing the buck" takes on a sinister meaning when this tangled web of deception is understood. In the words of Robert Hemphill, former Credit Manager of the Federal Reserve Bank of Atlanta:

> If all the bank loans were paid, no one could have a bank deposit, and there would not be a dollar of coin or currency in circulation. This is a staggering thought. We are completely dependent on the commercial banks. Someone has to borrow every dollar we have in circulation, cash, or credit. If the banks create ample synthetic money we are prosperous; if not, we starve. We are absolutely without a permanent money system. When one gets a complete grasp of the picture, the tragic absurdity of our hopeless situation is almost incredible — but there it is.[37]

Furthermore, if there is really no limit to the amount of FRNs which the Government can print and then borrow from the Fed, one might justifiably wonder why it even needs to tax its citizens at all. The fact is, there is no such need on the Government's part. In 1946, Beardsley Ruml, then Chairman of the Federal Reserve Bank of New York, wrote an article entitled, "Taxes For Revenue Are Obsolete," in which he argued that "given control of a central banking system and an inconvertible currency, a sovereign national government is finally free of money worries and needs no longer levy taxes for the purpose of providing

---

36. *Stanek v. White* (1927), 172 Minn. 390, 215 N.W. 784.

37. Robert Hemphill, "Foreword" in Irving Fisher, *100% Money* (New York: Adelphi Company, 1936), page xxii.

itself with revenue. All taxation, therefore, should be regarded from the point of view of social and economic consequences."[38] The "social consequences" are that continued taxation of the people has the effect of giving credibility to a system of fiat money which likely would not exist if its creation out of thin air were obvious to all. The fact that the fiat money can both be spent and used for the payment of taxes perpetuates the illusion that the Government is collecting something of value from its citizens without which it could not continue to operate. Periodic "shut downs" of the Government due to a "lack of money" are also useful tools to maintain this illusion.

Ruml went on to explain the "economic consequences" of taxation: "The dollars the government spends become purchasing power in the hands of the people who have received them. The dollars the government takes by taxes cannot be spent by the people, and therefore, these dollars can no longer be used to acquire the things which are available for sale. Taxation is, therefore, an instrument of the first importance in the administration of any fiscal and monetary policy."[39] Thus, the collection of taxes acts as a safety valve to relieve some of the pressure of an inflating currency and to keep prices rising at only a moderate rate rather than sky-rocketing out of control and causing a panic.

Does the Fed Cause War and Depressions?

Such is the tyrannical system which has been imposed on the American people by their supposed representatives in Congress. While the Federal Reserve System can be abolished by the same body of men who gave it life in 1913, it is not considered "in the public interest" to do so and every politician either goes to Washington, D.C. with this already fully understood, or quickly learns it after his arrival. Coming full circle back to the views of Alexander Hamilton, Lawrence C. Murdoch, Jr. of the Federal Reserve Bank of Philadelphia declared, "A large and growing number of analysts... now regard the national debt as something useful if not an actual blessing... and that the national debt need not be reduced at all."[40] Of course, the debt is "an actual blessing" only to the elite few who reap its bountiful harvest of interest, but it certainly is a curse to those who suffer under the burden of perpetual debt and increasing taxation.

Not surprisingly, the Courts have refused to rule the Fed system unconstitutional. Whereas the Constitution prohibits the Government from emitting "bills of credit," it does permit the Government to "borrow money on the credit of the United States." Since FRNs do not *technically* become "money" until they are borrowed, it is reasoned that the letter of

---

38. Beardsley Ruml, "Taxes For Revenue Are Obsolete," *American Affairs*, January 1946, page 35.

39. Ruml, *ibid.*, page 36.

40. Lawrence C. Murdoch, Jr., *The National Debt* (Philadelphia, Pennsylvania: Federal Reserve Bank of Philadelphia, 1970), pages 2, 11.

the Constitution is not *technically* violated by this arrangement. This was the same argument used to justify the issuance of bank notes by the first Bank of the United States back in 1791. Indeed, no other nation in the world has resorted to such chicanery in order to foist a central bank on its citizens. However, there is another and much darker side to the Federal Reserve which needs to be mentioned before we close this chapter: its instigation of economic depressions and war. According to John C. Redpath, "It has been the immemorial policy of the Money Power to foment wars among the nations; to edge on the conflict until both parties pass under the impending bankruptcy; to buy up the prodigious debt of both with a pail full of gold; to raise the debt to par; to invent patriotic proclamations for preserving the National Honor; and finally to hire the presses and pulpits of two generations to glorify a crime."[41]

The Fed opened its doors on 16 November 1914. On that date, Europe had already been embroiled in war for three months, but the American people had refused to finance the U.S. Government's involvement by purchasing its savings bonds. "Keep the Boys Home" was a popular political slogan at that time. However, since the Government now had another lending source other than its citizens, it is not surprising that in April of 1917, only one month after his second inauguration as the President who "kept us out of war," Woodrow Wilson sent a message to Congress requesting the involvement of the United States in World War I. Congress responded by declaring war on the sixteenth of April and the War Loan Act was passed scarcely a week later which extended $1 billion in credit to the Allied powers. During this time, nearly all of the Government's gold reserves were relocated to the vaults of the Federal Reserve. Lester Chandler explained what role the Fed played in the nation's war-time economy: "The Federal Reserve System became an integral part of the war financing machinery. The System's overriding objective, both as a creator of money and as fiscal agent, was to insure that the Treasury would be supplied with all the money it needed, and on terms fixed by Congress and the Treasury.... A grateful nation now hailed it as a major contributor to the winning of the war, an efficient fiscal agent for the Treasury, a great source of currency and reserve funds, and a permanent and indispensable part of the banking system."[42]

During World War I, on 6 October 1917, Congress also passed the Trading With the Enemy Act, which would provide a convenient foundation for the Fed's massive power grab still to come. According to Alan Greenspan, formerly the Chairman of the New York Federal Reserve, the Great Depression was caused when, in 1929, "the excessive credit which the Fed pumped into the economy spilled over into the stock market — triggering a fantastic

41. John C. Redpath, quoted by George R. Kirkpatrick, *War — What For?* (West Lafayette, Ohio: self-published, 1910), page 66.

42. Lester V. Chandler, *Benjamin Strong, Central Banker* (Washington, D.C.: Brookings Institution, 1958), pages 101-102.

speculative boon.... As a result, the American economy collapsed."[43] Public confidence in the system also collapsed, resulting in massive runs on the banks by panicked depositors. Of course, there was not enough gold in the vaults to cover all the inflated currency which the Fed had been putting into circulation and the scam was in danger of discovery. In an effort to preserve the system, the Federal Reserve Board of New York sent the following recommendation, written by Eugene Meyers, to President Herbert Hoover on the last day of his term:

> WHEREAS, In the opinion of the Board of Directors of the Federal Reserve Bank of New York, the continued and increasing withdrawal of currency and gold from the banks of the country has now created a national emergency, and
>
> WHEREAS, It is understood the adequate remedial measures cannot be enacted before tomorrow morning,
>
> NOW, THEREFORE, BE IT RESOLVED, That in this emergency the Federal Reserve Board is hereby requested to urge the President of the United States to declare a bank holiday Saturday, March 4, and Monday, March 6, in order to afford opportunity to governmental authorities and banks themselves to take such measures as may be necessary to protect the interests of the people and promptly to provide adequate banking and credit facilities for all parts of the country.

Proposed Executive Order

> WHEREAS the nation's banking institutions are being subjected to heavy withdrawals of currency for hoarding; and
>
> WHEREAS there is increasing speculative activity in foreign exchanges; and
>
> WHEREAS these conditions have created a national emergency in which it is in the best interest of all bank depositors that a period of respite be provided with a view to preventing further hoarding of coin, bullion or currency or speculation in foreign exchange, and permitting the application of appropriate measures for dealing with the emergency in order to protect the interests of all the people; and
>
> WHEREAS it is provided in Section 5 (b) of the Act of October 6, 1917, as amended, that *"The President may investigate, regulate, or prohibit, under such rules and regulations as he may prescribe, by means of licenses or otherwise, any transactions in foreign exchange and the export, hoarding, melting, or earmarking of gold or silver coin or bullion or currency * * *"*; and
>
> WHEREAS it is provided in Section 16 of the said Act that *"Whoever shall willfully violate any of the provisions of this Act or of any license, rule, or regulation issued thereunder, and whoever shall willfully violate, neglect, or refuse to comply with any order of the President issued in compliance with the provisions of this Act shall, upon conviction, be fined not more than $10,000, or, if a natural person, imprisoned for not more than ten years, or both * * *"* (emphasis in original)

---

43. Alan Greenspan, "Gold and Economic Freedom," in Ayn Rand (editor), *Capitalism: The Unknown Ideal* (New York: Signet Books, 1967), pages 99-100.

If these words sound familiar, they should; right down to the deceptive rewording of Section 5 of the Trading With the Enemy Act, they are the very words of Roosevelt's proclamation of 4 March 1933, in which he declared a national banking emergency and prohibited the private ownership of gold. Hoover, who was no friend of the Fed, refused to issue this executive order based on the 1917 Act after his legal advisors pointed out that the "war powers were apparently terminated" at the close of World War I, and that "there was danger that action under such doubtful authority would create a mass of legal conflicts in the country and would incur the refusal of the banks to comply."[44] In his letter of response to Meyers, Hoover wrote, "...I am at a loss to understand why such a communication should have been sent to me in the last few hours of this Administration, which I believe the Board must now admit was neither justified nor necessary." His confusion stemmed largely from the fact that President-elect Roosevelt had told him the previous night that "he did not wish such a proclamation issued." Immediately upon taking office, however, Roosevelt reversed his position and issued the proposed executive order in spite of its "doubtful authority." Consequently, by bailing out the Fed and covering up its misdeeds, Roosevelt instituted what was clearly a new deal for the bankers but a raw deal for the American people. As we will see in the next few chapters, we have lived under this banker-contrived national emergency ever since.

On 10 June 1932, Louis T. McFadden, Chairman of the House Banking and Currency Committee, stated:

> Mr. Chairman, we have in this country one of the most corrupt institutions the world has ever known. I refer to the Federal Reserve Board and the Federal Reserve banks. The Federal Reserve Board, a Government board, has cheated the Government of the United States and the people of the United States out of enough money to pay the national debt. The depredations and iniquities of the Federal Reserve Board and the Federal Reserve banks acting together have cost this country enough money to pay the national debt several times over. This evil institution has impoverished and ruined the people of the United States; has bankrupted itself, and has practically bankrupted our Government. It has done this through the defects of the law under which it operates, through the maladministration of that law by the Federal Reserve Board, and through the corrupt practices of the moneyed vultures who control it.
>
> Some people think the Federal Reserve banks are United States Government institutions. They are not Government institutions. They are private credit monopolies which prey upon the people of the United States for the benefit of themselves and their foreign customers; foreign and domestic speculators and swindlers; and rich and predatory are those who would cut a man's throat to get a dollar out of his pocket; there are those who send money into States to buy votes to control our legislation; and there are those who maintain an international propaganda for the purpose of deceiving us and wheedling us into the granting of new concessions which will permit them to cover up their past mis-

---

44. Herbert Hoover, *The Memoirs of Herbert Hoover, 1929-1941: The Great Depression* (New York: Macmillan Company, 1952), page 205.

deeds and set again in motion their gigantic train of crime.[45]

The following year, McFadden went on to say:

> Every effort has been made by the Federal Reserve to conceal its powers but the truth is — the Federal Reserve has usurped the government. It controls everything here and it controls all our foreign relations. It makes and breaks governments at will.
> [The Depression] was not accidental. It was a carefully contrived occurrence.... The international bankers sought to bring about a condition of despair here so they could emerge the rulers of us all....
> I charge them... with having brought repudiation of the national currency of the United States in order that the gold value of said currency might be given to private interests... with having arbitrarily and unlawfully raised and lowered the rates on money... increased and diminished the volume of currency in circulation for the benefit of private interests... with having brought about the decline in prices on the New York Stock Exchange... with the crime of having treasonably conspired and acted against the peace and security of the United States, and with having treasonably conspired to destroy constitutional government.[46]

McFadden, of course, need not have expended so much effort defending a Constitution and Government which had perished seventy-two years previous to his speech at the hands of the "party of Lincoln" — the Republicans. The twin tyrants of massive public debt and inflationary currency were already seated upon their imperial thrones and dissent in the chambers of Congress would not be tolerated. Representative McFadden was assassinated by poisoning not long afterward on 3 October 1936.[47]

---

45. Louis T. McFadden, *Congressional Record — House*, 10 June 1932, pages 12595-12596.

46. McFadden, *ibid.*, 9 March 1933.

47. The cause of death was officially listed as "intestinal flu," which McFadden had supposedly contracted after attending a public banquet. This was the third attempt on his life.

SUPPORTING DOCUMENT

Louis T. McFadden's Speech
in the House of Representatives
Congressional Record — 10 June 1932

Mr. Chairman, at the present session of Congress we have been dealing with emergency situations. We have been dealing with the effect of things rather than with the cause of things. In this particular discussion I shall deal with some of the causes that lead up to these proposals. There are underlying principles which are responsible for conditions such as we have at the present time and I shall deal with one of these in particular which is tremendously important in the consideration that you are now giving to this bill.

Mr. Chairman, we have in this country one of the most corrupt institutions the world has ever known. I refer to the Federal Reserve Board and the Federal Reserve Banks. The Federal Reserve Board, a Government board, has cheated the Government of the United States and the people of the United States out of enough money to pay the national debt. The depredations and iniquities of the Federal Reserve Board has cost this country enough money to pay the national debt several times over. This evil institution has impoverished and ruined the people of the United States, has bankrupted itself, and has practically bankrupted our Government. It has done this through the defects of the law under which it operates, through the maladministration of that law by the Federal Reserve Board, and through the corrupt practices of the moneyed vultures who control it.

Some people think the Federal Reserve banks are United States Government institutions. They are not Government institutions. They are private credit monopolies which prey upon the people of the United States for the benefit of themselves and their foreign customers; foreign and domestic speculators and swindlers; and rich and predatory money lenders. In that dark crew of financial pirates there are those who would cut a man's throat to get a

809

dollar out of his pocket; there are those who send money into States to buy votes to control our legislation; and there are those who maintain international propaganda for the purpose of deceiving us and of wheedling us into the granting of new concessions which will permit them to cover up their past misdeeds and set again in motion their gigantic train of crime.

These twelve private credit monopolies were deceitfully and disloyally foisted upon this country by the bankers who came here from Europe and repaid us for our hospitality by undermining our American institutions. Those bankers took money out of this country to finance Japan in a war against Russia. They created a reign of terror in Russia with our money in order to help that war along. They instigated the separate peace between Germany and Russia and thus drove a wedge between the Allies in the World War. They financed Trotsky's passage from New York to Russia so that he might assist in the destruction of the Russian Empire. They fomented and instigated the Russian revolution and they placed a large fund of American dollars at Trotsky's disposal in one of their branch banks in Sweden so that through him Russian homes might be thoroughly broken up and Russian children flung far and wide from their natural protectors. They have since begun the breaking up of American homes and the dispersal of American children.

It has been said that President Wilson was deceived by the attentions of these bankers and by the philanthropic poses they assumed. It has been said that when he discovered the manner in which he had been misled by Colonel House, he turned against that busybody, that "holy monk" of the financial empire, and showed him the door. He had the grace to do that, and in my opinion he deserves great credit for it.

President Wilson died a victim of deception. When he came to the Presidency, he had certain qualities of mind and heart which entitled him to a high place in the councils of this Nation; but there was one thing he was not and which he never aspired to be; he was not a banker. He said that he knew very little about banking. It was, therefore, on the advice of others that the iniquitous Federal Reserve act, the death warrant of American liberty, became law in his administration.

Mr. Chairman, there should be no partisanship in matters concerning the banking and currency affairs of this country, and I do not speak with any.

In 1912 the National Monetary Association, under the chairmanship of the late Senator Nelson W. Aldrich, made a report and presented a vicious bill called the National Reserve Association bill. This bill is usually spoken of as the Aldrich bill. Senator Aldrich did not write the Aldrich bill. He was the tool, but not the accomplice, of the European-born bankers who for nearly twenty years had been scheming to set up a central bank in this country and who in 1912 had spent and were continuing to spend vast sums of money to accomplish their purpose.

The Aldrich bill was condemned in the platform upon which Theodore Roosevelt was nominated in the year 1912, and in that same year, when Woodrow Wilson was nominated, the Democratic platform, as adopted at the Baltimore convention, expressly stated: "We are opposed to the Aldrich plan for a central bank." This was plain language. The men who ruled the Democratic Party then promised the people that if they were returned to power there would be no central bank established here while they held the reigns of government. Thirteen months later that promise was broken, and the Wilson administration, under the tutelage of those sinister Wall Street figures who stood behind Colonel House, established here in our free country the worm-eaten monarchical institution of the "king's bank" to control us from the top downward, and to shackle us from the cradle to the grave. The Federal Reserve act destroyed our old and characteristic way of doing business; it discriminated against our one-name commercial paper, the finest in the world; it set up the antiquated two-name paper, which is the present curse of this country, and which wrecked every country which has ever given it scope; it fastened down upon this country the very tyranny from which the framers of the Constitution sought to save us.

One of the greatest battles for the preservation of this Republic was fought out here in Jackson's day, when the Second Bank of the United States, which was founded upon the same false principles as those which are here exemplified in the Federal Reserve act, was hurled out of existence. After the downfall of the Second Bank of the United States in 1837, the country was warned against the dangers that might ensue if the predatory interests, after being cast out, should come back in disguise and unite themselves to the Executive, and through him acquire control of the Government. That is what the predatory interests did when they came back in the livery of hypocrisy and under false pretenses obtained the passage of the Federal Reserve act.

The danger that the country was warned against came upon us and is shown in the long train of horrors attendant upon the affairs of the traitorous and dishonest Federal Reserve Board and the Federal Reserve banks are fully liable. This is an era of financed crime and in the financing of crime, the Federal Reserve Board does not play the part of a disinterested spectator.

It has been said that the draughtsman who was employed to write the text of the Federal Reserve bill used a text of the Aldrich bill for his purpose. It has been said that the language of the Aldrich bill was used because the Aldrich bill had been drawn up by expert lawyers and seemed to be appropriate. It was indeed drawn up by lawyers. The Aldrich bill was created by acceptance bankers of European origin in New York City. It was a copy and in general a translation of the statutes of the Reichsbank and other European central banks.

Half a million dollars was spent one part of the propaganda organized by those same European bankers for the purpose of misleading public opinion in regard to it, and for the purpose of giving Congress the impression that there was an overwhelming popular demand for that kind of banking legislation and the kind of currency that goes with it, namely, an asset currency based on human debts and obligations instead of an honest currency based on gold and silver values. Dr. H. Parker Willis had been employed by the Wall Street bankers and propagandists and when the Aldrich measure came to naught and he obtained employment with Carter Glass to assist in drawing a banking bill for the Wilson administration, he appropriated the text of the Aldrich bill for his purpose. There is no secret about it. The text of the Federal Reserve act was tainted from the beginning.

Not all of the Democratic Members of the Sixty-third Congress voted for this great deception. Some of them remembered the teachings of Jefferson; and, through the years, there had been no criticisms of the Federal Reserve Board and the Federal Reserve banks so honest, so out-spoken, and so unsparingly as those which have been voiced here by Democrats. Again, although a number of Republicans voted for the Federal Reserve act, the wisest and most conservative members of the Republican Party would have nothing to do with it and voted against it. A few days before the bill came to a vote, Senator Henry Cabot Lodge, of Massachusetts, wrote to Senator John W. Weeks as follows:

New York City, December 17, 1913

My Dear Senator Weeks:

Throughout my public life I have supported all measures designed to take the Government out of the banking business.... This bill puts the Government into the banking business as never before in our history and makes, as I understand it, all notes Government notes when they should be bank notes.

The powers vested in the Federal Reserve Board seem to me highly dangerous, especially where there is political control of the Board. I should be sorry to hold stock in a bank subject to such domination. The bill as it stands seems to me to open the way to a vast inflation of the currency. There is no necessity of dwelling upon this point after the remarkable and most powerful argument of the senior Senator from New York. I can be content here to follow the example of the English candidate for Parliament who thought it enough "to say ditto to Mr. Burke." I will merely add that I do not like to think that any law can be passed which will make it possible to submerge the gold standard in a flood of irredeemable paper currency.

I had hoped to support this bill, but I can not vote for it as it stands, because it seems to me to contain features and to rest upon principles in the highest degree menacing to our prosperity, to stability in business, and to the general welfare of the people of the United States.

Very sincerely yours,
Henry Cabot Lodge

In eighteen years that have passed since Senator Lodge wrote that letter of warning all of his predictions have come true. The Government is in the banking business as never before. Against its will it has been made the backer of horsethieves and card sharps, bootleggers, smugglers, speculators, and swindlers in all parts of the world. Through the Federal Reserve Board and the Federal Reserve banks the riffraff of every country is operating on the public credit of this United States Government. Meanwhile, and on account of it, we ourselves are in the midst of the greatest depression we have ever known. Thus the menace to our prosperity, so feared by Senator Lodge, has indeed struck home. From the Atlantic to the Pacific our country has been ravaged and laid waste by the evil practices of the Federal Reserve Board and the Federal Reserve banks and the interests which control them. At no time in our history has the general welfare of the people of the United States been at a lower level or the mind of the people so filled with despair.

Recently in one of our States 60,000 dwelling houses and farms were brought under the hammer in a single day. According to the Rev. Father Charles E. Coughlin, who has lately testified before a committee of this House, 71,000 houses and farms in Oakland County, Michigan, have been sold and their erstwhile owners dispossessed. Similar occurrences have probably taken place in every county in the United States. The people who have thus been driven out are the wastage of the Federal Reserve act. They are the victims of the dishonest and unscrupulous Federal Reserve Board and Federal Reserve banks. Their children are the new slaves of the auction blocks in the revival here of the institution of human slavery.

In 1913, before the Senate Banking and Currency Committee, Mr. Alexander Lassen made the following statement:

> But the whole scheme of the Federal Reserve bank with its commercial-paper basis is an impractical, cumbersome machinery, is simply a cover, to find a way to secure the privilege of issuing money and to evade payment of as much tax upon circulation as possible, and then control the issue and maintain, instead of reduce, interest rates. It is a system that, if inaugurated, will prove to the advantage of the few and the detriment of the people of the United States. It will mean continued shortage of actual money and further extension of credits; for when there is a lack of real money people have to borrow credit to their cost.

A few days before the Federal Reserve act was passed Senator Elihu Root denounced the Federal Reserve bill as an outrage on our liberties and made the following prediction: "Long before we wake up from our dreams of prosperity through an inflated currency, our gold, which alone could have kept us from catastrophe, will have vanished and no rate of interest will tempt it to return."

If ever a prophecy came true, that one did. It was impossible, however, for those luminous and instructed thinkers to control the course of events. On December 23, 1913, the Federal Reserve bill became law, and that night Colonel House wrote to his hidden master in Wall Street as follows:

> I want to say a word of appreciation to you for the silent but no doubt effective work you have done in the interest of currency legislation and to congratulate you that the measure has finally been enacted into law. We all know that an entirely perfect bill, satisfactory to everybody, would have been an impossibility, and I feel quite certain that unless the President had stood as firm as he did we should likely have had no legislation at all. The bill is a good one in many respects; anyhow good enough to start with and to let experience teach us in what direction it needs perfection, which in due time we shall then get. In any event you have personally good reason to feel gratified with what has been accomplished.

The words "unless the President had stood as firm as he did we should likely have had no legislation at all," were a gentle reminder that it was Colonel House himself, the "holy monk," who had kept the President firm.

The foregoing letter affords striking evidence of the manner in which the predatory interests then sought to control the Government of the United States by surrounding the Executive with the personality and the influence of a financial Judas. Left to itself and to the conduct of its own legislative functions without pressure from the Executive, the Congress would not have passed the Federal Reserve act. According to Colonel House, and since this was his report to his master, we may believe it to be true, the Federal Reserve act was passed because Wilson stood firm; in other words because Wilson was under the guidance and control of the most ferocious usurers in New York through their hireling, House. The Federal Reserve act became law the day before Christmas Eve in the year 1913, and shortly afterwards the German international bankers, Kuhn, Loeb and Co., sent one of their partners here to run it.

In 1913, when the Federal Reserve bill was submitted to the Democratic caucus, there was a discussion in regard to the form the proposed paper currency should take. The proponents of the Federal Reserve act, in their determination to create a new kind of paper money, had not needed to go outside of the Aldrich bill for a model. By the terms of the Aldrich bill, bank notes were to be issued by the National Reserve Association and were to be secured partly by gold or lawful money and partly by circulating evidences of debt. The first draft of the Federal Reserve bill presented the same general plan, that is, for bank notes as opposed to Government notes, but with certain differences of regulation.

When the provision for the issuance of Federal Reserve notes was placed before President Wilson he approved of it, but other Democrats were more mindful of Democratic principles and a great protest greeted the plan. Foremost amongst those who denounced it was William Jennings Bryan, the Secretary of State. Bryan wished to have the Federal Reserve notes issued as Government obligations. President Wilson had an interview with him and found him adamant. At the conclusion of the interview Bryan left with the understanding that he would resign if the notes were made bank notes. The President then sent for his Secretary and explained the matter to him. Mr. Tumulty went to see Bryan and Bryan took from his library shelves a book containing all the Democratic platforms and read extracts from them bearing on the matter of the public currency. Returning to the President, Mr. Tumulty told him what had happened and ventured the opinion that Mr. Bryan was right and that Mr. Wilson was wrong. The President then asked Mr. Tumulty to show him where the Democratic Party in its national platforms had ever taken the view indicated by Bryan. Mr. Tumulty gave him the book, which he had brought from Bryan's house, and the President read very carefully plank after plank on the currency. He then said, "I am convinced there is a great deal in what Mr. Bryan says," and thereupon it was arranged that Mr. Tumulty should see the proponents of the Federal Reserve bill in an effort to bring about an adjustment of the matter.

The remainder of this story may be told in the words of Senator Glass. Concerning

Bryan's opposition to the plan of allowing the proposed Federal Reserve notes to take the form of bank notes and the manner in which President Wilson and the proponents of the Federal Reserve bill yielded to Bryan in return for his support of the measure, Senator Glass makes the following statement:

> The only other feature of the currency bill around which a conflict raged at this time was the note-issue provision. Long before I knew it, the President was desperately worried over it. His economic good sense told him the notes should be issued by the banks and not by the Government; but some of his advisers told him Mr. Bryan could not be induced to give his support to any bill that did not provide for a "Government note." There was in the Senate and House a large Bryan following which, united with a naturally adversary party vote, could prevent legislation. Certain overconfident gentlemen proffered their services in the task of "managing Bryan." They did not budge him.... When a decision could no longer be postponed the President summoned me to the White House to say he wanted Federal Reserve notes to "be obligations of the United States." I was for an instant speechless. With all the earnestness of my being I remonstrated, pointing out the unscientific nature of such a thing, as well as the evident inconsistency of it.
>
> "There is not, in truth, any Government obligation here, Mr. President," I exclaimed. "It would be a pretense on its face. Was there ever a Government note based primarily on the property of banking institutions? Was there ever a Government issue not one dollar of which could be put out except by demand of a bank? The suggested Government obligation is so remote it could never be discerned," I concluded, out of breath.
>
> "Exactly so, Glass," earnestly said the President. "Every word you say is true; the Government liability is a mere thought. And so, if we can hold to the substance of the thing and give the other fellow the shadow, why not do it, if thereby we may save our bill?"

Shadow and substance! One can see from this how little President Wilson knew about banking. Unknowingly, he gave the substance to the international banker and the shadow to the common man. Thus was Bryan circumvented in his efforts to uphold the Democratic doctrine of the rights of the people. Thus the "unscientific blur" upon the bill was perpetrated. The "unscientific blur," however, was not the fact that the United States Government, by the terms of Bryan's edict, was obliged to assume as an obligation whatever currency was issued. Mr. Bryan was right when he insisted that the United States should preserve its sovereignty over the public currency. The "unscientific blur" was the nature of the currency itself, a nature which makes it unfit to be assumed as an obligation of the United States Government. It is the worst currency and the most dangerous this country has ever known. When the proponents of the act saw that the Democratic doctrine would not permit them to let the proposed banks issue the new currency as bank notes, they should have stopped at that. They should not have foisted that kind of currency, namely, an asset currency, on the United States Government. They should not have made the Government liable on the private debts of individuals and corporations and, least of all, on the private debts of foreigners.

The Federal Reserve note is essentially unsound. As Kemmerer says: "The Federal

Reserve notes, therefore, in form have some of the qualities of Government paper money, but, in substance, are almost a pure asset currency possessing a Government guaranty against which contingency the Government has made no provision whatever." Hon. E.J. Hill, a former Member of the House, said, and truly: "They are obligations of the Government for which the United States has received nothing and for the payment of which at any time it assumes the responsibility looking to the Federal Reserve to recoup itself."

If the United States Government is to redeem the Federal Reserve notes when the general public finds out what it costs to deliver this flood of paper money to the twelve Federal Reserve banks, and if the Government has made no provision for redeeming them, the first element of unsoundness is not far to seek.

Before the Banking and Currency Committee, when the Federal Reserve bill was under discussion, Mr. Crozier, of Cincinnati, said:

> In other words, the imperial power of elasticity of the public currency is wielded exclusively by these central corporations owned by the banks. This is a life and death power over all local banks and all business. It can be used to create or destroy prosperity, to ward off or cause stringencies and panics. By making money artificially scarce, interest rates throughout the country can be arbitrarily raised and the bank tax on all business and cost of living increased for the profit of the banks owning these regional central banks, and without the slightest benefit to the people. These twelve corporations together cover the whole country and monopolize and use for private gain every dollar of the public currency and all public revenue of the United States. Not a dollar can be put into circulation among the people by their Government without the consent of and on terms fixed by these twelve private money trusts.

In defiance of this and all other warnings, the proponents of the Federal Reserve act created the twelve private credit corporations and gave them an absolute monopoly of the currency of the United States, not of the Federal Reserve notes alone, but of all the currency, the Federal Reserve act providing ways by means of which the gold and general currency in the hands of the American people could be obtained by the Federal Reserve banks in exchange for Federal Reserve notes, which are not money, but merely promises to pay money. Since the evil day when this was done the initial monopoly has been extended by vicious amendments to the Federal Reserve act and by the unlawful and treasonable practices of the Federal Reserve Board and the Federal Reserve banks.

Mr. Chairman, when a Chinese merchant sells human hair to a Paris wigmaker and bills him in dollars, the Federal Reserve banks can buy his bill against the wigmaker and then use that bill as collateral for the Federal Reserve notes. The United States Government thus pays the Chinese merchant the debt of the wigmaker and gets nothing in return except a shady title to the Chinese hair.

Mr. Chairman, if a Scottish distiller wishes to send a cargo of Scotch whiskey to the United States, he can draw his bill against the purchasing bootlegger in dollars; and after the bootlegger has accepted it by writing his name across the face of it, the Scotch distiller can send that bill to the nefarious open discount market in New York City, where the Federal Reserve Board and the Federal Reserve banks will buy it and use it as collateral for a new issue of Federal Reserve notes. Thus the Government of the United States pays the Scotch distiller for the whiskey before it is shipped; and if it is lost on the way, or if the Coast Guard seizes it and destroys it, the Federal Reserve banks simply write off the loss and the Government never recovers the money that was paid to the Scotch distiller. While we are attempting to enforce prohibition here, the Federal Reserve Board and the Federal Reserve banks are financing the distillery business in Europe and paying bootleggers' bills with the public credit of the United States Government.

Mr. Chairman, if a German brewer ships beer to this country or anywhere else in the world and draws his bill for it in dollars, the Federal Reserve banks will buy that bill and use it as collateral for Federal Reserve notes. Thus, they compel our Government to pay the German brewer for his beer. Why should the Federal Reserve Board and the Federal Reserve banks be permitted to finance the brewing industry in Germany, either in this way or as they do by compelling small and fearful United States banks to take stock in the Isenbeck brewery and in the German bank for brewing industries?

Mr. Chairman, if Dynamit Nobel of Germany wishes to sell dynamite to Japan to use in Manchuria or elsewhere, it can draw its bill against the Japanese customers in dollars and send that bill to the nefarious open discount market in New York City, where the Federal Reserve Board and Federal Reserve banks will buy it and use it as collateral for a new issue of Federal Reserve notes, while at the same time the Federal Reserve Board will be helping Dynamit Nobel by stuffing its stock into the United States banking system. Why should we send our representatives to the disarmament conference at Geneva while the Federal Reserve Board and the Federal Reserve banks are making our Government pay Japanese debts to German munition makers?

Mr. Chairman, if a bean grower of Chile wishes to raise a crop of beans and sell them to a Japanese customer, he can draw a bill against his prospective Japanese customer in dollars and have it purchased by the Federal Reserve Board and Federal Reserve banks and get the money out of this country at the expense of the American people before he has even planted the beans in the ground.

Mr. Chairman, if a German in Germany wishes to export goods to South America or anywhere else, he can draw his bill against his customer and send it to the United States and get the money out of this country before he ships or even manufactures the goods.

Mr. Chairman, why should the currency of the United States be issued on the strength of Chinese human hair? Why should it be issued on the trade whims of a wigmaker? Why should it be issued on the strength of German beer? Why should it be issued on the crop of unplanted beans to be grown in Chile for Japanese consumption? Why should the Government of the United States be compelled to issue many billions of dollars every year to pay the debts of one foreigner to another foreigner? Was it for this that our national-bank depositors had their money taken out of our banks and shipped abroad? Was it for this that they had to lose it? Why should the public credit of the United States Government and likewise money belonging to our national-bank depositors be used to support foreign brewers, narcotic drug vendors, whiskey distillers, wigmakers, human-hair merchants, Chilean bean growers, and the like? Why should our national-bank depositors and our Government be forced to finance the munition factories of Germany and Soviet Russia?

Mr. Chairman, if a German in Germany, wishes to sell wheelbarrows to another German, he can draw a bill in dollars and get the money out of the Federal Reserve banks before an American farmer could explain his request for a loan to move his crop to market. In Germany, when credit instruments are being given, the creditors say, "See you, it must be of a kind that I can cash at the reserve." Other foreigners feel the same way. The reserve to which these gentry refer is our reserve, which, as you know, is entirely made up of money belonging to American bank depositors. I think foreigners should cash their own trade paper and not send it over here to bankers who use it to fish cash out of the pockets of the American people.

Mr. Chairman, there is nothing like the Federal Reserve pool of confiscated bank deposits in the world. It is a public trough of American wealth in which foreigners claim rights equal to or greater than those of Americans. The Federal Reserve banks are agents of the foreign central banks. They use our bank depositors' money for the benefit of their foreign principals. They barter the public credit of the United States Government and hire it out to foreigners at a profit to themselves.

All this is done at the expense of the United States Government, and at a sickening loss to the American people. Only our great wealth enabled us to stand the drain of it as long as we did.

I believe that the nations of the world would have settled down after the World War more peacefully if we had not had this standing temptation here — this pool of our bank depositors' money given to private interests and used by them in connection with illimitable drafts upon the public credit of the United States Government. The Federal Reserve Board invited the world to come in and to carry away cash, credit, goods, and everything else of value that was movable. Values amounting to many billions of dollars have been taken out of this country by the Federal Reserve Board and the Federal Reserve banks for the benefit of their foreign principals. The United States has been ransacked and pillaged. Our structures have been gutted and only the walls are left standing. While this crime was being perpetrated everything the world could rake up to sell us was brought in here at our own expense by the Federal Reserve Board and the Federal Reserve banks until our markets were swamped with unneeded and unwanted imported goods priced far above their value and made to equal the dollar volume of our honest exports and to kill or reduce our favorable balance of trade. As agents of the foreign central banks, the Federal Reserve Board and the Federal Reserve banks try by every means within their power to reduce our favorable balance of trade. They act for their foreign principals and they accept fees from foreigners for acting against the best interests of the United States. Naturally there has been great competition among foreigners for the favors of the Federal Reserve Board.

What we need to do is to send the reserves of our national banks home to the people who earned and produced them and who still own them and to the banks which were compelled to surrender them to predatory interests. We need to destroy the Federal Reserve pool, wherein our national-bank reserves are impounded for the benefit of the foreigners. We need to make it very difficult for outlanders to draw money away from us. We need to save America for Americans.

Mr. Chairman, when you hold a $10 Federal Reserve note in your hand you are holding a piece of paper which sooner or later is going to cost the United States Government $10 in gold, unless the Government is obliged to give up the gold standard. It is protected by a reserve of 40 per cent. or $4 in gold. It is based on Limburger cheese, reputed to be in foreign warehouses; or on cans purported to contain peas but which may contain salt water instead; or on horse meat; illicit drugs; bootleggers' fancies; rags and bones from Soviet Russia of which the United States imported over a million dollars' worth last year; on wines, whiskey, natural gas, on goat or dog fur, garlic on the string, or Bombay ducks. If you like to have paper money which is secured by such commodities, you have it in the Federal Reserve note. If you desire to obtain the thing of value upon which this paper currency is based — that is, the Limburger cheese, the whiskey, the illicit drugs, or any of the other staples — you will have a very hard time finding them. Many of these worshipful commodities are in foreign countries. Are you going to Germany to inspect her warehouses to see if the specified things of value are there? I think not. And what is more, I do not think you would find them there if you did go.

Immense sums belonging to our national-bank depositors have been given to Germany on no collateral security whatever. The Federal Reserve Board and the Federal Reserve banks have issued United States currency on mere finance drafts drawn by Germans. Billions upon billions of our money has been pumped into Germany and money is still being pumped into Germany by the Federal Reserve Board and the Federal Reserve banks. Her worthless paper is still being negotiated here and renewed here on the public credit of the United States Government and at the expense of the American people. On April 27, 1932, the Federal Reserve outfit sent $750,000, belonging to American bank depositors, in gold to Germany. A week later, another $300,000 in gold was shipped to Germany in the same way. About the middle of May $12,000,000 in gold was shipped to Germany by the Federal Reserve Board and the Federal Reserve banks. Almost every week there is a shipment of gold to Germany. These shipments are not made for profit on the exchange since the German marks are below parity with the dollar.

Mr. Chairman, I believe that the national-bank depositors of the United States are entitled to know what the Federal Reserve Board and the Federal Reserve banks are doing with their money. There are millions of national-bank depositors in this country who do not know that a percentage of every dollar they deposit in a member bank of the Federal Reserve system goes automatically to American agents of the foreign banks and that all their deposits can be paid away to foreigners without their knowledge or consent by the crooked machinery of the Federal Reserve act and the questionable practices of the Federal Reserve Board and the Federal Reserve banks. Mr. Chairman, the American people should be told the truth by their servants in office.

In 1930 we had over half a billion dollars outstanding daily to finance foreign goods stored in or shipped between countries. In its yearly total, this item amounts to several billion dollars. What goods are those on which the Federal Reserve banks yearly pledge several billions of dollars of the public credit of the United States? What goods are those which are hidden in European and Asiatic storehouses and which have never been seen by any officer of this Government, but which are being financed on the public credit of the United States Government? What goods are those upon which the United States Government is being obligated by the Federal Reserve banks to issue Federal Reserve notes to the extent of several billions of dollars a year?

The Federal Reserve Board and the Federal Reserve banks have been international bankers from the beginning, with the United States Government as their enforced banker and supplier of currency. But it is none the less extraordinary to see those twelve private credit monopolies buying the debts of foreigners against foreigners in all parts of the world and asking the Government of the United States for new issues of Federal Reserve notes in exchange for them.

I see no reason why the American taxpayers should be hewers of wood and drawers of water for the European and Asiatic customers of the Federal Reserve banks. I see no reason why a worthless acceptance drawn by a foreign swindler as a means of getting gold out of this country should receive the lowest and choicest rate from the Federal Reserve Board and be treated as better security than the note of an American farmer living on American land.

The magnitude of the acceptance racket, as it has been developed by the Federal Reserve banks, their foreign correspondents, and the predatory European-born bankers who set up the Federal Reserve institution here and taught our own brand of pirates how to loot the people — I say the magnitude of this racket is estimated to be in the neighborhood of $9,000,000,000 a year. In the past ten years it is said to have amounted to $90,000,000,000. In my opinion, it has amounted to several times as much. Coupled with this you have, to the extent of billions of dollars, the gambling in the United States securities, which takes place in the same open discount market — a gambling upon which the Federal Reserve Board is now spending $100,000,000 per week.

Federal Reserve notes are taken from the United States Government in unlimited quantities. Is it strange that the burden of supplying these immense sums of money to the gambling fraternity has at last proved too heavy for the American people to endure? Would it not be a national calamity if the Federal Reserve Board and the Federal Reserve banks should again bind this burden down on the backs of the American people and, by means of the long rawhide whips of the credit masters, compel them to enter another seventeen years of slavery? They are trying to do that now. They are taking $100,000,000 of the public credit of the United States Government every week in addition to all their other seizures, and they are spending that money in the nefarious open market in New York City in a desperate gamble to reestablish their graft as a going concern.

They are putting the United States Government in debt to the extent of $100,000,000 a week, and with the money they are buying up our Government securities for themselves and their foreign principals. Our people are disgusted with the experiments of the Federal Reserve Board. The Federal Reserve Board is not producing a loaf of bread, a yard of cloth, a bushel of corn, or a pile of cordwood by its check-kiting operations in the money market.

A fortnight or so ago great aid and comfort was given to Japan by the firm of A. Gerli & Sons, of New York, an importing firm, which bought $16,000,000 worth of raw silk from the Japanese Government. Federal Reserve notes will be issued to pay that amount to the Japanese Government, and these notes will be secured by money belonging to our national-bank depositors.

Why should United States currency be issued on this debt? Why should United States currency be issued to pay the debt of Gerli & Sons to the Japanese Government? The Federal Reserve Board and the Federal Reserve banks think more of the silkworms of Japan than they do of American citizens. We do not need $16,000,000 work of silk in this country at the present time, not even to furnish work to dyers and finishers. We need to wear home-grown and American-made clothes and to use our own money for our own goods and staples. We could spend $16,000,000 in the United States of America on American children and that would be a better investment for us than Japanese silk purchased on the public credit of the United States Government.

Mr. Speaker, on the 13th of January of this year I addressed the House on the subject of the Reconstruction Finance Corporation. In the course of my remarks I made the following statement:

> In 1928 the member banks of the Federal Reserve system borrowed $60,598,690,000 from the Federal Reserve banks on their fifteen-day promissory notes. Think of it! Sixty billion dollars payable upon demand in gold in the course of one single year. The actual payment of such obligations calls for six times as much monetary gold as there is in the entire world. Such transactions represent a grant in the course of one single year of about $7,000,000 to every member bank of the Federal Reserve system. Is it any wonder that there is a depression in this country? Is it any wonder that American labor, which ultimately pays the cost of all banking operations of this country, has at last proved unequal to the task of supplying this huge total of cash and credit for the benefit of the stock-market manipulators and foreign swindlers?

Mr. Chairman, some of my colleagues have asked for more specific information concerning this stupendous graft, this frightful burden which has been placed on the wage earners and taxpayers of the United States for the benefit of the Federal Reserve Board and the Federal Reserve banks. They were surprised to learn that member banks of the Federal Reserve system had received the enormous sum of $60,598,690,000 from the Federal Reserve Board and the Federal Reserve banks on their promissory notes in the course of one single year, namely, 1928. Another Member of this House, Mr. Beedy, the honorable gentleman from Maine, has questioned the accuracy of my statement and has informed me that the

Federal Reserve Board denies absolutely that these figures are correct. This Member has said to me that the thing is unthinkable, that it can not be, that it is beyond all reason to think that the Federal Reserve Board and the Federal Reserve banks should have so subsidized and endowed their favorite banks of the Federal Reserve system. This Member is horrified at the thought of a graft so great, a bounty so detrimental to the public welfare as sixty and a half billion dollars a year and more shoveled out to favored banks of the Federal Reserve system.

In 1930, while the speculating banks were getting out of the stock market at the expense of the general public, the Federal Reserve Board and the Federal Reserve banks advanced them $13,022,782,000. This shows that when the banks were gambling on the public credit of the United States Government as represented by the Federal Reserve currency, they were subsidized to any amount they required by the Federal Reserve Board and the Federal Reserve banks. When the swindle began to fall, the bankers knew it in advance and withdrew from the market. They got out with whole skins and left the people of the United States to pay the piper.

On November 2, 1931, I addressed a letter to the Federal Reserve Board asking for the aggregate total of member bank borrowing in the years 1928, 1929, 1930. In due course, I received a reply from the Federal Reserve Board, dated November 9, 1931, the pertinent part of which reads as follows:

My Dear Congressman:

     In reply to your letter of November 2, you are advised that the aggregate amount of fifteen-day promissory notes of member banks during each of the past three calender years has been as follows:

1928 . . . . $60,598,690,000
1929 58,046,697,000
1930 13,022,782,000

     This will show the gentleman from Maine the accuracy of my statement. As for the denial of these facts made to him by the Federal Reserve Board, I can only say that it must have been prompted by fright, since hanging is too good for a Government board which permitted such a misuse of Government funds and credit.

My friend from Kansas, Mr. McGugin, has stated that he thought the Federal Reserve Board and the Federal Reserve banks lent money by rediscounting. So they do, but they lend comparatively little that way. The real rediscounting that they do has been called a mere penny in the slot business. It is too slow for genuine high flyers. They discourage it. They prefer to subsidize their favorite banks by making these $60,000,000,000 advances, and they prefer to acquire acceptances in the notorious open discount market in New York, where they can use them to control the prices of stocks and bonds on the exchanges. For every dollar they advanced on rediscounts in 1928 they lent $33 to their favorite banks for gambling purposes. In other words, their rediscounts in 1928 amounted to $1,814,271,000, while their loans to member banks amounted to $60,598,690,000. As for their open-market operations, these are on a stupendous scale, and no tax is paid on the acceptances they handle; and their foreign principals, for whom they do a business of several billion dollars every year, pay no income tax on their profits to the United States Government.

This is the John Law swindle all over again. The theft of Teapot Dome was trifling compared to it. What king ever robbed his subjects to such an extent as the Federal Reserve Board and the Federal Reserve banks have robbed us? Is it any wonder that there have lately been ninety cases of starvation in one of the New York hospitals? Is there any wonder that the children of this country are being dispersed and abandoned?

The Government and the people of the United States have been swindled by swindlers deluxe to whom the acquisition of American gold or a parcel of Federal Reserve notes presented no more difficulty than the drawing up of a worthless acceptance in a country not subject to the laws of the United States, by sharpers not subject to the jurisdiction of the United States courts, sharpers with a strong banking "fence" on this side of the water — a "fence" acting as a receiver of the worthless paper coming from abroad, endorsing it and getting the currency out of the Federal Reserve banks for it as quickly as possible, exchanging that currency for gold, and in turn transmitting the gold to its foreign confederates.

Such were the exploits of Ivar Kreuger, Mr. Hoover's friend, and his hidden Wall Street backers. Every dollar of the billions Kreuger and his gang drew out of this country on acceptances was drawn from the Government and the people of the United States through the Federal Reserve Board and the Federal Reserve banks. The credit of the United States Government was peddled to him by the Federal Reserve Board and the Federal Reserve banks for their own private gain. That is what the Federal Reserve Board and the Federal Reserve banks have been doing for many years. They have been peddling the credit of this Government and the signature of this Government to the swindlers and speculators of all nations. That is what happens when a country forsakes its Constitution and gives its sovereignty over the public currency to private interests. Give them the flag and they will sell it.

The nature of Kreuger's organized swindle and the bankrupt condition of Kreuger's combine was known here last June when Hoover sought to exempt Kreuger's loan to Germany of $125,000,000 from the operation of the Hoover moratorium. The bankrupt condition of Kreuger's swindle was known here last summer when $30,000,000 was taken from the American taxpayers by certain bankers in New York for the ostensible purpose of permitting Kreuger to make a loan to Colombia. Colombia never saw that money. The nature of Kreuger's swindle and the bankrupt condition of Kreuger was known here in January when he visited his friend, Mr. Hoover, at the White House. It was known here in March before he went to Paris and committed suicide there.

Mr. Chairman, I think the people of the United States are entitled to know how many billions of dollars were placed at the disposal of Kreuger and his gigantic combine by the Federal Reserve Board and the Federal Reserve banks and to know how much of our Government currency was issued and lost in the financing of that great swindle in the years during which the Federal Reserve Board and the Federal Reserve banks took care of

Kreuger's requirements.

Mr. Chairman, I believe there should be a congressional investigation of the operations of Kreuger and Toll in the United States and that Swedish Match, International Match, the Swedish-American Investment Corporation, and all related enterprises, including the subsidiary companies of Kreuger and Toll, should be investigated and that the issuance of United States currency in connection with those enterprises and the use of our national-bank depositors' money for Kreuger's benefit should be made known to the general public. I am referring, not only to the securities which were floated and sold in this country, but also to the commercial loans to Kreuger's enterprises and the mass financing of Kreuger's companies by the Federal Reserve Board and the Federal Reserve banks and the predatory institutions which the Federal Reserve Board and the Federal Reserve banks shield and harbor.

A few days ago, the President of the United States, with a white face and shaking hands, went before the Senate on behalf of the moneyed interests and asked the Senate to levy a tax on the people so that foreigners might know that the United States would pay its debt to them. Most Americans thought it was the other way around. What do the United States owe to foreigners? When and by whom was the debt incurred? It was incurred by the Federal Reserve Board and the Federal Reserve banks when they peddled the signature of this Government to foreigners for a price. It is what the United States Government has to pay to redeem the obligations of the Federal Reserve Board and the Federal Reserve banks. Are you going to let those thieves get off scot free? Is there one law for the looter who drives up to the door of the United States Treasury in his limousine and another for the United States veterans who are sleeping on the floor of a dilapidated house on the outskirts of Washington?

The Baltimore & Ohio Railroad is here asking for a large loan from the people and the wage earners and the taxpayers of the United States. It is begging for a hand-out from the Government. It is standing, cap in hand, at the door of the Reconstruction Finance Corporation, where all the other jackals have gathered to the feast. It is asking for money that was raised from the people by taxation, and wants this money of the poor for the benefit of Kuhn, Loeb, & Co., the German international bankers. Is there one law for the Baltimore & Ohio Railroad and another for the needy veterans it threw off its freight cars the other day? Is there one law for sleek and prosperous swindlers who call themselves bankers and another law for the soldiers who defended the United States flag?

Mr. Chairman, some people are horrified because the collateral behind Kreuger and Toll debentures was removed and worthless collateral substituted for it. What is this but what is being done daily by the Federal Reserve banks? When the Federal Reserve act was passed, the Federal Reserve banks were allowed to substitute "other like collateral" for collateral behind Federal Reserve notes but by an amendment obtained at the request of the corrupt and dishonest Federal Reserve Board, the act was changed so that the word "like" was stricken out. All that immense trouble was taken here in Congress so that the law would permit the Federal Reserve banks to switch collateral. At the present time behind the scenes in the Federal Reserve banks there is a night-and-day movement of collateral. A visiting Englishman, leaving the United States a few weeks ago, said that things would look better here after "they cleaned up the mess at Washington." Cleaning up the mess consists in fooling the people and making them pay a second time for the bad foreign investments of the Federal Reserve Board and the Federal Reserve banks. It consists in moving that heavy load of dubious and worthless foreign paper — the bills of wigmakers, brewers, distillers, narcotic-drug vendors, munition makers, illegal finance drafts, and worthless foreign securities, out of the banks and putting it on the back of American labor. That is what the Reconstruction Finance Corporation is doing now. They talk about loans to banks and railroads but they say very little about that other business of theirs which consists in relieving the swindlers who promoted investment trusts in this country and dumped worthless foreign securities into them and then resold that mess of pottage to American investors under cover of their own corporate titles. The Reconstruction Finance Corporation is taking over those worthless securities from those investment trusts with United States Treasury money at the expense of the American taxpayer and the wage earner.

It will take us twenty years to redeem our Government. Twenty years of penal servitude to pay off the gambling debts of the traitorous Federal Reserve Board and the Federal Reserve banks and to earn again that vast flood of American wages and savings, bank deposits, and United States Government credit which the Federal Reserve Board and the Federal Reserve banks exported out of this country to their foreign principals.

The Federal Reserve Board and the Federal Reserve banks lately conducted an anti-hoarding campaign here. Then they took that extra money which they had persuaded the American people to put into the banks and they sent it to Europe along with the rest. In the last several months, they have sent $1,300,000,000 in gold to their foreign employers, their foreign masters, and every dollar of that gold belonged to the people of the United States and was unlawfully taken from them.

Is not it high time that we had an audit of the Federal Reserve Board and the Federal Reserve banks and an examination of all our Government bonds and securities and public moneys instead of allowing the corrupt and dishonest Federal Reserve Board and the Federal Reserve banks to speculate with those securities and this cash in the notorious open discount market of New York City?

Mr. Chairman, within the limits of the time allowed me, I can not enter into a particularized discussion of the Federal Reserve Board and the Federal Reserve banks. I have singled out the Federal Reserve currency for a few remarks because there has lately been some talk here of "fiat money." What kind of money is being pumped into the open discount market and through it into foreign channels and stock exchanges? Mr. Mills of the Treasury has spoken here of his horror of the printing presses and his horror of dishonest money. He has no horror of dishonest money. If he had, he would be no party to the present gambling of the Federal Reserve Board and the Federal Reserve banks in the nefarious open discount market of New York, a market in which the sellers are represented by ten great discount dealer corporations owned and organized by the very banks which own and control the Federal Reserve Board and the Federal Reserve banks. Fiat money, indeed!

After the several raids on the Treasury Mr. Mills borrows the speech of those who protested against those raids and speaks now with pretended horror of a raid on the Treasury. Where was Mr. Mills last October when the United States Treasury needed $598,000,000 of the taxpayers' money which was supposed to be in the safe-keeping of Andrew W. Mellon in the designated depositories of Treasury funds, and which was not in those depositories when the Treasury needed it? Mr. Mills was the Assistant Secretary of the Treasury then, and he was at Washington throughout October, with the exception of a very significant week he spent at White Sulphur Springs closeted with international bankers, while the Italian minister, Signor Grandi, was being entertained — and bargained with — at Washington.

What Mr. Mills is fighting for is the preservation whole and entire of the banker's monopoly of all the currency of the United States Government. What Mr. Patman proposes is that the Government shall exercise its sovereignty to the extent of issuing some currency for itself. This conflict of opinion between Mr. Mills as the spokesman of the bankers and Mr. Patman as the spokesman of the people brings the currency situation here into the open. Mr. Patman and the veterans are confronted by a stone wall — the wall that fences in the bankers with their special privileges. Thus, the issue is joined between the host of democracy, of which the veterans are a part, and the men of the king's bank, the would-be aristocrats, who deflated American agriculture and robbed this country for the benefit of their foreign principals.

Mr. Chairman, last December, I introduced a resolution here asking for an examination and an audit of the Federal Reserve Board and the Federal Reserve banks and all related matters. If the House sees fit to make such an investigation, the people of the United States will obtain information of great value. This is a Government of the people, by the people, for the people. Consequently, nothing should be concealed from the people. The man who deceives the people is a traitor to the United States. The man who knows or suspects that a crime has been committed and who conceals or covers up that crime is an accessory to it. Mr. Speaker, it is a monstrous thing for this great Nation of people to have its destinies presided over by a traitorous Government board acting in secret concert with international usurers. Every effort has been made by the Federal Reserve Board to conceal its power but the truth is the Federal Reserve Board has usurped the Government of the United States. It controls everything here and it controls all our foreign relations. It makes and breaks governments at will. No man and no body of men is more entrenched in power than the arrogant credit monopoly which operates the Federal Reserve Board and the Federal Reserve banks. These evil-doers have robbed this country of more than enough money to pay the national debt. What the National Government has permitted the Federal Reserve Board to steal from the people should now be restored to the people. The people have a valid claim against the Federal Reserve Board and the Federal Reserve banks. If that claim is enforced, Americans will not need to stand in the breadlines or to suffer and die of starvation in the streets. Homes will be saved, families will be kept together, and American children will not be dispersed and abandoned. The Federal Reserve Board and the Federal Reserve banks owe the United States Government an immense sum of money. We ought to find out the exact amount of the people's claim. We should know the amount of the indebtedness of the Federal Reserve Board and the Federal Reserve banks to the people and we should investigate this treacherous and disloyal conduct of the Federal Reserve Board and the Federal Reserve banks.

Here is a Federal Reserve note. Immense numbers of these notes are now held abroad. I am told that they amount to upwards of a billion dollars. They constitute a claim against our Government and likewise a claim against the money our people have deposited in the member banks of the Federal Reserve system. Our people's money to the extent of $1,300,000,000 which has within the last few months been shipped abroad to redeem Federal Reserve notes and to pay other gambling debts of the traitorous Federal Reserve Board and the Federal Reserve banks. The greater part of our monetary stock has been shipped to foreigners. Why should we promise to pay the debts of foreigners to foreigners? Why should our Government be put into the position of supplying money to foreigners? Why should the Federal Reserve Board and the Federal Reserve banks be permitted to finance our competitors in all parts of the world? Do you know why the tariff was raised? It was raised to shut out the flood of Federal Reserve goods pouring in here from every quarter of the globe — cheap goods, produced by cheaply paid foreign labor on unlimited supplies of money and credit sent out of this country by the dishonest and unscrupulous Federal Reserve Board and the Federal Reserve banks. Go out in Washington to buy an electric light bulb and you will probably be offered one that was made in Japan on American money. Go out to buy a pair of fabric gloves and inconspicuously written on the inside of the gloves that will be offered to you will be found the words "made in Germany" and that means "made on the public credit of the United States Government paid to German firms in American gold taken from the confiscated bank deposits of the American people."

The Federal Reserve Board and the Federal Reserve banks are spending $100,000,000 a week buying Government securities in the open market and are making a great bid for foreign business. They are trying to make rates so attractive that the human-hair merchants and distillers and other business entities in foreign lands will come here and hire more of the public credit of the United States Government and pay the Federal Reserve outfit for getting it for them.

Mr. Chairman, when the Federal Reserve act was passed, the people of the United States did not perceive that a world system was being set up here which would make the savings of an American school-teacher available to a narcotic-drug vendor in Macao. They did not perceive that the United States were to be lowered to the position of a coolie country which has nothing but raw materials and heavy goods for export; that Russia was destined to supply the man power and that this country was to supply financial power to an international superstate — a superstate controlled by international bankers and international industrialists acting together to enslave the world for their own pleasure.

The people of the United States are being greatly wronged. If they are not, then I do not know what "wronging the people" means. They have been driven from their employments. They have been dispossessed of their homes. They have been evicted from their rented quarters. They have lost their children. They have been left to suffer and to die for lack of shelter, food, clothing, and medicine.

The wealth of the United States and the working capital of the United States has been taken away from them and has either been locked in the vaults of certain banks and the great corporations or exported to foreign countries for the benefit of the foreign customers of those banks and corporations. So far as the people of the United States are concerned, the cupboard is bare. It is true that the warehouses and coal yards and grain elevators are full, but the warehouses and coal yards and grain elevators are padlocked and the great banks and corporations hold the keys. The sack of the United States by the Federal Reserve Board and the Federal Reserve banks is the greatest crime in history.

Mr. Chairman, a serious situation confronts the House of Representatives to-day. We are trustees of the people and the rights of the people are being taken away from them. Through the Federal Reserve Board and the Federal Reserve banks, the people are losing the rights guaranteed to them by the Constitution. Their property has been taken from them without due process of law. Mr. Chairman, common decency requires us to examine the public accounts of the Government and see what crimes against the public welfare have and are being committed.

What is needed here is a return to the Constitution of the United States. We need to have a complete divorce of Bank and State. The old struggle that was fought out here in Jackson's day must be fought over again. The independent United States Treasury should be re-established and the Government should keep its own money under lock and key in the building the people provided for that purpose. Asset currency, the device of the swindler, should be done away with. The Government should buy gold and issue United States currency on it. The business of the independent bankers should be restored to them. The State banking systems should be freed from coercion The Federal Reserve districts should be abolished and the State boundaries should be respected. Bank reserves should be kept within the borders of the States whose people own them, and this reserve money of the people should be protected so that the international bankers and acceptance bankers and discount dealers can not draw it away from them. The exchanges should be closed while we are putting our financial affairs in order. The Federal Reserve act should be repealed and the Federal Reserve banks, having violated their charters, should be liquidated immediately. Faithless Government officers who have violated their oaths of office should be impeached and brought to trial. Unless this is done by us, I predict that the American people, outraged, robbed, pillaged, insulted, and betrayed as they are in their own land, will rise in their wrath and send a President here who will sweep the money changers out of the temple.

SUPPLEMENTARY ESSAY
The Unconstitutionality of the National Debt
by Henry Clay Dean

The War Debt is Not a Just Debt

What is a just and what is an unjust debt? To fasten upon thirty millions of people, by a minority of votes, and transmit to their posterity in the most palpable case, will always be a matter of doubt which can never be satisfactorily determined either by the contention of debate or the conflict of war.

There never yet has been a party in power in any government which excited or prosecuted a war, whether to satiate revenge or gratify ambition, that did not at the same time assume the contest as not only justifiable, but just; not only necessary, but holy. Such is the brief epitome of the arguments upon all wars. Such were declared the character and purposes of the wars of the Stuarts to crush the proud spirit of liberty in the English people, the war of King George to enslave America, wars against Ireland, Scotland and the East Indies by Great Britain — indeed all wars by all tyrants.

Every war has been the heated theme of songs and prayers, thanksgiving and praise, on every side, by all parties engaged; has been used as the machinery by which the human passions might be inflamed to their highest pitch of intensity; and religious sentiment used as the vehicle in which tyrants rode into power, and the habiliments worn by demons to enter the high priesthood, bearing the palm-wreath of victory or making their mournful dirge as victory or defeat befell them or the other army in conflict. This evident consciousness of right was not confined to one party alone. Each contending side was alike appealing to heaven for vindication of their mottoes, and denunciation of the wickedness of their enemies. Indeed, it is the common and remarkable feature of the history of all wars, that the same self-

829

adulatory harangues in very nearly the same phraseology, making due allowance for the difference of language and the habits, passions or customs of the people, have been employed in every country only with the slightest difference in America and Russia, England and China, Spain and Judea. The same imprecations of those they met in battle seem stereotyped in the mind, and painted only in new colors, without a change of feature.

Held by the light of Christianity, all wars are wicked. They are doubly wicked when Christians are engaged in mutual destruction; but they are atrocious beyond all power of expression when they involve people of a common blood, brethren in the flesh and in the spirit. It is only when pervading infidelity and thorough corruption coalesce to destroy the Church and State together that such wars can transpire and escape the opprobrium of both civilization and Christianity. All such wars are at best but organized systems of robbery with a common tendency and common end to the ruin of the country, the overthrow of just government, and the robbery and degradation of the people.

In full view of the wrongs and evils of war, the self-evident rights of man, and the clearly wicked and spiteful character of this war, what authority will be called in requisition to justify the attempt to bind generation after generation, loaded with an immoveable debt, to the cart-wheel of bankruptcy, and destroy our form of government? This debt was incurred to carry on a war conceived in the foulest passions of depraved human nature, carried on for the mercenary purposes of personal gain by a systematized corruption, cruelty and crime; condemned by every conception of justice, and outdoing in all of the elements of wrong the startling crimes charged by Edmund Burke against Warren Hastings (whilst Governor of India) in the British Parliament. In all of this wicked, cruel war, there has been but these unchangeable objects in view: to glut the avarice of the rich, to satiate the vengeance of the spiteful, and minister to the most grovelling appetites of the victims; to make the people the slaves of money and their armies the tools of tyrants.

This argument in behalf of the late civil war is somewhat changed, but is not strengthened, when the proposition assumes that the war was carried on (which is now upon all hands conceded) to abolish the system of African servitude in the United States. The argument concedes two points presented in this review:

1. There was no evil in slavery which could be abolished by war, to give it efficiency in times of peace. This is quite clear in itself, but it is fully conceded in the fact of the government by the change demanded in the Constitution, and through duress and fraud added to it.

2. The great improvement in the condition of the negro by his transfer from Africa to America will place it beyond cavil in history that he suffered no evil in the exchange of countries, conditions and character. It is quite as apparent that he has received no benefit from the late transition from organized protection to social anarchy.

3. Whatever may have been the will of the people — which is the great common law of America when legally expressed — concerning the status of the negro, there has been nothing done for his benefit by war which might not have been far better done peaceably, without the shedding of blood, the destruction of property, and the overthrow of the republi-

can form of government, the triple enormities perpetrated by the late revolution.

The debt is not just in this, we have had no *quid pro quo*. *The people are not bound in justice to pay this debt.* We have received nothing in return for it. Our currency is destroyed, our liberties gone, our institutions overthrown, leaving us nothing for all that we have lost, all that we have squandered, and all that we have surrendered, to say nothing of the enormous debt that we have contracted and yet hangs over us. The eternal law that every sale implies a price, the *quid pro quo* leaves this debt without approximating a material consideration, adequate or inadequate to its payment.

This debt might have been avoided. The evidence is everywhere at hand. By a strict adherence to the Constitution in the enunciation of political principles, it never could have transpired. An honest, earnest address to the people from President Lincoln after his election would have thoroughly settled the public mind, quieted excitement, and prevented civil war, with the consequent blood, carnage, and crime. Upon the inauguration of the President, a clear and implicit declaration of his purposes and constitutional integrity would have disarmed those already in arms, restored quiet to the country, and utterly ruined the leaders of the secession movement by destroying the pretexts for secession.

Congress could have arrested the war by manly avowals in the beginning of its session in 1861, notwithstanding the well-grounded distrust which had fixed itself in the public mind. By the least exhibition of justice upon the part of the administration, the war would have been avoided. The administration of Lincoln saw the absolute necessity of general public bribery to make the shadows of money abundant among the people and intoxicate them with the appearances of wealth, and postpone taxation to posterity. They used no more restraints upon expenditures than the profligate libertine, who measures his extravagance by his power to destroy property and capacity to create debt.

It was in view of creating war and preventing the exposure of the nakedness of the administration that presses were destroyed, free speech prohibited and elections treated as a farce, to destroy the liberties of the people, with all of the solemn forms of law. The administration of the government forced issues between capital and labor, arbitrary power and rational government. It has been made our duty in self-preservation to teach tyrants that all elections shall be fair and free, to teach usurpers that the will of the people shall be the supreme law of the land, and that no debt contracted to enslave them shall be paid. Self-respect imposes this duty upon the people to impress this lesson upon despots, that legislation shall be pure and untrammelled. It is a duty that we owe to free government that no statute enacted, no debt contracted, no obligation imposed by corrupt or unfair legislation, shall be of such binding force as that a failure in the courts to declare them void shall prevent the people at their will from repudiating them. This will instruct capitalists and gamblers in stocks, who swindle themselves into wealth, that they may not trample labor into the dust with impunity, nor safely connive at the overthrow of constitutional government to amass immense wealth.

The War Debt is Unconstitutional

By what authority did the President destroy State government? "The United States shall guarantee to every State in this Union a republican form of government, and shall protect each of them against invasion, and, on application of the Legislature, from domestic violence" (U.S. Constitution, Article IV, Section 4). What Governor or Legislature of what State applied to the President to protect them against domestic violence? On the contrary, when the President asked the Governors of Tennessee, Virginia, Missouri, and Kentucky to do this, they indignantly declined the work of butchery proposed; the President had no right to invade any State. There was no domestic violence; the operation of law was unclogged until the President commenced the work of disintegration. There were no changes made in the State laws and State constitutions, which were not made in conformity with the organic laws.

By what authority did the President imprison the Legislature of Maryland? incarcerate the Judges of the several States of the Union? "The judicial power of the United States shall not be construed to extend to any suit of law or equity, commenced or to be prosecuted against one of the United States by citizens of another State or by subjects of a foreign power" (*Ibid.*, Amendment XI). How much less the right to wage war against a State. What may not be done peaceably may not be forcibly done. Judgment always precedes execution. A war levied against a State is unconstitutional. A debt contracted for such purpose is likewise unconstitutional. No such war could grow out of the Constitution, nor the debt be of valid obligation. The people are not bound by the Constitution to pay this debt because it was entirely unauthorized by the Constitution. It was created in violation of the Constitution for the purpose of overthrowing the Constitution.

From the beginning there was scarcely anything lawfully done; and what was otherwise lawfully done, was done in an unlawful manner. The general emulation in civil and military life was to see who could set the laws most at defiance. These factors are conceded by the authors and instigators of the war. 1. They passed acts of immunity to cover their crimes; 2. They offered amendments to the Constitution to legalize their usurpations; and 3. They propose amendments to make the debt obligatory upon the country.

How can a debt bind a people which is not made according to law? *We are not bound by the theory of our Government to pay this debt.* The war was waged in violation of the theory of our government by consent in the exact form, spirit, and purpose of arbitrary government, to destroy the republican system. How then can such a debt have constitutional force or obligation to bind any one, since it was made in the interest of self-destruction and to pay for violence done to and butchery of the people?

In its stead was a monarchy in everything but the name, in which the President was guarded, in the style of the Czar and Sultan, with all of the brutality of the one and the pomp of the other; with all of the trappings of monarchy and the violence of despotism. With the overthrow of our system and theory of government, and the adoption of the imperial style and military guard, the most intimate friend of Washington, Jefferson or Monroe would have entirely failed to recognize the old and familiar forms that gave us characteristic distinction everywhere. A new and unique system was substituted. We had the forms of republican government enforced or obstructed, or both, as occasion might demand or necessity might justify. It was not republican, for nobody was free. The citizens and soldiers were alternately arrested, and State and military officers were spending their terms in guard-houses or military prisons as whim, interest, or caprice might suggest, at the will of their masters who were not always known, for it was as difficult to learn who directed affairs as it was to know who was loyal. Everybody was conscripted; everybody was an officer; everybody was arrested; everybody was removed from office; everybody was reinstated in turn, just as the President might be persuaded by the last committee of merchants, ministers, loyal leaguers, free negroes or ruling madams of the sanitary commission or sewing society. Never was there such a medley of tragedy and farce, murder and mockery, of grave pronunciations and the most ridiculous government follies. Anarchy, which knows no law, was reduced to a system by which anarchies were to be let loose and restrained as occasion might require, or circumstances might dictate. From the government nothing could be known of its character except occasionally an act in lucid intervals.

The War Debt is a Breach of Trust

A debt may be contracted under such systematic breaches of trust upon the part of public officers as to have no moral binding force upon the people, though ostensibly for the most unquestionable public good. This is especially true where the contractors were privy to the fraud. The only security that popular governments have for the faithful performance of contracts is that nothing stronger than public opinion is held for the payment of debts, because no suits can be entertained by a sovereign power to coerce itself.

When the questions which originate war and public debts largely divide the public mind, then the justice and probabilities of its liquidation become a matter just as doubtful as the vagaries of human opinion and political integrity. But the question may be evenly balanced in the public judgment. Public opinion may be restrained concerning it. It becomes still more uncertain how far the public conscience may feel bound for the payment; but each succeeding decade, with its accumulating responsibilites, will feel less and less bound in honor to meet an obligation which, at the best, holds but a feeble grasp upon the public responsibility.

When it is clear that the majority of a full million and a half of actual voters, not engaged in war, were opposed to the war as a remedy for existing evils, or that the debt and war are both frauds upon the public credulity and destructive of our system of government, then the payment of the debt becomes impossible. This is precisely the case of our war and war debt. Abraham Lincoln reached the Presidency by a great minority in both the first and second elections. In the second election, the minority was even greater than in the first, amounting to 1,200,000 less than a majority of the votes of the people, not accounting the fraud and force applied to divest the election of every attribute of choice. But the strength of this argument is irresistible. Every vote cast at the election of 1860 was given to candidates pledged in public professions of political faith, including the ablest speeches of Mr. Lincoln himself, against coercion or war. He had, in the most public manner avowed, and in the most solemn oaths sworn before heaven and earth, not to interfere with the existing condition of things in the government. The right of one-half of the States to overrun and destroy the other half had been denied by all of the leading statesmen, North and South, in every period of our history, and by the courts in the exercise of their plenary powers.

We Are Unable to Pay This Debt

There is no subject upon which even statesmen are so frequently the victims of delusion as that of the resources of their own country. Whether in regard to the relation which their wealth bears to their indebtedness, or the relation which their resources bear to that of other nations; and quite as vague are their notions about their ability to pay enormous debts. One source of this deception is the value which they attach to property, based upon the crazy inflation of the currency and the corrupt imaginations of speculators engaged in stock-gambling.

This delusion is not peculiar to the financiers of our own age and country. It has been universal. Such is the intoxicating nature of trade and commerce in the height of a paper bubble. Just before the outbreak of the French Revolution, which was precipitated by national bankruptcy and the reckless violence which always accompanies bold loaning and extravagant living, even the most illustrious English statesmen were dazzled and carried away with the grandeur of its profligacy, and for a time believed the French finances solid and immoveable because the national credit was pledged for its redemption. Edmund Burke was so completely captivated with Necker's theory that when Necker wrote a history of his political views and administration, confessing his failure and the fallacies of his opinion, Burke was dismayed and mortified at his own simplicity in being the victim of such hollow expedients; nearly every one of which remind one of the present times. Indeed, in all times, these expedients and subterfuges are the same. The younger William Pitt, the most searching analytical mind of his day, saw entirely through Necker's financial scheme and the ruin that would follow it, and in consequence, refused the tempting offer of the hand of Necker's gifted daughter, Madame de Stael.

It would be amazing were it not sorrowful to contemplate the picture which Secretary Chase has drawn of his financial plans in the ruin of the country. A complete detail of the financial history of the Treasury and the currency, with the shame, tricks, and villanies consequent upon them, practiced by himself, would rival in romance the confessions of Barnum in the exhibition of his Japanese Mermaid, Joyce Heath, Tom Thumb, the wooly horse, and "What is it?" — the low artifices to which they both resorted to deceive the people; the one in shows for their amusement, the other in falsehoods to overthrow their liberty.

We have never duly considered the present condition of our resources since the conclusion of the war, and the preliminary questions to be settled before we commence our calculation.

1. The war drove out of the country thousands of millions of capital, much of its own bullion, in consequence of its general unsafety.

2. It destroyed thousands of millions of dollars of capital in the Southern States which could no longer be taxed.

3. The destruction of hundreds of millions of dollars in the Confederate States rendered unavailable other hundreds of millions of dollars in the Northern States which were dependent upon the South for a market.

4. There has been no increase of a single article produced in the United States which could be exported or added to the financial prosperity of the country except kerosene oil, which is a late discovery and an insignificant matter.

A blind, stupid and destructive fanaticism assumes that our resources are incomparably greater than at any time heretofore. This they demonstrate by the magnitude of our public debt, which they denominate as so much active capital; and the destruction of public and private property, which they parade as a triumph over treason. The chief source of this delusion is that they account our money as capital, when in fact it is the certified evidence of our debt and poverty. The bonds held are simply the amount of debt which we hold against ourselves.

There is no more common expression or delusion in regard to the public debt than this. The bonds are not all due among ourselves; but upon the contrary, they were directly sold to European capitalists, as far as it was possible to get them into that market, where they are quoted from the market reports of London, Amsterdam, and Paris; but millions of these bonds were bought in America by European capitalists and re-invested in bank stocks under European auspices. It was this investment of European capital in America securities which was the most complete solution of the visit of the European capitalists to this country which excited as much curiosity and elicited as much parade as did Japanese Tommy's advent into the city of New York.

It is the most disgusting form of balderdash to maintain that poor men own bonds, or any other interest-bearing securities in America, any more than in Europe. The mere fact that some of these bonds are the property of American citizens makes it in no sense different from their ownership abroad. Once cast upon the market, they will seek the idle capital of the world and absorb it.

The debt is an offset to the resources of the country and must be deducted from them in the calculation of our wealth. It injures every department of wealth, commerce, manufactures, agriculture and navigation. It withdraws from active business to positive idleness all of the capital to the full extent of the funding system. The conversion of the bonds into bank notes is the destruction of the resources of the people. Not one dollar passes out of the bonds into National bank currency which does not cost the public nearly one hundred per cent. in interest on the bonds, on the bank notes and the ruinous premium paid upon the depreciated currency with which they bought their bonds, besides the extravagant bonus which was given as an inducement to purchase them. Every bondholder realizes this amount of money for his bonds. Against such profits in investment there can be no successful competition. Railroads cannot be built. How is it possible for them to offer an equivalent security to these bonds? Commerce is checked, because the bonds are proof against shipwreck; and who can invest in the legitimate trade of the ocean against such odds? The Western people cannot hope for the usual improvement of their lands, because no investment in improvements can justify the payment of more than six per cent., and scarcely that amount can be realized in agricultural pursuits with the entire destruction of our exports and commerce, and a most extraordinary increase of our current government expenses. Our standing army is quadrupled. The expenses of each soldier is twice as much as formerly. The clerical force of every department is more than duplicated. This is the financial condition of the country and a fair exhibit of its resources and capacity to liquidate its debt. It is a most notable fact that during the administration of Mr. Buchanan, the chief tangible accusation against him was the extravagance with which he administered the government and the exceeding great difficulty with which the money was raised, and that he left the treasury empty at the end of his term. Mr. Buchanan left the country free from debt, in the most healthy industrial condition; the people not only in comfortable, but in affluent circumstances. Such is the contrast.

What has been added to the productive wealth of the country to meet the additional expenditures? It may be safely assumed that no one branch of industry has been increased in the last five years, except that used or destroyed in the military service, consisting of arms, ammunition, artillery, *etc*. We have lost without any compensation whatever. 2,600,000 able-bodied men were taken from actual productive business; from the plough, the loom, the anvil and buildings of the country, whose daily labor added millions to the stock of American capital. The horses, mules, cattle, sheep, hogs, wagons, and gears necessary to the support of such armies during four years of uninterrupted and constantly augmenting warfare, the entire value of which has been scarcely less than $5,000,000,000, which may be added to the calculation, but does not present the full extent of the loss we suffer.

No nation or man has ever trampled with impunity upon the clearly written law of God, or the well-defined rights of man, without answering directly for his crime. The law of God is a crystal mirror which reflects back upon the soul of every rational being the exact character of the motives of his heart and the action of his life. No man, nation or age ever committed a crime or perpetrated an enormity, which did not fling its monstrous image back upon its guilty perpetrator. Nor have we escaped in either morals or finances this clearly marked law of the living God. When Sheridan's highwaymen carried the torch through Virginia, and the hordes of Sherman's incendiaries were turned loose upon the defenceless people of Georgia, the United States were the sufferers. The cotton-fields destroyed made our corn-fields worthless and the very same communities which sent armies to burn cotton-fields had to burn their corn-fields for fuel. The poor man in the army burned the clothes of his family under the delusion that he was impoverishing the cotton planters, and did not discover his mistake until he returned from the war and found that the cotton goods which he used to buy for ten cents now cost him fifty. He was wild with excitement over the fires that swept down the sugar-house, and never dreamed of his own suffering, until his children were crying for syrups which he could not buy.

Such has been the complete work of destruction and the entire mutilation of our available resources that nearly every article which secured to us the balance of trade abroad, hemp — cotton, rice, sugar and tobacco, with tar, resin and turpentine — was destroyed by our own hands and our resources cut off by our own folly. The cotton plant supplied the people with its fibre for clothing. The regular supply of this staple was bought by the people of the North and West, and paid for by the products of their cattle, horses, hogs, sheep and agriculture. When the Southern States ceased to produce cotton, the Northern people had to rely upon the production of wool. The ancient habits of the American Revolution were revived in the Southern States. Women went to the loom and the spinning-wheel, and every thriving household became a primitive manufactory. In the Northern States woolen manufactories of great extent were kept in operation, and the demand for wool became absorbent. In less than four years, the whole agricultural aspect of the country was changed. Sheep took the place of horses and cattle in the mountain districts, and supplanted the culture of swine in the Western States, until horses commanded the most extravagant prices, and meat cattle sold at the former prices for hogs, and a single hog sold at the price formerly paid for a yoke of oxen or an ordinary horse. This process of depletion went on until a famine stared the people in the face. The introduction of sheep into the country drove the cattle out, for neither cattle nor horses will thrive in the same pasturage with sheep. During all this time of general depletion, the people believed themselves in the height of prosperity. They mistook their own debt for their own wealth, as though the mortgage upon their farms, created by government liabilities, was actual wealth. This delusion, kept up by the system of Secretary Chase, had a powerful agency in the protraction of the war and did much to conciliate those time-serving statesmen who knew that ruin must follow such political economy, but hoped to indemnify themselves for all losses in the general plunder in which they might share.

In addition to the men in military life, the war employed quite three millions of producers out of a population of twenty millions. The labor and wages of this vast army of men would have built railroads as a net-work in the States from which they were dragged away. Their idleness would have been a calamity, a severe blow, from which it would require a great State an age to recover. If these men had been idle, our ships of war safely anchored, and our costly armaments scattered to the winds, the loss would have been comparatively small; but added to this was the loss to the whole country of the labor of nearly one million of men during the same period. The cost of their arms, ammunition, artillery, clothing and all incidental expenses to defend against this invasion of the vast army arrayed in the North, by both sea and land, added to the entire destruction of the exports of cotton, rice, tobacco, sugar, molasses and everything grown and exported in the Confederate States. The daily occurring losses from idle men and idle hands, with the daily accruing expenses of military rule, are increasing these losses and impairing our power to recuperate our exhaustive system.

Matthew F. Maury, who, at the commencement of the rebellion, was in charge of the National Observatory in Washington, has written a three column letter to the London *Morning Herald*, in which he gives the following estimate of the losses of the South caused by the war:

> I estimate the amount of the pecuniary losses incurred by the people of the Southern Confederacy, in their late attempt at independence, to be not less than $7,000,000,000 (seven thousand millions of dollars) viz:
>
> By emancipation $3,000,000,000
> Expenses of the war 2,000,000,000
> Destruction of private property 1,000,000,000
> Additional taxation imposed by the victor
> for payment of Federal war debt, say
> $10,000,000 per annum, equal to interest on . . 1,000,000,000
> _____
> Total $7,000,000,000
>
> This loss falls upon less than eight millions of whites, who have, moreover, in addition, to contribute largely to the support of the four millions of blacks who have been suddenly turned loose among them, and who, for the present at least, are incapable of caring for themselves.
>
> This $7,000,000,000 of money was the accumulated wealth of centuries; it constituted nearly the whole industrial plan and capital of the South.

> The debt could not be paid if it were just and desirable to pay it:
> 1. The experience of the world has been that no people have been able to lay up anything above their current expenses, and such repairs and improvements as the increase of population and the accumulating demands of society render necessary.
> 2. That the increase of population of every country brings with it a *pro rata* diminution of wealth *per capita*.
> 3. That every generation of people are better able to pay the debts of their own creation than the generations which succeed them.
> 4. That the growing age of every country carries with it more than an equal growth of expenditures, and to that extent incapacitates it to pay the debts of its own creation, and makes the payment of prior debts impossible.
> 5. This has always been the condition of society and will continue to be.
> 6. Each generation will have its wars and consequent expenses and cannot, nor ought not to bear the expenses of wars of preceding generations.
> There are three ways of disposing of such a debt, each of which has its conveniences:
> 1. By repudiating the obligations of the debt entirely, which would bring the burden of the evil upon the rich who have hoarded their means and invested them in government

credits.

2. By funding the debt and paying the interest on it after the manner of British debt. This impoverishes the poor and places them where the British have left their poor, in perpetual servitude; or

3. By abolishing the funding system and banking system built upon it, freeing the people from its onerous burdens and in its stead issuing certificates, entitling the holder to such share *pro rata* as he may be entitled to upon a final settlement, in which the public lands or a part of them may be hypothecated for the redemption of these certificates.

The liberty of the people demands an immediate abolition of the whole funding system.

One Generation Cannot Bind Another to Its Debts

By what right can any one generation contract to enslave successive generations, and mortgage the labor of future centuries to pay a debt created to satiate hate and aggrandize a lawless cupidity? All just debts are based upon mutual honor and mutual benefit; upon the *quid pro quo*; but the very essence of the contract is that both parties are capable of contracting, and give a rational assent to the obligations which bind them.

What is a debt? "Any kind of a just demand" (*Bouvier Dictionary*). It is that obligation which one person may voluntarily lay himself under to another to be computed by the standards of value then in vogue. The voluntary repudiation of a just debt is no less a crime than the robbery of honest creditors by any other means of fraud or force.

A contract cannot be voluntary or of binding obligation upon the next generation which has been entered into by this generation. It is impossible; the contract had no consent of the party upon whom the obligation falls. To this rule, founded in justice, there can be no variations, except in the following cases:

1st. When a debt shall have been contracted for the erection of some public improvement necessary to the permanent administration of justice, or the maintenance of law among the people, such as court houses, jails, *etc.*

2d. A canal dug or railroad built at the public expense, fastened upon the property of the country, inures to the benefit of posterity, and is the representative to future generations of the energy, genius and enterprize of their ancestry. But the most magnificent monuments ever reared to the honor of human genius and mechanical skill have been justly accounted too costly for the endorsement and redemption of future generations. But in all such cases the creditors may have justly no other security for the payment of what may remain due upon it than that which is afforded in the value, use, and the profits of the public improvement itself.

This maxim must hold good in all just governments. A contract made by past generations cannot even bind the honor of the present generation, who may have declared against the justice of the act for which the debt has been contracted. It may have been a vision or a whim in which the persons engaged by contract robbed the public. It may have been unjust or unnecessary. What is true in the private affairs of men must be true of their public matters, since the public is but the aggregate of the private. If a banker builds a great house for his business, or a miller establishes his mill at great expense and involves a debt which he is unable to liquidate, no one dreams of entailing this debt upon his children, although his estate should pay but a trifling portion of the encumbrance which passes away with his property. The son can, in no sense, be responsible because he had no voice in the contract; and elects to waive his rights in the inheritance, and is under no obligation to consider the action of his father as binding upon his honor or conscience. This is the law of every free country; freedom demands this much, otherwise the son would be a slave to the improvidence of the father. A very few generations would create caste in society that would make slavery absolute, which time could not efface without revolution.

What may not be done by the individual, may not justly be done by the government. The golden rule, *"whatsoever ye would have men do unto you, do even so unto them,"* was given for nations as well as for men, and is alike obligatory upon both. There is no application of the principle that "all just powers of government are derived from the consent of the governed," more forcible or just than to that of taxation. No one generation of men have the right of contract or can bind the succeeding generations to pay a debt contracted to maintain any religious or political party or any system of religion and politics.

Every system of government is comparatively good or evil, as it expresses the wishes of the people, who are the source of just power; or as it conforms or disagrees with those fundamental self-evident rights of man which are elevated above the legitimate reach of legislation, and the violation of which is an unpardonable trespass upon the prerogative of human nature. Each generation for itself has the right to make, alter, amend, or conform the existing system to its will, and is under personal obligations to pay all of the expenses incident to and consequent upon the conduct or change of the government. The reasons for this are two-fold and apparent. First, they are the only persons interested in the change, for if the generation which preceded us are not competent judges of the laws for this generation, how is it possible for us to be infallible arbiters of the opinions of the next generation? and by what right do they assume to mortgage their soul, understanding and conscience, to particular doctrines in advance, and mortgage their labor to the heirs of bondholders in all future time? The principle is not only absurd and dangerous, but it is the most complete system of slavery imaginable, by which each generation in advance of its birth is assigned to labor — the kind, amount, when, where and how, beforehand — to pay the expense of the riot, profligacy, debauchery of thieving contractors, loathsome prostitutes, and effeminate military officers. The immediate offspring of the shavers, usurers, extortioners and misers who grew fat upon the blood of the sires, is the grief of their mothers and the destitution of themselves, now doomed to perpetual taxation.

The second reason is even stronger than the first. It is the duty of every man to pay for what he receives. This is the touchstone of honesty itself that he does it willingly. Then they who work a violent revolution are, by common consent, the only ones benefitted by it;

they are under obligations to defray its expenses, and immediate levies of tax as the revolution transpires, is the only legitimate mode of paying it.

The old maxim, "in times of peace prepare for war," was the fixed law of governments among our fathers, and each generation transmitted to its successor a treasury filled with money, as the means of carrying on wars in national defence which was often diverted to the purpose of civil wars and squandered in the enslavement and degradation of the people. But in such a war as that which has just closed, payment of the debt resolves itself into two very plain questions:

1. If it has been a blessing to the people or a public benefit, then those receiving the benefit ought not to hesitate cheerfully to bear the expenses; much more, they ought to forgive the indebtedness incurred as held by them in notes or bonds.

2. But if the revolution is a great public curse and has destroyed all that is sacred in principle and desirable in property, how wicked a crime must it be, against natural justice, to ask an injured people to pay a debt consequent upon a contract forced upon them to consummate their own degradation, slavery and utter ruin.

No debt incurred by a war of any kind can possibly bind the succeeding generation. First, they have not consented to it, which is the essence of the contract, and without which the parties held obliged to pay are in the very same condition of the traveler met by the highwaymen, who cry, "Stand and deliver" — "Your money or your life." It is the application of force purely as a means of taking and applying property.

Second, the war which may seem just to the fathers, may seem unjust to the children, and the children may contract a debt equal to that contracted by the fathers for the purpose of subverting the very system established by them, and leave a double debt upon the grandchildren, who disagree with both the father and grandfather, and believe that both wars were unnecessary, unjust, cruel and disgraceful, and that their causes might have been readily removed by the slightest forbearance and the simplest appeal to reason.

Third, if the claims upon which a transmitted debt are based be the self-sacrifice of those who contracted it, then let it be verified by the sacrifice; for if the debt is transmitted there has been no equal sacrifice. It is a sacrifice of the lives of the poor, but not of the wealth of the rich. If it were just and necessary that the poor people, who always fight the battles of a country, should sacrifice their property in a common cause, then how very unjust is it that the property and labor of the surviving soldiers and their children, in all time to come, should be held in perpetual mortgage to pay the debt and accruing interest to those who made merchandise of the blood and treasures of their comrades and parents. These reasons are not only just, but they are conclusive against the entailment of such debt upon posterity.

This is the chief corner-stone of our government, that there can be no hereditary rulers, either of kings or nobility, transmitted from one generation to another; neither by succession nor appointment by birth or condition. The second great principle and corollary of the first, is that no one generation has the power to bind an organic law irrevocably upon a succeeding generation, any more than kings have the right to appoint successors, or the people may be governed by the laws of royal descent. The third great principle and corollary of the first and second is that there is no just power in any one generation to mortgage the labor of a succeeding generation, without transmitting the means of payment; and then it is purely optional with the succeeding generations, whether they will accept the conditions upon which it is done. The debt is represented as "a first mortgage upon the property of the United States," but it is rather a bill of credit drawn upon the prosperity of the people which they will repudiate and send to protest in eternity.

The power to create and transmit such a debt is a most terrible revival of the old hard-hearted Jewish doctrine that *"the father ate sour grapes and put the children's teeth on edge."* We are met with the philanthropic argument that the debt was a contract to give to the country liberty. This is impossible. For the very taxation necessary to pay the interest on the debt is itself a slavery intolerable and insupportable, from which the people will be forced to fly to strange lands and seek refuge in perpetual alienage; or, as the alternative demand, repudiation of both principal and interest as the only remaining remedy.

The great idea upon which the late civil war was waged was that no one man may enslave his contemporary under any pretence whatever. It is the acme of the triumph claimed by its friends and instigators that this great question was settled by the force of arms and sealed with the richest blood of a whole generation of civilized men, that innocent involuntary servitude shall find no legal tolerance among us. But what a fatal conclusion to this argument is it that we may transmit slavery and unrequited obligations to be exacted by unborn generations from each other, through the funding system. Sifted of their sophistry, the arguments used to extenuate the crime of transmitting mortgages to posterity would as well apologize for the transmission of scrofula, consumption or other diseases. Carried to its legitimate results, the present system assumes that the profligacy of each generation may mortgage the prosperity and labor of all generations succeeding it until the full value of the property is exhausted, the labor absorbed in advance, and capital as effectually owns labor as the grazier owns the bullock, or the mule only, awaiting the time when age will consign them to the collar and the yoke. Deducting food, raiment and shelter, the owner pockets the earnings of the poor very much in the same manner.

The Duty to Repudiate War Debts

All wars of modern times have been under the control of capitalists. In Europe, the moneyed kings dictate terms to their political sovereigns, control wars and make peace. In America, the bankers contrived the late civil war. It was quite as much a scheme of money as of policy. War would not have been created if the banks had refused to engage in it. It could not have been carried on if the capital of the country had manfully opposed it. The liberty of the people, the peace of the world, and material prosperity of the poor would have been undisturbed, and even the condition of the negroes would have been better than now, but for these men.

The capitalists and stock-gamblers in Europe, by their alliance with the political adventurers of America, carefully planned this war in the interest of despotism and the funding system. They anticipated every argument and prepared the public mind for war in advance. During the war they prepared for the debt and continued the war that the debt might reach its present enormous extent. These gamesters upon human life and public misfortune have fattened upon the bloody conflicts of emperors and kings, and inherit fortunes coined out of the most frightful battles of modern times. Austria, France, Prussia and England have been fettered by the mortgages entailed by these brokers upon their property and industry.

Such is the perfection of the conspiracy against the property of the world, entered into by these stock gamblers, that war is always precipitated upon a particular country whenever it is believed to be ripe for revolution or fat enough to enrich the money trade. For the purpose of creating civil war, destroying the agriculture of the South, entailing a debt upon the people and, if possible, the utter destruction of Republican government in the United States, English emissaries were, by the monied interests of Europe, under religious guise, sent to America to stir up civil war. Pamphleteers added their wicked labors to the work. Sumner's celebrated visit to Europe was in the same general interest, and when Gen. James Shields of the United States Army had left the valley of the Shenandoah, Sumner assured him that he was glad that the rebels were not entirely defeated because his great object would not be accomplished if they were. The destruction of our prosperity, the ultimatum of the stock gamblers, had not been reached. The raid of John Brown and the partizan conflicts were but incidents in the grand purpose to create war and base a funding system upon it.

Such has been the unbroken success of the professional mischief-makers of the world, that they have succeeded in Europe for a full half century in fastening ruin and bankruptcy upon every sovereignty which was directed by their counsels or fell into their grasp. Bonaparte eluded their machinations; this only provoked their wrath and drove them to the combinations which culminated at Waterloo in the destruction of his empire and liberty.

The Mexican war was the first game played by the American stockbrokers, upon which the general peace of the Western Hemisphere was staked and lost. The late civil war has been a success, and if the stakes are delivered up by the ruined people to the stockgamblers, permanent peace in the United States is gone forever.

The successes have emboldened the stockbrokers and given them possession of every avenue to popular favor and power. The pulpit, the press and the army have been used as their instrument to secure their prize in the blood market of the world. These instruments of popular favor speak of war as the only means of government to be used upon every occasion to gratify spites, to punish indignities, or secure plunder. Unless this spirit be arrested promptly, our peace is imperilled and will be destroyed.

There is only one way to counteract this wicked spirit; and that is to give notice to the world that debts contracted in such an enterprize bind no one and cannot be collected. If it be wicked to engage in wars it is also unjust to pay money to carry on wars; but if it be unjust to carry on wars by ready money, how much more atrocious to carry them on by anticipating the credit of generations. It is the duty of all sincere peace men to make a demonstration against this usurpation; and let it be understood that no debt made in the interest of a war of premeditated plunder can be enforced upon a free people, or be sanctioned by the friends of peace.

There is an Equity which, in all public affairs, looks to the purposes, the mode and the application of monies in the creation of debts, when debts have been created in fraud, for purposes of corruption, and the parties issuing evidences of debt were *particeps criminis* and beneficiaries, then the question goes back to the legislatures, which must levy taxes before they can be collected. The new legislature must be elected by the people. The people of no country hasten to pay the debts known to be fraudulent or unjust. Against the indiscriminate payment of no debt ever contracted has there been so many conclusive arguments for utter repudiation as the debt now claimed by the foreign capitalists and domestic speculators, holding bonds and certificates of indebtedness against the United States, as the basis of a perpetual system of gambling upon the labor and commerce of the country.

Every consistent friend of peace must oppose the payment of the debt. If it be wrong to engage in a war of unparalleled cruelty and horror, it cannot be right to compensate the worst participants in it; men whose business is to inflame wars to fatten upon the blood of the innocent, and hoard up the treasure gained by the slaughter of hundreds of thousands of human beings, hurried into the presence of God without thought or preparation. What care these men — the brokers in immortal souls — for the burning of cities, barns, mills, and the desolation of whole regions of cultivated lands; with the food and raiment of decrepit old men, feeble women, and helpless children; the razing of churches and desecration of cemeteries?

Experience for the last three centuries demonstrates that the capitalists of the world hold the peace and the destiny of nations in their hands; they create war and make peace. The superstitions of religion and the malignity of politics are under the mercenary control of capital. The payment of this debt is a test question of civilization which the gamblers in public stocks watch with an intense interest that Christians might well emulate in the propagation of the gospel. Wars in Europe have placed their mercenary bankers in princely opulence. They furnish the sinews of war and command peace whenever they have sufficiently involved the imperial powers to secure an increase of annuities, and kings quiescently yield to their behests.

These kingly brokers watch the probabilities of war with the same keen scent that vultures follow the camp of moving armies to fatten on the offal. Such has been their success and sagacity that whilst kings exercise arbitrary power over the lives and liberties of their subjects by war and conscription, these bankers divide the regal power by subsidizing the labor of the subjects of kings in advance, absorbing it in taxations levied at their dictation, purchasing kings, bribing judges, suborning witnesses, entering into partnerships with legislatures, commissioning military officers, and hiring standing armies to stamp out the liberties of the people, who are forced to support all of these by taxation.

The United States have laid the foundation for just such a comprehensive system of monied oligarchy. There is now thrust into our faces the frightful picture by every newspaper under the control of capital, predictions of war and clamoring for blood as the remedy for every trivial evil, that adventurers may reap a rich harvest from the vices of the wicked, the follies of the weak, and the general profligacy of society. Such is the spirit of fanaticism, and the maddened temper of bad men aspiring to power, that all argument is ridiculed, except that which opens up a new field of plunder, or draws new victims into the net of their insatiate lust of gain.

If such men succeed in funding and consolidating the public debt made during the war, they have established a precedent which will assure them the power to incite a war at any time hereafter, when whim, interest or bad feeling may indicate either its profit or necessity. A strict and rigid settlement, according to the equities of eternal justice, is the only remedy for the great evil upon us. This is the clearest and most direct way to teach these gentlemen what they may not do, although they inflame the vilest passions of human nature into war; yet they must be taught that they cannot control the public conscience to enslave itself, and enforce perpetual bondage upon a people born free; that they cannot safely create and carry on wars, wicked and destructive in themselves, which might averted, but for the persistent chicanery of capital, which uses all of the well known arts of diplomacy to involve the people in civil war; which, failing in every other means to precipitate their revolutionary ends upon the country, connive at war, eschew compromise, and mob and murder the friends of peace.

The only hope of peace is in the destruction of the prosperity of mercenaries engaged in provoking civil wars. He is neither an intelligent nor a true friend of peace who will not boldly repudiate every illegal, fraudulent and vicious claim against the labor of the people to satiate the venality of capital, fattened on blood. This style of mortgaging labor in anticipated taxation is a wicked device of modern times to carry on wars of conquest, wars of subjugation, wars of plunder and wars to feed the malignity of bad men. It has never been successfully carried out to ensure more than annually accruing interest on the debt, and then only at reduced rates, and when it could be made the ministering servant of a system of aristocracy and overbearing power. Let it be an avowed article of American faith that no war of money, no war for money can be successfully prosecuted and carried on under the auspices of a free people; henceforth capitalists will have neither the will nor power to involve a peaceful people in universal carnage. Such has been the work of war upon our social system, sought to be ratified by the sanction of the people in the submission to this debt, that it binds us hand and foot and adds to war slavery, and to slavery all of its concomitant degradation.

The preceding essay was extracted from Henry Clay Dean, Crimes of the Civil War and Curse of the Funding System *(Baltimore, Maryland: J. Wesley Smith and Brothers, 1869).*

CHAPTER TWENTY-THREE
The Socialist Utopia of Federal Insurance

The Social Security Act of 1935

The state cannot aid men without enfeebling their energies and imperiling their self-reliance. Such a condition goes on for a century or so, and by and by the people, who gradually have been losing independence and self-initiative, become an easy prey to the man on horseback....

The Treasury of the United States has been opened wide by distributing money into every part of the country for purposes with which the national government has nothing to do, with the intention of directing the attention of the people to the all-wise providence of Congress and of the Executive. A hundred years ago, our people asked no favors from government, but only for a fair, square deal, each man confident in his ability to win by his own brain and his own hand. To-day, under this paternal rule, everybody is in the habit of looking to the President and Congress for relief from every evil....

Now such government is destructive of public virtue. The function of democracy is not alone to make government good, but to make men strong by intensifying their individual responsibility. The belief that the President or government has the power to make everybody comfortable or happy, and the inclination of the people to depend upon our government as the people of France and Germany depend upon theirs, is a tendency destructive of liberty and individual initiative. Paternalism is the dry rot of government, and as surely brings paralysis through all its members as the law of gravitation controls the universe....

The people must fight their own battles for better conditions. Every time they call upon that great central deity, the Government, to fight an evil, they surrender their God-given right to grow strong by fighting it themselves. By and by, if recent tendencies continue, they will surrender all their duties and all their rights, so dearly bought, to their rulers. By and by the government, like that of Germany, will dog the citizen's footsteps at every turn, provide him with old-age pensions, recompense him for all injuries received through negligence, destroy his manhood while alive, and bury him when dead. Let us go on at the same rate we have been during the last five years, and the sole idea of our country will be a divinely inspired President whose authority, as guardian of the people, insures their general felicity. This evolution will consist in erecting an absolutely central power over the ruins of state and local life.[1]

The above words were written in 1908 by New York attorney, Franklin Pierce, as a warning of what the future would hold for the American people should they continue to allow their leaders to provide for them. What was in his day a mere tendency toward subservience has now, over a century later, become a way of life for millions. The shift of the American mindset from self-reliance, or mutual cooperation within small communities, to a dependence upon the Government for subsistence is a striking illustration of how far removed we are from our hardy forefathers who endured disease, starvation, and even death to carve out a new civilization on this continent in the Seventeenth Century. To even attempt to live as though the Government is not Providence itself is to invite social ostracism and even outright persecution as a public enemy. Even the memory of manhood has all but perished in this country and in its place stands an impotent nation of groveling slaves whose gaze is ever fixed eastward to the Potomac for their master's benevolent care.

This slavish mentality is perhaps no better illustrated than by the Social Security system. On 14 August 1935, the Seventy-Fourth Congress passed what is commonly known as the Social Security Act: "To provide for the general welfare by establishing a system of Federal old-age benefits, and by enabling the several States to make more adequate provision for aged persons, blind persons, dependent and crippled children, maternal and child welfare, public health, and the administration of their unemployment compensation laws; to establish a Social Security Board; to raise revenue; and for other purposes."[2] There is a blatant falsehood right here in the Act's title: "To provide for the general welfare...." This was a reference to Article I, Section 8, Clause 1 of the U.S. Constitution, which delegated to Congress power "to lay and collect taxes, duties, imposts, and excises to pay the debts and provide for the common defence and general welfare of the United States." This clause applied only to the general welfare of the States within the Union; as such it had no reference whatsoever to the establishment of a welfare program for individual citizens, which the federal Government had no authority under the Constitution to do. In fact, the only contact that the Government had with the Citizen of one of the States was through the general post office, when the Citizen enlisted in the military, or when the able-bodied men comprising the State militias were called into actual service of the United States. In all other instances, the State Citizen was essentially a foreigner to the general Government in Washington, D.C. and he would

---

1. Pierce, *Federal Usurpation*, pages 128, 132, 133, 134-135.

2. Social Security Act, Public Law 74-271 (14 August 1935).

have looked with horror upon any legislation which proposed to make him anything less than a responsible and self-sufficient provider for his own well-being and that of his family. A "wise and frugal Government," according to Thomas Jefferson, was one "which shall restrain men from injuring one another, [and] leave them otherwise free to regulate their own pursuits of industry and improvement."[3] Rexford G. Tugwell, who served the Roosevelt Administration as a member of the "New Deal Brains Trust," commented on this view:

> The Constitution was a negative document, meant mostly to protect citizens from their government.... It would have been... fantastic to suggest that individuals ought to be made secure from the risks of their occupations, or to be protected from the hazards of life. Among the Framers there was no concern for the welfare of citizens as welfare is now conceived. Opportunities were open to all, and if they were not taken advantage of, or if an individual lost out to a more enterprising competitor, it was his own fault.... The laws would maintain order but would not touch the individual who behaved reasonably. He must pay taxes to support a smallish government and he must not interfere with commerce; but otherwise laws would do him neither good nor ill. The government of the Constitution was this kind of government.[4]

However, in the midst of the economic crisis of the 1930s, a social welfare program was much more attractive than in the better days of the Republic. In the words of Franklin Roosevelt prior to the passage of the Social Security Act:

> Next winter we may well undertake the great task of furthering the security of the citizen and his family through social insurance. This is not an untried experiment. Lessons of experience are available from States, from industries, and from many nations of the civilized world. The various types of social insurance are inter-related; and I think it is difficult to attempt to solve them piecemeal. Hence I am looking for a sound means which I can recommend to provide at once security against several of the great disturbing factors in life — especially those which relate to unemployment and old age.[5]

Like the rest of the New Deal package, Social Security was specifically designed to meet the demands of the "national emergency." As before, Roosevelt had a basic outline of what he wanted to implement, and he relied on select advisors to fill in the details. The

---

3. Jefferson, First Inaugural Address, 4 March 1801; in Richardson, *Messages and Papers of the Presidents*, Volume I, page 323.

4. Rexford G. Tugwell, "Rewriting the Constitution," *The Center Magazine* (Los Angeles, California: Center for the Study of Democratic Institutions, March 1968), Volume I, Number 3, pages 19-20.

5. Roosevelt, address to Congress on 8 June 1934; quoted by Arthur J. Altmeyer, *The Formative Years of Social Security* (Madison, Wisconsin: The University of Wisconsin Press, 1968), page 3.

Committee on Economic Security was thus created by Executive Order 6757 on 29 June 1934, the basis of which was Section 5(b) of the Trading With the Enemy Act. The Committee was composed of five top-ranking members of Roosevelt's Cabinet, all of whom were either former members of the defunct Progressive (Socialist) party or avowed sympathizers with socialism: Secretary of Labor Frances Perkins of Boston, Massachusetts,[6] Secretary of the Treasury Henry Morgenthau, Jr. of New York city, Attorney General Homer Cummings of Chicago, Illinois, Secretary of Agriculture Henry A. Wallace of Orient, Iowa, and Federal Emergency Relief Administrator Harry L. Hopkins of Sioux City, Iowa. The Committee in turn appointed a staff of advisors borrowed from other Government agencies to assist it in drafting the legislation which would become the Social Security bill.

Roosevelt's plan was a comprehensive "cradle to the grave" insurance program. In fact, in discussion with members of the Committee, he voiced his desire to issue an "insurance policy" to every child at birth "to protect him against all the major economic misfortunes which might befall him during his lifetime."[7] Supposedly, this would implement "the ideal objective of a government to assure the 'Good Life' in all its phases for all its citizens," and thus, "the term [social security] is even more sweeping, if that is possible, than the term 'welfare state.'"[8] After signing the Act into law, Roosevelt described its foreseen effects as follows: "This law... represents a cornerstone in a structure which is being built but is by no means complete — a structure intended to lessen the force of possible future depressions, to act as a protection to future administrations of government against the necessity of going deeply into debt to furnish relief to the needy — a law to flatten out the peaks and valleys of deflation and of inflation — in other words, a law that will take care of human needs and at the same time provide for the United States an economic structure of

---

6. Arthur Schlesinger, Jr. described Perkins, the Committee Chairman as follows: "Brisk and articulate, with vivid dark eyes, a broad forehead and a pointed chin, usually wearing a felt tricorn hat, she remained a Brahmin reformer, proud of her New England background... and intent on beating sense into the heads of those foolish people who resisted progress. She had pungency of character, a dry wit, an inner gaiety, an instinct for practicality, a profound vein of religious feeling, and a compulsion to instruct...." (*The Age of Roosevelt: The Coming of the New Deal* [Boston: Houghton-Mifflin Company, 1958]). Perkins herself stated that she had come to Washington "to work for God, FDR, and the millions of forgotten, plain common workingmen." In previous chapters, we have seen what disastrous results were wrought by such New England "reformers" with their "religious feelings" when they took up the cause of the "workingmen" of the antebellum South. They, too, sought to "beat sense" into the heads of "foolish people who resisted progress" — Southerners who saw in Abolitionism a resurrection of the theological and sociological heresies of eighteenth-century French humanism. As will be shown, this is precisely the ideological foundation of the Social Security system.

7. Altmeyer, *Formative Years of Social Security*, page 5.

8. Altmeyer, *ibid*.

vastly greater soundness."[9]

Roosevelt's enthusiasm was far from unanimous. For example, in the House debate pending passage of the bill, Representative Allan Towner Treadway of Massachusetts noted, "The Federal Government has no express or inherent power under the Constitution to set up such a scheme as is proposed. No one knows this any better than the administration and the Democratic majority of the committee. They have been working for months trying to give titles II and VIII some color of constitutionality." These attempts, said Treadway, constituted "outright deception." He continued, "Either the Federal Government has the power to set up this compulsory-insurance system or it has not. The Constitution should be either respected or abolished. What is the sense of having it if we are going to spend most of our time trying to devise ways and means to circumvent it?"[10]

Republican Representative Daniel Reed of New York predicted, "The lash of the dictator will be felt and 25 million free American citizens will for the first time submit themselves to a fingerprint test."[11] The prognostication of Representative James Wolcott Wadsworth, also of New York, was equally dire:

> I know the appeal this bill has to every human being, that it appeals to the humane instincts of men and women everywhere. We will not deny, however, that it constitutes an immense, immense departure from the traditional functions of the Federal Government... pensioning the individual citizens of the several States. It launches the Federal Government into an immense undertaking which in the aggregate will reach dimensions none of us can really visualize and which in the last analysis, you will admit, affects millions and millions of individuals. Remember, once we pay pensions and supervise annuities, we cannot withdraw from the undertaking no matter how demoralizing and subversive it may become. Pensions and annuities are never abandoned; nor are they ever reduced. The recipients ever clamor for more. To gain their ends they organize politically. They may not constitute a majority of the electorate, but their power will be immense. On more than one occasion we have witnessed the political achievements of organized minorities. This bill opens the door and invites the entrance into the political field of a power so vast, so powerful as to threaten the integrity of our institutions and to pull the pillars of the temple down upon the heads of our descendants.
>
> We are taking a step here today which may well be fateful. I ask you to consider it, to reexamine the fundamental philosophy of this bill, to estimate the future and ask yourselves the questions, "In what sort of country shall our grandchildren live? Shall it be a free country or one in which the citizen is a subject taught to depend upon

---

9. Roosevelt, speech delivered 14 August 1935; in J.B.S. Hardman (editor), *Rendezvous With Destiny: Addresses and Opinions of Franklin Delano Roosevelt* (New York: The Dryden Press, 1944), page 310.

10. Allan Towner Treadway, *Congressional Record — House*, 2 April 1935, page 5530.

11. Daniel Reed, quoted by Altmeyer, *Formative Years of Social Security*, page 38.

government?"[12]

    Within the first decade or so after its enactment, several more voices were raised in opposition to the Social Security Act. It was declared by one U.S. Supreme Court justice that the Act was a direct attack on State rights in that it "was intended to enable federal officers virtually to control the exertion of powers of the States in a field in which they alone have jurisdiction and from which the United States is by the Constitution excluded."[13] Marjorie Shearon, who had served in the Bureau of Research and Statistics of the Social Security Board in 1946, warned two years later that if the Social Security Act was not repealed by Congress, the country would be "entirely engulfed by the legislative program" and that it would usher in "State Socialism and dictatorship via a comprehensive scheme of National Compulsory Social Security for the entire population."[14] Likewise, in his 1946 book entitled *Our Enemy the State*, Albert Jay Nock wrote:

> Heretofore in this country sudden crises of misfortune have been met by a mobilization of social power. In fact (except for certain institutional enterprises like the home for the aged, the lunatic-asylum, city-hospital and county-poorhouse) destitution, unemployment, "depression," and similar ills, have been no concern of the State, but have been relieved by the application of social power. Under Mr. Roosevelt, however, the State assumed this function, publicly announcing the doctrine, brand-new in our history, that the State owes its citizens a living. Students of politics, of course, saw in this merely an astute proposal for a prodigious enhancement of State power; merely what, as long ago as 1794, James Madison called "the old trick of turning every contingency into a resource for accumulating force in the government"; and the passage of time has proved that they were right.[15]

Social Security as a National Identification System

    Thirty years after the Act became law, Rexford G. Tugwell, who was an advisor to Roosevelt in the 1930s, admitted that the President had purposefully misled the American public with the "constantly reiterated intention that what was being done was in pursuit of

---

12. James W. Wadsworth, quoted by Altmeyer, *ibid*.

13. *Steward Machine Company v. Davis* (1937), 301 U.S. 618.

14. Marjorie Shearon, testimony before the Senate Committee on Education and Labor on 30 January 1948; quoted by William Haber and Wilbur J. Cohen, *Readings in Social Security* (New York: Prentice-Hall, Inc., 1948), page vii.

15. Albert Jay Nock, *Our Enemy the State* (Caldwell, Idaho: The Caxton Printers, Ltd., 1946), page 5.

the aims embodied in the Constitution of 1787, when obviously it was in contravention of them."[16] When the Social Security system was originally introduced, concerns were immediately raised that the number would eventually evolve into a national identification number by which the privacy of the citizen would be undermined. Not only did the Government solemnly promise the American people that such would never happen, but up to 1972, all Social Security cards contained the phrase "Not For Identification Purposes" on their face.

The first step taken in the direction of changing Social Security into a national identification system was Executive Order 9397, signed on 22 November 1943 by Franklin Roosevelt. This order required all Federal agencies to use the Social Security number (SSN) in order to create "a single unduplicated numerical identification system of accounts." In 1961, the Internal Revenue Service began to use it as a taxpayer identification number and, with the passage of the Tax Reform Act of 1976, State and local tax, welfare, driver's license, or motor vehicle registration authorities were authorized by Congress to use the SSN to likewise establish identities. Over time, Americans have grown accustomed to Social Security and to being branded for life with its number; it is now required in order to register to vote, to obtain a marriage license, a business license, a driver's license, open a bank account, and even in most cases, to obtain employment. Just as its opponents had warned so long ago, nearly every aspect of the individual's life is open for investigation by any governmental agency, or even any interested individual, because of this intrusive welfare system.

It is a fact that the origins and purposes of Social Security are little known, much less understood, by the vast majority of its participants. The stated intent of this Act was to extend the "general welfare" clause of the Constitution to the "persons" who were declared to be "citizens of the United States" in Section One of the Fourteenth Amendment.[17] These were the same "persons" referred to in the Emancipation Proclamation of 1863, in the Freedman's Bureau Act of 1865, and in the Civil Rights Act of 1866. As previously discussed, the American people were originally led to believe that these provisions were "war measures" meant to apply only to the former Negro slaves and their descendants. As such, the Social Security Act could not have been other than an enactment of martial rule. This should be obvious when it is remembered that this Act was passed as part of Roosevelt's New Deal legislation in which the "ordinary course of judicial proceedings" were interrupted by the declaration of a national emergency.

There are several notable similarities between the Freedmen's Bureau Act and the Social Security Act. The opening section of the Freedmen's Bureau Act stated, "That there is hereby established in the War Department... a bureau of refugees, freedmen, and abandoned lands, to which shall be committed... the control of all subjects relating to refugees and freedmen... under such rules and regulations as may be prescribed by the head of the bureau and approved by the President. The said bureau shall be under the management and control

16. Tugwell, "Rewriting the Constitution," page 20.

17. Title 26, *Code of Federal Regulations*, Section 36.3121(1).

of a commissioner to be appointed by the President, by and with the advice and consent of the Senate...." The Social Security Act likewise provided, "There is hereby established a Social Security Board (in this Act referred to as the Board) to be composed of three members to be appointed by the President, by and with the advice and consent of the Senate." In addition, "[t]he Social Security Administration is headed by a Commissioner of Social Security, appointed by the President."[18] Finally, the reader should remember Andrew Johnson's warning that the Freedmen's Bureau Act would create Executive military zones within the several States:

> The bill proposes to establish by authority of Congress military jurisdiction over all parts of the United States containing refugees and freedmen. It would by its very nature apply with most force to those parts of the United States in which the freedmen most abound, and it expressly extends the existing temporary jurisdiction of the Freedmen's Bureau, with greatly enlarged powers, over those States "in which the ordinary course of judicial proceedings has been interrupted by the rebellion." The source from which this military jurisdiction is to emanate is none other than the President of the United States, acting through the War Department and the Commissioner of the Freedmen's Bureau. The agents to carry out this military jurisdiction are to be selected either from the Army or from civil life; the country is to be divided into districts and sub-districts, and the number of salaried agents to be employed may be equal to the number of counties or parishes in all the United States where freedmen and refugees are to be found.

Since the Social Security Act deals with the same subject matter as did the Freedmen's Bureau Act, it would seem logical to assume that the ten regions into which the country is now divided are also military districts under the supervision of the President in his capacity as Commander-in-Chief.

The question may be asked, Why would Roosevelt be so anxious to establish an expensive national welfare program such as Social Security at a time when the U.S. Government supposedly had no money? The answer, of course, is that such a program created yet another revenue source outside of those allotted to it by the Constitution. Those who were formerly beyond the reach of the Government's taxing power are brought therein whenever they accept any of its benefits or privileges. A contractual relationship for the purpose of tax liability is therefore established whenever someone registers or is registered in the Social Security program: "Liability to taxation is... based on the individual's reciprocal enjoyment of the benefits of government... [P]ersons who are clearly beyond the reach of governmental benefits are likewise beyond the scope of the taxing power."[19] In other words, there would

---

18. Charles I. Schottland, *The Social Security Program in the United States* (New York: Meredith Publishing Company, 1963), page 73.

19. Arnold G. Ginnow and Milorad Nikolic (editors), *Corpus Juris Secundum* (St. Paul, Minnesota: West Publishing Company, 1988), Volume LXXXIV, Section 59, "Taxation."

be no income tax liability for most Americans if not for the Social Security number. It is interesting to note that prior to the implementation of the Social Security scheme in 1936, only five million tax returns were filed with 2.1 million of those filed reporting income taxes owed. Thus, out of a population of 125 million, a scant four percent of Americans were liable to the income tax, with only 1.6 percent of those liable actually owing the tax. In 1937, after the Roosevelt Administration had sponsored a month-long media campaign to coerce the American people into Social Security, over 22 million citizens were required to file a tax return. By 1944, nearly 80 million tax returns were filed — an astounding 1600 percent increase in the taxing power of the central Government in just eight years. It is hard to understand how Roosevelt can still be viewed as a national hero today.

The Myth of Social Security as Insurance

It has been historically true throughout history that people are prone to willingly surrender their liberty in exchange for security. The American people have proven themselves not to be immune to this malady. Of course, as revealed before the Joint Economics Committee by W. Allen Wallis, Chairman of the 1975 Advisory Council on Social Security, the "social insurance" offered to the American people in exchange for their degradation is anything but secure:

> Many people think that the Social Security taxes taken out of their wages and sent to Washington each month provide for their old-age pensions and other Social Security benefits. This simply is not the case. Those taxes are levied on workers in order to pay benefits to people who have already retired and are drawing their Social Security pensions....
>
> When you pay Social Security taxes you are in no way making provision for your own retirement. You are paying the pensions of those who already are retired.
>
> Once you understand this, you see that whether you will get the benefits you are counting on when you retire, depends on whether the Congress will levy enough taxes, borrow enough, or print enough money, and whether it will authorize the level of benefits you are counting on.
>
> The situation is in no way analogous to putting money each month into a private insurance company which invests it and undertakes to pay you an annuity.
>
> Misunderstanding of the pay-as-you-go nature of Social Security is widespread among journalists and the public. Indeed, this misunderstanding seems to have been deliberately cultivated sometimes, in the belief that it makes the Social Security System more palatable to the public.[20]

---

20. W. Allen Wallis, testimony of 27 May 1976; quoted by Irwin Schiff, *The Social Security Swindle* (Hamden, Connecticut: Freedom Books, 1984), page 131.

The U.S. Supreme Court likewise observed:

> [Social Security taxes] are to be paid into the Treasury at Washington, and thereafter are subject to appropriation like public moneys generally. They are not ear-marked in any way....[21]

> They enter the Treasury as free funds set apart to no special use and subject to be applied to any congressional appropriation.[22]

After conducting a protracted study of the Social Security program, Bryce Webster and Robert L. Perry even more recently concluded that "every working person faces the same sober fact he or she faced in 1935; you must provide for your own retirement."[23] Moreover, unlike policy holders in a true insurance program, participants in Social Security have absolutely no contractual rights to their "contributions" once they have been collected because Congress "included in the original act, and since retained a claim expressly reserving to it the right to alter, amend, or repeal any provision of the act" at its own discretion: "To engraft upon the Social Security System a concept of 'accrued property rights' would deprive it of the flexibility and boldness in adjustment to ever-changing conditions which it demands.... [D]espite their own and their employers' payments, the Government, in paying the beneficiaries out of the fund, is merely giving them something for nothing and can stop doing so when it pleases."[24] Consequently, what the worker of today is really doing is paying for the benefits of the retired workers of yesterday and thus providing for *their* security, not his own. Candid admissions to this fact are easily located in numerous Government documents, especially the *Congressional Record*.[25]

---

21. *Helvering v. Davis* (1937), 301 U.S. 619.

22. *Stewart Machine v. Davis*, at 548.

23. Bryce Webster and Robert L. Perry, *The Complete Social Security Handbook* (New York: Dodd, Mead and Company, 1983), page 297.

24. *Flemming v. Nestor* (1960), 363 U.S. 624. See also Title 42, United States Code, Section 1304.

25. The following exchange occurred in 1965 between two members of the House Ways and Means Committee:

> Mr. Byrnes, So that fundamentally what we are doing here is not prepaying, but what we are doing here is having the people who are currently working finance the benefits of those currently over 65?
> Mr. Myers. I think it can be viewed that way, just as the old-age and survivors insurance trust fund can, or else you can also view that it is prepayment in advance on a collective group basis, so that the younger contributors are making their contributions with the expectation that they will receive the benefits in the future — and not necessarily with the thought that their money is being put aside and earmarked for them, but rather that later there will be current income to the system

A perfect example of the injustice of the system is found in the case of the first recipient of Social Security benefits — Ida May Fuller, of Ludlow, Vermont. After working under the Social Security system as a legal secretary for less than three years, Fuller retired at the age of 65 having paid a mere $24.75 in taxes. Her first benefit check for $22.54 was issued on 31 January 1940, and she continued to draw monthly benefits until her death at age 100 in 1975. In all, she received a total of $22,888.92 — $22,864.17 of which she did not work for and which was unjustly extracted from the wages of other people whom she never met. The same scenario played itself out repeatedly in the earlier days of Social Security, but there were, at that time, more workers paying into the system than those drawing benefits. Today, as more and more of the "baby boom" generation are retiring, the burden placed upon the shoulders of current workers is becoming more and more oppressive.[26] Arthur J. Altmeyer, who is sometimes credited as the "father of Social Security" for his contributions to the early stages of the system,[27] wrote, "The people with larger incomes and larger resources ought to contribute for the people with the lower incomes and resources. While it is important to maintain financing [of Social Security] on a basis that insures adequacy of benefits and adaptability of the benefits to income loss, it is also important to make sure that we accomplish something by way of distribution of welfare among the various economic groups of this country, through a redistribution of some of the income and resources."[28] The system is thus exposed by one of its framers as a massive Government-enforced confiscation of wealth "without just compensation" contrary to the Fifth Amendment.

---

for their benefits.

 Mr. Byrnes. In other words, on the theory that if I am going to be asked to pay for a tax today for a benefit that is available to people over 65, then when I get to 65, somebody who is then working ought to do the same thing for me? Is that it?

 Mr. Myers. Yes. I would say that is the way it is, and this is a reasonable group prepayment basis, I think you can call it, because of the compulsory nature of the tax for now and for all time to come on people in covered employment (House Ways and Means Committee Executive Hearings on Medical Care for the Aged [Eighty-Ninth Congress, First Session], Part I, page 20).

26. In 1937, no one paid more than $30.00 in F.I.C.A. taxes; within thirty years, that amount had increased ten times. Since Congress is constantly raising the level of benefits for current recipients, the level of "contributions" extracted from current workers must also continue to rise.

27. Altmeyer was one of the chief advisors to the President's Committee on Economic Security that drafted the original legislative proposal in 1934. He was also a member of the three-person Social Security Board created to run the new program, and thereafter served as Chairman of the Board and Commissioner for Social Security from 1937 to 1953.

28. Altmeyer, quoted by Abraham Ellis, *The Social Security Fraud* (New Rochelle, New York: Arlington House, 1971), page 55.

A Socialist Scheme for the Re-Distribution of Wealth

That Social Security is pure socialism — a redistribution of wealth from one class of citizens (the "haves") to another (the "have-nots")[29] — is beyond reasonable dispute. In his 1936 book entitled *Fool's Gold*, Fred R. Marvin pointed out that the provisions of the Social Security system mirror the fifth, sixth, and seventh planks of the National Platform of the Socialist Party of 1932 which called for the establishment of "a compulsory system of unemployment compensation with adequate benefits, based on contributions by the government and by employers," "old-age pensions for men and women sixty years of age and over," and "health and maternity insurance."[30] In fact, nearly every aspect of the New Deal legislation followed the Socialist platform very closely while bearing little resemblance to the Democratic platform on which Roosevelt had been elected:

> One finds, upon investigation, that not only is the legislation in question out of harmony with the 1932 platform declarations of the Democratic party, but that the persons selected to administer this legislation are not Democrats....
>
> One is forced to the conclusion, after a careful study of the facts, that what is now termed the New Deal party... is but the Progressive (Socialist) party of 1924 seeking to conceal its identity by wearing stolen clothing. This conclusion is forced both by the nature of the legislation adopted, and by the personnel of those holding key positions in the federal government. The number of persons who supported the Progressive (Socialist) ticket in 1924 now on the federal payroll is rather impressive....[31]

Ardent supporters of Social Security, such as Altmeyer, have been unabashed in their admission that the system has its roots in European socialist theory, particularly that of Jean-Jacques Rousseau and Claude Henri de Saint-Simon.[32] A devout Unitarian, Altmeyer made it very clear in his writings on the subject that he was operating within the philosophical context of humanism — "faith [in] man's infinite perfectibility"[33] — when he advised Roosevelt's Committee in drafting the original legislation. Altmeyer was joined in this task by

---

29. W. Barnard Faraday, *Democracy and Capital* (London: John Murray Publishers, Ltd., 1921), page 236.

30. Fred R. Marvin, *Fool's Gold: An Expose of Un-American Activities and Political Action in the United States Since 1860* (New York: Madison and Marshall, Inc., 1936), page 10.

31. Marvin, *ibid.*, pages 16, 17.

32. Arthur Altmeyer, "Ten Years of Social Security," in Haber and Cohen, *Readings in Social Security*, pages 80, 81.

33. Altmeyer, *ibid.*, page 80.

Representative Thomas Eliot of Massachusetts, who was also a Unitarian.[34] Members of the Committee itself held similar religious and political views. For example, Harry Hopkins, former member of the Progressive party and a Fabian socialist,[35] was vocally pro-Soviet, as was Henry Wallace, another former Progressive. Hopkins was known as Roosevelt's "alter ego"[36] and Wallace would later serve under Roosevelt as Vice-President in 1940.

The roots of the Soviet Communism which both these men held in such high esteem went deep into the same soil from whence sprang the socialist theory — the Humanist religion of the evolution and self-perfectibility of man.[37] In fact, both Karl Marx and

---

34. It should be remembered that Unitarianism was the driving theological force behind the Northern Abolitionist movement of the Nineteenth Century.

35. The Fabians accepted the basic premises of Marxism, but rejected violent revolution as the necessary means to implement them, believing instead that socialism should and could be achieved peacefully through legislation and endless taxation:

> Step by step, land, mines, railways, ships, banks, shops — everything — will be nationalised, municipalised, socialised. Private enterprise will be slowly but completely squeezed out of existence; competition will be imperceptibly but entirely eliminated. And the funds to achieve these ends will not be seized by lawless force; they will be quietly but remorselessly extracted from private enterprise and competitive industry themselves by a graduated system of predatory taxation. Nothing will be confiscated; everything will be purchased and paid for. The members of the possessing classes will, by some ingenious device or other, compensate one another, until (again gradually) their funds run out, when they will, to their great advantage, be compelled to resort to work, even if it be only to "earn a precarious livelihood by taking in one another's washing." Meantime the proletariat will rejoice. They will all be servants of the beneficent state; their wages will go up, for they will fix them themselves through their elected representatives; their hours of labour will go down, for they will no longer have to maintain capitalists and landlords in luxury; they will begin to draw large old-age pensions whilst they still have youth and energy to enjoy them; education, medical attendance, amusements, recreations, transport — all will be free and unrestricted. In the end, every one will be a blessed pauper, paying away all his earnings in rates and taxes, and in return being luxuriously maintained (so long as he does not display any recrudescence of individualism) on outdoor relief (F.J.C. Hearnshaw, *A Survey of Socialism: Analytical, Historical and Critical* [London: Macmillan and Company, Ltd., 1929], pages 298-299).

With this description in mind, it is apparent that Washington, D.C. has become the bastion of modern-day Fabianism with Social Security as its crown jewel.

36. Flynn, *Roosevelt Myth*, page 11.

37. The religious nature of Humanism is easily established. For example, in the preface to the *Humanist Manifestoes I and II*, noted Humanist Paul Kurtz wrote, "Humanism is a philosophical, religious, and moral point of view" (Buffalo, New York: Prometheus Books, 1980, page 3). In its 1961 decision in *Torcaso v. Watkins*, the U.S. Supreme Court included "Secular Humanism" in a list of "religions in this country which do not teach what would be generally be considered a belief in the existence of God...." Four years later in *United States v. Seeger*, the Court granted Daniel Seeger

Vladamir Lenin viewed socialism as "a transitional state" between Western capitalism and full-blown communism.[38] Wallace, "the most controversial figure of the regime,"[39] was also an admirer, if not an actual member, of the Theosophical Society, an occult group founded on the esoteric teachings of a nineteenth-century Russian spirit-medium named Helena Petrovna Blavatsky.[40] It would be naive to think that the philosophical and religious presup-

---

conscientious objector status on the basis of his "religious belief" — which Seeger himself identified as Humanism.

38. Kenneth Neill Cameron, *Marxism: The Science of Society* (Boston: Bergin and Garvey, 1985), page 85; Vladimir I. Lenin, *Collected Works* (Moscow: Progress Publishers, 1980), Volume XXV, page 468.

39. Flynn, *Roosevelt Myth*, page 11.

40. In her book entitled, *The Secret Doctrine* (Pasadena, California: Theosophical University Press, 1963), Blavatsky taught that mankind's evolution is being directed by "Ascended Masters" from their highly-advanced plane of existence called "Shamballah," located in the Tibetan Himalayas. At the head of this "hierarchy" is an entity which Blavatsky frequently identified as "Satan," the "God of Wisdom," (*Secret Doctrine*, Volume II, page 237), "the most wise and spiritual spirit of all" (page 378), and the great benefactor of mankind who led our Edenic parents to spiritual enlightenment, contrary to the wishes of the evil "Jehovah," the true "adversary of men" (page 387). Blavatsky insisted that the spiritual evolution of which she wrote may rightly be labelled "satanic" because "it is owing to the prototype of that which became in time the Christian Devil — to the Radiant Archangel who wanted Man to become his own creator and an immortal god — that men can reach Nirvana and the haven of heavenly divine Peace...." (pages 245-246).

   Blavatasky's writings heavily influenced Adolph Hitler and provided the philosophical basis of the Nazi's fascination with the "Aryan superman." *The Secret Doctrine* also supplied German National Socialism with its most cherished symbol — the swastika — which Blavatsky believed was "pregnant with real occult meaning" (page 587). Occultists such as the Theosophists certainly know the importance of symbolism in communicating their ideology to an unsuspecting public. It was Henry Wallace, the disciple of Blavatsky, who was mainly responsible for the inclusion of the so-called "reverse" of the Great Seal on the back of the $1 Federal Reserve Note. Though it had been ignored since its creation in the Eighteenth Century, Wallace saw in the design a symbolic depiction of what the Roosevelt Administration was attempting to do through Social Security and other New Deal legislation. He pointed in particular to the two Latin phrases, *Annuit Caeptis* and *Novus Ordo Seclorum*. The first phrase is translated, "He favors our undertaking." This phrase was taken from Virgil's epic poem, *The Aeneid*, and refers to the pagan sun-deity, Jupiter, which is represented by the "All-Seeing Eye" overseeing the construction of a *novus ordo seclorum* ("New Order of the Ages"), symbolized by the unfinished pyramid. Michael Howard wrote, "Wallace's reasons for wanting to introduce the Great Seal onto the American currency were based on his belief that America was reaching a turning point in her history and that great spiritual changes were imminent. He believed that the 1930s represented a time when a great spiritual awakening was going to take place which would precede the creation of the one-world state" (*The Occult Conspiracy: Secret Societies and Their Influence and Power in World History* [Rochester, Vermont: Destiny Books,

positions held by these men did not have a significant impact upon their work.

One critic of Social Security described the system as "merely a political mechanism designed for persons who can be lulled into believing that the police power of government is the proper moral and financial base on which to build a sound retirement program."[41] Altmeyer himself, quoting with approval the communist dictum, "From each according to his ability and to each according to his need," claimed, "A society successfully built on that foundation would be a rather fine one in which to live."[42] However, as we have seen, Social Security is not *"merely* a political mechanism" to bring about this promised utopia, because it is also religious to the core and involves at least an implicit worship of the State as the embodiment of Rousseau's "collective soul" of divine humanity: "The golden calf now is the Welfare State — or Big Brother. Pay your taxes, make your sacrifices, and have unquestioning faith. Do your worshipping and your prayers will be answered. The checks will roll out for everyone. Above all, do not doubt the gods in Washington.... The State sees all, knows all, and has eternal life."[43] As such, Social Security — and socialism in general — stands in direct opposition to Christianity, which views God alone as the rightful recipient of faith and worship, and the God-ordained mandate of honest work as the only legitimate means of daily subsistence.

It is therefore not surprising that Socialists in the past have usually been very candid in acknowledging their antagonism towards Christianity. For example, in a statement uncannily reminiscent of the cry of the heathen in the second Psalm, the International Congress of Socialists which met in Geneva in 1868 declared:

> God and Christ, these citizen-Providences, have been at all times the armour of Capital, and the most sanguinary enemies of the working classes. It is owing to God and to Christ that we remain to this day in slavery. It is by deluding us with lying hopes, that the priests have caused us to accept all the sufferings of this earth.
>
> It is only after sweeping away all religion and after tearing up even to the roots every religious idea, Christian and every other whatsoever, that we can arrive at our political and social ideal. Let Jesus look after his heaven. We believe only in humanity. It would be but to fail in all our duties were we to cease, even for a second, to pursue the monsters

---

1989], page 95).

Both Wallace and Roosevelt were Thirty-Second Degree Masons; Homer Cummings and Henry Morgenthau, Jr., two other members of the Committee which concocted Social Security, were also Freemasons. For an exposition of the occult religion of the Masonic Lodge and its self-proclaimed connection to pagan sun-worship, see Greg Loren Durand, *Communion With the Gods: The Pagan Altar of Freemasonry* (Dahlonega, Georgia: Crown Rights Book Company, 2006).

41. Dr. Dean Russell, quoted by Ellis, *Social Security Fraud*, pages 70-71.

42. Altmeyer, "Ten Years of Social Security," page 81.

43. Ellis, *Social Security Fraud*, pages 115-116.

who have tortured us. Down, then, with God and with Christ! Down with the despots of Heaven and Earth! Death to the Priests! Such is the motto of our grand crusade.[44]

More recently, Emelyan Yaroslavsky, President of the League of Militant Atheists of the Soviet Union, declared, "Remember that the struggle against religion is a struggle for Socialism!"[45] It should be kept in mind that when Socialists and Communists attack "religion," it is primarily Christianity that they have in mind. In the Christian worldview, social and economic inequality is inescapable because not all men have the same abilities and talents, the same level of intelligence, or even the same drive to work hard; in the Socialist worldview, this inequality is the ultimate evil and must be eradicated. Those who have acquired wealth by industry and thrift must surrender it to those who have failed to acquire wealth through slothfulness or have squandered it through foolish spending and waste. Upon this premise is founded the Social Security system in this country:

> [S]ocialism runs directly counter to all the dominant human instincts which cause men to produce. In the name of equality it destroys the freedom which is necessary for effective activity; in the name of co-operation it puts an end to that healthy competition which is the bracing air of industrial activity, and the main means by which the community secures efficient service; in the name of community it deprives men of the capacity to acquire property, and so removes the chief incentive to labour; in the name of nationalisation it appropriates successful private businesses, and thus damps down energy and initiative; in the name of public assistance it discourages both thrift and self-help; in the name of readjusted taxation it institutes a vindictive spoliation of those who, by diligence and self-restraint, have managed to save; in the name of capital levy it projects an orgy of legalised loot. In short, all the principles and all the devices of socialism seem to be as carefully contrived as though they had been designed in Bedlam, to depress labour, discourage enterprise, damp initiative, discountenance forethought, prevent the accumulation of capital, encourage recklessness and extravagance, foster parasitism, ruin industry. In the supposed interests of the proletariat, socialism tends to drag the whole community down to one disastrous level of laziness, incompetence, and destitution.[46]

A Test Run For Compulsory Global Socialism?

Of course, the proponents of government-enforced socialism will never be satisfied

---

44. Manifesto of the International Congress, held in Geneva in 1868; quoted by Marvin, *Fool's Gold*, page 170.

45. Emelyan Yaroslavsky, quoted by Elizabeth Dilling, *The Roosevelt Red Record and its Background* (Kenilworth, Illinois: self-published, 1936), page 14.

46. F.J.C. Hearnshaw, *Democracy and Labour* (London: Macmillan and Company, Ltd., 1924), page 171.

until they have eliminated the inequalities of human society from the entire world. They insist that this plan will necessarily involve the termination of national sovereignty and the subjugation of all countries to some form of centralized global government. Most of the industrialized nations of the world already have in place some form of compulsory social security and it requires little imagination to foresee a day when these programs, which are already very similar to one another, may be merged together under the administration of a single "health and human services" organization that will dictate to the erstwhile nations how they can and will provide for their citizens:

> The Humanist is truly global in his concern for he realizes that no man is a separate island and that we are all part of the mainland of humanity. Thus the idea of mankind as a whole and of one world, is a profound moral vision that sustains and nourishes the Humanist morality. And this can be achieved only by some degree of rule of law, some measure of peace and economic well-being and cultural enrichment for all men, who may share experience and a sense of brotherhood with others.... We nevertheless recognize the need for the human race to transform blind social force into rational control and to build a world community.[47]

> The problems of economic growth and development can no longer be resolved by one nation alone; they are worldwide in scope. It is the moral obligation of the developed nations to provide — through an international authority that safeguards human rights — massive technical, agricultural, medical, and economic assistance, including birth control techniques, to the developing portions of the globe. World poverty must cease. Hence extreme disproportions in wealth, income, and economic growth should be reduced on a worldwide basis.[48]

At this point in time, the United Nations is the only likely candidate for such a job of enforcing global socialism. However, the American people at present would not tolerate on an international scale the socialism which they already embrace on a national scale, so that day may yet be far in the future. What should concern us now is the serious threat that Social Security poses to what is left of our individual liberties as Americans. While it is technically a voluntary system in that no one is yet required to get a number,[49] those who have conscientious objections to Social Security — whether they be political or religious in

47. Paul Kurtz, *The Humanist Alternative* (Buffalo, New York: Prometheus Books, 1973), page 179.

48. Raymond B. Bragg, Paul Kurtz and Edwin H. Wilson, *Humanist Manifesto II* (Buffalo, New York: Prometheus Books, 1980), page 22.

49. Title 42, United States Code, Section 405(c)(2)(B)(i) requires the issuance of Social Security Numbers only to resident aliens who are seeking employment within the United States and applicants for benefits under any program which is financed in whole or in part by Federal funds.

nature[50] — are finding it increasingly difficult to maintain the most minimal participation in modern society without this "voluntary," "not for identification" number. One is immediately reminded of a similar situation which was faced by Christians in the waning years of the imperial Roman. In the Book of Revelation, the empire is described as a "beast" which, in claiming for itself the worship which belongs to God alone, "opened his mouth in blasphemy against God, to blaspheme his name, and his tabernacle, and them that dwell in heaven" (Revelation 13:6). All those who lived under the military jurisdiction of Rome were required by law to publicly proclaim their "orthodox State Paganism"[51] by burning a pinch of incense before the image of the emperor and declaring *"kaiser kurios"* (Caesar is lord). Upon compliance with this law, the citizens and subjects were given a papyrus document called a *libellus*, which they were required to present when either stopped by the police or attempting to engage in commerce in the marketplace. According to Scripture, "the beast causeth all, both small and great, rich and poor, free and bond, to receive a mark in their right hand, or in their foreheads: and that no man might buy or sell, save he that had the mark, or the name of the beast, or the number of his name" (Revelation 13:16-17). In this way, Roman society became, for all intents and purposes, closed to anyone not willing to adhere himself and his family to the established religion of Caesar-worship (statism). In addition, such refusal carried the death sentence (Revelation 13:15). Consequently, Christians by the hundreds were singled out for persecution because they refused to offer up even a tiny pinch of incense to a man and proclaim that he, not Christ, was Lord. Lest the idea seem ridiculous that modern America is well on her way to mimicking ancient Rome in this regard, the skeptic would do well to remember the words of King Solomon: "The thing that hath been, it is that which shall be; and that which is done is that which shall be done: and there is no new thing under the sun. Is there any thing whereof it may be said, See, this is new? It hath been already of old time, which was before us" (Ecclesiastes 1:9-10).

---

50. *David Stevens v. Stephen Berger* (1977), 428 F.Supp. 896.

51. H. Donald M. Spence, *Ancient Christianity and Paganism* (London: Cassell and Company, 1902), page 349.

SUPPORTING DOCUMENT
Daniel Reed's Speech in the
House of Representatives
Congressional Record — 17 April 1935

Mr. Chairman, the economic security bill now before us raises grave constitutional questions. More and more as the proposals of this administration are presented and the motives behind them are revealed, thoughtful citizens turn to the Supreme Court as the one dependable instrumentality of Government to hold the rudder of the Constitution true.

Recent decisions of this great bulwark of liberty and justice have inspired new hope in the hearts and minds of those who believe in the principles of constitutional government.

Two comparatively recent and notable decisions of the Supreme Court ought to exert a restraining influence on the Congress as well as the executive branch of the Government. The economic security bill now before us is evidence that another attempt is to be made to evade constitutional limitations and invade the rights reserved to the States. This Congress, under irresponsible executive leadership, has already attempted to delegate its legislative power in violation of the Federal Constitution, and under the same leadership it has attempted to repudiate the promises of the Government to its citizens. The same leadership that has brought the stigma of repudiation upon this Congress may be satisfied to dismiss this ugly word by issuing a statement from the White House that "the President is gratified," but the responsibility for this injustice to the citizens of the Nation rests upon Congress.

The executive branch of the Government for the past two years has made a spineless rubber stamp of this legislative body, and it has done so to the humiliation of the self-respecting Members of Congress and to the detriment of the Nation.

It may require a more blistering rebuke from the Supreme Court and the pressure of an aroused and enraged public opinion to restrain this Congress from continuing to be the tool of those who would destroy the Constitution; but the time is not far distant when those who believe in constitutional government will speak with force and with finality.

There are times when I enjoy to turn back the pages of our history and examine the philosophy of those who framed the Constitution, and to compare it with the philosophy of the ardent advocates of the new deal who have all but destroyed it.

One of the framers of the Federal Constitution, in commenting on the advantages to be derived from having two branches of our National Legislature, made these interesting observations:

> Each House will be cautious and careful and circumspect in those proceedings, which they know must undergo the strict and severe criticism of judges, whose inclination will lead them, and whose duty will enjoin them, not to leave a single blemish unnoticed or uncorrected.
>
> Every bill will, in some one or more steps in its progress, undergo the keenest scrutiny. Its relations, whether near or remote, to the principles of freedom, jurisprudence, and the Constitution will be accurately examined; and its effects upon laws already existing will be maturely traced. In this manner rash measures, violent innovations, crude projects, and partial contrivances will be stifled in the attempt to bring them forth.

When the distinguished statesman and jurist made this statement he did not have in contemplation the time when a Chief Executive would usurp the functions of Congress, bend it to his will, make the legislative committees subservient to him, formulate the legislative program, draft the bills both as to substance and form, and then demand enactment of them into laws without change. It did not occur to him, I venture to say, that legislators elected to the Congress of the United States would ever become so servile. Moreover, I dare say the thought never entered his mind that a Chief Executive would engage adroit counsel and assign to them the specific task of so formulating legislative measures as to evade the spirit and intent of the Federal Constitution. Few bills that have come before Congress, I am sure, have had more time spent upon them by legal talent in an attempt to evade and circumvent constitutional barriers than has the economic-security bill now before this House.

The provisions have been cut, carved, sawed, assembled, and reassembled in an effort to make it constitutionally presentable to the Supreme Court. A resort has finally been had to an ingenious mechanical arrangement of title II and title VIII as the most likely means of diverting the attention of the Supreme Court from the real issue, viz. that these two titles are the same in purpose, spirit, intent, and substance. This clever scheme may succeed, but I do not believe this mechanical subterfuge will deceive the Court. If the purpose sought to be accomplished does escape the scrutiny of the Court because of the mere juggling of titles, then other police powers reserved to the States may in the same manner be taken over and operated by the Federal Government without let or hindrance.

But, Mr. Chairman, the courts are not dumb when it comes to detecting legislative subterfuges, even when such attempted evasions are drawn by the "brain trust" counselors.

We have evidence of this in a recent opinion written by Federal Judge Charles I. Dawson in support of a decision adverse to new-deal legislation. The language and the logic expressed in the opinion are appropriate and applicable to title II and title VIII in the bill before us. Judge Dawson writes, "It is impossible for anyone who has any respect for constitutional limitations to contemplate this law with complacency.... It is the plainest kind of an attempt to accomplish an unconstitutional purpose by the pretended exercise of constitutional powers."

In this same opinion, Judge Dawson said that if the act itself shows that "subterfuges were resorted to to circumvent constitutional limitations, no judge who respects his oath to support and defend the Constitution will hesitate to strike it down, it matters not how great may be the demand for such legislation."

Executive domination is responsible for including in this economic-security bill subject matter that should have been brought in under separate measures. Never under any circumstances, except under present dictatorial pressure, would the Ways and Means Committee have brought a bill in here loaded down with subject matter some of which ought to receive profound study before being launched in perilous times like these. There would be little if any opposition to Federal aid to the humanitarian subjects, such as adequate aid to the aged, grants to States for dependent children, grants in aid of maternal and child-health service, grants to aid crippled children, aid to child-welfare services, support to vocational rehabilitation, and to public-health work.

But there is included in this bill, by the direction and at the command of the President, the compulsory contributory old-age-annuity provision. As I have stated, it raises a grave constitutional question, and, beyond all this, it lays a heavy tax burden on employers and employees alike when they are least able to bear it, not to meet an emergency or to furnish immediate relief to those in need. Titles II and VIII, I repeat, were placed in this bill and kept in this bill because you were ordered and commanded to do it by the President.

This measure, like so many complex bills that have preceded it, was not brought here, and you did not dare bring it here, until it had run the gamut of administration approval. First it had to satisfy the "brain trust." Next it had to receive the benediction of the President. When the press announced that the majority members of the Ways and Means Committee had been to the White House to obtain the consent of the President to bring the economic-security bill before the House of Representatives for consideration, I was reminded of the truth that history repeats itself. Almost six centuries ago, when the King of England convened Parliament, the sole duty of the Commons was to consent to taxes. Later on, in 1354, Edward III, for some reason not revealed, asked the Commons their opinion of the French war which he was then carrying on, and this was their reply: "Most dreaded lord, as to this war and the equipment needed for it we are so ignorant and simple that we do not know how nor have we the power to decide. We, therefore, pray your grace to excuse us in the matter."

The parallel is in the procedure only — not a reflection upon the intellectual capacity of my colleagues. I want it distinctly understood that I have a profound admiration and respect for the character and intelligence of my associates on the Ways and Means Committee. What I deplore is the lack of legislative independence so much needed to prevent constant dictatorial Executive interference with the legislative branch of the Government. A great statesman has said, "The true danger is when liberty is nibbled away for expedients and by parts."

The centralization of power in the executive branch of the Government is a menace of major proportions. I know that the admonitions of George Washington on this point will fall on deaf ears, but I hope you will indulge me while I quote from his Farewell Address. He said:

> It is important, likewise, that the habits of thinking in a free country should inspire caution in those intrusted with its administration to confine themselves within their respective constitutional spheres, avoiding in the exercise of the powers of one department to encroach upon another. The spirit of encroachment tends to consolidate the powers of all the departments in one, and thus to create, whatever the form of government, a real despotism.
>
> A just estimate of that love of power and proneness to abuse it which predominate in the human heart is sufficient to satisfy us of the truth of this position.
>
> The necessity of reciprocal checks in the exercise of political power by dividing and distributing it into different depositories, and constituting each the guardian of the public weal against invasions of the others, has been evinced by experiments, ancient and modern; some of them in our country and under our own eyes. To preserve them must be as necessary as to institute them.
>
> If in the opinion of the people the distribution or modification of the constitutional powers be in any particular wrong, let it be corrected by an amendment in the way which the Constitution designates. But let there be no change by usurpation; for though this in one instance may be the instrument of good, it is the customary weapon by which free governments are destroyed. The precedent must always greatly overbalance in permanent evil any partial or transient benefit which the use can at any time yield.

Again let me remind the members of the majority that even though you enact title II and title VIII as commanded by President Roosevelt, the responsibility for an adverse decision by the Supreme Court as to the constitutionality of these two titles will rest upon you. It will not relieve you from it to say, We obeyed our master's voice. Will he come to your rescue? Not at all. What will his answer be? Is he not in a position to say this: "My fellow countrymen, I made my position clear on this subject when I was Governor of New York State. In a radio address broadcast on March 2, 1930, I then said —

> "As a matter of fact and law the governing rights of the States are all of those which have not been surrendered to the National Government by the Constitution or its amendments. Wisely or unwisely, people know that under the eighteenth amendment Congress has been given the right to legislate on this particular subject [prohibition]; but this is not the case in the matter of a great number of other vital problems of government, such as the conduct of public utilities, of banks, of insurance, of business, of agriculture,

of education, of social welfare, and of a dozen other important features. In these Washington must not be encouraged to interfere.

"Federal Government costs us now $3,5000,000,000 every year, and if we do not halt this steady process of building commissions and regulatory bodies and special legislation like huge inverted pyramids over every one of the simple constitutional provisions, we will soon be spending many billions of dollars more."

Mr. Chairman, what is the situation? It is this: Five years ago in the broadcast from which I have quoted, Governor Roosevelt stressed his opposition to the type of Federal legislation which you now seek to enact. His reasons then given were, viz, that "the governing rights of the States are all those which have not been surrendered to the National Government by the Constitution or its amendments." That among the governing rights of the States not so surrendered are insurance, social welfare, business, and others.

You on the majority side say that you cannot understand our position with reference to title II and title VIII. I venture to suggest that the minority has a clearer conception of where the President stands with reference to the unconstitutional aspects of title II and VIII than do you on the majority side. The position taken by President Roosevelt, when he was Governor of New York State, as to the constitutional questions involved in legislation of the character of the bill now before us, was sound then, and it is sound now, and you know it and he knows it. We know it, and under our oath of office we shall support the Constitution.

You may manipulate, distort, and butcher this bill in an endeavor to evade the fundamental law of the land, but you cannot change the fundamental purpose, the facts, nor the law.

The tenth amendment to the Constitution provides that the powers not delegated to the United States by the Constitution, nor prohibited by it to the States, are reserved to the States, respectively, or to the people.

The fourteenth amendment does not take from the States police powers reserved to them at the time of the adoption of the Constitution. Furthermore, the Supreme Court of the United States has steadfastly adhered to the principle that the States possess, because they have never surrendered, the power to protect the public health, morals, and safety by any legislation appropriate to that end, which does not encroach upon the rights guaranteed by the National Constitution. What is more, as stated by Judge Cooley in his great work, *Constitutional Limitations*:

In the American constitutional system, the power to establish the ordinary regulations of police has been left with the individual States, and it cannot be taken away from them, either wholly or in part, and exercised under legislation of Congress.

Neither can the National Government, through any of its departments or officers, assume any supervision of the police regulations of the States.

Furthermore, the distinguished author makes this additional observation: "And neither the power [police power] itself, nor the discretion to exercise it as need may require, can be bargained away by the State."

Aside from insurmountable constitutional objections, there are practical reasons that ought to deter you from enacting titles II and VIII. Under these two titles the Congress proposes to compel the employers and employees to assume a financial burden that will ultimately amount to over $32,000,000,000. It is proposed to set up a bureaucratic scheme like this when 12,000,000 wage earners are without employment, when one-sixth of our population is on the relief rolls, when our national and State debts are appalling, and in face of the fact that it will be years before benefits will be paid.

Mr. Chairman, speaking of the present plight of the country brings me to a discussion of title III and title IX, which deal with unemployment insurance. This is another compulsory pay-roll tax. The system that is proposed to coerce the States to adopt by means of a 3-percent pay-roll tax, imposed on employers who employ ten or more persons, is a State function as distinguished from a Federal function. The States may or may not set up an unemployment system, but in a State that fails to do so the employers who fall within the purview of titles III and IX will receive no unemployment benefits for their employees from the 3-percent tax imposed. In such a case it is not a tax but a penalty, and, therefore, discriminatory as well.

The problem before the Nation today is to find work — not public work paid out of the taxpayers' money — but work in private industry. Private business and industry should be encouraged, not discouraged. What has been the philosophy under which our Government has operated for the past 150 years, until recently? It has been the nonintervention of government in competition with private business. When social or economic legislation has been presented the practice heretofore has been for Congress to ascertain whether the ideas proposed would produce useful or injurious results, without troubling about their theoretical value. Now all this is reversed by the apostles of Government intervention, who maintain that the brain trust, by reason of the intellectual superiority of its members, ought to control the whole complex of the Nation's industrial and commercial activities, even though it may deprive the citizen of initiative and therefore of liberty.

The gradual replacement of private initiative by that of Government domination is apparent to those whose intellectual and moral senses have not been dulled by Federal doles and assurance of "a more abundant life."

Steadily and gradually, under the powers granted by Congress to the executive branch of the Government, it is beginning to direct everything, manage everything, and monopolize everything. Day by day the Government will intervene more and more in the most trivial activities of its citizens.

The Congress has appropriated millions of dollars, in fact billions of dollars, of the taxpayers' money and made them available to Government functionaries to spend in developing Government plants and commercial activities to compete with private enterprise.

The United States of America, under constitutional government, has for 144 years, until the advent of the "new deal," surpassed every other nation in the creation of wealth and in the wide distribution of it among the masses. The American philosophy of government has permitted the activity of the individual to reach its maximum and that of the Government to be reduced to a minimum. It is proposed now to reverse the American policy of private initiative and, instead, to make the Federal Government preponderant in the daily affairs of every individual.

Unemployment insurance is dependent on the pay rolls of private industry, not on Government pay rolls. Private pay rolls are a condition precedent to the success of the plan embodied in titles III and IX of the bill before us.

It has been truly said that "the man who is trying to make a living for his family and pay taxes to city, State, and Nation, always loses if he has a government for a competitor." Mr. Chairman, the small-business man, the one who falls within the purview of titles III and IX, is sorely pressed at the present time to maintain his solvency. These small concerns can meet this new burden of taxation only by either going out of business or by cutting expenses. How will the man employing twelve or fifteen men reduce his expenses? He will, if possible, reduce the number of his employees to nine to escape the tax burden.

Much has been said about the unemployment systems of foreign governments; that the United States is a backward nation in this field of social legislation. The experience of some of the other nations with unemployment insurance demonstrates clearly that if such a system is launched on a large scale during a period of depression, all that can save it from financial disaster is the Treasury of the Federal Government. The burden of keeping the system solvent will first fall on the wage earner.

Gustav Hertz, German labor economist, in a recent work on social insurance, states this:

> In Germany no one any longer doubts the fact that the employer's share of the premium is taken from the workman's wages. What the employer pays as his contribution to social insurance he cannot pay the workmen in the form of wages.
>
> Some years ago a well-known unionist even had to admit that countries without social insurance have higher real wages than Germany [United States, Holland, Scandinavia], while another said, "High wages are the best social policy."
>
> In other words, social insurances handicap wage development. But not only this, they also intensify wage struggles.

Mr. Hertz states that under the German system, "premiums started on a modest basis. The first were 1½ percent for employee and three-fourths of 1 percent for employer. Today the entire premium averages almost one-fifth of the amount of the wages, and for miners it is nearly 30 percent."

Mr. Chairman, I am not hostile to unemployment insurance, but I do maintain that such a system, to succeed, must be put in operation when the unemployment fund can be built up without retarding recovery.

British experience with unemployment insurance demonstrates the advantage of starting such a plan under auspicious circumstances. The British National Insurance Act went into effect December 16, 1911. It covered only 2,000,000 manual workers in "seven of the more unstable industries." After the outbreak of the World War, 1,500,000 were added to the insurance list. The scheme operated successfully from 1911 up to 1920. It could not do otherwise, because during that time there was practically no unemployment. Because of the war activities, it was almost impossible to find men to fill available jobs.

In November 1920 the unemployment scheme was expanded to cover a total of 12,000,000 workers. Then came the depression of 1920, followed by unemployment. What happened?

The fund of £22,000,000, accumulated prior to the depression, was exhausted by the middle of 1921. Then the unemployment system had to borrow from the Treasury, and by 1922 a debt of £14,3000,000 had be incurred.

The employment-fund debt in March 1927 had increased to £24,710,000, more than twice what it had been previous year.

Then contributions were increased and benefits reduced.

It became necessary in 1929 to borrow £10,000,000 more from the Treasury.

The annual cost in 1930 increased £13,000,000 more. The debt doubled in the next twelve months, and in March 1931 stood a £73,600,000 — all this drawn from the Treasury and as an added burden to the taxpayers.

The indebtedness of the unemployment fund increased steadily at the rate of £1,000,000 a month.

In September 1931 the debt had reached £101,910,000.

Mr. Chairman, is this the record and this experience of Great Britain to be ignored by the Members of this House? Theorists may do so, but ought we, as responsible representatives of the people, to do so?

It cannot be successfully disputed that the national budgetary crisis of Great Britain in 1931 was largely due from financing the unemployment system.

I want to impress on the Members of the House that during the calender year 1931 the British Treasury paid out £16,000,000 in contributions, £28,000,000 in transitional benefits, and also loaned in addition to these fifty million to the unemployment fund.

Mr. Chairman, only last year, 1934, one of the great problems of the British Parliament was to find some way to establish the unemployment system on a solvent and self-supporting basis. It still remains an unsolved problem in Great Britain.

I urge you not to disregard the facts. The greatest boon that can come to the wage earners of this Nation is industrial and business recovery. The unemployed want jobs and not doles. Recovery cannot come by plunging the Nation further and further into debt by increasing Government bureaus and commissions and by imposing taxes. The way to confidence and recovery is not by squandering money on experiments that have been tried and have failed.

Let us replace experiments with experience. "Experience," says Wendell Phillips, "is a safe light to work by, and he is not a rash man who expects success in the future by the same means which secured it in the past."

SUPPLEMENTARY ESSAY
The Redistribution of Power From Society to the State
by Albert Jay Nock

If we look beneath the surface of our public affairs, we can discern one fundamental fact, namely: a great redistribution of power between society and the State. This is the fact that interests the student of civilization. He has only a secondary or derived interest in matters like price-fixing, wage-fixing, inflation, political banking, "agricultural adjustment," and similar items of State policy that fill the pages of newspapers and the mouths of publicists and politicians. All these can be run up under one head. They have an immediate and temporary importance, and for this reason they monopolize public attention, but they all come to the same thing; which is, an increase of State power and a corresponding decrease of social power.

It is unfortunately none too well understood that, just as the State has no money of its own, so it has no power of its own. All the power it has is what society gives it, plus what it confiscates from time to time on one pretext or another; there is no other source from which State power can be drawn. Therefore every assumption of State power, whether by gift or seizure, leaves society with so much less power; there is never, nor can be, any strengthening of State power without a corresponding and roughly equivalent depletion of social power.

Moreover, it follows that with any exercise of State power, not only the exercise of social power in the same direction, but the disposition to exercise it in that direction, tends to dwindle. Mayor Gaynor astonished the whole of New York when he pointed out to a correspondent who had been complaining about the inefficiency of the police, that any citizen has the right to arrest a malefactor and bring him before a magistrate. "The law of England and of this country," he wrote, "has been very careful to confer no more right in that respect upon policemen and constables than it confers on every citizen." State exercise of that right through a police force had gone on so steadily that not only were citizens indisposed to exercise it, but probably not one in ten thousand knew he had it.

Heretofore in this country sudden crises of misfortune have been met by a mobilization of social power. In fact (except for certain institutional enterprises like the home for the aged, the lunatic-asylum, city-hospital and county-poorhouse) destitution, unemployment, "depression" and similar ills, have been no concern of the State, but have been relieved by the application of social power. Under Mr. Roosevelt, however, the State assumed this function, publicly announcing the doctrine, brand-new in our history, that the State owes its citizens a living. Students of politics, of course, saw in this merely an astute proposal for a prodigious enhancement of State power; merely what, as long ago as 1794, James Madison called "the old trick of turning every contingency into a resource for accumulating force in the government"; and the passage of time has proved that they were right. The effect of this upon the balance between State power and social power is clear, and also its effect of a general indoctrination with the idea that an exercise of social power upon such matters is no longer called for.

It is largely in this way that the progressive conversion of social power into State power becomes acceptable and gets itself accepted. When the Johnstown flood occurred, social power was immediately mobilized and applied with intelligence and vigour. Its abundance, measured by money alone, was so great that when everything was finally put in order, something like a million dollars remained. If such a catastrophe happened now, not only is social power perhaps too depleted for the like exercise, but the general instinct would be to let the State see to it. Not only has social power atrophied to that extent, but the disposition to exercise it in that particular direction has atrophied with it. If the State has made such matters its business, and has confiscated the social power necessary to deal with them, why, let it deal with them. We can get some kind of rough measure of this general atrophy by our own disposition when approached by a beggar. Two years ago we might have been moved to give him something; today we are moved to refer him to the State's relief-agency. The State has said to society, You are either not exercising enough power to meet the emergency, or are exercising it in what I think is an incompetent way, so I shall confiscate your power, and exercise it to suit myself. Hence when the beggar asks us for a quarter, our instinct is to say that the State has already confiscated our quarter for his benefit, and he should go to the State about it.

Every positive intervention that the State makes upon industry and commerce has a similar effect. When the State intervenes to fix wages or prices, or to prescribe the conditions of competition, it virtually tells the enterpriser that he is not exercising social power in the right way, and therefore it proposes to confiscate his power and exercise it according to the State's own judgment of what is best. Hence the enterpriser's instinct is to let the State look after the consequences. As a simple illustration of this, a manufacturer of a highly specialized type of textiles was saying to me the other day that he had kept his mill going at a loss for five years because he did not want to turn his workpeople on the street in such hard times, but now that the State had stepped in to tell him how he must run his business, the State might jolly well take the responsibility.

The process of converting social power into State power may perhaps be seen at its simplest in cases where the State's intervention is directly competitive. The accumulation of State power in various countries has been so accelerated and diversified within the last twenty years that we now see the State functioning as telegraphist, telephonist, matchpedlar, radio-operator, cannon-founder, railway-builder and owner, railway-operator, wholesale and retail tobacconist, shipbuilder and owner, chief chemist, harbour-maker and dockbuilder, housebuilder, chief educator, newspaper-proprietor, food-purveyor, dealer in insurance, and so on through a long list. It is obvious that private forms of these enterprises must tend to dwindle in proportion as the energy of the State's encroachments on them increases, for the competition of social power with State power is always disadvantaged, since the State can arrange the terms of competition to suit itself, even to the point of outlawing any exercise of social power whatever in the premises; in other words, giving itself a monopoly. Instances of this expedient are common; the one we are probably best acquainted with is the State's monopoly of letter-carrying. Social power is estopped by sheer fiat from application to this form of enterprise, notwithstanding it could carry it on far cheaper, and, in this country at least, far better. The advantages of this monopoly in promoting the State's interests are peculiar. No other, probably, could secure so large and well-distributed a volume of patronage, under the guise of a public service in constant use by so large a number of people; it plants a lieutenant of the State at every country-crossroad. It is by no means a pure coincidence that an administration's chief almoner and whip-at-large is so regularly appointed Postmaster-general.

Thus the State "turns every contingency into a resource" for accumulating power in itself, always at the expense of social power; and with this it develops a habit of acquiescence in the people. New generations appear, each temperamentally adjusted — or as I believe our American glossary now has it, "conditioned" — to new increments of State power, and they tend to take the process of continuous accumulation as quite in order. All the State's institutional voices unite in confirming this tendency; they unite in exhibiting the progressive conversion of social power into State power as something not only quite in order, but even as wholesome and necessary for the public good.

In the United States at the present time, the principal indexes of the increase of State power are three in number. First, the point to which the centralization of State authority has been carried. Practically all the sovereign rights and powers of the smaller political units — all of them that are significant enough to be worth absorbing — have been absorbed by the federal unit; nor is this all. State power has not only been thus concentrated at Washington, but it has been so far concentrated into the hands of the Executive that the existing regime is a regime of personal government. It is nominally republican, but actually monocratic; a curious anomaly, but highly characteristic of a people little gifted with intellectual integrity. Personal government is not exercised here in the same ways as in Italy, Russia or Germany, for there is as yet no State interest to be served by so doing, but rather the contrary; while in those countries there is. But personal government is always personal government; the mode of its exercise is a matter of immediate political expediency, and is determined entirely by circumstances.

This regime was established by a *coup d'Etat* of a new and unusual kind, practicable only in a rich country. It was effected, not by violence, like Louis-Napoleon's, or by terrorism, like Mussolini's, but by purchase. It therefore presents what might be called an American variant of the *coup d'Etat*. Our national legislature was not suppressed by force of arms, like the French Assembly in 1851, but was bought out of its functions with public money; and as appeared most conspicuously in the elections of November, 1934, the consolidation of the *coup d'Etat* was effected by the same means; the corresponding functions in the smaller units were reduced under the personal control of the Executive. This is a most remarkable phenomenon; possibly nothing quite like it ever took place; and its character and implications deserve the most careful attention.

A second index is supplied by the prodigious extension of the bureaucratic principle that is now observable. This is attested *prima facie* by the number of new boards, bureaux and commissions set up at Washington in the last two years. They are reported as representing something like 90,000 new employees appointed outside the civil service, and the total of the federal pay-roll in Washington is reported as something over three million dollars per month. This, however, is relatively a small matter. The pressure of centralization has tended powerfully to convert every official and every political aspirant in the smaller units into a venal and complaisant agent of the federal bureaucracy. This presents an interesting parallel with the state of things prevailing in the Roman Empire in the last days of the Flavian dynasty, and afterwards. The rights and practices of local self-government, which were formerly very considerable in the provinces and much more so in the municipalities, were lost by surrender rather than by suppression. The imperial bureaucracy, which up to the second century was comparatively a modest affair, grew rapidly to great size, and local politicians were quick to see the advantage of being on terms with it. They came to Rome with their hats in their hands, as governors, Congressional aspirants and such-like now go to Washington. Their eyes and thoughts were constantly fixed on Rome, because recognition and preferment lay that way; and in their incorrigible sycophancy they became, as Plutarch says, like hypochondriacs who dare not eat or take a bath without consulting their physician.

A third index is seen in the erection of poverty and mendicancy into a permanent political asset. Two years ago, many of our people were in hard straits; to some extent, no doubt, through no fault of their own, though it is now clear than in the popular view of their case, as well as in the political view, the line between the deserving poor and the undeserving poor was not distinctly drawn. Popular feeling ran high at that time, and the prevailing wretchedness was regarded with undiscriminating emotion, as evidence of some general wrong done upon its victims by society at large, rather than as the natural penalty of greed, folly or actual misdoings; which in large part it was. The State, always instinctively "turning every contingency into a resource" for accelerating the conversion of social power into State power, was quick to take advantage of this state of mind. All that was needed to organize these unfortunates into an invaluable political property was to declare the doctrine that the

State owes all its citizens a living; and this was accordingly done. It immediately precipitated an enormous mass of subsidized voting-power, an enormous resource for strengthening the State at the expense of society.

There is an impression that the enhancement of State power which has taken place since 1932 is provisional and temporary, that the corresponding depletion of social power is by way of a kind of emergency-loan, and therefore is not to be scrutinized too closely. There is every probability that this belief is devoid of foundation. No doubt our present regime will be modified in one way or another; indeed, it must be, for the process of consolidation itself requires it. But any essential change would be quite unhistorical, quite without precedent, and is therefore most unlikely; and by an essential change, I mean one that will tend to redistribute actual power between the State and society. In the nature of things, there is no reason why such a change should take place, and every reason why it should not. We shall see various apparent recessions, apparent compromises, but the one thing we may be quite sure of is that none of these will tend to diminish actual State power.

For example, we shall no doubt shortly see the great pressure-group of politically-organized poverty and mendicancy subsidized indirectly instead of directly, because State interest can not long keep pace with the hand-over-head disposition of the masses to loot their own Treasury. The method of direct subsidy, or sheer cash-purchase, will therefore in all probability soon give way to the indirect method of what is called "social legislation"; that is, a multiplex system of State-managed pensions, insurances and indemnities of various kinds. This is an apparent recession, and when it occurs it will no doubt be proclaimed as an actual recession, no doubt accepted as such; but is it? Does it actually tend to diminish State power and increase social power? Obviously not, but quite the opposite. It tends to consolidate firmly this particular fraction of State power, and opens the way to getting an indefinite increment upon it by the mere continuous invention of new courses and developments of State-administered social legislation, which is an extremely simple business. One may add the observation for whatever its evidential value may be worth, that if the effect of progressive social legislation upon the sum-total of State power were unfavourable or even nil, we should hardly have found Prince de Bismark and the British Liberal politicians of forty years ago going in for anything remotely resembling it.

When, therefore, the inquiring student of civilization has occasion to observe this or any other apparent recession upon any point of our present regime, he may content himself with asking the one question, *What effect has this upon the sum-total of State power?* The answer he gives himself will show conclusively whether the recession is actual or apparent, and this is all he is concerned to know.

There is also an impression that if actual recessions do not come about of themselves, they may be brought about by the expedient of voting one political party out and another one in. This idea rests upon certain assumptions that experience has shown to be unsound; the first one being that the power of the ballot is what republican political theory makes it out to be, and that therefore the electorate has an effective choice in the matter. It is a matter of open and notorious fact that nothing like this is true. Our nominally republican system is

actually built on an imperial model, with our professional politicians standing in the place
of the praetorian guards; they meet from time to time, decide what can be "got away with,"
and how, and who is to do it; and the electorate votes according to their prescriptions. Under
these conditions it is easy to provide the appearance of any desired concession of State
power, without the reality; our history shows innumerable instances of very easy dealing with
problems in practical politics much more difficult than that. One may remark in this
connexion also the notoriously baseless assumption that party-designations connote principles, and that party-pledges imply performance. Moreover, underlying these assumptions and
all others that faith in "political action" contemplates, is the assumption that the interests of
the State and the interests of society are, at least theoretically, identical; whereas in theory
they are directly opposed, and this opposition invariably declares itself in practice to the
precise extent that circumstances permit.

However, without pursuing these matters further at the moment, it is probably enough
to observe here that in the nature of things the exercise of personal government, the control
of a huge and growing bureaucracy, and the management of an enormous mass of subsidized
voting-power, are as agreeable to one stripe of politician as they are to another. Presumably
they interest a Republican or a Progressive as much as they do a Democrat, Communist,
Farmer-Labourites, Socialist, or whatever a politician may, for electioneering purposes, see
fit to call himself. This was demonstrated in the local campaigns of 1934 by the practical
attitude of politicians who represented nominal opposition parties. It is now being further
demonstrated by the desirable haste that the leaders of the official opposition are making
towards what they call "reorganization" of their party. One may well be inattentive to their
words; their actions, however, mean simply that the recent accretions of State power are here
to stay, and that they are aware of it; and that, such being the case, they are preparing to
dispose themselves most advantageously in a contest for their control and management. This
is all that "reorganization" of the Republican party means, and all it is meant to mean; and
this is in itself quite enough to show that any expectation of an essential change of regime
through a change of party-administration is illusory. On the contrary, it is clear that whatever
party-competition we shall see hereafter will be on the same terms as heretofore. It will be
a competition for control and management, and it would naturally issue in still closer centralization, still further extension of the bureaucratic principle, and still larger concessions to
subsidized voting-power. This course would be strictly historical, and is furthermore to be
expected as lying in the nature of things, as it so obviously does.

Indeed, it is by this means that the aim of the collectivists seems likeliest to be attained in this country; this aim being the complete extinction of social power through absorption by the State. Their fundamental doctrine was formulated and invested with a quasi-
religious sanction by the idealist philosophers of the last century; and among peoples who
have accepted it in terms as well as in fact, it is expressed in formulas almost identical with
theirs. Thus, for example, when Hitler says that "the State dominates the nation because it
alone represents it," he is only putting into loose popular language the formula of Hegel, that
"the State is the general substance, whereof individuals are but accidents." Or, again, when

Mussolini says, "Everything for the State; nothing outside the State; nothing against the State," he is merely vulgarizing the doctrine of Fichte, that "the State is the superior power, ultimate and beyond appeal, absolutely independent."

It may be in place to remark here the essential identity of the various extant forms of collectivism. The superficial distinctions of Fascism, Bolshevism, Hitlerism, are the concern of journalists and publicists; the serious student sees in them only the one root-idea of a complete conversion of social power into State power. When Hitler and Mussolini invoke a kind of debased and hoodwinking mysticism to aid their acceleration of this process, the student at once recognizes his old friend, the formula of Hegel, that "the State incarnates the Divine Idea upon earth," and he is not hoodwinked. The journalist and the impressionable traveller may make what they will of "the new religion of Bolshevism"; the student contents himself with remarking clearly the exact nature of the process which this inculcation is designed to sanction.

This process — the conversion of social power into State power — has not been carried as far here as it has elsewhere; as it has in Russia, Italy or Germany, for example. Two things, however, are to be observed. First, that it has gone a long way, at a rate of progress which has of late been greatly accelerated. What has chiefly differentiated its progress here from its progress in other countries is its unspectacular character. Mr. Jefferson wrote in 1823 that there was no danger he dreaded so much as "the consolidation [*i.e.*, centralization] of our government by the noiseless and therefore unalarming instrumentality of the Supreme Court." These words characterize every advance that we have made in State aggrandizement. Each one has been noiseless and therefore unalarming, especially to a people notoriously preoccupied, inattentive and incurious, Even the *coup d'Etat* of 1932 was noiseless and unalarming. In Russia, Italy, Germany, the *coup d'Etat* was violent and spectacular; it had to be; but here it was neither. Under cover of a nation-wide, State-managed mobilization of insane buffoonery and aimless commotion, it took place in so unspectacular a way that its true nature escaped notice, and even now is not generally understood. The method of consolidating the ensuing regime, moreover, was also noiseless and unalarming; it was merely the prosaic and unspectacular "higgling of the market," to which a long and uniform political experience had accustomed us. A visitor from a poorer and thriftier country might have regarded Mr. Farley's activities in the local campaign of 1934 as striking or even spectacular, but they made no such impression on us. They seemed so familiar, so much the regular thing, that one heard little comment on them. Moreover, political habit led us to attribute whatever unfavourable comment we did hear, to interest; either partisan or monetary interest, or both. We put it down as the jaundiced judgment of persons with axes to grind; and naturally the regime did all it could to encourage this view.

The second thing to be observed is that certain formulas, certain arrangements of words, stand as an obstacle in the way of our perceiving how far the conversion of social power into State power has actually gone. The force of phrase and name distorts the identification of our own actual acceptances and acquiescences. We are accustomed to the rehearsal of certain poetic litanies, we are indifferent to their correspondence with truth and fact. When

Hegel's doctrine of the State, for example, is restated in terms by Hitler and Mussolini, it is distinctly offensive to us, and we congratulate ourselves on our freedom from the "yoke of a dictator's tyranny." No American politician would dream of anything of the kind. We may imagine, for example, the shock to popular sentiment that would ensue upon Mr. Roosevelt's declaring publicly that "the State embraces everything, and nothing has value outside the State. The State creates right." Yet an American politician, as long as he does not formulate that doctrine in set terms, may go further with it in a practical way than Mussolini has gone, and without trouble or question. Suppose Mr. Roosevelt should defend his regime by publicly reasserting Hegel's dictum that "the State alone possesses rights, because it is the strongest." One can hardly imagine that our public would get that down without a great deal of retching. Yet how far, really, is that doctrine alien to our public's actual acquiescences? Surely not far.

The point is that in respect of the relation between the theory and the actual practice of public affairs, the American is the most unphilosophical of beings. The rationalization of conduct in general is most repugnant to him; he prefers to emotionalize it. He is indifferent to the theory of things, so long as he may rehearse his formulas; and so long as he can listen to the patter of his litanies, no practical inconsistency disturbs him — indeed, he gives no evidence of even recognizing it as an inconsistency.

The ablest and most acute observer among the many who came from Europe to look us over in the early part of the last century was the one who is for some reason the most neglected, notwithstanding that in our present circumstances, especially, he is worth more to us than all the de Tocquevilles, Bryces, Trollopes and Chateaubriands put together. This was the noted St.-Simonien and political economist, Michel Chevalier. Professor Chinard, in his admirable biographical study of John Adams, has called attention to Chevalier's observation that the American people have "the morale of an army on the march." The more one thinks of this, the more clearly one sees how little there is in what our publicists are fond of calling "the American psychology" that it does not exactly account for; and it exactly accounts for the trait that we are considering.

An army on the march has no philosophy; it views itself as a creature of the moment. It does not rationalize conduct except in terms of an immediate end. As Tennyson observed, there is a pretty strict official understanding against its doing so; "theirs not to reason why." Emotionalizing conduct is another matter, and the more of it the better; it is encouraged by a whole elaborate paraphernalia of showy etiquette, flags, music, uniforms, decorations, and the careful cultivation of a very special sort of comradery. In every relation to "the reason of the thing," however — in the ability and eagerness, as Plato puts it, "to see things as they are" — the mentality of an army on the march is merely so much delayed adolescence; it remains persistently, incorrigibly and notoriously infantile.

Past generations of Americans, as Martin Chuzzlewit left record, erected this infantilism into a distinguishing virtue, and they took great pride in it as the mark of a chosen people, destined to live forever amidst the glory of their own unparalleled achievements *wie Gott in Frankreich*. Mr. Jefferson Brick, General Choke and the Honourable Elijah Pogram made a first-class job of indoctrinating their countrymen with the idea that a philosophy is wholly unnecessary, and that a concern with the theory of things is effeminate and unbecoming. An envious and presumably dissolute Frenchman may say what he likes about the morale of an army on the march, but the fact remains that it has brought us where we are, and has got us what we have. Look at a continent subdued, see the spread of our industry and commerce, our railways, newspapers, finance-companies, schools, colleges, what you will! Well, if all this has been done without a philosophy, if we have grown to this unrivalled greatness without any attention to the theory of things, does it not show that philosophy and the theory of things are all moonshine, and not worth a practical people's consideration? The morale of an army on the march is good enough for us, and we are proud of it.

The present generation does not speak in quite this tone of robust certitude. It seems, if anything, rather less openly contemptuous of philosophy; one even sees some signs of a suspicion that in our present circumstances the theory of things might be worth looking into, and it is especially towards the theory of sovereignty and rulership that this new attitude of hospitality appears to be developing. The condition of public affairs in all countries, notably in our own, has done more than bring under review the mere current practice of politics, the character and quality of representative politicians, and the relative merits of this-or-that form or mode of government. It has served to suggest attention to the one institution whereof all these forms or modes are but the several, and, from the theoretical point of view, indifferent, manifestations. It suggests that finality does not lie with consideration of species, but of genius; it does not lie with consideration of the characteristic marks that differentiate the republican State, monocratic State, constitutional, collectivist, totalitarian, Hitlerian, Bolshevist, what you will. It lies with consideration of the State itself.

There appears to be a curious difficulty about exercising reflective thought upon the actual nature of an institution into which one was born and one's ancestors were born. One accepts it as one does the atmosphere; one's practical adjustments to it are made by a kind of reflex. One seldom thinks about the air until one notices some change, favourable or unfavourable, and then one's thought about it is special; one thinks about purer air, lighter air, heavier air, not about air. So it is with certain human institutions. We know that they exist, that they affect us in various ways, but we do not ask how they came to exist, or what their original intention was, or what primary function it is that they are actually fulfilling; and when they affect us so unfavourably that we rebel against them, we contemplate substituting nothing beyond some modification or variant of the same institution. Thus colonial America, oppressed by the monarchical State, brings in the republican State; Germany gives up the republican State for the Hitlerian State; Russia exchanges the monocratic State for the collectivist State; Italy exchanges the constitutionalist State for the "totalitarian" State.

It is interesting to observe that in the year 1935 the average individual's incurious attitude towards the phenomenon of the State is precisely what his attitude was towards the phenomenon of the Church in the year, say, 1500. The State was then a very weak institution; the Church was very strong. The individual was born into the Church, as his ancestors had been for generations, in precisely the formal, documented fashion in which he is now born into the State. He was taxed for the Church's support, as he now is for the State's support. He was supposed to accept the official theory and doctrine of the Church, to conform to its discipline, and in a general way to do as it told him; again, precisely the sanctions that the State now lays upon him. If he were reluctant or recalcitrant, the Church made a satisfactory amount of trouble for him, as the State now does. Notwithstanding all this, it does not appear to have occurred to the Church-citizens of that day, any more than it occurs to the State-citizen of the present, to ask what sort of institution it was that claimed his allegiance. There it was; he accepted its own account of itself, took it as it stood, and at its own valuation.

It appears to me that with the depletion of social power going on at the rate it is, the State-citizen should look very closely into the essential nature of the institution that is bringing it about. He should ask himself whether he has a theory of the State, and if so, whether he can assure himself that history supports it. He will not find this a matter that can be settled offhand; it needs a good deal of investigation, and a stiff exercise of reflective thought. He should ask, in the first place, how the State originated, and why; it must have come about somehow, and for some purpose. This seems an extremely easy question to answer, but he will not find it so. Then he should ask what it is that history exhibits continuously as the State's primary function. Then, whether he finds that "the State" and "government" are strictly synonymous terms; he uses them as such, but are they? Are there any invariable characteristic marks that differentiate the institution of government from the institution of the State? Then finally he should decide whether, by the testimony of history, the State is to be regarded as, in essence, a social or an anti-social institution?

It is pretty clear now that if the Church-citizen of 1500 had put his mind on questions as fundamental as these, his civilization might have had a much easier and pleasanter course to run; and the State-citizen of today may profit by his experience.

The preceding essay was extracted from Albert Jay Nock, Our Enemy the State *(New York: William Morrow & Company, 1937).*

CHAPTER TWENTY-FOUR
A Permanent State of National Emergency

The Admissions of the Ninety-Third Congress

In the United States at the present time... [p]ractically all the sovereign rights and powers of the smaller political units — all of them that are significant enough to be worth absorbing — have been absorbed by the federal unit; nor is this all. State power has not only been thus concentrated at Washington, but it has been so far concentrated into the hands of the Executive that the existing regime is a regime of personal government. It is nominally republican, but actually monocratic; a curious anomaly, but highly characteristic of a people little gifted with intellectual integrity....

This regime was established by a *coup d'Etat* of a new and unusual kind, practicable only in a rich country. It was effected, not by violence, like Louis-Napoleon's, or by terrorism, like Mussolini's, but by purchase. It therefore presents what might be called an American variant of the *coup d'Etat*. Our national legislature was not suppressed by force of arms, like the French Assembly in 1851, but was bought out of its functions with public money.... This is a most remarkable phenomenon; possibly nothing quite like it ever took place; and its character and implications deserve the most careful attention.[1]

One does not have to rely upon conjecture or doubtul conspiracy theories to substantiate the assertions contained in the above quote. Indeed, the subjugation of the American people by their leaders "for filthy lucre's sake" is a matter of public record. It is also clear that those in positions of authority know exactly what they are doing and how they have come to possess the power to do it. For example, in late 1973, the Ninety-Third Congress

---

1. Nock, *Our Enemy the State*, pages 10-12.

formed the Special Committee on the Termination of the National Emergency.[2] Co-chaired by Senators Charles Mathias Jr. and Frank Church, the purpose of the Committee, as stated in its report entitled *Emergency Powers Statutes* — otherwise known as *Senate Report 93-549* — was "to examine the consequences of terminating the declared states of national emergency that now prevail; to recommend what steps the Congress should take to ensure that the termination can be accomplished without adverse effect upon the necessary tasks of governing; and, also, to recommend ways in which the United States can meet future emergency situations with speed and effectiveness but without relinquishment of congressional oversight and control."[3] Furthermore, the Committee was charged with the task of determining "the most reasonable ways to restore normalcy to the operations of our Government."[4]

What was this national emergency which required termination in 1973 before the normal operations of the U.S. Government could be restored? The very first sentence in the "Foreword" of *Senate Report 93-549* provided the answer: "Since March 9, 1933, the United States has been in a state of declared national emergency."[5] What the Senate Special Committee was admitting was that the national emergency of the Great Depression, in which the American people lost what was left of their constitutional liberties to Roosevelt's socialist "New Deal" democracy, was still in force forty years later, long after the economic crisis had ended. Even more astonishing are the following admissions:

> In fact, there are now in effect four presidentially proclaimed states of national emergency: In addition to the national emergency declared by President Roosevelt in 1933, there are also the national emergency proclaimed by President Truman on December 16, 1950, during the Korean conflict, and the states of national emergency declared by President Nixon on March 23, 1970, and August 15, 1971.
>
> These proclamations give force to 470 provisions of Federal law. These hundreds of statutes delegate to the President extraordinary powers, ordinarily exercised by Congress, which affect the lives of American citizens in a host of all-encompassing manners. This vast range of powers, taken together, confer enough authority to rule this country without reference to normal constitutional processes.
>
> Under the powers delegated by these statutes, the President may: seize property; organize and control the means of production; seize commodities; assign military forces abroad; institute martial law; seize and control all transportation and communication; regulate the operation of private enterprise; restrict travel; and, in a plethora of particular

---

2. *Senate Resolution 9* (Ninety-Third Congress, First Session).

3. U.S. Senate, "Foreword," *Emergency Powers Statutes*, page iii.

4. U.S. Senate, *ibid.*, page iv.

5. U.S. Senate, *ibid.*, page iii.

ways, control the lives of all American citizens.[6]

When compared with the limited confederated system chartered by our forefathers in the Constitution of 1787, the Government described above appears much like an Orwellian nightmare of centralized despotism. This means that while the country's young men were overseas supposedly fighting to "make the world safe for democracy" in the second World War, in the Korean War, and in the Vietnam War, Americans themselves were being deprived of the most basic constitutional liberties by their own Government. In its "Introduction," *Senate Report 93-549* went on to state:

> A majority of the people of the United States have lived all their lives under emergency rule. For almost 40 years, freedoms and governmental procedures guaranteed by the Constitution have, in varying degrees, been abridged by laws brought in force by states of national emergency. The problem of how a constitutional democracy reacts to great crises, however, far antedates the Great Depression. As a philosophical issue, its origins reach back to the Greek city-states and the Roman Republic. And, in the United States, actions taken by the Government in times of great crises have — from, at least, the Civil War — in important ways shaped the present phenomenon of a permanent state of national emergency....[7]

Over the next two pages, the report briefly discussed Woodrow Wilson's efforts to "expand executive emergency powers enormously" during the first World War. As mentioned in Chapter Twenty, it was declared at that time that a national emergency could only be met by the President acting as "supreme dictator." The astute reader should not be surprised to read the observation that "this expansion of powers in wartime was based on precedents set by Lincoln decades earlier."[8] The report continued:

> Over the course of at least the last 40 years, then, Presidents have had available an enormous — seemingly expanding and never-ending — range of emergency powers. Indeed, at their fullest extent and during the height of a crisis, these "prerogative" powers appear to be virtually unlimited.... Because Congress and the public are unaware of the extent of emergency powers, there has never been any notable congressional or public objection made to this state of affairs. Nor have the courts imposed significant limitations.
> During the New Deal, the Supreme Court initially struck down much of Roosevelt's emergency economic legislation [citation omitted]. However, political pressures, a change in personnel, and presidential threats of court-packing, soon altered this course of decisions [citation omitted]. Since 1937, the Court has been extremely reluctant to invalidate any congressional delegation of economic powers to the President. It appears that this

---

6. U.S. Senate, *ibid.*

7. U.S. Senate, "Introduction, " *ibid.*, page 1.

8. U.S. Senate, *ibid.*, page 3.

will not change in the foreseeable future.[9]

In other words, not only had Congress abdicated its responsibilities into the hands of the President, but the Supreme Court had also been failing to do its job since 1937. In these few paragraphs, the Senate Special Committee had indicted all three branches of the Government for dereliction of their constitutional duties. However, since the attention of the American people was being diverted at the time by the war in Vietnam and a looming energy crisis, the shocking admissions contained in *Senate Report 93-549* went largely unnoticed. Consequently, the situation remained in which "too few are aware of the existence of emergency powers and their extent, and the problem has never been squarely faced."[10]

A year later, the same Senate, in its second session, produced a working paper entitled *A Brief History of Emergency Powers in the United States* which elaborated on the previous report:

> ...[I]t has been Congress' habit to delegate extensive emergency authority — which continues even when the emergency has passed — and not to set a terminating date. The United States thus has on the books at least 470 significant emergency powers statutes without time limitations delegating to the Executive extensive discretionary powers, which affect the lives of American citizens in a host of all-encompassing ways. This vast range of powers, taken together, confer enough authority to rule this country without reference to normal constitutional processes. These laws make no provision for congressional oversight nor do they reserve to Congress a means for terminating the "temporary" emergencies which trigger them into use. No wonder the distinguished political scientist, the late Clinton Rossiter, entitled his post-World War II study on modern democratic states, "Constitutional Dictatorship." Emergency government has become the norm....[11]

National Emergencies Declared a Necessity

In the "Foreword" to *Senate Report 93-549*, Senators Mathias and Church wrote, "[T]here is no present need for the United States Government to continue to function under emergency conditions." Later, in the body of the report, they added, "In the view of the Special Committee, an emergency does not now exist. Congress, therefore, should act in the near future to terminate officially the states of national emergency now in effect."[12] The U.S. Attorney General, however, was of a different opinion:

---

9. U.S. Senate, *ibid.*, page 6.

10. U.S. Senate, *ibid.*

11. U.S. Senate, *Brief History of Emergency Powers*, page v.

12. U.S. Senate, *Emergency Powers Statutes*, pages iii, 12.

The Trading With the Enemy Act of 1917 has been amended frequently, and in the process its original purpose and effect have been altered significantly. The Act was originally intended to "define, regulate, and punish trading with the enemy." 40 Stat. 415. Directed primarily to meeting the exigencies of World War I, its drafters intended the Act to remain on the books for future *war* situations. 55 Cong. Rec. 4908. Accordingly, when other war powers were terminated in 1921 an exception was made for the Act and it remained valid law. 41 Stat. 1359.

On March 5, 1933, President Roosevelt relied on Sec. 5(b) of the Trading With the Enemy Act as authority for his Proclamation 2039 which closed all banks for five days. This was clearly a time of financial crisis, not of war, and hence was not within the literal terms and purposes of the Act. Congress rectified the situation five days later when it ratified the President's proclamation and amended Sec. 5(b) to give the President the broad wartime powers of that section in times of declared national emergency as well. 48 Stat. 1. The desperate economic circumstances of the time dictated the passage of this sweeping change....

Another declaration of national emergency was made in Proclamation 2914 of December 16, 1950 during the Korean War. Trading With the Enemy Act powers were exercised pursuant to this proclamation throughout the war. Because the state of emergency so declared has never been terminated, however, this proclamation has continued to serve as the basis for invocation of powers under the Act. Most notably, President Johnson used Sec. 5(b) as authority for Executive Order 11837 of January 1, 1968, imposing controls over transfers of private capital to foreign countries....

On August 15, 1971, President Nixon, in Proclamation 4074, declared an emergency concerning America's declining worldwide economic position. He imposed an import surcharge and devalued the dollar, among other things. One year later, when the Export Control Act lapsed for a month, he invoked Sec. 5(b) to regulate exports, basing his authority to do so both on his Proclamation 4074 and on President Truman's proclamation of 1950.

The current law, which has thus accreted over a period of 50 years, gives the President a wide range of powers, but only in time of war or declared national emergency. Although the Korean war has ended, those powers are being exercised solely on the basis of the 1950 emergency; or, on the basis of the President's unilaterally designating as "emergencies" situations which have only the most tenuous relationship to the serious national crises for which the Trading With the Enemy Act was originally intended. The President, with the approval of Congress,[13] has thus used as authority for extraordinary actions laws which have no real relationship whatsoever to existing circumstances. As a

---

13. This is a sophism. Neither Lincoln nor Roosevelt waited to receive the approval of Congress, but both sought Congress' approval *after the fact*. There is nothing under an Executive dictatorship to stop the current President from doing the same thing. In fact, standing approval of anything the President may choose to do in the exercise of his "emergency powers" is found at 12 USC 95(a). In *Pike v. United States* it was declared, "The power conferred upon the President by 12 USCS 95(a)1 was not confined to the 1933 banking crisis, but extended to any national emergency proclaimed by the President" ([1965], CA 9 Cal. 340 F2d 487).

consequence, a "national emergency" is now a practical necessity in order to carry out what has become the regular and normal method of governmental action. What were intended by Congress as delegations of power to be used only in the most extreme situations and for the most limited durations have become everyday powers; and a state of "emergency" has become a permanent condition (emphasis in original).[14]

The importance of the above words must not be missed. What the Attorney General was saying is that the Government has operated for so long under the auspices of a national emergency, that an attempt to terminate that emergency status would itself inaugurate a crisis of monumental proportions. For example, most, if not all, of the welfare programs upon which millions of Americans depend for their sustenance — the most notable of which is Social Security — would cease to exist without the emergency powers which gave them life. More importantly, the entire credit-based economy is also firmly rooted in emergency powers and would instantly collapse should the Government be "restored to normalcy." Americans have become accustomed to using Federal Reserve Notes in their everyday transactions, and since gold and silver have long ago gone out of circulation, nearly every business in the country would have to close its doors should paper money lose its emergency "legal tender" status. Unemployment on a much larger scale than during the Great Depression would also result, because employers would no longer have a way to pay their employees. It may seem fantastic to some that nearly the entire social, political, and economic structure of the country is balanced precariously on a single subsection of an obsolete Act from the first World War — but it is true nonetheless. Because of the unchecked wickedness of their late leaders, Americans are caught on the horns of a dilemma very much like that which the institution of slavery presented to Southerners in the Nineteenth Century; to quote Thomas Jefferson, "We have the wolf by the ears and can neither hold him nor safely let him go. Justice is in one scale, and self-preservation in the other."

In an effort to "end a potentially dangerous situation,"[15] Congress passed the National Emergencies Act of 14 September 1976 which stated, "All powers and authorities possessed by the President, any other officer or employee of the Federal Government, or any executive agency... as a result of the existence of any declaration of national emergency in effect on the date of enactment of this Act are terminated two years from the date of such enactment."[16] However, the four existing national emergencies were not terminated, but merely rendered

14. U.S. Attorney General, quoted by U.S. Senate, *Emergency Powers Statutes*, pages 182-184.

15. United States Senate Special Committee on National Emergencies and Delegated Emergency Powers, *National Emergencies and Delegated Emergency Powers* (Senate Report No. 94-922, Ninety-Fourth Congress, Second Session; Washington, D.C.: Government Printing Office, 1976), page 19.

16. National Emergencies Act (Public Law 94-412; Statutes at Large, Volume XC, page 1255), Title I, Section 101. This Act was statutized at 50 USC 1622(d).

dormant. Furthermore, in Title II, the same Act gave back what it appeared to take away in Title I: "With respect to Acts of Congress authorizing the exercise, during the period of a national emergency, of any special or extraordinary power, the President is authorized to declare such national emergency. Such proclamation shall immediately be transmitted to the Congress and published in the Federal Register."[17] Predictably, every year since 1976, the President of the United States has availed himself of this loophole and proclaimed a new or reaffirmed an existing state of national emergency.[18]

---

17. *Ibid.*, Title II, Section 202(d).

18. For example, on 12 November 1997, President William J. Clinton issued a *Notice of the Continuation of the National Emergency Regarding Weapons of Mass Destruction*:

> On November 14, 1994, by Executive Order 12938, I declared a national emergency with respect to the unusual and extraordinary threat to the national security, foreign policy, and economy of the United States posed by the proliferation of nuclear, biological, and chemical weapons ("weapons of mass destruction") and the means of delivering such weapons. Because the proliferation of weapons of mass destruction and the means of delivering them continue to pose an unusual and extraordinary threat to the national security, foreign policy, and economy of the United States, the national emergency declared on November 14, 1994, and extended on November 14, 1995 and November 14, 1996, must continue in effect beyond November 14, 1997. Therefore, in accordance with section 202(d) of the National Emergencies Act (50 U.S.C. 1622(d)), I am continuing the national emergency declared in Executive Order 12938.
>
> This notice shall be published in the Federal Register and transmitted to the Congress (66 Fed.Reg.48197-48199).

Under Clinton's successor, George W. Bush, Americans continued to live under a series of declared national emergencies, beginning on 11 September 2001 when the World Trade Center in New York city was destroyed by high-jacked airliners. The following Declaration of National Emergency By Reason of Certain Terrorist Attacks was issued on 14 September:

> A national emergency exists by reason of the terrorist attacks at the World Trade Center, New York, New York, and the Pentagon, and the continuing and immediate threat of further attacks on the United States.
>
> NOW THEREFORE, I, GEORGE W. BUSH, President of the United States of America, by virtue of the authority vested in me as President by the Constitution and the laws of the United States, I hereby declare that the national emergency has existed since September 11, 2001, and, pursuant to the National Emergencies Act (50 U.S.C. 1601 *et seq.*), I intend to utilize the following statutes: sections 123, 123a, 527, 2201(c), 12006, and 12302 of title 10, United States Code, and sections 331, 359, and 367 of title 14, United States Code.
>
> This proclamation immediately shall be published in the Federal Register or disseminated through the Emergency Federal Register, and transmitted to the Congress.

Under this latest national emergency, the Department of Homeland Security was created and the Uniting and Strengthening America by Providing Appropriate Tools Required to Intercept and Obstruct Terrorism Act (USA PATRIOT) was pushed through Congress on 21 October 2001, the

It has been over thirty years since *Senate Report 93-549* was published and it now sits forgotten and gathering dust on law library shelves.[19] Rather than slowing down the Executive grab for power, the tyranny to which the American people have become subjected has instead gained alarming momentum and shows no signs of slowing down. It should also be noted that "Congress has made little or no distinction between a 'state of emergency' and a 'state of war.'"[20] The existence of a "state of war" requires the array of co-belligerents against one another. We have already seen, and will see in even greater detail in the next chapter, whom the U.S. Government views as its primary belligerent.

---

latter of which significantly increased the surveillance and investigative powers of law enforcement agencies against persons living within the country — whether U.S. citizens or foreign nationals — particularly in regard to their transmission of information through e-mail and the internet. As with the sweeping emergency legislation of 1933, this Act originated with the Executive administration and, under pressure from U.S. Attorney-General John Ashcroft, was passed with little congressional debate and with no accompanying House or Senate report explaining its contents. The critics of the Act have pointed out that it permits the search of homes and offices without a warrant and without notification ("sneak and peak"), grants the FBI access to personal information such as banking, educational, medical, dental, and library records without the constitutional requirement of probable cause, and allows for the detention by the Attorney-General of persons suspected of a vaguely-defined "terrorist activity" or intentions without the benefit of a trial. For a detailed analysis of this Act, see http://www.epic.org/privacy/terrorism/usapatriot.

19. It is really the American people who have forgotten this report, assuming that they ever knew it existed. Those in authority certainly have not forgotten it, as evidenced by Harold C. Relyea's report entitled *National Emergency Powers* (98-505 GOV), which was researched and published under the authority of the Congressional Research Service on 18 September 2001 in response to the terrorist attack on the World Trade Center in New York city. Relyea quoted and expounded upon *Senate Report 93-549* throughout his report.

20. *Brown v. Bernstein* (1943), D.C. Pa., 49 F.Supp. 732.

SUPPORTING DOCUMENT
Emergency Powers Statutes
93d Congress, 1st Session
Report No. 93-549

EMERGENCY POWERS STATUTES:

PROVISIONS OF FEDERAL LAW
NOW IN EFFECT DELEGATING TO THE
EXECUTIVE EXTRAORDINARY AUTHORITY
IN TIME OF NATIONAL EMERGENCY

REPORT OF THE SPECIAL COMMITTEE ON THE
TERMINATION OF THE NATIONAL EMERGENCY

UNITED STATES SENATE

NOVEMBER 19, 1973

U.S. GOVERNMENT PRINTING OFFICE
WASHINGTON : 1973
24-509 O

FRANK CHURCH, Idaho Co-Chairman
PHILIP A. HART, Michigan
CLAIBORNE PELL, Rhode Island

ADLAI E. STEVENSON III, Illinois
CHARLES MC MATHIAS, Jr., Maryland
CLIFFORD P. CASE, New Jersey
JAMES B. PEARSON, Kansas
CLIFFORD P. HANSEN, Wyoming

WILLIAM G. MILLER, Staff Director
THOMAS A. DINE, Professional Staff

FOREWORD

Since March 9, 1933, the United States has been in a state of declared national emergency. In fact, there are now in effect four presidentially-proclaimed states of national emergency: In addition to the national emergency declared by President Roosevelt in 1933, there are also the national emergency proclaimed by President Truman on December 16, 1950, during the Korean conflict, and the states of national emergency declared by President Nixon on March 23, 1970, and August 15, 1971.

These proclamations give force to 470 provisions of Federal law. These hundreds of statutes delegate to the President extraordinary powers, ordinarily exercised by the Congress, which affect the lives of American citizens in a host of all-encompassing manners. This vast range of powers,
taken together, confer enough authority to rule the country without reference to normal Constitutional processes.

Under the powers delegated by these statutes, the President may: seize property; organize and control the means of production; seize commodities; assign military forces abroad; institute martial law; seize and control all transportation and communication; regulate the operation of private enterprise; restrict travel; and, in a plethora of particular ways, control the lives of all American citizens.

With the melting of the cold war — the developing detente with the Soviet Union and China, the stable truce of over 20 years duration between North and South Korea, and the end of U.S. involvement in the war in Indochina — there is no present need for the United States Government to continue to function under emergency conditions.

The Special Committee on the Termination of the National Emergency was created to examine the consequences of terminating the declared states of national emergency that now prevail; to recommend what steps the Congress should take to ensure that the termination can be accomplished without adverse effect upon the necessary tasks of governing; and, also, to recommend ways in which the United States can meet future emergency situations with speed and effectiveness but without relinquishment of congressional oversight and control.

In accordance with this mandate, the Special Committee — in conjunction with the Executive branch, expert constitutional authorities, as well as former high officials of this

Government — is now engaged in a detailed study to determine the most reasonable ways to restore normalcy to the operations of our Government.

A first and necessary step was to bring together the body of statutes, which have been passed by Congress, conferring extraordinary powers upon the Executive branch in times of national emergency.

This has been a most difficult task. Nowhere in the Government, in either the Executive or Legislative branches, did there exist a complete catalog of all emergency statutes. Many were aware that there had been a delegation of an enormous amount of power but, of how much power, no one knew. In order to correct this situation, the Special Committee staff was instructed to work with the Executive branch, the Library of Congress, and knowledgeable legal authorities to compile an authoritative list of delegated emergency powers.

This Special Committee study, which contains a list of all provisions of Federal law, except the most trivial, conferring extraordinary powers in time of national emergency, was compiled by the staff under the direction of Staff Director William G. Miller, and Mr. Thomas A. Dine; utilizing the help of the General Accounting Office, the American Law Division of the Library of Congress, the Department of Justice, the Department of Defense, and the Office of Emergency Planning.

The Special Committee is grateful for the assistance provided by Jack. Goldklang of the Office of Legal Counsel, Department of Justice; Lester S. Jayson, the director of the Congressional Research Service of the Library of Congress; Joseph E. Ross, head of the American Law Division of CRS; and especially Raymond Celada of the American Law Division and his able assistants, Charles V. Dale and Grover S. Williams; Paul Armstrong of the General Accounting Office; Linda Lee, Patrick Norton, Roland Moore, William K. Sawyer, Audrey Hatry, Martha Mecham, and David J. Kyte.

The Special Committee will also publish a list of Executive Orders, issued pursuant to statutes brought into force by declared states of emergency, at a later date.

CHARLES M. MATHIAS, JR.
FRANK CHURCH, *Co-Chairmen.*

EMERGENCY POWERS STATUTES:
PROVISIONS OF FEDERAL LAW NOW IN EFFECT DELEGATING
TO THE EXECUTIVE EXTRAORDINARY AUTHORITY
IN TIME OF NATIONAL EMERGENCY

November 19, 1973. Ordered to be printed.

Mr. MATHIAS (for Mr. CHURCH) as co-chairman of the Special Committee on the Termination of the National Emergency, submitted the following:

REPORT
[Pursuant to S. Res. 9, 93d Cong.]

INTRODUCTION

(A) A BRIEF HISTORICAL SKETCH OF THE ORIGINS
OF EMERGENCY POWERS NOW IN FORCE

A majority of the people of the United States have lived all of their lives under emergency rule. For 40 years, freedoms and governmental procedures guaranteed by the Constitution have, in varying degrees, been abridged by laws brought into force by states of national emergency. The problem of how a constitutional democracy reacts to great crises, however, far antedates the Great Depression. As a philosophical issue, its origins reach back to the Greek city-states and the Roman Republic. And, in the United States, actions taken by the Government in times of great crises have — from, at least, the Civil War — in important ways, shaped the present phenomenon of a permanent state of national emergency.

American political theory of emergency government was derived and enlarged from John Locke, the English political-philosopher whose thought influenced the authors of the Constitution. Locke argued that the threat of national crisis — unforeseen, sudden, and potentially catastrophic — required the creation of broad executive emergency powers to be exercised by the Chief Executive in situations where the legislative authority had not provided a means or procedure of remedy. Referring to emergency power in the 14th chapter of his *Second Treatise on Civil Government* as "prerogative," Locke suggested that it:

> ...should be left to the discretion of him that has the executive power... since in some governments the lawmaking power is not always in being and is usually too numerous, and so too slow for the dispatch requisite to executions, and because, also it is impossible to foresee and so by laws to provide for all accidents and necessities that may concern the public, or make such laws as will do no harm, if they are executed with an inflexible rigour on all occasions and upon all persons that may come in their way, therefore there is a latitude left to the executive power to do many things of choice; which the laws do not prescribe.

To what extent the Founding Fathers adhered to this view of the executive role in emergencies is a much disputed issue. Whatever their conceptions of this role, its development in practice has been based largely on the manner in which individual Presidents have viewed their office and its functions. Presidents Theodore Roosevelt and William Howard Taft argued the proper role of the President and, perhaps, their debate best expounds diametrically-opposed philosophies of the presidency. In his autobiography, Roosevelt asserted his "stewardship theory":

> My view was that every Executive officer... was a steward of the people bound

actively and affirmatively to do all he could for the people and not to content himself with the negative merit of keeping his talents undamaged in a napkin.... My belief was that it was not only [the President's] right but his duty to do anything that the needs of the Nation demanded unless such action was forbidden by the Constitution or by the laws. Under this interpretation of executive power I did and caused to be done many things not previously done by the President and the heads of departments. I did not usurp power but I did greatly broaden the use of executive power. In other words, I acted for the common well being of all our people whenever and whatever measure was necessary, unless prevented by direct constitutional or legislative prohibition.

Roosevelt compared this principle of "stewardship" to what he called the Jackson-Lincoln theory, and contrasted it to the theory ascribed to William Howard Taft.

Roosevelt's ideas on the limit of presidential authority and responsibility were vigorously disputed by Taft. In lectures on the presidency — delivered at Columbia University in 1915-1916 — Taft responded that: "... the wide field of action that this would give to the Executive one can hardly limit. A President can exercise no power which cannot fairly and reasonably be traced to some specific grant of power." And he cautioned that: "...such specific grants must be either in the Federal Constitution, or in any act of Congress passed in pursuance thereof. There is no undefined residuum of power which he can exercise because it seems to him to be in the public interest."

In recent years, most scholars have interpreted the Roosevelt-Taft dispute in Roosevelt's favor. In the prevailing academic view, Roosevelt is described as "active," "expansionist," and "strong." The historical reality, in fact, does not afford such a sharp distinction either between the actions of these two Presidents, or between their analysis of the problem of emergency powers. Taft, in his concluding remarks to his Columbia lectures, said: "Executive power is limited, so far as it is possible to limit such a power consistent with that discretion and promptness of action that are essential to preserve the interests of the public in times of emergency or legislative neglect or inaction." Thus, even Taft was disposed to employ emergency power when the need arose, but, he did not wish to go beyond his own narrower, conservative conception of what was meant by constitutional and legal bounds. Thus, the dispute was over where those bounds lay, rather than the nature of the office itself.

Taft's successor, Woodrow Wilson, was no less zealous in observing what he thought the Constitution demanded. Faced with the exigencies of World War I, Wilson found it necessary to expand executive emergency powers enormously. In many respects, this expansion of powers in wartime was based on precedents set by Lincoln decades earlier. Unlike Lincoln, however, Wilson relied heavily on Congress for official delegations of authority no matter how broadly these might be.

Wilson's exercise of power in the First World War provided a model for future Presidents and their advisors. During the preparedness period of 1915-1916, the submarine crisis in the opening months of 1917, and the period of direct involvement of U.S. armed forces from April 1917 to November 1918, Wilson utilized powers as sweeping as Lincoln's. Because governmental agencies were more highly organized and their jurisdictions wider, presidential powers were considerably more effective than ever before. Yet, perhaps, because of Wilson's scrupulous attention to obtaining prior congressional concurrence, there was only one significant congressional challenge to Wilson's wartime measures.

That challenge came in February-March 1917, following the severance of diplomatic relations with Germany. A group of Senators successfully filibustered a bill authorizing the arming of American merchant ships. In response — records American historian Frank Freidel in his book *Roosevelt: The Apprenticeship* — Assistant Secretary of the Navy Franklin D. Roosevelt found an old statute under which the President could proceed without fresh authorization from Congress. Roosevelt, impatient for action, was irritated because Wilson waited a few days before implementing the statute.

Lincoln had drawn most heavily upon his power as Commander-in-Chief; Wilson exercised emergency power on the basis of old statutes and sweeping new legislation — thus drawing on congressional delegation as a source of authority. The most significant Wilsonian innovations were economic, including a wide array of defense and war agencies, modeled to some extent upon British wartime precedents. In August 1916, just prior to the United States' entry into the war, Congress at Wilson's behest established a Council of National Defense — primarily advisory. In 1917, a War Industries Board, also relatively weak, began operating. The ineffectiveness of the economic mobilization led Republicans in Congress in the winter of 1917-1918 to demand a coalition War Cabinet similar to that in England. Wilson forestalled Congress by proposing legislation delegating him almost total economic power and, even before legislative approval, authorized the War Industries Board to exercise extensive powers. Subsequently Congress enacted Wilson's measure, the Overman Act, in April 1918. Other legislation extended the economic authority of the Government in numerous directions.

Following the allied victory, Wilson relinquished his wartime authority and asked Congress to repeal the emergency statutes, enacted to fight more effectively the war. Only a food-control measure and the 1917 Trading With the Enemy Act were retained. This procedure of terminating emergency powers when the particular emergency itself has, in fact, ended has not been consistently followed by his successors.

The next major development in the use of executive emergency powers came under Franklin D. Roosevelt. The Great Depression had already overtaken the country by the time of Roosevelt's inauguration and confronted him with a totally different crisis. This emergency, unlike those of the past, presented a nonmilitary threat. The Roosevelt administration, however, conceived the economic crisis to be a calamity equally as great as a war and employed the metaphor of war to emphasize the depression's severity. In his inaugural address, Roosevelt said: "I shall ask the Congress for the one remaining instrument to meet the crisis — broad executive power to wage a war against the emergency, as great as the power that would be given me if we were in fact invaded by a foreign foe."

Many of the members of the Roosevelt administration, including F.D.R. himself, were veterans of the economic mobilization of World War I and drew upon their experiences to combat the new situation. The first New Deal agencies, indeed, bore strong resemblance to wartime agencies and many had the term "emergency" in their titles — such as the Federal Emergency Relief Administration and the National Emergency Council.

In his first important official act, Roosevelt proclaimed a National Bank Holiday on the basis of the 1917 Trading With the Enemy Act — itself a wartime delegation of power. New Deal historian William E. Leuchtenburg writes:

> When he sent his banking bill to Congress, the House received it with much the same ardor as it had greeted Woodrow Wilson's war legislation. Speaker Rainey said the situation reminded him of the late war when "on both sides of this Chamber the great war measures suggested by the administration were supported with practical unanimity.... Today we are engaged in another war, more serious even in its character and presenting greater dangers to the Republic."
>
> After only thirty-eight minutes of debate, the House passed the administration's banking bill, sight unseen.

The Trading With the Enemy Act had, however, been specifically designed by its originators to meet only wartime exigencies. By employing it to meet the demands of the depression, Roosevelt greatly extended the concept of "emergencies" to which expansion of executive powers might be applied. And in so doing, he established a pattern that was followed frequently: In time of crisis the President should utilize any statutory authority readily at hand, regardless of its original purposes, with the firm expectation of *ex post facto* congressional concurrence.

Beginning with F.D.R., then, extensive use of delegated powers exercised under an aura of crisis has become a dominant aspect of the presidency. Concomitant with this development has been a demeaning of the significance of "emergency." It became a term used to evoke public and congressional approbation, often bearing little actual relation to events. Roosevelt brain-truster, Rexford G. Tugwell, has described the manner in which Roosevelt used declarations of different degrees of emergency: "The 'limited emergency' was a creature of Roosevelt's imagination, used to make it seem that he was doing less than he was. He did not want to create any more furor than was necessary. The qualifying adjective had no limiting force. It was purely for public effect. But the finding that an emergency existed opened a whole armory of powers to the Commander-in-Chief, far more than Wilson had had."

Roosevelt and his successor, Harry S. Truman, invoked formal states of emergency to justify extensive delegations of authority during actual times of war. The Korean war, however, by the fact of its never having been officially declared a "war" as such by Congress, further diluted the concept of what constituted circumstances sufficiently critical to warrant the delegation of extraordinary authority to the President.

At the end of the Korean war, moreover, the official state of emergency was not terminated. It is not yet terminated. This may be primarily attributed to the continuance of the Cold War atmosphere which, until recent years, made the imminent threat of hostilities an accepted fact of everyday life, with "emergency" the normal state of affairs. In this, what is for all practical purposes, permanent state of emergency, Presidents have exercised numerous powers — most notably under the Trading With the Enemy Act — legitimated by that ongoing state of national emergency. Hundreds of others have lain fallow, there to be exercised at any time, requiring only an order from the President.

Besides the 1933 and Korean war emergencies, two other states of declared national emergency remain in existence. On March 23, 1970, confronted by a strike of Postal Service employees, President Nixon declared a national emergency. The following year, on August 15, 1971, Nixon proclaimed another emergency under which he imposed stringent import controls in order to meet an international monetary crisis. Because of its general language, however, that proclamation could serve as sufficient authority to use a substantial proportion of all the emergency statutes now on the books.

Over the course of at least the last 40 years, then, Presidents have had available an enormous — seemingly expanding and never-ending — range of emergency powers. Indeed, at their fullest extent and during the height of a crisis, these "prerogative" powers appear to be virtually unlimited, confirming Locke's perceptions. Because Congress and the public are unaware of the extent of emergency powers, there has never been any notable congressional or public objection made to this state of affairs. Nor have the courts imposed significant limitations.

During the New Deal, the Supreme Court initially struck down much of Roosevelt's emergency economic legislation (*Schecter v. United States*, 295 U.S. 495). However, political pressures, a change in personnel, and presidential threats of court-packing, soon altered this course of decisions (*NLRB v. Jones & Laughlin Steel Corp.*, 301 U.S. 1). Since 1887, the Court has been extremely reluctant to invalidate any congressional delegation of economic powers to the President. It appears that this will not change in the foreseeable future.

In a significant case directly confronting the issue of wartime emergency powers, *Youngstown Steel & Tube Co. v. Sawyer* (343 U.S. 579), the Court refused to allow the President to rely upon implied constitutional powers during a crisis. The action at issue involved presidential seizure of steel plants in a manner apparently directly at odds with congressional policy, Justice Black's plurality opinion specifically acknowledges that if Congress delegates powers to the President for use during an emergency those powers are absolutely valid within constitutional restraints on Congress' own power to do so. Concurring opinions appear to agree on this point. It should be noted, therefore, that all statutes in this compilation are precisely these kinds of specific congressional delegations of power.

The 2,000-year-old problem of how a legislative body in a democratic republic may extend extraordinary powers for use by the executive during times of great crisis and dire emergency — but do so in ways assuring both that such necessary powers will be terminated immediately when the emergency has ended and that normal processes will be resumed — has not yet been resolved in this country. Too few are aware of the existence of emergency powers and their extent, and the problem has never been squarely faced.

(B) SUMMARY VIEWS OF THE PRESENT STATUS
OF EMERGENCY POWERS STATUTES

A review of the laws passed since the first state of national emergency was declared in 1933, reveals a consistent pattern of lawmaking. It is a pattern showing that the Congress, through its own actions, transferred awesome magnitudes of power to the executive ostensibly to meet the problems of governing effectively in times of great crisis. Since 1933, Congress has passed or recodified over 470 significant statutes delegating to the President powers that had been the prerogative and responsibility of the Congress since the beginning of the Republic. No charge can be sustained that the Executive branch has usurped powers belonging to the Legislative branch; on the contrary, the transfer of power has been in accord with due process of normal legislative procedures.

It is fortunate that at this time that, when the fears and tensions of the Cold War are giving way to relative peace and detente is now national policy, Congress can assess the nature, quality, and effect of what has become known as emergency powers legislation. Emergency powers make up a relatively small but important body of statutes — some 470 significant provisions of law out of the total of tens of thousands that have been passed or recodified since 1933. But emergency powers laws are of such significance to civil liberties, to the operation of domestic and foreign commerce, and the general functioning of the U.S. Government, that, in microcosm, they reflect dominant trends in the political, economic, and judicial life in the United States.

A number of conclusions can be drawn from the Special Committee's study and analysis of emergency powers laws now in effect. Congress has in most important respects, except for the final action of floor debate and the formal passage of bills, permitted the Executive branch to draft and in large measure to "make the laws." This has occurred despite the constitutional responsibility conferred on Congress by Article I Section 8 of the Constitution which states that it is Congress that "makes all Laws...."

Most of the statutes pertaining to emergency powers were passed in times of extreme crisis. Bills drafted in the Executive branch were sent to Congress by the President and, in the case of the most significant laws that sat on the books, were approved with only the most perfunctory committee review and virtually no consideration of their effect on civil liberties or the delicate structure of the U.S. Government of divided powers. For example, the economic measures that were passed in 1933 pursuant to the proclamation of March 5, 1933, by President Roosevelt, asserting that a state of national emergency now existed, were enacted in the most turbulent circumstances. There was a total of only eight hours of debate in both houses. There were no committee reports; indeed, only one copy of the bill was available on the floor.

This pattern of hasty and inadequate consideration was repeated during World War II when another group of laws with vitally significant and far reaching implications was passed. It was repeated during the Korean war and, again, in most recent memory, during the debate on the *Tonkin Gulf Resolution* passed on August 6, 1964.

On occasion, legislative history shows that during the limited debates that did take place, a few, but very few, objections were raised by Senators and Congressmen that expressed serious concerns about the lack of provision for congressional oversight. Their speeches raised great doubts about the wisdom of giving such open-ended authority to the President, with no practical procedural means to withdraw that authority once the time of emergency had passed.

For example, one of the very first provisions passed in 1933 was the Emergency Banking Act based upon Section 5(b) of the Trading With the Enemy Act of 1917. The provisions gave to President Roosevelt, with the full approval of the Congress, the authority to control major aspects of the economy, an authority which had formerly been reserved to the Congress. A portion of that provision, still in force, is quoted here to illustrate the kind of open-ended authority Congress has given to the President during the past 40 years:

> (b)(1) During the time of war or during any other period of national emergency declared by the President, the President may, through any agency that he may designate, or otherwise, and under such rules and regulations as he may prescribe, by means of instructions, licenses, or otherwise —
>
>> (A) investigate, regulate, or prohibit, any transactions in foreign exchange, transfers of credit or payments between, by, through, or to any banking institution, and the importing, exporting, hoarding, melting, or earmarking of gold or silver coin or bullion, currency or securities, and
>>
>> (B) investigate, regulate, direct and compel, nullify, void, prevent or prohibit, any acquisition, holding, withholding, use, transfer, withdrawal, transportation, importation or exportation of, or dealing in, or exercising any right, power, or privilege with respect to, or transactions involving, any property in which any foreign country or a national thereof has any interest.
>
> by any person, or with respect to any property, subject to the jurisdiction of the United States; and any property or interest of any foreign country or national thereof shall vest, when, as, and upon the terms, directed by the President, in such agency or person as may be designated from time to time by the President, and upon such terms and conditions as the President may prescribe such interest or property shall be held, used, administered, liquidated, sold, or otherwise dealt with in the interest of and for the benefit of the United States, and such designated agency or person may perform any and all acts incident to the accomplishment or furtherance of these purposes; and the President shall, in the manner hereinabove provided, require any person to keep a full record of, and to furnish under oath, in the form of reports or otherwise, complete information relative to any act or transaction referred to in this subdivision either before, during, or after the completion thereof, or relative to any interest in foreign property, or relative to any property in which any foreign country or any national thereof has or has had an interest, or as may be otherwise necessary to enforce the provisions of this subdivision, and in any case in which a report could be required, the President may, in the manner hereinabove provided, receive the production, or if necessary to the national security or defense, the seizure, of any books of account, records, contracts, letters, memoranda, or other papers, in the custody or control of such person; and the President may, in the manner hereinabove provided, take

other and further measures not inconsistent herewith for the enforcement of this subdivision.

(2) Any payment, conveyance, transfer, assignment, or delivery of property or interest therein, made to or for the account of the United States, or as otherwise directed, pursuant to this subdivision or any rule, regulation, instruction, or direction issued hereunder shall to the extent thereof be a full acquittance and discharge for all purposes of the obligation of the person making the same; and no person shall be held liable in any court for or in respect to anything done or omitted in good faith in connection with the administration of, or in pursuance of and in reliance on, this subdivision, or any rule, regulation, instruction, or direction issued hereunder.

To cite two further examples: In the context of the war powers issue and the long debate of the past decade over national commitments, 10 U.S.C. 712 is of importance:

10 U.S.C. 712. Foreign governments: detail to assist.
(a) Upon the application of the country concerned, the President, whenever he considers it in the public interest, may detail members of the Army, Navy, Air Force, and Marine Corps to assist in military matters —
(1) any republic in North America, Central America, or South America;
(2) the Republic of Cuba, Haiti, or Santo Domingo and
(3) during a war or a declared national emergency, any other country that he considers it advisable to assist in the interest of national defense.
(b) Subject to the prior approval of the Secretary of the military department concerned, a member detailed under this section may accept any office from the country to which he is detailed. He is entitled to credit for all service while so detailed, as if serving with the armed forces of the United States. Arrangements may be made by the President, with countries to which such members are detailed to perform functions under this section, for reimbursement to the United States or other sharing of the cost of performing such functions.

The Defense Department, in answer to inquiries by the Special Committee concerning this provision, has stated that it has only been used with regard to Latin America, and interprets its applicability as being limited to noncombatant advisers. However, the language of Section 712 is wide open to other interpretations. It could be construed as a way of extending considerable military assistance to any foreign country. Since Congress has delegated this power, arguments could be made against the need for further congressional concurrence in a time of national emergency.

The repeal of almost all of the Emergency Detention Act of 1950 was a constructive and necessary step, but the following provision remains:

18. U.S.C. 1383. Restrictions in military areas and zones.
Whoever, contrary to the restrictions applicable thereto, enters, remains in, leaves, or commits any act in any military area or military zone prescribed under the authority of

an Executive order of the President, by the Secretary of the Army, or by any military commander designated by the Secretary of the Army, shall, if it appears that he knew or should have known of the existence and extent of the restrictions or order and that his act was in violation thereof, be fined not more than $5,000 or imprisoned not more than one year, or both.

18 U.S.C. 1383 does not appear on its face to be an emergency power. It was used as the basis for internment of Japanese-Americans in World War II. Although it seems to be cast as a permanent power, the legislative history of the section shows that the statute was intended as a World War II emergency power only, and was not to apply in "normal" peace-time circumstances. Two years ago, the Emergency Detention Act was repealed, yet 18 U.S.C. 1383 has almost the same effect.

Another pertinent question among many, that the Special Committee's work has revealed, concerns the statutory authority for domestic surveillance by the FBI. According to some experts, the authority for domestic surveillance appears to be based upon an Executive Order issued by President Roosevelt during an emergency period. If it is correct that no firm statutory authority exists, then it is reasonable to suggest that the appropriate committees enact proper statutory authority for the FBI with adequate provision for oversight by Congress.

What these examples suggest and what the magnitude of emergency powers affirm is that most of these laws do not provide for congressional oversight or termination. There are two reasons which can be adduced as to why this is so. First, few, if any, foresaw that the temporary states of emergency declared in 1938, 1939, 1941, 1950, 1970, and 1971 would become what are now regarded collectively as virtually permanent states of emergency (the 1939 and 1941 emergencies were terminated in 1952). Forty years can, in no way, be defined as a temporary emergency. Second, the various administrations who drafted these laws for a variety of reasons were understandably not concerned about providing for congressional review, oversight, or termination of these delegated powers which gave the President enormous powers and flexibility to use those powers.

The intense anxiety and sense of crisis was contained in the rhetoric of Truman's 1950 proclamation:

> Whereas recent events in Korea and elsewhere constitute a grave threat to the peace of the world and imperil the efforts of this country and those of the United Nations to prevent aggression and armed conflict; and
>
> Whereas world conquest by communist imperialism is the goal of the forces of aggression that have been loosed upon the world; and
>
> Whereas, if the goal of communist imperialism were to be achieved, the people of this country would no longer enjoy the full and rich life they have with God's help built for themselves and their children; they would no longer enjoy the blessings of the freedom of worshipping as they severally choose, the freedom of reading and listening to what they choose, the right of free speech, including the right to criticize their Government, the right

to choose those who will conduct their Government, the right to engage freely in collective bargaining, the right to engage freely in their own business enterprises, and the many other freedoms and rights which are a part of our way of life; and

Whereas, the increasing menace of the forces of communist aggression requires that the national defense of the United States be strengthened as speedily as possible:

Now, therefore, I, Harry S. Truman, President of the United States of America, do proclaim the existence of a national emergency, which requires that the military, naval, air, and civilian defenses of this country be strengthened as speedily as possible to the end that we may be able to repel any and all threats against our national security and to fulfill our responsibilities in the efforts being made through the United Nations and otherwise to bring about lasting peace.

I summon all citizens to make a united effort for the security and well-being of our beloved country and to place its needs foremost in thought and action that the full moral and material strength of the Nation may be readied for the dangers which threaten us.

I summon our farmers, our workers in industry, and our businessmen to make a mighty production effort to meet the defense requirements of the Nation and to this end to eliminate all waste and inefficiency and to subordinate all lesser interests to the common good.

I summon every person and every community to make, with a spirit of neighborliness, whatever sacrifices are necessary for the welfare of the Nation.

I summon all State and local leaders and officials to cooperate fully with the military and civilian defense agencies of the United States in the national defense program.

I summon all citizens to be loyal to the principles upon which our Nation is founded, to keep faith with our friends and allies, and to be firm in our devotion to the peaceful purposes for which the United Nations was founded.

I am confident that we will meet the dangers that confront us with courage and determination, strong in the faith that we can thereby "secure the Blessings of Liberty to ourselves and our Posterity."

In witness whereof, I have hereunto set my hand and caused the Seal of the United States of America to be affixed. Done at the City of Washington this 16th day of December (10:90 a.m.) in the year of our Lord nineteen hundred and fifty, and of the Independence of the United States of America the one hundred and seventy-fifth.

HARRY S. TRUMAN
[SEAL]

By the President:
DEAN ACHESON,
Secretary of State

The heightened sense of crisis of the cold war so evident in Truman's proclamation has fortunately eased. The legislative shortcomings contained in this body of laws can be corrected on the basis of rational study and inquiry.

In the view of the Special Committee, an emergency does not now exist. Congress, therefore, should act in the near future to terminate officially the states of national emergency now in effect.

At the same time, the Special Committee is of the view that it is essential to provide the means for the Executive to act effectively in an emergency. It is reasonable to have a body of laws in readiness to delegate to the President extraordinary powers to use in times of real national emergency. The portion of the concurring opinion given by Justice Robert Jackson in the *Youngstown Steel* case with regard to emergency powers provides sound and pertinent guidelines for the maintenance of such a body of emergency laws kept in readiness to be used in times of extreme crisis. Justice Jackson, supporting the majority opinion that the "President's power must stem either from an act of Congress or from the Constitution itself" wrote:

> The appeal, however, that we declare the existence of inherent powers *ex necessitate* to meet an emergency asks us to do what many think would be wise, although it is something the forefathers omitted. They knew what emergencies were, knew the pressures they engender for authoritative action, knew, too, how they afford a ready pretext for usurpation. We may also suspect that they suspected that emergency powers would tend to kindle emergencies. Aside from suspension of the privilege of the writ of *habeas corpus* in time of rebellion or invasion, when the public safety may require it, they made no express provision for exercise of extraordinary authority because of a crisis. I do not think we rightfully may so amend their work, and, if we could, I am not convinced it would be wise to do so, although many modern nations have forthrightly recognized that war and economic crises may upset the normal balance between liberty and authority. Their experience with emergency powers may not be irrelevant to the argument here that we should say that the Executive, of his own volition, can invest himself with undefined emergency powers.
>
> Germany, after the First World War, framed the Weimar Constitution, designed to secure her liberties in the Western tradition. However, the President of the Republic, without concurrence of the Reichstag, was empowered temporarily to suspend any or all individual rights if public safety and order were seriously disturbed or endangered. This proved a temptation to every government, whatever its shade of opinion, and in 13 years suspension of rights was invoked on more than 250 occasions. Finally, Hitler persuaded President Von Hindenburg to suspend all such rights, and they were never restored.
>
> The French Republic provided for a very different kind of emergency government known as the "state of siege." It differed from the German emergency dictatorship particularly in that emergency powers could not be assumed at will by the Executive but could only be granted as a parliamentary measure. And it did not, as in Germany, result in a suspension or abrogation of law but was a legal institution governed by special legal rules and terminable by parliamentary authority.
>
> Great Britain also has fought both World Wars under a sort of temporary dictatorship created by legislation. As Parliament is not bound by written constitutional limitations, it established a crisis government simply by delegation to its Ministers of a larger measure than usual of its own unlimited power, which is exercised under its supervision by Ministers whom it may dismiss. This has been called the "high-water mark in the

voluntary surrender of liberty," but, as Churchill put it, "Parliament stands custodian of these surrendered liberties, and its most sacred duty will be to restore them in their fullness when victory has crowned our exertions and our perseverance." Thus, parliamentary controls made emergency powers compatible with freedom.

This contemporary foreign experience may be inconclusive as to the wisdom of lodging emergency powers somewhere in a modern government. But it suggests that emergency powers are consistent with free government only when their control is lodged elsewhere than in the Executive who exercises them. That is the safeguard that would be nullified by our adoption of the "inherent powers" formula.

Nothing in my experience convinces me that such risks are warranted by any real necessity, although such powers would, of course, be an executive convenience.

In the practical working of our Government we already have evolved a technique within the framework of the Constitution by which normal executive powers may be considerably expanded to meet an emergency. Congress may and has granted extraordinary authorities which lie dormant in normal times but may be called into play by the Executive in war or upon proclamation of a national emergency. In 1939, upon congressional request, the Attorney General listed ninety-nine such separate statutory grants by Congress of emergency or wartime executive powers. They were invoked from time to time as need appeared. Under this procedure we retain Government by law — special, temporary law, perhaps, but law nonetheless. The public may know the extent and limitations of the powers that can be asserted, and persons affected may be informed from the statute of their rights and duties.

In view of the ease, expedition and safety with which Congress can grant and has granted large emergency powers, certainly ample to embrace this crisis, I am quite unimpressed with the argument that we should affirm possession of them without statute. Such power either has no beginning or it has no end. If it exists, it need submit to no legal restraint. I am not alarmed that it would plunge us straightway into dictatorship, but it is at least a step in that wrong direction.

But I have no illusion that any decision by this Court can keep power in the hands of Congress if it is not wise and timely in meeting its problems. A crisis that challenges the President equally, or perhaps primarily, challenges Congress. If not good law, there was worldly wisdom in the maxim attributed to Napoleon that "The tools belong to the man who can use them." We may say that power to legislate for emergencies belongs in the hands of Congress, but only Congress itself can prevent power from slipping through its fingers.

The essence of our free Government is "leave to live by no man's leave, underneath the law" — to be governed by those impersonal forces which we call law. Our Government is fashioned to fulfill this concept so far as humanly possible. The Executive, except for recommendation and veto, has no legislative power. The executive action we have here originates in the individual will of the President and represents an exercise of authority without law. No one, perhaps not even the President, knows the limits of the power he may seek to exert in this instance and the parties affected cannot learn the limit of their rights. We do not know today what powers over labor or property would be claimed to flow from Government possession if we should legalize it, what rights to compensation would be claimed or recognized, or on what contingency it would end. With all its defects, delays and inconveniences, men have discovered no technique for long preserving free government except that the Executive be under the law, and that the law be made by parliamentary deliberations.

   Such institutions may be destined to pass away. But it is the duty of the Court to be last, not first, to give them up.

   With these guidelines and against the background of experience of the last 40 years, the task that remains for the Special Committee is to determine — in close cooperation with all the Standing Committees of the Senate and all Departments, Commissions, and Agencies of the Executive branch — which of the laws now in force might be of use in a future emergency. Most important, a legislative formula needs to be devised which will provide a regular and consistent procedure by which any emergency provisions are called into force. It will also be necessary to establish a means by which Congress can exercise effective oversight over such actions as are taken pursuant to a state of national emergency as well as providing a regular and consistent procedure for the termination of such grants of authority.

SUPPLEMENTARY ESSAY
An Essay on Constitutional Dictatorship
by Clinton L. Rossiter

Constitutional dictatorship is a rag-bag phrase, and into it can be tossed all sorts of different institutions and procedures of emergency government. In general, all institutions and techniques of constitutional dictatorship fall into one of two related, yet reasonably distinct categories: emergency action of an executive nature, and emergency action of a legislative nature. The crisis of rebellion is dealt with primarily in an executive fashion and calls for the institution of some form of military dictatorship. The crisis of economic depression is dealt with primarily through emergency laws (although these too have to be executed) and calls for lawmaking by the executive branch of government. The crisis of war, at least total war, is dealt with in both ways. If a situation can be dealt with judicially, it is probably not a crisis.

The basis institution of constitutional dictatorship of an executive nature is *martial rule*; in one form or another it has existed in all constitutional countries. Martial rule is an emergency device designed for use in the crises of invasion or rebellion. It may be most precisely defined as an extension of military government to the civilian population, the substitution of the will of a military commander for the will of the people's elected government. In the event of an actual or imminent invasion by a hostile power, a constitutional government may declare martial rule in the menaced area. The result is the transfer of all effective powers of government from the civil authorities to the military, or often merely the assumption of such powers by the latter when the regular government has ceased to function. In the event of a rebellion its initiation amounts to a governmental declaration of war on those citizens in insurrection against the state. In either case it means military dictatorship — government by the army, courts-martial, suspension of civil liberties, and the whole range of dictatorial

907

action of an executive nature. In the modern democracies the military exercises such dictatorship while remaining subordinate and responsible to the executive head of the civil government. Martial rule has a variety of forms and pseudonyms, the most important of which are martial law, as it is known in the common law countries of the British Empire and the United States, and *the state of siege*, as it is known in the civil law countries of continental Europe and Latin America. The state of siege and martial law are two edges to the same sword, and in action they can hardly be distinguished. The institution of martial rule is a recognition that there are times in the lives of all communities when crisis has so completely disrupted the normal workings of government that the military is the only power remaining that can restore public order and secure the execution of the laws.

The outstanding institution of constitutional dictatorship of a legislative nature is *the delegation of legislative power*. What this amounts to is a voluntary transfer of lawmaking authority from the nation's representative assembly to the nation's executive, a frank recognition that in many kinds of crisis (particularly economic depressions) the legislature is unequal to the task of day-to-day, emergency lawmaking, and that it must therefore hand over its functions to someone better qualified to enact arbitrary crisis laws. On its face this would not seem to be a procedure of a particularly dictatorial character. When the age-old battles fought in all constitutional countries to thrust the executive out of the field of lawmaking are recalled to mind, however, it is obvious indeed that the transfer of legislative power from Parliament to Prime Minister or Congress to President is a highly unusual and even dictatorial method of government. The delegation of power may be limited in time, made in and for a particular crisis, or it may be permanent, to be exercised by the executive in the event of some future crisis. Permanent delegations for emergency purposes have in modern times been cast in the form of statutes enacted by the national legislature. In some countries, however, the constitution itself has granted the executive branch of the government a provisional power of issuing emergency ordinances with the force of law. When the delegation of lawmaking power is a large scale proposition, that is, when the executive is empowered to make emergency laws for the solution of some or all of the nation's major problems, this device may be known as *the enabling act*.

Martial rule and executive lawmaking are both marked by a correlative technique or characteristic of constitutional dictatorship, *the governmental invasion of political or economic liberties*. The crisis expansion of power is generally matched by a crisis contraction of liberty. When a censorship of the press is instituted in time of war, when public meetings are absolutely forbidden in an area racked by rebellion, when a man's house can be legally searched without warrant, when a national legislature itself postpones the elections which it is supposed to face, or when a barkeeper is told in 1944 that he cannot sell a glass of whisky for more than he charged in 1942 — then political and economic rights of free men have been definitely abridged. That all these invasions of liberty and many more like them have been effected in periods of crisis by constitutional governments will shortly become apparent, and the ultimate reason in each case was apparently good and sufficient — the preservation of the state and the permanent freedom of its citizens.

There are many other devices and techniques of constitutional dictatorship: the cabinet dictatorship, the presidential dictatorship, the wartime expansion of administration, the peacetime emergency planning agency, the "war cabinet," the congressional investigating committee, the executive dominance of the legislative process — just to mention a few. Not all of them are necessarily dictatorial, but each can be regarded as an institution of constitutional dictatorship — a technique or device to which a constitutional government may resort in time of emergency. It is important to realize that they all overlap one another, and that there have been plenty of crisis governments, particularly those engaged in total war, which have made use of all of them at once. It is equally important to realize that they are legal and constitutional, that the people of the constitutional democracies have recognized openly that their leaders should have extraordinary power in extraordinary times.

It is perhaps unfortunate that the controversial *law of necessity* has to be mentioned at all. Actually this well-known doctrine is little better than a rationalization of extra-constitutional, illegal emergency action. The fact remains that there have been instances in the history of every free state when its rulers were forced by the intolerable exigencies of some grave national crisis to proceed to emergency actions for which there was no sanction in law, constitution, or custom, and which indeed were directly contrary to all three of these foundations of constitutional democracy. When Abraham Lincoln said, "Often a limb must be amputated to save a life, but a life is never wisely given to save a limb,"[1] he was grounding a number of unconstitutional and dictatorial actions on the law of necessity. The Constitution and certain statutes told him that he could not raise the limits of the army and navy, pay money to persons unauthorized by law to receive it, or contract a public debt for the United States — but Mr. Lincoln decided and candidly declared that the necessity of preserving the Union was sufficient cause for him to go ahead and do these things anyway:

> Every man thinks he has a right to live and every government thinks it has a right to live. Every man when driven to the wall by a murderous assailant will override all laws to protect himself, and this is called the great right of self-defense. So every government, when driven to the wall by a rebellion, will trample down a constitution before it will allow itself to be destroyed. This may not be constitutional law, but it is fact.[2]

> The law is made for the state, not the state for the law. If the circumstances are such that a choice must be made between the two, it is the law which must be sacrificed to the state. *Salus populi suprema lex esto.*[3]

---

1. Lincoln to Hodges, J.G. Nicolay and John Hay (editors), *Complete Works of Abraham Lincoln* (New York, 1905), Volume II, page 508.

2. Fisher, "Suspension of Habeas Corpus," page 485.

3. Joseph Barthelemy, *Problemes de Politique et Finances de Guerres* (Alcan, 1915), page 121.

This is the theory of *Not kennt kein Gebot*, necessity knows no law.[4] It isn't a pleasant theory, because Hitler could shout "necessity!" as easily as Lincoln, but there is no denying the fact that responsible statesmen in every free country have broken the law in order to protect the nation in time of serious national emergency, and responsible statesmen will do it again. And the nation was always pretty solidly behind them. In Rousseau's words: "In such a case there is no doubt about the general will, and it is clear that the people's first intention is that the State shall not perish."[5]

There is one other feature of constitutional dictatorship that should be explained here, an obvious and even axiomatic feature, yet still deserving of passing mention. In the last resort, it is always the executive branch in the government which possesses and wields the extraordinary powers of self-preservation of any democratic, constitutional state. Whether the crisis demands the initiation of martial rule or an enabling act or a full-blown war regime, it will be to the executive branch that the extraordinary authority and responsibility for prosecuting the purposes of the constitutional dictatorship will be consigned. *Crisis government is primarily and often exclusively the business of presidents and prime ministers.* Where the forms of constitutional dictatorship have been worked out and given a legal or constitutional basis — as in the state of siege, the enabling act, or the statutes which give the President of the United States certain emergency powers — it is always the executive organ which is selected by the legislators to be the spearhead of crisis action. Where the forms have not been worked out, it is still the executive, this time selected by nature and expediency, which must shoulder the burden and deal with the emergency under the law of necessity. Locke could champion the supremacy of the legislature and bespeak the Whig fear of overweening executive power, but even he had to admit that it was the undefined power of this organ — the Crown's prerogative "to act according to discretion for the public good, without the prescription of the law and sometimes even against it" — that was the ultimate repository of the nation's will and power to survive. It is never so apparent as in time of crisis that the executive is the aboriginal power of government.

The preceding essay was extracted from Constitutional Dictatorship: Crisis Government in the Modern Democracies *(Princeton, New Jersey: Princeton University Press, 1948).*

---

4. The law of necessity was particularly dear to the German jurists of the pre-1914 era, and received its classic statement (complete, with authorities) in Josep Kohler's controversial *Not kennt kein Gebot* (Berlin, 1915), in which a famous legal authority set forth the philosophical justification of the German invasion of Belgium. The law of necessity found its practical application in the vindication of emergency executive law-making in the absence of the legislature. The best statement of this doctrine is, strangely enough, by the French writer L. Duguit, *Traite de Droit Constitutionnel* (2nd ed., Paris, 1921-1925), III, pages 700ff. See also W. Jellinek, *Gesetz und Verordnung* (Vienna, 1887), pages 376ff; J.K. Bluntschli, *Allgemeines Staatsrecht* (Munich, 1857), II, page 109.

5. *Social Contract*, IV, page 6.

CHAPTER TWENTY-FIVE
The Cold War in the United States

Americans Are a Subjugated People

The basic institution of constitutional dictatorship of an executive nature is *martial rule*.... Martial rule is an emergency device designed for use in the crises of invasion or rebellion. It may be most precisely defined as an extension of military government to the civilian population, the substitution of the will of a military commander for the will of the people's elected government.... [I]t means military dictatorship — government by the army, courts-martial, suspension of civil liberties, and the whole range of dictatorial action of an executive nature....

Martial rule and executive lawmaking are both marked by a correlative technique or characteristic of constitutional dictatorship, *the government invasion of political or economic liberties*. The crisis expansion of power is generally matched by a crisis contraction of liberty (emphasis in original).[1]

In a very real sense, the non-flagrant war against the American people begun during the Reconstruction period in the mid-1860s and continued in the early 1930s is still being waged today. In light of what has been documented in this book, it should be obvious that efforts to "preserve our rights" via constitutional arguments in the courts, or by electing "the right man" to office, or asserting State sovereignty under the Tenth Amendment, or creating new political parties, are all a futile waste of valuable time and resources. As stated by William Whiting, "While war is raging, many of the rights held sacred by the Constitution — rights which cannot be violated by any acts of Congress — may and must be suspended

---

1. Rossiter, *Constitutional Dictatorship*, pages 9-10.

and held in abeyance,"[2] and *"None of these rights, guaranteed to peaceful citizens, by the Constitution belong to them after they have become belligerents against their own government"* (emphasis in original).[3] The constitutional protection of property against confiscation "without due process of law"[4] is now non-existent within the United States because "nothing in the Constitution interferes with the belligerent right of confiscation of enemy property," and "no judicial process is necessary to give the government full title thereto...."[5] According to the laws of war, "the property of persons residing in the enemy's country is deemed, in law, hostile, and subject to condemnation without any evidence as to the opinions or predilections of the owner,"[6] and "the title to such real property remains in abeyance during military occupation, and until the conquest is made complete."[7] In the words of William Birkhimer, "The government of military occupation has complete control of lands and immovable property of the enemy in the occupied district. The fruits, rents, and profits issuing therefrom are therefore under the control of that government, whose officials may lawfully claim and receive them."[8] Consequently, a report commissioned by the U.S. Senate in 1933 declared, "The ultimate ownership of all property is in the State; individual so-called 'ownership' is only by virtue of Government, *i.e.* law, amounting to mere user; and use must be in accordance with law [public policy] and subordinate to the necessities of the State."[9] Furthermore, since "a victorious army appropriates all public money,"[10] the wealth of the people has also been seized and substituted with "legal tender" paper instruments of exchange, known today as Federal Reserve Notes, which completely lack any backing in gold or silver.

The right of the people of the several States to govern themselves has been superceded by a perpetual state of declared national emergency which "confers upon the government... the right to seize and hold conquered territory by military forces, and of instituting and maintaining military government over it, thereby suspending in part, or in whole,

---

2. Whiting, *War Powers of the President*, page 59.

3. Whiting, *ibid.*, page 51.

4. U.S. Constitution, Fifth Amendment.

5. Whiting, *War Powers of the President.*, pages 52, 54.

6. Whiting, *ibid.*, page 57.

7. Francis Lieber, LL.D., *Instructions for the Government of Armies of the United States in the Field* (Gen. Orders No. 100, Adjutant-General's Office, 1863), Section II, Clause 31.

8. Birkhimer, *Military Government*, pages 191-192.

9. George Cyrus Thorpe, *Contracts Payable in Gold* (Washington, D.C.: Government Printing Office, 1933; Senate Document No. 43).

10. Lieber, *Instructions for Armies in the Field*, Section II, Clause 31.

the ordinary civil administration,"[11] the functions of which "cease under martial law, or continue only with the sanction, or, if deemed necessary, the participation of the occupier or invader."[12] The presence of "a military commander in a district which is the theatre of war" is a public notice to the effect that "the laws of war apply to that district," and "by the laws of war, an invaded country has all its laws and municipal institutions swept by the board, and martial law takes the place of them."[13] To put it simply, the republican form of government guaranteed to the several States by Article IV, Section 4 of the Constitution is denied to them under the laws of conquest. According to the Supreme Court in *Dooley v. U.S.*, "We therefore do not look to the constitution or political institutions of the conqueror for authority to establish a government for the territory of the enemy in his possession, during its military occupation, nor for the rules by which the powers of such government are regulated and limited. Such authority and such rules are derived directly from the laws of war."[14]

Because "martial law affects chiefly the police and collection of public revenue and taxes,"[15] the various "law enforcement" agencies within the States, Counties, and Cities serve to "police" military districts, insuring that "public policy" is obeyed by all within their respective jurisdictions, and collecting reparations from offenders.[16] That public policy is not really law at all is seen in the following definition: "Public policy is a variable quantity; it must and does vary with the habits, capacities, and opportunities of the public."[17] When the public capacity is that of subjugation to an occupying military force, public policy can only be interpreted as the exercise of an unlimited police power against a conquered people. As pointed out by F. Harold Essert in 1933:

> The police power of the state has been called the "dark continent" of American constitutional law, and rightly so, for this section of the law is the most vague and difficult to define of all over the courts have labored. To attempt to convey a true concept of its nature and its limitations involves many problems.... The power is, and must be from its nature, incapable of any very exact definition or limitation, for it is that function of government which has for its direct and primary purpose the promotion of public welfare

---

11. Whiting, *War Powers of the President*, pages 54-55.

12. Lieber, *Instructions for Armies in the Field*, Section I, Clause 6.

13. John Quincy Adams, speech delivered in the United States House of Representatives, 14 and 15 April 1842; quoted by Whiting, *War Powers of the President*, page 80.

14. *Dooley v. U.S.* (1901), 182 U.S. 222.

15. Lieber, *Instructions for Armies in the Field*, Section I, Clause 10.

16. It is significant to note that the Federal Law Enforcement Training Center is under the U.S. Department of the Treasury, rather than the Department of Justice.

17. 38 Ch. Div. 359; *Chaffee v. Farmer's Co-Op Elevator Co.* (1918), 93 N.D. 585, 168 N.W. 616, 618.

through the means of compulsion and restraint over private rights. Who shall say what constitutes the public welfare? Who shall say where the limits of compulsion and restraint should end? As each tomorrow shall offer different social, political, and economic conditions, so there shall be a totally different interpretation of the police power for each circumstance....[18]

The chilling reality of Essert's description of an unlimited Executive police power is seen in the Ninety-Third Congress' admission that such power "originates in the individual will of the President and represents an exercise of authority without law. No one, perhaps not even the President, knows the limits of the power he may seek to exert in this instance and the parties affected cannot learn the limit of their rights."[19] Furthermore, "no person [Executive agent] shall be held liable in any court for or in respect to anything done or omitted in good faith in connection with the administration of, or in pursuance of" the declared state of national emergency.[20] Those found within the venue of the Fourteenth Amendment and who are thus "subject to the jurisdiction of the United States," have nothing at all with which to shield themselves from "an enormous — seemingly expanding and never-ending — range of emergency powers."[21] Hence, they are taxed in their enjoyment of what would normally be constitutionally protected rights, such as travel, labor, ownership of property, inheritance, marriage, and so forth. It is not a coincidence that the Bureau of Internal Revenue, which became the Internal Revenue Service in 1953, was birthed by the Lincoln Administration in 1862 when the whole country had been placed under martial law. Although the collection of a direct tax from the people of the several States without apportionment is prohibited in the Constitution,[22] no such provision applies to the collection of taxes from those who have either lost their citizenship by conquest or have voluntarily surrendered the same through their own negligence:

> Enforced contributions from the enemy are equally authorized whether required during the progress of the war for the sustenance and transportation of the conqueror's army, or after the conclusion thereof, as one of the terms of peace....
> Those upon whom contributions are levied during the progress of war are not the armies of the enemy.... They are, as a rule, non-combatants, peaceable citizens, and corpo-

---

18. F. Harold Essert, "What is Meant By the 'Police Power'"? *Nebraska Law Bulletin* (Lincoln, Nebraska: College of Law, The University of Nebraska, 1933), Volume XII, page 208.

19. U.S. Senate, "Introduction," *Emergency Powers Statutes*, page 14.

20. U.S. Senate, *ibid*.

21. U.S. Senate, *ibid*.

22. U.S. Constitution, Article I, Section 2, Clause 3.

rations, all of whom the demands of the times have thrown into financial straits.[23]

Viewed in this light, the so-called Sixteenth Amendment does indeed legally establish the income tax, its dubious "ratification" and the complaints of the "tax protest movement" notwithstanding.[24] In the words of Charles Edward Merriam, "Under this [police] power it

---

23. Birkhimer, *Military Government*, pages 204, 207. The reader should take special note of the term "enforced contributions" in this quote. One of the taxes levied against employees within the United States — the Social Security tax — originated in the Federal Insurance Contribution Act (F.I.C.A.).

24. Bill Benson and M.J. Beckman, *The Law That Never Was: The Fraud of the Sixteenth Amendment and Personal Income Tax* (South Holland, Illinois: Constitutional Research Association, 1985). In 1986, the "never ratified" arguments of Benson and Beckman were examined by the 7th Circuit Court and dismissed as frivolous. The ruling of *U.S. v. Thomas* stated in part:

> Benson and Beckman did not discover anything; they rediscovered something that Secretary Knox considered in 1913. Thirty-eight states ratified the sixteenth amendment, and thirty-seven sent formal instruments of ratification to the Secretary of State. (Minnesota notified the Secretary orally, and additional states ratified later; we consider only those Secretary Knox considered.) Only four instruments repeat the language of the sixteenth amendment exactly as Congress approved it. The others contain errors of diction, capitalization, punctuation, and spelling. The text Congress transmitted to the states was: "The Congress shall have power to lay and collect taxes on incomes, from whatever source derived, without apportionment among the several States, and without regard to any census or enumeration."
>
> Many of the instruments neglected to capitalize "States," and some capitalized other words instead. The instrument from Illinois had "remuneration" in place of "enumeration"; the instrument from Missouri substituted "levy" for "lay"; the instrument from Washington had "income" not "incomes"; others made similar blunders.
>
> Thomas insists that because the states did not approve exactly the same text, the amendment did not go into effect. Secretary Knox considered this argument. The Solicitor of the Department of State drew up a list of the errors in the instruments and — taking into account both the triviality of the deviations and the treatment of earlier amendments that had experienced more substantial problems — advised the Secretary that he was authorized to declare the amendment adopted. The Secretary did so.
>
> Although Thomas urges us to take the view of several state courts that only agreement on the literal text may make a legal document effective, the Supreme Court follows the "enrolled bill rule." If a legislative document is authenticated in regular form by the appropriate officials, the court treats that document as properly adopted. *Field v. Clark*, 143 U.S. 649, 36 L.Ed. 294, 12 S.Ct. 495 (1892). The principle is equally applicable to constitutional amendments. See *Leser v. Garnett*, 258 U.S. 130, 66 L.Ed. 505, 42 S.Ct. 217 (1922), which treats as conclusive the declaration of the Secretary of State that the nineteenth amendment had been adopted. In *United States v. Foster*, 789 F.2d. 457, 462-463, n.6 (7th Cir. 1986), we relied on *Leser*, as well as the inconsequential nature of the objections in the face of the 73-year acceptance of the effectiveness of the sixteenth amendment, to reject a claim similar to Thomas's. See also *Coleman v. Miller*, 307 U.S. 433, 83 L. Ed. 1385, 59 S. Ct. 972 (1939) (questions about ratification of amendments may be nonjusticiable). Secretary Knox declared that enough states had ratified the sixteenth amendment. The Secretary's decision is not transparently defective. We need not decide when, if ever, such a decision may be

is possible to take the most of a man's income, and to do it in a perfectly legal manner."[25]

Licenses are also required for all commercial activity because "all intercourse between the territories occupied by belligerent[s], whether by traffic, by letter, by travel, or in any other way, ceases," except "according to agreement approved by the government, or by the highest military authority [the Commander-in-Chief]."[26] The Government's definition of what constitutes "intercourse" is quite exhaustive:

> The question of what is commerce is to be approached both affirmatively and negatively, that is, from the points of view as to what it includes and what it excludes. While commerce includes trade, traffic, the purchase, sale, or exchange of commodities, and the transportation of persons or property, whether on land or water or through the air, according to various definitions of the term, and according to judicial exposition apart from formal definitions, nevertheless commerce is broader than, and is not limited to trade, transportation, or the purchase, sale, or exchange of goods or commodities.
>
> Commerce is more than any one of these things in that it is intercourse. The terms "commerce," "interstate commerce," and "commerce among the states" or "commerce among the several states," embrace business and commercial intercourse in any and all of its forms and branches and all its component parts between citizens of different states, and may embrace purely social intercourse between citizens of different states, as over the telephone, telegraph, or radio, or the mere passage of persons from one state to another for social intercourse and traffic, but also the subject matter thereof, which may be either things, goods, chattels, merchandise, or persons.[27]

Commenting on the Trading With the Enemy Act, the U.S. Senate likewise stated:

> The trade or commerce regulated or prohibited is defined in Subsections (a), (b), (c), (d) and (e), page 4. This trade covers almost every imaginable transaction, and is forbidden and made unlawful except when allowed under the form of licenses issued by the Secretary of Commerce (p. 4, sec. 3, line 18). This authorization of trading under licenses constitutes the principal modification of the rule of international law forbidding

---

reviewed in order to know that Secretary Knox's decision is now beyond review (*U.S. v. Thomas*, 788 F.2d 1253).

The fact that arguments based on the supposed defects of the ratification of the Sixteenth Amendment have been ruled frivolous and the matter declared to be "beyond review" has not deterred the countless "gurus" in the so-called "patriot" movement from continuing to extract exorbitant fees from their gullible followers for their "untax" schemes.

25. Charles Edward Merriam, *The Written Constitution and the Unwritten Attitude* (New York: Richard R. Smith, Inc., 1931), page 14.

26. Lieber, *Instructions for Armies in the Field*, Section V, Clause 86.

27. Ginnow and Nikolic, *Corpus Juris Secundum*, Volume XV, pages 383-385.

trade between the citizens of belligerents, for the power to grant such licenses, and therefore exemption from the operation of law, is given by the bill.[28]

To this end, "military commanders under such circumstances [are] sometimes led to assume a licensing authority."[29] To find out for themselves whether or not they are considered to be the enemy by the U.S. Government, Americans need look no further than their own wallets for the evidence.

The Suspension of Lawful Courts

According to the *Lieber Code*, which was originally promulgated in 1863 under Lincoln's direction as General Orders No. 100, "Whenever feasible, martial law is carried out in cases of individual offenders by military courts.... Military jurisdiction is of two kinds: first, that which is conferred and defined by statute; second, that which is derived from the common law of war.... In the armies of the United States the first is exercised by courts-martial...."[30] In the 1867 case *Hefferman v. Porter* it was likewise declared:

> The right of a military occupant to govern, implies the right to determine in what manner, and through what agency.... The municipal laws of the place may be left in operation, or suspended, and others enforced. The administration of justice, may be left in the hands of the ordinary officers of the law; or these may be suspended, and others appointed in their place. Civil rights and civil remedies may be suspended, and military laws and courts and proceedings, may be substituted for them, or new legal remedies and civil proceedings, may be introduced.[31]

More recently, the U.S. Supreme Court declared:

> The jurisdiction of United States courts-martial is limited to serving in the armed forces, certain categories of reserve and retired personnel, prisoners of war... and persons employed by or accompanying the armed forces beyond the continental limits of the United States of America. Nevertheless, where martial law has been declared and the privilege of the writ of *habeas corpus* suspended, any civilian may find himself amenable to trial not before the regular civil courts, but by the order of or under regulations promulgated by a military commander, by one of a miscellany of *ad hoc* tribunals composed of officers of the armed services and usually designated as provost courts, military commis-

---

28. Senate Report 113.

29. Birkhimer, *Military Government*, pages 277-278.

30. Lieber, *Instructions for Armies in the Field*, Section I, Clauses 12-13.

31. *Hefferman v. Porter* (1867), 6 Coldw. (46 Tenn.) 391.

sions, or military boards....[32]

Likewise, the *Law of Land Warfare* manual states:

> ...[I]n practice, offenders who are not subject to the *Uniform Code of Military Justice* but who by the law of war are subject to trial by military tribunals, are tried by military commissions, provost courts, or other forms of military tribunals.
>
> In areas occupied by United States forces, military jurisdiction over individuals, other than members of the Armed Forces, who are charged with violating legislation or orders of the occupant is usually exercised by military government courts. Although sometimes designated by other names, these tribunals are actually military commissions. They sit in and for the occupied area and thus exercise their jurisdiction on a territorial basis.[33]

The gold-fringed military flag which was carried by the Army of the Potomac during its war against the Southern people now stands in American courtrooms as a public proclamation of the military occupation and government of the former States. The spearhead finial is used in the traffic and justice (provost) courts, in which the summary trials proceed upon charges and specifications rather than an indictment. The eagle finial is used in the larger civil courts which are organized under the authority of the President in times of national emergency or when the normal courts of the States are closed.[34] Both of these are courts-martial of the occupying power, not lawful courts of the State. For those tempted to think that the gold fringe is mere decoration, the following quote is provided:

> From a military standpoint flags are of two classes, those flown from stationary masts over army posts, and those carried by troops in formation. The former are referred to by the general name flags. The latter are called colors when carried by mounted troops. Colors and standards are... made of silk with a knotted fringe of yellow on three sides.
>
> Use of the flag. The most general and appropriate use of the flag is as a symbol of authority and power.[35]

Elsewhere, we are told that, "within the discretion of the President as Commander-in-

---

32. *Duncan v. Kahanamoku* (1946), 327 U.S. 304.

33. *The Law of Land Warfare: Army Field Manual 27-10* (Washington, D.C.: Government Printing Office, 1983 O-381-647 [5724]), page 11.

34. *United States Army Regulations* (Washington, D.C.: Government Printing Office, 1 October 1979; AR 840-10), Chapter 8.

35. Henry Suzzallo, Ph.D., Sc.D., LL.D. (editor), *The National Encyclopedia* (New York: P.F. Collier and Son Corporation, 1944), Volume IV, page 326.

Chief of the Army and Navy,"[36] the gold-fringed United States flag is "flown indoors, only in military courtrooms" and "[d]isplay or use of flags, guidons, and streamers or replicas thereof, including those presently or formerly carried by U.S. Army units, by other than the office, individual, or organization for which authorized, is prohibited except [by]... [r]ecognized United States Army division associations...."[37] It is very clear that the display or use of a military flag outside a military venue is strictly prohibited.

It is commonly asserted within the so-called Patriot movement that the gold-fringe indicates admiralty jurisdiction. However, courts which hear cases of admiralty jurisdiction fall within the venue of Article III of the Constitution and are therefore part of the constitutional function of the Judicial Branch of the Government, whereas "Military courts are not Article III courts but agencies established pursuant to Article I."[38] The origin of these courts can be located in the unconstitutional Acts of the Reconstruction period, and as such, they exist solely to enforce the "appropriate legislation" and "military jurisdiction" of those Acts — in other words, the "Rules concerning Captures on Land and Water."[39]

Remedy is Denied to the People

The arbitrary nature of the present-day legal system as the mere collection of war reparations from the conquered enemies of the U.S. Government is further evident from the following: "New administrative undertakings of the war and post-war years introduced the National Government permanently into fresh areas of activity. Among these [was]... in 1870 [during Reconstruction] the creation, under the Attorney-General, of a Department of Justice to supervise from Washington the activities of the United States attorneys in the field."[40] "In the field" is defined as "[a]ny place, on land or water, apart from permanent cantonments or fortifications, where military operations are being conducted."[41] Furthermore, according to

---

36. 34 Ops. Atty. Gen. 483.

37. *Army Regulations*, Chapter 2. This flag also appears as a shoulder patch on law enforcement uniforms, even those of police at the municipal (city) level — additional evidence that such men are agents of the occupying military force rather than the servants of the people.

38. U.S. Senate, "The War Power," *The Constitution of the United States: An Analysis and Interpretation* (U.S. Senate Document No. 92-82, Ninety-Second Congress, Second Session; Washington, D.C.: U.S. Government Printing Office, 1972), page 334.

39. U.S. Constitution, Article I, Section 8, Clause 11.

40. U.S. Government, *Report of the Commission of Intergovernmental Relations* (Washington, D.C.: Government Printing Office, 1955), pages 24-25.

41. *Ex parte Gerlach* (D.C.) 247 F. 616, 617; *Ex parte Jochen* (D.C.) 257 F. 200, 205; *Ex parte Mikell* (D.C.) 253 F. 817, 819; *Hines v. Mikell* (C.C.A.) 259 F. 28, 30.

the Uniform Code of Military Justice Act of 5 May 1950, "The words 'in the field' imply military operations with a view to an enemy..., and it has been said that in view of the technical and common acceptation of the term, the question of whether an armed force is 'in the field' is not to be determined by the activity in which it may be engaged at any particular time...."[42] It is not surprising, therefore, to find that all other administrative workers who are employed or commissioned by the Government to collect reparations from its citizens or otherwise monitor and regulate their activities, such as Internal Revenue, Bureau of Alcohol, Tobacco, and Firearms (BATF), or Federal Bureau of Investigation (FBI)[43] agents, are also referred to as "agents in the field."

That this is what is really going on in the courts is kept hidden from the ignorant public by the illusion of jury trials. As noted in a previous chapter, Lincoln had justified the removal of the courts from their constitutional foundation by an appeal to "necessity" and the "public welfare" — both of which he reserved the right to define himself. He even ordered the arrest of the Chief Justice of the Supreme Court for opposing his policies. Consequently, the judge which presides in such courts is seated at the pleasure of the Executive police power and since he is bound only by what is deemed to be beneficial to the public welfare, he may overturn a jury's verdict as he pleases. The old constitutional doctrine of jury nullification cannot co-exist with such an arbitrary system because the jury members no longer take the law with them into the courtroom, but instead have it delivered to them from the mouth of the judge, who decides what it shall be as the necessity of the moment or his own personal discretion dictates.[44] Since panel members must be "U.S. citizens" under the Fourteenth Amendment (themselves "completely subject" to all the codes and regulations arising therefrom) and they are carefully screened to weed out those who may hold political or religious views contrary to the purpose of the court-martial (*i.e.* those who still believe the Constitution to be "the supreme law of the land" will rarely make it through this screening process to sit on a panel), it is impossible for the accused to be guaranteed a trial by "an

---

42. Uniform Code of Military Justice Act, 5 May 1950; Statutes at Large, Volume LXIV, page 108; Title 50 United States Code, Sections 551-736.

43. In *Emergency Powers Statutes* report of 1973, the U.S. Senate wrote the following: "Another pertinent question among many, that the Special Committee's work has revealed, concerns the statutory authority for domestic surveillance by the FBI. According to some experts, the authority for domestic surveillance appears to be based upon an Executive Order issued by President Roosevelt during an emergency period. If it is correct that no firm statutory authority exists, then it is reasonable to suggest that the appropriate committees enact proper statutory authority for the FBI with adequate provision for oversight by Congress" (page 10). Thus, as late as the 1970s, the FBI did not even have a statutory basis for its existence. This was yet another example of Congress' *ex post facto* rubber-stamping the unconstitutional activities of the Executive branch during a contrived national emergency.

44. "[I]f the judge's opinion in matter of law must rule the issue of fact submitted to the jury, the trial by jury would be useless" (*Sparf v. United States* [1895] 156 U.S. 51).

impartial jury of his peers" as stated in the Sixth Amendment.[45] Consequently, the presence of a jury in a court-martial is nothing more than a formality, for the proceedings are conducted on "principles of public policy as distinguished from the common law."[46] Elsewhere, we read:

> ...[T]he courts are selected from among the ranks of men filled with the spirit of the times. We are certain to find the Constitution a growing and expanding instrument. For that very reason it is a living and not a dead Constitution. By suiting itself to different times and circumstances it lives.
>
> So, too, the police power must continue to be elastic — capable of development — as economic, social, and political conditions vary. Therefore the rule of precedent, *Stare Decisis*, is not a sufficient basis upon which to judge the present-day meaning of this term, nor the extent of its scope.[47]

We must not overlook the above admission: modern American courts have rejected *stare decisis*, which simply means that they are not bound "to abide by, or adhere to, decided cases."[48] This malady of capriciousness extends even to the Supreme Court, which, as evidenced by Lincoln's utter contempt for the Court of his day and by Roosevelt's "court packing" in the 1930s, has little function under an Executive dictatorship other than "a fairly harmless observer of the emergency activities of the President...."[49] Willam J. Millard of the Washington State supreme court commented:

> The Supreme Court of the United States has "rendered it impossible for the practicing lawyer to advise his client as to what the law is today, or even to offer a guess as to what it will be tomorrow...." The court repeatedly has overruled decisions, precedents and landmarks of the law of long standing without assigning any valid reason therefore, dismissing the question with a wave of the hand, and contenting itself with the assertion that these precedents have been eroded by the processes of the years; or basing its decision on casuistry and sophistry rather than by logic.... By this conduct [the court] has subjected itself to the suspicion, widely held, that it speaks, or undertakes to speak, in the voice of

---

45. According to Patrick Henry, a man's peers are "those who reside near him, his neighbors, and who are well acquainted with his character and situation in life" (Elliott, *Debates in the Several State Conventions*, Volume III, page 579).

46. *Prize Cases* (1862), 2 Black, 674.

47. Essert, "Police Power," pages 214-215.

48. *Black's Law Dictionary* (Sixth Edition), page 1406.

49. Rossiter, *Constitutional Dictatorship*, page 264.

the appointing [Executive] power, rather than by the voice of the law.[50]

The American people have been duped into placing their trust in a legal profession which is impotent to even inform them "what the law is today," much less to shield them from the abuses of a government freed from all constitutional restraint. To say that there is no remedy in the courts for a people subjected to military occupation would be an understatement. According to the *Manual for Courts Martial*, an "act of war" exists "in virtually every act conceivable by any person, against which the United States Government has made a law, rule, or regulation."[51] As we have seen above in the admissions of the Ninety-Third Congress, the codes, rules, and regulations promulgated by Congress under the direction of the President acting as Commander-in-Chief are so voluminous that it is impossible for any U.S. citizen to understand, much less to comply with them at all times. Of course, it is not intended for the citizens to do so; indeed, the very existence of the system depends upon "criminal activity" to carry on its "war on crime," its "war on drugs," its "war on poverty," its "war on terror," or any other artificial war or national emergency that is concocted by the current Administration to justify the continued derogation of constitutional rights.

According to the laws of war, the military authority in an occupied country has the right "to search by day or night the homes of citizens.... to order the surrender of arms and stores, and to proceed to search and seize them; [and] to prohibit publications and meetings that it judges to be of a nature tending to incite and maintain disorder."[52] The military siege and subsequent summary execution without a trial of over eighty men, women, and children in Waco, Texas in 1993 was a brazen exercise of the President's assumed power under martial law to wage war against belligerent citizens, as are the many other examples of Executive tyranny which have occurred with increasing frequency in our day. It is time that Americans wake up and face the truth that the "land of the free" is a thing of the past, and that the celebration sanctioned by the United States Government each year on the Fourth of July is not the independence of the people, but its own "new birth of freedom" from the "chains" of the Constitution which was won for it by the "father" of the "new nation" — Abraham Lincoln.

The American Republic is Dead

In 1987, Thurgood Marshall, the first Black Supreme Court Justice, admitted:

---

50. J. Millard, dissenting opinion in *Southwest Washington Production Credit Assn. v. Fender* (1944) 21 Wash. 2d 349, 363-364.

51. *Manual for Courts Martial*, page IV-4, Article 104(C)(6)(c). The offenses that may be committed by a civilian, which are classified as "Acts of War," cover one hundred and twenty-five pages in this manual.

52. *Laws Regarding the State of Siege of 9th August, 1849*, Chapter III, Article IX.

...I do not believe that the meaning of the Constitution was forever "fixed" at the Philadelphia Convention. Nor do I find the wisdom, foresight, and sense of justice exhibited by the Framers particularly profound. To the contrary, the government they devised was defective from the start, requiring several amendments, a civil war, and momentous social transformation to attain the system of constitutional government, and its respect for the individual freedoms and human rights, we hold as fundamental today. When contemporary Americans cite "The Constitution," they invoke a concept that is vastly different from what the Framers barely began to construct two centuries ago....

While the Union survived the civil war, the Constitution did not. In its place arose a new, more promising basis for justice and equality, the 14th Amendment, ensuring protection of the life, liberty, and property of all persons against deprivations without due process, and guaranteeing equal protection of the laws.[53]

Even more revealing is the following statement by George P. Fletcher:

The "original republic" — the one for which our "forefathers" fought "face to face — hand to hand" — exists only in the minds of academics and fundamentalist patriots. The republic created in 1789 is long gone. It died with 600,000 Americans killed in the Civil War. That conflict decided once and forever that the People and the States do not have the power to govern their local lives apart from the nation as a whole. The People have no power either to secede as states or to abolish the national government.

The new Constitution — the one that shapes and guides the national government and disturbs the new patriots to their core — begins to take hold in the Gettysburg Address, in which Lincoln skips over the original Constitution and reconstitutes it according to the principles of equality articulated in the Declaration of Independence. This short speech functions as the Preamble to a new charter that crystalizes after the war in the Thirteenth, Fourteenth, and Fifteenth Amendments. The Gettysburg Address signals the beginning of a new Constitution. The language is so familiar that we do not realize the implicit transformation.[54]

Fletcher is Professor of Jurisprudence at Columbia University and the author of several books and over sixty major articles on criminal law, comparative law, torts, and jurisprudence, and so his words should not be taken lightly. It was also not a mere metaphor when he referred to "the new Constitution" as distinguished from the "original Constitution." As he stated in the article quoted above, "the new Constitution" is founded in the Reconstruction amendments, which were nothing more than war measures used to establish a "new jurisdiction" — U.S. citizenship — which can be regulated and taxed without limitation in

---

53. Thurgood Marshall, bicentennial speech given at Maui, Hawaii on 6 May 1987; online at www.thurgoodmarshall.com/speeches/constitutional_speech.htm.

54. Fletcher, "Unsound Constitution," pages 14-15. For a good response to Fletcher's arguments, see Ron Paul, "Original Intent," *Congressional Record — House* (1 August 1997), page H6710. This speech is available at www.c-spanvideo.org/videolibrary

order to prop up the debt-ridden Federal behemoth. Back in the early Nineteenth Century, the able and respected jurist William Rawle warned the American people of the dangers of departing from a written and permanent constitution as the security of their rights:

> It is not necessary that a constitution should be in writing; but the superior advantages of one reduced to writing over those which rest on traditionary information, or which are to be collected from the acts and proceedings of the government itself, are great and manifest. A dependence on the latter is indeed destructive of one main object of a constitution, which is to check and restrain governors. If the people can only refer to the acts and proceedings of the government to ascertain their own rights, it is obvious, that as every such act may introduce a new principle, there can be no stability in the government. The order of things is inverted; what ought to be the inferior, is placed above that which should be the superior, and the legislature is enabled to alter the constitution at its pleasure.
>
> This is admitted by English jurists to be the case in respect to their own constitution, which in all its vital parts may be changed by an act of parliament; that is, the king, lords, and commons may, if they think proper, abrogate and repeal any existing laws, and pass any new laws in direct opposition to that which the people contemplate and revere as their ancient constitution. No such laws can be resisted or disobeyed by the subject, nor declared void by their courts of justice as unconstitutional. A written constitution which may be enforced by the judges and appealed to by the people, is therefore most conducive to their happiness and safety.[55]

With this in mind, we can see why "public servants" and "law enforcement officers" remain unimpressed when informed by "Patriots," "sovereign state Citizens," "Christian Coalitions," or any other political faction or party, that they have acted unconstitutionally. The oath sworn by these men is to "support and defend the Constitution of the United States against all enemies, foreign and domestic." This is no longer "the original Constitution" — the written document ratified by the several States for their own general welfare, now declared to be a "dead constitution" — but the ever-growing and ever-changing mass of codes, rules, regulations, Executive Orders, international treaties (*e.g.* N.A.F.TA., G.A.T.T., the United Nations charter, *etc.*) that have their basis in military law, not the Common Law.

A Bankrupt Corporation is Owned By its Creditors

We have seen very clear evidence that by 1933, the U.S. Government was completely bankrupt. This fact was declared in 1934 by Representative William Lemke of North Dakota:

> This nation is bankrupt; every State in this Union is bankrupt; the people of the United States, as a whole, are bankrupt. The public and private debts of this Nation, which are evidenced by bonds, mortgages, notes, or other written instruments amount to about

---

55. Rawle, *View of the Constitution*, pages 15-16.

$250,000,000,000, and it is estimated that there is about $50,000,000,000 of which there is no record, making in all about $300,000,000,000 of public and private debts. The total physical cash value of all the property in the United States is now estimated at about $70,000,000,000.

That is more than it would bring if sold at public auction. In this we do not include debts or the evidence of debts, such as bonds, mortgages, and so forth. These are not physical property. They will have to be paid out of the physical property. How are we going to pay $300,000,000,000 with only $70,000,000,000?[56]

Representative McFadden believed that this bankruptcy was caused by "the corrupt and dishonest Federal Reserve," but the roots of the problem, though certainly exasperated by the passage of the Federal Reserve Act of 1913, actually go back much further in American history. The U.S. Treasury had been bankrupt in 1861 and it is impossible to believe that a protracted and costly war of four years' duration could have improved the situation at all. According to the candid admission of Representative James Trafficant, Jr. of Ohio in 1993, "We are now in chapter 11 [bankruptcy]" and those who write and pass the laws in this country are merely "official trustees presiding over the greatest reorganization of any bankrupt entity in world history, the U.S. Government."[57] The importance of this statement must not be missed:

The debtor rehabilitation provisions of the [Bankruptcy] Code (Chapters 11, 12 and 13) differ, however, from the straight bankruptcy in that the debtor looks to rehabilitation and reorganization, rather than liquidation, and the creditor looks to future earnings of the bankrupt, rather than property held by the bankrupt to satisfy their claims....

When a debtor business entity realizes it will become insolvent or will be unable to pay its debts as they mature, it can petition for reorganization under Chapter 11 of the Bankruptcy Code. The debtor business normally is permitted to continue its operations under court supervision until some plan of reorganization is approved by two-thirds of the creditors.[58]

The "future earnings of the bankrupt" can be none other than the future earnings of the American people and their posterity collected by the Government through taxation. Furthermore, a "bankruptcy trustee" is a "person appointed by the Bankruptcy Court to take charge of the debtor estate, [and] to collect assets...."[59] Are we to conclude, then, that our supposed representatives in Congress are nothing more than collection agents? One thing that can be stated with certainty is that a bankrupt corporation, which is considered *civiliter*

---

56. William Lemke, *Congressional Record — House*, 3 March 1934.

57. James Traficant, Jr., *ibid.*, 17 March 1993, page H 1303.

58. *Black's Law Dictionary* (Sixth Edition), page 147.

59. *Ibid.*

mortuus (civilly dead), can make no law, enter no contract, or do anything other than what its creditors will allow.[60] As mentioned before, it is "public policy" that is the "law" being enforced in America today in order to promote "public safety" — the "public" being, not the American people, but the bondholders, corporations and big business interests, and ultimately, the international bankers behind the Federal Reserve system who control the President, the Congress, and the entire judicial system, through the national debt created by the Lincoln Administration and legalized by the Fourteenth Amendment. If it was impossible for the combined debt of the country in 1934, which totaled between $250 and $300 billion, to be paid even if all property owned by every citizen had been sold at auction, how is it possible that the current debt of nearly $17 trillion[61] can be paid when there is no longer any property to be sold? Every "dollar" in the pocket of every American is owned by the Federal Reserve, and thus every piece of property, every stock, every asset, and every service which has been purchased with such "money" is likewise owned by the Federal Reserve. A more complete slavery could not be imagined.

This is all anything but a conspiracy which only the John Birch Society has uncovered, since it has had full and open disclosure in the public record for the past one-hundred and fifty years — and yet the American people go about their daily lives for the most part unconcerned about their own condition, and even contributing with patriotic zeal to further their own oppression. Rather than enjoying the "more perfect Union" envisioned by our forefathers, it is obvious that we, their posterity, are instead living examples of the effectiveness of the primary weapon of conquest — deception:

> ...[A]llow them [the conquered] to live under their own laws, taking tribute of them, and creating within the country a government composed of a few who will keep it friendly to you.... A city used to liberty can be more easily held by means of its citizens than in any other way....
>
> ...[T]hey must at least retain the semblance of the old forms; so that it may seem to the people that there has been no change in the institutions, even though in fact they are entirely different from the old ones. For the great majority of mankind are satisfied with appearances, as though they were realities, and are often even more influenced by the things that seem than by those that are.... [The conqueror should] not wish that the people... should have occasion to regret the loss of any of their old customs....[62]

---

60. *Ibid.*, pages 245, 246.

61. National Debt Clock at www.brillig.com/debt_clock. For a shocking dose of reality, the reader is encouraged to go to this site and repeatedly hit the "refresh" button on the keyboard. As of this writing, the amount of the debt increases by increments of at least 100,000 "dollars" every two or three seconds and 2.5 billion every day.

62. Niccolo Machiavelli, *The Prince and the Discourses* (New York: Random House, 1950), pages 18, 182-183.

SUPPORTING DOCUMENT
The Original Draft of the Declaration of Independence
June 1776

A Declaration by the Representatives of the United States of America, in General Congress assembled.

When in the course of human events, it becomes necessary for one people to dissolve the political bands which have connected them with another, and to assume among the powers of the earth the separate and equal station to which the laws of nature and of nature's God entitle them, a decent respect to the opinions of mankind requires that they should declare the causes which impel them to the separation.

We hold these truths to be self evident: that all men are created equal; that they are endowed by their Creator with inherent and inalienable rights; that among these are life, liberty, and the pursuit of happiness; that to secure these rights, governments are instituted among men, deriving their just powers from the consent of the governed; that whenever any form of government becomes destructive of these ends, it is the right of the people to alter or to abolish it, and to institute new government, laying its foundation on such principles, and organizing its powers in such form, as to them shall seem most likely to effect their safety and happiness. Prudence, indeed, will dictate that governments long established should not be changed for light and transient causes; and accordingly all experience hath shown that mankind are more disposed to suffer while evils are sufferable, than to right themselves by abolishing the forms to which they are accustomed. But when a long train of abuses and usurpations, begun at a distinguished period and pursuing invariably the same object, evinces a design to reduce them under absolute despotism, it is their right, it is their duty to throw off such government, and to provide new guards for their future security. Such has been the patient sufferance of these colonies; and such is now the necessity which constrains them to expunge their former systems of government. The history of the present king of Great Britain is a history of unremitting injuries and usurpations, among which appears no solitary fact to contradict the uniform tenor of the rest, but all have in direct object the establishment of an absolute tyranny over these states. To prove this, let facts be submitted to a candid world for the truth of which we pledge a faith yet unsullied by falsehood.

He has refused his assent to laws the most wholesome and necessary for the public good.

He has forbidden his governors to pass laws of immediate and pressing importance, unless suspended in their operation till his assent should be obtained; and, when so suspended, he has utterly neglected to attend to them.

He has refused to pass other laws for the accommodation of large districts of people, unless those people would relinquish the right of representation in the legislature, a right inestimable to them, and formidable to tyrants only.

He has called together legislative bodies at places unusual, uncomfortable, and distant from the depository of their public records, for the sole purpose of fatiguing them into compliance with his measures.

He has dissolved representative houses repeatedly and continually for opposing with manly firmness his invasions on the rights of the people.

He has refused for a long time after such dissolutions to cause others to be elected, whereby the legislative powers, incapable of annihilation, have returned to the people at large for their exercise, the state remaining, in the meantime, exposed to all the dangers of invasion from without and convulsions within.

He has endeavored to prevent the population of these states; for that purpose obstructing the laws for naturalization of foreigners, refusing to pass others to encourage their migrations hither, and raising the conditions of new appropriations of lands.

He has suffered the administration of justice totally to cease in some of these states, refusing his assent to laws for establishing judiciary powers.

He has made our judges dependent on his will alone for the tenure of their offices, and the amount and payment of their salaries.

He has erected a multitude of new offices, by a self-assumed power and sent hither swarms of new officers to harass our people and eat out their substance.

He has kept among us in times of peace standing armies and ships of war without the consent of our legislatures.

He has affected to render the military independent of, and superior to, the civil power.

He has combined with others to subject us to a jurisdiction foreign to our constitutions and unacknowledged by our laws, giving his assent to their acts of pretended legislation for quartering large bodies of armed troops among us; for protecting them by a mock trial from punishment for any murders which they should commit on the inhabitants of these states; for cutting off our trade with all parts of the world, for imposing taxes on us without our consent; for depriving us in many cases of the benefits of trial by jury; for transporting us beyond seas to be tried for pretended offences; for abolishing the free system of English laws in a neighboring province, establishing therein an arbitrary government, and enlarging its boundaries, so as to render it at once an example and fit instrument for introducing the same absolute rule into these states; for taking away our charters, abolishing our most valuable laws, and altering fundamentally the forms of our governments; for suspending our own legislatures, and declaring themselves invested with power to legislate for us in all cases whatsoever.

He has abdicated government here withdrawing his governors, and declaring us out of his allegiance and protection, and waging war against us.

He has plundered our seas, ravaged our coasts, burnt our towns, and destroyed the lives of our people.

He is at this time transporting large armies of foreign mercenaries to complete the works of death, desolation and tyranny already begun with circumstances of cruelty and perfidy, unworthy the head of a civilized nation.

He has constrained our fellow citizens taken captive on the high seas, to bear arms against their country, to become the executioners of their friends and brethren, or to fall themselves by their hands.

He has endeavored to bring on the inhabitants of our frontiers, the merciless Indian savages, whose known rule of warfare is an undistinguished destruction of all ages, sexes and conditions of existence.

He has incited treasonable insurrections of our fellow citizens, with the allurements of forfeiture and confiscation of our property.

He has waged cruel war against human nature itself, violating its most sacred rights of life and liberty in the persons of a distant people who never offended him, captivating and carrying them into slavery in another hemisphere, or to incur miserable death in their transportation thither. This piratical warfare, the opprobrium of infidel powers, is the warfare of the christian king of Great Britain. Determined to keep open a market where men should be bought and sold, he has prostituted his negative for suppressing every legislative attempt to prohibit or to restrain this execrable commerce. And that this assemblage of horrors might want no fact of distinguished die, he is now exciting those very people to rise in arms among us, and to purchase that liberty of which he has deprived them, by murdering the people for whom he also obtruded them: thus paying off former crimes committed against the liberties of one people, with crimes which he urges them to commit against the lives of another.

In every stage of these oppressions we have petitioned for redress in the most humble terms: our repeated petitions have been answered only by repeated injuries.

A prince whose character is thus marked by every act which may define a tyrant is unfit to be the ruler of a people who mean to be free. Future ages will scarcely believe that the hardiness of one man adventured, within the short compass of twelve years only, to lay a foundation so broad and so undisguised for tyranny over a people fostered and fixed in principles of freedom.

Nor have we been wanting in attentions to our British brethren. We have warned them from time to time of attempts by their legislature to extend a jurisdiction over these our states. We have reminded them of the circumstances of our emigration and settlement here, no one of which could warrant so strange a pretension: that these were effected at the expense of our own blood and treasure, unassisted by the wealth or the strength of Great Britain: that in constituting indeed our several forms of government, we had adopted one common king, thereby laying a foundation for perpetual league and amity with them: but that submission to their parliament was no part of our constitution, nor ever in idea, if history may be credited: and, we appealed to their native justice and magnanimity as well as to the ties of our common kindred to disavow these usurpations which were likely to interrupt our connection and correspondence. They too have been deaf to the voice of justice and of consanguinity, and when occasions have been given them, by the regular course of their laws, of removing from their councils the disturbers of our harmony, they have, by their free election, reestablished them in power. At this very time too, they are permitting their chief magistrate to send over not only soldiers of our common blood, but Scotch and foreign mercenaries to invade and destroy us. These facts have given the last stab to agonizing affection, and manly spirit bids us to renounce forever these unfeeling brethren. We must endeavor to forget our former love for them, and hold them as we hold the rest of mankind, enemies in war, in peace friends. We might have been a free and a great people together; but a communication of grandeur and of freedom, it seems, is below their dignity. Be it so, since they will have it. The road to happiness and to glory is open to us, too. We will tread it apart from them, and acquiesce in the necessity which denounces our eternal separation!

We therefore the representatives of the United States of America in General Congress assembled, do in the name, and by the authority of the good people of these states reject and renounce all allegiance and subjection to the kings of Great Britain and all others who may hereafter claim by, through or under them; we utterly dissolve all political connection which may heretofore have subsisted between us and the people or parliament of Great Britain: and finally we do assert and declare these colonies to be free and independent states, and that as free and independent states, they have full power to levy war, conclude peace, contract alliances, establish commerce, and to do all other acts and things which independent states may of right do.

And for the support of this declaration, we mutually pledge to each other our lives, our fortunes, and our sacred honor.

SUPPLEMENTARY ESSAY
A Treatise on Military Government
by William E. Birkhimer

The Constitution has placed no limits upon the war powers of the government, but they are regulated and limited by the laws of war. One of these powers is the right to institute military governments.

First — over conquered foreign territory: The erection of such governments over the persons and territory of a public enemy is an act of war; is in fact the exercise of hostilities without the use of unnecessary force. It derives its authority from the customs of war, and not the municipal law. It is a mode of retaining a conquest, of exercising a supervision over an unfriendly population, and of subjecting malcontent non-combatants to the will of a superior force, so as to prevent them from engaging in hostilities, or inciting insurrections or breaches of the peace, or from giving aid and comfort to the enemy. Large numbers of persons may thus be held morally and physically in subjection to a comparatively small military force. Contributions may be levied, property be appropriated, commerce may be restrained or forbidden, for the same reasons which would justify the repression of the open hostilities of the inhabitants by force of arms.

Those who institute or enforce military government should have a care to base their exercise of authority upon the certain ground of belligerent right or its necessary incidents. Military commanders, under these circumstances, should avoid the meshes of either constitutional or civil law; first, because such complications are unnecessary; second, because facilities for securing good advice on constitutional and legal matters generally are very poor amidst the clang of armies in the field. So long as military government lasts the will of the commander should be the supreme law. Constitutional and civil lawyers have their day in court after civil law has been established. By following this simple and sound principle many military commanders and some Administrations would have been saved a great deal of unnecessary trouble.

The instituting military government in any country by the commander of a foreign army there is not only a belligerent right, but often a duty. It is incidental to the state of war, and appertains to the law of nations. "The rights of occupation," says Hall, "may be placed upon the broad foundation of simple military necessity."[1] The commander of the invading, occupying, or conquering army rules the country with supreme power, limited only by international law and the orders of his government. For, by the law of nations, the *occupatio bellica* transfers the sovereign power of the enemy's country to the conqueror. An army in the enemy's country may do all things allowed by the rules of civilized warfare, and its officers and soldiers will be responsible only to their own government. The same rule applies to our own territory permanently occupied by the enemy. Castine, Maine was occupied by the British September 1st, 1814, and retained by them until after the treaty of peace, February, 1815. By this conquest and military occupation the enemy acquired that firm possession which enabled him to exercise the fullest rights of sovereignty over that place. The sovereignty of the United States over the territory was, for the time being, of course, suspended.

As commander-in-chief the President is authorized to direct the movements of the naval and military forces, and to employ them in the manner he may deem most effectual to harass, conquer, and subdue the enemy. He may invade the hostile country and subject it to the sovereignty and authority of the United States. When Tampico, Mexico had been captured and the State of Tamaulipas subjugated, other nations were bound to regard the country, while our possession continued, as the territory of the United States and respect it as such. For, by the laws and usages of nations, conquest gives a valid title while the victor maintains the exclusive possession of the conquered country. The power of the President, under which this conquest was made, was that of a military commander prosecuting a war waged against a public enemy by the authority of his government.

Upon the acquisition, in the year 1846, by the arms of the United States of the Territory of New Mexico, the officer holding possession for the United States, by virtue of the power of conquest and occupancy, and in obedience to the duty of maintaining the security of the inhabitants in their persons and property, ordained under the sanction and authority of the President a provisional or temporary government for the country. Nor does it signify what name is given a government established by arms. Its essence is military; it is a government of force. In *Cross v. Harrison* the Supreme Court of the United States, first calling attention to the fact that California, or the port of San Francisco, had been conquered by the arms of the United States as early as 1846; that shortly afterwards the United States had military possession of all of Upper California; that early in 1847 the President, as constitutional commander-in-chief of the Army and Navy, authorized the military and naval commanders there to exercise the belligerent right of a conqueror, to form a civil government for the conquered country, and to impose duties on imports and tonnage as military contributions

---

1. 23 Opinions Attorneys-General, page 430.

for the support of the government and of the army which had the conquest in possession; observed as to this that no one could doubt that these orders of the President, and the action of our army and navy commanders in California in conformity with them, were according to the law of arms and the right of conquest.

The governments thus established in New Mexico and California were indeed styled "civil"; but they were in fact military. The milder name was a matter of state policy. The government of the United States had resolved to wrest those Territories from Mexico and annex them to the Federal domain. By the use of gentle terms the inhabitants were to be conciliated, the weight of the mailed hand rendered seemingly less oppressive, though its grasp was never relaxed.

The rulings of State courts are to the same effect. The Supreme Court of Tennessee, in *Rutlege v. Fogg*,[2] remarked that ordinarily the right of one belligerent nation to occupy and govern territory of the other while in its military possession is one of the incidents of the war and flows directly from the fact of conquest; that the authority for this is derived directly from the laws of war, as established by the usage of the world, confirmed by the writings of publicists and the decisions of courts; and that the constitution of political institutions of the conqueror are not, therefore, looked to directly for authority to establish a government for the territory of the enemy in his possession during his military occupation. It is a power that appertains to the fact of adverse military possession. On this ground that tribunal upheld the decisions of the military commissions convened at Memphis, Tennessee in 1803, by the commanding general of the Union forces.

Title by conquest is acquired and maintained by force of arms. The conqueror prescribes its limits. Humanity, however, acting on public opinion, has established, as a general rule, that the conquered shall not be wantonly oppressed, and that their condition shall remain as eligible as is compatible with the objects of the conquest.

When in the House of Commons, May 1851, it was said that martial law had been established by the British commander in 1814 in the south of France, military government, and not martial law, in the sense we use it, was meant. And so of the remarks of the Duke of Wellington, the commander referred to, in the House of Lords, April 1, 1851, in the debate on the Ceylon rebellion, when he said: "I contend that martial law is neither more nor less than the will of the general who commands the army. In fact, martial law means no law at all. Therefore, the general who declares it, and commands that it be carried into execution, is bound to lay down distinctly the rules and regulations and limits according to which his will is to be carried out."

Plainly what the Duke of Wellington here referred to was not martial law as a domestic fact, and as the term is used in this treatise; he was speaking of his conduct in foreign territory, and the methods there pursued to establish and enforce the rule of the conqueror.

In *Thorington v. Smith* the Supreme Court of the United States, adverting to the fact that military governments were classed by publicists as *de facto*, observed that they more

---

2. 3 Coldwell 554.

properly might be denominated governments of paramount force. Their characteristics were said to be (1) that their existence is maintained by active military power, and (2) that while they exist they must necessarily be obeyed in civil matters by private citizens who, by acts of obedience, rendered in submission to such force, do not become responsible, as wrong-doers, for these acts, though not warranted by the laws of the rightful government; that actual governments of this sort are established over districts differing greatly in extent and conditions; and that they are usually administered directly by military authority, but they may be administered, also, by civil authority, supported more or less directly by military force. By "rightful government" is here meant that to which the permanent allegiance of the people is due.

Such, then, is the authority, under the laws of war and the war powers of the government, for the establishment of military governments without the boundaries of the United States.

Second — within districts occupied by rebels treated as belligerents: The constitutional power to establish such governments within States or districts occupied by rebels treated as belligerents is as clear as the right to so govern foreign territory. The experience of the Civil War of 1861-65 frequently, indeed constantly, furnished illustrations of this branch of military government.

The object of the national government in that contest was neither conquest nor subjugation, but the overthrow of the insurgent organization, the suppression of insurrection, and the re-establishment of legitimate authority. In the attainment of these ends it became the duty of the Federal authorities whenever the insurgent power was overthrown, and the territory which had been dominated by it was occupied by the national forces, to provide as far as possible, so long as the war continued, for the security of persons and property and for the administration of justice. The duty of the National Government, in this respect, was no other than that which, as just shown, devolves upon the government of a regular belligerent occupying, during war, the territory of another independent belligerent. It was a military duty, to be performed by the President as commander-in-chief, and entrusted as such with the direction of the military force by which the occupation was held. So long as the war continued it can not be denied that the President might institute temporary governments within insurgent districts occupied by the national forces. In carrying them into effect he acted through his duly constituted subordinates. Although that war was not between independent nations, but between factions of the same nation, yet, having taken the proportions of a territorial war, the insurgents having become formidable enough to be recognized as belligerents, the doctrine of international law regarding the military occupation of enemy's country was held to apply.

The character of government to be established over conquered territory depends entirely upon the laws of the dominant power, or the orders of the military commander. Against the persons and property of rebels to whom belligerent rights have been conceded, the President may adopt any measures authorized by the laws of war, unless Congress otherwise determines. The protection of loyal citizens and their property located within the rebellious district is not a right which they can demand, but entirely a matter of expediency.

From the day that the military authorities obtained a firm foothold in the Philippine Islands, which may be considered as the 13th of August, 1898, when Manila was captured, the executive power unaided ruled the archipelago for upwards of two years. By act of March 2d, 1901, Congress lent the aid of its assistance. On the 4th of July, 1901, the plainly military gave way to the civil rule as announced, but the government in its essence remained a politico-military one, and, though styled civil, was upheld only by force of arms — in lesser degree, of the constabulary; in greater degree, of the nation.

It is well settled that where the rebels are conceded belligerent rights a civil domestic war will, during its continuance, confer all the rights and be attended by all the incidents of a contest between independent nations. One object of military government is to render the hold of the conqueror secure and enable him to set the seal on his success, and it must, therefore, in common with every other recognized means of war, be at the command of a legitimate government endeavoring to subdue an insurrection. As the army advances into the rebellious territory, a hostile may be replaced by a loyal magistracy, and a provisional government established to preserve order and administer justice until the courts can be reopened on the return of peace. It is true that as such a war is not prosecuted with a view of conquest, but to restore the normal condition which the rebellion interrupts, the right to employ force for the purpose indicated might be thought to cease with the suppression of the rebellion. It must still, however, be in the discretion of the legitimate government, if successful, to determine when the war is at an end; also whether the insurgents are sincere in their submission or intend to renew the contest at the first favorable opportunity, and while this uncertainty continues military government and occupation may be prolonged on the ground of necessity.

As was remarked by the Supreme Court of the United States in *Horn v. Lockhart*, "The existence of a state of insurrection and war does not loosen the bonds of society or do away with civil government, or the regular administration of the laws. Order must be preserved, police regulations maintained, crime prosecuted, property protected, contracts enforced, marriages celebrated, estates settled, and the transfer and descent of property regulated precisely as in time of peace."[3] These considerations led to the recognition as valid of those judicial and legislative acts in the insurrectionary States touching the enumerated and kindred subjects, where they were not hostile in purpose or mode of enforcement to the authority of the National Government, or did not impair contracts entered into under the Federal Constitution. This being true of insurrectionary districts, however far removed from the scene of contest, so much the more necessary is it, when armies have overrun the country, that some government be instituted to protect life and property and preserve society. And as the military power alone is competent to do this, the government so established must of necessity be military government.

It is of little consequence whether it be called by that name. Its character is the same whatever it may be called. Its source of authority is the same in any case. It is imposed by the

---

3. 17 Wallace 580.

conqueror as a belligerent right, and, in so far as the inhabitants of said territory or the rest of the world are concerned, the laws of war alone determine the legality or otherwise of acts done under its authority. But the conquering State may of its own will, and independently of any provisions in either its constitution or laws, impose restrictions or confer privileges upon the inhabitants of the rebellious territory so occupied which are not recognized by the laws of war. If the government of military occupation disregard these, it is accountable to the dominant government only whose agent it is, and not to the rest of the world.

No proclamation on the part of the victorious commander is necessary to the lawful inauguration and enforcement of military government. That government results from the fact that the former sovereignty is ousted, and the opposing army now has control. Yet the issuing such proclamation is useful as publishing to all living in the district occupied those rules of conduct which will govern the conqueror in the exercise of his authority. Wellington, indeed, as previously mentioned, said that the commander is bound to lay down distinctly the rules according to which his will is to be carried out. But the laws of war do not imperatively require this, and in very many instances it is not done. When it is not, the mere fact that the country is militarily occupied by the enemy is deemed sufficient notification to all concerned that the regular has been supplanted by a military government. In our own experience the practice has widely differed. Neither at Castine, Maine in 1814, by the British, nor at Tampico, Mexico in 1840, or in numerous cases during the Civil War when territory was wrested from the enemy, was any proclamation issued; while in other cases, as New Mexico in 1846, California in 1847, and New Orleans in 1862, proclamations were formally promulgated, announcing the principles by which the country would be governed while subject to military rule.

These proclamations may become very important, because, if approved by the government of the commanders making them, they assume in equity and perhaps in law the scope and force of contracts between the government and that people to whom they are addressed, and who in good faith accept and observe their terms. Thus when New Orleans was captured in 1862, the Federal commander, in his proclamation dated May 1st and published May 6th, that year, announced among other things that "all the rights of property of whatever kind will be held inviolate, subject only to the laws of the United States." The Supreme Court afterwards held that this was a pledge, binding the faith of the government, and that no subsequent commander had a right to seize private property within the district over which the proclamation extended as booty of war; consequently, that an order issued by a subsequent Federal commander in August, 1863, while the military occupation continued, requiring the banks of New Orleans to pay over to the quartermaster all moneys standing on their books to the credit of any corporation, association, or government in hostility to the United States, or person being an enemy of the United States, was illegal and void.[4]

New Mexico was not only conquered, but remained thereafter under the dominion of the United States. The provisional government established therein ordained laws and

---

4. 16 Wallace 483.

adopted a judicial system suited to the needs of the country. The Supreme Court of the United States held that these laws and this system legally might remain in force after the termination of the war and until modified either by the direct legislation of Congress or by the territorial government established by its authority.[5] We have had the same experiences in Cuba, Porto Rico, and the Philippines.

It has been observed, and the observation has the sanction of numerous expressions emanating from the Supreme Court, that those who quietly remain in the occupied district, transacting their ordinary business, should receive the care of, and they owe temporary allegiance to, the government established over them.[6] Allegiance is a duty owing by citizens to their government, of which, so long as they enjoy its benefits, they can not divest themselves. It is the obligation they incur for the protection afforded them. It varies with, and is measured by, the character of that protection. That allegiance and protection are reciprocal obligations binding mutually upon citizens and the government is the fundamental principle upon which society rests.

Under military government this allegiance is said to be temporary only. It is not wholly different in kind, but in degree falls far short of that owing by native-born or naturalized subjects to their permanent government. A consideration of the character of military as contradistinguished from regular governments will show that this distinction rests upon a proper basis. The consent of the people is the foundation-stone of governments having even a semblance of permanency. This is theoretically true at least, and generally is so practically. The proposition rests on observed facts, otherwise revolution would follow revolution and there could be no stability; but this in the more fully established States we know is contrary to experience. Moreover, should the factions, exhausted by internal discord, erect at last a regular government, it would be done only with the consent of the people.

The Declaration of Independence of the United States laid it down as a political maxim that governments derived their just powers from the governed, and that it is the right of a people to alter or abolish their form of government and institute a new one, laying its foundations in such principles and organizing its powers in such form as to them shall seem most likely to effect their safety and happiness. This doctrine, however, is no more applicable in the United States than elsewhere. The history of the world illustrates at once its antiquity and universality. When a people have become tired of their government, it has been their custom to change it. And while many governments have been built and perpetuated on force and fraud perhaps, yet even these may be considered as resting upon the tacit consent or acquiescence of the governed. Society can not exist without government, which is necessary to preserve and keep that society in order. To be effective it must be entrusted with supreme authority. This is necessary, not for the gratification of those who may be entrusted with the reins of power, but for the safety of that society, for the protection and preservation of which

---

5. *Leitensdorfer v. Webb*, 20 Howard 186.

6. 8 Wallace 10; 4 Wheaton 253; 9 Howard 615.

government is instituted. "And," says Blackstone, "this authority is placed in those hands wherein (according to the opinions of the founders of States, either expressly given or collected from their tacit approbation), the qualities requisite for supremacy, wisdom, goodness, and power are the most likely to be found."

As government is based on the necessities of society, affording the only practicable means by which the rights of its members may be secured and their wrongs redressed, its formation is regarded as the highest privilege and most important work of man. When formed — when, after the long, probationary, changeful periods which usually precede the accomplished fact, governments have been instituted — they have ever been regarded as worthy the reverence, the homage, and loyal support of those for whose benefit they were brought into existence.

From the earliest records of established governments it has been held the first duty of those who received their protection to support and defend them. Those who rebel against their authority are regarded as deserving severest punishment. These are universal principles, based on the instincts of rational beings and the experience of mankind. Having established government, having performed that supreme act, mankind have uniformly insisted that, so long as it performed its proper functions, those subjected to its authority and who enjoy its benefits are bound, if need be, to support it to the utmost of their ability. Any other principle would sanction revolution, with its attendant misery, upon the slightest pretext; an experience characteristic, not of States which have proved to be the blessings, but the curse of mankind. Considerations like these, based upon human nature, and the demands of society, have unalterably established the principle that allegiance and protection are reciprocal duties as between subject and government.

In a modified degree these principles are applicable to military government, and this leads to corresponding modifications of the allegiance of the subject. And first, let it be observed, that consent of the people freely given, so far from being the basis on which military government is founded, the very opposite is true. It is the rule of force imposed on subjects by paramount military power. That primary element of stability — a confidence grounded in the mutual interests of the people and their rulers self-imposed for the benefit of all — is here wanting. Yet it is the modern practice for the government of military occupation to protect the people in their rights of person and property. When this is not done, it is because the success of military measures renders such a course unadvisable. Here, as elsewhere, it is found to be for the best interests of all concerned to cultivate a feeling of good-will between rulers and subjects.

By the English law it is high treason to compass or imagine the death of the king, his lady the queen, or their eldest son and heir. The king here intended is the king in possession, without regard to his title. "For," says Blackstone, "it is held that a king *de facto* and not *de jure*, or, in other words, a usurper that hath got possession of the throne, is a king within the meaning of the statute, as there is a temporary allegiance due to him for his administration of the government and temporary protection of the public."[7] And so far was this principle carried that, though Parliament had declared the line of Lancaster to be usurpers, still, treasons committed against Henry VI. were punished, under Edward IV. By a subsequent statute all persons who, in defense of the king for the time being, wage war against those who endeavor to subvert his authority by force of arms, though the latter may be aiding the lawful monarch, are relieved from penalties for treason.[8] This is declaratory of the common law.[9] Being in possession, allegiance is due to the usurper as king *de facto*.[10] To this height has the duty of allegiance to *de facto* government been carried by the English law. Another illustration, differing in its incidents, yet based on the same principle, is found in the government of England under the Commonwealth, first by Parliament, and afterwards by Cromwell as protector. It was indeed held otherwise by the judges by whom Sir Henry Vane was tried for treason in the year following the restoration. "But," as has been justly remarked, "such a judgment, in such a time, has little authority."

The principle here involved, and which is equally applicable to both regular and temporary governments, is the simple one of mutuality of allegiance and protection. In this regard military government is on the same footing with any other. To the extent that it assumes and discharges these obligations of a regular government, it is entitled to the obedience of those who are recipients of its bounty. But as military government is at best but transient, the allegiance due to it is correspondingly temporary. It becomes complete only on the confirmation of the conquest with the consent, express or implied, of the displaced government.

Under the modern rules of warfare between civilized nations, this temporary transfer of allegiance carries in a qualified manner the reciprocal rights and duties of government and subject respectively. If, after military government is set up over them, the people attempt to leave the district to join the enemy, they will be repressed with utmost vigor. This transfer of allegiance takes place only to the extent mentioned, and operates only on those who at the time come actually under the new dominion. Mere paper government is not a valid one. To be so it must be capable of enforcing its decrees. And this will be only as by gradual conquest the victor extends the supremacy of his arms.

Hence the untenableness of the proposition that the Spanish sovereignty was ousted from the Philippine Archipelago, and that of the United States extended over it, by the capture alone of the capital and commercial emporium, Manila. The change of temporary allegiance extended no further than effectually could be maintained by the arms of the invader: the permanent change did not take place until the ratification of the treaty of peace.

7. Blackstone, *Commentaries*, Volume IV, page 77.

8. II Henry VII., Ch. 1.

9. Blackstone, *Commentaries*, Volume IV, page 77.

10. *Thorington v. Smith*, 8 Wallace 8.

Though it is a legitimate use of military power to secure undisturbed the possession of that which has been acquired by arms, yet it is difficult, by aid of any moderate number of troops, to guard and oversee an extended conquered territory; and it is practically impossible for any army to hold and occupy all parts of it at the same moment. Therefore, if the inhabitants are to be permitted to remain in their domiciles unmolested, some mode must be adopted of controlling their movements, and of preventing their committing acts of hostility against the dominant power, or of violence against each other. The disorganization resulting from civil war requires, more than that following from any other, those restraints which the dominant military alone can impose. In countries torn by intestine commotions neighbors become enemies, all forms of lawless violence are but too apt to be common, and in the absence of military rule would be unrestrained. Hence, to ensure quiet within rebellious districts when reduced into control during a civil war, it becomes all the more necessary to establish there a rigorous government, that life and property may be rendered secure and crime be either prevented or promptly punished. Firm possession of a conquered province can be held only by establishing a government which shall control the inhabitants thereof. And that there exists in the opinion of the Supreme Court of the United States no distinction as to the rights in this regard of the conqueror, whether the subjugated territory be foreign or that of rebels treated as belligerents, clearly appears from the language in the case of *Tyler v. Defrees*. "We do not believe," said the court in that case, "that the Congress of the United States, to which is confided all the great powers essential to a perpetual union, the power to make war, to suppress insurrection, to levy taxes, to make rules concerning captures on land and sea, is deprived of these powers when the necessity for their exercise is called out by domestic insurrection and internal civil war; when States, forgetting their constitutional obligations, make war against the nation, and confederate together for its destruction."[11]

The question, What legally, under the customs of war, shall constitute "military occupation"? was one of the important matters which the conference at Brussels in 1874 tried, but failed to decide.

The conference concluded that "a territory is considered as occupied when it finds itself placed in fact under the authority of the hostile army. The occupation extends only to territory where this authority is established and in condition to be exercised." The German view of occupation was that it did not always manifest itself by exterior signs, like a place blockaded; that, for instance, a town in the conquered district left without troops ought nevertheless to be considered as occupied, and all risings there should be severely repressed.

The English took a different view of the subject — that government holding, in brief, that, to be militarily occupied, a territory should be held firmly in the conqueror's grasp, and that if he did not keep a military force at any particular point, the people living there were under no obligations to remain quiet, but properly might rise against the occupying power without incurring the penalties meted out to insurgents.

It is plain that the latter (English) view would favor risings of the people *en masse*

---

11. 11 Wallace 331, 345.

to strike at the occupying power; a right for which that government strenuously contends. It is naturally the contention of a power having a comparatively small standing army, and whose policy it is to encourage so-called patriotic risings of the people, to make headway against the invader. The German view, on the contrary, is favorable to the government with a large regular army. According to this idea of "military occupation," risings of the people are proscribed even if no enemy be present to keep them in subjection, the army having just passed through on its career of conquest. The foundation for this theory maintained by such a people is not difficult to understand: if the enemy have but a small regular force, and it can be made outlawry for the people to rise against the authority of even an absent foe, that enemy will not contend long against a large standing army which not only fights its antagonist in front, but *constructively* controls enemy territory that it has only traversed. This is a constructive occupation, something like the constructive blockades of the beginning of the century.

The truth must be that a territory is militarily occupied when the invader dominates it to the exclusion of the former and regular government. The true test is exclusive possession.

Such was the rule established by the Hague Peace Conference, July 29, 1899, to which the United States was a party. Under Article XLII, Section 3, military occupation is limited to the district over which its authority can be asserted. During the Russo-Japanese war the Russian commander gave this a broad construction in Manchuria in favor of the Czar's authority.

A determination of the time when military government becomes operative is important. As the military dominion rests on force alone, it will receive recognition only from the time when, the original governmental authorities having been expelled, the commander of the occupying army is able to cause his authority to be respected. No presumptions exist in favor of a change from old to new government. Whatever rights are claimed for the latter must be clearly shown to belong to it.

When New Orleans was captured in 1862, the Federal general issued a proclamation announcing the fact of occupation, and setting forth the administrative principles which would regulate the United States authorities in governing the district occupied and the rules of conduct to be observed by the people. The Supreme Court of the United States, referring to this, said: "We think the military occupation of the city of New Orleans may be considered as substantially complete from the date of this publication; and that all the rights and obligations resulting from such occupation, or from the terms of the proclamation, may be properly regarded as existing from that time."[12] Firm possession of the enemy's country in war suspends his power and right to exercise sovereignty over the occupied place, and gives those rights, temporarily at least, to the conqueror; rights which all nations recognize and to which all loyal citizens may submit.

Acts of Congress take effect from date of signature unless there be something in their

---

12. 2 Wallace 276.

terms to modify the rule. In contemplation of law those are the dates of promulgation to persons interested, and rights accruing under them vest accordingly. The general rule is that retroactive construction is never favored. The same principles apply when a conqueror announces by proclamation his assumption of the reins of government; observing that, if the dates of signing and promulgation differ, the latter governs. And this is reasonable because, as this announcement on the part of the conqueror under the strict laws of war is unnecessary — the mere fact of occupation serving on the people sufficient notice that the will of the conqueror is for the time their law — a proclamation setting forth in terms what that will is gives rise to mutual rights and obligations as between the conqueror and the conquered; and therefore the date of promulgation which makes that will known is properly taken as the point of time from which rights vest and obligations are incurred.

"The port of Tampic," said the Supreme Court of the United States in *Fleming v. Page*, referring to the establishment of military government in Mexico, "and the Mexican State of Tamaulipas, in which it is situated, were subject to the sovereignty and dominion of the United States. The Mexican authorities had been driven out, or had submitted to our army and navy, and the country was in the firm and exclusive possession of the United States and governed by its military authorities, acting under the orders of the President." The criterion of conquest here announced is the driving out of enemy authorities, or their submission to the dominant power. It is a proper test and must receive a reasonable construction. Its meaning is that from the instant the authorities surrender to the invader the duty of protecting the people in their rights of person and property, the allegiance of the latter is temporarily transferred from their former to their new rulers.

The territorial extent of military government can not be greater than that of conquest, and generally will be coincident with it. Its basis being overpowering force, its ability to exercise that force and the extent to which that ability is recognized by the people of the district occupied determine the limits of its authority. The conqueror can not demand that temporary transfer of allegiance which is one feature of military government, unless, in return therefor, he can and does protect the people throughout the occupied district in those rights of person and property which it is binding on government to secure to them.

Unless confirmed by treaty, such acquisitions are not considered permanent. Yet for every commercial and belligerent purpose they are considered as part of the domain of the conqueror so long as he retains the possession and government.

The fifth section of the Act of July 13, 1861, for the collection of duties and other purposes, looking to the suppression of the then existing rebellion, provided that, under certain conditions, the President, by proclamation, might declare the inhabitants of a State or any section or part thereof to be in a state of insurrection against the United States. In pursuance of this act the President, on the 16th of August following, issued a proclamation declaring the inhabitants of certain States, excepting designated districts, as well as those "from time to time occupied and controlled by forces of the United States engaged in dispersing the insurgents," to be in a condition of rebellion. Referring to these measures, the Supreme Court of the United States said:

This legislative and executive action related, indeed, mainly to trade and intercourse between the inhabitants of loyal and the inhabitants of insurgent parts of the country; but, by excepting districts occupied and controlled by national troops from the general prohibition of trade, it indicated the policy of the Government not to regard such districts as in actual insurrection as enemies. Military occupation and control, to work this exception, must be actual; that is to say, not illusory, not imperfect, not transient; but substantial, complete, and permanent. Being such, it draws after it the full measure of protection to person and property consistent with a necessary subjection to military government. It does not, indeed, restore peace, or, in all respects, former relations; but it replaces rebel by national authority, and recognizes, to some extent, the conditions and responsibilities of national citizenship.[13]

The case here considered was one of government dealing with rebellious subjects; but it clearly sets forth the general principles of military government, under the rules of modern war, when control has become substantial, complete, if not permanent. The inhabitants pass under the government of the conqueror, and are bound by such laws, and such only, as it chooses to recognize and impose.

In this connection the remarks of Chancellor Kent, when treating of the obligations arising out of blockades, are interesting: "A blockade must be existing in point of fact; and in order to constitute that existence, there must be a power present to enforce it. All decrees and orders declaring extensive coasts and whole countries in a state of blockade, without the presence of an adequate naval force to support it, are manifestly illegal and void, and have no sanction in public law." These remarks are equally applicable to military occupation of enemy country. To extend the rights of such occupation by mere intention, implication, or proclamation, without the military power to enforce it, would be establishing a paper conquest infinitely more objectionable in its character and effects than a paper blockade. The occupation, however, of part by right of conquest, with intent and power to appropriate the whole, gives possession of the whole, if the enemy maintain military possession of no portion of the residue. But if any part hold out, so much only is possessed as is actually conquered. Forcible possession extends only so far as there is an absence of resistance.

It must not be inferred from what has just been said that the conqueror can have no control or government of hostile territory unless he actually occupies it with an armed force. It is deemed sufficient if it submits to him and recognizes his authority as conqueror; for conquests are, indeed, in this way extended over the territory of an enemy without actual occupation by an armed force. But so much of such territory as refuses to submit or to recognize the authority of the conqueror, and is not forcibly occupied by him, can not be regarded as under his control or within the limits of his conquest; and he therefore can not pretend to govern it or to claim the temporary allegiance of its inhabitants, or in any way to divert or restrict its intercourse with neutrals. It remains as the territory of its former sovereign, hostile to the would-be conqueror as a belligerent and friendly to others as neutrals. The government

---

13. 2 Wallace 277.

of the conqueror being *de facto* and not *de jure* in character, it must always rest upon the fact of possession, which is adverse to the former sovereign, and therefore can never be inferred or presumed. Not only must the possession be actually acquired, but it must be maintained. The moment possession is lost the rights of military occupation are also lost. By the laws and usages of nations conquest is a valid title only while the victor maintains the exclusive possession of the conquered country.

The preceding essay was extracted from William E. Birkhimer, LL.B., Military Government and Martial Law *(Kansas City, Missouri: Franklin Hudson Publishing Company, 1914).*

CONCLUSION

Conquest Does Not Grant Indefeasible Title

In the "Address to the People" which accompanied the Virginia Resolutions of 1798, the State legislature warned:

If measures can mould Governments, and if an uncontrolled power of construction is surrendered to those who administer them, their progress may be easily foreseen and their end easily foretold. A lover of monarchy who opens the treasures of corruption by distributing emoluments among devoted partisans, may at the same time be approaching his object, and deluding the people with professions of republicanism. He may confound monarchy and republicanism by the art of definition. He may varnish over the dexterity which ambition never fails to display, with the pliancy of language, the seduction of expediency, or the prejudices of the times. And he may come at length to avow that so extensive a territory as that of the United States can only be governed by the energies of monarchy, that it cannot be defended except by standing armies, and that it cannot be united except by consolidation. Measures have already been adopted which may lead to these consequences. They consist:

In fiscal systems and arrangements, which keep an host of commercial and wealthy individuals embodied and obedient to the mandates of the treasury.

In armies and navies, which will, on the one hand, enlist the tendency of man to pay homage to his fellow-creature who can feed or honour him; and on the other, employ the principle of fear by punishing imaginary insurrections, under the pretext of preventive justice.

In swarms of officers, civil and military, who can inculcate political tenets, tending to consolidation and monarchy, both by indulgences and severities, and can act as spies over the free exercise of human reason.

In restraining the freedom of the press, and investing the Executive with legislative, executive, and judicial powers over a numerous body of men.

And, that we may shorten the catalogue, in establishing, by successive precedents, such a mode of construing the Constitution as will rapidly remove every restraint upon the Federal power.[1]

These dire predictions are vindicated by a review of American history and the decline and fall of the erstwhile Republic. Today, there is no longer any substantial restraint, constitutional or otherwise, upon the central Government. A nation established upon the principles of usurpation and coercion will never, of its own accord, move onto a foundation of law. It must demand "unqualified allegiance" from its citizens because it cannot allow them to think for themselves — after all, a thinking populace is harder to control because they tend to resist tyranny. Having abandoned forever the concept of "inherent, natural, human rights," which it views as "at best a useful myth in the days of yore... with all the vulnerability that this implies,"[2] such a government seats itself in the place of God, dispensing "civil rights" to its conquered subjects which it may reclaim anytime it deems it necessary — usually during a state of emergency which it has engineered in a grab for more power. Knowing nothing else, such a government can only continue to resort to increased coercion to achieve its end until it either forces the people to rebel or it collapses from its own top-heaviness. Edmund Burke's comments on the French Revolution of 1787 have uncanny application to our own situation in America today:

There is no safety for honest men, but by believing all possible evil of evil men, and by acting with promptitude, decision, and steadiness on that belief....

I find, that some persons entertain other hopes, which I confess appear more specious than those by which at first so many were deluded and disarmed. They flatter themselves that the extreme misery brought upon the people by their folly, will at last open the eyes of the multitude, if not of their leaders. Much the contrary, I fear. As to the leaders in this system of imposture, you know, that cheats and deceivers never can repent. The fraudulent have no resource but in fraud. They have no other goods in their magazine. They have no virtue or wisdom in their minds, to which, in a disappointment concerning the profitable effects of fraud and cunning, they can retreat. The wearing out of an old, serves only to put them upon the invention of a new delusion. Unluckily too, the credulity of dupes is as inexhaustible as the invention of knaves. They never give the people possession; but they always keep them in hope....

Those who have been once intoxicated with power, and have derived any kind of emolument from it, even though but for one year, never can willingly abandon it. They

1. "An Address to the People of Virginia," 21 December 1798; in Elliott, *Debates in the Several State Conventions*, Volume IV, page 530.

2. Delos B. McKown, "Demythologizing Natural Human Rights," *The Humanist*, May/June 1989, page 34.

may be distressed in the midst of all their power; but they will never look to any thing but power for their relief.[3]

The situation in America indeed looks grim, but it is not hopeless. Beneath the din of endless campaigning, lobbying, and bowing and scraping to a system that never changes, and indeed is *incapable* of change, there remains a remedy waiting to be understood and put into practice. According to the U.S. Supreme Court in *Fleming v. Page*:

> The duty of allegiance is reciprocal to the duty of protection. When, therefore, a nation is unable to protect a portion of its territory from the superior force of an enemy, it loses its claim to the allegiance of those whom it fails to protect, and the conquered inhabitants pass under a temporary allegiance to the conqueror, and are bound by such laws, and such only, as he may choose to impose. The sovereignty of the nation which is thus unable to protect its territory is displaced, and that of the successful conqueror is substituted in its stead.
>
> The jurisdiction of the conqueror is complete. He may change the form of government and the laws at his pleasure, and may exercise every attribute of sovereignty. The conquered territory becomes a part of the domain of the conqueror, subject to the right of the nation to which it belonged to recapture it if they can. By reason of this right to recapture, the title of the conqueror is not perfect until confirmed by treaty of peace.... As long as he retains possession he is sovereign; and not the less sovereign because his sovereignty may not endure for ever.
>
> ...[B]y conquest and firm military occupation of a portion of an enemy's country, the sovereignty of the nation to which the conquered territory belongs is subverted, and the sovereignty of the conqueror is substituted in its place.... [A]lthough this sovereignty, until cession by treaty, is subject to be ousted by the enemy, and therefore does not give an indefeasible title for purposes of alienation, yet while it exists it is supreme, and confers jurisdiction without limit over the conquered territory, and the right to allegiance in return for protection.[4]

In the words of the 1880 *Institut de Droit International*: "A territory is considered to be occupied where, as the result of its invasion by an enemy's force, the state to which it belongs has ceased in fact to exercise its ordinary authority within it and the invading state is alone in a position to maintain order. The extent and duration of the occupation are determined by the limits of space and time within which this state of things exists."[5] Finally, William Birkhimer, the late authority on military government and martial law, wrote:

---

3. Edmund Burke, "A Letter to a Member of the National Assembly," *Further Reflections on the Revolution in France* (Indianapolis, Indiana: Liberty Fund, 1992), pages 33-35.

4. *Fleming v. Page* (1850), 50 U.S. 603.

5. *The Laws of War*, Oxford, September 1880.

The government of the conqueror being *de facto* and not *de jure* in character, it must always rest upon the fact of possession, which is adverse to the former sovereign, and therefore can never be inferred or presumed. Not only must the possession be actually acquired, but it must be maintained. The moment possession is lost the rights of military occupation are also lost. By the laws and usages of nations conquest is a valid title only while the victor maintains the exclusive possession of the conquered country.

The fundamental rule [is] that to render military government legal there must be an armed force in the territory occupied capable of enforcing its "adverse possession" against all disputants....

...[B]y the laws and usages of nations, conquest is a valid title while the victor maintains exclusive possession of the conquered country....

...[A]lthough acts done in a country by an invader cannot be nullified in so far as they have produced effects during the occupation, they become inoperative so soon as the legitimate government is restored....

As under military government the conqueror rules by virtue of the sword alone, his title extends no further and lasts no longer than his physical force excludes the enemy. While he thus rules he can do with property found in the territory as either inclination or policy dictates. That which he can seize, convert to his own use on the spot, sell to others, or carry away, he can make his own absolutely. But the rule of superior force marks the limitation of his right. When he ceases to exercise that force and retires from the country all rights he had acquired over immovable property at once cease. The ancient owner, if it has been disposed of, now may return to claim and re-possess what of real property belongs to him.[6]

As we have seen, two different theories were presented by Northern authorities regarding the political status of the Southern States in the 1860s. The first, as expressed by Lincoln in his first Inaugural Address and his 4 July 1861 address to Congress, was that the secession ordinances of these States were all null and void, and that each of them continued to be a State within the Union, albeit in a condition of insurrection. This view was also the basis for Salmon Chase's 1867 opinion in *Texas v. White*. The opposing theory, held by Thaddeus Stevens, Charles Sumner, and the other Radicals in Congress, was that the Southern States had indeed seceded from the Union and they therefore constituted a foreign power subject to conquest by the U.S. Government. Whereas the war between North and South was waged for four years on the assumption that Lincoln's theory was correct, the legislation of the Reconstruction period rested completely on the assumption that the Radical theory was correct. Reconstruction was therefore an open repudiation of the congressionally-declared purpose of the war and a complete break with the former constitutional Union. Not only were the people of the South deprived of their right of self-government, but the sovereignty of the Northern States was also destroyed as a result.

The entire modern American political system is inextricably connected to the Radical theory of conquest. As such, it cannot be republican in nature, but is instead a despotism

6. Birkhimer, *Military Government*, pages 77, 83, 195, 233.

forced upon the people against their will. The mere passage of time cannot make such a government lawful. Southern Presbyterian theologian, Robert Lewis Dabney, wrote:

>...[T]he pretended legislations of the Washington government, in organizing spurious State governments, contrary to the Constitution, within the territories of the Confederate States and without their consent, were all illegal and void. They rest, to this day, on no better basis than the right of conquest. But this is a ground which cannot be righteous or valid for a power which solemnly declares that "all just government rests upon the consent of the governed."

>...[T]he real overthrow, which the Northern people, in their lust of aggrandizement and fury, inflicted by force of arms, was not only of the Confederacy, but of the whole liberties of themselves and their children. ...[T]he equitable, Constitutional, and federal government created by the Fathers, has been annihilated, and is replaced by a consolidated democracy, which, under the name of a "Republic," is in fact a virtual oligarchy of demagogues and capitalists.

>...[T]he so-called "reconstruction measures" were the crowning and most violent usurpations of all. For the Washington government had declared all along, that there was no way under heaven by which a State could cease to be a member of the Union; that the States called Confederate had been in and under the Union during the whole time of their attempted secession, and at and after the end of the war.

>But these State governments, declared indestructible, were annihilated by the United States Congress two years after [the ending of hostilities], without any crime or offense of the States, or of a single person in them. While there was not a hand lifted against the United States, while the conquered population were submissively obeying all laws, even the illegal laws, the States were thrust out of the Union, every magistrate and citizen in them was disfranchised without trial or even indictment; and all were stripped of the inalienable rights of trial by jury and *habeas corpus*, and thrust under a bayonet government.

>No invasion of human right, as monstrous and sweeping as these, over so many millions of human beings, has ever before been perpetrated in time of peace, by any usurper, military emperor, or arbitrary conqueror. This crime, committed by a democracy, under universal suffrage, proves that this government of a popular majority, now dominant in place of the Constitution and the States, is capable of just as enormous outrages as any other despot.

>Of course, every clear mind sees, that if those views... are just, the current boasts as to the results of the war are precisely the reverse of truth. "That the war has, forever settled the question of unity, *etc*." Rather the war has forever unsettled the unity of the country, as well as every other institution. For, just as soon as any section feels again the pressure of a grievance and thinks of any power to escape it, that section will of course pronounce — what everybody knows to be true in fact — that the war of 1861-5, substituted a government of brute force for one of right and popular consent; that force, as everybody but robbers confesses, settles no question of morals, and grounds no claim of right; and that the domination of the Washington government has therefore always been illegal and invalid ever since the fraudulent "reconstruction," which any section has a right

to reject it, whenever strong enough to do so.[7]

The above assertion that Americans are not bound to recognize the Government in Washington, D.C. as legal and valid, and that they, as a people, even have the right to reject its authority, may sound strange to the modern ear. Some may even suggest that the subjection of our Southern forefathers to the military governments forced upon them somehow binds their posterity to the same subjection. Consider, in response, the following statements of Scottish theologian Samuel Rutherford:

> Conquest without the consent of the people is but royal robbery....
>
> ...[A] conquered kingdom is but *continuata injuria*, a continued robbery.... Now, in reason, we cannot think that a tyrannous and unjust domineering can be God's lawful mean of translating kingdoms; and, for the other part, the conqueror cannot domineer as king over the innocent, and especially the children not yet born....
>
> If the act of conquering be violent and unjust, it is no manifestation of God's regulating and approving will, and can no more prove a just title to a crown, because it is an act of divine providence, than Pilate and Herod's crucifying of the Lord of glory, which was an act of divine providence, flowing from the will and decree of divine providence (Acts ii.23; iv.28) is a manifestation that it was God's approving will, that they should kill Jesus Christ. Though the consent be some way over-awed, yet is it a sort of contract and covenant of loyal subjection made to the conqueror, and therefore sufficient to make the title just; otherwise, if the people never give their consent, the conqueror, domineering over them by violence, hath no just title to the crown....
>
> No lawful king may be dethroned, nor lawful kingdom dissolved.... Though conquerors extort consent and oath of loyalty, yet that maketh not over a royal right to the conqueror to be king over their posterity without their consent....
>
> What compelled people may do to redeem their lives, with loss of liberty, is nothing to the point; such a violent conqueror who will be a father and a husband to a people, against their will, is not their lawful king; and that they may sell the liberty of their posterity, not yet born, is utterly denied as unlawful... and the posterity may vindicate their own liberty given away unjustly, before they were born.[8]

Rutherford went on to state that "nature in a forced people, so soon as they can escape from a violent conqueror, maketh them a free people."[9] However, it cannot be stressed enough that this escape may only be achieved by the people acting as an organized political community, and not by private individuals acting on their own initiative. The former is what

7. Robert Lewis Dabney, "The Rise and Fall of the Confederate Government," in *The Southern Presbyterian Review*, Volume XXXII, Number 2 (April 1882), page 290.

8. Samuel Rutherford, *Lex, Rex* (Harrisonburg, Virginia: Sprinkle Publications [1644], 1982), pages 8, 48-50, 66.

9. Rutherford, *ibid.*, page 67.

has historically been known as the "right of revolution,"[10] while the latter is mere anarchy and can only lead to a tightening of the conqueror's grip on his victims. This fact was demonstrated by the Government's reaction to the bombing of the Murrah Federal Building in Oklahoma City in 1995 and by the terrorist attacks on the World Trade Center in New York city in 2001. What is needed is an awakening of the American people to what has been done to their country under the guise of "necessity," and their united demand that constitutional government be restored, first in the several States, and then in Washington, D.C.

Apart from the direct intervention of Divine Providence, the road to recovery will be a long and arduous one, but we are nevertheless duty-bound to at least turn our backs on the attractions of the American Vanity Fair and commence the journey. Should it please God to bless our efforts, we can begin to reclaim our respective States from our imperial occupier if we will only educate ourselves and our children regarding the basis of our own oppression and cease to partake of the benefits by which it lulls to sleep the indolent. Not only does the *de facto* military government which occupies the seat of authority in the District of Columbia have "the right to allegiance in return for protection," but "those subjected to its authority and who enjoy its benefits are bound, if need be, to support it to the utmost of their ability."[11] Sadly, the majority of Americans, both in the North *and* in the South, are more than happy to pledge such allegiance in exchange for security from "the cradle to the grave." There must be a mass exodus from the Executive "plantation" if we ever expect to see things change for the better in our lifetimes. The alternative is a slavery beyond remedy for generations to come.

The Cause of the South is the Cause of All

A story is told of one woman inquiring of Benjamin Franklin the nature of the new government created that summer of 1787 in Philadelphia. "We have given you a republic," he answered, adding, "if you can keep it." We have seen that the system of government established under the Constitution did not work; a mere document simply could not act as a barrier to the natural depravity of the human heart. Albert Taylor Bledsoe wrote, "The fathers, in one word, did not begin to foresee the weakness, the folly, the madness, and the wickedness of their descendants. Hence, their sublime attempt to 'establish justice, ensure domestic tranquility, promote the general welfare, and secure the blessings of liberty to their posterity,' proved an awful failure."[12] Indeed, the new system of government fulfilled to the letter the many prognostications made against it by the Anti-Federalists. The "glorious Union" lasted but for a mere seventy-two years before its light was extinguished by a military

---

10. See Appendix Seven: "Civil Government and the Right of Revolution."

11. Birkhimer, *Military Government*, page 66.

12. Bledsoe, *Is Davis a Traitor?*, page 255.

despotism perhaps more monstrous than has existed in the history of the world since the darkest days of the Roman Empire under Nero Caesar.

We, the people of America, are, without a doubt, at a crossroads. We may continue to live our lives as if nothing is seriously amiss in this country, or we may heed the many voices of the past which echo throughout the corridors of time with the warning that a new dark age of unspeakable horrors may be on the horizon for our children or our grandchildren. History provides us with innumerable illustrations of fallen nations which we cannot afford to ignore — peoples once free who slept the deadly sleep of complacency as their enemies crept in among them to destroy them. Since even the divinely-chosen nation of Israel is no more, let us not fool ourselves any longer that we have been somehow blessed with immunity to such a calamity of extinction. Those who now hold us in chains have only their own selfish interests to prevent their implementing our destruction immediately; today, they stroke the heads of their captives in feigned benevolence because it so suits their momentary purposes, but it is only a matter of time before the iron fist will be pulled from its velvet glove.

It has been stated, and correctly so, that "Imperialists always look on the people as sheep, to be deceived and driven."[13] However, the blame for our condition lies not with our oppressors, but with ourselves, for it is we who have allowed the ruination of the constitutional Republic at times when popular opinion, and fidelity of our elected representatives to their oath of office, could have prevented it.[14] Furthermore, "To commit an act, and not to prohibit one when in your power, is the same thing; and he who does not prohibit or forbid when he can prevent it is in fault, or does the same thing as ordering it to be done."[15] We, the

---

13. Edmonds, *Facts and Falsehoods*, page 157.

14. In his report, *National Emergency Powers*, Harold Relyea wrote:

> In the case of Lincoln, the opinion of scholars and experts is "that neither Congress nor the Supreme Court exercised any effective restraint upon the President." The emergency actions of the Chief Executive were either unchallenged or approved by Congress, and were either accepted or, because of almost no opportunity to render judgment, went largely without notice by the Supreme Court. The President made a quick response to the emergency at hand, a response which Congress or the courts might have rejected in law, but which, nonetheless, had been made in fact and with some degree of popular approval. Similar controversy would arise concerning the emergency actions of Presidents Woodrow Wilson and Franklin D. Roosevelt. Both men exercised extensive emergency powers with regard to world hostilities, and Roosevelt also used emergency authority to deal with the Great Depression. Their emergency actions, however, were largely supported by statutory delegations and a high degree of approval on the part of both Congress and the public (pages 6-7).

15. *Coke's Institutes: Coke on Magna Charta and Old Acts*, 146,308.

descendants of a once proud[16] and free people, no longer know how to assume the awesome responsibility of self-government and have contented ourselves to, as Patrick Henry so eloquently stated, "lie supinely on our backs, hugging the delusive phantom of hope, until our enemies... have bound us hand and foot." As Confederate Vice-President Alexander Hamilton Stephens so long ago declared, "There will come a time when the cry will ring out across this land, 'The cause of the South is the cause of us all!'"[17] That time has now come.

---

16. The common understanding of the word "proud" as "of great dignity, honored, spirited, brave, and virtuous" is that which is meant in this context.

17. Stephens, *Constitutional View of the War Between the States*, Volume II, page 666.

APPENDICES

APPENDIX ONE
The Nature of Civil Liberty
by Albert Taylor Bledsoe

Few subjects, if any, more forcibly demand our attention, by their intrinsic grandeur and importance, than the great doctrine of human liberty. Correct views concerning this are, indeed, so intimately connected with the most profound interests, as well as with the most exalted aspirations, of the human race, that any material departure therefrom must be fraught with evil to the living, as well as to millions yet unborn. They are so inseparably interwoven with all that is great and good and glorious in the destiny of man, that whosoever aims to form or to propagate such views should proceed with the utmost care, and, laying aside all prejudice and passion, be guided by the voice of reason alone.

Hence it is to be regretted — deeply regretted — that the doctrine of liberty has so often been discussed with so little apparent care, with so little moral earnestness, with so little read energetic searching and longing after truth. Though its transcendent importance demands the best exertion of all our powers, yet has it been, for the most part, a theme for passionate declamation, rather than of severe analysis or of protracted and patient investigation. In the warm praises of the philosopher, no less than in the glowing inspirations of the poet, it often stands before us as a vague and ill-defined *something* which all men are required to worship, but which no man is bound to understand. It would seem, indeed, as if it were a mighty something not to be clearly seen, but only to be deeply felt. And felt it has been, too, by the ignorant as well as by the learned, by the simple as well as by the wise: felt as a fire in the blood, as a fever in the brain, and as a phantom in the imagination, rather than as a form of light and beauty in the intelligence. How often have the powers of darkness surrounded its throne, and desolation marked its path! How often from the altars of this *unknown idol* has the blood of human victims streamed! Even here, in this glorious land of ours, how often do the *too-religious* Americans seem to become deaf to the most appalling lessons of the past, while engaged in the frantic worship of this their tutelary deity! At this very moment, the highly-favored land in which we live is convulsed from its centre to its circumference by the agitations of these pious devotees of freedom; and how long ere scenes like those which called forth the celebrated exclamation of Madame Roland — "O Liberty, what crimes are perpetuated in thy name!" — may be enacted among us, it is not possible for human sagacity or foresight to determine.

If no one would talk about liberty except those who had taken the pains to understand it, then would a perfect calm be restored, and peace once more bless a happy people. But there are so many who imagine they understand liberty as Falstaff knew the true prince, namely, by instinct, that all hope of such a consummation must be deferred until it may be shown that their instinct is a blind guide, and its oracles are false. Hence the necessity of a close study and of a clear analysis of the nature and conditions of civil liberty, in order to a distinct delineation of the great idol, which all men are so ready to worship, but which so few are willing to take the pains to understand. In the prosecution of such an inquiry, we intend to consult neither the pecuniary interests of the South nor the prejudices of the North; but calmly and immovably proceed to discuss, upon purely scientific principles, this great problem of our social existence and national prosperity, upon the solution of which the hopes and destinies of mankind in no inconsiderable measure depend. We intend no appeal to passion or to sordid interest, but only to the reason of the wise and good. And if justice, or mercy, or truth, be found at war with the institution of slavery, then, in the name of God, let slavery perish. But however guilty, still let it be tried, condemned, and executed according to law, and not extinguished by a despotic and lawless power more terrific than itself.

"Civil liberty," says Blackstone, "is no other than natural liberty so far restrained as is necessary and expedient for the general advantage." This definition seems to have been borrowed from Locke, who says that, when a man enters into civil society, "he is to part with so much of his natural liberty, in providing for himself, as the good, prosperity, and safety of the society shall require." So, likewise, say Paley, Berlamaqui, Rutherforth, and a host of others. Indeed, among jurists and philosophers, such seems to be the commonly-received definition of civil liberty. It seems to have become a political maxim that civil liberty is no other than a certain portion of our natural liberty, which has been carved therefrom, and secured to us by the protection of the laws.

But is this a sound maxim? Has it been deduced from the nature of things, or is it merely a plausible show of words? Is it truth — solid and imperishable truth — or merely one of those fair semblances of truth, which, through the too hasty sanction of great names, have obtained a currency among men? The question is not what Blackstone, or Locke, or Paley may have thought, but what is truth? Let us examine this point, then, in order that our decision may be founded, not upon the authority of man, but, if possible, in the wisdom of God.

Before we can determine whether such be the origin of civil liberty, we must first ascertain the character of that natural liberty out of which it is supposed to be reserved. What, then, is natural liberty? What is the nature of the material out of which our civil liberty is supposed to be fashioned by the art of the political sculptor? It is thus defined by Locke: "To understand political power right, and derive it from its original, we must consider what state all men are naturally in; and that is a state of perfect freedom to order their actions and dispose of their possessions and persons as they think fit, *within the bounds of the law of nature*, without asking leave or depending upon the will of any other man."

In perfect accordance with this definition, Blackstone says: "This natural liberty consists in a power of acting as one thinks fit, without any restraint or control, unless by the laws of nature, being a right inherent in us by birth, and one of the gifts of God to man at his creation, when he endowed him with the faculty of free-will."

Such, according to Locke and Blackstone, is that natural liberty, which is limited and abridged, as they suppose, when we enter into the bonds of civil society.

Now mark its features: it is the gift of God to man at his creation; that by which he is distinguished from the lower animals and raised to the rank of moral and accountable beings. Shall we sacrifice this divine gift, then, in order to secure the blessings of civil society? Shall we abridge or mutilate the image of God, stamped upon the soul at its creation, by which we are capable of knowing and obeying his law, in order to secure the aid and protection of man? Shall we barter away any portion of this our glorious birthright for any poor boon of man's devising? Yes, we are told — and why? Because, says Blackstone, "Legal obedience and conformity is infinitely more valuable than *the wild and savage liberty which is sacrificed to obtain it.*"

But how is this? *Now* this natural liberty is a thing of light, and *now* it is a power of darkness. Now it is the gift of God, that moves within a sphere of light, and breathes an atmosphere of love; and anon, it is a wild and savage thing that carries terror in its train. It would be an angel of light, if it were not a power of darkness; and it would be a power of darkness, if it were not an angel of light. But as it is, it is both by turns, and neither long, but runs through its Protean changes, according to the exigencies of the flowing discourse of the learned author. Surely such inconsistency, so glaring and so portentous, and all exhibited on one and the same page, is no evidence that the genius of the great commentator was as steady and profound as it was elegant and classical.

The source of this vacillation is obvious. With Locke, he defines natural liberty to be a power of acting as one thinks fit, *within the limits prescribed by the law of nature*; but he soon loses sight of this all-important limitation, from which natural liberty derives its form and beauty. Hence it becomes in his mind a power to act as one pleases, without the restraint or control of any law whatever, either human or divine. The sovereign will and pleasure of the individual becomes the only rule of conduct, and lawless anarchy the condition which it legitimates. Thus, having loosed the bonds and marred the beauty of natural liberty, he was prepared to see it, now become so "wild and savage," offered up as a sacrifice on the altar of civil liberty.

This, too, was the great fundamental error of Hobbes. What Blackstone thus did through inadvertency, was knowingly and designedly done by the philosopher of

Malmesbury. In a state of nature, says he, all men have a right to do as they please. Each individual may set up a right to all things, and consequently to the same things. In other words, in such a state there is no law, except that of force. The strong arm of power is the supreme arbiter of all things. Robbery and outrage and murder are as lawful as their opposites. That is to say, there is no such thing as a law of nature; and consequently all things are, in a state of nature, equally allowable. Thus it was that Hobbes delighted to legitimate the horrors of a state of nature, as it is called, in order that mankind might, without a feeling of indignation or regret, see the wild and ferocious liberty of such a state sacrificed to despotic power. Thus it was that he endeavoured to recommend the "Leviathan," by contrasting it with the huger monster called Natural Liberty.

This view of the state of nature, by which all law and the great Fountain of all law are shut out of the world, was perfectly agreeable to the atheistical philosophy of Hobbes. From one who had extinguished the light of nature, and given dominion to the powers of darkness, no better could have been expected; but is it not deplorable that a Christian jurist should, even for a moment, have forgotten the great central light of his own system, and drawn his arguments from such an abyss of darkness?

Blackstone has thus lost sight of truth, not only in regard to his general propositions, but also in regard to particular instances. "The law," says he, "which restrains a man from doing mischief to his fellow-citizens diminishes the natural liberty of mankind." Now, is this true? The doing of mischief is contrary to the law of nature, and hence, according to the definition of Blackstone himself, the perpetration of it is not an exercise of any natural right. As no man possesses a natural right to do mischief, so the law which forbids it does not diminish the natural liberty of mankind. The law which forbids mischief is a restraint not upon the *natural liberty*, but upon the *natural tyranny*, of man.

Blackstone is by no means alone in the error to which we have alluded. By one of the clearest thinkers and most beautiful writers of the present age, it is argued, "that as government implies restraint, it is evident we give up a certain portion of our liberty by entering into it." This argument would be valid, no doubt, if there was nothing in the world beside liberty to be restrained; but the evil passions of men, from which proceed so many frightful tyrannies and wrongs, are not to be identified with their rights or liberties. As government implies restraint, it is evident that something is restrained when we enter into it; but it does not follow that this something must be our natural liberty. The argument in question proceeds on the notion that government can restrain nothing, unless it restrain the natural liberty of mankind; whereas, we have seen, the law which forbids the perpetration of mischief, or any other wrong, is a restriction, not upon the *liberty*, but upon the *tyranny*, of the human will. It sets a bound a limit, not to any right conferred on us by the Author of nature, but upon the evil thoughts and deeds of which we are the sole and exclusive originators. Such a law, indeed, so far from restraining the natural liberty of man, recognises his natural rights, and secures his freedom, by protecting the weak against the injustice and oppression of the strong.

The way in which these authors show that natural liberty is, and of right ought to be, abridged by the laws of society, is, by identifying this natural freedom, not with a power to act as God wills, but with a power in conformity with our own sovereign will and pleasure. The same thing is expressly done by Paley. "To do what we will," says he, "is natural liberty." Starting from this definition, it is no wonder that he should have supposed that natural liberty is restrained by civil government. In like manner, Burke first says, "That the effect of liberty to individuals is, *that they may do what they please;*" and then concludes, that in order to "secure some liberty," we make "a surrender in trust of the whole of it." Thus the natural rights of mankind are first caricatured, and then sacrificed.

If there be no God, if there be no difference between right and wrong, if there be no moral law in the universe, then indeed would men possess a natural right to do mischief or to act as they please. Then indeed should we be fettered by no law in a state of nature, and liberty therein would be coextensive with power. Right would give place to might, and the least restraint, even from the best laws, would impair our natural freedom. But we subscribe to no such philosophy. That learned authors, that distinguished jurists, that celebrated philosophers, that pious divines, should thus deliberately include the enjoyment of our natural rights and the indulgence of our evil passions in one and the same definition of liberty, is, it seems to us, matter of the most profound astonishment and regret. It is to confound the source of all tyranny with the fountain of all freedom. It is to put darkness for light, and light for darkness. And it is to inflame the minds of men with the idea that they are struggling and contending for liberty, when, in reality, they may be only struggling and contending for the gratification of their malignant passions. Such an offence against all clear thinking, such an outrage against all sound political ethics, becomes the more amazing when we reflect on the greatness of the authors by whom it is committed, and the stupendous magnitude of the interests involved in their discussions.

Should we, then, exhibit the fundamental law of society, and the natural liberty of mankind, as antagonistic principles? Is not this the way to prepare the human mind, at all times so passionately, not to say so madly, fond of freedom, for a repetition of those tremendous conflicts and struggles beneath which the foundations of society have so often trembled, and some of its best institutions been laid in the dust? In one word, is it not high time to raise the inquiry, Whether there be, in reality, any such opposition as is usually supposed to exist between the law of the land and the natural rights of mankind? Whether such opposition be real or imaginary? Whether it exists in the nature of things, or only in the imagination of political theorists?

By the two great leaders of opposite schools, Locke and Burke, it is contended that when we enter into society the natural right of self-defence is surrendered to the government. If any natural right, then, be limited or abridged by the laws of society, we may suppose the right of self-defence to be so; for this is the instance which is always selected to illustrate and confirm the reality of such a surrender of our natural liberty. It has, indeed, become a sort of maxim, that when we put on the bonds of civil society, we give up the natural right of self-defence.

But what does this maxim mean? Does it mean that we transfer the right to repel force by force? If so, the proposition is not true; for this right is as fully possessed by every individual after he has entered into society as it could have been in a state of nature. If he is assailed, or threatened with immediate personal danger, the law of the land does not require him to wait upon the strong but slow arm of government for protection. On the contrary, it permits him to protect himself, to repel force by force, in so far as this may be necessary to guard against injury to himself; and the law of nature allows no more. Indeed, if there be any difference, the law of the land allows a man to go farther in the defence of self than he is permitted to go by the law of God. Hence, in this sense, the maxim under consideration is not true; and no man's natural liberty is abridged by the State.

Does this maxim mean, then, that in a state of nature every man has a right to redress his own wrongs by the *subsequent* punishment of the offender, which right the citizen has transferred to the government? It is clear that this must be the meaning, if it have any correct meaning at all. But neither in this sense is the maxim or proposition true. The right to punish an offender must rest upon the one or the other of two grounds: either upon the ground that the offender deserves punishment, or that his punishment is necessary to prevent similar offences. Now, upon neither of these grounds has any man, even in a state of nature, the right to punish an offence committed against himself.

First, he has no right to punish such an offence on the ground that it deserves punishment. No man has, or ever had, the right to wield the awful attribute of retributive justice; that is, to inflict so much pain for so much guilt or moral turpitude. This is the prerogative of God alone. To his eye, all secrets are known, and all degrees of guilt perfectly apparent; and to him alone belongs the vengeance which is due for moral ill-desert. His law extends over the state of nature as well as over the state of civil society, and calls all men to account for their evil deeds. It is evident that, in so far as the intrinsic demerit of actions is concerned, it makes no difference whether they be punished here or hereafter. And besides, if the individual has possessed such a right in a state of nature, he has not transferred it to society; for society neither has nor claims any such right. Blackstone but utters the voice of the law when he says, "The end or final cause of human punishment is not by way of atonement or expiation, for that must be left to the just determination of the supreme Being, but as a precaution against future offences of the same kind."

The exercise of retributive justice belongs exclusively to the infallible Ruler of the world, and not to frail, erring man, who himself so greatly stands in need of mercy. Hence, the right to punish a transgressor on the ground that such punishment is deserved, has not been transferred from the individual to civil society: first, because he had no such natural right to transfer; and, secondly, because society possesses no such right.

In the second place, if we consider the other ground of punishment, it will likewise appear that the right to punish never belonged to the individual, and consequently could not have been transferred by him to society. For, by the law of nature, the individual has no right to punish an offence against himself *in order to prevent future offences of the same kind*. If the object of human punishment be, as indeed it is, to prevent the commission of crime, by holding up examples of terror to evil-doers, then it is evidently no more the natural right of the party injured to redress the wrong, than it is the right of others. All men are interested in the prevention of wrongs, and hence all men should united to redress them. All men are endowed by their Creator with a sense of justice, in order to impel them to secure its claims, and throw the shield of its protection around the weak and oppressed.

The prevention of wrong, then, is clearly the natural duty, and consequently the natural right, of all men.

This duty should be discharged by others, rather than by the party aggrieved. For it is contrary to the law of nature itself, as both Locke and Burke agree, that any man should be "judge in his own case;" that any man should, by an *ex post facto* decision, determine the amount of punishment due to his enemy, and proceed to inflict it upon him. Such a course, indeed, so far from preventing offences, would inevitably promote them; instead of redressing injuries, would only add wrong to wrong; and instead of introducing order, would only make confusion worse confounded, and turn the moral world upside down.

On no ground, then, upon which the right to punish may be conceived to rest, does it appear that it was ever possessed, or could ever have been possessed, by the individual. And if the individual never possessed such a right, it is clear that he has never transferred it to society. Hence, this view of the origin of government, however plausible at first sight, or however generally received, has no real foundation in the nature of things. It is purely a creature of the imagination of theorists; one of the phantoms of that manifold, monstrous, phantom deity called Liberty, which has been so often invoked by the *pseudo* philanthropists and reckless reformers of the present day to subvert not only the law of capital punishment, but also other institutions and laws which have received the sanction of both God and man.

The simple truth is, that we are all bound by the law of nature and the law of God to love our neighbor as ourselves. Hence it is the duty of every man, in a state of nature, to do all in his power to protect the rights and promote the interests of his fellow-men. It is the duty of all men to consult together, and concert measures for the general good. Right here it is, then, that the law of man, the constitution of civil society, comes into contact with the law of God and rests upon it. Thus, civil society arises, not from a surrender of individual rights, but from a right originally possessed by all; nay, from a solemn duty originally imposed upon all by God himself — a duty which must be performed, whether the individual gives his consent or not. The very law of nature itself requires, as we have seen, not only the punishment of the offender, but also that he be punished according to the pre-established law, and by the decision of an impartial tribunal. And in the enactment of such law, as well as in the administration, the collective wisdom of society, or its agents, moves in obedience to the law of God, and not in pursuance of rights derived from the individual.

In the foregoing discussion we have, in conformity to the custom of others, used the terms *rights* and *liberty* as words of precisely the same import. But, instead of being convertible terms, there seems to be a very clear difference in their significance. If a man be taken, for example, and without cause thrown into prison, this deprives him of his *liberty*, but not of his *right*, to go where he pleases. The right still exists; and his not being allowed to enjoy this right, is precisely what constitutes the oppression in the case supposed. If there were no right still subsisting, then there would be no oppression. Hence, as the *right* exists, while the *liberty* is extinguished, it is evident they are distinct from each other. The liberty of a man in such a case, as in all others, would consist in an opportunity to enjoy his right, or in a state in which it might be enjoyed if he so pleased.

This distinction between rights and liberty is all-important to a clear and satisfactory discussion of the doctrine of human freedom. The great champions of that freedom, from a Locke down to a Hall, firmly and passionately grasping the natural rights of man, and confounding these with his liberty, have looked upon society as the restrainer, and not as the author, of that liberty. On the other hand, the great advocates of despotic power, from a Hobbes down to a Whewell, seeing that there can be no genuine liberty — that is, no secure enjoyment of one's rights — in a state of nature, have ascribed, not only our liberty, but all our existing rights also, to the State.

But the error of Locke is a noble and generous sentiment when compared with the odious dogma of Hobbes and Whewell. These learned authors contend that we derive all our existing rights from society. Do we, then, live and move and breathe and think and worship God only by rights derived from the State? No, certainly. We have these rights from a higher source. God gave them, and all the powers of earth combined cannot take them away. But as for our liberty, this we freely own is, for the most part, due to the sacred bonds of civil society. Let us render unto Caesar the things that are Caesar's, and unto God the things that are God's.

Herein, then, consists the true relation between the *natural* and the *social* states. Civil society does not abridge our natural rights, but secures and protects them. She does not assume our right of self-defence — she simply discharges the duty imposed by God to defend us. The original right is in those who compose the body politic, and not in any individual. Hence, civil society does not impair our natural liberty, as actually existing in a state of nature, or as it might therein exist; for, in such a state, there would be no real liberty, no real enjoyment of natural rights.

Mr. Locke, as we have seen, defines the state of nature to be one of "perfect freedom." Why then should we leave it? Says he:

> If man, in the state of nature, be so free, why will he part with his freedom? To which it is obvious to answer, that though, in the state of nature, he hath such a right, *yet the enjoyment of it is very uncertain*, and constantly exposed to the invasion of others; for all being kings as much as he, every man his equal, and the greater part not strict observers of equity and justice, the enjoyment of the property he has in this state is very unsafe, very insecure. This makes him willing to quit a condition which, however free, is full of fears and continual dangers; and it is not without reason that he seeks out, and is willing to join in society with, others who are already united, or have a mind to unite, for the mutual preservation of their lives, liberties and estates, which I call by the general name property.

What! Can that be a state of perfect freedom which is subject to fears and perpetual dangers? In one word, can a reign of terror be the reign of liberty? It is evident, we think, that

Locke has been betrayed into no little inaccuracy and confusion of thought from not having distinguished between rights and liberty.

The truth seems to be that, in a state of nature, we would possess rights, but we could not enjoy them. That is to say, notwithstanding all our rights, we should be destitute of freedom or liberty. Society interposes the strong arm of the law to protect our rights, to secure us in the enjoyment of them. She delivers us from the alarms, the dangers, and the violence of the natural state. Hence, under God, she is the mother of our peace and joy, by whose sovereign rule anarchy is abolished and liberty established. Liberty and social law can never be dissevered. Liberty, robed in law, and radiant with love, is one of the best gifts of God to man. But liberty, despoiled of law, is a wild, dark, fierce spirit of licentiousness, which tends "to uproar the universal peace."

Hence it is a frightful error to regard the civil state or government as antagonistic to the natural liberty of mankind; for this is, indeed, the author of the very liberty we enjoy. Good government it is that restrains the elements of tyranny and oppression, and introduces liberty into the world. Good government it is that shuts out the reign of anarchy, and secures the dominion of equity and goodness. He who would spurn the restraints of law, then, by which pride, and envy, and hatred, and malice, ambition, and revenge, are kept within the sacred bounds of eternal justice — he, we say, is not the friend of human liberty. He would open the flood-gates of tyranny and oppression; he would mar the harmony and extinguish the light of the world. Let no such man be trusted.

If the foregoing remarks be just, it would follow that the state of nature, as it is called, would be one of the most unnatural states in the world. We may conceive it to exist, for the sake of illustration or argument; but if it should actually exist, it would be at war with the law of nature itself. For this requires, as we have seen, that men should unite together, and frame such laws as the general good demands.

Not only the law, but the very necessities of nature, enjoin the institution of civil government. God himself has thus laid the foundations of civil society deep in the nature of man. It is an ordinance of heaven, which no human decree can reverse or annul. It is not a thing of compacts, bound together by promises and paper, but is itself a law of nature as irreversible as any other. Compacts may give it one form or another, but in one form or another it must exist. It is no accidental or artificial thing, which may be made or unmade, which may be set up or pulled down, at the mere will and pleasure of man. It is a decree of God; the spontaneous and irresistible working of that nature, which, in all climates, through all ages, and under all circumstances, manifests itself in social organizations.

Much has been said about inherent and inalienable rights, which is either unintelligible or rests upon no solid foundation. "The inalienable rights of men" is a phrase often brandished by certain reformers, who aim to bring about "the immediate abolition of slavery." Yet, in the light of the foregoing discussion, it may be clearly shown that the doctrine of inalienable rights, if properly handled, will not touch the institution of slavery.

An inalienable right is either one which the possessor of it himself cannot alienate or transfer, or it is one which society has not the power to take from him. According to the import of the terms, the first would seem to be what is meant by an inalienable right; but in this sense it is not pretended that the right to either life or liberty has been transferred to society or alienated to the individual. And if, as we have endeavored to show, the right, or power, or authority of society is not derived from a transfer of individual rights, then it is clear that neither the right to life nor liberty is transferred to society. That is, if no rights are transferred, than these particular rights are still untransferred, and, if you please, untransferable. Be it conceded, then, that the individual has never transferred his right to life or liberty to society.

But it is not in the above sense that the abolitionist uses the expression, *inalienable rights*. According to his view, an inalienable right is one of which society itself cannot, without doing wrong, deprive the individual, or deny the enjoyment of it to him. This is evidently his meaning; for he complains of the injustice of society, or civil government, in depriving a certain portion of its subjects of civil freedom, and consigning them to a state of servitude. "Such an act," says he, "is wrong, because it is a violation of the inalienable rights of all men." But let us see if his complaint be just or well founded.

It is pretended by no one that society has the right to deprive any subject of either life or liberty, *without good and sufficient cause or reason*. On the contrary, it is on all hands agreed that it is only for good and sufficient reasons that society can deprive any portion of its subjects of either life or liberty. Nor can it be denied, on the other side, that a man may be deprived of either, or both, by a preordained law, in case there be a good and sufficient reason for the enactment of such law. For the crime of murder, the law of the land deprives the criminal of life: *a fortiori*, might it deprive him of liberty. In the infliction of such a penalty, the law seeks, as we have seen, not to deal out so much pain for so much guilt, nor even to deal out pain for guilt at all, but simply to protect the members of society, and *secure the general good*. The general good is the sole and sufficient consideration which justifies the state in taking either the life or the liberty of its subjects.

Hence, if we would determine in any case whether society is justified in depriving any of its members of civil freedom by law, we must first ascertain whether the general good demands the enactment of such a law. If it does, then such a law is just and good — as perfectly just and good as any other law which, for the same reason or on the same ground, takes away the life or liberty of its subjects. All this talk about the inalienable rights of men may have a very admirable meaning, if one will only be at the pains to search it out; but is it not evident that, when searched to the bottom, it has just nothing at all to do with the great question of slavery?

This great problem, as we have seen, is to be decided, not by an appeal to the inalienable rights of men, but simply and solely by a reference to the general good. It is to be decided, not by the aid of abstractions alone; a little good sense and *practical sagacity* should be allowed to assist in its determination. There are inalienable rights, we admit — inalienable both because the individual cannot transfer them, and because society can never rightfully deprive any man of their enjoyment. But life and liberty are *not* "among these." There are inalienable rights, we admit, but then such abstractions are the edge-tools of political science, with which it is dangerous for either men or children to play. They may inflict deep wounds on the cause of humanity; they can throw no light on the great problem of slavery.

One thing seems to be clear and fixed; and that is, that the rights of the individual are subordinate to those of the community. *An inalienable right is a right coupled with a duty; a duty with which no other obligation can interfere.* But, as we have seen, it is the *duty*, and consequently, the *right*, of society to make such laws as the general good demands. This inalienable right is conferred, and its exercise enjoined, by the Creator and Governor of the universe. All individual rights are subordinate to this inherent, universal, and inalienable right. It should be observed, however, that in the exercise of this paramount right, this supreme authority, no society possesses the power to contravene the principles of justice. In other words, it should be observed that no unjust law can ever promote the public good. Every law, then, which is not unjust, and which the public good demands, should be enacted by society.

But we have already seen and shall still more fully see, that the law which ordains slavery is not unjust in itself, or, in other words, that it interferes with none of the inalienable rights of man. Hence, if it be shown that the public good, and especially the good of the slave, demands such a law, then the question of slavery will be settled.

In conclusion, we shall merely add that if the foregoing remarks be just, it follows that the great problem of political philosophy is not precisely such as it is often taken to be by statesmen and historians. This problem, according to Mackintosh and Macaulay, consists in finding such an adjustment of the antagonistic principles of public order and private liberty, that neither shall overthrow or subvert the other, but each be confined within its own appropriate limits. Whereas, if we are not mistaken, these are not *antagonistic*, but *co-ordinate*, principles. The very law which institutes public order is that which introduces private liberty, since no secure enjoyment of one's rights can exist where public order is not maintained. And, on the other hand, unless private liberty be introduced, public order cannot be maintained, or at least such public order as should be established; for, if there be not private liberty, if there be no secure enjoyment of one's rights, then the highest and purest elements of our nature would have to be extinguished, or else exist in perpetual conflict with the surrounding despotism. As license is not liberty, so despotism is not order, nor even friendly to that enlightened, wholesome order, by which the good of the public and the individual are at the same time introduced and secured. In other words, what is taken from the one of these principles is not given to the other; on the contrary, every additional element of strength and beauty which is imparted to the one is an accession of strength and beauty to the other. Private liberty, indeed, lives and moves and has its very being in the bosom of public order. On the other hand, that public order alone which cherishes the true liberty of the individual is strong in the approbation of God and in the moral sentiments of mankind. All else is weakness, and death, and decay.

The true problem, then, is, not how the conflicting claims of these two principles may be adjusted, (for there is no conflict between them,) but how a real public order, whose claims are identical with those of private liberty, may be introduced and maintained. The practical solution of this problem, for the heterogeneous population of the South imperatively demands the institution of slavery; and that without such an institution it would be impossible to maintain either a sound public order or a decent private liberty. The very laws or institution which is supposed by fanatical declaimers to shut out liberty from the Negro race among us, really shuts out the most frightful *license* and disorder from society. In one word, we shall endeavor to show that in preaching up liberty *to and for* the slaves of the South, the abolitionist is "casting pearls before swine," that can neither comprehend the nature, nor enjoy the blessings, of the freedom which is so officiously thrust upon them. And if the Negro race should be moved by their fiery appeals, it would only be to rend and tear in pieces the fair fabric of American liberty, which, with all its shortcomings and defects, is by far the most beautiful ever yet conceived or constructed by the genius of man.

APPENDIX TWO
Lincoln and Democracy
by Paul S. Whitcomb

Nothing so intrigues the mind of the people of the Northern States of the American Republic as the personality of Abraham Lincoln and the imperial American Union. For sixty-two years the crescendo of laudation of Lincoln has been steadily rising, and the end is not yet. For Lincoln was the central figure and the dominating personality in one of the greatest wars of history and, in spite of all the theories of democracy, nothing so appeals to the emotions of men, which are the well-springs of eulogy, as martial and imperial glory. People are not given to repudiating the wars they wage or those who lead them into war. Lincoln, himself, was retired from Congress for eight years because of his opposition to the Mexican War.

It is an interesting question as to what Lincoln's place in history would have been if there had been no Civil War with its lurid glow to silhouette his eccentric personality for future generations. At the time of his election to the Presidency he was scarcely more than a local character. He had served in Congress without rising above mediocrity. He had played fast and loose with the questions of slavery and secession without contributing anything original or constructive to the discussion, and what he said only served to further agitate the South and to so compromise his own public position as to make secession inevitable when the Black Republicans came into power.

He has been called a great thinker, but his attitude toward both slavery and secession was at once doctrinaire and the result of mechanistic logic which failed to recognize the distinction between the laws of physical science and the laws of human action. With regard to the slaves he appealed from their legal status to the "higher" law, but with regard to secession and the rights of the free and highly civilized White people of the South he argued their rights on the basis of those maxims of despotism which were invented for the express purpose of denying to the people their rightful liberties. He argued that the principles of the Declaration of Independence applied to the Negro but denied that they applied to the free White inhabitants of the States in whose favor they were originally promulgated. He failed to discern that the independence of the slave and the independence of the States involved the same fundamental principle, that the right of secession was absolute and unqualified and no more required oppressive acts to justify it than did the right of the slave to secede from his master. He failed to see that those same class of arguments which denied freedom to the South also denied freedom to all men "and undermined the very foundation of free society."

The indiscriminate and uncritical eulogies which have been heaped upon Lincoln have been pronounced in the face of all but the most superficial facts and as though all the rest of the world was composed of brutes, knaves and fools. There is no evidence that Lincoln was any more honest, kind, accommodating or sagacious than the ordinary run of men. His waging of the Civil War was the very antithesis of common sense and statesmanship. There was no catastrophe potential in secession that in any way justified the waging of the war, viewed simply as a matter of State policy, without reference to the moral and human aspect of the war. It was one of the most colossal bankruptcies of common sense and humane statesmanship known to modern history. As the situation stood in 1860, it were better for the North and the South both that they should separate. The prosperity which followed in the wake of the Civil War was not due to keeping the South in the Union but to the development of the West. But even if it was, it is a Prussian, and not an American, doctrine that war is a legitimate agent of national progress, that the end justifies the means. We have no right to do evil that good may abound.

Lincoln has been acclaimed the great democrat,[1] yet the greatest act of his career was the very antithesis of democracy. Washington was infinitely a greater statesman and a greater democrat. Robert E. Lee was greater in all around character. It has been too readily assumed that lowliness of birth is evidence of greater democracy. But the man of lowly birth can be no more than a democrat and it is no particular credit to him that he is. But the man of aristocratic birth, who has the privilege and opportunity of being more than a democrat, and yet who remains one, not only in simulation but at heart, can truly claim the title of being a great democrat. The purpose of democracy is not to drag the few down but to lift the many up. It is not to make all common but to make all aristocrats, to diffuse the benefits of culture and good breeding throughout the community. And Washington, who was an aristocrat by birth, because of the largeness of his heart and the breadth of his character became the first democrat through choice and affection. Never can it be truthfully charged against the man who subordinated the military to the civil through seven long miserable, heartbreaking years of revolutionary struggle and at the finish scornfully spurned the crown, that he was lacking in

---

1. In politics Lincoln was a Whig.

all the great qualities of a democrat.[2]

When Lincoln said that the question of union or disunion could only be settled by war, and ridiculed those who decried force as a legitimate and lawful means of maintaining the Union, arguing that "their idea of means to preserve the object of their great affection would seem to be exceedingly thin and airy" and compared them to free lovers, Washington said, "Let us erect a standard to which the wise and the just can repair — the result is in the hands of God"; and of the accomplished Union he said that it was "the offspring of our own choice, uninfluenced and unawed, adopted upon full investigation and mature deliberation, completely free in its principles." Washington based the Union upon the democratic principle of free consent. Lincoln ridiculed the basis of democracy, spoke of it as exceedingly thin and airy, likened it to a free love arrangement and asserted that force was the only sound basis of government. He appealed from the basis of democracy to the basis of despotism, from the ballot to the bullet. The Civil War was the result of the putting the new wine of democracy into the old skins of despotism.

The responsibility for the Civil War has been laid at the door of the South on the grounds that they fired the first shot against Fort Sumter. But the grounds beg the question and the responsibility for the war must await the determination of the question as to whether or not the South had the right to secede. If South Carolina had a right to secede she had a right to take Fort Sumter. Lincoln's policy in sitting tight and forcing the South to make the first move was identical with that of Bismarck. "Success," Bismark said, "essentially depends upon the impression which the origination of the war makes upon us and others; it is important that we should be the party attacked."

But the attack of South Carolina upon Fort Sumter was not an attack upon the North in any such a sense as the attack which Bismarck maneuvered an all too willing Napoleon into making upon Prussia. Fort Sumter was historically and geographically an integral part of the soil of South Carolina. It was there, as Lincoln said in his special message to Congress, for the protection of the people of South Carolina. It was an integral and vital part of their system of common defense. It symbolized the right of these people to defend themselves, a right which is basic to all other rights and which is the very test of manhood. Deny a man or a group of men the right to defend themselves and you deny them all other rights, for what a man has not the right to protect it cannot be reasonably and intelligently argued that he has a right to at all.

Fundamentally and vitally the fort belonged to the people of South Carolina. The site of the fort had been ceded to the Federal Government for the protection of the City of Charleston, and the moneys with which the fort had been constructed were drawn by taxation from the people of the States by methods to which all the States had agreed in ratifying the

---

2. It is a remarkable confirmation of this character of Washington that Col. Landon Carter, of Sabine Hall, Virginia used the following language on 3 May 1776, before Washington had been called to the command of the American armies, "I never knew but one man who resolved not to forget the citizen in the soldier or ruler, and that is G.W., and I am afraid I shall not know another" (Tyler).

Constitution. South Carolina had contributed her share and was morally entitled to a division of the common property. As to the legal phase of it there was none, for there was no law governing the subject, regardless of the fact that no technical, legal grounds can justify such a social catastrophe as war. War defeats the very end of law and government, which is the conservation of human values.

In spite of the persistent attempt, carried on through school histories and by partisan historians in general, to brand the people of the South in general, and of South Carolina in particular, as so many hell-bent hotheads, the fact is that the secession movement was done "decently and in order." They did not wantonly and in undue haste fire upon Fort Sumter. They sent a commission to Washington to negotiate a peaceful settlement of all questions arising from secession.[3] The assertion that secession was an essentially war-like act was a Federal doctrine and not a Southern doctrine. It was not until this commission had been snubbed on the narrow, childish legalism that the people of the South had no right to speak for themselves, that the people of South Carolina took the only other course open to them and asserted their rights by force of arms.[4]

In general principle the right of the people of South Carolina to dispossess the Federal Government of Fort Sumter involves no more than the right of any property owner to discharge a watchman hired to protect his property. The Federal Government had no more reasonable or moral right to wage war against the people of South Carolina and destroy their lives and property than a discharged watchman would have to destroy the property he was hired to protect. The authority of government is not an end in itself but a means to an end. The attempt to give to civil authority a special extra moral status is without ethical or social warrant and is simply one of the superstitions invented by despots as a means of awing the people and maintaining themselves in power.

Unionists would deny that two times two make four if it were necessary to vindicate the Civil War. To them no statement of principle is valid in favor of the independence of the South and against the war. Secession itself is a true principle when exercised in favor of the Union as Lincoln declared in the case of the secession of the forty-nine counties of Old Virginia.

The issues involved in the Civil War were not of concern solely to the generation which fought the war but are questions of eternal right and wrong and are subject to the law of Lincoln's doctrine that no question is settled until it is settled right. The objection that the war is water over the dam and that the problems of the present demand our attention is valid

---

3. They offered to pay the cost of construction of the fort, *etc.*

4. This does not state the full case. Not only were commissioners snubbed and denied audience, but no attack took place till Lincoln sent an armed squadron to supply the Fort with men and provisions. On this very question he took the advice of his Cabinet on 15 March 1861 and only one of them favored the movement. The rest in effect declared that the measure would inaugurate civil war, and it must be remembered that Mr. Hallam in his constitutional *History of England* states that "the aggressor in a war is not the first who uses force, but the first who renders force necessary." (Tyler)

providing that history is all bunk and that there is nothing to learn from our past. But the problems of the present are largely the legacy of the past, and if the past had settled them right they wouldn't confront us at the present time. It has only been since the late war that an English Premier has quoted the arguments of Lincoln against secession as an answer to the principles of the Declaration of Independence as put forward in defense of the right of the Irish to freedom. And the struggle of Ireland for freedom antedates our Revolutionary War by a century and a half and involved and involves the same questions.

It is thus that our past rises up to meet us and, as Lincoln said of slavery, "deprives our republican example of its just influence in the world." In setting up the sovereignty of the Union as a basis for making war against the seceding States and as a fence against European interference, he was acting upon the same principle that if one man chooses to kill another, neither that man nor any third man has a right to object. The logic of the Civil War was that the right to govern is paramount over the right to live, that man is made for government, rather than that government is made for man, and that for men to claim the right of self-government is to deserve and incur the death penalty.

Lincoln's arguments against the right of the South to independence were drawn from baseless exaggerations, the fatalistic sequence of mechanistic logic, an imperial and authoritarian interpretation of the Constitution which ignored its humanitarian purpose, a strange hodgepodge of the maxims of monarchical political science, and an instinctive metaphysical attitude toward government.

Lincoln said of slavery that it was the only thing that endangered the perpetuity of the Union and that it was the *sine qua non* of secession, but from the constitutional and historical standpoint this is not true. Slavery, as he admitted, was "indeed older than the Revolution." It existed previous to the Constitution and the Union was formed in spite of it. Both from the standpoint of the Constitution and sound statesmanship it was not slavery but the intemperate fanatical Abolition movement that endangered the Union. These Abolitionists proposed to apply all the principles of the Declaration of Independence to a race of people that were totally unprepared for self-government.

It was the intemperate, arrogant, self-righteous and academic attitude of the Abolitionists that made any constructive solution of the slavery question impossible and led the six cotton States to withdraw from the Union. The right to withdraw was early claimed. As a matter of historical fact South Carolina had threatened to secede over the tariff. The Colonies seceded from Britain over a question of local self-government. Belgium seceded from Holland and Norway from Sweden, where no question of slavery was involved.

Lincoln said of secession that it was the destruction of the country, of the Union, of the nation, and of the liberties of the people and of the institutions of the country. He said, "We have, as all will agree, a free government, where every man has a right to be equal with every other man. In this great struggle, this form of government and every form of human right is endangered if our enemies succeed."

The argument was absolutely senseless. One would think to read the argument that some Napoleon, Caesar or Alexander the Great were attempting to conquer the Southern people and set up a despotism and that Lincoln was waging a war in aid and defense of those people, rather than that those people were seeking to do nothing more than govern themselves and that Lincoln was warring to conquer them, to keep them from exercising their rightful liberties.

Secession was not, in any substantial sense, the destruction of the nation, nor was it in a proper sense the destruction of the Union. A nation is simply a corporation through which men exercise certain of their rights, just as they exercise other of their rights through their other organizations. Secession did not destroy the nation, but merely altered it. The Union existed when there were only thirteen States composing it,[5] and it would have continued to exist when there were twenty States left with a boundless public domain.

As for the liberties of the people, all their liberties would have remained intact. Furthermore, in spite of the gravity of the situation as it existed in 1789, Washington never proposed to use force to compel a Union.

In his Missouri Compromise speech Lincoln said:

> I trust I understand and truly estimate the right of self-government. My faith in the proposition that each man should do precisely as he pleases with all which is exclusively his own lies at the foundation of all the sense of justice there is in me. I extend the principle to communities of men as well as to individuals. I so extend it because it is politically wise, as well as naturally just; politically wise in saving us from broils about matters which do not concern us — the doctrine of self-government is right — absolutely and eternally right.

No argument could give any stronger support to the right of secession than this argument in favor of freedom for the slave. If the inhabitants of the States are men, is it not to that extent a total destruction of self-government to say that they shall not govern themselves? When the people of the North govern themselves that is self-government; but when they govern themselves and also govern the people of the South, that is more than self-government — that is despotism.

The Negro was the beneficiary rather than the victim of slavery, as Booker T. Washington has admitted. Lincoln's talk about "unrequited toil" ignores the fact that the condition of the Negro was better under slavery than it was in Africa, it ignores the fact that as compared to White laborers of equal mentality he was not deprived of any substantial rights, it ignores the economic and social status of northern so-called "free" labor which bordered closely upon serfdom, and it ignores the contribution of management to production. The strong probability is that the Negro received at least as great a share, in proportion to what he contributed to production, as did the technically free Northern laborer.

In any event civil war was no more a legitimate remedy for slavery than were the

---

5. As a matter of fact it existed when only eleven States were members of it — before North Carolina and Rhode Island joined.

reputedly revolutionary methods of the I.W.W. a proper remedy for the wrongs inflicted upon free labor by Northern capitalists.

In his first inaugural address Lincoln said:

> I hold that in contemplation of universal law and of the Constitution, the Union of these States is perpetual. Perpetuity is implied, if not expressed, in the fundamental law of all national governments. It is safe to assert that no government proper ever had a provision in its organic law for its own termination. Continue to execute all the express provision of our National Constitution, and the Union will endure forever — it being impossible to destroy it except by some action not provided for in the instrument itself.

The argument views States simply as political abstractions. It ignores "States" as denoting an organization of men. It assumes that there is some authority capable of making a contract binding upon all generations of men which shall, throughout the course of time, inhabit a certain territory. It assumes that a few hundred thousand voters living along the Atlantic seaboard a century and a half ago possessed authority over all generations of men which may throughout the course of time inhabit all the country from the Atlantic to the Pacific seaboard.

The Southern people of 1860 had never entered into "a clear compact of government." It is true that a generation of men previously inhabiting the same territory had done so, but that was not their affair. One generation possesses no such authority over future generations. Political theorists may call this anarchy, but they take their theories too seriously. Men do not maintain government because their granddaddy said they should any more than they live in homes, or eat three square meals a day, or go to church because their granddaddy said they should. In some notes on government Lincoln said, "Most governments have been based, practically, on the denial of the equal rights of men, as I have, in part stated them; ours began by affirming those rights."

In asserting that if we continue to execute all the express provisions of the Constitution the Union will last forever, Lincoln asserted no more than is true of any institution whose charter runs in perpetuity. But the assertion contains no argument against secession. Theorize, as men will, with regard to the basis of government it must conform to rational and moral reasoning, and there is no rational and moral reasoning to support the assumption that one generation can bind another generation in any such a way as is implicit in Lincoln's interpretation of the idea of perpetuity as applied to the Union.

Lincoln neglected to draw the distinction between the right to dissolve an organization and the right to withdraw or secede from it. The one is a right which belongs to the members as a whole while the other is a right inherent if not expressed in the laws of any organization except as membership therein partakes of the nature of a contractual obligation involving a consideration. But the Union is not of such a nature and there is no authority by which such a perpetual obligation could be established.

In arguing that secession was the essence of disintegration and anarchy Lincoln asked:

Why may not any portion of a new confederacy — arbitrarily secede again.... Is there such perfect identity of interests among the States to compose a new union, as to produce harmony only, and prevent renewed secession? Plainly, the central idea of secession is the essence of anarchy. A majority, held in restraint by constitutional checks and limitations — is the only true sovereign of a free people.

Grant has admitted in his *Memoirs* that if the Southern States had been allowed to secede, they would have set up a government that would have been real and respected, and the assertion that secession was the essence of anarchy was purely academic. The essence of secession is not anarchy but freedom, independence, and nationalism.

Lincoln asserted that, "All who cherish disunion sentiments are now being educated to the exact temper of doing this [continuous disintegration]." He could have better argued that all who cherish warlike sentiments were being educated to the temper of conquest. His argument that secession was the essence of anarchy and that the movement could end only in the complete disintegration of society is answered by his own words that "happily the human mind is not so constituted."

But while the central idea of secession is not the essence of anarchy, war is anarchy. "It is the essence of war to summon force to decide questions of justice -- a task for which it has no pertinence."

After being brought up to the idea that the Southern leaders were so many hasty hotheads, it is disconcerting to read in the speeches of their real leaders the fairness, calmness and friendliness with which they faced the situation. And this attitude was not only in their speeches but in their actions as well. They took only those measures which any people who had determined upon their course, would have taken as a matter of good judgment and precaution.

Lincoln asked, "Why should there not be a patient confidence in the ultimate justice of the people," and again, "Will you hazard so desperate a step while there is any possibility that any portion of the ills you fly from have no real existence?" He had better have asked why he should not have a patient confidence in the ultimate justice of the Southern people and why he would hazard so desperate a step as war while there was any possibility that the evils of secession had no real existence. He had said of the Southern people that in point of justice he did not consider them inferior to any people and that devotion to the Constitution was equally great on both sides.[6]

The South in seceding did not take anything that by any moral principle belonged to the North, and if the Civil War is to be justified, either upon policy or principle, it must be upon a showing that secession was an invasion of the rights of the people of the North that

---

6. At this point the author overlooks the circumstance that only the cotton States acted on their rights of secession prior to President Lincoln's making war on them — then the other States united in resisting the invading armies.

justified the taking of human life.[7] No abstract, highly synthetic and controversial theories of sovereignty can justify the taking of human life. Man acting gregariously possesses no other right to take life than is possessed by the individual. Murder is murder whether it is committed by one man or twenty millions of men and the empiricisms of political so-called "science" constitute no authority for murder. The idea that a "nation" can commit murder in order to achieve a fancied destiny is the essence of immorality and imperialism.

Lincoln said, "This country, with its institutions belongs to the people who inhabit it. Whenever they shall grow weary of the existing government, they can exercise their constitutional right of amending it, or their revolutionary right to dismember or overthrow it." His theory was that the territory of the United States belonged to the people as a whole as sovereign proprietor. That the soil of South Carolina did not belong to the people of South Carolina, who inhabit it, but to the people of the United States as a whole. The theory is a legacy from feudalism and monarchy and as applied to a republican Union or State is the essence of communism. Democracy is an association of equals. Under monarchy or feudalism the title to both person and property ultimately resided in the monarch or lord. It was this principle which was the cause of the War of 1812 when England asserted that once a subject always a subject, just as Lincoln claimed that once a State in the Union always a State in the Union. The right of expatriation, which is simply a right of personal secession, is an acknowledged American right and has ever been since Jefferson directed the affairs of the nation. We fought over it in the War of 1812 and incorporated it in the Burlingame treaty with China. This right is absolutely inconsistent with the description of the Southern peoples as rebels and traitors and the calling of them to return to their "allegiance" to the Federal Government. The idea of "allegiance" is that of the relation of an inferior to a superior and not of the citizens of a republic to their republican society.

Certainly there is a territorial consideration in the formation of civil society, but that consideration is born of practical necessity and must end with the necessity. But no such consideration was involved in the secession of the Southern States. They were as able to govern themselves as were the people of the North or of England or of France or any other State. There are however no constitutional grounds for the pretense of territorial sovereignty on the part of the United States Government. The Government of the United States is simply the joint and common agent of the States, members of the Union, just as a farmers co-operative is the agent of its members. The basic principles involved in the Union of the States are the same as those involved in the agricultural co-operatives. And as I have previously observed, the United States cannot, under the Constitution, exercise exclusive legislative

---

7. The New York *Times*, in a remarkable editorial dated 9 September 1864, justified the war not on slavery or the restoration of the Union, but on the threatened danger to the Northern people. It passed a tremendous eulogy on the resistance which had disintegrated the Southern people beyond any in the world, rendering their conquest absolutely necessary, lest in the future the Northern States themselves might become subject to their terrible neighbors. In other words, the more evidence the Southerners gave of their right to self-government, the more it was denied to them.

jurisdiction over the site for its own capitol, or the sites for forts, dockyards or other needful public buildings without first getting the consent of the legislature in which the site is situated. To call such a government a territorial sovereign is absurd.

The people of South Carolina possess exactly the same natural, moral and fundamental rights as against the people of the State of New York that the people of Canada do.

Lincoln spoke of the people as possessing a revolutionary right, but such talk is to deny their sovereignty and imply the sovereignty of the Constitution. Revolution is the overthrow of the sovereign, not of the Constitution or of the Government. The people do not derive their sovereign authority from the Constitution. It is not the Constitution of the people but of the Federal Government and is also the record of a compact between the States.

Lincoln admitted that the Government could be overthrown and the Union dismembered. A successful rebel becomes a revolutionist and his success vindicates his rebellion. It is a curious doctrine that success vindicates what would otherwise be a crime.

As a matter of historical fact these rebellions were generally efforts on the part of the people to regain their rightful liberties. As to whether or not secession was revolution depends upon whether the people of the seceding States possessed the right to run their own business.

Lincoln said of secession that "it recognizes no fidelity to the Constitution, no obligation to maintain the Union," but the fact is, there is no obligation on the part of the States to maintain the Union. He said, "Surely each man has as strong a motive now to preserve our liberties as each had then to establish them," but in order to justify war he must have a stronger motive, for the Union wasn't established by force and the war overthrew those very liberties for which the Revolutionary War was fought and the Union created — the right of each State to govern itself. He said, "This Union shall never be abandoned, unless the possibility of its existence shall cease to exist without the necessity of throwing passengers and cargo overboard." A more accurate analogy would be to compare the Union to a fleet of ships sailing in voluntary convoy for mutual protection and Lincoln's act in waging war to the act of the elected commander of such a convoy in sinking any ship that seceded from the convoy.

Of the States Lincoln said:

> They have their status in the Union, and they have no other legal status. If they break from this, they can do so only against law and by revolution. This Union, and not themselves separately, procured their independence and their liberty.... The Union is older than any of the States and, in fact, it created them as States. Originally some dependent Colonies made the Union, and, in turn, the Union threw off their old dependence for them, and made them States, such as they are.

Lincoln here pretends to be arguing upon legal grounds. The force of his argument lies in the implication that the Union had the legal authority to create those "dependent colonies, States, such as they are." But the Union of which he speaks possessed no legal status or authority whatever. It was purely an illegal, revolutionary Union whose acts depended for their force upon ratification by the respective Colonies represented in the Continental Congress or tacit consent. It was ridiculous for Lincoln to impute legality to such a Union while denying it to the Confederacy which was established upon the same legal authority as was the United States.

Lincoln hypostatizes the Union and speaks of it achieving the independence of the States. But the Union was not a personality or an entity but simply a condition of co-operation.[8] Water cannot rise higher than its source; derived power cannot be superior to the power from which it is derived and the Federal Union cannot be superior to the States that created it. The Constitution is supreme only in the sense that the laws of any organization are supreme over its members, so long as they remain members.

Contrary to Webster's assertion and the language of the enacting clause of the Constitution, it was not ratified either by the authority of the people of the United States or directly by the people of the States.[9] The phrase, "people of the United States," does not bear out the argument of Webster and the imperialists, that the people of the United States are united. The phrase is not "united people" but "United States." The present Constitution was ratified when the Union was still based upon the Articles of Confederation. The mode of ratification ignored the Articles entirely and referred back to the prime authority of the State legislature.

It is only in a subjective or administrative sense that the people of the United States constitute one people. In the exercise of their sovereign powers they do, and always have resolved themselves into sovereign States. Marshall argued that the United States was sovereign to the extent of its authority, but is no more sovereign than any agent is sovereign. Its powers are delegated powers. In waging the Revolutionary War, the men of 1776 were fighting for everything that Webster and Lincoln argued against. The men of 1776 denied the rightfulness of the asserted British sovereignty. They asserted that they were men with all the rights of men, and Englishmen with all the constitutional rights of Englishmen, and that their colonial situation had no political significance, that it was not a crime for which they could be punished by depriving them of their rights of self-government.

They claimed for their colonial legislature a constitutional parity with Parliament, possessed of exclusive legislative jurisdiction within its respective colony and that the

---

8. There was no Union in existence before 1781. There was a congress of delegates who acted as allowed or directed by the several Colonies or States. In 1781, Maryland having agreed, the congress then became a Congress of the States — and the confederation became operative. Then by Article VII of the proposed Constitution: "The ratification of nine states shall be sufficient for the establishment of the constitution between the States so ratifying the same"; and, when nine States ratified, it went into effect between them; and it went into practical effect, leaving out some of the States. The ratifying States had broken up the old confederacy — agreed to be "perpetual."

9. The Constitution was to take effect between the States just as the "perpetual confederation" of 1781 was — not *over* the States, but *between* the States — and Virginia and each other State was, by the Treaty of Peace with Great Britain, declared to be — each separately — "free sovereign and independent States"; and so in subsequent treaties. Nor was their condition altered by the Constitution of 1787.

Empire was bound simply by the theoretical sovereignty of the Crown. They did not fight for union, but for the right of each Colony to complete self-government.

The question as to whether the Union is a league, confederation, federation or nation, is not a vital one, but is purely technical and is simply a matter of the mode of administration, of the extent of organization, not of obligation. Because it employs some machinery of government also used in its national organizations is no more reason for calling it a "nation" than there would be for calling a gasoline engine a steam engine because of certain features they possess in common.

The assertion that secession is treason is not borne out by the nature of the Union, by the constitutional definition of treason or the nature of treason itself, or by the principles of democracy. Treason is a crime against the "sovereign." The Union is an association of co-equal States and the Federal Government is simply the common agent of those States. The Constitution says that, "Treason against the United States shall consist in levying war against them, or in adhering to their enemies," *etc*. It uses the plural "them" and "their" denoting an association of sovereigns rather than a unitary sovereign. It was Lincoln who committed treason and not the States. Lincoln overthrew eleven sovereign States and State governments, which even according to Webster were the equal of the Federal Government. The idea of the sovereignty of the whole people of the United States is purely an imperialistic dogma. Analyzed, it means that the people of Oregon are sovereign over the people of South Carolina and that the people of South Carolina are sovereign over the people of Oregon. The people of Oregon possess no more sovereign rights in the government of the people of South Carolina than they do in the government of the people of Canada or Mexico. The doctrine is indefensible by the principles of democracy.

Lincoln has been put forward as the great exemplar of Christianity, but the Civil War was fought in diametrical opposition not only to every principle of democracy, but of Christianity. What he said of John Brown may also be said of Lincoln that "it could avail himself nothing that he might think himself right." That cannot excuse violence, bloodshed, and treason.

Like the enthusiast, of whom Lincoln said that he "broods over the oppression of a people till he fancies himself commissioned by Heaven to liberate them," so Lincoln brooded until he fancied himself commissioned by Heaven as a modern Moses raised up to lead the "oppressed" slaves to freedom, and when the war had brought such misery and destruction that it could no longer be justified upon the original object of saving the Union, he then attributed to it the added character of a divinely appointed means of punishing the North and the South for "the bondsman's two hundred and fifty years of unrequited toil."

But, regardless of the fact that slavery was in no sense a unique crime, Christ said that He came, not to judge the world, but that the world through Him might be saved. The Civil War was a greater crime than slavery. Both were a denial of the right of self-government, but where slavery simply took away the unrestrained barbaric freedom of the negro and put him to constructive employment, the war destroyed the very lives of those who had been previously denied the right of self-government. Lord Morley has said that it is not enough that we should do good. We must do it in the right way. War was no more a righteous method of perpetuating the Union than it would have been a righteous method of originally forming the Union. It was no more a righteous method of keeping the Southern States inside the Union than it would be a righteous method for bringing Canada into the Union or the United States into the League of Nations. The end does not justify the means.

Lincoln would have been a true democrat if he had perpetuated the Union by the method by which Washington formed it. He would have been a true Christian if he had followed the example of that other Abraham who said to his kinsman: *"Let there be no strife I pray the between me and the — for we be brethren. Is not the whole land before thee? Separate thyself, I pray thee, from me; if thou wilt take the left hand, then I will go to the right, or if thou depart to the right hand, then I will go to the left."*

APPENDIX THREE
The Permanent Constitution of the
Confederate States of America (1861)

We, the people of the Confederate States, each State acting in its sovereign and independent character, in order to form a permanent federal government, establish justice, insure domestic tranquility and secure the blessings of liberty to ourselves and our posterity — invoking the favor and guidance of Almighty God — do ordain and establish this constitution for the Confederate States of America.

ARTICLE I

Section One

All legislative powers herein delegated shall be vested in a Congress of the Confederate States, which shall consist of a Senate and House of Representatives.

Section Two

1. The House of Representatives shall be composed of members chosen every second year by the people of the several States; and the electors in each State shall be citizens of the Confederate States, and have the qualifications requisite for electors of the most numerous branch of the State Legislature; but no person of foreign birth, not a citizen of the Confederate States, shall be allowed to vote for any officer, civil or political, State or federal.

2. No person shall be a Representative who shall not have attained the age of twenty-

five years, and be a citizen of the Confederate States, and who shall not, when elected, be an inhabitant of that State in which he shall be chosen.

3. Representatives and Direct Taxes shall be apportioned among the several States, which may be included within this Confederacy, according to their respective numbers, which shall be determined by adding to the whole number of free persons, including those bound to service for a term of years, and excluding Indians not taxed, three-fifths of all slaves. The actual enumeration shall be made within three years after the first meeting of the Congress of the Confederate States, and within every subsequent term of ten years, in such manner as they shall by law direct. The number of Representatives shall not exceed one for every fifty thousand, but each State shall have at least one Representative; and until such enumeration shall be made, the State of South Carolina shall be entitled to choose six — the State of Georgia ten — the State of Alabama nine — the State of Florida two — the State of Mississippi seven — the State of Louisiana six, and the State of Texas six.

4. When vacancies happen in the representation from any State, the Executive authority thereof shall issue writs of election to fill such vacancies.

5. The House of Representatives shall choose their speaker and other officers; and shall have the sole power of impeachment; except that any judicial or other federal officer, resident and acting solely within the limits of any State, may be impeached by a vote of two-thirds of both branches of the Legislature thereof.

Section Three

1. The Senate of the Confederate States shall be composed of two Senators from each State, chosen for six years by the Legislature thereof, at the regular session next immediately preceding the commencement of the term of service; and each Senator shall have one vote.

2. Immediately after they shall be assembled, in consequence of the first election, they shall be divided as equally as may be into three classes. The seats of the Senators of the first class shall be vacated at the expiration of the second year; of the second class at the expiration of the fourth year; and of the third class at the expiration of the sixth year; so that one-third may be chosen every second year; and if vacancies happen by resignation, or otherwise, during the recess of the Legislature of any State, the executive thereof may make temporary appointments until the next meeting of the Legislature which shall then fill such vacancies.

3. No person shall be a Senator who shall not have attained the age of thirty years, and be a citizen of the Confederate States; and who shall not, when elected, be an inhabitant of the State for which he shall be chosen.

4. The Vice President of the Confederate States shall be President of the Senate, but shall have no vote, unless they be equally divided.

5. The Senate shall choose their officers; and also a President *pro tempore* in the absence of the Vice President, or when he shall exercise the office of President of the Confederate States.

6. The Senate shall have the sole power to try all impeachments. When sitting for that

purpose, they shall be on oath or affirmation. When the President of the Confederate States is tried, the Chief Justice shall preside; and no person shall be convicted without the concurrence of two-thirds of the members present.

7. Judgment in cases of impeachment shall not extend further than to removal from office, and disqualification to hold and enjoy any office of honor, trust or profit, under the Confederate States; but the party convicted shall, nevertheless, be liable and subject to indictment, trial, judgment and punishment according to law.

Section Four

1. The times, place and manner of holding elections for Senators and Representatives, shall be prescribed in each State by the Legislature thereof, subject to the provisions of this Constitution; but the Congress may, at any time, by law, make or alter such regulations, except as to the times and places of choosing Senators.

2. The Congress shall assemble at least once in every year; and such meeting shall be on the first Monday in December, unless they shall, by law, appoint a different day.

Section Five

1. Each House shall be the judge of the elections, returns and qualifications of its own members, and a majority of each shall constitute a quorum to do business; but a smaller number may adjourn from day to day, and may be authorized to compel the attendance of absent members, in such manner and under such penalties as each House may provide.

2. Each House may determine the rules of its proceedings, punish its members for disorderly behavior, and with the concurrence of two-thirds of the whole number expel a member.

3. Each House shall keep a journal of its proceedings, and from time to time punish the same, excepting such parts as may in their judgment require secrecy; and the yeas and nays of the members of either House, on any question, shall, at the desire of one-fifth of those present, be entered on the journal.

4. Neither House, during the session of Congress, shall, without the consent of the other, adjourn for more than three days, nor to any other place than that in which the two Houses shall be sitting.

Section Six

1. The Senators and Representatives shall receive a compensation for their services, to be ascertained by law, and paid out of the Treasury of the Confederate States. They shall, in all cases, except treason, felony, and breach of the peace, be privileged from arrest during their attendance at the session of their respective Houses, and in going to and returning from the same; and for any speech or debate in either House, they shall not be questioned in any

other place.

2. No Senator or Representative shall, during the time for which he was elected, be appointed to any civil office under the authority of the Confederate States, which shall have been created, or the emoluments whereof shall have been increased during such time; and no person holding any office under the Confederate States shall be a member of either House during his continuance in office. But Congress may, by law, grant to the principal officer in each of the Executive Departments a seat upon the floor of either House, with the privilege of discussing any measures appertaining to his department.

Section Seven

1. All bills for raising the revenue shall originate in the House of Representatives; but the Senate may propose or concur with amendments, as on other bills.

2. Every bill which shall have passed both Houses, shall, before it becomes a law, be presented to the President of the Confederate States; if he approve, he shall sign it; but if not, he shall return it, with his objections, to that House in which it shall have originated, who shall enter the objections at large on their journal, and proceed to reconsider it. If, after such reconsideration, two-thirds of that House shall agree to pass the bill, it shall be sent, together with the objections, to the other House, by which it shall likewise be reconsidered, and if approved by two-thirds of that House, it shall become a law. But in all such cases, the votes of both Houses shall be determined by yeas and nays, and the names of the persons voting for and against the bill shall be entered on the journal of each House respectively. If any bill shall not be returned by the President within ten days (Sundays excepted) after it shall have been presented to him, the same shall be a law, in like manner as if he had signed it, unless the Congress, by their adjournment, prevent its return; in which case it shall not be a law. The President may approve any appropriation and disapprove any other appropriation in the same bill. In such case he shall, in signing the bill, designate the appropriations disapproved; and shall return a copy of such appropriations, with his objections, to the House in which the bill shall have originated; and the same proceedings shall then be had as in case of other bills disapproved by the President.

3. Every order, resolution or vote, to which the concurrence of both Houses may be necessary, (except on a question of adjournment,) shall be presented to the President of the Confederate States; and before the same shall take effect, shall be approved by him; or being disapproved, shall be re-passed by two-thirds of both Houses, according to the rules and limitations prescribed in case of a bill.

Section Eight

The Congress shall have power —

1. To lay and collect taxes, duties, imposts, and excises, for revenue necessary to pay the debts, provide for the common defence, and carry on the Government of the Confederate

States; but no bounties shall be granted from the treasury; nor shall any duties or taxes on importations from foreign nations be laid to promote or foster any branch of industry, and all duties, imposts, and excises shall be uniform throughout the Confederate States:

2. To borrow money on the credit of the Confederate States:

3. To regulate commerce with foreign nations, and among the several States, and with the Indian tribes; but neither this, nor any other clause contained in the constitution, shall ever be construed to delegate the power to Congress to appropriate money for any internal improvement intended to facilitate commerce; except for the purpose of furnishing lights, beacons, and buoys, and other aid to navigation upon the coasts, and the improvement of harbors and the removing of obstructions in river navigation, in all which cases, such duties shall be laid on the navigation facilitated thereby, as may be necessary to pay the costs and expenses thereof:

4. To establish uniform laws of naturalization, and uniform laws on the subject of bankruptcies, throughout the Confederate States; but no law of Congress shall discharge any debt contracted before the passage of the same:

5. To coin money, regulate the value thereof and of foreign coin, and fix the standard of weights and measures:

6. To provide for the punishment of counterfeiting the securities and current coin of the Confederate States:

7. Establish post-offices and post-routes; but the expenses of the Post-office Department, after the first day of March in the year of our Lord eighteen hundred and sixty-three, shall be paid out of its own revenues:

8. To promote the progress of science and useful arts, by securing for limited times to authors and inventors the exclusive right to their respective writings and discoveries:

9. To constitute tribunals inferior to the Supreme Court:

10. To define and punish piracies and felonies committed on the high seas, and offences against the law of nations:

11. To declare war, grant letters of marque and reprisal, and make rules concerning captures on land and on water:

12. To raise and support armies; but no appropriation of money to that use shall be for a longer term than two years:

13. To provide and maintain a navy:

14. To make rules for the government and regulation of the land and naval forces:

15. To provide for calling forth the militia to execute the laws of the Confederate States, suppress insurrections, and repel invasions:

16. To provide for organizing, arming, and disciplining the militia, and for governing such part of them as may be employed in the service of the Confederate States; reserving to the States, respectively, the appointment of the officers, and the authority of training the militia according to the discipline prescribed by Congress:

17. To exercise exclusive legislation, in all cases whatsoever, over such district (not exceeding ten miles square) as may, by cession of one or more States and the acceptance of

Congress, become the seat of the Government of the Confederate States; and to exercise like authority over places purchased by the consent of the Legislature of the State in which the same shall be, for the erection of forts, magazines, arsenals, dockyards, and other needful buildings:

and

18. To make all laws which shall be necessary and proper for carrying into execution the foregoing powers, and all other powers vested by this Constitution in the government of the Confederate States, or in any department or officer thereof.

Section Nine

1. The importation of negroes of the African race, from any foreign country other than the slaveholding States or Territories of the United States of America, is hereby forbidden; and Congress is required to pass such laws as shall effectually prevent the same.

2. Congress shall also have power to prohibit the introduction of slaves from any State not a member of, or Territory not belonging to, this Confederacy.

3. The privilege of the writ of habeas corpus shall not be suspended, unless when in case of rebellion or invasion the public safety may require it.

4. No bill of attainder, *ex post facto* law, or law denying or impairing the right of property in negro slaves shall be passed.

5. No capitation or other direct tax shall be laid, unless in proportion to the census or enumeration hereinbefore directed to be taken.

6. No tax or duty shall be laid on articles exported from any State, except by a vote of two-thirds of both Houses.

7 . No preference shall be given by any regulation of commerce or revenue to the ports of one State over those of another.

8. No money shall be drawn from the treasury, but in consequence of appropriations made by law; and a regular statement and account of the receipts and expenditures of all public money shall be published from time to time.

9. Congress shall appropriate no money from the treasury except by a vote of two-thirds of both Houses, taken by yeas and nays, unless it be asked and estimated for by some one of the heads of departments, and submitted to Congress by the President; or for the purpose of paying its own expenses and contingencies; or for the payment of claims against the Confederate States, the justice of which shall have been judicially declared by a tribunal for the investigation of claims against the Government, which it is hereby made the duty of Congress to establish.

10. All bills appropriating money shall specify in federal currency the exact amount of each appropriation and the purposes for which it is made; and Congress shall grant no extra compensation to any public contractor, officer, agent or servant, after such contract shall have been made or such service rendered.

11. No title of nobility shall be granted by the Confederate States; and no person

holding any office of profit or trust under them, shall, without the consent of the Congress, accept of any present, emolument, office or title of any kind whatever, from any king, prince, or foreign State.

12. Congress shall make no law respecting an establishment of religion, or prohibiting the free exercise thereof; or abridging the freedom of speech, or of the press; or the right of the people peaceably to assemble and petition the Government for a redress of grievances.

13. A well-regulated militia being necessary to the security of a free State, the right of the people to keep and bear arms shall not be infringed.

14. No soldier shall, in time of peace, be quartered in any house without the consent of the owner; nor in time of war, but in a manner to be prescribed by law.

15. The right of the people to be secure in their persons, houses, papers, and effects, against unreasonable searches and seizures, shall not be violated; and no warrants shall issue but upon probable cause, supported by oath or affirmation, and particularly describing the place to be searched, and the persons or things to be seized.

16. No person shall be held to answer for a capital or otherwise infamous crime, unless on a presentment or indictment of a grand jury, except in cases arising in the land or naval forces, or in the militia, when in actual service in time of war or public danger; nor shall any person be subject for the same offence to be twice put in jeopardy of life or limb; nor be compelled, in any criminal case, to be a witness against himself; nor be deprived of life, liberty, or property, without due process of law; nor shall private property be taken for public use, without just compensation.

17. In all criminal prosecutions, the accused shall enjoy the right to a speedy and public trial, by an impartial jury of the State and district wherein the crime shall have been committed, which district shall have been previously ascertained by law, and to be informed of the nature and cause of the accusation; to be confronted with the witness against him; to have compulsory process for obtaining witnesses in his favor; and to have the assistance of counsel for his defence.

18. In suits at common law, where the value in controversy shall exceed twenty dollars, the right of trial by jury shall be preserved; and no fact so tried by jury shall be otherwise re-examined in any court of the Confederacy, than according to the rules of the common law.

19. Excessive bail shall not be required, nor excessive fines imposed, nor cruel and unusual punishment inflicted.

20. Every law, or resolution having the force of law, shall relate to but one subject, and that shall be expressed in the title.

Section Ten

1. No State shall enter into any treaty, alliance, or confederation; grant letters of marque and reprisal; coin money: make any thing but gold and silver coin a tender in payment of debts; pass any bill of attainder, or *ex post facto* law, or law impairing the obligation

of contracts; or grant any title of nobility.

2. No State shall, without the consent of the Congress, lay any imposts or duties on imports or exports, except what may be absolutely necessary for executing its inspection laws; and the nett produce of all duties and imposts, laid by any State on imports or exports, shall be for the use of the treasury of the Confederate States, and all such laws shall be subject to the revision and control of Congress.

3. No State shall, without the consent of Congress, lay any duty on tonnage, except on sea-going vessels, for the improvement of its rivers and harbors navigated by the said vessels; but such duties shall not conflict with any treaties of the Confederate States with foreign nations; and any surplus revenue, thus derived, shall, after making such improvement, be paid into the common treasury. Nor shall any State keep troops or ships of war in time of peace, enter into any agreement or compact with another State, or with a foreign power, or engage in war, unless actually invaded, or in such imminent danger as will not admit of delay. But when any river divides or flows through two or more States, they may enter into compacts with each other to improve the navigation thereof.

ARTICLE II

Section One

1. The executive power shall be vested in a President of the Confederate States of America. He and the Vice President shall hold their offices for the term of six years; but the President shall not be re-eligible. The President and Vice President shall be elected as follows:

2. Each State shall appoint, in such manner as the Legislature thereof may direct, a number of electors equal to the whole number of Senators and Representatives to which the State may be entitled in the Congress; but no Senator or Representative, or person holding an office of trust or profit under the Confederate States, shall be appointed an elector.

3. The electors shall meet in their respective States and vote by ballot for President and Vice President, one of whom, at least, shall not be an inhabitant of the same State with themselves; they shall name in their ballots the person voted for as President, and in distinct ballots the person voted for as Vice President, and they shall make distinct lists of all persons voted for as President, and of all persons voted for as Vice President, and of the number of votes for each, which lists they shall sign and certify, and transmit, sealed, to the seat of government of the Confederate States, directed to the President of the Senate; the President of the Senate shall, in the presence of the Senate and House of Representatives; open all the certificates, and the votes shall then be counted; the person having the greatest number of votes for President shall be the President, if such number be a majority of the whole number of electors appointed; and if no person have such majority, then, from the persons having the highest numbers, not exceeding three, on the list of those voted for as President, the House of Representatives shall choose immediately, by ballot, the President. But in choosing the

President, the votes shall be taken by States — the representation from each State having one vote. A quorum for this purpose shall consist of a member or members from two-thirds of the States, and a majority of all the States shall be necessary to a choice. And if the House of Representatives shall not choose a President, whenever the right of choice shall devolve upon them, before the fourth day of March next following, then the Vice President shall act as President, as in case of the death, or other constitutional disability of the President.

4. The person having the greatest number of votes as Vice President, shall be the Vice President, if such number be a majority of the whole number of electors appointed; and if no person have a majority, then, from the two highest numbers on the list, the Senate shall choose the Vice President. A quorum for the purpose shall consist of two-thirds of the whole number of Senators, and a majority of the whole number shall be necessary to a choice.

5. But no person constitutionally ineligible to the office of President shall be eligible to that of Vice President of the Confederate States.

6. The Congress may determine the time of choosing the electors, and the day on which they shall give their votes; which day shall be the same throughout the Confederate States.

7. No person except a natural born citizen of the Confederate States, or a citizen thereof at the time of the adoption of this Constitution, or a citizen thereof born in the United States prior to the 20th of December, 1860, shall be eligible to the office of President; neither shall any person be eligible to that office who shall not have attained the age of thirty-five years, and been fourteen years a resident within the limits of the Confederate States, as they may exist at the time of his election.

8. In case of the removal of the President from office, or of his death, resignation, or inability to discharge the powers and duties of the said office, the same shall devolve on the Vice President; and the Congress may, by law, provide for the case of removal, death, resignation, or inability, both of the President and Vice President, declaring what officer shall then act as President; and such officers shall act accordingly, until the disability be removed or a President shall be elected.

9. The President shall, at stated times, receive for his services a compensation, which shall neither be increased nor diminished during the period for which he shall have been elected; and he shall not receive within that period any other emolument from the Confederate States, or any of them.

10. Before he enters on the execution of his office, he shall take the following oath or affirmation: "I do solemnly swear (or affirm) that I will faithfully execute the office of President of the Confederate States of America, and will, to the best of my ability, preserve, protect and defend the Constitution thereof."

Section Two

1. The President shall be commander-in-chief of the army and navy of the Confederate States, and of the militia of the several States, when called into the actual service of the

Confederate States; he may require the opinion, in writing, of the principal officer in each of the executive departments, upon any subject relating to the duties of their respective offices; and he shall power to grant reprieves and pardons for offences against the Confederacy, except in cases of impeachment.

2. He shall have power, by and with the advice and consent of the Senate, to make treaties; provided two-thirds of the Senators present concur: and he shall nominate, and by and with the advice and consent of the Senate, shall appoint ambassadors, other public ministers and consuls, judges of the Supreme Court, and all other officers of the Confederate States whose appointments are not herein otherwise provided for, and which shall be established by law. But the Congress may, by law, vest the appointment of such inferior officers, as they may think proper, in the President alone, in the courts of law, or in the heads of departments.

3. The principal officer in each of the executive departments, and all persons connected with the diplomatic service, may be removed from office at the pleasure of the President. All other civil officers of the executive departments may be removed at any time by the President, or other appointing power, when their services are unnecessary, or for dishonesty, incapacity, inefficiency, misconduct, or neglect of duty; and when so removed, the removal shall be reported to the Senate, together with the reasons therefor.

4. The President shall have the power to fill all vacancies that may happen during the recess of the Senate, by granting commissions which shall expire at the end of their next session; but no person rejected by the Senate shall be re-appointed to the same office during their ensuing recess.

Section Three

1. The President shall, from time to time, give to the Congress information of the state of the Confederacy, and recommend to their consideration such measures as he shall judge necessary and expedient; he may, on extraordinary occasions, convene both Houses, or either of them; and in case of disagreement between them, with respect to the time of adjournment, he may adjourn them to such time as he shall think proper; he shall receive ambassadors and other public ministers; he shall take care that the laws be faithfully executed, and shall commission all the officers of the Confederate States.

Section Four

1. The President, Vice President, and all civil officers of the Confederate States, shall be removed from office on impeachment for, and conviction of, treason, bribery, or other high crimes and misdemeanors.

ARTICLE III

Section One

1. The judicial power of the Confederate States shall be vested in one Supreme Court, and in such inferior courts as the Congress may, from time to time, ordain and establish. The judges, both of the Supreme and inferior courts, shall hold their offices during good behavior, arid shall, at stated times, receive for their services a compensation which shall not be diminished during their continuance in office.

Section Three

1. The judicial power shall extend to all cases arising under this Constitution, the laws of the Confederate States, and treaties made, or which shall be made, under their authority; to all cases affecting ambassadors, other public ministers and consuls; to all cases of admiralty and maritime jurisdiction; to controversies to which the Confederate States shall be a party; to controversies between two or more States; between a State and a citizen of another State, where the State is plaintiff; between citizens claiming lands under grants of different States; and between a State or the citizens thereof, and foreign States, citizens or subjects; but no State shall be sued by a citizen or subject of any foreign State.

2. In all cases affecting ambassadors, other public ministers and consuls, and those in which a State shall be a party, the Supreme Court shall have original jurisdiction. In all the other cases before mentioned, the Supreme Court shall have appellate jurisdiction both as to law and fact, with such exceptions and under such regulations as the Congress shall make.

3. The trial of all crimes, except in cases of impeachment, shall be by jury, and such trial shall be held in the State where the said crimes shall have been committed; but when not committed within any State, the trial shall be at such place or places as the Congress may by law have directed.

Section Three

1. Treason against the Confederate States shall consist only in levying war against them, or in adhering to their enemies, giving them aid and comfort. No person shall be convicted of treason unless on the testimony of two witnesses to the same overt act, or on confession in open court.

2. The Congress shall have power to declare the punishment of treason; but no attainder of treason shall work corruption of blood, or forfeiture, except during the life of the person attainted.

ARTICLE IV

Section One

1. Full faith and credit shall be given in each State to the public acts, records, and judicial proceedings of every other State. And the Congress may, by general laws, prescribe the manner in which such acts, records, and proceedings shall be proved, and the effect thereof.

Section Two

1. The citizens of each State shall be entitled to all the privileges and immunities of citizens in the several States; and shall have the right of transit and sojourn in any State of this Confederacy, with their slaves and other property; and the right of property in said slaves shall not be thereby impaired.

2. A person charged in any State with treason, felony, or other crime against the laws of such State, who shall flee from justice, and be found in another State, shall, on demand of the executive authority of the State from which he fled, be delivered up, to be removed to the State having jurisdiction of the crime.

3. No slave or other person held to service or labor in any State or Territory of the Confederate States, under the laws thereof, escaping or lawfully carried into another, shall, in consequence of any law or regulation therein, be discharged from such service or labor; but shall be delivered up on claim of the party to whom such slave belongs, or to whom such service or labor may be due.

Section Three

1. Other States may be admitted into this Confederacy by a vote of two-thirds of the whole House of Representatives and two-thirds of the Senate, the Senate voting by States; but no new State shall be formed or erected within the jurisdiction of any other State; nor any State be formed by the junction of two or more States, or parts of States, without the consent of the Legislatures of the States concerned, as well as of the Congress.

2. The Congress shall have power to dispose of and make all needful rules and regulations concerning the property of the Confederate States, including the lands thereof.

3. The Confederate States may acquire new territory; and Congress shall have power to legislate and provide governments for the inhabitants of all territory belonging to the Confederate States, lying without the limits of the several States; and may permit them at such times, and in such manner as it may by law provide, to form States to be admitted into the Confederacy. In all such territory, the institution of negro slavery, as it now exists in the Confederate States, shall be recognized and protected by Congress and by the territorial government: and the inhabitants of the several Confederate States and Territories shall have

the right to take to such territory any slaves lawfully held by them in any of the States or Territories of the Confederate States.

4. The Confederate States shall guaranty to every State that now is, or hereafter may become, a member of this Confederacy, a republican form of government; and shall protect each of them against invasion; and on application of the legislature, (or of the executive, when the legislature is not in session,) against domestic violence.

ARTICLE V

Section One

1. Upon the demand of any three States, legally assembled in their several conventions, the Congress shall summon a convention of all the States, to take into consideration such amendments to the Constitution as the said States shall concur in suggesting at the time when the said demand is made; and should any of the proposed amendments to the Constitution be agreed on by the said convention — voting by States — and the same be ratified by the legislature of two-thirds of the several States, or by conventions in two-thirds thereof — as the one or the other mode of ratification may be proposed by the general convention — they shall thenceforward form a part of this Constitution. But no State shall, without its consent, be deprived of its equal representation in the Senate.

ARTICLE VI

1. The Government established by this Constitution is the successor of the Provisional Government of the Confederate States of America, and all the laws passed by the latter shall continue in force until the same shall be repealed or modified; and all the officers appointed by the same shall remain in office until their successors are appointed and qualified, or the offices abolished.

2. All debts contracted and engagements entered into before the adoption of this Constitution shall be as valid against the Confederate States under this Constitution as under the Provisional Government.

3. This Constitution, and the laws of the Confederate States made in pursuance thereof, and all treaties made or which shall be made under the authority of the Confederate States, shall be the supreme law of the land; and the judges in every State shall be bound thereby, any thing in the Constitution or laws of any State to the contrary notwithstanding.

4. The Senators and Representatives before mentioned, and the members of the several State Legislatures, and all executive and judicial officers, both of the Confederate States and of the several States, shall be bound by oath or affirmation to support this Constitution; but no religious test shall ever be required as a qualification to any office or public trust under the Confederate States.

5. The enumeration, in the Constitution, of certain rights, shall not be construed to

deny or disparage others retained by the people of the several States.

6. The powers not delegated to the Confederate States by the Constitution, nor prohibited by it to the States, are reserved to the States, respectively, or to the people thereof.

ARTICLE VII

1. The ratification of the Convention of five States shall be sufficient for the establishment of this Constitution between the States so ratifying the same.

2. When five States shall have ratified this Constitution, in the manner before specified, the Congress under the Provisional Constitution shall prescribe the time for holding the election of President and Vice President, and for the meeting of the Electoral College, and for counting the votes, and inaugurating the President. They shall also prescribe the time for holding the first election of members of Congress under this Constitution, and the time for assembling the same. Until the assembling of such Congress, the Congress under the Provisional Constitution shall continue to exercise the Legislative powers granted them; not extending beyond the time limited by the Constitution of the Provisional Government.

APPENDIX FOUR
A View of the Permanent Confederate Constitution
by Alexander Hamilton Stephens

Here is the Constitution for the Permanent Government as finally unanimously adopted by the seven States. It is, as will be seen, based on the general principles of the Federal Constitution, framed by the Philadelphia Convention, in 1787, with the amendments thereafter adopted. Several changes in the details appear. Some of the more prominent of these may very properly be specially noted.

The first is the Preamble. In this, the words "each State acting in its Sovereign and Independent character" were introduced to put at rest forever the argument of the Centralists, drawn from the Preamble of the old Constitution, that it had been made by the people of all the States collectively, or in mass, and not by the States in their several Sovereign character.

The official term of the President was extended, in the new Constitution, to six years instead of four, with a disqualification for re-election.

The question of the "Protective Policy," as it was called, under the old Constitution, was put to rest under the new, by the express declaration that no duties or taxes on importations from foreign nations should be laid to promote or foster any branch of industry. Under the new Constitution, Export duties were allowed to be levied with the concurrence of two-thirds of both Houses of Congress.

In passing acts of Bankruptcy, it was expressly declared that no law of Congress should discharge any debt contracted before the passage of the same. Considerable controversy had existed on this point under the old Constitution.

The President, under the new Constitution, was empowered to approve any appropriation, and disapprove any other appropriation in the same bill, returning to the House those portions disapproved as in other like cases of veto.

The impeachment of any judicial, or other Federal officer, resident and acting solely within the limits of any State, was allowed by a vote of two-thirds of both branches of the Legislature thereof, as well as by the House of Representatives of Congress. The Senate of the Confederate States, however, still having the sole power to try all impeachments.

No general appropriation of money was allowed, unless asked and estimated for by some one of the Heads of Departments, except by a two-thirds vote in both branches of Congress. The object of this was to make, as far as possible, each Administration responsible for the public expenditures.

All extra pay or extra allowance to any public contractor, officer, agent, or servant, was positively prohibited as well as all bounties. Great abuses had grown up under the old system in this particular.

Internal improvements by Congress, another subject which had given rise to great controversy under the old, were prohibited by the new Constitution, but Congress was empowered to lay local duties, to support lights, beacons, buoys, and for the improvement of harbors, the expenses to be borne by the navigation facilitated thereby.

The general power of the President to remove from office was restricted to the extent that he could remove for special cause only, and in all cases of removal, he was required to report the same to the Senate, with his reasons, except in the case of the principal officer in each of the Executive Departments, and all persons connected with the Diplomatic service. These, and these only, he could remove at pleasure, and without assigning any reasons therefore.

Citizens of the several States, under the new Constitution, were not permitted to sue each other in the Federal Courts, as they are under the old Constitution. They were left to their actions in the State Courts.

The right of any citizen of one State to pass through or sojourn in another with his slaves or other property, without molestation, was expressly guaranteed.

The admission of other States into the Confederacy required a vote of two-thirds of the whole House of Representatives, and two-thirds of the Senate, the Senate voting by States, instead of a bare majority of each.

A Convention of the States to consider proposed amendments of the Constitution was to be assembled for that purpose upon the call of any three States legally assembled in their several Conventions; and if a Convention so called should agree to the proposed amendments, the vote on them being taken by States, and the same should afterwards be ratified by the Legislatures of two-thirds of the several States, or by Conventions in them, then the proposed amendments were to form a part of the Constitution.

Congress was authorized by law to grant to the principal officer in each of the Executive Departments a seat upon the floor of either House, with the privilege of discussing any measures appertaining to his Department.

And, lastly, the power of Congress over the Territories was settled, in express language, in opposition both to the doctrine of the Centralists and the doctrine of "Squatter Sovereignty," so called.

There are the more prominent of the changes made. Several others will be seen upon a close examination. Some of them, however, verbal merely. Most of the prominent ones noticed emanated from Mr. (Robert Barnwell) Rhett, the Chairman. A few of them from Mr. (Robert Augustus) Toombs. Those proposed by Mr. Toombs were the ones prohibiting bounties, extra allowances, and internal improvements, with some others of less importance. The leading changes proposed by Mr. Rhett, were the ones in relation to the Protective policy, the Presidential term, the modification upon the subject of removal from office, and the mode provided for future amendments. The clause in relation to the admission of new States occupied the special attention of Mr. (John) Perkins, (Jr.) of Louisiana. The change in the old Constitution, which authorized Congress to pass a law to allow Cabinet Ministers to occupy seats in either House of Congress, and to participate in debates on subjects relating to their respective Departments, was the one in which I took the most interest. The clause, as it stands, did not go as far as I wished. I wanted the President to be required to appoint his Cabinet Ministers from Members of one or the other Houses of Congress. This feature in the British Constitution, I always regarded as one of the most salutary principles in it. But enough on this subject.

All of these amendments were decidedly of a conservative character. It is true, I did not approve of all of them. They were all, however, such as in the judgment of a majority of these States, the experience of seventy years had shown were proper and necessary for the harmonious working of the system. The whole document utterly negatives the idea which so many have been active in endeavoring to put in the enduring form of history, that the Convention at Montgomery was nothing but a set of "Conspirators," whose object was the overthrow of the principles of the Constitution of the United States, and the erection of a great "Slavery Oligarchy," instead of the free Institutions thereby secured and guaranteed. This work of the Montgomery Convention, with that of the Constitution for a Provisional Government, will ever remain not only as a monument of the wisdom, forecast and statesmanship of the men who constituted it, but an everlasting refutation of the charges which have been brought against them. These works together show clearly that their only leading object was to sustain, uphold, and perpetuate the fundamental principles of the Constitution of the United States.

APPENDIX FIVE
The Cult of Lincoln

How Lincoln Was Viewed By His Contemporaries

The real Lincoln will probably never be known, for his picture is now so completely encrusted with a patina of stained glass fictions and apocryphal rubbish that nobody knows where truth ends and myth begins.

His canonization as an American saint and hero took place after his death. While he was alive nobody of importance whom I have been able to discover, except James Russell Lowell and a few abolitionists, considered him a really great man. The intellectual class looked upon him as an unfortunate choice that had to be endured.[1]

The American obsession with the sixteenth President of the United States can rightly be described as a cult — not merely a political cult, but an idolatrous religious cult wherein Abraham Lincoln is literally worshiped as a god. His deified likeness seated upon its marble throne in Washington, D.C. is but a symbol of the sublime place of adoration he occupies in the hearts of his admirers everywhere. In the words of the St. Louis *Globe-Democrat*: "Abraham Lincoln has long since entered the sublime realm of apotheosis. Where now is the man so rash as to warmly criticise Abraham Lincoln?"[2]

The cult of Lincoln was founded on 15 April 1865 when a single bullet altered what otherwise would have been his rightful place alongside history's bloodiest rulers. Up until

1. W.E. Woodward, *Meet General Grant* (New York: The Literary Guild of America, 1928), page 277.

2. St. Louis *Globe-Democrat*, 6 March 1898.

the time of his death, Lincoln was denounced by nearly everyone in Washington, including the men of his own party and the members of his own Cabinet, as "a more unlimited despot than the world knows this side of China,"[3] "a despicable tyrant,"[4] "that original gorilla,"[5] and "a low, cunning clown."[6] He was ridiculed for his "halting imbecility,"[7] and his Administration was criticized for its "feebleness, faithlessness and incapacity,"[8] for being "an insult to the flag, and a traitor to their God,"[9] and for "dragging the Union to ruin."[10] Of "Ol' Honest Abe" it was asserted that "a hound might hunt Mr. Lincoln, and never find him by an honest scent."[11] Wendell Phillips, a leading Republican Abolitionist, viewed Lincoln as "a mere convenience [who was] waiting, like any other broomstick, to be used."[12]

In an editorial entitled "Lincoln and Johnson," the editors of the New York *World* wrote in 1864:

> The age of rail splitters and tailors, of buffoons, boors and fanatics has succeeded. Mr. Lincoln and Mr. Johnson are both men of mediocre talent, neglected education, narrow views, deficient information and of course, vulgar manners. A statesman is supposed to be a man of some depth of thought and extent of knowledge. Has this country with so proud a record been reduced to such intellectual poverty as to be forced to present two such names as Abraham Lincoln and Andrew Johnson for the highest stations in this most trying crisis of its history? It is a cruel mockery and bitter humiliation. Such nominations at this juncture are an insult to the common sense of the people.[13]

Apotheotized By the Republican Leaders

These denunciations ceased with Lincoln's last breath when the real Lincoln suddenly

3. Wendell Phillips, quoted by Woodward, *Meet General Grant*, page 276.

4. New York *World*, 26 October 1864.

5. Edwin Stanton, quoted by Edmonds, *Facts and Falsehoods*, page 18.

6. Stanton, quoted by Minor, *Real Lincoln*, page 42.

7. "A Yearning for the Democratic Party," New York *World*, 15 April 1864.

8. *New York World*, 2 June 1864.

9. Alfred R. Wooten, Attorney-General of Delaware, quoted by New York *Tribune*, 4 June 1863.

10. Wendell Phillips, *ibid*.

11. Wooten, *ibid*.

12. Phillips, speech delivered on 1 August 1862; quoted by Edmonds, *Facts and Falsehoods*, page 16.

13. "Lincoln and Johnson," New York *World*, 9 June 1864.

vanished from the public record to be replaced by a figure resembling the mythical gods of pagan Rome more than a man. The editors of the Saint Louis *Globe-Democrat* stated, "One thing is certain, Lincoln was apotheosized after his death. Had he lived 4000 years ago his name would now be enrolled among the gods of Greece and Rome."[14] In the words of Charles L.C. Minor, "The Real Lincoln was a very different man, in his private and in his public life, from what the world's verdict has pronounced him to be."[15] Ward H. Lamon, who was one of Lincoln's closest friends during his stay in the White House, stated:

> The ceremony of Mr. Lincoln's apotheosis was planned and executed by men who were unfriendly to him while he lived. The deification took place with showy magnificence; men who had exhausted the resources of their skill and ingenuity in venomous detractions of the living Lincoln were the first, after his death, to undertake the task of guarding his memory, not as a human being, but as a god.
>
> There was the fiercest rivalry as to who should canonize Mr. Lincoln in the most solemn words; who should compare him to the most sacred character in all history. He was prophet, priest and king, he was Washington, he was Moses, he was likened to Christ the Redeemer, he was likened to God. After that came the ceremony of apotheosis.
>
> For days and nights after the President's death it was considered treason to be seen in public with a smile on your face. Men who ventured to doubt the ineffable purity and saintliness of Lincoln's character, were pursued by mobs of men, beaten to death with paving stones, or strung up by the neck to lamp posts until dead.[16]

Since American society at that time was still dominated by an external form of Christianity, one of the main features of Lincoln's apotheosis was to declare his eminent religious character. Journalist J.G. Holland eulogized his dead hero with these words:

> The power of a true-hearted Christian man, in perfect sympathy with a true-hearted Christian people, was Mr. Lincoln's power. Open on one side of his nature to all descending influences from him to whom he prayed, and open on the other to all ascending influences from the people whom he served, he aimed simply to do his duty to God and man. Acting rightly he acted greatly.... Moderate, frank, truthful, gentle, forgiving, loving, just, Mr. Lincoln will always be remembered as eminently a Christian President; and the almost immeasurably great results which he had the privilege of achieving were due to the fact that he was a Christian President.[17]

---

14. *The Globe-Democrat*, quoted by Edmonds, *Facts and Falsehoods*, page 2.

15. Minor, *Real Lincoln*, page 1.

16. Lamon, *Life of Abraham Lincoln*; quoted by Edmonds, *Facts and Falsehoods*, pages 2-3, 9, 10.

17. Holland, *Life of Lincoln*, page 542.

Likewise, when Lincoln's alleged birthplace in Kentucky[18] was dedicated as a national monument, Henry Watterson, a Southern-born man and a former Confederate soldier, stated:

> You lowly cabin which is to be dedicated on the morrow may well be likened to the Manger of Bethlehem, the boy that went thence to a God-like destiny, to the Son of God, the Father Almighty of Him and us all. Whence his prompting except from God? His tragic death may be likened also to that other martyr whom Lincoln so closely resembled.
>
> There are utterances of his which read like rescripts from the Sermon on the Mount. Reviled as Him of Galilee, slain, even as Him of Galilee, yet as gentle and as unoffending a man who died for men.[19]

Today, over 140 years after his death, the myth of Lincoln's moral character and faith in Christianity continues to be perpetuated. In his lectures and writings, David Barton of Wallbuilders, Inc. often cites Lincoln's ambiguous religious statements as supporting evidence of "America's Christian Heritage." A Presbyterian church in Pennsylvania recently published a booklet entitled *Freedom's Holy Light*, in which an entire chapter is devoted to the claim that Lincoln was "almost like a national saint" whose "heroic work and tragic death create a sense of awe," and whose "faith in the transcendent purposes of a God of Providence gave him hope in his quest to try to heal the torn and wounded nation."[20] In the words of popular Southern Baptist minister, Dr. Charles Stanley:

> Despite his Christian upbringing, Lincoln did not accept Christ as his Savior until later in life. While he governed the nation by many of the principles written in God's Word, he lacked a personal relationship with Jesus Christ. After the death of his son, Willie, Lincoln heard for the first time of Christ's personal love and forgiveness for each man and woman.
>
> He wrote: "When I left Springfield, I asked the people to pray for me; I was not a Christian. When I buried my son — the severest trial of my life — I was not a Christian. But when I went to Gettysburg, and saw the graves of thousands of our soldiers, I then and there consecrated myself to Christ."
>
> Finally, Lincoln had found the inner peace he longed for all his life. Following his

---

18. Lincoln was actually born in the western North Carolina home of Abraham Enloe, for whom his mother, Nancy Hanks, worked as a servant and with whom she had an adulterous affair. Because of the reproach thus brought upon the family, Nancy and her infant son were sent by Enloe to Kentucky, where she eventually married Thomas Lincoln (James H. Cathey, *The Genesis of Lincoln* [Atlanta, Georgia: Franklin Printing and Publishing Company, 1899]; James Caswell Coggins, *The Eugenics of President Abraham Lincoln* [Elizabethton, Tennesse: Goodwill Press, 1940]).

19. Henry Watterson, quoted by Rutherford, *True Estimate of Abraham Lincoln*, page 73.

20. Dr. Peter A. Lillback, *Freedom's Holy Light* (Bryn Mawr, Pennsylvania: The Providence Forum, 2000), page 23.

salvation experience, he worshiped regularly at the New York Avenue Presbyterian Church and planned to make a public confession of his faith. The war was winding down. Lee surrendered to Grant on April 9 — Palm Sunday, and Lincoln was re-elected President. He gave thanks to God for bringing a close to the war and began turning the nation's interest toward reconciliation and reconstruction. However, five days later on Good Friday, he was shot by an assassin's bullet.

Throughout his life, Lincoln suffered many defeats — enough to make most men give up. But not Abraham Lincoln. His dedication and commitment found merit in heaven. He believed he was chosen "for such a time as this."[21]

"He Lived and Died a Deep-Grounded Infidel"

Was Lincoln indeed a Christian? Is it true that he accepted Jesus Christ as Savior, even if only in the last days of his life? To answer these questions, we must not turn to the tall tales that were concocted following Lincoln's death by ambitious Republican radicals and later permanently etched in the historical record by endless repetition, but to the testimonies of those who knew him personally, both before and during his tenure as President of the United States. In the suppressed biography entitled *The Life of Lincoln*, by William H. Herndon, who was "for Twenty Years His Friend and Partner," we find the following description of the sixteenth President:

Lincoln was a deep-grounded infidel. He disliked and despised churches. He never entered a church except to scoff and ridicule. On coming from a church he would mimic the preacher. Before running for any office he wrote a book against Christianity and the Bible. He showed it to some friends and read extracts. A man named Hill was greatly shocked and urged Lincoln not to publish it. Urged it would kill him politically. Hill got this book in his hands, opened the stove door, and it went up in flames and ashes. After that, Lincoln became more discreet, and when running for office often used words and phrases to make it appear that he was a Christian. He never changed on this subject. He lived and died a deep-grounded infidel.[22]

Herndon was so outraged by the "pretended biographies" of his late friend that he wrote the following article which appeared in the Toledo (Ohio) *Index* in 1870:

I became acquainted with Mr. Lincoln in 1834, and I think I knew him well to the day of his death.... He came to Illinois in 1830, and, after some little roving, settled in New Salem, now in Menard county and state of Illinois... It was here that Mr. Lincoln became acquainted with a class of men the world never saw the like of before or since.... They

---

21. Charles F. Stanley, "Abraham Lincoln: For Such a Time as This," online at www.intouch.org/myintouch/mighty/portraits/abraham_lincoln_213718.html.

22. William H. Herndon, quoted by Edmonds, *Facts and Falsehoods*, pages 54-55.

were a bold, daring, and reckless sort of men; they were men of their own minds — believed what was demonstrable; were men of great common sense. With these men Mr. Lincoln was thrown; with them he lived, and with them he moved and almost had his being. They were skeptics all — scoffers some. These scoffers were good men, and their scoffs were protests against theology — loud protests against the follies of Christianity.... They declared that Jesus was an illegitimate child.... They riddled all divines, and not infrequently made them skeptics, disbelievers as bad as themselves....

In 1835 he wrote out a small work on Infidelity, and intended to have it published. This book was an attack upon the whole grounds of Christianity, and especially was it an attack upon the idea that Jesus was the Christ, the true and only-begotten son of God, as the Christian world contends. Mr. Lincoln was at that time in New Salem, keeping store for Mr. Samuel Hill, a merchant and postmaster of that place. Lincoln and Hill were very friendly. Hill, I think, was a skeptic at this time. Lincoln, one day after the book was finished, read it to Mr. Hill, his good friend. Hill tried to persuade him not to make it public, not to publish it. Hill at that time saw in Mr. Lincoln a rising man, and wished him success. Lincoln refused to destroy it — said it should be published. Hill swore it should never see light of day. He had an eye on Lincoln's popularity — his present and future success; and believing that if the book was published it would kill Lincoln forever, he snatched it from Lincoln's hand when Lincoln was not expecting it, and ran it into an old-fashioned tinplate stove, heated as hot as a furnace; and so Lincoln's book went up to the clouds in smoke....

When Mr. Lincoln was a candidate for our Legislature, he was accused of being an Infidel and of having said that Jesus Christ was an illegitimate child. He never denied his opinions nor flinched from his religious views....

Mr. Lincoln ran for Congress against the Rev. Peter Cartwright in the year 1846. In that contest he was accused of being an Infidel, if not an Atheist. He never denied the charge.... In the first place, because he knew it could and would be proved on him; and in the second place, he was too true to his own convictions, to his own soul, to deny it.

When Mr. Lincoln left this city for Washington, I knew he had undergone no change in his religious opinions or views. He held many of the Christian ideas in abhorrence, and among them there was this one, namely, that God would forgive the sinner for a violation of his laws. Lincoln maintained that God could not forgive; that punishment has to follow the sin; that Christianity was wrong in teaching forgiveness.[23]

Herndon explained why the word "God" appeared so often in Lincoln's speeches:

No man had a stronger or firmer faith in Providence — God — than Mr. Lincoln, but the continued use by him late in life of the word God must not be interpreted to mean that he believed in a personal God. In 1854 he asked me to erase the world God from a speech which I had written and read to him for criticism, because my language indicated

23. Herndon, letter to Toledo (Ohio) *Index* on 18 February 1870; quoted by John E. Remsburg, *Abraham Lincoln: Was He a Christian?* (New York: The Truth Seeker Company, 1906), pages 99-103.

a personal God, whereas he insisted that no such personality ever existed.[24]

Two years later Lincoln's former associate, Ward Lamon, corroborated Herndon's testimony: "Mr. Lincoln was never a member of any church, nor did he believe in the divinity of Christ, or the inspiration of the Scriptures in the sense understood by evangelical Christians."[25] In her biography entitled *Life of Abraham Lincoln*, Ida Tarbell declared, "If Mr. Lincoln was not strictly orthodox, he was profoundly religious. He was a regular and reverent attendant at church."[26] However, Lincoln's "regular and reverent" church attendance was seen in a different light by Lamon:

> At an early age he began to attend the "preachings" roundabout, but principally at the Pigeon Creek church, with a view to catching whatever might be ludicrous in the preacher's air or matter, and making it the subject of mimicry as soon as he could collect an audience of idle boys and men to hear him....
> When he went to church at all, he went to mock, and came away to mimic....[27]

John Matthews, who described himself as Lincoln's "personal and political friend," testified that he "attacked the Bible and the New Testament," and "would come into the clerk's office where I and some young men were writing... and would bring a Bible with him; would read a chapter and argue against it."[28] John G. Nicolay, who was Lincoln's private secretary throughout his Presidency, and who "probably was closer to the martyred [sic] President than any other man,"[29] declared in a letter written just six weeks after Lincoln's death, "Mr. Lincoln did not, to my knowledge, in any way change his religious views, opinions or beliefs from the time he left Springfield till the day of his death."[30] Even Lincoln's own widow confessed in a letter to family friend Lamon that, "Mr. Lincoln had no hope and no faith in the usual acceptance of these words."[31] Finally, we have the testimony of Lincoln himself, who, following the death of his son Willie in 1862, wrote in a letter to Judge J.S. Wakefield these words: "My earlier views of the unsoundness of the Christian scheme of salvation and the human origin of the scriptures have become clearer and stronger with

---

24. Herndon, *Life of Lincoln*, pages 445-446.

24. Lamon, *Life of Lincoln*, page 486.

26. Ida Tarbell, *Life of Abraham Lincoln* (New York: Doubleday and McClure Company, 1900).

26. Lamon, *Life of Lincoln*, pages 55, 486.

27. John Matthews, quoted by Edmonds, *Facts and Falsehoods.*, page 56; Minor, *Real Lincoln*, pages 28-29.

28. *Cosmopolitan* of March 1901, quoted by Minor, *ibid.*, page 30.

29. John G. Nicolay, letter to Lamon, 27 May 1865; quoted by Lamon, *Life of Lincoln*, page 492.

30. Mary Todd Lincoln, quoted by Lamon, *ibid.*, page 489.

advancing years, and I see no reason for thinking I shall ever change them."

A Lover of Vulgar Stories

It is beyond comprehension how a professing Christian, such as Lincoln is said to have been, would have engaged in the vulgar manner of behavior that he did. According to William Herndon, "Lincoln could never realize the impropriety of telling vulgar yarns in the presence of a minister of the gospel," and "Lincoln's highest delight was to get a rowdy crowd in groceries or on street corners and retell vulgar yarns too coarse to put in print."[32] A.Y. Ellis, who was a friend of Lincoln's, said, "On electioneering trips Mr. Lincoln told stories which drew the boys after him. I remember them, but modesty forbids me to repeat them."[33] Ward Lamon likewise stated, "His humor was not of a delicate quality; it was chiefly exercised in telling and hearing stories of the grossest sort. Mr. Lincoln's habit of relating vulgar yarns (not one of which will bear printing) was restrained by no presence and no occasion."[34] In a rare moment of honesty, Lincoln-worshiper J.G. Holland wrote:

> It is useless for Mr. Lincoln's biographers to ignore this habit; the whole West, if not the whole country, is full of these stories, and there is no doubt at all that he indulged in them with the same freedom that he did in those of a less objectionable character.... Men who knew him throughout all his professional and political life... have said that "he was the foulest in his jests and stories of any man in the country."[35]

Following the bloody battle of Antietam in 1862, the Sussex, New Jersey *Statesman* published the following account:

> We see that many papers are referring to the fact that Lincoln ordered a comic song to be sung upon the battlefield. We have known the facts of the transaction for some time, but have refrained from speaking about them. As the newspapers are stating some of the facts, we will give the whole. Soon after one of the most desperate and sanguinary battles, Mr. Lincoln visited the Commanding General [George McClellan], who, with his staff, took him over the field, and explained to him the plan of the battle, and the particular places where the battle was most fierce. At one point the Commanding General said: "Here on this side of the road five hundred of our brave fellows were killed, and just on the other side of the road four hundred and fifty more were killed, and right on the other side of that well five hundred rebels were destroyed. We have buried them where they fell." "I de-

---

31. Herndon, quoted by Edmonds, *Facts and Falsehoods*, pages 68, 69.

32. A.Y. Ellis, quoted by Edmonds, *ibid.*, page 69.

33. Lamon, *Life of Lincoln*, page 480.

34. J.G. Holland, quoted by Minor, *Real Lincoln*, pages 31-32.

clare," said the President, "this is getting gloomy; let us drive away." After driving a few rods the President said: "Jack," speaking to his companion [Ward Lamon], "can't you give us something to cheer us up? Give us a song, and a lively one." Whereupon, Jack struck up, as loud as he could bawl, a comic negro song, which he continued to sing while they were riding off from the battle ground, and until they approached a regiment drawn up, when the Commanding General said: "Would it not be well for your friend to cease his song till we pass this regiment? The poor fellows have lost more than half their number. They are feeling very badly, and I should be afraid of the effect it would have on them." The President asked his friend to stop singing until they passed the regiment.

　　　　When this story was told to us we said: "It is incredible, it is impossible, that any man could act so over the fresh-made graves of the heroic dead." But the story is told on such authority we know it to be true. We tell the story now that the people may have some idea of the man elected to be President of the United States.[36]

　　　　Above we have read the alleged and undocumented testimony of Lincoln that he "consecrated his life to Christ" on the battlefield of Gettysburg, Pennsylvania. However, despite its uncritical endorsement by Charles Stanley's organization, such is merely a myth drawn from one of the many stories that were fabricated about Lincoln as part of his apotheosis ceremony. Indeed, it does not coincide with the testimonies of eyewitnesses of Lincoln's conduct at Gettysburg while the ground was still wet from the blood of both Union and Confederate soldiers. General Donn Piatt, who was present as Lincoln toured the battlefield, referred to Gettysburg as "the field that he shamed with a ribald song."[37] One observer of Lincoln's lack of respect for those who died for their convictions voiced his disgust in verse: "Abe may crack his jolly jokes/Over bloody fields of battle/While yet the ebbing life tide smokes/From men who die like butchered cattle/And even before the guns grow cold/To pimps and pet Abe cracks his jokes."[38] Lincoln's last words were a joke told at the expense of the conquered and devastated Southern people. In fulfillment of the promise of Psalm 7:11-16, the foul tongue of the reprobate President was forever silenced by the assassin's bullet as he sat in the audience of — fittingly — a comedy play at Ford's Theater in the capital of a country he had destroyed.

Opposed By Springfield's Christian Leaders

　　　　It is noteworthy that during Lincoln's campaign for the Presidency, twenty out of the twenty-three Christian ministers in his home town of Springfield, Illinois, opposed him

35. Sussex (New Jersey) *Statesman*, quoted by Edmonds, *Facts and Falsehoods*, pages 73-74.

36. Piatt, *Men Who Saved the Union*, page 35.

37. Editorial: "One of Mr. Lincoln's Jokes," New York *World*, 9 September 1864.

because "in religious views" he was "an open and avowed Infidel."[39] The closest that Lincoln ever came to a denial of this consensus was in the handbill that was circulated during his campaign for re-election in 1864:

TO THE VOTERS OF THE SEVENTH CONGRESSIONAL DISTRICT:

FELLOW CITIZENS:

A charge having got into circulation in some of the neighborhoods of this district in substance that I am an open scoffer at Christianity. I have by the advice of some friends concluded to notice the subject in this form. That I am not a member of any Christian church is true; but I have never denied the truth of the Scripture; and I have never spoken with intentional disrespect of religion in general, or of any denomination, of Christians in particular. It is true that in early life I was inclined to believe in what I understand is called the "Doctrine of Necessity,"   that is, that the human mind is impelled to action or held in rest by some power, over which the mind itself has no control; and I have sometimes (with one, two, or three, but never publicly) tried to maintain this opinion in argument. The habit of arguing thus, however, I have entirely left off for more than five years; and I add here I have always understood this same opinion to be held by several of the Christian denominations. The foregoing is the whole truth, briefly stated in relation to myself on this subject.[40]

Lincoln was the consummate politician and a master of rhetoric, so his "denial" of the charges against him need to be carefully dissected. Lincoln claimed that he had "never spoken with intentional disrespect of religion in general." Technically, this was true. He could not afford to speak with disrespect for "religion in general" since the Republican party upon which his political career depended was dominated by Unitarians, who, like himself, held to a form of "natural religion" which found the "spark of divinity" in all mankind and denied the unique Divinity of Jesus Christ. The "Scripture" of such people was nature itself, which human reason was capable of comprehending without the aid of divine revelation, and the Bible was derided, in the words of Thaddeus Stevens, as "nothing but obsolete history of a barbarous people."[41] Such was the basis of the Abolition movement that declared war on the Christian South.

Furthermore, Lincoln did not directly lie when he claimed that he had never spoken with disrespect for "any denomination, of Christians in particular." As seen in the above testimonies of his closest friends and associates, his disdain was voiced for Christianity *in*

---

38. T. Charlton Henry, letter to Lincoln, 26 May 1860.

39. Lincoln, quoted by Roy P. Basler, *A Touchstone For Greatness* (Westport, Connecticut: Greenwood, 1973), page 61.

40. Thaddeus Stevens, quoted by Edmonds, *Facts and Falsehoods*, page 59.

general, rather than for denominations "in particular." Finally, Lincoln's claim that his "Doctrine of Necessity" was "held by several of the Christian denominations" was an outright lie. This doctrine, in which events are predetermined by "some power over which the mind has no control," was nothing more than a pagan fatalism upon which Lincoln could rely to relieve himself of the responsibility for the deaths of 600,000 American men and the destruction of the Union and its Constitution which he had been sworn to uphold and defend. After all, reasoned Lincoln, "What is to be will be and no prayers of ours can arrest the decree."[42] This was not the predestination taught in the Bible and held by the Presbyterian and Reformed churches, but was the doctrine espoused by the apostate Abolitionists at the helm of Lincoln's Republican party, who merely used religious rhetoric to conceal their true character from their deceived constituents. It was only later, in his second Inaugural Address, that Lincoln attempted to pin the blame for the horrific carnage which he had caused on the righteous Judge of men, for which blasphemy he was not long thereafter summoned before the Heavenly Bench to give an account.

It is a travesty indeed that Abraham Lincoln, the infidel, is mythologized by so many today as "Abraham Lincoln, the Christian." As this book was written to prove, the sixteenth U.S. President was no friend to the Union he professed to save, no friend to the slaves he professed to emancipate, and no friend to his "fellow countrymen" for whom he professed no malice. It is time for History to execute her long overdue sentence of infamy against the tyrant who, with the wave of his executive scepter, nearly single-handedly destroyed the remnants of a centuries-old social and law order and plunged America into the dark abyss of pagan despotism from which we have yet to recover.

We conclude here with the following comparison of the American "Caesar" of the Nineteenth Century to his ancient Roman counterpart in the First Century:

> There was a singular resemblance between Claudius Nero, and Abraham Lincoln.
>
> In early life, Nero was remarkable for his jovial habit of illustration. Lincoln's whole field of logic, illustration, ridicule and satire, was anecdote and stories.
>
> Nero proposed many reforms under Seneca and Burrhus, and grew in popularity among the people, until he was accounted a god. Lincoln commenced his administration as a benevolent reformer, under the auspices of all the reformers of the country.
>
> Nero's subjects rebelled against his usurpation. Lincoln's subjects anticipated his usurpation. Such rulers always create rebellions and excite resistance.
>
> Nero played the drama of the destruction of Troy, during the seven days' burning of Rome. Lincoln attended balls and engaged in festivities during the five years' conflagration of the country, and the wanton, bloody slaughter of his countrymen; and had vile songs sung among his dying armies.
>
> Nero rebuilt Rome at his own expense, by extortion and robbery, and the tyrant was liberal to the sufferers. In this Nero excelled Lincoln, who repaired no damages of burning cities.

---

41. Lincoln, quoted by Lamon, *Life of Lincoln*, page 503.

Nero threw prisoners to wild beasts; Lincoln kept prisoners confined in cold prisons, where their limbs were frozen; in filthy prisons where they were eaten up with vermin; starved them until they died of scurvy and other loathsome diseases, after months of terror, torture and cruelty.

Nero put Christians to death under false pretenses, to gratify the worshippers of the Pantheon. Lincoln corrupted one part of the Church to engage in warfare with the other part, and burned twelve hundred houses of worship; mutilated grave-yards; and left whole cities, churches and all in ashes; dragged ministers from their knees in the very act of worship; tied them up by their thumbs; had their daughters stripped naked by negro soldiers, under the command of white officers.

Suetonius, under Nero, butchered eighty thousand Britons, defended by Queen Boadicea. His officers flogged Boadicea and ravished her daughters; and lost thousands of Romans in the attempt to subdue the Britons, who were defending their homes, altars and grave-yards. Lincoln let loose Turchin to ravish the women of Athens, Alabama; Banks and Butler to rob New Orleans; Sheridan to burn up Virginia; Sherman to ravage the South with desolating fires; Payne and Burbridge to murder in Kentucky; Neil, Strachan and the vagabond thieves, to murder, rob and destroy Missouri, until one million of his murdered countrymen butchered each other by his command.

Every department of Nero's government was signalized by licentiousness and debauchery, nameless and loathsome. Lincoln's court was the resort of debauchees; the Treasury Department was a harem; the public officers were one great unrestrained multitude who yielded to the coarsest appetites of nature, stimulated by strong drinks and inflamed by the indulgence of every other vice.

In this did Nero, to his credit, differ from Lincoln. The generals of Nero respected the works of arts, the paintings, poems and manuscripts of the learned, and the discoveries of genius. Upon the other hand, Lincoln destroyed everything that indicated superior civilization. In one instance, a general officer of scientific pretension, arrayed his daughter in the stolen garments of the wife of C.C. Clay, an old Senator of Alabama. During the invasion of Huntsville, Mr. Clay's house was robbed of its jewelry, the heir-looms of three generations, taken against the tearful prayers of his black servant. The exquisitely beautiful statute of his dead babe, was ground to powder before his eyes. An appeal to Lincoln's men, that any object was of scientific value, only hastened its destruction; his wars were directed against civilization.

Nero fled before the judgment of the Senate, and died by his own hand. Lincoln could not have survived his crimes, so unrelenting is the retributive justice of God.[43]

---

42. Dean, *Crimes of the Civil War*, pages 172-174.

APPENDIX SIX

The Duty of the Hour
by Robert Lewis Dabney

Young gentlemen of the Eumenean and Philanthropic Societies: I am here to-day in response not only to your call, but to an imperative sentiment. This the sense of the value of the young men of the South, and their claims upon every patriot. When I remember how your class has lately striven and died for us — how this seat of learning, like every other shrine of the Muses, was emptied at the call of a bleeding country, I feel that you have earned a claim upon our sympathies and aid, which cannot be refused. Nor was this devotion of our youth the less admirable — in my eyes it is only the more touching — because it has pleased the divine disposer, in his mysterious and awful providence, to deny you that success which you hoped. It has pleased Heaven that you should be so disappointed of your deserved victory, as that fools should say you have bled in vain.

But be assured, that as the afflicted child is ever dearest to the mother's heart, your disasters only cause your country to press you closer to her bosom. Amid her cruel losses, her children alone remain her last, as her most precious possession; and it is only from their energies, their virtues, their fortitude under obloquy and oppression, that she hopes for restoration. We assuredly believe, young gentlemen, that no drop of blood, generously shed in the right, ever wets our mother earth in vain.

The vision of the harvest from this precious seed may tarry, but in the end it will not fail; and we wait for it. The holy struggle may meet with seeming overthrow. But if our immediate hope is denied, amidst the manifold alternatives of Almighty Providence, some other recompense is provided, which will gladden and satisfy the hearts of our children, if not ours, in God's own time and place.

Now that this expectation may not fail, it is needful that you cherish jealously, the virtues and principles which ennoble your cause. Your steadfast and undebauched hearts must be the nurturing soil to preserve the precious seed of martyr blood, during this winter of disaster, to the appointed summer of its resurrection. The urgency, the solemnity of this season of darkness and danger, warn me that it is no mere literary pastime, but a high and serious duty which should occupy this hour. Pardon me, then, for passing to a topic which is fundamental, at once to the dearest hopes of your country and of its dead heroes. I would employ this season of communion with my young fellow-citizens, in uttering my earnest warning to them of a danger and a duty arising out of the misfortunes of our country — a danger most portentious to a thoughtful mind, a duty peculiarly incumbent on educated men.

This danger may be expressed by the fearful force of conquest and despotism to degrade the spirit of the victims. The correlated duty is that of anxiously preserving our integrity and self-respect. A graphic English traveller in the East describes the contrast, so striking to us, between the cowering spirit of the Orientals, and the manly independence of the citizens of free States in Western Europe. These have been raised in commonwealths which avouch and protect the rights of individuals. They are accustomed to claim their chartered liberties as an inviolable heritage. The injuries of power are met by them with moral indignation and the high purpose of resistance.

But the abject Syrian or Copt is affected no otherwise by Turkish oppressions than by the incursions of nature's resistless forces; the whirlwind or the thunderbolt. The only emotion excited is that of passive terror. He accepts the foulest wrong as his destiny and almost his right. He has no other thought than to crouch and disarm the lash by his submissiveness. And if any sentiment than that of helpless panic is excited, it is rather admiration of superior power than righteous resentment against wrong. He who is the most ruthless among his masters is in his abject view the greatest.

When we remember the ancestry of these Orientals, we ask with wonder what has wrought this change? These are the children of those Egyptians who under Sesostris pushed their conquests from Thrace to furthest Ind, beyond the utmost march of Alexander and who, under the Pharoahs, so long contested the empire of the world with the Assyrian. Or they are the descendants of the conquering Saracens, who in later ages made all Europe tremble. Or these Jews who now kiss the sword that slays them are the posterity of the heroes who, under the Macabees, wrested their country from Antiochus against odds even more fearful than Southern soldiers were wont to breast. Whence, then, the change?

The answer is, this mournful degeneracy is the result of ages of despotism. These base children of noble sires are but living examples of the rule that not only the agents, but the victims of unrighteous oppression, are usually degraded by their unavenged wrongs: a law which our times renders so significant to us.

Illustrations of the same rule also may be found in the more familiar scenes of domestic life. Few observing men can live to middle life without witnessing sad instances of it. We recall, for instance, some nuptial scene, from the distance of a score of years. We remember how the bridegroom led his adored prize to the altar, elate with proud affection. We recall the modest, trembling happiness of the bride, as she confidently pledged away her heart, her all, to the chosen man whom she trusted with an almost religious faith. Her step, diffident yet proud, the proprieties of her tasteful dress, her spotless purity of person, her sparkling eyes, all bespoke self-respect, aspiration, high hope, and noble love. They revealed the thoughts of generous devotion with which her gentle breast was filled.

Had one whispered at that hour that the trusted man would one day make a brutal use of the power she now so confidently gave, she would have resented it as the foulest libel on humanity. Had the prophet added that she was destined to submit, tamely and basely, to such brutality, she would have repudiated this prediction also with scorn as an equal libel on herself. But we pass over a score of years. We find the same woman sitting in an untidy cabin, with a brood of squalid, neglected children around her knees; her shoulders scantily covered with tawdry calico, her once shining hair now wound like a wisp of hay into a foul knot. She is without aspiration, without hope, without self-respect, almost without shame. What is the explanation? She has been for years a drunkard's wife. She was wholly innocent of her husband's fall. Long has she endured unprovoked tyranny and abuse. Not seldom has she been the helpless victim of blows from the hand which was sworn to cherish her. Often has she meditated escape from her degrading yoke; but the unanswerable plea of her helpless children arrested her always. She has found herself tied to a bondage where there was neither escape nor resistance; and these wrongs, this misery, has at last crushed her down into the degraded woman we see. The truthfulness of this picture will only be denied by those who judge from romance without experience, not from facts.

We need only to look a little at the operations of moral causes on man's nature to find the solution of these cases. We are creatures of imitation and habit. Familiarity with any object accustoms us to its lineaments. The effect of this acquaintanceship to reconcile us to vice has been expressed by Pope in words too trite to need citation. And the fact that one is the injured object of repeated crime does not exempt him from this law, but, as will be shown, only subjects him the more surely to it. Not only is every act of oppression a crime, but the seasons of despotism are usually eras of profuse and outbreaking crime. The baleful shadow of the tyrant's throne is the favorite haunt of every unclean bird and beast. And if the oppressing power be the many-headed monster, a tyrant faction, this is only more emphatically true. At such a time the moral atmosphere is foul with evil example. The vision of conscience is darkened and warped. The very air is unhealthy even for the innocent soul.

For the common mind the standard of rectitude is almost overthrown in the guilty confusion. But this is the consideration of least weight. A more momentous one is found in the law of man's sensibilities. The natural reflex of injury or assault upon us is resentment. This instinctive emotion has evidently been designed by our Creator as the protector of man in this world of injustice. Its function is to energize his powers for self defense. But its nature is active; in exertion is its life. Closely connected with this is the sentiment of moral disapprobation for the wrong character of the act.

This emotion is the necessary correlative to approbation for the right: so that the former cannot be blunted without equally blaming the latter. The man who has ceased to feel moral indignation for wrong has ceased to feel the claims of virtue. Nor is there a valid reason for your insensibility to evil in the fact that you yourself are the object of it.

Now when a man is made the helpless victim of frequent wrongs when his misfortunes allow him nothing but passive endurance, resentment and moral indignation give place to simple fear. And this by two sure causes; not only is the very power of sensibility worn away by these repeated and violent abrasions; not only is the nature dulled by the perpetual violences to which it is subjected, but that activity being denied which is the necessary scope of these sentiments of resistance, they are extinguished in their birth. The soul which first rose against injustice with the quick and keen sense of wrong and heroic self-defense; at last brutalized by its very injuries, subsides into dull indifference or abject panic. Should it not make the thoughtful patriot shudder to compare the present temper of the people with that of the revolutionary sires who bequeathed to us the liberties we have forfeited? With how quick and sensitive a jealousy, with what generous disdain did they spurn at the imposition of a tax of a few pence, against their rights as Englishmen; while we seek to reconcile ourselves with a jest or sophism to wrongs a thousand fold as onerous. In the words of Burke, "In other countries the people judge of an ill principle in government only by an actual grievance; here they anticipated the evil, and judged of the pressure of misgovernment at a distance, and snuffed the reproach of tyranny in every tainted breeze." But we, their miserable children, are compelled to inhabit the very miasm and stench of extreme oppression until our tainted nostrils almost refuse the office and leave us unconscious, while stifled by the pollution.

We need not go so far to find this startling contrast; we have only to compare our present selves with ourselves a few years ago to find fearful illustrations of the working of these influences. Let us suppose that on the evening of July 21, 1861, I had stood before that panting citizen soldiery which had just hurled back the onset of our gigantic foe, and that I had denounced to them that seven short years would find them tamely acquiescing in the unutterable wrongs since heaped upon us: in the insolent violation of every belligerent right, in the sack of their homes, in the insult of their females, in the treacherous arming of their own slaves, in their subjection to them; with what anger and incredulity would they not have repelled me? Let us suppose that I had made the imputation that some day they would consent to survive such infamy: that it would be possible for them to make any other election than that of death, with their faces to the foe rather than such a fate; would they not have declared it a libel upon the glories of that day, and upon the dead heroes even then lying with their faces to the sky? But we have consented to live under all this and are even now persuading ourselves to submit to yet more! Do you remember that unutterable swelling of indignation aroused in us by the first rumor of outrage to Southern women? How that you felt your breasts must rend with anguish unless it were solaced by some deeds of defense and righteous retribution? But we have since had so illstarred a tuition by a multitude of more monstrous wrongs that the slavish pulse is now scarcely quickened by the story of the foulest iniquities heaped upon a defenseless people. Thus does our own melancholy experience verify the reasonings given.

But, my hearers, this determination of the moral sensibilities does not place man above the promptings of selfishness: it rather subjects him more fully to them. We may not expect that the sense of helplessness and fear will reconcile him to suffer with passive fortitude without a struggle. As well might we look to see the panting stag bear the bit and spur with quietude. The instinct of self-preservation goads the oppressed to attempt some evasion from their miseries; but the only remaining means is that common weapon of the weak against the strong — artifice. Every down-trodden people is impelled almost irresistibly to seek escape from the injustice which can no longer be resisted by force through the agency of concealments, of duplicity, of lies, or perjuries. The government of the oppressor is therefore a school to train its victims in all the arts of chicanery and meanness. Mark, I pray you, the cruel alternative to which it shuts them up. They must suffer without human help or remedy evils unrighteous, relentless, almost intolerable; evils which outrage at once their well-being and their moral sense; or they must yield to temptation and seek deceitful methods of escape. And the only motives to move them to elect suffering rather than dishonor are the power of conscience, the fear of God, and faith in the eventual awards of His justice. What portion of any people may be expected to persevere in this passive heroism without other support?

In answering this question we must not forget the inexpressible seductiveness and plausibility of that temptation. It pleads with the injured victim of wrong that his oppressors had no moral right to inflict these evils: That their injustice and treachery forfeit all claim upon his conscience: That to deceive them is but paying them as they deserve in their own coin. An embittered hatred, which pleads its excuse from a thousand unprovoked injuries, impels the sufferer by a sting as keen as living fire, to seek the revenge of deception: the only one in his reach. And last, the specious maxim, "That necessity knows no law," completes the triumph of the temptation with the plea that the endurance of this tyrant's unmitigated will is impossible, and therefore the case justifies the means of evasion.

Now I need hardly pause, before this assembly, to say that all this pretended argument is a guilty sophism. You know that, however plausible it may be, it is grounded in a profane forgetfulness of God, of his holy will, and of his omnipotent government over oppressors and oppressed. You see how it involves that maxim of delusion, of whose advocates the Apostle declared "their damnation is just"; that the end sanctifies the means. At the day when God shall bring him into judgment, no man will dare to obtrude these specious pleas for his violation of the eternal principles of truth and right — principles on which repose the welfare of all creatures and the honor of God, principles whose sanctity only finds illustrations in the very evils which man experiences from the breach. But none the less do we find anticipations of seductions verified by ten thousand lamentable lapses from honor among our suffering people: in their tampering with ensnaring and oppressive oaths; in the evasion of pecuniary obligations; in the deceitful avowal of pretenses abhorrent at once to the political pride and principles of our country. The facts are too melancholy to be pursued.

Meantime the efficiency of all these seductions is made more fearful by the causes which hedge our young men up from wholesome activities. There is no longer a career for their individual energies. Scarcely any profession offers a prize worthy of their exertions. If they turn to agriculture, or the pursuits of the merchant or artisan, the ruin of trade and the crushing burden of unequal taxation compel them to labor for a pittance. Hence the danger that they will succumbing to an apathetic despair. We see too many of our youth whose fortitude should sustain a fainting, sinking country, sitting down in skeptical doubt to question the control of Divine Providence, or sinking into an indolence which they persuade themselves is inevitable, and seeking a degrading solace in epicurean ease. Take heed, gentlemen, lest these insidious discouragements transmute the sons of the heroes of Manassas and Shiloh, as the despotism of arbitrary rulers has charge, into the modern Roman. In the Eternal city we see the descendants of that race which gave laws and civilization to a conquered world, now in the words of their own sensual poet, *"Porci de grege Epicuri, cut bene curata,"* filling their idleness with the criticism of cooks and singing women. Rather than risk the yielding to this, arise and go forth, sturdy exiles, to carve out a new career on some more propitious soil.

It has been made my duty by my appointed pursuits to examine the history of previous conquests; and it is my deliberate conviction that no civilized people have ever been subjected to an ordeal of oppression so charged as ours with all the elements of degradation. I have explained how the unrighteousness of the despotism becomes a potent influence for temptation. We experience a domination, the iniquity of which is declared by every patriot of every previous party, and constantly avowed by the very men that impose it up to the day, when their reason was swept away by the torrent of revenge and the lust of domination. Our people have been violently thrust down from the proudest ancestral traditions, and highest freedoms boasted by any commonwealth on earth, to the deepest humiliations and most grinding exactions. They have been overpowered, not by manly force, but by filthy lucre, which bribed the prolitaries of the whole world to crush us. We stooped our banners, not like the conquered Gaul and Briton to one who knew how, *debellare uperbos, forcere victis*; but to a rabble who are not ashamed to confess that their fourfold numbers and ten fold resources were unable to subdue us until they had armed against us all the mercenaries of Europe and our own poor slaves besides. And to crown all, the favorite project is to subject us, not to the conqueror only, but to these alien serfs, to be invested with our plundered franchises. Thus are our people robbed not only of their possessions and rights, but of their dearest point of honor. Now, every one experienced of human nature knows that when you break down the chosen point of honor, the man is degraded to a brute unless he is sustained by the vital grace of God. Thus it appears that the influence and temptations by which conquest depraves its victims are now applied to our people in their most malignant efficacy. The lesson which we should learn from this fact is that we should be watchful in an equal degree to preserve our own rectitude and honor.

For, young gentlemen, as the true dishonor of defeat lies only in this determination of spirit, so it is the direct wrong which the injustice of the conqueror can inflict. A brave people may, for a time, be overpowered by brute force, and be neither dishonored nor destroyed. Its life is not in the outward organization of its institutions. It may be stripped of these and clothe itself in some diverse garb, in which it may resume its growth. But if the spirit of independence and honor be lost among the people, this is the death of the common weal: a death on which there waits no resurrection. Dread, then, this degradation of spirit as worse than defeat, than subjugation, than poverty, than hardship, than prison, than death.

The law on which I have commented has ever appeared to me the most awful and obscure of all those which regulate the divine providence over men and nations. That the ruthless wrong-doer should be depraved in his own soul by his crimes, that he should find a part of his just penalty in the disorders and remorse infused in his own nature by his acts; this is a dispensation as adorably righteous as it is terrible. But that not only guilty agent, but guiltless victim should, by a law, almost natural, find his moral being broken down; that a necessity which his will had no agency in procuring should subject his heart to an ordeal so usually disastrous — this is indeed fearful. "Clouds and darkness" here surround him. Yet "justice and judgment are the habitation of his throne." One thing I clearly infer hence, that he has ordained the virtuous man's life in this wicked world to be often a battle in which he may be called "to resist unto blood, striving against sin." We learn from these mournful histories how it may be our duty to surrender life, rather than conscience and moral independence. Man's first duty to himself is the preservation of his own virtue. His prime duty to his God may be said to be the same. For how shall the depraved creature fulfill that "chief end," glorifying God? With no little seeming then was it argued of old that a dishonored life was no life indeed; so that the imposition of unavoidable degradation of soul was equivalent to the Maker's decree dismissing us out of the scene of defiled existence. Here is the most plausible excuse of that antique self-sacrifice, by which the heroic souls of the Pagan world claimed the privilege of escaping subjugation, and defying the oppressor by a voluntary grave. For they knew not the only power by which the inward strain of oppression can be countervailed. They had never heard of gospel grace; of regeneration and adoption; of a hope anchored beyond the grave; of a reward in glory ennobling all suffering and endurance for conscience sake. Let us not, however, palliate the error of those who thus retired from life's battle without the word of supreme command of the Captain. But from this danger of the soul's subjugation along with that of the body, we may infer the duty and privilege of preferring the surrender of life to the desertion of duty.

It is yours, young gentlemen, to boast among the alumni of your college, more than one illustrious instance of this fate, which may prove so enviable compared with ours. First among these, I am reminded of one, whose youthful face, then ruddy as that of the hero of Bethlehem, is filed in the memories of my first visit here, General Ramseur. Nowhere in the rich record of Southern chivalry can there be found the name of one who more deliberately resolved for death rather than forfeiture of duty and honor. Twice within a few weeks, at Winchester and Fisher's Hill, his command had yielded to numbers, in spite of his most strenuous and daring exertion. On the morning of the battle of Belle Plain, which began so gloriously for the Confederates, while marshalling his troops for the strife, he exhorted them to stand to their colors, and calmly declared that if they had any value for his life they would henceforward be staunch; for he was resolved never to participate with them in another flight from their foes. It was with this deliberate purpose he joined battle. But as the bravest are ever the most gentle, this stern resolve did not exclude the thought of the domestic tie, which his country's call had sundered almost as soon as it was bound around his heart, and of the infant which had never received its father's kiss. His courage was only reinforced by these remembrances. For, as he began the onset, in the second movement of the tragedy, he exclaimed to the officers near him, "Now, gentlemen, let us so fight to-day as to finish this campaign; I want to see my first born." After performing his whole duty during the changeful day, he saw all the line upon his left giving way. With his own command he strove to stem the torrent of enemies; and when they, too, broke in panic he refused to flee with them, but busied himself in rallying a few determined spirits like himself. When the last fugitive left the field they saw him with a handful, breasting the whole pursuing host, until, according to his pledge, he fell with his face to the foe. Let this example inspire you to *endure* as he *fought*, and you will be secure against all the degradations of defeat.

This degradation, then, does not necessarily accompany our prostrate condition. Divine Providence often makes the furnace of persecution the place of cleansing for individual saints. Why may it not be so for a Christian people? Why may not a race of men come forth from their trials, like the gold seven times refined in the fire, with their pride chastened, and yet their virtues purified? This can be from the only cause which sanctifies the sufferings of the Christian, the inworkings of the grace of God. Nothing is more true than that the natural effect of mere pain is not to purify, but to harden the sinful heart of man, exasperating at once its evils and its miseries. The cleansing Word and Spirit of God alone interpret its sufferings to it and convert them into healthful medicines of its faults. So it is the power of true Christianity, and that alone, which can minister to us as a people the wholesome uses of adversity. The salvation of the life of the Southern society must be found by taking the Word of God as our constant guide. But it may be asked: To what course of action should this spirit of unyielding integrity prompt us? The answer from those infallible oracles is easy. While you refrain from the suggestion of revenge and despair, and give place as of necessity to inexorable force, resolve to abate nothing, to concede nothing of righteous conviction. Truckle to no falsehood and conceal no true principle; but ever assert *the right* with such means of endurance, self-sacrifice and passive fortitude as the dispensation of Providence has left you. If wholesale wrongs must be perpetrated, if wholesale rights must be trampled on, let our assailants do the whole work and incur the whole guilt. Resolve that no losses, nor threats, nor penalties, shall ever make you yield one jot or tittle of the true or just in principle, or submit to personal dishonor. And let us remember, young gentlemen, that while events, the successes of ruthless power, the overthrow of innocence may greatly modify the *expedient*, they have no concern whatever in determining the *right*. The death of a beloved child may determine its mother to bury its decaying body out of sight, even to hide in the wintry earth that which before she cherished in her bosom; but its death will never make the true mother repudiate its relation of paternity to it, or deny its memory, or to acquiesce in any slander upon its filial loveliness. You must decide, then, each one for himself, what things must be conceded to the necessities of new events, and what things must be disclaimed as contaminating to the unconquered soul. May I not safely advise, that, in making these decisions you should always refer them to that standard of judgment which we held before our disasters, as the truer and worthier one; rather than to that standard to which we are seduced by their humiliations? Judge then from the same principles (however new their special application) from which you have judged in happier years when your souls were inspired by the glorious traditions of your free forefathers, and saw the truth in the clear light of your conscious manhood; not as men would have you judge, from hearts debauched by defeat, and clouded with shame and despair.

We are a beaten, conquered people, gentlemen, and yet if we are true to ourselves, we have no cause for humiliation, however much for deep sorrow. It is only the atheist who adopts success as the criterion of right. It is not a new thing in the history of men that God appoints to the brave and true the stern task of contending and falling in a righteous quarrel. Would you find the grandest of all names upon the roll of time? You must seek them among this "noble army of martyrs," whose faith in God and the right was stronger than death and defeat. Let the besotted fools say that our dead have fallen in a "lost cause." Let abandoned defamers and pulpit buffoons say that theirs are "dishonored graves." I see them lie in their glory with an illustrious company: with the magnanimous Prince Jonathan, on Mount Gilboa, and the good king Josiah in the vale of Megiddo; with Demosthenes and Philopoemen; with Hannibal, the pillar of Carthage; with Brutus and Cato; with the British Queen, Boadicea; with the Teuton Herman; with Harold, the Saxon, on Hastings field; with Wallace, with Kosciusko; with one grander than all, our own Jackson. We have no need, sirs, to be ashamed of our dead; let us see to it that they be not ashamed of us. They have won the happier fate, "taken away from the evil to come, they have entered into peace; they rest in their beds, each one walking in their uprightness." To us they have bequeathed the sterner trial of asserting, by our unshaken fortitude under overthrow, the principles which they baptized with their blood. Let the same spirit which nerved them to do, nerve us to endure for the right; and they will not disdain our companionship on the rolls of fame. Before I end, let me invoke the aid of the gentler sex, whose sympathizing presence I see gracing our solemnities. The high mission of woman in society has been often and justly argued. But never before was the welfare of a people so dependent on their mothers, wives and sisters, as now and here. I freely declare that under God my chief hope for my prostrate country is in their women. Early in the war, when the stream of our noblest blood began to flow so liberally in battle, I said to an honored citizen of my State that it was so uniformly our best men who were made the sacrifice there was reason to fear that the staple and pith of the people of the South would be permanently depreciated. His reply was: "There is no danger of this while the women of the South are what they are. Be assured the mothers will not permit the offspring of such martyr-sires to depreciate."

But since, this river of generous blood has swelled into a flood. What is worse, the remnant of the survivors, few, subjugated, disheartened, almost despairing and, alas, dishonored, because they have not disdained life, on such terms as are left us; are subjected to every influence from without, which can be malignantly devised to sap the foundations of their manhood and degrade them into fit materials for slaves. If our women do not sustain them they will sink. Unless the spirits which rule and cheer their homes can reanimate their self-respect, confirm their resolve, and sustain their personal honor, they will at length become the base serfs their enemies desire. Outside their homes, everything conspires to depress, to tempt, to seduce them. Do they advert to their business affairs? They see before them only loss, embarrassment, and prospective destitution. To the politics of their country? They witness a scheme of domination and mercenary subserviency where the sacrifice of honor is the uniform condition of success. Only within their homes is there, beneath the skies, one ray of light or warmth to prevent their freezing into despair.

There, in your homes, is your domain. There *you* rule with the sceptre of affection, and not our conquerors. We beseech you, wield that gentle empire in behalf of the principles, the patriotism, the religion, which we inherited from our mothers. Teach our ruder sex that only by a deathless love to these can woman's dear love be deserved or won. Him who is true to these crown with your favor. Let the wretch who betrays them be exiled forever from the paradise of your arms. Then shall we be saved, saved from a degradation fouler than the grave. Be it yours to nurse with more than a vestal's watchfulness the sacred flame of our virtue now so smothered. Your task is unobtrusive; it is performed in the privacy of home, and by the gentle touches of daily love. But it is the noblest work which mortal can perform, for it furnishes the polished stones with which the temple of our liberties must be repaired. We have seen men building a lofty pile of sculptured marble, where columns with polished shafts pointed to the skies, and domes reared their arches on high like mimic heavens. They swung the massive blocks into their places on the walls with cranes and cables, with shouts and outcries, and hugh creaking of the ponderous machinery. But these were not the true artisans: they were but rude laborers. The true artists, whose priceless cunning was to give immortal beauty to the pile, and teach the dead stones to breathe majesty and grace were not there. None saw or heard their labors. In distant and quiet workrooms, where no eye watched them, and no shout gave signal of their motions, they plied their patient chisels slowly with gentle touches, evoking the forms of beauty which lay hid in the blocks before them. Such is your work; the home and fireside are the scenes of your industry. But the materials which you shape are the souls of men, which are to compose the fabric of our church and state. The politician, the professional man, is but the cheap, rude, day laborer who moves and lifts the finished block to its place. You are the true artists, who endue it with fitness and beauty; and therefore yours is the nobler task.

APPENDIX SEVEN
Civil Government and the Right of Revolution
by Charles Hodge

Our design is to state in few words in what sense government is a divine institution, and to draw from that doctrine the principles which must determine the nature and limits of the obedience which is due the laws of the land.

That the Bible, when it asserts that all power is of God, or that the powers that be are ordained of God, does not teach that any one form of civil government has been divinely appointed as universally obligatory, is plain because the scriptures contain no such prescription. There are no directions given as to the form which civil governments shall assume. All the divine commands on this subject, are as applicable under one form as another. The direction is general; Obey the powers that be. The proposition is unlimited. All power is of God; *i.e.* government, whatever its form, is of God. He has ordained it. The most pointed scriptural injunctions on this subject were given during the usurped or tyrannical reign of military despots. It is plain that the sacred writers did not, in such passages, mean to teach that a military despotism was the form of government which God had ordained as of perpetual and universal obligation. As the Bible enjoins no one form, so the people of God in all ages, under the guidance of his Spirit, have lived with a good conscience, under all the diversities of organization of which human government is susceptible. Again, as no one form of government is prescribed, so neither has God determined preceptively who are to exercise civil power. He has not said that such power must be hereditary, and descend on the principle of primogeniture. He has not determined whether it shall be confined to males to the exclusion of females; or whether all offices shall be elective. These are not matters of divine appointment, and are not included in the proposition that all power is of God. Neither is it included in this proposition that government is in such a sense ordained of God that the people have no control in the matter. The doctrine of the Bible is not inconsistent with the right of the people, as we shall endeavour to show in the sequel, to determine their own form of government and to select their own rulers.

When it is said government is of God, we understand the scriptures to mean, first, that it is a divine institution and not a mere social compact. It does not belong to the category of voluntary associations such as men form for literary, benevolent, or commercial purposes. It is not optional with men whether government shall exist. It is a divine appointment, in the same sense as marriage and the church are divine institutions. The former of these is not a mere civil contract, nor is the church as a visible spiritual community a mere voluntary society. Men are under obligation to recognise its existence, to join its ranks, and submit to its laws. In like manner it is the will of God that civil government should exist. Men are bound by his authority to have civil rulers for the punishment of evil doers and for the praise of them that do well. This is the scriptural doctrine, as opposed to the deistical theory of a social compact as the ultimate ground of all human governments.

It follows from this view of the subject that obedience to the laws of the land is a religious duty, and that disobedience is of the specific nature of sin, this is a principle of vast importance. It is true that the law of God is so broad that it binds a man to every thing that is right, and forbids every thing that is wrong; and consequently that every violation even of a voluntary engagement is of the nature of an offence against God. Still there is a wide difference between disobedience to an obligation voluntarily assumed, and which has no other sanction than our own engagement, and disregard of an obligation directly imposed of God. St. Peter recognises this distinction when he said to Ananias, "Thou hast not lied unto men but unto God." All lying is sinful, but lying to God is a higher crime than lying to men. There is greater irreverence and contempt of the divine presence and authority, and a violation of an obligation of a higher order. Every man feels that the marriage vows have a sacred character which could not belong to them, if marriage was merely a civil contract. In like manner the divine institution of government elevates it into the sphere of religion, and adds a new and higher sanction to the obligations which it imposes. There is a specific difference, more easily felt than described, between what is religious and what is merely moral; between disobedience to man and resistance to an ordinance of God.

A third point included in the scriptural doctrine on this subject is, that the actual existence of any government creates the obligation of obedience. That is, the obligation does not rest either on the origin or the nature of the government, or on the mode in which it is administered. It may be legitimate or revolutionary, despotic or constitutional, just or unjust, so long as it exists it is to be recognised and obeyed within its proper sphere. The powers that be are ordained of God in such sense that the possession of power is to be referred to his providence. It is not by chance, nor through the uncontrolled agency of men, but by divine ordination that any government exists. The declaration of the apostle just quoted was uttered under the reign of Nero. It is as true of his authority as of that of the Queen of England, or of that of our own President, that it was of God. He made Nero emperor. He required all within the limits of the Roman empire to recognise and obey him so long as he was allowed to occupy the throne. It was not necessary for the early Christians to sit in judgment on the title of every new emperor, whenever the pretorian guards chose to put down one and put up another; neither are God's people now in various parts of the world called upon to discuss the titles and adjudicate the claims of their rulers. The possession of civil power is a providential fact, and is to be regarded as such. This does not imply that God approves of every government which he allows to exist. He permits oppressive rulers to bear sway, just as he permits famine or pestilence to execute his vengeance. A good government is a blessing, a bad government is a judgment; but the one as much as the other is ordained of God, and is to be obeyed not only for fear but also for conscience sake.

A fourth principle involved in the proposition that all power is of God is, that the magistrate is invested with a divine right. He represents God. His authority is derived from Him. There is a sense in which he represents the people and derives from them his power; but in a far higher sense he is the minister of God. To resist him is to resist God, and "they that resist shall receive unto themselves damnation." Thus saith the Scriptures. It need hardly be remarked that this principle relates to the nature, and not to the extent, of the power of the magistrate. It is as true of the lowest as of the highest; of a justice of the peace as of the President of the United States; of a constitutional monarch as of an absolute sovereign. The principle is that the authority of rulers is divine, and not human, in its origin. They exercise the power which belongs to them of divine right. The reader, we trust will not confound this doctrine with the old doctrine of "the divine right of kings." The two things are as different as day and night. We are not for reviving a defunct theory of civil government; a theory which perished, at least among Anglo-Saxons, at the expulsion of James II. from the throne of England. That monarch took it with him into exile, and it lies entombed with the last of the Stuarts. According to that theory God had established the monarchical form of government as universally obligatory. There could not consistently with his law be any other. The people had no more right to renounce that form of government than the children of a family have to resolve themselves into a democracy. In the second place, it assumed that God had determined the law of succession as well as the form of government. The people could not change the one any more than the other; or any more than children could change their father, or a wife her husband. And thirdly, as a necessary consequence of these principles, it inculcated in all cases the duty of passive obedience. The king holding his office immediately from God, held it entirely independent of the will of the people, and his responsibility was to God alone. He could not forfeit his throne by any injustice however flagrant. The people if in any case they could not obey, were obliged to submit; resistence or revolution was treason against God. We have already remarked that the scriptural doctrine is opposed to every one of these principles. The Bible does not prescribe any one form of government; it does not determine who shall be depositories of civil power; and it clearly recognises the right of revolution. In asserting, therefore, the divine right of rulers, we are not asserting any doctrine repudiated by our forefathers, or inconsistent with civil liberty in its widest rational extent.

Such, as we understand it, is the true nature of civil government. It is a divine institution and not a mere voluntary compact. Obedience to the magistrate and laws is a religious duty; and disobedience is a sin against God. This is true of all forms of government. Men living under the Turkish Sultan are bound to recognise his authority, as much as the subjects of a constitutional monarch, or the fellow citizen of an elective president, are bound to recognise their respective rulers. All power is of God, and the powers that be are ordained of God, in such sense that all magistrates are to be regarded as his ministers, acting in his name and with his authority, each within his legitimate sphere; beyond which he ceases to be a magistrate.

That this is the doctrine of the scriptures on this subject can hardly be doubted. The Bible never refers to the consent of the governed, the superiority of the rulers, or to the general principles of expediency, as the ground of our obligation to the higher powers. The obedience which slaves owe their masters, children their parents, wives their husbands, people their rulers, is always made to rest on the divine will as its ultimate foundation. It is part of the service which we owe to God. We are required to act, in all these relations, not as men-pleasers, but as the servants of God. All such obedience terminates on our Master who is in heaven. This gives the sublimity of spiritual freedom even to the service of a slave. It is not in the power of man to reduce to bondage those who serve God, in all the service they render their fellow-men. The will of God, therefore, is the foundation of our obligation to obey the laws of the land. His will, however, is not an arbitrary determination; it is the expression of infinite intelligence and love. There is the most perfect agreement between all the precepts of the Bible and the highest dictates of reason. There is no command in the word of God of permanent and universal obligation, which may not be shown to be in accordance with the laws of our own higher nature. This is one of the strongest collateral arguments in favour of the divine origin of the scriptures. In appealing therefore to the Bible in support of the doctrine here advanced, we are not, on the one hand appealing to an arbitrary standard, a mere statute-book, a collection of laws which create the obligations they enforce; nor, on the other hand, to "the reason and nature of things" in the abstract, which after all is only our own reason; but we are appealing to the infinite intelligence of a personal God, whose will because of his infinite excellence, is necessarily the ultimate ground and rule of all moral obligation. This, however, being the case, whatever the Bible declares to be right is found to be in accordance with the constitution of nature and our own reason. All that the scriptures, for example, teach of the subordination of children to their parents, of wives to their husbands, has not its foundation, but its confirmation, in the very nature of the relation of the parties. Any violation of the precepts of the Bible, on these points, is found to be a violation of the laws of nature, and certainly destructive. In like manner it is clear from the social nature of man, from the dependence of men upon each other, from the impossibility of attaining the end of our being in this world, otherwise than in society and under an ordered government, that it is the will of God that such society should exist. The design of God in this matter is as plain as is the constitution of the universe. We might as well maintain that the laws of nature are the result of chance, or that marriage and parental authority have no other foundation than human law, as to assert that civil government has no firmer foundation than the will of man or the quicksands of expediency. By creating men social beings, and making it necessary for them to live in society, God has made his will as thus revealed the foundation of all civil government.

This doctrine is but one aspect of the comprehensive doctrine of Theism, a doctrine which teaches the existence of a personal God, a Spirit infinite, eternal and unchangeable, in his being, wisdom, power, justice, holiness, goodness and truth; a God who is everywhere present upholding and governing all his creatures and all their actions. The universe is not a machine left to go of itself. God did not at first create matter and impress upon it certain laws and then leave it to their blind operation. He is everywhere present in the material world, not superseding secondary causes, but so upholding and guiding their operations, that the intelligence evinced is the omnipresent intelligence of God, and the power exercised is the *potestas ordinata* of the Great First Cause. He is no less supreme in his control of intelligent agents. They indeed are free, but not independent. They are governed in a manner consistent with their nature; yet God turns them as the rivers of waters are turned. All events depending on human agency are under his control. God is in history. Neither chance nor blind necessity determine the concatenation or issues of things, Nor is the world in the hands of its inhabitants. God has not launched our globe on the ocean of space and left its multitudinous crew to direct its course without his interference. He is at the helm. His breath fills the sails. His wisdom and power are pledged for the prosperity of the voyage. Nothing happens, even to the falling of a sparrow, which is not ordered by him. He works all things after the counsel of his will. It is by him that kings reign and princes decree justice. He puts down one, and raises up another. As he leads out the stars by night, marshalling them as a host, calling each one by its name, so does he order all human events. He raises up nations and appoints the bounds of their habitation. He founds the empires of the earth and determines their form and their duration. This doctrine of God's universal providence is the foundation of all religion. If this doctrine be not true, we are without God in the world. But if it is true, it involves a vast deal. God is everywhere in nature and in history. Every thing is a revelation of his presence and power. We are always in contact with him. Everything has a voice, which speaks of his goodness or his wrath; fruitful seasons proclaim his goodness, famine and pestilence declare his displeasure. Nothing is by chance. The existence of any particular form of government is as much his work, as the rising of the sun or falling of the rain. It is something he has ordained for some wise purpose, and it is to be regarded as his work. If all events are under God's control, if it is by him that kings reign, then the actual possession of power is as much a revelation of his will that it should be obeyed, as the possession of wisdom or goodness is a manifestation of his will that those endowed with those gifts, should be reverenced and loved. It follows, therefore, from the universal providence of God, that "the powers that be are ordained of God." We have no more right to refuse obedience to an actually existing government because it is not to our taste, or because we do not approve of its measures, than a child has the right to refuse to recognise a wayward parent; or a wife a capricious husband.

The religious character of our civil duties flows also from the comprehensive doctrine that the will of God is the ground of all moral obligation. To seek that ground either in "the reason and nature of things," or in expediency, is to banish God from the moral world, as effectually as the mechanical theory of the universe banishes him from the physical universe and from history. Our allegiance on that hypothesis is not to God but to reason or to society. This theory of morals therefore, changes the nature of religion and of moral obligation. It modifies and degrades all religious sentiment and exercises; it changes the very nature of sin, of repentance and obedience, and gives us, what is a perfect solecism, a religion without God. According to the Bible, our obligation to obey the laws of the land is not founded on the fact that the good of society requires such obedience, or that it is a dictate of reason, but on the authority of God. It is part of the service which we owe to him. This must be so if the doctrine is true that God is our moral governor, to whom we are responsible for all our acts, and whose will is both the ground and the rule of all our obligations.

We need not, however, dwell longer on this subject. Although it has long been common to look upon civil government as a human institution, and to represent the consent of the governed as the only ground of the obligation of obedience, yet this doctrine is so notoriously of infidel origin, and so obviously in conflict with the teachings of the Bible, that it can have no hold on the convictions of a Christian people. It is no more true of the state than it is of the family, or of the church. All are of divine institution. All have their foundation in his will. The duties belonging to each are enjoined by him and are enforced by his authority. Marriage is indeed a voluntary covenant. The parties select each other, and the state may make laws regulating the mode in which the contract shall be ratified; and determining its civil effects. It is, however, none the less an ordinance of God. The vows it includes are made to God; its sanction is found in his law; and its violation is not a mere breach of contract or disobedience to the civil law, but a sin against God. So with regard to the church, it is in one sense a voluntary society. No man can be forced by other men to join its communion. If done at all it must be done with his own consent, yet every man is under the strongest moral obligation to enter its fold. And when enrolled in the number of its members his obligation to obedience does not rest on his consent; it does not cease should that consent be withdrawn. It rests on the authority of the church as a divine institution. This is an authority no man can throw off. It presses him everywhere and at all times with the weight of a moral obligation. In a sense analogous to this the state is a divine institution. Men are bound to organize themselves into a civil government. Their obligation to obey its laws does not rest upon their compact in this case, any more than in the others above referred to. It is enjoined by God. It is a religious duty, and disobedience is a direct offence against him. The people have indeed the right to determine the form of the government under which they are to live, and to modify it from time to time to suit their changing condition. So, though to a less extent, or within narrower limits, they have a right to modify the form of their ecclesiastical governments, a right which every church has exercised, but the ground and nature of the obligation to obedience remains unchanged. This is not a matter of mere theory. It is of primary practical importance and has an all-pervading influence on national character. Everything indeed connected with this subject depends on the answer to the question, Why are we obliged to obey the laws? If we answer because we made them; or because we assent to them, or framed the government which enacts them; or because the good of society enjoins obedience, or reason dictates it, then the state is a human institution; it has no religious sanction; it is founded on the sand; it ceases to have a hold on the conscience and to commend itself as a revelation of God to be reverenced and obeyed as a manifestation of his presence and will. But, on the other hand, if we place the state in the same category with the family and the church, and regard it as an institution of God, then we elevate it into a higher sphere; we invest it with religious sanctions and it becomes pervaded by a divine presence and authority, which immeasurably strengthens, while it elevates its power. Obedience for conscience sake is as different from obedience from fear, or from voluntary consent, or regard to human authority, as the divine from the human.

Such being, as we conceive, the true doctrine concerning the nature of the state, it is well to enquire into the necessary deductions from this doctrine. If government be a divine institution, and obedience to the laws a matter resting on the authority of God, it might seem to follow that in no case could human laws be disregarded with a good conscience. This, as we have seen, is in fact the conclusion drawn from these premises by the advocates of the doctrine "of passive obedience." The command, however, to be subject to the higher powers is not more unlimited in its statement than the command, "children obey your parents in all things." From this latter command no one draws the conclusion that unlimited obedience is due from children to their parents. The true inference doubtless is, in both cases, that obedience is the rule and disobedience the exception. If in any instance a child refuse compliance with the requisition of a parent, or a citizen with the law of the land, he must be prepared to justify such disobedience at the bar of God. Even divine laws may in some cases be dispensed with. Those indeed which are founded on the nature of God, such as the command to love him and our neighbour, are necessarily immutable. But those which are founded on the present constitution of things, though permanent as general rules of action, may on adequate grounds, be violated without sin. The commands, Thou shalt not kill, Thou shalt not steal, Remember the sabbath day to keep it holy, are all of permanent authority; and yet there may be justifiable homicide, and men may profane the sabbath and be blameless. In like manner the command to obey the laws, is a divine injunction, and yet there are cases in which disobedience is a duty. It becomes then of importance to determine what these cases are; or to ascertain the principles which limit the obedience which we owe to the state. It follows from the divine institution of government that its power is limited by the design of God in its institution, and by the moral law. The family, the church and the state are all divine institutions, designed for specific purposes. Each has its own sphere, and the authority belonging to each is necessarily confined within its own province. The father appears in his household as its divinely appointed head. By the command of God all the members of that household are required to yield him reverence and obedience. But he cannot carry his parental authority into the church or the state; nor can he appear in his family as a magistrate or church officer. The obedience due to him is that which belongs to a father, and not to a civil or ecclesiastical officer, and his children are not required to obey him in either of those capacities. In like manner the officers of the church have within their sphere a divine right to rule, but they cannot claim civil authority on the ground of the general command to the people to obey those who have the care of souls. Heb. xiii. 17. As the church officer loses his power when he enters the forum; so does the civil magistrate when he enters the church. His right to rule is a right which belongs to him as representing God in the state — he has no commission to represent God either in the family or the church; and therefore, he is entitled to no obedience if he claims an authority which does not belong to him. This is a very obvious principle, and is of wide application. It not only limits the authority of civil officers to civil affairs, but limits the extent due to the obedience to be rendered even in civil matters to the officers of the state. A justice of the peace has no claim to the obedience due to a governor of a state; nor a governor of a state to that which belongs to the President of the Union; nor the president of the Union to that which may be rightfully claimed by an absolute sovereign. A military commander has no authority over the community as a civil magistrate, nor can he exercise such authority even over his subordinates. This principle applies in all its force to the law-making power. The legislature can not exercise any power which does not belong to them. They cannot act as judges or magistrates unless such authority has been actually committed to them. They are to be obeyed as legislators; and in any other capacity their decisions or commands do not bind the conscience. And still further, their legislative enactments have authority only when made in the exercise of their legitimate powers. In other words, an unconstitutional law is no law. If our congress, for example, were to pass a bill creating an order of nobility, or an established church, or to change the religion of the land, or to enforce a sumptuary code, it would have no more virtue and be entitled to no more deference than a similar enactment intended to bind the whole country passed by a town council. This we presume will not be denied. God has committed unlimited power to no man and to no set of men, and the limitation which he has assigned to the power conferred, is to be found in the design for which it was given. That design is determined in the case of the family, the church, and the state, by the nature of these institutions, by the general precepts of the Bible, or by the providence of God determining the peculiar constitution under which these organizations are called to act. The power of a parent was greater under the old dispensation than it is now; the legitimate authority of the church is greater under some modes of organization than under others; and the power of the state as represented in its constituted authorities is far more extensive in some countries than in others. The theory of the British government is that the parliament is the whole state in convention, and therefore it exercises powers which do not belong to our congress, which represents the state only for certain specified purposes. These diversities, however, do not alter the general principle, which is that rulers are to be obeyed in the exercise of their legitimate authority; that their commands or requirements beyond their appropriate spheres are void of all binding force. This is a principle which no one can dispute.

A second principle is no less plain. No human authority can make it obligatory on us to commit sin. If all power is of God it cannot be legitimately used against God. This is a dictate of natural conscience, and is authenticated by the clearest teachings of the word of

God. The apostles when commanded to abstain from preaching Christ refused to obey and said, "Whether it be right in the sight of God to hearken unto you more than unto God, judge ye." No human law could make it binding on the ministers of the gospel, in our day, to withhold the message of salvation from their fellow-men. It requires no argument to prove that men cannot make it right to worship idols, to blaspheme God, to deny Christ. It is sheer fanaticism thus to exalt the power of the government above the authority of God. This would be to bring back upon us some of the worst doctrines of the middle ages as to the power of the pope and of earthly sovereigns. Good men in all ages of the world have always acted on the principle that human laws cannot bind the conscience when they are in conflict with the law of God. Daniel openly in the sight even of his enemies, prayed to the God of heaven in despite of the prohibition of his sovereign. Sadrach, Mesheck and Abednego refused to bow down, at the command of the king, to the golden image. The early Christians disregarded all those laws of Pagan Rome requiring them to do homage to false gods. Protestants with equal unanimity refused to submit to the laws of their papal sovereigns enjoining the profession of Romish errors. That these men were right no man, with an enlightened conscience, can deny; but they were right only on the principle that the power of the state and of the magistrate is limited by the law of God. It follows then from the divine institution of government that its power to bind the conscience to obedience is limited by the design of its appointment and the moral law. All its power being from God, it must be subordinate to him. This is a doctrine which, however, for a time and in words, it may be denied, is too plain and too important not to be generally recognised. It is a principle too which should at all times be publicly avowed. The very sanctity of human laws requires it. Their real power and authority lie in their having a divine sanction. To claim for them binding force when destitute of such sanction, it is to set up a mere semblance for a reality, a suit of armour with no living man within. The stability of human government and the authority of civil laws require that they should be kept within the sphere where they repose on God, and are pervaded by his presence and power. Without him nothing human can stand. All power is of God; and if of God divine; and if divine in accordance with his holy law.

But who are the judges of the application of these principles? Who is to determine whether a particular law is unconstitutional or immoral? So far as the mere constitutionality of a law is concerned, it may be remarked, that there is in most states, as in our own, for example, a regular judicial tribunal to which every legislative enactment can be submitted, and the question of its conformity to the constitution authoritatively decided. In all ordinary cases, that is, in all cases not involving some great principle or some question of conscience, such decisions must be held to be final, and to bind all concerned not only to submission but obedience. A law thus sanctioned becomes instinct with all the power of the state, and further opposition brings the recusants into conflict with the government; a conflict in which no man for light reasons can with a good conscience engage. Still it cannot be denied, and ought not to be concealed, that the ultimate decision must be referred to his own judgment. This is a necessary deduction from the doctrine that obedience to law is a religious duty. It is a primary principle that the right of private judgment extends over all questions of faith and morals. No human power can come between God and the conscience. Every man must answer for his own sins, and therefore every man must have the right to determine for himself what is sin. As he cannot transfer his responsibility, he cannot transfer his right of judgment. This principle has received the sanction of good men to every age of the world. Daniel judged for himself of the binding force of the command not to worship the true God. So did the apostles when they continued to preach Christ, in opposition to all the constituted authorities. The laws passed by Pagan Rome requiring the worship of idols had the sanction of all the authorities of the empire, yet on the ground of their private judgment the Christians refused to obey them. Protestants in like manner refused to obey the laws of Papal Rome, though sustained by all the authority both of the church and state. In all these cases the right of private judgment cannot be disputed. Even where no question of religion or morality is directly concerned, this right is undeniable. Does any one now condemn Hampden for refusing to pay "ship-money?" Does any American condemn our ancestors for resisting the stamp-act though the authorities of St. Stephens and Westminster united in pronouncing the imposition constitutional? However this principle may be regarded when stated in the abstract, every individual instinctively acts upon it in his own case. Whenever a command is issued by one in authority over us, we immediately and almost unconsciously determine for ourselves, first, whether he had a right to give the order; and secondly, whether it can with a good conscience be obeyed. If this decision is clearly in the negative, we at once determine to refuse obedience on our own responsibility. Let any man test this point by an appeal to his own consciousness. Let him suppose the President of the United States to order him to turn Romanist or Pagan; or Congress to pass a bill requiring him to blaspheme God; or a military superior to command him to commit treason or murder — does not his conscience tell him he would on the instant refuse? Would he, or could he wait until the constitutionality of such requisitions had been submitted to the courts? or if the courts should decide against him, would that at all alter the case? Men must be strangely oblivious of the relation of the soul to God, the instinctive sense which we possess of our allegiance to him, and of the self-evidencing power with which his voice reaches the reason and the conscience, to question the necessity which every man is under to decide all questions touching his duty to God for himself.

It may indeed be thought that this doctrine is subversive of the authority of government. A moment's reflection is sufficient to dispel this apprehension. The power of laws rests on two foundations, fear and conscience. Both are left by this doctrine in their integrity. The former, because the man refuses obedience at his peril. His private conviction that the law is unconstitutional or immoral does not abrogate it, or impede its operation. If arraigned for its violation, he may plead in his justification his objections to the authority of the law. If these objections are found valid by the competent authorities, he is acquitted; if otherwise, he suffers the penalty. What more can the State ask? All the power the State, as such, can give its laws, lies in their penalty. A single decision by the ultimate authority in favour of a law, is a revelation to the whole body of the people that it cannot be violated with impunity. The sword of justice hangs over every transgressor. The motive of fear in securing obedience, is therefore, as operative under this view of the subject, as it can be under any other. What, however, is of far more consequence, the power of conscience is left in full force. Obedience to the law is a religious duty, enjoined by the word of God and enforced by conscience. If, in any case, it be withheld it is under a sense of responsibility to God; and under the conviction that if this conscientious objection be feigned, it aggravates the guilt of disobedience as a sin against God an hundred fold; and if it be mistaken, it affords no palliation of the offence. Paul was guilty in persecuting the church, though he thought he was doing God service. And the man, who by a perverted conscience, is led to refuse obedience to a righteous law, stands without excuse at the bar of God. The moral sanction of civil laws, which gives them their chief power and without which they must ultimately become inoperative, cannot possibly extend further than this. For what is that moral sanction? It is a conviction that our duty to God requires our obedience; but how can we feel that duty to God requires us to do what God forbids? In other words, a law which we regard as immoral, cannot present itself to the conscience as having divine authority. Conscience, therefore, is on the side of the law wherever and whenever this is possible from the nature of the case. It is a contradiction to say that conscience enforces what conscience condemns. This then is all the support which laws of the land can possibly derive from our moral convictions. The allegiance of conscience is to God. It enforces obedience to all human laws consistent with that allegiance; further than this it cannot by possibility go. And as the decisions of conscience are, by the constitution of our nature, determined by our own apprehensions of the moral law, and not by authority, it follows of necessity that every man must judge for himself, and on his own responsibility, whether any given law of man conflicts with the law of God or not. We would further remark on this point that the lives and property of men have no greater protection than that which, on this theory, is secured for the laws of the state. The law of God says: Thou shalt not kill. Yet every man does, and must judge when and how far this law binds his conscience. It is admitted, on all hands, that there are cases in which its obligation ceases. What those cases are each man determines for himself, but under his two-fold responsibility to his country and to God. If through passion or any other cause, he errs as to what constitutes justifiable homicide, he must bear the penalty attached to murder by the law of God and man. It is precisely so in the case before us. God has commanded us to obey the magistrate as his minister and representative. If we err in our judgment as to the cases in which that command ceases to be binding, we fall into the hands of justice both human and divine. Can more than this be necessary? Can any thing be gained by trying to make God require us to break his own commands? Can conscience be made to sanction the violation of the moral law? Is not this the way to destroy all moral distinctions, and to prostrate the authority of conscience, and with it the very foundation of civil government? Is not all history full of the dreadful consequences of the doctrine that human laws can make sin obligatory, and that those in authority can judge for the people what is sin? What more than this is needed to justify all the persecutions for righteousness sake since the world began? What hope could there be, on this ground, for the preservation of religion or virtue in any nation on the earth? If the principle be once established that the people are bound to obey all human laws, or that they are not to judge for themselves when their duty to God requires them to refuse such obedience, then there is not only an end of all civil and religious liberty, but the very nature of civil government as a divine institution is destroyed. It becomes first atheistical, and then diabolical. Then the massacre of St. Bartholomew's, the decrees of the French National Assembly, and the laws of Pagan Rome against Christians, and of its Papal successor against Protestants, were entitled to reverent obedience. Then too may any infidel party which gains the ascendency in a state, as has happened of late in Switzerland, render it morally obligatory upon all ministers to close their churches, and on the people to renounce the gospel. This is not an age or state of the world in which to advance such doctrines. There are too many evidences of the gathering powers of evil to render it expedient to exalt the authority of man above that of God, or emancipate men from subjection to their Master in heaven, that they may become more obedient to their masters on earth. We are advocating the cause of civil government, of the stability and authority of human laws, when we make every thing rest on the authority of God, and when we limit every human power by subordinating it to him. We hold, therefore, that it is not only one of the plainest principles of morals that no immoral law can bind the conscience, and that every man must judge of its character for himself and on his own responsibility, but that this doctrine is essential to all religious liberty and to the religious sanction of civil government. If you deny this principle, you thereby deny that government is a divine institution, and denying that, you deprive it of its vital energy, and send it tottering to a dishonoured grave.

But here the great practical question arises, What is to be done when the law of the land comes into conflict with the law of God — or, which is to us the same thing, with our convictions of what that law demands? In answer to this question we would remark, in the first place, that in most cases the majority of the people have nothing to do, except peaceably to use their influence to have the law repealed. The mass of the people have nothing actively to do with the laws. Very few enactments of the government touch one in a thousand in the population. We may think a protective tariff not only inexpedient, but unequal and therefore unjust. But we have nothing to do with it. We are not responsible for it, and are not called upon to enforce it. The remark applies even to laws of a higher character, such, *e. g.* as a law proclaiming an unjust war; forbidding the introduction of the Bible into public schools; requiring homage or sanction to be given to idolatrous services by public officers, *&c., &c.* Such laws do not touch the mass of the people. They do not require them either to do or to abstain from doing, any thing which conscience forbids or enjoins; and therefore their duty in the premises may be limited to the use of legitimate means to have laws of which they disapprove repealed.

In the second place, those executive officers who are called upon to carry into effect a law which requires them to do what their conscience condemns, must resign their office, if they would do their duty to God. Some years since, General Maitland (if we remember the name correctly) of the Madras Presidency, in India, resigned a lucrative and honourable post, because he could not conscientiously give the sanction to the Hindu idolatry required by the British authorities. And within the last few months, we have seen hundreds of Hessian officers throw up their commissions rather than trample on the constitution of their country.

On the same principles the non-conformists in the time of Charles II. and the ministers of the Free Church of Scotland, in our day, gave up their stipends and their positions, because they could not with a good conscience carry into effect the law of the land. It is not intended that an executive officer should, in all cases, resign his post rather than execute a law which in his private judgment he may regard as unconstitutional or unjust. The responsibility attaches to those who make, and not to those who execute the laws. It is only when the act, which the officer is called upon to perform, involves personal criminality, that he is called upon to decline its execution. Thus in the case of war; a military officer is not the proper judge of its justice. That is not a question between him and the enemy, but between his government and the hostile nation. On the supposition that war itself is not sinful, the act which the military officer is called upon to perform is not criminal, and he may with a good conscience carry out the commands of his government, whatever may be his private opinion of the justice of the war. All such cases no doubt are more or less complicated, and must be decided each on its own merits. The general principle, however, appears plain, that it is only when the act required of an executive officer involves personal criminality, that he is called upon to resign. This is a case that often occurs. In Romish countries, as Malta, for example, British officers have been required to do homage to the host, and on their refusal have been cashiered. An instance of this kind occurred a few years ago, and produced a profound sensation in England. This was clearly a case of great injustice. The command was an unrighteous one. The duty of the officer was to resign rather than obey. Had the military authorities taken a fair view of the question, they must have decided that the command to bow to the host, was not obligatory, because *ultra vires*. But if such an order was insisted upon, the conscientious Protestant must resign his commission.

The next question is, What is the duty of private citizens in the case supposed, *i.e.* when the civil law either forbids them to do what God commands, or commands them to do what God forbids? We answer, their duty is not obedience, but submission. These are different things. A law consists of two parts, the precept and the penalty. We obey the one, and submit to the other. When we are required by the law to do what our conscience pronounces to be sinful, we cannot obey the precept, but we are bound to submit without resistance to the penalty. We are not authorized to abrogate the law; nor forcibly to resist its execution, no matter how great its injustice or cruelty. On this principle holy men have acted in all ages. The apostles did not obey the precept of the Jewish laws forbidding them to preach Christ, but neither did they resist the execution of the penalty attached to the violation of those laws. Thus it was with all the martyrs; they would not offer incense to idols, but refused not to be led to the stake. Had Cranmer, on the ground of the iniquity of the law condemning him to death, killed the officers who came to carry it into effect, he would have been guilty of murder. Here is the great difference which is often overlooked. The right of self-defence is appealed to as justifying resistance even to death against all attempts to deprive us of our liberty. We have this right in reference to unauthorized individuals, but not in reference to the officers of the law. Had men without authority entered Cranmer's house and attempted to take his life, his resistance, even if attended with the loss of life, would have been justifi-

able. But no man has the right to resist the execution of the law. What could be more iniquitous than the laws condemning men to death for the worship of God. Yet to these laws
Christians and Protestants yielded unresisting submission. This an obvious duty flowing from
the divine institution of government. "There is no power but of God, and the powers that be
are ordained of God. Whosoever, therefore, resisteth the power resisteth the ordinance of
God; and they that resist shall receive to themselves damnation." Thus Paul reasoned. If the
power is of God, it cannot be rightfully resisted; it must be obeyed or submitted to. Are
wicked, tyrannical, pagan powers of God? Certainly they are. Does not he order all things?
Does any man become a king without God's permission granted in mercy or in judgment?
Was not Nero to be recognised as emperor? Would it not be a sin to refuse submission to
Nicholas of Russia, or to the Sultan of Turkey? Are rulers to be obeyed only for their goodness? Is it only kind and reasonable masters, parents, or husbands who are to be recognised
as such? It is no doubt true that in no case is unlimited authority granted to men; and that
obedience to the precepts of our superiors is limited by the nature of their office, and by the
moral law; but this leaves their authority untouched, and the obligation to submission where
we cannot obey, unimpaired.

Have we then got back to the old doctrine of "passive obedience" by another route?
Not at all. The scriptural rule above recited relates to individuals. It prescribes the duty of
submission even to unjust and wicked laws on the part of men in their separate capacity; but
it does not deny the right of revolution as existing in the community. What the scriptures
forbid is that any man should undertake to resist the law. They do not forbid either change
in the laws or change in the government. There is an obvious difference between these two
things, viz: the right of resistance on the part of individuals, and the right of revolution on
the part of the people. This latter right we argue from the divine institution of government
itself. God has revealed his will that government should exist, but he has not not prescribed
the form which it shall assume. In other words he has commanded men to organize such
government, but has left the form to be determined by themselves. This is a necessary inference. It follows from the mere silence of scripture and nature on this subject, that it is left
free to the determination of those to whom the general command is given. In the next place,
this right is to be inferred from the design of civil government. That design is the welfare of
the people. It is the promotion of their physical and moral improvement; the security of life
and property; the punishment of evil doers, and the praise of those who do well. If such is
the end which God designs government to answer, it must be his will that it should be made
to accomplish that purpose, and consequently that it may be changed from time to time so
as to secure that end. No one form of government is adapted to all states of society, any more
than one suit of clothes is proper to all stages of life. The end for which clothing is designed,
supposes the right to adapt it to that end. In like manner the end government is intended to
answer, supposes the right to modify it whenever such modification is necessary. If God
commands men to accomplish certain ends, and does not prescribe the means, he does
thereby leave the choice of the means to their discretion. And any institution which fails to
accomplish the end intended by it, if it has not a divine sanction as to its form, may lawfully

be so changed as to suit the purpose for which it was appointed. We hold therefore that the people have by divine right the authority to change, not only their rulers but their form of government, whenever the one or the other, instead of promoting the well-being of the community, is unjust or injurious. This is a right which, like all other prerogatives may be exercised unwisely, capriciously, or even unjustly, but still it is not to be denied. It has been recognised and exercised in all ages of the world, and with the sanction of the best of men. It is as unavoidable and healthful as the changes in the body to adapt it to the increasing vigour of the mind, in its progress from infancy to age. The progress of society depends on the exercise of this right. It is impossible that its powers should be developed, if it were to be forever wrapt up in its swaddling clothes, or coffined as a mummy. The early Christians submitted quietly to the unjust laws of their Pagan oppressors, until the mass of the community become Christians, and then they revolutionized the government. Protestants acted in the same way with their papal rulers. So did our forefathers, and so may any people whose form of government no longer answers the end for which God has commanded civil government to be instituted. The Quakers are now a minority in all the countries in which they exist, and furnish an edifying example of submission to laws which they cannot conscientiously obey. But should they come, in any political society, to be the controlling power, it is plain they would have the right to conduct it on their own principles.

The right of revolution therefore is really embedded in the right to serve God. A government which interferes with that service, which commands what God forbids, or forbids what he commands, we are bound by our duty to him to change as soon as we have the power. If this is not so, then God has subjected his people to the necessity of always submitting to punishment for obeying his commands, and has cut them off from the only means which can secure their peaceful and secure enjoyment of the liberty to do his will. No one, however, in our land, or of the race to which we belong, will be disposed to question the right of the people to change their form of government. Our history forbids all diversity of sentiment on this subject. We are only concerned to show that the scriptural doctrine of civil government is perfectly consistent with that right; or rather that the right is one of the logical deductions from that doctrine.

What we have had most at heart in the preparation of this article, is the exhibition of the great principle that; all authority reposes on God; that all our obligations terminate on him; that government is not a mere voluntary compact, and obedience to law an obligation which rests on the consent of the governed. We regard this as a matter of primary importance. The character of men and of communities depends, to a great extent, on their faith. The theory of morals which they adopt determines their moral character. If they assume that expediency is the rule of duty, that a thing is right because it produces happiness, or wrong because it produces misery, that this tendency is not merely the test between right and wrong, but the ground of the distinction, then, the specific idea of moral excellence and obligation is lost. All questions of duty are merged into a calculation of profit and loss. There is no sense of God; reason or society takes his place, and an irreligious, calculating cast of character is the inevitable result. This is counteracted in individuals and the community by various causes, for neither the character of a man nor that of a society is determined by any one opinion; but its injurious influence may nevertheless be most manifest and deplorable. No man can fail to see the deteriorating influence of this theory of morals on public character both in this country and in England. If we would make men religious and moral, instead of merely cute, let us place God before them; let us teach them that his will is the ground of their obligations; that they are responsible to him for all their acts; that their allegiance as moral agents is not to reason or to society, but to the heart-searching God; that the obligation to obey the laws of the land does not rest on their consent to them, but to the fact government is of God; that those who resist the magistrate, resist the ordinance of God, and that they who resist, shall receive unto themselves damnation. This is the only doctrine which can give stability either to morals or to government. Man's allegiance is not to reason in the abstract, nor to society, but to a personal God, who has power to destroy both soul and body in hell. This is a law revealed in the constitution of our nature, as well as by the lips of Christ. And to no other sovereign can the soul yield rational obedience. We might as well attempt to substitute some mechanical contrivance of our own, for the law of gravitation, as a means of keeping the planets in their orbits, as to expect to govern men by any thing else than the fear of an Infinite God.

BIBLIOGRAPHY

General World History

Allison, Archibald, *The History of Europe From the Commencement of the French Revolution to the Restoration of the Bourbons* (Four Volumes; London: Eilliam Blackwood, 1848).

Burke, Edmund, *Further Reflections on the Revolution in France* (Indianapolis, Indiana: Liberty Fund, 1992).

Heinl, Robert and Heinl, Nancy, *Written in Blood: The Story of the Haitian People, 1492-1971* (Boston: Houghton Mifflin Company, 1978).

Howard, Michael, *The Occult Conspiracy: Secret Societies and Their Influence and Power in World History* (Rochester, Vermont: Destiny Books, 1989).

General American History

Angle, Paul M. (editor), *The American Reader* (New Brunswick, New Jersey: Rutgers University Press, 1947).

Bancroft, George, *A History of the United States* (six volumes; Boston: Little, Brown and Company, 1846).

Barker, Eugene C. and Commager, Henry Steele, *Our Nation*, (Evanston, Illinois: Row, Peterson and Company, 1942).

Binkley, Wilfred E., *American Political Parties* (New York: Alfred A. Knopf, 1943).

Binney, Horace, *The Privilege of the Writ of Habeas Corpus Under the Constitution* (Philadelphia, Pennsylvania: C. Sherman, Son and Company, 1862).

Bowden, Witt, *The Industrial History of the United States* (New York: Adelphi Company, 1930).

Bradford, Gamaliel, *The Lesson of Popular Government* (two volumes; New York: Harper and Brothers, 1899).

Bryce, James, *The American Commonwealth* (two volumes; London and New York: Macmillan Company, 1891).

Burnet, Jacob, *Notes on the Early Settlement of the North-Western Territory* (Cincinnati, Ohio: Derby, Bradley and Company, 1847).

Chesteron, Cecil, *History of the United States* (London: Chatto and Windus, 1919).

Donovan, Robert J., *The Assassins* (New York: Harper and Brothers, 1952).

Fehrenbach, T.R., *Greatness to Spare* (Princeton, New Jersey: D. Van Nostrand, 1968).

Fiske, John, *History of the United States For Schools* (Boston: Houghton, Mifflin and Company, 1899).

Garnett, Muscoe Russell Hunter, *The Union, Past and Future: How It Works and How to Save It* (Charleston, South Carolina: Walker and James Press, 1850).

Heitman, F.B., *Historical Register and Dictionary of the United States Army* (Washington, D.C.: Government Printing Office, 1903).

Hyman, Harold, *A More Perfect Union* (New York: Charles Scribner's Sons, 1973).

Lillback, Dr. Peter A., *Freedom's Holy Light* (Bryn Mawr, Pennsylvania: The Providence Forum,

2000).

Lodge, Henry Cabot, *A Short History of the English Colonies in America* (Boston: Harper and Brothers, 1881).

McDonald, Forrest, *E Pluribus Unum: The Formation of the American Republic, 1776-1790* (Indianapolis, Indiana: Liberty Fund, Inc., 1979).

McHenry, George, *The Position and Duty of Pennsylvania: A Letter Addressed to the President of the Philadelphia Board of Trade* (London: Henry F. Mackintosh, 1863).

Miner, Louie M., *Our Rude Forefathers American Political Verse 1783-1788* (Cedar Rapids, Iowa: Torch Press, 1937).

Oberholtzer, Ellis P., *A History of the United States Since the Civil War* (New York: Macmillan Company, 1917).

Ramsay, David, *The History of the American Revolution* (Trenton, New Jersey: James J. Wilson, 1811).

Rhodes, James Ford, *History of the United States* (seven volumes; New York: Harper Brothers, 1893).

Shenkman, Richard, *Legends, Lies, and Myths of American History* (New York William Morrow and Company, 1988).

Sparks, Edwin Earle, *Expansion of the American People* (Chicago, Illinois: Scott, Foresman and Company, 1901).

Tocqueville, Alexis, *Democracy in America* (London: George Allard, 1838).

General Southern History

Curry, Jabez L.M., *The Southern States of the American Union* (Richmond, Virginia: B.F. Johnson Publishing Company, 1895).

Dunning, William Archibald, *Studies in Southern History and Politics* (New York: Columbia University Press, 1914).

Hening, William Waller (editor), *The Statutes at Large: A Collection of All the Laws of Virginia From the First Session of the Legislature in the Year 1619* (New York: W.G. Bartow, 1823).

Selph, Fannie Eoline, *The South in American Life and History* (Nashville, Tennessee: McQuiddy Printing Company, 1928).

Woodward, C. Vann, *The Burden of Southern History* (Baton Rouge, Louisiana: Louisiana State University Press, 1960).

United States Constitution, State Constitution, and Conventions

Adams, John Quincy, *The Jubilee of the Constitution* (New York: Samuel Coman, 1839).

Beard, Charles Austin, *An Economic Interpretation of the Constitution of the United States* (New York: The Macmillan Company, 1935).

Benson, Bill and Beckman, M.J., *The Law That Never Was: The Fraud of the Sixteenth Amendment and Personal Income Tax* (South Holland, Illinois: Constitutional Research Association, 1985).

Benton, Thomas Hart (editor), *Abridgement of the Debates of Congress 1789 to 1856* (sixteen volumes; New York: D. Appleton and Company, 1857-1861).

Burgess, John W., *Political Science and Comparative Constitutional Law* (Boston: Ginn and Company, 1896).

Burnett, Edmund C. (editor), *Letters and Correspondence of Members of the Continental Congress* (eight volumes; Washington, D.C.: Carnegie Institution of Washington, 1921).

Curtis, George Ticknor, *History of the Origin, Formation, and Adoption of the Constitution of the United States* (New York: Harper and Brothers, 1855).

Elliott, Jonathan (editor), *The Debates in the Several State Conventions on the Adoption of the Federal Constitution* (five volumes; Washington, D.C.: Self-published, 1837).

Farrand, Max (editor), *The Records of the Federal Convention of 1787* (New Haven, Connecticut: Yale University Press, 1913).

Madison, James (editor), *Notes of Debate in the Federal Convention of 1787* (New York: W.W. Norton and Company, 1966).

Madison, James (editor), *Journal of the Federal Convention* (two volumes; Chicago, Illinois: Albert, Scott and Company, 1893).

Merriam, Charles Edward, *The Written Constitution and the Unwritten Attitude* (New York: Richard R. Smith, Inc., 1931).

Rawle, William, *A View of the Constitution of United States of America* (Philadelphia, Pennsylvania: Philip H. Nicklin and Company, 1829).

Rutland, Robert Allen, *The Ordeal of the Constitution* (Boston: Northern University Press, 1983).

Spooner, Lysander, *No Treason: The Constitution of No Authority* (Boston: Self-Published, 1870).

Story, Joseph, *Commentaries on the Constitution* (Boston: Hilliard, Gray and Company, 1833).

Thorpe, Francis Newton, *The Constitutional History of the United States* (Chicago, Illinois: Callahan and Company, 1901).

Thorpe, Francis Newton, *The Federal and State Constitutions* (seven volumes; Washington, D.C.: Government Printing Office, 1906).

United States Government and State Governments

Abraham, Henry J., *Justices, Presidents, and Senators: A History of the U.S. Supreme Court Appointments from Washington to Clinton* (Lanham, Maryland: Rowman and Littlefield, 1999).

Blaine, James G., *Twenty Years of Congress: From Lincoln to Garfield* (two volumes; Norwich, Connecticut: The Henry Bill Publishing Company, 1884).

Holst, H. Von, *The Constitutional and Political History of the United States* (Chicago, Illinois: Callahan and Company, 1889).

Landon, Judson A., *The Constitutional History and Government of the United States* (Boston: Hougton, Mifflin and Company, 1905).

McClure, Alexander K., *Our Presidents and How We Make Them* (New York: Harper and Brothers, 1900).

Moore, John West, *The American Congress: A History of National Legislation and Political Events, 1774-1895* (New York: Harper and Brothers, 1895).

Pierce, Franklin, *Federal Usurpation* (New York: D. Appleton and Company, 1908).

Richardson, James D., *Messages and Papers of the Presidents* (ten volumes; Washington, D.C.:

Government Printing Office, 1897).

Schattschneider, E.E., *Two Hundred Million Americans in Search of a Government* (New York: Holt, Rinehart and Winston, 1969).

Schlesinger, Jr., Arthur M., *The Imperial Presidency* (Boston: Houghton Mifflin Company, 1973).

Small, Norman J., *Some Constitutional Interpretations of the Presidency* (Baltimore, Maryland: John Hopkins Press, 1932).

Stanwood, Edward, *A History of the Presidency* (Boston: Houghton, Mifflin and Company, 1906).

Upshur, Abel P., *The True Nature and Character of Our Federal Government* (New York: Van Evrie, Horton, and Company, [1840] 1868).

Upham, Warren, *Minnesota in Three Centuries: 1655 to 1908* (Mankato, Minnesota: The Publishing Society of Minnesota, 1908).

Warren, Charles, *The Supreme Court in United States History* (two volumes; Boston: Little, Brown and Company, 1924).

Wilson, Woodrow, *Constitutional Government in the United States* (New York: Columbia University Press, 1908).

Political Parties and Sectionalism

Adams, Henry (editor), *Documents Relating to New-England Federalism* (Boston: Little, Brown and Company, 1877).

Banner, James, *To the Hartford Convention: The Federalists and the Origins of Party Politics in Massachusetts* (New York: Alfred A. Knopf, Inc., 1970).

Baxter, Maurice, *Henry Clay and the American System* (Lexington, Kentucky: University of Kentucky Press, 1995).

Carey, Matthew, *The Olive Branch* (Philadelphia, Pennsylvania: M. Carey and Son, 1818).

Carey, Jr., Matthew, The Democratic Speaker's Handbook (Cincinnati, Ohio: Miami Printing and Publishing, 1868).

Carpenter, Jesse T., *The South as a Conscious Minority, 1789-1861* (New York: New York University Press, 1930).

Collins, Charles Wallace, *Whither Solid South? A Study in Politics and Race Relations* (New Orleans, Louisiana: Pelican Publishing Company, 1947).

Curtis, Francis, *The Republican Party: A History of its Fifty Years' Existence and a Record of its Measures and Leaders* (New York: G.P. Putnam's Sons, 1904).

Cussons, John, *United States "History" As the Yankee Makes and Takes It* (Glen Allen, Virginia: Cussons, May and Company, 1900).

Johannsen, Robert W. (editor), *The Lincoln-Douglas Debates of 1858* (New York: Oxford University Press, 1965).

McKee, Thomas Hudson, *National Conventions and Platforms of All Political Parties 1789-1900* (Baltimore, Maryland: Friedenwald Company, 1900).

Schlesinger, Jr., Arthur M., *The Age of Jackson* (New York: Mentor Books, 1945).

Scott, John, *The Lost Principle: The Sectional Equilibrium, How It Was Created, How It Was Destroyed, and How It May Be Restored* (Richmond, Virginia: James Woodhouse and Company, 1860).

Taylor, John, *Tyranny Unmasked* (Indianapolis, Indiana: Liberty Fund, Inc., 1992).

Van Deusen, John G., *Economic Bases of Disunion in South Carolina* (New York: AMS Press, Incorporated, 1928).

Slavery and Abolitionism

Adams, Nehemiah, *A Southside View of Slavery* (Boston: T.R. Marvin and B.B. Mussey and Company, 1854).

Ballagh, James Curtis, *History of Slavery in Virginia* (Baltimore, Maryland: Johns Hopkins Press, 1902).

Berlin, Ira, *et. al.* (editors), *Free at Last: A Documentary History of Slavery, Freedom, and the Civil War* (New York: The New Press, 1992).

Bledsoe, Albert Taylor, *Liberty and Slavery* (Philadelphia, Pennsylvania: J.B. Lippincott and Company, 1856).

Buckingham, James S., *The Slave States of America* (two volumes; London: Fisher, Son and Company, 1841).

Carpenter, Stephen D., *The Logic of History: Five Hundred Political Texts Being Concentrated Extracts of Abolitionism* (Madison, Wisconsin: self-published, 1864).

Cole, Arthur Charles, *The Irrepressible Conflict: 1850-1865* (New York: Macmillan Company, 1934).

Dabney, Robert Lewis, *A Defense of Virginia and the South* (New York: E.J. Hale and Son, 1867).

DuBois, W.E. Burghardt, *The Suppression of the American Slave Trade to the United States of America 1638-1870* (New York: Longmans, Green and Company, 1896).

Ewing, Elbert William R., *The Legal and Historical Status of the Dred Scott Decision* (Washington, D.C.: Cobden Publishing Company, 1908).

Helper, Hinton Rowan, *The Impending Crisis of the South: How To Meet It* (New York: A.B. Burdick, Publishers, 1857).

Helper, Hinton Rowan, *Black Negroes in Negroland* (New York: Carleton, 1868).

Hildreth, Richard, *Despotism in America: An Inquiry Into the Nature and Results of the Slave-Holding System in the United States* (Boston: Anti-Slavery Society, 1840).

Hopkins, John Henry, *A Scriptural, Ecclesiastical, and Historical View of Slavery* (New York: W.I. Pooley and Company, 1864).

Hosmer, William, *The Higher Law in its Relation to Civil Government With Particular Reference to Slavery and the Fugitive Slave Act* (Auburn, New York: Derby and Miller, 1852).

Jenkins, William Sumner, *Pro-Slavery Thought in the Old South* (Chapel Hill, North Carolina: The University of North Carolina Press, 1960).

Koger, Larry, *Black Slaveowners in South Carolina, 1790-1860* (Jefferson, North Carolina: McFarland and Company, Inc., 1985).

McCabe, James Dabney, *Fanaticism and Its Results* (Baltimore, Maryland: James Robinson, 1860).

Merk, Frederick W., *Slavery and the Annexation of Texas* (New York: Alfred A. Knopf, 1972).

Munford, Beverley, *Virginia's Attitude Toward Slavery and Secession* (New York: Longmans, Green and Company, 1909).

Page, Thomas Nelson, *The Negro: The Southerner's Problem* (New York: Charles Scribner's Sons, 1904).

Phillips, Ulrich B., *American Negro Slavery* (New York: D. Appleton and Company, 1918).

Phillips, Ulrich B., *Life and Labor in the Old South* (Boston: Little, Brown, and Company, 1929).

Phillips, Wendell, *The Constitution a Pro-Slavery Compact: Extracts From the Madison Papers* (New York: American Anti-Slavery Society, 1856).

Pickett, William P., *The Negro Problem: Abraham Lincoln's Solution* (New York: G.P. Putnam's Sons, 1909).

Scott, Otto, *The Secret Six* (Murphys, California: Uncommon Books, 1979).

Sewell, Richard H., *Ballots For Freedom: Antislavery Politics in the United States, 1837-1860* (New York: W.W. Norton, 1976).

Smedes, Susan Dabney, *Memorials of a Southern Planter* (Baltimore, Maryland: Cushings and Bailey, 1888).

Smith, William A., *The Philosophy and Practice of Slavery in the United States* (Nashville, Tennessee: Stevensen and Evans, 1856).

Smith, William Henry, *A Political History of Slavery* (New York: G.P. Putnam's Sons, 1903).

Spears, John Randolph, *The American Slave Trade: An Account of Its Origin, Growth and Suppression* (New York: Charles Scribner's Sons, 1900).

Spooner, Lysander, *The Unconstitutionality of Slavery* (Boston: Bela Marsh, Publisher, 1846).

Stampp, Kenneth, *The Peculiar Institution: Slavery in the Antebellum South* (New York: Alfred A. Knopf, 1956).

Stowe, Harriet Beecher, *Uncle Tom's Cabin, or Life Among the Lowly* (Boston: John P. Jewitt and Company, 1853).

Vallandigham, Clement Laird, *Abolition, the Union, and the Civil War* (Columbus, Ohio: J. Walter and Company, 1863).

Van Evrie, J.H., *White Supremacy and Negro Subordination* (New York: Van Evrie, Horton and Company, 1868).

Weld, Theodore Dwight, *American Slavery As It Is: Testimony of a Thousand Witnesses* (New York: American Anti-Slavery Society, 1839).

Whitfield, Theodore M., *Slavery Agitation in Virginia, 1829-1832* (Baltimore, Maryland: The Johns Hopkins Press, 1930).

Williams, George W., *History of the Negro Race in America* (two volumes; New York: G.P. Putnam's Sons, 1885).

Wilson, Henry, *History of the Rise and Fall of the Slave Power in America* (Boston: James R. Osgood and Company, 1874).

State Rights and Secession

Bledsoe, Albert Taylor, *Is Davis a Traitor?* (Richmond, Virginia: The Hermitage Press, Inc., 1907).

Dumond, Dwight Lowell (editor), *Southern Editorials on Secession* (New York: The Century Company, 1931).

Sage, Bernard Janin, *The Republic of Republics: A Retrospect of Our Century of Federal Liberty* (Philadelphia, Pennsylvania: William W. Harding, 1878).

Stephens, Alexander Hamilton, *A Constitutional View of the War Between the States* (two volumes; Philadelphia, Pennsylvania: National Publishing Company, 1868, 1870).

War Between the States

Adams, Charles, *When in the Course of Human Events: Arguing the Case For Southern Secession* (Lanham, Maryland: Rowman and Littlefield Publishers, Inc., 2000).

Adams, Ephraim D., *Great Britain and the American Civil War* (two volumes; London, England: Longmans, Green, and Company, 1925).

Ashe, S.A., *A Southern View of the Invasion of the Southern States and War of 1861-65* (Raleigh, North Carolina: self-published, 1938).

Burgess, John W., *The Civil War and the Constitution* (New York: Charles Scribner's Sons, 1901).

Chadwick, French Ensor, *Causes of the Civil War* (New York: Harper and Brothers Publishers, 1906).

Cole, Arthur Charles, *The Era of the Civil War, 1848-1870* (Springfield, Illinois: Illinois Centennial Commission, 1919).

Crawford, Samuel W., *Genesis of the Civil War* [New York: J.A. Hill and Company, 1887.

Curry, Leonard P., *Blueprint for Modern America: Nonmilitary Legislation of the First Civil War Congress* (Nashville, Tennessee: Vanderbilt University Press, 1968).

Curtis, Benjamin Robbins, *Executive Power* (Boston: Little, Brown and Company, 1862).

Davis, Jefferson, *The Rise and Fall of the Confederate Government* (two volumes; New York: D. Appleton and Company, 1881).

Davis, Jefferson, *A Short History of the Confederate States of America* (New York: Belford, Clarke and Company, 1890).

Davis, William C., *Brother Against Brother: The War Begins* (Alexandria, Virginia: Time-Life Books, 1983).

Davis, William C. and Wiley, Bell I. (editors), *Photographic History of the Civil War: Fort Sumter to Gettysburg* (New York: Black Dog and Leventhal Publishers, 1994).

Dean, Henry Clay, *Crimes of the Civil War and Curse of the Funding System* (Baltimore, Maryland: J. Wesley Smith and Brothers, 1869).

Edmonds, George, *Facts and Falsehoods Concerning the War on the South 1861-1865* (Memphis, Tennessee: A.R. Taylor and Company, 1904).

Eisenschiml, Otto, *Why Was Lincoln Murdered?* (New York: Grosset and Dunlap, 1937).

Foner, Philip, *Business and Slavery: The New York Merchants and the Irrepressible Conflict* (Chapel Hill, North Carolina: University of North Carolina Press, 1941).

Gallagher, Gary, *The Confederate War* (Cambridge, Massachusetts: Harvard University Press, 1997).

Garrison, Webb, *Lincoln's Little War* (Nashville, Tennessee: Rutledge Hill Press, 1997).

Gordon, John Brown, *Reminiscences of the Civil War* (New York: Charles Scribner's Sons, 1903).

Gragg, Rod (editor), *The Illustrated Confederate Reader* (New York: Gramercy Books, 1998).

Greeley, Horace, *The American Conflict* (Hartford, Connecticut: O.D. Chase, 1866).

Henderson, G.F.R., *Stonewall Jackson and the American Civil War* (two volumes; New York: Longmans, Green and Company, 1902).

Hendrick, Burton J., *Statesmen of the Lost Cause: Jefferson Davis and His Cabinet* (New York: The Literary Guild of America, Inc., 1939).

Henry, Robert Selph, *The Story of the Confederacy* (New York: Garden City Publishing Company, 1931).

Horton, R.G., *A Youth's History of the Great Civil War of the United States From 1861 to 1865*

(New York: Van Evrie, Horton and Company, 1868).

Hummel, Jeffrey Rogers, *Emancipating Slaves, Enslaving Free Men* (Chicago, Illinois: Open Court Publishing Company, 1996).

Johnstone, H.W., *Truth of the War Conspiracy of 1861* (Idylwild, Georgia: self-published, 1921).

Lunt, George, *The Origin of the Late War* (New York: D. Appleton and Company, 1866).

Mahony, Dennis A., *Prisoner of State* (New York: G.W. Carleton and Company, 1863).

Marshall, John A., *American Bastile* (Philadelphia, Pennsylvania: Thomas W. Hartley and Company, 1881).

Marx, Karl and Engels, Friedrich, *The Civil War in the United States* (New York: International Publishers, 1937).

McClure, Alexander K., *Abraham Lincoln and Men of War Times* (Philadelphia, Pennsylvania: Times Publishing, 1892).

McGuire, Hunter and Christian, George L., *The Confederate Cause and Conduct in the War Between the States* (Richmond, Virginia: L.H. Jenkins, Inc., 1907).

McHenry, George, *The Cotton Trade: Its Bearing Upon the Prosperity of Great Britain and Commerce of the American Republics* (London: Saunders, Otley, and Company, 1863).

McPherson, James M., *Abraham Lincoln and the Second American Revolution* (New York: Oxford University Press, 1990).

Moore, Frank (editor), *The Rebellion Record: A Diary of American Events* (New York: G.P. Putnam's Sons, 1861).

Neely, Jr., Mark E., *The Fate of Liberty: Abraham Lincoln and Civil Liberties* (New York: Oxford University Press, 1991).

Owsley, Frank Lawrence, *King Cotton Diplomacy: Foreign Relations of the Confederate States of America* (Chicago, Illinois: University of Chicago Press, 1931).

Perkins, Howard Cecil, *Northern Editorials on Secession* (two volumes; New York: D. Appleton and Company, 1942).

Piatt, Donn, *Memories of the Men Who Saved the Union* (New York: Butler Brothers, 1887).

Pollard, Edward A., *The Lost Cause* (New York: E.B. Treat and Company, 1866).

Pollard, Edward A., *A Southern History of the War* (New York: Charles B. Richardson, Publisher, 1866).

Putnam, Sallie B., *Richmond During the War: Four Years of Personal Observation* (New York: C.W. Carleton and Company, Publishers, 1867).

Randall, James G., *The Civil War and Reconstruction* (Boston: D.C. Heath and Company, 1937).

Richardson, Heather Cox, *The Greatest Nation on the Earth: Republican Economic Policies During the Civil War* (Cambridge, Massachusetts: Harvard University Press, 1997).

Rutherford, Mildred Lewis, *Truths of History* (Athens, Georgia: self-published, 1920).

Russell, William Howard, *My Diary North and South* (Boston: T.O.H.P. Burnam, 1863).

Semmes, Raphael, *Memoirs of Service Afloat* (Baltimore, Maryland: Kelly, Piet and Company, 1869).

Shaffner, Taliaferro P., *The Secession War in America* (London: Hamilton, Adams and Company, 1862).

Silliker, Ruth L. (editor), *The Rebel Yell and Yankee Hurrah* (Camden, Maine: Down East Books, 1985).

Simms, William Gilmore, *The Sack and Destruction of Columbia, South Carolina* (Columbia, South Carolina: Power Press of the Daily Phoenix, 1865).

Smith, Robert Hardy, *An Address to the Citizens of Alabama on the Constitution and Laws of the Confederate States of America* (Mobile, Alabama: Mobile Daily Register, 1861).

Sons of Confederate Veterans, *The Gray Book* (Columbia, Tennessee: The Gray Book Committee, 1935).

Spence, James, *The American Union: Its Effect on National Character and Policy* (London: Richard Bentley and Son, 1862).

Stampp, Kenneth, *The Causes of the Civil War* (Inglewood, New Jersey: Spectrum Books, 1960).

Stiles, Robert, *Four Years Under Marse Robert* (New York: The Neale Publishing Company, 1904).

Thomas, Emory M., *The Confederacy as a Revolutionary Experience* (Englewood Cliffs, New Jersey: Prentice-Hall, 1971).

Tilley, John Shipley, *Lincoln Takes Command* (Chapel Hill, North Carolina: The University of North Carolina Press, 1941).

Tyler, Lyon Gardiner, *John Tyler and Abraham Lincoln: Who Was the Dwarf?* (Richmond, Virginia: Richmond Press, Inc., 1929).

Reconstruction

Avary, Myrta Lockett, *Dixie After the War* (New York: Doubleday, Page, and Company, 1906).

Barnes, William H., *History of the Thirty-Ninth Congress of the United States* (New York: Harper and Brothers, Publishers, 1868).

Beale, Howard K., *The Critical Year: A Study of Andrew Johnson and Reconstruction* (New York: Harcourt, Brace and Company, 1930).

Bowers, Claude G., *The Tragic Era: The Revolution After Lincoln* (New York: Blue Ribbon Books, 1940).

Boyard, Thomas, *Ku Klux Klan Organization* (Washington, D.C.: U.S. Government Printing Office, 1871).

Burgess, John W., *Reconstruction and the Constitution* (New York: Charles Scribner's Sons, 1902).

Collins, Charles Wallace, *The Fourteenth Amendment and the States* (Boston: Little, Brown and Company, 1912).

Davis, Susan Lawrence, *Authentic History of the Ku Klux Klan, 1865-1877* (New York: American Library Service, 1924).

Dunning, William Archibald, *Reconstruction: Political and Economic, 1865-1877* (New York: Harper and Brothers, Publishers, 1907).

Eckenrode, H.J., *A Political History of Virginia During Reconstruction* (Baltimore, Maryland: Johns Hopkins Press, 1904).

Fleming, Walter L., *Documents Relating to Reconstruction* (Morgantown, West Virginia: Self-published, 1904).

Fleming, Walter L., *Documentary History of Reconstruction* (two volumes; Cleveland, Ohio: The Arthur H. Clarke Company, 1907).

Foner, Eric, *Reconstruction: America's Unfinished Revolution 1863-1877* (New York: Harper and Row, 1988).

Garner, James Wilford, *Reconstruction in Mississippi* (New York: Macmillan Company, 1901).

Henry, Robert Selph, *The Story of Reconstruction* (New York: Grosset and Dunlap, 1938).

Hirshson, Stanley P., *Farewell to the Bloody Shirt: Northern Republicans and the Southern Negro,*

1877-1893 (Chicago, Illinois: Quadrangle Press, 1968).

Horn, Stanley F., *The Invisible Empire: The Story of the Ku Klux Klan, 1866-1871* (Boston: Houghton Mifflin Company, 1935).

McPherson, James M., *The Struggle For Equality: Abolitionists and the Negro in the Civil War and Reconstruction* (Princeton, New Jersey: Princeton University Press, 1964).

Reid, Whitelaw, *After the War: A Southern Tour, May 1, 1865 to May 1, 1866* (Cincinnati, Ohio: Moore, Wilstach, and Baldwin, 1866).

Reynolds, John S., *Reconstruction in South Carolina, 1865-1877* (Columbia, South Carolina: The State Company, 1905).

Stampp, Kenneth M., *The Era of Reconstruction, 1865-1877* (New York: Random House, 1965).

Thompson, Henry T., *Ousting the Carpetbagger From South Carolina* (Columbia, South Carolina: R.L. Bryan Company, 1927).

Thompson, C. Mildred, *Reconstruction in Georgia* (New York: Columbia University Press, 1915).

Trowbridge, John Thompson, *The South: A Tour of its Battlefields and Ruined Cities* (Hartford, Connecticut: L. Stebbins, 1866).

Tourgee, Albion Winegar, *A Fool's Errand* (New York: Fords, Howard and Hulbert, 1880).

Wallace, John, *Carpetbag Rule in Florida* (Jacksonville, Florida: Da Costa Printing and Publishing House, 1888).

Wood, Fernando, *Alleged Ku Klux Outrages* (Washington, D.C.: U.S. Government Printing Office, 1971).

World War One

Frederic L. Paxson, Edward S. Corwin, and Samuel B. Harding (editors), *War Cyclopedia: A Handbook for Ready Reference on the Great War* (Washington, D.C.: Government Printing Office, 1918).

The New Deal

Altmeyer, Arthur J., *The Formative Years of Social Security* (Madison, Wisconsin: The University of Wisconsin Press, 1968).

Dilling, Elizabeth, *The Roosevelt Red Record and its Background* (Kenilworth, Illinois: Self-published, 1936).

Ellis, Abraham, *The Social Security Fraud* (New Rochelle, New York: Arlington House, 1971).

Flynn, John T., *The Roosevelt Myth* (San Francisco, California: Fox and Wilkes, 1998).

Haber, William and Cohen, Wilbur J., *Readings in Social Security* (New York: Prentice-Hall, Inc., 1948).

Leuchtenburg, William E., *The Supreme Court Reborn: The Constitutional Revolution in the Age of Roosevelt* (New York: Oxford University Press, 1995).

Lindley, Ernest K., *Half Way With Roosevelt* (New York: Viking Press, 1946).

Marvin, Fred R., *Fool's Gold: An Expose of Un-American Activities and Political Action in the United States Since 1860* (New York: Madison and Marshall, Inc., 1936).

Nock, Albert Jay, *Our Enemy the State* (Caldwell, Idaho: The Caxton Printers, Ltd., 1946).

Roosevelt, Franklin Delano, *On Our Way* (New York: The John Day Company, 1934).

Schiff, Irwin, *The Social Security Swindle* (Hamden, Connecticut: Freedom Books, 1984).

Schlesinger, Arthur M., Jr., *The Age of Roosevelt: The Coming of the New Deal* (Boston: Houghton-Mifflin Company, 1958).

Schottland, Charles I., *The Social Security Program in the United States* (New York: Meredith Publishing Company, 1963).

Webster, Bryce and Perry, Robert L., *The Complete Social Security Handbook* (New York: Dodd, Mead and Company, 1983).

Communism and Socialism

Cameron, Kenneth Neill, *Marxism: The Science of Society* (Boston: Bergin and Garvey, 1985).

Hearnshaw, F.J.C., *Democracy and Labour* (London: Macmillan and Company, Ltd., 1924).

Hearnshaw, F.J.C., *A Survey of Socialism: Analytical, Historical and Critical* (London. Macmillan & Company, Ltd., 1929).

Kirkpatrick, George R., *War — What For?* (West Lafayette, Ohio: self-published, 1910).

Lenin, Vladimir I., *Collected Works* (Moscow: Progress Publishers, 1980), Volume XXV.

Humanism

Bragg, Raymond B., Kurtz, Paul and Wilson, Edwin H., *Humanist Manifesto II* (Buffalo, New York: Prometheus Books, 1980).

Kurtz, Paul, *The Humanist Alternative* (Buffalo, New York: Prometheus Books, 1973).

Banking and Finance

Chandler, Lester V., *Benjamin Strong, Central Banker* (Washington, D.C.: Brookings Institution, 1958).

Faraday, W. Barnard, *Democracy and Capital* (London: John Murray Publishers, Ltd., 1921).

Fisher, Irving, *100% Money* (New York: Adelphi Company, 1936).

Galbraith, John Kenneth, *Money: Whence It Came, Where It Went* (Boston: Houghton Mifflin Company, 1975).

Griffin, G. Edward, *The Creature From Jekyll Island* (Westlake Village, California: American Media, 1998).

Josephson, Matthew, *The Robber Barons: The Great American Capitalists 1861-1901* (New York: Harcourt, Brace and Company, 1934).

Krooss, Herman E. (editor), *Documentary History of Banking and Currency in the United States* (four volumes; New York: Chelsea House, 1983).

Lindburgh, Charles A., *Banking and Currency and the Money Trust* (Washington, D.C.: National Capital Press, 1913).

Lundberg, Ferdinand, *America's Sixty Families* (New York: Vanguard Press, 1937).

Makin, John H., *The Global Debt Crisis: America's Growing Involvement* (New York: Basic Books, 1984).

Mullins, Eustace, *Secrets of the Federal Reserve* (Staunton, Virginia: Bankers Research Institute, 1984).

Murdoch, Jr., Lawrence C., *The National Debt* (Philadelphia, Pennsylvania: Federal Reserve Bank of Philadelphia, 1970).

Myers, Gustavus, *History of the Great American Fortunes* (New York: Random House, 1936).

Owen, Robert L., *National Economy and the Banking System* (Washington, D.C.: U.S. Government Printing Office, 1939).

Rand, Ayn (editor), *Capitalism: The Unknown Ideal* (New York: Signet Books, 1967).

Richardson, Heather Cox, *The Greatest Nation on the Earth: Republican Economic Policies During the Civil War* (Cambridge, Massachusetts: Harvard University Press, 1997).

Rothbard, Murry N., *The Mystery of Banking* (New York: Richardson and Snyder, 1983).

Smith, Adam, *An Inquiry into the Nature and Causes of the Wealth of Nations* (Indianapolis, Indiana: The Liberty Fund, [1776], 1981).

Thorpe, George Cyrus, *Contracts Payable in Gold* (Washington, D.C.: Government Printing Office, 1933; Senate Document No. 43).

Military Government, Martial Law, and Emergency Powers

Birkhimer, William E., *Military Government and Martial Law* (Kansas City, Missouri: Franklin Hudson Publishing Company, 1914).

Lieber, Francis, *Instructions for the Government of Armies of the United States in the Field* (Gen. Orders No. 100, Adjutant-General's Office, 1863).

Rossiter, Clinton L., *Constitutional Dictatorship: Crisis Government in the Modern Democracies* (Princeton, New Jersey: Princeton University Press, 1948).

Sheffer, Martin S., *The Judicial Development of Presidential War Powers* (Westport, Connecticut: Praeger Publishers, 1999).

Whiting, William, *The War Powers of the President* (Boston: John L. Shorey, 1862).

Autobiographies, Biographies, Speeches, and Collected Writings

Abbot, W.W., *The Papers of George Washington: Confederation Series* (Charlottesville, Virginia: University Press of Virginia, 1994).

Baker, George (editor), *The Works of William Seward* (four volumes; Boston: Houghton, Mifflin and Company, 1884).

Basler, Roy P. (editor), *The Collected Works of Abraham Lincoln* (eight volumes; New Brunswick, New Jersey: Rutgers University Press, 1953).

Bell, Howard Wilford (editor), *Letters and Addresses of Abraham Lincoln* (New York: Unit Book Publishing Company, 1905).

Beveridge, Albert J., *The Life of John Marshall* (two volumes; Boston: Houghton Mifflin Company, 1916).

Boyd, Julian P. (editor), *The Papers of Thomas Jefferson* (twenty-one volumes; Princeton, New Jersey: Princeton University Press, 1950-1984).

Browning, Orville H., *Diary* (Springfield, Illinois: Illinois State Historical Library, 1933).

Buchanan, James, *Mr. Buchanan's Administration on the Eve of the Rebellion* (New York: D. Appleton and Company, 1866).

Butler, Benjamin F., *Butler's Book: Autobiography and Personal Reminiscences of Major-General Benjamin F. Butler* (two volumes; Boston: A.M. Thayer and Company, 1892).

Cathey, James H., *The Genesis of Lincoln* (Atlanta, Georgia: Franklin Printing and Publishing Company, 1899).

Chambers, Richard (editor), *Speeches of the Honorable Henry Clay of the Congress of the United States* (Cincinnati, Ohio: Shepard and Stearns, 1842).

Coggins, James Caswell, *The Eugenics of President Abraham Lincoln* (Elizabethton, Tennesse: Goodwill Press, 1940).

Conway, Moncure Daniel, *Omitted Chapters of History Disclosed in the Life and Papers of Edmund Randolph* (New York: G.P. Putnam's Sons, 1888).

Cralle, Richard K. (editor), *The Works of John C. Calhoun* (six volumes; New York: Appleton and Company, 1851-1856), Volume VI.

Curtis, George Ticknor, *Life of Daniel Webster* (two volumes; New York: D. Appleton and Company, 1870).

Curtis, George Ticknor, *Life of James Buchanan, Fifteenth President of the United States* (New York: D. Appleton and Company, 1883).

Dickinson, John, *The Political Writings of John Dickinson, Esquire* (Wilmington, Delaware: Bonsol and Niles, 1801).

Dwight, Theodore, *The Character of Thomas Jefferson Exhibited in His Own Writings* (Boston: Weeks, Jordan and Company, 1839).

Everett, Edward, *Address of His Excellency Edward Everett to the Two Branches of the Legislature on the Organization of the Government for the Political Year Commencing January 6, 1836* (Boston: Dutton and Wentworth, 1837).

Ford, Paul Leicester (editor), *The Writings of Thomas Jefferson* (ten volumes; New York: G.P. Putnam and Sons, 1892-1899), Volume X.

Garrison, Wendell Phillips and Garrison, Francis Jackson, *William Lloyd Garrison, 1805-1870* (Boston: Houghton, Mifflin Company, 1894).

Hapgood, Norman, *Abraham Lincoln: The Man of the People* (New York: The Macmillan Company, 1913).

Hardman, J.B.S. (editor), *Rendezvous With Destiny: Addresses and Opinions of Franklin Delano Roosevelt* (New York: The Dryden Press, 1944).

Hart, Albert Bushnell, *Salmon P. Chase* (Boston: Houghton Mifflin Company, 1899).

Herndon, William H. and Weik, Jesse William, *Life of Lincoln* (two volumes; Chicago, Illinois: Bedford, Clark and Company, 1889).

Hinton, Richard J., *John Brown and His Men* (New York: Funk and Wagnall's Company, 1894).

Holland, Josiah Gilbert, *Life of Abraham Lincoln* (Springfield, Massachusetts: Gurdon Bill, 1866).

Hoover, Herbert, *The Memoirs of Herbert Hoover, 1929-1941: The Great Depression* (New York: Macmillan Company, 1952).

Jefferson, Thomas, *Memoirs, Correspondence, and Miscellanies From the Papers of Thomas Jefferson* (Charlottesville, Virginia: F. Carr and Company, 1829).

Johannsen, Robert W., *Lincoln, the South, and Slavery: The Political Dimension* (Baton Rouge, Louisiana: Louisiana State University Press, 1991)

Kussiel, Saul (editor), *Karl Marx on the American Civil War* (New York: McGraw Hill Company, 1972).

Lamon, Ward H., *Life of Abraham Lincoln* (Boston: James R. Osgood and Company, 1872).

Lee, Jr., Robert E., *Recollections and Letters of General Robert E. Lee* (Garden City, New York: Garden City Publishing Company, 1924).

Leland, Charles Godfrey, *Abraham Lincoln* (New York: G.P. Putnam's Sons, 1881).

Lence, Ross M. (editor), *Union and Liberty: The Political Philosophy of John C. Calhoun* (Indianapolis, Indiana: Liberty Fund, 1992).

Lipscomb, Andrew and Bergh, Albert Ellery (editors), *The Writings of Thomas Jefferson* (twenty volumes; Washington, D.C.: Jefferson Memorial Association, 1903-1905).

Lodge, Henry Cabot, *Daniel Webster* (Boston: Houghton, Mifflin, and Company, 1899).

Malin, James C., *John Brown and the Legend* (Philadelphia, Pennsylvania: American Philosophical Society, 1942).

Mason, Virginia, *The Public Life and Diplomatic Correspondence of James M. Mason* (New York: Neal Publishing Company, 1906).

Meriwether, Robert L. (editor), *The Papers of John C. Calhoun* (twenty-six volumes; Columbia, South Carolina: University of South Carolina Press, 1959-2001).

Meyers, Marvin (editor), *The Mind of the Founder: Sources of the Political Thought of James Madison* (Indianapolis, Indiana: The Bobbs-Merrill Company, 1973).

Minor, Charles L.C., *The Real Lincoln* (Richmond, Virginia: Everett Waddey Company, [1904] 1928).

Morse, Jr., John T., *Abraham Lincoln* (two volumes; Boston: Houghton, Mifflin and Company, 1892).

Nicolay, John G. and Hay, John (editors), *Abraham Lincoln: Complete Works Comprising His Speeches, Letters, State Papers and Miscellaneous Writings* (eleven volumes; New York: The Century Company, 1984-1902).

Nicolay, John G. and Hay, John, *Abraham Lincoln: A History* (ten volumes; New York: The Century Company, 1886-1890).

Nicolay, John G., *A Short Life of Abraham Lincoln* (New York: The Century Company, 1911).

Oldroyd, Osborn H., *The Lincoln Memorial* (New York: American Union Publishing Company, 1882).

Peterson, Merril D. (editor), *Thomas Jefferson: Writings* (New York: Library of America, 1984).

Phillips, Wendell, *Speeches, Lectures, and Letters* (Boston: Walker, Wise and Company, 1864).

Raymond, Henry J., *The Life and Public Services of Abraham Lincoln Together With His State Papers* (New York: Derby and Miller, 1865).

Redpath, James, *The Public Life of Captain John Brown* (Boston: Thayer and Eldridge, 1860).

Remsburg, John E., *Abraham Lincoln: Was He a Christian?* (New York: The Truth Seeker Company, 1906).

Rosenman, Samuel Irving (editor), *The Public Papers and Addresses of Franklin D. Roosevelt* (five volumes; New York: Random House, 1938).

Rowland, Dunbar (editor), *Jefferson Davis, Constitutionalist: His Letters, Papers, and Speeches* (Jackson, Mississippi: Mississippi Department of Archives and History, 1923).

Rutland, Robert Allen (editor), *The Papers of George Mason* (three volumes; Chapel Hill, North Carolina: The University of North Carolina Press, 1970).

Sanborn, F.B. (editor), *The Life and Letters of John Brown, Liberator of Kansas and Martyr of Virginia* (Boston: Roberts Brothers, 1888).

Schuckers, J.W., *Life and Public Services of Salmon P. Chase, United States Senator and Governor of Ohio, Secretary of the Treasury, and Chief Justice of the Supreme Court* (New York: D.

Appleton and Company, 1874).

Sparks, Jared, *Life of Gouverneur Morris With Selections From His Correspondence and Miscellaneous Papers* (Boston: Gary and Bowen, 1832).

Stowe, Charles Edward (editor), *The Life of Harriet Beecher Stowe Compiled from Her Letters and Journals* (Boston: Houghton, Mifflin and Company, 1889).

Sumner, Charles, *The Works of Charles Sumner* (Boston: Lee and Shepherd, 1880).

Tarbell, Ida, *Life of Abraham Lincoln* (two volumes; New York: Lincoln Memorial Association, 1900).

Thoreau, Henry David, *The Writings of Henry David Thoreau* (Cambridge, Massachusetts: Riverside Press, 1894).

Villard, Oswald Garrison, *John Brown, 1800-1859* (Garden City, New York: Doubleday, Nolan and Company, 1929).

Viola, Herman J., *Andrew Jackson* (New York: Chelsea House, 1986).

Weiss, John (editor), *The Life and Correspondence of Theodore Parker* (D. Appleton and Company, 1864), two volumes.

Welles, Gideon, *Diary of Gideon Welles* (three volumes; Boston: Houghton, Mifflin and Company, 1911).

Willis, Garry, *Cincinnatis: George Washington and the Enlightenment* (Garden City, New York: Doubleday and Company, 1984).

Woodward, W.E., *Meet General Grant* (New York: The Literary Guild of America, 1928).

Government Publications and Reports (arranged by date of publication)

American State Papers: Foreign Relations (four volumes; Washington, D.C.: Gales and Seaton, Printers, 1832).

The Statutes at Large of South Carolina (Columbia, South Carolina: A.S. Johnston, 1836).

Statutes at Large of the Provisional Government of the Confederate States of America (Richmond, Virginia: R.M. Smith, Printer to Congress, 1864).

Report of the Joint Committee on Reconstruction (Washington, D.C.: U.S. Government Printing Office, 1866).

Report of the Joint Congressional Committee on Affairs in the Insurrectionary States (Washington, D.C.: Government Printing Office, 1872).

Official Records of the Union and Confederate Armies in the War of the Rebellion (seventy volumes; Washington, D.C.: Government Printing Office, 1880-1901).

Official Records of the Union and Confederate Navies in the War of the Rebellion (thirty volumes; Washington, D.C.: Government Printing Office, 1894-1922).

Documentary History of the Constitution of the United States (three volumes; Washington, D.C.: Government Printing Office, 1904).

Slave Narratives: A Folk History of Slavery in the United States From Interviews With Former Slaves (Washington, D.C.: Government Printing Office, 1934).

Report of the Commission of Intergovernmental Relations (Washington, D.C.: Government Printing Office, 1955).

Money Facts (Washington, D.C.: House Banking and Currency Committee; Eighty-Eighth Congress, Second Session, 1964).

The Constitution of the United States: An Analysis and Interpretation (U.S. Senate Document No. 92-82, Ninety-Second Congress, Second Session; Washington, D.C.: U.S. Government Printing Office, 1972).

Emergency Powers Statutes: Provisions of Federal Law Now in Effect Delegating to the Executive Authority in Time of National Emergency: Report of the Special Committee on the Termination of the National Emergency (United States Senate Report No. 93-549, Ninety-Third Congress, First Session; Washington, D.C.: U.S. Government Printing Office, November 19, 1973; #24-509).

A Brief History of Emergency Powers in the United States: A Working Paper (Special Committee on National Emergencies and Delegated Emergency Powers, 93rd Congress, 2nd Session; Washington, D.C.: U.S. Government Printing Office, July, 1974).

Official Opinions of the Attorney General of the United States Advising the Presidents and Heads of Departments in Relation to their Official Duties (Washington, D.C.: U.S. Government Printing Office, 1974).

National Emergencies and Delegated Emergency Powers (Senate Report No. 94-922, Ninety-Fourth Congress, Second Session; Washington, D.C.: Government Printing Office, 1976).

United States Army Regulations (Washington, D.C.: Government Printing Office, 1 October 1979; AR 840-10).

The Law of Land Warfare: Army Field Manual 27-10 (Washington, D.C.: Government Printing Office, 1983 O-381-647 [5724]).

Inaugural Addresses of the Presidents of the United States From George Washington to George Bush (Washington, D.C.: Government Printing Office, 1989).

Miscellaneous Reference Works

American Annual Cyclopedia and Register of Important Events of the Year 1861 (New York: D. Appleton and Company, 1862).

American Annual Cyclopedia and Register of Important Events of the Year 1867 (New York: D. Appleton and Company, 1868).

American Annual Cyclopedia and Register of Important Events of the Year 1863 (New York: D. Appleton and Company, 1870).

American Annual Cyclopedia and Register of Important Events of the Year 1867 (New York: D. Appleton and Company, 1870).

Black, Henry Campbell, *Black's Dictionary* (St. Paul, Minnesota: West Publishing Company, 1990; Sixth Edition).

Blackstone, William, *Commentaries on the Laws of England* (four volumes; Chicago, Illinois: University of Chicago Press, 1979).

Bouvier, John, *A Law Dictionary Adapted to the Constitution and Laws of the United States of America and of the Several States of the American Union* (two volumes; Philadelphia, Pennsylvania: J. B. Lippincott Company, 1839).

A Collection of All Such Acts of the General Assembly of Virginia of a Public and Permanent Nature as are Now in Force (Richmond, Virginia: Samuel Pleasants, Jr., 1803).

Ginnow, Arnold G. and Nikolic, Milorad (editors), *Corpus Juris Secundum* (one hundred and one volumes; St. Paul, Minnesota: West Publishing Company, 1988).

Hill, Frederick Trevor, *Decisive Battles of the Law* (New York: Harper and Brothers, 1907).

Journal of the Constitutional Convention of the State of Illinois (Springfield, Illinois: C.H. Lanphier, 1862).

Lalor, John J. (editor), *Cyclopedia of Political Science, Political Economy, and of the Political History of the United States* (three volumes; Chicago, Illinois: Rand McNally, 1881-1890).

Lieber, Francis, *Civil Liberty and Self Government* (Philadelphia, Pennsylvania: J.B. Lippincott and Company, 1859).

Rawle, Francis (editor), *Bouvier's Law Dictionary* (Kansas City, Missouri: Vernon Law Book Company, 1914).

Suzzallo, Henry (editor), *The National Encyclopedia* (ten volumes; New York: P.F. Collier and Son Corporation, 1936-1944).

Wheaton, Henry (W.B. Lawrence, editor), *Elements of International Law* (Boston: Little, Brown and Company, 1863).

Essays and Articles

Boughter, I.F., "Western Pennsylvania and the Morrill Tariff," *Western Pennsylvania Historical Magazine* (April, 1923), Volume VI.

Burr, Charles Chauncey, "Political History of William H. Seward," *The Old Guard* (New York: Van Evrie, Horton and Company, 1866), Volume IV.

Robert Lewis Dabney, "The Rise and Fall of the Confederate Government," in *The Southern Presbyterian Review*, Volume XXXII, Number 2 (April 1882).

Dowlet, Robert, "The Right to Arms: does the Constitution or the Predilection of Judges Reign?" *Oklahoma Law Review* [1983], Vol. 36, No. 1.

DuBois, W.E. Burghardt, "The Freedmen's Bureau," *Atlantic Monthly*, Volume LXXXVII (1901).

Dudley, Edgar S., "Was 'Secession' Taught at West Point?", *The Century Magazine* (New York, 1909), Volume LXXVIII.

Essert, F. Harold, "What is Meant By the 'Police Power'"? *Nebraska Law Bulletin* (Lincoln, Nebraska: College of Law, The University of Nebraska, 1933), Volume XII.

Fisher, Sydney G., "The Suspension of Habeas Corpus During the War of the Rebellion," *Political Science Quarterly* (1888), Volume III.

Fletcher, George P., "Unsound Constitution," *The New Republic*, 23 June 1997.

Howe, W.A. DeWolfe, "General Sherman's Letters Home," *Scribner's Magazine*, April 1909.

Luthin, Reinhard H., "Abraham Lincoln and the Tariff," *The American Historical Review* (July, 1944), Volume XLIX, Number 4.

McDonald, Forrest, "Was the Fourteenth Amendment Constitutionally Adopted?" *Georgia Journal of Southern Legal History*, Volume One, Number One (Spring/Summer 1991).

McKown, Delos B., "Demythologizing Natural Human Rights," *The Humanist*, May/June 1989.

Ramsdell, Charles Williams., "The Natural Limits of Slavery Expansion," *Mississippi Valley Historical Review* (September 1929), Volume XVI, Number 2.

Ramsdell, Charles William, "Lincoln and Fort Sumter," in *The Journal of Southern History*, February-November 1937.

Ruml, Beardsley, "Taxes For Revenue Are Obsolete," *American Affairs*, January 1946.

Spence, James, "The American Republic: Resurrection Through Dissolution," *Northern British*

Review, February 1862.

Sturm, Albert L., "Emergencies and the Presidency," *Journal of Politics*, February 1949.

Sumner, Charles, "Our Domestic Relations: How to Treat the Rebel States," *Atlantic Monthly* (September, 1863), Volume XII, Number 71.

Tugwell, Rexford G., "Rewriting the Constitution," *The Center Magazine* (Los Angeles, California: Center for the Study of Democratic Institutions, March 1968), Volume I, Number 3.

Whitcomb, Paul S., "Lincoln and Democracy," *Tyler's Quarterly Magazine*, July 1927.

NAME INDEX

SUBJECT INDEX

Underground Railroad, 215
Uniform Code of Military Justice, 918, 920
Union

an experiment, 33, 118, 119, 142, 231ff, 426
dissolution of, 44, 49, 50, 51, 52, 59, 60,
70, 74, 76, 117, 118, 128, 140ff,
254, 287, 292, 312, 315, 330, 393,
419, 420, 431, 477
nature of, 15, 19, 45, 61ff, 194, 231, 238,
259ff, 715, 980
Union League, 603, 606ff, 609, 610, 629, 639
Unitarianism, 77, 140, 145, 859, 1010
Universalism, 617

V
Vietnam War, 885
Virginia Peace Conference, 346
Virginia Resolutions, 238, 273, 945

W
War powers (see Emergency powers)
West Point Military Academy, 235, 292
Whig party, 166, 191, 194, 340, 341, 359, 431,
437, 910
Whiskey Rebellion, 396, 397
Wilmot Proviso, 162, 181, 190
World War One, 715, 727, 755, 759, 761, 805,
807, 810, 818, 871, 885, 887, 888, 895,
896, 904
World War Two, 886, 899, 902

Y
YMCA, 723

NOTES

NOTES

NOTES

NOTES

NOTES

NOTES

NOTES

NOTES

NOTES

NOTES

NOTES

NOTES

NOTES

NOTES

NOTES

Proof

Made in the USA
Charleston, SC
26 June 2013

20086331R00292